Cost Accounting for Managerial Planning, Decision Making and Control

Sixth Edition

Woody Liao,
Hsihui Chang,
Andrew Schiff and
Stacy Kline

Bassim Hamadeh, CEO and Publisher
Christopher Foster, General Vice President
Michael Simpson, Vice President of Acquisitions
Jessica Knott, Managing Editor
Kevin Fahey, Cognella Marketing Manager
Jess Busch, Senior Graphic Designer
Melissa Barcomb, Acquisitions Editor
Sarah Wheeler, Project Editor
Stephanie Sandler, Licensing Associate
Kate McKellar, Interior Designer

First published in the United States of America in 2013 by Cognella, Inc.

Printed in the United States of America

ISBN: 978-1-62131-102-7 (pbk)/ 978-1-62131-103-4 (br)

www.cognella.com 800.200.3908

Contents

1. *To distinguish between financial accounting and cost accounting.*
2. *To describe the organizational environment of the accounting function.*
3. *To discuss the role of an accountant in an organization.*
4. *To discuss management accounting as a professional discipline.*

1 The Role of Cost Accounting

Accountability has become an important concern in our society. Corporate managers are accountable to stockholders and governments, political leaders are accountable to those who are led, employees are accountable to their employers, and students are accountable to their teachers for their performances in each of these roles. Accountability is achieved and performance is measured by some method of accounting; that is, a method of converting to quantitative measures the results of activities over a period of time. The most commonly used methods in modern organizations attempt to measure activities in terms of their monetary impact; this is the foundation of the study of accounting with which all readers of this book are familiar.

The need for accountability in modern organizations has created the body of knowledge known as cost accounting. The existence of cost accounting systems for determining product costs can be traced to medieval times, but they only became widely used with the arrival of the industrial revolution. The development of large, widely dispersed organizations made the problem of maintaining accountability more difficult. As a result, the purposes of cost accounting systems have been extended beyond their initial objective of recording and summarizing data on product costs. Cost accounting systems now provide information for managerial planning and control. Managerial *control* is concerned with making individual managers accountable for their performance. Information for *planning* and *decision-making* aids managers in improving performance in carrying out their individual responsibilities. The methods and principles of cost accounting have evolved in response to this need for management accountability.

Who should undertake a study of cost accounting? Future accountants in industry and government will be required to design cost accounting systems and to utilize many of the methods described in this book. Future public accountants will be required to review existing cost accounting systems and may have the opportunity to advise clients on the development of new systems, or on improvements to existing ones. Future managers will be evaluated using cost accounting systems, and will rely on cost accounting data in making many of their decisions. When making a decision, a manager must decide, not only on the action to be taken, but also on the information on which to rely in choosing a course of action. A study of cost accounting will enable a future manager to be an intelligent consumer of accounting information.

As will be discussed throughout this book, accounting information exists for many different purposes. Any user of accounting information must be able to select the information which is appropriate for his or her immediate purpose. And an accountant, as a supplier of information, must be able to advise management on the appropriate uses of it.

Cost Accounting and Financial Accounting

Accounting systems provide information of many different kinds. A distinction is commonly made between *cost* accounting and *financial* accounting. Each is concerned with providing measures of accountability; however, these fields of study are distinguished by the entities for which accountability is measured and the entities to which accountability is provided.

Objectives of Financial Accounting

Financial accounting is concerned with measuring, in monetary terms, the activities of an entire business over an annual reporting period. The principles and methods followed are based on a set of concepts including those of conservatism, the business as an entity and a going concern, consistency and materiality. These methods are collectively referred to as *generally accepted accounting principles* (GAAP). Financial accounting principles have been developed for reporting to parties external to the organization on its financial state and the custodianship of its management. These external parties include stockholders, creditors, and governmental agencies.

Because of this external reporting objective, many practices are followed in financial accounting that may not be appropriate for other objectives. Financial accounting measures are based on historical costs, which sometimes are not relevant for managerial planning and decision-making. Financial accounting principles also require cost allocations of various forms.

Allocations frequently are highly dependent on an accountant's judgment. Although acceptable for the objectives of external reporting, they may produce results which are misleading for other purposes. These differences do not mean that one accounting method is correct and another is incorrect, but rather that any accounting method should be selected to achieve its proper objectives. An accountant must have a thorough understanding of the different objectives of accounting information and the principles which are appropriate for each objective.

Objectives of Cost Accounting

Whereas financial accounting has a single objective, the principles of cost accounting have been developed to serve a dual set of objectives. Cost accounting systems must serve the external reporting objective by recording data on the costs of products or services rendered by the accounting entity. These costs are then used for purposes of inventory valuation and income determination in the financial statements prepared for external parties. As a result, the methods of accounting for product costs normally are subjected to the requirements of GAAP.

Cost accounting systems also provide data for internal reporting to managers and employees of the accounting entity. Internal reports may be produced on a periodic basis to aid in planning and controlling the operations of the organization. Cost accounting information is also used on a non-periodic basis in making managerial decisions of a non-routine nature. Accounting principles and methods that are appropriate for planning, control, and making special decisions may differ from those used for the external reporting objective. Again, the issue of concern to an accountant is not if an accounting method is correct, but rather whether or not a method is proper for its intended use.

Cost accounting principles for internal reporting are not required to be in accordance with GAAP. More frequently they are selected to reflect the methods which management and cost accountants think are appropriate for the organization. As a result, different organizations commonly approach the same accounting problem with different underlying assumptions and using different methods. Many times these methods are not those which are generally accepted for external reporting. For example, many cost accountants prefer to avoid certain types of cost allocations, feeling that they have a detrimental effect on management control and are not appropriate for planning. Sometimes, in making special managerial decisions, costs are recognized that are not costs in a traditional accounting sense because they do not represent expenditures. Major differences in accounting methods for internal reporting exist in different organizations, and these differences will be described throughout this book.

The Organizational Environment of Accounting

Cost accounting systems for planning and control are developed within the context of a particular organization. Because organizations differ, the methods of cost accounting employed may differ from one to the next. Yet most organizations are organized in a traditional manner which clearly distinguishes lines of authority and responsibility. In such companies, the relationships between the accounting function and the other functional areas may be described as follows.

Traditional Organization Structure

Traditionally the formal relationship between the employees of a company is a hierarchical one. At the top of the hierarchy is the company president to who report several vice-presidents responsible for the major functional areas of the business. The decision-makers at this level constitute *executive management* because as officers of the company they are responsible for the planning and coordination of all of its activities. Reporting to each vice-president are one or more members of *middle management*. Middle managers typically have specific duties within a functional business division, such as manager of a production facility, a sales region, or a product line. And finally, those decision-makers at the lowest levels in the hierarchy are known as *operating management*. These managers have responsibility for controlling the daily operations of the organization and monitoring the performance of most of the company's non-managerial employees. An accounting system used for internal reporting is designed to establish operating objectives for managers at all levels in the organization and to provide measures of their performance.

Executive, middle, and operating managers constitute what is frequently referred to as *line management*. These are the people who on a regular basis make decisions affecting other employees' actions and the company's overall profitability. Line managers daily utilize the internal reporting system because it provides them with summaries reflecting past activities and plans for those in the future. The performance of a line manager is measured by the cost accounting system. The manager in turn uses the system to evaluate the performance of his or her subordinates. As will be discussed in later chapters, the design of the cost accounting system can have a significant impact on the ability and desire of line managers to achieve the objectives of the organization.

Many companies also have non-managerial employees who are not involved in day-to-day operations, but rather serve as advisors to line management. These employees are said to fill *staff functions*, because they are part of an advisory staff for the president or some other decision-maker. Staff employees are generally equivalent to operating managers in terms of salary, education, and experience. However, they do not have decision-making responsibility and normally report directly to an executive at higher levels in the organization. Staff personnel are hired to advise line management in many specialized areas of concern to the entire company. They include the corporate planning, public relations, and internal audit staffs. Frequently corporate budgets are developed by a budgetary staff reporting to a controller or financial vice-president. Certain staff personnel may work closely with the cost accounting system when it is used for purposes of planning and control.

An organization chart for a typical company structured in this fashion is shown in Illustration 1-1. There are, of course, many variations of this basic structure found in practice. Nevertheless, this chart illustrates the organizational environment in which accountants and the accounting system must operate.

Organization of the Accounting Function

The chief accounting manager in a company normally has the title of *controller*. The controller may be a part of middle management and report to a financial vice-president as shown in Illustration 1-1. In some organizations, particularly in very large corporations, the controller will be an officer of the company and a member of executive management. The duties of the controller may vary widely depending on the size and the management philosophy of the company. In a very large company a corporate controller may supervise the work of several divisional controllers. In a small company the controller may assume many duties commonly assigned to a treasurer, or may function primarily as a bookkeeper. As a minimum, the job's duties generally include those summarized in Illustration 1-2. Depending on the company and the individual filling the job, the controller's duties as an advisor to management and an interpreter of accounting data may represent a significant part of his or her responsibilities.

In carrying out these responsibilities, the controller is usually aided by a number of other employees with accounting, bookkeeping and clerical duties. Frequently an accounting department will be divided into four major sections as shown in Illustration 1-3. The *general accounting* section is responsible for processing all accounting transactions on a daily basis, and may be composed of a supervisory bookkeeper and other clerical personnel assigned to specific types of processing. The *cost accounting* group is charged with determining product costs. These accountants may additionally aid in the preparation of reports for control purposes or of analyses for special managerial decisions.

A *budgeting* section works with managers in the organization on the preparation of the company, divisional, and departmental budgets. In some companies, this group of accountants may

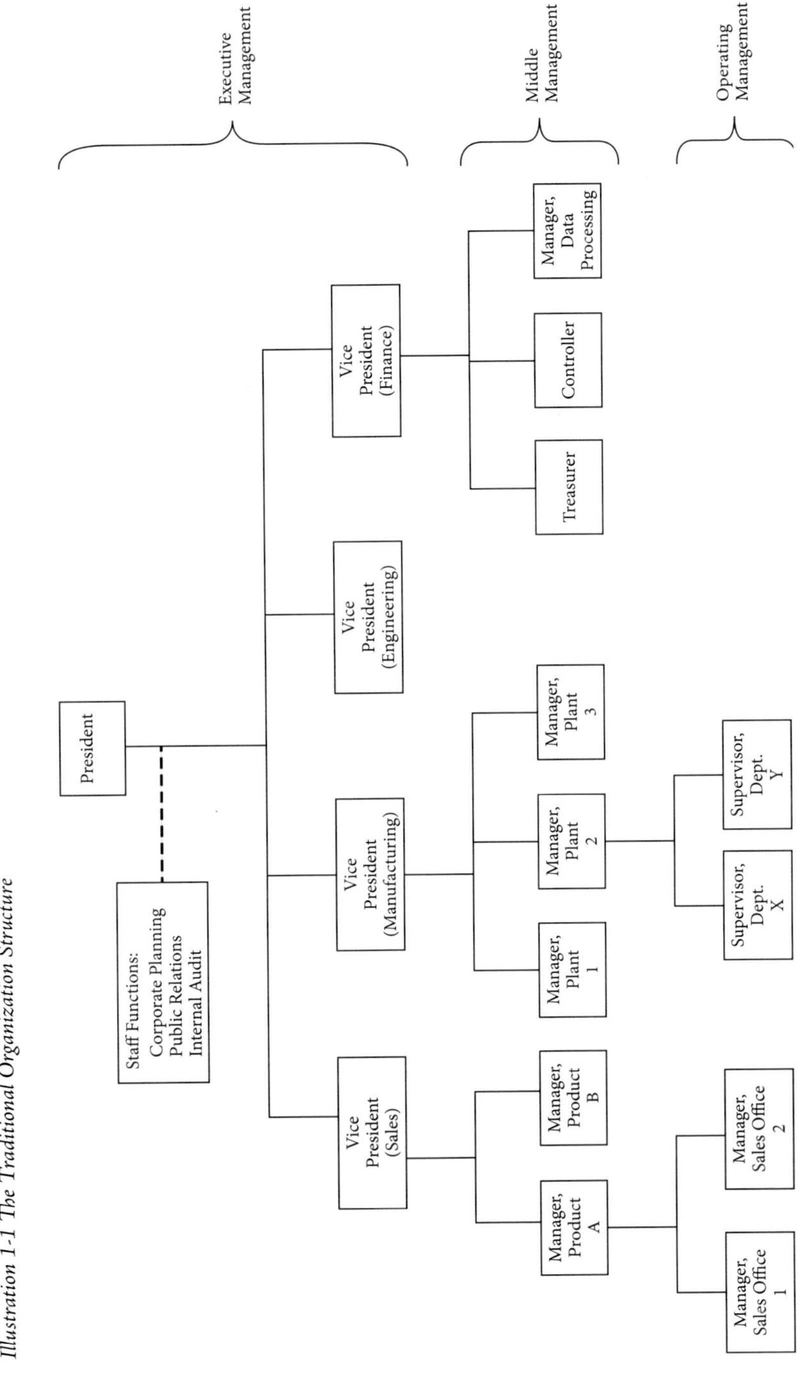

Illustration 1-1 The Traditional Organization Structure

Illustration 1-2 Duties of the Controller

1. Supervise the maintenance of the accounting records
2. Income tax planning and preparation
3. Establishing and supervising systems for management control
4. Supervise preparation of financial reports to external parties
5. Advise executive management on accounting and reporting policies
6. Provide and interpret data for special managerial decisions.

Illustration 1-3 Organization of the Accounting Department

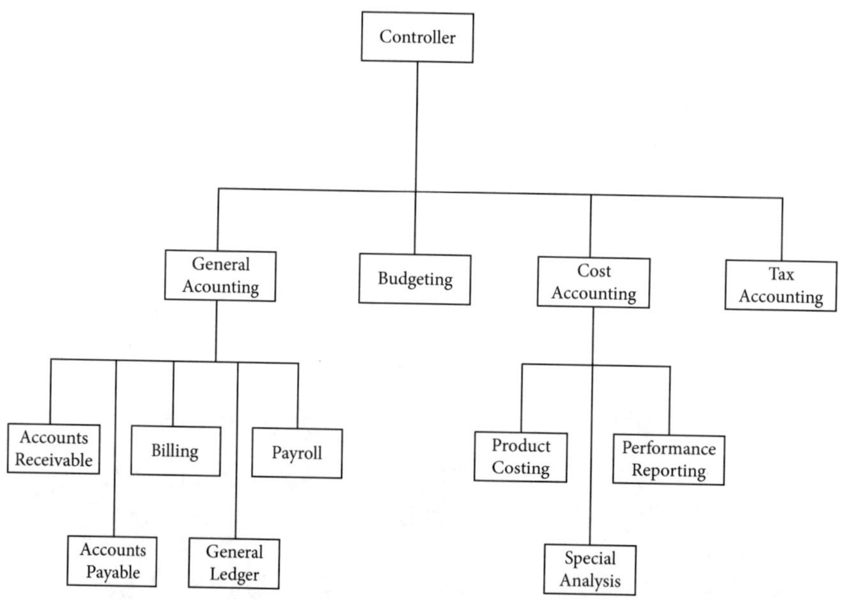

constitute a staff function reporting directly to the president or vice-president for finance. The **tax *accounting*** group is responsible for preparing and filing periodic tax returns and reports.

The Profession of Management Accounting

As has been discussed, a wide range of alternative methods exist in cost accounting. The controller must be able to adopt accounting methods which are appropriate for the organization using them. Furthermore, the cost accounting system must provide information that is useful for both the external and the internal reporting objectives. As a result, developing and maintaining a cost accounting system is indeed a very complex task.

The complexities of corporate accounting systems have created a body of professionals with special expertise in the area. These professionals are referred to as management accountants, and their discipline is called management accounting. The profession of management accounting has evolved in response to the special knowledge requirements that an accountant in industry must possess.

The Institute of Management Accountants (IMA) has issued the following definition of management accounting:

> Management accounting is the process of identification, measurement, accumulation, analysis, preparation, interpretation, and communication of financial information used by management to plan, evaluate, and control within an organization and to assure appropriate use of and accountability for its resources. Management accounting also comprises the preparation of financial reports for non-management groups such as shareholders, creditors, regulatory agencies, and tax authorities.

In this definition, financial information comprises that information necessary to interpret the cause and effect of actual or planned business activities and economic circumstances. The term *management accountant* then refers to persons involved in a broad range of functions. These include controller-ship, treasury, financial analysis, planning and budgeting, cost accounting, internal audit, systems, and general accounting.

This definition has been taken from *Statement on Management Accounting Number IB*, "Objectives of Management Accounting," dated June 17, 1982. Much of this statement has been reproduced in the Appendix to this chapter. It is available in its entirety from IMA at 10 Paragon Drive, Montvale, New Jersey 07645-1759.

Body of Knowledge for Management Accounting

From the preceding discussion, it is clear that a management accountant must have some knowledge in many different fields. Historically, the accountant has been the organization's expert on accounting procedures. However, in modern corporations the knowledge requirements extend far beyond this narrow area.

The management accountant is involved in developing systems of internal reporting for planning and control. As a result, he or she must have a thorough understanding of the operations of the organization in which these systems are implemented. Because most companies utilize computer-based systems to prepare this information, the management accountant must be familiar with the methods and internal control measures which relate to electronic data processing. Systems for planning and control may have a significant effect on the motivation and performance of line managers in the company. As a consequence, the management accountant must also have some knowledge of the principles underlying the fields of psychology, sociology, and human behavior in complex organizations.

An accountant in industry must also provide information for reporting to external parties. Thus, an understanding is required of generally accepted accounting principles as they apply in his or her particular organization. The management accountant is concerned with the laws and procedures relating to taxation, so that returns and reports will be filed promptly and correctly.

Perhaps the greatest challenge to the management accountant lies in his or her role as an advisor to management. Accounting information has some impact on virtually all decisions made in a modern business. But to adequately serve in an advisory capacity, the accountant must be able to approach decisions from the perspective of management. It is necessary that he or she develop a concern for the financial and social implications of decisions, and knowledge of the economic environment in which the business operates. The management accountant should be familiar with the variety of quantitative techniques that are used by managers in evaluating decision alternatives. In addition, the implications of legal and ethical constraints on business and accounting decisions must be understood. Because of the breadth of knowledge required in management accounting, it is not surprising that members of the profession have advanced to the top executive positions in some of the world's largest companies.

The role of management accounting as a professional discipline has been enhanced by the creation of the Institute of Management Accounting and its certification program. Many accountants have chosen to demonstrate their achievements in the field by earning the Certificate in Management Accounting.

The Certificate in Management Accounting

The Certificate in Management Accounting (CMA) has become widely recognized as the professional designation for management accountants. It is granted to those who have met certain educational and moral standards, have at least two years of related work experience, and have passed a comprehensive examination in the field. The CMA program is actively promoted by many large companies who recognize it as evidence of an accountant's abilities and motivation.

The CMA program is administered by the Institute of Certified Management Accountants (ICMA) which was established by the Institute of Management Accountants in 1972. Its objectives, as stated by the ICMA, are as follows:

1. To establish management accounting as a profession by identifying the role of the management accountant and the underlying body of knowledge;
2. To foster higher educational standards in the field of management accounting; and
3. To establish an objective measure of an individual's knowledge and competence in the field of management accounting.

The objective measure of competence referred to in these objectives is the CMA examination. It is administered twice each year over a two and a half day period at many locations in the United States. The examination consists of five parts, each of which must be passed within a three-year period. Each part covers one or more major topic areas in the body of knowledge which has been identified for management accountants; the parts of the CMA examination are listed in Illustration 1-4. Successful completion of the exam is a significant accomplishment, and indicates that a person has the ambition and qualifications to become a successful member of the management accounting profession.

Ethical Behavior for Management Accountants

Management accountants, like everyone in modern society, face ethical dilemmas. They must make decisions and take actions based on personal evaluations of what is good and bad or what is right and wrong. Furthermore, they sometimes work in situations where their short-term interests may seem inconsistent with accepted accounting practice. This makes the management accountant's ethical choices especially difficult.

Illustration 1-4 Certificate in Management Accounting Examination Topical Coverage

1. Economics, finance, and management
2. Financial accounting and reporting
3. Management reporting, analysis, and behavioral issues
4. Decision analysis and information systems

For example, an accountant's supervisor may tell the accountant to record the physical inventory at its original cost when the accountant knows that the inventory is obsolete and should be recorded at a reduced value. Refusal to do so may result in the accountant's discharge, but compliance will result in misstated financial reports. What should the accountant do?

To aid management accountants in such decisions, the IMA has developed a set of standards for ethical conduct. Such a set of standards are a characteristic of most professions. Those for the management accounting profession describe how to resolve ethical conflicts and identify responsibilities in four areas: competence, confidentiality, integrity, and objectivity.

Ethical Responsibilities of Management Accountants

In the area of *competence*, management accountants have a responsibility to:

1. Maintain an appropriate level of professional competence by ongoing development of their knowledge and skills.
2. Perform their professional duties in accordance with relevant laws, regulations, and technical standards.
3. Prepare complete and clear reports and recommendations after appropriate analysis of relevant and reliable information.

In the area of *confidentiality*, management accountants have a responsibility to:

1. Refrain from disclosing confidential information acquired in the course of their work except when authorized, unless legally obligated to do so.
2. Inform subordinates as appropriate regarding the confidentiality of information acquired in the course of their work and monitor their activities to assure the maintenance of that confidentiality.
3. Refrain from using or appearing to use confidential information acquired in the course of their work for unethical or illegal advantage either personally or through third parties.

Regarding *integrity*, management accountants have a responsibility to:

1. Avoid actual or apparent conflicts of interest and advise all appropriate parties of any potential conflict.
2. Refrain from engaging in any activity that would prejudice their ability to carry out their duties ethically.
3. Refuse any gift, favor, or hospitality that would influence or would appear to influence their actions.

4. Refrain from either actively or passively subverting the attainment of the organization's legitimate and ethical objectives.
5. Recognize and communicate professional limitations or other constraints that would preclude responsible judgment or successful performance of an activity.
6. Communicate unfavorable as well as favorable information and professional judgments or opinions.
7. Refrain from engaging in or supporting any activity that would discredit the profession.

Finally, concerning *objectivity*, management accountants have a responsibility to:

1. Communicate information fairly and objectively
2. Disclose fully all relevant information that could reasonably be expected to influence an intended user's understanding of the reports, comments, and recommendations presented.

Resolving Ethical Conflicts

When faced with significant ethical decisions, management accountants should follow the established policies of their organizations affecting the decision. When these policies do not resolve the conflict, they should consider one of the following courses of action.

Refer to Higher Management. The management accountant should discuss the ethical conflict with the immediate superior unless the superior is involved. When this is the case, the discussion should be with someone at the next higher management level. If this discussion does not resolve the issue, then the management accountant refers the problem to the next higher management level.

Discuss With an Objective Advisor. The management accountant should clarify relevant concepts by confidential discussions with an objective advisor, such as a lawyer or trusted friend. This provides an understanding of possible courses of action.

Resignation. When a significant ethical conflict still exists after exhausting all levels of internal review, the management accountant may have no other choice but to resign from the organization. In this case, an informative memorandum should be submitted to an appropriate representative of the organization. This may include a member of executive management, the audit committee, the board of directors, the board of trustees, or the owners.

Except where required by law, communication of ethical conflicts to authorities or individuals outside of the organization is inappropriate.

Summary

The field of cost accounting is concerned with providing accounting information for both external and internal reporting purposes. Cost accounting methods developed in response to the industrial revolution and were initially concerned only with determining the costs of products and services. Later the applications of cost accounting in planning and control were recognized, and cost accounting systems evolved which aided in making decision-makers accountable for their performances. In most organizations, cost accounting is a responsibility of the controller. Many important uses of cost accounting information, and the complexities of developing adequate internal reporting systems, have created the discipline of management accounting.

Professional recognition in this discipline can be achieved by earning the Certificate in Management Accounting.

Key Definitions

Controller	The chief accounting manager in a company. The controller serves as an advisor to management and supervises all accounting, record-keeping, and reporting activities.
Cost accounting	The branch of accounting which is concerned with maintaining accountability for product costs and managerial performance.
Executive management	The officers of a company, who are responsible for the planning and coordination of its activities.
Financial accounting	The branch of accounting which is concerned with maintaining accountability to external parties, including stockholders, creditors, and governmental agencies.
Line management	The people in a company who regularly make decisions affecting its profitability and the actions of other employees.
Management accounting	A professional discipline which is concerned with providing information that is useful to management.
Middle management	Line managers who have duties within specific functional divisions of a company.
Operating management	Line managers who control the daily operations of a business, and supervise non-managerial employees.
Staff functions	Employees of an organization who serve as advisors to line management, but do not make decisions.

Appendix

Excerpts from Statement on Management Accounting No. 1B: Objectives of Management Accounting

Objectives

In fulfilling the objectives of management accounting, management accountants:

1. Provide information, and
2. Participate in the management process.

Providing Information

Management accountants select and provide, to all levels of management, information needed for (a) planning, evaluating, and controlling operations; (b) safeguarding the organization's assets; and (c) communicating with interested parties outside the organization, such as shareholders and regulatory bodies.

Participating in the Management Process

Management accountants at appropriate levels are involved actively in the process of managing the entity. This process includes making strategic, tactical, and operating decisions and helping to coordinate the efforts of the entire organization. The management accountant participates, as part of management, in assuring that the organization operates as a unified whole in its long-run, intermediate, and short-run best interests.

Responsibilities

To fulfill the objectives, management accountants accept certain major responsibilities. They establish and maintain the necessary practices and techniques to provide essential information to management, and they fulfill external reporting requirements. The responsibilities of management accountants are as follows:

1. Planning-Quantifying and interpreting the effects on the organization of planned transactions and other economic events. The planning responsibility, which includes strategic, tactical, and operating aspects, requires that the accountant provide quantitative historical and prospective information to facilitate planning. It includes participation in developing the planning system, setting obtainable goals, and choosing appropriate means of monitoring the progress toward the goals.
2. Evaluating-Judging implications of historical and expected events and helping to choose the optimum course of action. Evaluating includes translating data into trends and relationships. Management accountants must communicate effectively and promptly the conclusions derived from the analyses.
3. Controlling-Assuring the integrity of financial information concerning an organization's activities and resources; monitoring and measuring performance and inducing any corrective actions required to return the activity to its intended course. Management accountants provide information to executives operating in functional areas who can make use of it to achieve desirable performance.
4. Assuring accountability of resources-Implementing a system of reporting that is aligned with organizational responsibilities. This reporting system will contribute to the effective use of resources and measurement of management performance. The transmission of management's goals and objectives throughout the organization in the form of assigned responsibilities is a basis for identifying accountability. Management accountants must provide an accounting and reporting system that will accumulate and report appropriate revenues, expenses, assets, liabilities, and related quantitative information to managers. Managers then will have better control over these elements.
5. External reporting-Preparing financial reports based on generally accepted accounting principles, or other appropriate bases, for non-management groups such as shareholders,

creditors, regulatory agencies, and tax authorities. Management accountants should participate in the process of developing the accounting principles that underlie external reporting.

Activities

Management accountants discharge their responsibilities by organizing and implementing activities in seven principal categories: reporting, interpretation, resource management, information systems development, technological implementation, verification, and administration.

Reporting

Reporting relates to both internal and external needs for information about past or future events and circumstances. Management accountants make available to managers timely reports that provide the information and perspective necessary for them to make decisions in a goal congruent manner. The reports may concern financial, physical, and human resources and the markets and regulatory environments in which entities operate. In addition to reporting internally, management accountants make appropriate information available to shareholders, creditors, and governmental regulatory agencies and tax authorities.

Interpretation

Management accountants interpret all forms of internal and external information pertinent to the various segments of the organization and communicate the implications of the information being reviewed, including its relevance and reliability. Management accountants thus must understand both the sources and uses of the information.

Resource Management

Management accountants must establish systems which facilitate planning and control of the organization's resources to ensure that their use is consistent with established policies. These systems also should meet the needs of management, investors, creditors, and other interested parties. Some of these needs are:

- Custody and management of working capital, including credit and collections and inventory management.
- Creating and maintaining the most appropriate debt and equity capital structure.
- Developing and implementing a system to control plant, property, and equipment.
- Administering a pension or similar plan.
- Tax planning and compliance.
- Insurance management.
- Creating and operating a system of internal accounting control that can detect misuses of assets, taking into account the cost/benefit aspects of the control system.

Information Systems Development

Design and development of the overall management information system implies:

1. Determining the output required by users
2. Specifying the data inputs needed to obtain the required output
3. Developing the requirements for a processing system that converts input to output
4. Managing and securing the data bases

Technological Implementation

Modern equipment and techniques should be employed to facilitate the selection, accumulation, transmission, analysis, and safeguarding of information. Management accountants therefore should be familiar with current technology relative to information processing and the accounting techniques appropriate to controlling and using the information. Some examples are:

- Computer applications—basic accounting functions and data-base management techniques in financial planning and decision making, such as models for optimizing asset utilization and resource allocation.
- Network and communications systems.

Verification

Management accountants assure the accuracy and reliability of information derived from the accounting system or related sources that is used throughout the organization. They also must be satisfied that actions taking place throughout the entity are consistent with policies of the organization. Both of these activities use the internal control system and are reviewed by internal audit.

Administration

Administration includes development and maintenance of an effective and efficient management accounting organization. This organization addresses and resolves issues relevant to the accounting and financial structure such as:

- Assignment of management accounting responsibilities
- Interface between accounting and other operations
- Delegation of authority and determinations relevant to centralization or decentralization
- Recruiting, training, and developing personnel in the various areas of responsibility
- Separation of duties

Other important administrative activities performed by management accountants include the development and maintenance of:

- Accounting policy and procedure manuals
- A cost-effective records management program
- Records adequate to meet the requirements of tax laws, other laws and regulatory agencies, and independent auditors

Processes

Certain operational processes are inherent throughout the range of activities described in the preceding section. These include:

1. Identification-recognition and evaluation of business transactions and other economic events for appropriate accounting action.
2. Measurement-quantification, including estimates, of business transactions or other economic events that have occurred or forecasts of those that may occur.
3. Accumulation-disciplined and consistent approaches to recording and classifying appropriate business transactions and other economic events.
4. Analysis-determination of the reasons for the reported activity and its relationship with other economic events and circumstances.
5. Preparation and Interpretation-meaningful coordination of accounting and/or planning data to provide information, presented logically, and including, if appropriate, the conclusions drawn from those data.
6. Communication-reporting pertinent information to management and others for internal and external uses.

Questions

1-1. Why should a Certified Public Accountant (CPA) know the principles and methods of cost accounting?

1-2. What is meant by "an intelligent consumer of accounting information"?

1-3. What external objectives does cost accounting serve? What internal objectives?

1-4. Accounting principles for external reporting are incorporated in Generally Accepted Accounting Principles (GAAP). What are the accounting principles for internal reporting called?

1-5. Name some accounting practices which are used for external reporting that may not be appropriate for internal reporting.

1-6. Classify each of the following positions in an organization as either a line or a staff position:

a. President

b. Controller

c. Production manager

d. Budgetary accountant

e. Sales manager

f. Corporate planner

g. Production scheduler

h. Engineering manager

i. Salesperson

1-7. What distinguishes operating management from middle management?

1-8. Describe the major duties of the controller.

1-9. Who typically reports to the controller? To whom does the controller report?

1-10. Management accounting is considered a profession. What distinguishes a profession from a vocation?

1-11. Why is the term "management accountant" a more appropriate title for an accountant in industry than the term "cost accountant"?

1-12. What knowledge should a management accountant have to effectively serve as an advisor to management?

1-13. Why should a management accountant consider becoming a CMA?

1-14. Objectives of Management Accounting

There has been a significant expansion of the responsibilities of management accounting and the management accountant over the past 30 years. This expansion that has evolved in practice has been well documented in current accounting and business periodicals as well as modern cost and managerial accounting textbooks. In fact, the Management Accounting Practices Committee of the Institute of Management Accountants issued a statement in 1982 entitled, ***Objectives of Management Accounting*** that identified and described major responsibilities of the management accounting function:

Required:

(a) Identify and describe five major areas of responsibility for the management accounting function.

(b) Describe how effective performances of these major areas of responsibility contribute to the success of an organization.

(*IMA adapted*)

1. *To discuss cost accounting objectives and relate them to different management information needs.*
2. *To distinguish different classifications of costs based on their characteristics.*
3. *To show the flow of manufacturing costs.*
4. *To introduce the statement of cost of goods manufactured.*
5. *To compare the financial statements of manufacturing firms and merchandising firms.*

2

Cost Accounting and Objectives and Cost Classifications

Costs are resources sacrificed or foregone to achieve a specific objective. Cost accounting measures the amount of resources sacrificed or foregone for an activity, a need, or a plan. As was discussed in Chapter One, different measurements of cost are needed for different purposes. The purpose of this chapter is to present a number of important concepts in cost accounting theory and practice. The different cost accounting objectives are described. Some cost classifications and terms are discussed in order to provide a working knowledge of different cost measurements for different purposes. A comparison of the financial statements prepared by a manufacturing firm and those prepared by a merchandising firm is presented. While the discussion will center around manufacturing activities, the concepts discussed in this chapter can be applied to service activities as well.

Cost Accounting Objectives

Cost accounting systems are designed to serve management's information needs; thus, cost accounting objectives are derived from those needs. In general, cost accounting objectives may be grouped into three areas:

1. Product costing for inventory valuation and income determination,
2. Providing information for planning and control of operations,
3. Providing cost data for managerial decision making.

Product Costing

An important objective of cost accounting is to provide unit product costs for internal and external reporting purposes. Unit product costs are used within the organization for pricing decisions. They are used in external reporting for inventory valuation and the determination of cost of goods sold. In current cost accounting practice, the product costing objective is achieved by different costing procedures and alternative systems for accumulating, recording, and analyzing cost data.

Planning and Control of Operations

Another objective of cost accounting is to provide information for management's planning and control of operations. Planning of operations is a basic management process that goes on at all levels in an organization. In the planning function, cost accounting provides budgets for each functional area of activity and for a firm's overall operations for a future period of time. Budgets are used to provide guidelines for operations and benchmarks for evaluating managerial performance. Control of operations involves monitoring the activities of the organization and reporting deviations of actual results from those budgeted. In the control function, cost accounting provides management with performance reports, variance analysis, and other forms of feedback. Control is intended to achieve conformity between actual results and the plans that have been incorporated in budgets.

Relevant Information for Decisions

Another important objective of cost accounting is to provide cost data for management's decisions in evaluating alternative courses of action. Adding or dropping a product line, making or buying a component part, replacing old equipment, and accepting or rejecting an order are some of the special decisions for which cost accounting provides useful information.

Cost Classifications

Production of goods or services requires the consumption of resources such as materials, labor, and fixed assets. The use of these resources in any activity results in a cost. Management requires information on costs for purposes of planning, control and decision-making. However, no single kind of cost measure is useful in all managerial planning and control situations; different concepts of cost exist for different managerial purposes. It is important for the users and providers of cost data to understand the basic cost terminology and classification systems for different cost accounting objectives. The following discussion provides a description of various cost classification systems that have been developed by accountants to satisfy management information needs. These classification systems are not mutually exclusive; a cost may be classified according to any one of them.

Variable Costs, Fixed Costs, Semi-Fixed Costs, and Mixed Costs

By observing the relationship between the behavior of a total cost and changes in the measure of activity (such as units produced, units sold, labor hours, and machine hours), a cost can be classified as variable, fixed, semifixed, or mixed.

Variable costs are those total costs that change in direct proportion to changes in the activity level. When the activity level is zero, the total variable cost is equal to zero. As the activity level increases, the total cost increases at a constant rate. However, the cost per unit stays the same. Examples of variable costs include costs of materials and parts, assembly labor costs, sales commissions, and some supplies. Illustration 2-1 shows the relationship between a specific example of variable cost, the cost of direct material, and activity measured in units produced.

Fixed costs are those in which total cost remains constant over a given range of output, while the cost per unit varies inversely with output. For example, the fixed costs identified in Illustration 2-2 will remain at $2,000 a year if production is between 0 and 40 units. At 25 units of production, the fixed cost is $2,000 or $80 per unit ($2,000/25). At 40 units of production, the fixed cost remains at $2,000, but the fixed cost per unit reduced to only $50 ($2,000/40). Straight-line depreciation, property taxes, rent, salaries of top management, and insurance are some examples of fixed costs.

For purposes of planning and control, fixed costs are sometimes identified as "committed fixed costs" or "discretionary fixed costs." Committed fixed costs are those fixed costs that the firm will incur because of commitments made by management. Essentially, committed fixed costs represent the long-term costs that must be incurred if the firm is to maintain its planned volume or level of activity. Typical committed fixed costs include depreciation, rental on buildings or equipment, property taxes and insurance, and salaries of key personnel. Discretionary fixed costs (also referred to as programmed or managed fixed costs) are those fixed costs that arise from periodic management appropriation decisions. This type of fixed costs does not necessarily relate to the anticipated level of activity. Examples of discretionary fixed costs include research and development, advertising, public relations, employee training programs, and management consulting services.

Semi-fixed costs vary in stairstep fashion and thus do not fit the definitions of either variable costs or fixed costs. Semi-fixed costs remain unchanged only over a limited range of activity. Inspection costs and supervisor's salaries are examples of costs which behave in this manner. To illustrate, assume that an inspector can inspect 1,000 units a month. If 2,000 units are to be inspected each month, two inspectors would be needed. If more than 2,000 units are to be inspected, additional inspector(s) must be added. Although an inspector's monthly salary,

Illustration 2-1 Variable Cost-Material Costs ($2 per unit produced)

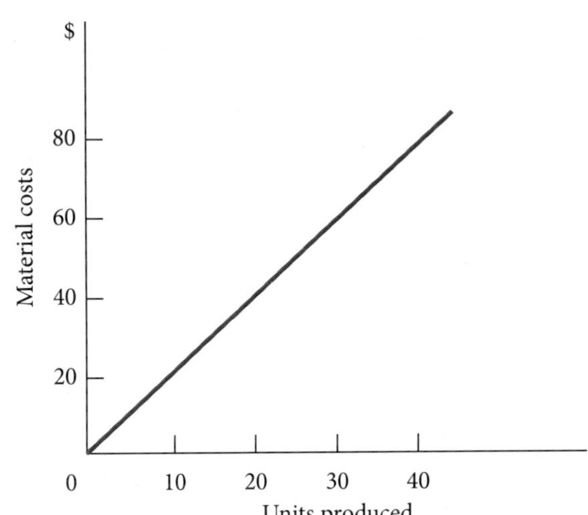

Illustration 2-2 Fixed Costs and Activity ($2,000 a year)

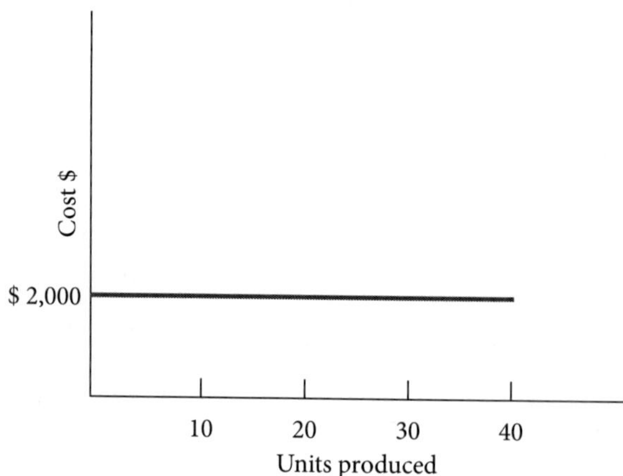

say $1,500 is fixed, the number of inspectors may vary. Thus, total inspection costs are fixed within an activity range of 1,000 units. The range of activity over which a semifixed cost remains constant is called the *relevant range.* This example of semi-fixed inspection costs is depicted graphically in Illustration 2-3.

In practice, when the steps for a semi-fixed cost are relatively small, the cost is treated as a variable cost. If the steps are very large, the step cost is treated as a fixed cost.

Mixed or *semi-variable costs* are those costs that include a fixed element and a variable element. The fixed cost element is the minimum cost incurred, which occurs at zero activity. The variable cost element is the portion of the mixed cost that is caused by changes in activity. Mixed costs, as the term implies, do not fit the definition of variable costs because they are not equal to zero when the activity is zero. Nor are they considered fixed costs because they change when the activity level changes. Car rentals, telephone expenses and a salesperson's pay consisting of a fixed salary plus commission are examples of mixed costs. Illustration 2-4 provides an example where the fixed element is $15,000 and the variable element is $5 per unit.

Period Costs and Product Costs

Theoretically all costs begin their existence in a business as assets, that are acquired by a business because they have potential value in producing future revenues. They are matched against revenue when consumed in producing the revenue. In practice, some goods and services are consumed entirely or substantially in the accounting period in which they are purchased. In cost accounting such costs are called *period costs* and are recorded as expenses in the period in which the resources are consumed. Salesperson's and top executives' pay, utility services used in administrative buildings, and repairs to office furniture are examples. Other costs such as inventory of sales supplies and office furniture are recorded as assets but become expenses (period costs) as they are used up or depreciated. Period costs typically appear in the selling and administrative expenses section of the income statement.

All costs incurred in the manufacturing processes of a business are recorded as assets and are called *product costs* because they can be readily associated with the finished products. In addition to direct materials, all wages in a factory, including those of workers, janitors, and supervisors, are product costs and become a part of the cost of the inventory of finished goods. Product costs remain an asset until the finished product is sold to the customer. At that time

Illustration 2-3 Semi-Fixed Cost of Inspection ($1,500 a month for 1,000 units)

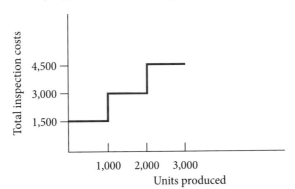

Illustration 2-4 Mixed Cost (Total Costs = $15,000 + $5 per Unit)

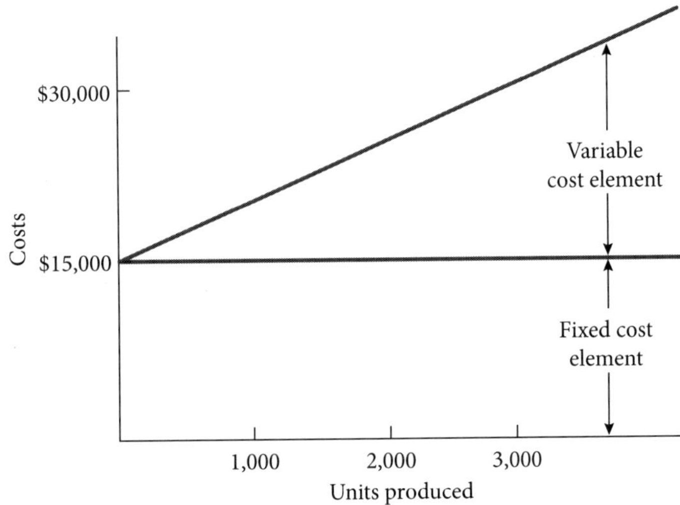

they are included in cost of goods sold and their costs are matched against revenue. This approach is followed whether the finished product is sold several months later or, in certain cases, as soon as it is completed.

MANUFACTURING COSTS AND NON-MANUFACTURING COSTS

Costs can be classified according to management function as either manufacturing costs or non-manufacturing costs. All manufacturing costs are considered as product costs. The costs of unsold products are treated as assets and appear in the balance sheet. The costs of products sold are included in cost of goods sold and appear in the income statement. Non-manufacturing costs include selling and administrative expenses, and are generally treated as period costs in the income statement.

Manufacturing costs are those costs that are associated with the output from a production process. Traditionally, manufacturing costs are classified into three elements: (1) direct materials, (2) direct labor, and (3) factory overhead.

Direct Materials are raw materials that become an integral part of the finished product. For example, in manufacturing furniture the wood is a direct material. Conceptually, minor items such as glue, nails, and screws used to assemble the furniture are also direct materials because they are an integral part of the furniture. In practice, they are not treated as direct materials because the cost of tracing minor items is not worth the benefit of having more accurate product costs. Minor material items are usually considered as supplies or indirect materials and are included in factory overhead.

Direct Labor costs are those costs associated with labor involved directly in production of the output. Examples of direct labor costs include the wages of machine operators and assemblers in a furniture factory. The wages of personnel indirectly involved in the production of a product, such as inspectors and plant guards, are called *indirect labor* and are included in factory overhead. Three labor related costs (overtime premium, idle time, and payroll fringe benefits) need further discussion.

Overtime premium paid to factory workers is usually treated as a part of factory overhead. Even though overtime is spent on a particular job or product, production is normally scheduled on a random basis. In this situation it would be unfair to charge an overtime premium to a particular job or product. The overtime premium should be regarded as factory overhead and borne by all jobs and units produced during the period. In some cases, overtime is needed for a particular job because of rush order. Then the overtime premium associated with the job should be treated as direct labor and assigned to the products which required the rush order.

The cost of idle time represents wages paid for unproductive labor arising from machine breakdowns, materials shortages, power failures, faulty production scheduling or bad weather. This cost should be treated as indirect labor and included in factory overhead.

The following example illustrates the allocation of labor costs to direct labor, overtime premium, and idle time. Assume that a machine operator earns $10 per hour and works 42 hours during a given week, including idle time of 4 hours due to materials shortages. The allocation of the operator's gross earnings, $10 (42) + $5 (2) = $430, would be as follows:

Direct labor	$10 (38) = $380
Overtime Premium (factory overhead)	$ 5 (2) = 10
Idle time (factory overhead)	$10 (4) = 40
Gross earnings	$430

Payroll fringe benefits include items such as employer contributions to FICA, life insurance, hospitalization plans, pension plans, vacation pay, and other employee benefits. In most companies, they are treated as factory overhead. However, some companies distinguish between fringe benefits relating to direct labor and those relating to indirect labor. In this case, the portion relating to direct labor is treated as direct labor costs and the portion relating to indirect labor is considered a part of factory overhead.

Factory Overhead Costs include all manufacturing costs other than direct materials and direct labor, and are sometimes referred to as *indirect manufacturing costs.* Examples are indirect materials, indirect labor, rent, taxes, insurance, depreciation on equipment, water, electricity, and power used in the production process. Factory overhead may be subclassified into two categories depending on cost behavior. They are:

1. Variable factory overhead—Examples are utilities, supplies, indirect materials, and indirect labor which varies in direct proportion to the activity level, and
2. Fixed factory overhead—Examples are rent, insurance, property taxes, depreciation, and supervisory salaries. They do not change as the activity level changes.

Prime Costs and Conversion Costs

Direct materials and direct labor are called the *prime cost* of a product. These two cost elements can be directly associated with the product and are the major part of its cost. On the other hand, labor and factory overhead together are called the *conversion costs* (or the processing costs) of the product. These two cost elements are incurred to convert raw materials into finished products. Direct labor is both a prime cost and a conversion cost as shown below.

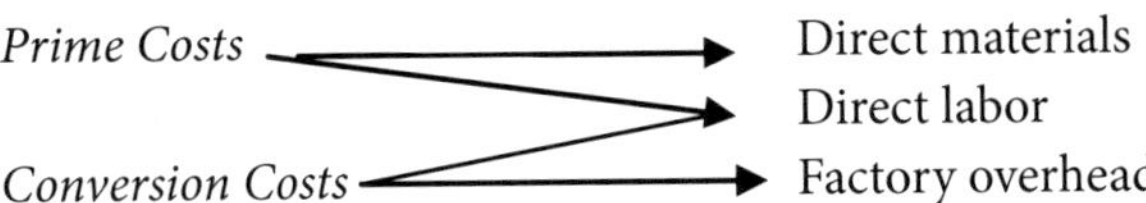

In the case of a service organization, direct labor would be the major prime cost.

Direct Costs and Indirect Costs

The manner in which costs are associated with products, activities, or departments determines whether they will be classified as direct costs or indirect costs. *Direct costs* are those costs that can be directly associated with a product, an activity, or a department. For example, the costs of direct materials and labor are direct costs of a production department. The cost of labor for repairs and maintenance are a direct cost of a maintenance department. *Indirect costs* are those costs that cannot be directly associated with a product, an activity, or a department. These costs can be associated with such cost objects only through allocation. For example, the cost of above maintenance department is an indirect cost to each production department, and will be allocated to the production departments. The procedures to accomplish this will be described in a later chapter.

The distinction between a direct cost and an indirect cost depends upon the unit of product, activity, or organization under consideration. A cost could be a direct cost to one unit and an indirect cost to another unit. For example, a supervisor's salary may be a direct cost to the production department but an indirect cost to the product being produced in the department.

Controllable and Uncontrollable Costs

In order to evaluate a manager's performance, accountants may classify costs as being either controllable or uncontrollable. *Controllable costs* are those that may be regulated by a given manager in the organization. When the amount of a cost is under a manager's control, it is considered a controllable cost by that manager. For example, if the manager of a production department has control over the amount of a material used in the manufacturing process, the raw material cost is controllable by the manager. However, if a manager has no control over the rental expense on equipment, the rent is not a controllable cost for the manager.

All costs are controllable to some extent by someone in the organization. Thus, it is incorrect to say that all variable costs are controllable and all fixed costs are uncontrollable. For example, rental expense for equipment is a fixed cost which may be uncontrollable by the production manager, but is a controllable cost to the executive vice-president. One should also not conclude that direct costs are controllable and indirect costs are uncontrollable. For example, if the company president undertakes an advertising campaign for Product A, the advertising cost is a direct cost to Product A but it is not controllable by the manager of Product A.

Cost Classifications for Decision Making

Decision making by management is essentially a process of choosing among alternatives. Usually, alternative courses of action are first identified. Costs associated with each alternative are then estimated. The most desirable alternative is selected from a comparison of net benefits expected from the alternatives. Some cost terms that are useful to management in making decisions are: (1) incremental costs, (2) sunk costs, and (3) opportunity costs.

Incremental costs are defined as the difference in total costs between two decision alternatives. For example, suppose management wishes to choose between two production levels. The cost of producing 1,000 units is $15,000, and of producing 2,000 units is $30,000. Then, the incremental production cost associated with the additional 1,000 units is $15,000.

Used in this context, incremental costs in accounting are similar in concept to marginal costs in economics. However, a marginal cost is associated with a single additional unit of output. Incremental costs of production may refer to major changes in production levels.

Sunk costs are costs that have already been incurred and result from management's decisions in the past. They are irrelevant for making decisions about the future. For example, the original cost of a machine is a sunk cost in a decision to keep a machine or to replace it. The cost of the machine cannot be changed and thus is irrelevant to the decision making process except in the calculation of any income tax liability from a gain or loss.

Opportunity costs are the benefits of an alternative that is given up when a different decision alternative is chosen. Opportunity costs are not recorded in formal accounting systems, but may be significant in evaluating an alternative course of action. For example, suppose a firm can either use its current extra capacity of 10,000 machine hours to process a product further or rent the extra capacity to another firm for $15,000. In this case, the $15,000 is an opportunity cost of choosing to further process the product. Opportunity costs are defined in relation to the best alternative that is available to the firm. In the previous example, if there is a third alternative that will provide $20,000 of profit, then the opportunity cost of utilizing the facility to further process the product is $20,000. If there is no other alternative to utilize the capacity, there will be no opportunity costs.

Manufacturing Cost Flows

The accounting process for recording manufacturing costs parallels the actual physical flow of the products being manufactured. Certain costs such as prepaid insurance, manufacturing supplies, raw materials, buildings, machinery and tools are first recorded as assets in appropriate accounts. As these assets are consumed in the manufacturing process, they are classified as direct materials or manufacturing overhead items. Direct labor is recorded when the factory wages are accrued. These three types of costs, direct materials, direct labor, and factory overhead are then transferred to the work-in-process inventory account. Schematically this flow may be represented as follows:

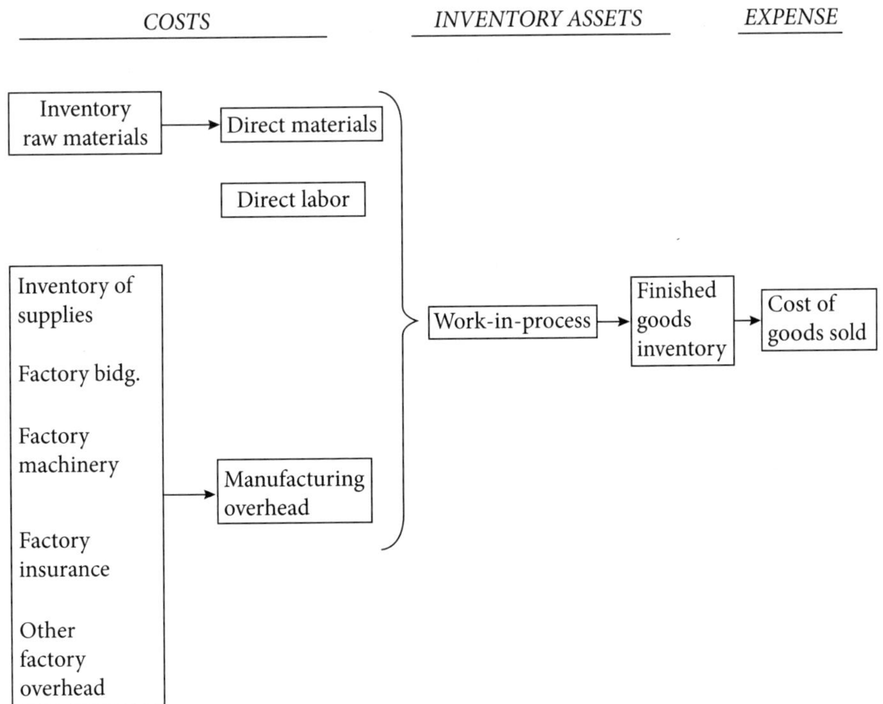

As direct materials, direct labor, and factory overhead costs are incurred in the manufacturing process, they are classified as work-in-process. At the end of any period, some of these costs generally will be retained in the work-in-process inventory account to represent costs of incomplete products. As the products are completed and transferred to the finished goods warehouse, their costs are transferred to the finished goods inventory account. At the end of any period, some finished products will be on hand and the finished goods inventory account will contain the total manufacturing costs of these items. When the finished products are sold and delivered to the customer, their costs are recorded as a part of cost of goods sold for the period.

Financial Statements for a Manufacturing Firm

The purpose of a manufacturing process is to convert raw materials into finished products by using services from labor and production facilities. Accounting for a manufacturing process utilizes many cost terms that are not present in a merchandising or retail business. Thus, the financial statements prepared by a manufacturing firm are more complex than those prepared by a merchandising firm.

The Income Statement

Illustration 2-5 compares the income statement of a manufacturing firm to the income statement of a merchandising firm. The major difference between the income statements is in the computation of cost of goods sold. In a merchandising firm, the cost of goods sold is determined by adding purchases to the beginning merchandise inventory and subtracting from this total the ending merchandise inventory. In a manufacturing firm, the *cost of goods manufactured* must be calculated, and is usually supported by a separate schedule. This schedule contains the three elements of manufacturing costs and the beginning and the ending work-in-process. The three elements of manufacturing costs are direct materials, direct labor, and factory overhead which were discussed earlier in this chapter. Work-in-process represents the cost of partially completed goods which still remain in production at the end of a period.

The periodic method of calculating the cost of inventory used appears in three places in the cost of goods manufactured statement and in the income statement of a manufacturing firm, as shown below (the amounts are from Illustration 2-5):

> Direct Materials Used (50,000) = Beginning DM Inventory (30,000) + DM Purchases (40,000) – Ending DM (20,000)
>
> Cost of Goods Manufactured (80,000) = Beginning Work-in-Process (20,000) + DM Used (50,000) + Direct Labor (40,000) + Factory Overhead (10,000) – Ending Work-in-Process (40,000)
>
> Cost of Goods Sold (60,000) = Beginning Finished Goods (20,000) + Cost of Goods Manufactured (80,000) – Ending Finished Goods Inventory (40,000)

Cost of goods manufactured represents the total cost of all units that have been completed during the period.

The income statement of a service organization is similar to that of a manufacturing organization, but differs in several important respects. First, supplies are also a part of services rendered, but a separate calculation of direct material and supplies used does not appear if the amount is insignificant. If this is the case, any material and supplies used are treated as part of overhead. Second, while a cost of goods manufactured calculation appears, a cost of goods sold calculation is not necessary. This is because service organizations usually invoice their customers as soon as the work is done, and do not maintain an "inventory" of finished services. The cost of goods manufactured is therefore the same as cost of goods sold, and is renamed cost of services.

Illustration 2-5 Comparison of Income Statements

Income Statement for a Manufacturing Firm

Sales		$100,000
Less: Cost of Goods Sold:		
Finished Goods (Beg.)	$20,000	
Cost of Goods Manufactured (See Schedule)	80,000	
Finished Goods (Ending)	(40,000)	60,000
Gross Margin		40,000
Less: Selling and Administrative Expenses		10,000
Operating Income		$30,000

Schedule of Cost of Goods Manufactured

Direct Materials:		
Inventory (Beginning)	$30,000	
Purchases	40,000	
Inventory (Ending)	(20,000)	
Direct Materials Used		$ 50,000
Direct Labor		40,000
Factory Overhead:		
Indirect Materials	$ 2,000	
Indirect Labor	1,000	
Utilities	1,500	
Insurance	500	
Property Taxes	2,000	
Depreciation-Equipment	1,000	
Depreciation-Plant Building	1,500	
Miscellaneous	500	10,000
Total Manufacturing costs incurred during the period		100,000
Add: Work-in-process (Beginning)		20,000
Less: Work-in-process (Ending)		(40,000)
Cost of Goods Manufactured		$ 80,000

Income Statement for a Merchandising firm

Sales		$50,000
Less: Cost of Goods Sold:		
Merchandise Inventory (Beg.)	$10,000	
Purchases	30,000	
Merchandising Inventory (Ending)	(5,000)	35,000
Gross Margin		15,000
Less: Selling and Administrative Expenses		5,000
Operating Income		$10,000

Illustration 2-6 Comparison of Current Asset Sections of Balance Sheets

For a Manufacturing Firm			*For a Merchandising Firm*	
Cash..		$ 5.000	Cash..	S 5,000
Accounts Receivable..............		20,000	Accounts Receivable.....................	10,000
Inventories:			Merchandise Inventories.............	13,000
Materials and Supplies.........	$21,000			
Work-in-Process.....................	40.000			
Finished Goods.......................	40,000	$101,000		
Prepaid Expenses....................		4,000	Prepaid Expenses............................	1,000
Total Current Assets..............		5130,000	Total Current Assets......................	S31,000

The Balance Sheet

Illustration 2-6 compares the current asset section of the balance sheet of a manufacturing firm with that of a merchandising firm. The manufacturing firm reports three classes of inventory: materials and supplies inventory, work-in-process inventory, and finished goods inventory. The balance sheet of the merchandising firm has only one class-merchandise inventory. The balance sheet of a service organization would show work-in-process inventory, and it would also show materials and supplies inventory if the amount was significant.

Summary

Cost accounting recognizes three primary objectives: (1) product costing, (2) providing information for planning and control of operations, and (3) providing information for managerial decision making. A cost accounting system should be designed to serve each of these objectives. However, there is no single concept of cost that is appropriate for all of the purposes. This chapter has presented some basic cost terms and cost classifications that have been developed by accountants to satisfy management information needs. Additional cost terms will be introduced in later chapters. An understanding of these cost terms and classifications is essential to an understanding of cost accounting.

Key Definitions

Committed fixed costs Fixed costs that the firm will incur because of commitments made by management.

Controllable costs Costs that can be directly regulated by a given manager in the organization.

Conversion cost Direct labor and factory overhead costs associated with a product.

Cost of goods manufactured	The cost of all goods completed during a period.
Direct cost	Costs that can be directly associated with a product, an activity, or a department.
Direct materials	Raw materials that become an integral part of the finished product.
Direct labor	The wages paid to workers directly involved in the production process.
Discretionary fixed costs	Fixed costs that arise from periodic management appropriation decisions.
Factory overhead	All manufacturing costs other than direct materials and direct labor.
Fixed costs	Costs that remain the same in total regardless of changes in the level of activity.
Incremental costs	The difference in total costs between two decision alternatives.
Indirect costs	Costs that cannot be directly associated with a product, an activity, or a department.
Indirect labor	Wages paid to workers indirectly involved in the production of a product, such as materials handling and supervisory wages. Indirect labor is treated as factory overhead.
Manufacturing costs	Costs that are associated with the output from a production process. They are considered as product costs and inventoriable costs.
Mixed (Semi-variable) costs	Costs that include a variable cost element and a fixed cost element.
Non-manufacturing costs	Costs that are associated with non-manufacturing functions such as selling and administration. These costs are generally treated as period costs.
Opportunity costs	The benefit given up with the choice of a decision alternative. Period costs Costs that are recorded as expenses and matched against revenue in the period in which they are incurred.
Prime costs	Direct materials and direct labor costs of a product.
Product costs	Costs that can be readily associated with units of product. They are matched against revenue when the products are sold.
Relevant range	A range of activity over which a fixed cost remains unchanged.
Semi-fixed costs	Costs that remain unchanged over a limited range of activity.
Sunk costs	Costs that have already been incurred and are not affected by the choice among alternatives.
Variable costs	Costs that change in total in direct proportion to changes in the activity level.
Work-in-process	The cost of partially completed goods that are still in the production process at the end of a period.

Questions

2-1 Discuss three cost accounting objectives.

2-2 Define the relevant range of activity.

2-3 Distinguish between product costs and period costs.

2-4 What are the three major components of manufacturing costs?

2-5 Distinguish between direct materials and indirect materials; between direct labor and indirect labor.

2-6 Define prime costs and conversion costs.

2-7 Distinguish between variable factory overhead and fixed factory overhead.

2-8 What are direct costs? What are indirect costs?

2-9 What are controllable costs? What are uncontrollable costs? Why is it important to distinguish controllable costs and uncontrollable costs?

2-10 Is a fixed cost an incremental cost? Give an example in which a fixed cost is an incremental cost.

2-11 What are sunk costs?

2-12 What are opportunity costs?

2-13 Describe the flow of costs in a manufacturing company.

2-14 What is the major difference between the balance sheets of manufacturing firms and of merchandising firms?

2-15 What is the major difference between the income statements of manufacturing firms and of merchandising firms?

Problems

2-16 *Terminology*

Match each of the following lettered terms on the left with the appropriate numbered definition on the right.

a. Conversion cost
b. Factory overhead
c. Fixed cost
d. Incremental cost
e. Mixed cost
f. Opportunity cost
g. Period cost
h. Product cost
i. Relevant range
j. Variable cost

1. A cost that is directly associated with the finished product
2. Direct labor and factory overhead
3. Total costs remain constant while cost per unit varies with output
4. Recorded as expenses in the period in which they are consumed
5. Total costs that change in direct proportion to changes in the activity level
6. The difference in total costs between two decision alternatives
7. Inspection costs, supervisor salaries
8. A range of activity over which a fixed cost remains unchanged
9. The benefit given up with the choice of an alternative
10. All manufacturing costs other than direct material and direct labor

2-17 *Cost Classification*

The following items are product costs of the Pretex Manufacturing Corp. Classify each item first as a variable, mixed, or fixed cost and, second, as a direct or indirect product cost.

1. Insurance on factory equipment
2. Maintenance of factory building
3. Subcontract cost of part for product
4. Labor for painting product
5. Factory time clerk's wages
6. Factory electricity cost
7. Hardware for product
8. Sandpaper used on product
9. Factory water cost
10. Vacation pay to factory workers

2-18 *Cost Classification*

The Florida Manufacturing Corporation produces desks. Prepare a work sheet with the following columns: Product cost, Period cost, Direct cost, Indirect cost, Fixed cost, Variable cost. Classify each of the following cost items. Any cost item may appear in different columns, but only a product cost may be classified as direct or indirect.

1. Factory telephone base monthly charge
2. Property tax on factory building
3. Transportation-in
4. Transportation-out
5. Desk legs
6. Wage of tool room attendant
7. Salary of vice-president of manufacturing
8. Glue to be used to bind legs to each desk
9. Apprentice workmen training program costs
10. Manufacturing process patent charge based upon number of units produced

2-19 *Controllable Costs and Uncontrollable Costs*

Classify the following costs as controllable or uncontrollable by *the production manager* of the Best Furniture Company.

1. Heat, light and power
2. Straight-line depreciation on production equipment
3. Repairs and maintenance on production equipment
4. Scrap and spoiled goods
5. Amount of materials used
6. Materials purchase cost
7. Overtime and idle time costs (due to scheduling problems)

8. Shipping costs
9. Inspection and supervision
10. Property tax and insurance on the factory

2-20 *Overtime Premium and Idle Time Pay*

Bob Bonds works on the assembly line in the Chicago Company. During the past week, he worked a total of 46 hours including 4 hours of idle time. His hourly wage rate is $8.

Required:

(1) Calculate Bob Bonds' wages for the week.

(2) Allocate the wages between direct labor cost and factory overhead.

2-21 *Opportunity Costs*

Mr. Hilton has been operating a bookstore as a single proprietorship. Recently he has received an offer of $20,000 for the net assets of the bookstore business. He is considering whether to sell the bookstore or to continue to operate it. Assume that: (a) the bookstore annual income is $15,000, (b) Mr. Hilton could find another job and earn $14,000 a year, and (c) Mr. Hilton could invest the offer of $20,000 on bonds yielding 8% per year.

Required: (ignore the gain or loss on sale of assets):

(1) What is the opportunity cost per year for operating the bookstore?

(2) Should Mr. Hilton sell the bookstore? Why?

2-22 *Incremental Costs*

An engineering study has developed the following cost data for the production of product A:

	Factory Overhead		Direct	Direct
Production	Fixed (total)	Variable	Labor	Materials
0–1,000 units	$1,000	$1/unit	$2/unit	$3/unit
1,001–2,000 units	$1,000	$1/unit	$2/unit	$3/unit
2,001–3,000 units	$2,000	$1/unit	$2/unit	$3/unit

(1) If the current production level is 1,500 units, what is the incremental cost of producing an additional 200 units?
(2) If the current production level is 1,500 units, what is the incremental cost of producing an additional 1,000 units?
(3) What is the total prime costs and the total conversion costs for the production of 2,500 units?
(4) If the current production level is 1,500 units, should the firm accept a special order of 1,500 additional units at a unit price of $7?

2-23 *Incremental Costs*

The Benson Company has collected the following production cost data:

	Production		
	0 Units	10 Units	20 Units
Depreciation	$1,000	$1,000	$1,000
Supplies	0	800	1,600
Property Taxes	500	500	500
Labor	0	2,000	4,000
Materials	0	3,000	6,000

In addition, the company has found that repair and maintenance expense follows the following *step* behavior:

Production	Repair and Maintenance Expense
0–5 units	$ 400
6–10 units	800
11–15 units	1,200
16–20 units	1,600

Required:

What would be the incremental production costs for an additional 10 units after the Benson Company has produced 8 units?

2-24 *Statement of Cost of Goods Manufactured*

The following data relate to the Denver Company's operations for the year ended December 31, 20XX:

Direct materials purchases	$100,000
Indirect material usage	10,000
Indirect labor	10,000
Direct labor	300,000
Sales salaries	100,000
Administrative salaries	50,000
Factory water and electricity	20,000
Advertising expenses	60,000
Depreciation-sales and general office	40,000
Depreciation-factory	50,000
Beginning Inventories:	
Direct materials	$20,000
Work-in-process	60,000
Finished goods	80,000
Ending Inventories:	
Direct materials	$30,000
Work-in-process	50,000
Finished goods	60,000

Required:

Prepare a statement of cost of goods manufactured.

2-25 *Manufacturing Costs*

Mat Company's cost of goods sold for the month ended March 31, 20XX, was $345,000. Ending work-in-process inventory was 90% of beginning work-in-process inventory. Factory overhead was $80,000. Other information pertaining to Mat Company's inventories and production for the month of March is as follows:

Beginning inventories—March 1:	
Direct materials	$20,000
Work-in-process	40,000
Finished goods	102,000
Purchases of direct materials during March	110,000
Ending inventories—March 31:	
Direct materials	26,000
Work-in-process	?
Finished goods	105,000

Required:

Prepare a schedule of cost of goods manufactured for the month of March.
Prepare a schedule to compute the prime cost incurred during March.

(*AICPA adapted*)

2-26 *Determining Direct Materials Usage and Work-in-Process*

The Virginia Company is a manufacturing firm. The following data relate to the month of March:

(1) Total manufacturing cost incurred during the month was $100,000,
(2) Cost of goods manufactured was $90,000,
(3) Factory overhead was $20,000 which is equal to 40% of direct labor costs,
(4) Work-in-process at the beginning of the month was 80% of work-in-process at the end of the month.

Required:

Determine direct materials usage during the month.
Determine the beginning and ending work-in-process.

2-27 *Statement of Cost of Goods sold and Income Statement*

The Houston Company, a manufacturer, had the following beginning and ending inventory for the year ending December 31, 20XX:

	Beginning	*Ending*
Raw materials	$12,000	$ 20,000
Work-in-process	30,000	38,000
Finished goods	20,000	13,000
Indirect materials and supplies	20,000	10,000

During the year the following transactions occurred:

Sales	$700,000
Raw materials purchased	320,000
Indirect materials and supplies purchased	30,000
Direct labor cost	100,000
Indirect labor cost	50,000
Property taxes and depreciation on factory building	20,000
Property taxes and depreciation on sales office and general office	10,000
Utilities (60% to factory; 40% to sales office and general office)	40,000
Sales staff's salaries	30,000
Office salaries	34,000
Sales staff's commission	7,000

Required:

(1) Prepare a statement of cost of goods manufactured for the year.

(2) Prepare an income statement for the year.

2-28 *Cost of Goods Manufactured and Sold (Spreadsheet)*

Gay's Auto Repair Shop had the following inventory balances during July 2006:

Inventories	*July 1, 2006*	*July 31, 2006*
Direct Materials	$150,000	$178,000
Work in process	200,000	210,000
Finished goods	70,000	52,000

During the month of July the company purchased $50,000 of direct materials and incurred $13,000 of direct labor costs. Factory overhead was 75% of direct labor costs.

Required:

(a) Using a computer spreadsheet program, prepare a schedule which computes the cost of goods manufactured and the cost of goods sold for July. Follow the format shown in the chapter for the income statement of a manufacturing firm.

(b) Use this schedule to show the effect on cost of goods manufactured and sold if purchases of direct materials increases to $60,000 and ending finished goods inventory decreases to $48,000.

2-29 *Statement of Costs of Goods Manufactured*

The following data have been collected for a manufacturing company for the year ending December 31, 20XX:

Inventories	*January 1, 20XX*	*December 31, 20XX*
Raw materials	$ 40,000	$45,000
Work-in-process	20,000	15,000
Finished goods	60,000	50,000

Other items recorded during the year:

Purchases of raw materials	$120,000
Factory overhead costs	80,000
Cost of goods sold	400,000

Required:

Prepare a statement of costs of goods manufactured for the year ending December 31, 20XX.

1. *To illustrate how cost behavior patterns can be used in estimating future costs.*
2. *To study the common accounting and statistical techniques which are useful in determining cost behavior patterns.*
3. *To discuss the advantages and weaknesses of each cost estimation technique.*

3 Cost Estimation

In the discussion of cost classifications in Chapter Two, we stated that costs can be classified by cost behavior patterns. Cost behavior shows how a cost will change with changes in the level of activity. A proper analysis of cost behavior patterns is the foundation for the planning and control of operations. An analysis of cost behavior patterns is also useful for some special managerial decisions.

The cost behavior patterns discussed in Chapter 2 were variable, fixed, semi-fixed, and mixed. For purposes of planning and controlling operations and certain types of special decisions, mixed costs are separated into fixed cost components and variable cost components; semi-fixed costs are treated as fixed costs. In this way all costs are classified as either fixed or variable costs. The purpose of this chapter is to introduce some methods that can be used by accountants to determine cost behavior patterns (or cost functions) for purposes of estimating future costs.

In general, methods used to estimate costs can be classified into two broad categories: the engineering approach and the analysis of historical cost approach. The engineering approach relies on an engineering study to specify the physical relationship between the input and the output of the manufacturing process. In contrast, analysis of historical costs yields cost estimates based on past experience about different levels of costs and different levels of activity. According to the degree of difficulty and sophistication, the analysis of historical cost approach can be subdivided into several methods: the account classification method, the high-low method, the scattergraph method, simple regression analysis, and multiple regression analysis.

The Engineering Approach

The engineering approach derives the physical relationships between inputs and outputs in a manufacturing process from an engineering study. The engineering study involves a quantitative analysis of what costs should be. This analysis is usually based upon the engineer's evaluation of the production method, the materials specifications, labor and equipment requirements, and efficiency of production. Once the relationships between the production factors and outputs are established, the production cost can be estimated by assigning the unit cost of a production factor to the quantity required. For example, if the raw material requirement for producing a product is specified by an engineering study to be 5 pounds of material A and the accounting record shows that the unit cost of material A is $10/lb., the total material cost of producing one unit of the product will be:

$$\$10 \text{ x } 5 = \$50.$$

The engineering approach may be used in situations where no past experience is available with the relationship between costs and the activity level. It may be particularly useful in estimating the relationships between a prime cost (direct materials or direct labor) and activity because this relationship can be directly observed and measured. However, the engineering approach is not useful in estimating those costs that cannot be directly associated with an activity base, such as the costs of utilities, supervision, repairs and maintenance. The engineering approach may tend to be an expensive method because extensive analysis is necessary to specify the relationship between production factors and the units produced.

Analysis of Historical Costs

The analysis of historical cost approach obtains cost estimates based on the relationship between costs and activity in past periods. The usefulness of approach depends upon the consistency of the historical relationship between the cost and activity. If the underlying cost structure remains unchanged over periods of time, the historical relationship between the cost and activity should be reliable as a basis for estimating future costs. If the underlying cost structure changes, the historical relationship without adjustment may be inappropriate for cost estimation.

Regardless of which method is used to analyze historical cost data, certain steps are necessary before reliable results can be obtained. These include:

1. Selection of Independent Variable-The independent variable used for cost estimation should be an activity measure that causes the major effect (or change) in the cost to be estimated. The most widely used variables are direct labor hours, the number of units produced, and machine hours. The independent variable must first be selected before the analysis can be carried further. Selection of the independent variable is normally based upon the manager's or accountant's belief that some relationship exists between the independent variable and the cost to be estimated.
2. Observation and Examination of Historical Data-A number of observations are made from accounting records of past costs at varying values of the independent variable. The number of observations should be large enough and the time period under consideration should be long enough to permit collection of meaningful data. The observations should

cover a wide range of values of the independent variable and of costs. If the range of observations is not wide enough, variation from period to period in cost and in the independent variable may be insignificant. Without an adequate range of observations, the relationship between cost and the independent variable cannot be estimated effectively. An analyst should make sure that the cost and activity data that are recorded have been incurred in the same accounting period.

3. Observation of Data for Homogeneity-Data must be collected under the same conditions. For example, changes in price level during the time period being analyzed may require adjustment to insure that the cost data under consideration are on the same purchasing power base. Observations made under a different production technology should be excluded from the analysis.
4. Determination of the Usefulness of the Data-Cost observations should be plotted against the observed activity on a scatter diagram to determine the usefulness of data. Any unusual or extreme observation should be excluded from analysis.

The Account Classification Method

This method is also referred to as the "accountant's approach" because it relies heavily on the accountant's professional judgment. According to this method, the accountant first obtains the actual activity and cost data for a period and then classifies each cost (including mixed costs) into variable and fixed categories. The total cost in the fixed cost category provides the estimated fixed cost. The total cost in the variable cost category divided by activity in the period provides the estimated variable unit cost. Then the cost estimate for an output level X is given by the following formula:

$$TC = a + bX$$

where
TC = estimated total cost
a = estimated fixed cost
b = estimated variable cost per unit
X = number of units to be produced

Illustration 3-1 demonstrates the account classification method of cost estimation, in which an accountant estimated the fixed and variable portion of the total cost.

Actual production = 1,000 units
a = \$ 8,000
b = \$37,000/1,000 = \$37

The cost-estimating equation for the example would be:

$$TC = \$8{,}000 + \$37\,(X).$$

Based on this estimating equation, the estimated total cost of a production of 1,100 units for the example is:

$$TC = \$8{,}000 + \$37\,(1{,}100) = \$48{,}700.$$

Illustration 3-1 The Account Classification Method

Account	Actual Cost	Variable	Fixed
Direct Materials	$10,000	$10,000	
Direct Labor	20,000	20,000	
Factory Overhead			
Indirect Labor	2,000	1,000	1,000
Indirect Materials	1,000	1,000	
Utilities	5,000	4,000	1,000
Depreciation (Straight line)	4,000		4,000
Repairs and Maintenance	2,000	1,000	1,000
Miscellaneous	1,000		1,000
Total	$45,000	$37,000	$8,000

Advantages and Weaknesses The primary advantage of the account classification method is that the technique is easy and inexpensive. It is particularly suited for new products because it requires only one period's production data. However, the method has weaknesses:

1. It is subjective. It relies heavily on the initial judgment of the accountant to classify a cost into fixed or variable costs. Different accountants may develop different cost estimates from the same data.
2. It relies on a single observation to develop the cost-estimating equation. The method ignores the possibility of variations in the cost-volume relationships from one period to another.
3. The data used in the analysis may reflect inefficient operations. In this case, the method is not appropriate for determining standard costs which may be used for evaluating performance.

The High-Low Method

The high-low method is a simple and basic procedure for cost estimation. It requires only two observations of activity and cost data. One observation is at the highest activity level and the other is at the lowest activity level within a relevant range of activity. The estimate of unit variable cost is obtained by dividing the difference in the two observed costs by the difference in level of activity. An estimate of fixed costs is obtained by subtracting total variable costs at the highest (or lowest) activity from the total costs at the highest (or lowest) activity. The equations for estimating unit variable costs and fixed costs are:

$$b = \frac{TC_k - TC_l}{X_k - X_l}$$

$$a = TC_h - b(X_h) \text{ or}$$
$$= TC_i - b(X_l)$$

where

TC_h = total costs at the highest level of activity

TC_l = total costs at the lowest level of activity

X_h = the highest activity level
X_l = the lowest activity level.

For example, assume that the total production costs and the number of units produced were observed for twelve months. The observations are given in Illustration 3-2.

The month of August shows the highest level of activity with 80 units of production and the associated production cost of $2,300. The month of May is the lowest activity month with 30 units of production and $1,000 of production cost. Using the high-low method, the estimated variable cost and the estimated fixed cost are determined as follows:

$$b = \frac{\$2,300 - \$1,000}{80\,units - 30\,units} = \$26 \ per\ unit$$

a = $2,300 – $26(80) = $220 per month
or = $1,000 – $26(30) = $220 per month.

The equation for estimating the monthly production cost in the example is:

TC = $220 + $26(X).

Advantages and Weaknesses The high-low method is simple and fast. It provides a quick estimate of the cost function. Since the method requires no accountant's judgments to classify costs into fixed and variable, it is more objective than the account classification method. However, the method has several weaknesses. The estimating equation is solely dependent on two observations of production data and ignores information contained in any other observations. Furthermore, the high-low method may overstate or understate the variable cost rate. For example, in the following diagram the unit variable cost rate is overstated.

The method relies on two extreme points and may represent abnormal rather than normal operating conditions.

Illustration 3.2 Production Data for Twelve Months

Month	Production Costs	Units Produced
January	$1,300	40
February	1,800	60
March	2,000	70
April	1,600	50
May	1,000	30 (low)
June	1,900	60
July	2,100	70
August	2,300	80 (high)
September	2,000	60
October	1,950	70
November	1,400	40
December	1,500	50

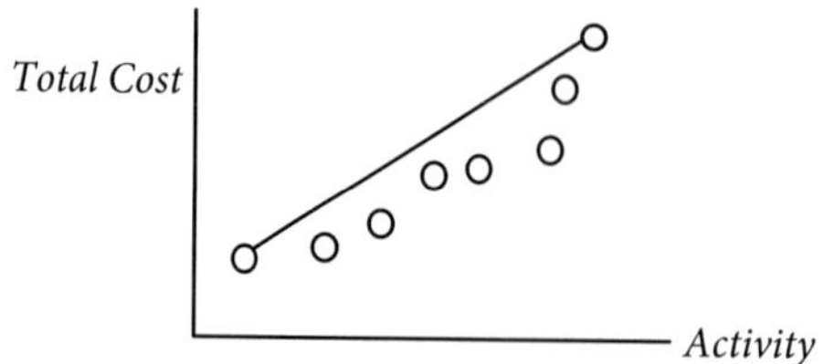

The Scattergraph Method

The scattergraph method requires a plot of cost and activity observations on a graph. The accountant's judgment is used to determine visually a line on the graph that best explains the relationship between changes in cost and changes in the level of activity. Once the line has been determined, any two points on the line are then selected to estimate the fixed cost and the variable cost rate using a procedure similar to the high-low method. Illustration 3-3 presents an example of the scattergraph method of cost estimation.

$$\text{Variable cost per unit, } b = \frac{\$1,000 - \$800}{15 - 5} = \$20$$

Fixed cost, a = \$1,000 – \$20(15) = \$700
or = \$ 800 – \$20(5) = \$700.

The cost-estimating equation for the example is:

$$\text{TC} = \$700 + \$20(\text{X}).$$

Advantages and Weaknesses The graphical presentation provides insight into the strength of the relationship between costs and the activity measure. Thus this method is frequently used in preliminary analyses of possible relationships between the dependent and independent variables. In addition, plotting observed data on a graph helps in determining whether a linear cost function is appropriate and in locating any unusual data points. The major weakness of the method is that it lacks objectivity, and is limited by the judgment of the accountant. Given the same observed data, different accountants may choose different lines to describe the relationship

Illustration 3-3 The Scattergraph Method

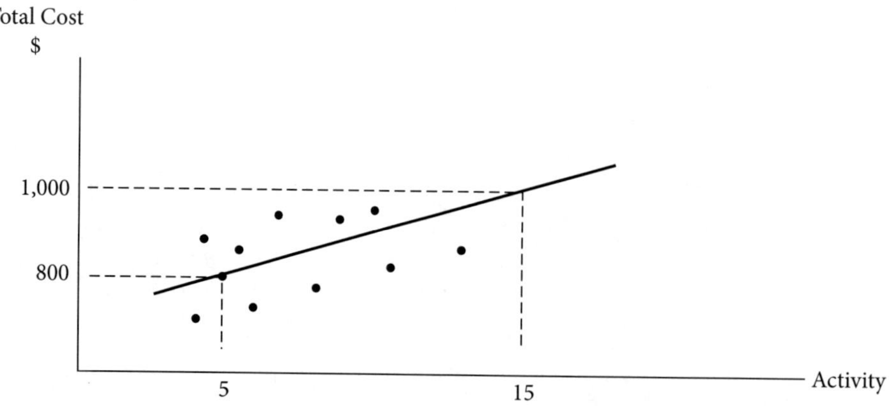

between the dependent and independent variables. Although the method may provide more accurate estimates than the account classification method and the high-low method, it provides no objective tests to evaluate the usefulness of the predicting equation. A more systematic approach to cost estimation is regression analysis which will be discussed in the next section.

Simple Regression Analysis

Regression analysis is a statistical method of measuring the relationship between a dependent variable and one or more independent variables. When the relationship between a dependent variable and one independent variable is studied, the analysis is called *simple regression analysis.* When more than one independent variable is considered, the analysis is called *multiple regression analysis.* This section provides a discussion of simple regression analysis. Multiple regression analysis will be discussed in the Appendix to this chapter.

Regression analysis involves employing a set of mathematical procedures to derive an estimating equation. The first step in simple regression analysis is to identify the independent variable and to plot a set of observations of cost and activity on a scatter diagram. The objective of this step is to determine the form of the relationship between the dependent and d independent variables. If the points that represent the observed data are widely dispersed, there is apparently no relationship between the variables. If the points are in close proximity, a high degree of correlation exists between the variables. In some cases, the points follow a curvilinear relationship. When the points follow a straight line pattern, there is a linear relationship. For example, in Illustration 3-4 a linear relationship has been found between the total cost and the activity level for the data given in Illustration 3-2.

The second step in simple regression analysis is to apply the mathematical method of least squares. This procedure can be easily performed by many widely available standardized computer programs or on some programmed calculators.

The method of least squares determines the equation of the line which provides the best fit to a set of observations. This equation is of the form Y' = a + bX, where Y' is an estimate of total costs, "a" is the fixed cost per time period, and "b" is the unit variable cost. The parameters a and b are selected in order to minimize the sum of the squares of the vertical distances between each observation (Y) and its estimated value (Y). Mathematically, it is denoted as

$$\sum_{i=1}^{n}(Y_i - Y_i')^2$$

Illustration 3-4 Scatter Diagram of Observed Data

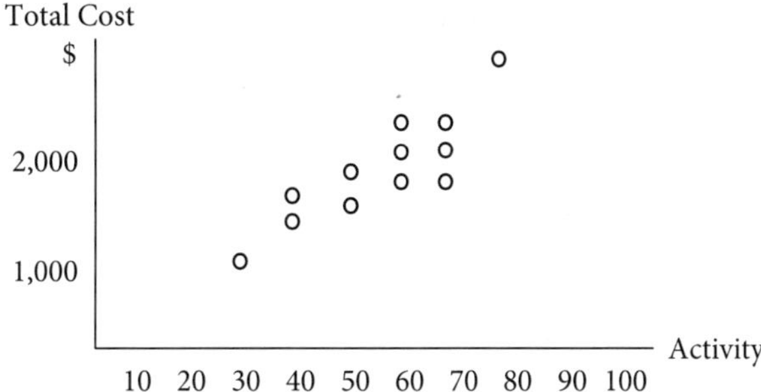

The values of a and b that minimize the sum of squares can be determined by the simultaneous solution of the following two *normal equations:*

$$\Sigma Y = na + b\Sigma$$
$$\Sigma XY = a\Sigma X + b\Sigma X^2$$

In these equations, n is the number of observations from which the line is being constructed. The normal equations can be solved by computing the values of ΣX, ΣY, ΣXY, and ΣX^2 for the set of observations, and then using simultaneous solution techniques. Illustration 3-5 shows the calculation of these values for the data of Illustration 3-2.

Using the values from Illustration 3-5 and substituting them into the normal equations, we obtain two simultaneous equations:

$$20{,}850 = 12a + 680b$$
$$1{,}242{,}500 = 680a + 41{,}000b$$

The simultaneous solution is a = 336.15 and b = 24.73. An alternative approach is to derive equations for a and b:

$$a = \frac{(\Sigma Y)(\Sigma X^2) - (\Sigma X)(\Sigma XY)}{n(\Sigma X^2) - (\Sigma X)^2}$$

$$b = \frac{n(\Sigma XY) - (\Sigma X)(\Sigma Y)}{n(\Sigma X^2) - (\Sigma X)^2}$$

Therefore, the predicting equation for the data in Illustration 3-2 is:

$$Y' = 336.15 + 24.73(X)$$

This predicting equation can be applied to estimate the total production cost for the next period if the expected level of activity is known. For example, if X = 65 units, the estimated total production cost based on the regression equation is:

Illustration 3.5 Computations for Least Squares

Period	*Activity* X	*Cost* Y	XY	X^2
1	40	1,300	52,000	1,600
2	60	1,800	108,000	3,600
3	70	2,000	140,000	4,900
4	50	1,600	80,000	2,500
5	30	1,000	30,000	900
6	60	1,900	114,000	3,600
7	70	2,100	147,000	4,900
8	80	2,300	184,000	6,400
9	60	2,000	120,000	3,600
10	70	1,950	136,500	4,900
11	40	1,400	56,000	1,600
12	50	1,500	75,000	2,500
Total	$\Sigma X = 680$	$\Sigma Y = 20{,}850$	$\Sigma XY = 1{,}242{,}500$	$\Sigma X^2 = 41{,}000$

$$Y' = \$336.15 + \$24.73(65) = \$1{,}943.60$$

Coefficient of Determination and Coefficient of Correlation. An interesting question may be addressed here: How well does the regression line fit to the observations? The question can be answered by calculating the coefficient of determination and the coefficient of correlation. The coefficient of determination, r^2, is a measure of the percent of the total variance that is explained by the variation in the independent variable, X. The total variance, $\Sigma(Y - \bar{Y})^2$ can be separated into an explained variance and an unexplained variance. The explained variance, the difference between the average cost $(\bar{Y})$ and the predicted value Y', represents the variation in Y explained by the variation in X. The unexplained variance is the difference between Y and Y'. Illustration 3-6 shows the variances from one cost observation to the regression line in a diagram.

Mathematically, their relationships can be expressed as:
Total Variance = Explained Variance + Unexplained Variance

$$\text{i.e., } \Sigma(Y - \bar{Y})^2 = \Sigma(Y' - \bar{Y})^2 + \Sigma(Y - Y')^2$$

$$\text{or } 1 = \frac{\Sigma(Y' - \bar{Y})^2}{\Sigma(Y - \bar{Y})^2} + \frac{\Sigma(Y - Y')^2}{\Sigma(Y - \bar{Y})^2}$$

Therefore, the coefficient of determination, r^2, can be determined by:

$$r^2 = \frac{\Sigma(Y' - \bar{Y})^2}{\Sigma(Y - \bar{Y})^2} = \frac{\textit{Explained Variance}}{\textit{Total Variance}}$$

$$\text{or } r^2 = 1 - \frac{\Sigma(Y - Y')^2}{\Sigma(Y - \bar{Y})^2} = 1 - \frac{\textit{Un exp lained Variance}}{\textit{Total Variance}}$$

The range of r^2 is from 0 to 1. When all values of Y' equal $\bar{Y}$, $r^2 = 0$ and no portion of the total variance is explained by the variation in X. On the other hand, when all values of Y' equal Y, $r^2 = 1$. In this case, the total variance is entirely explained by the variation in X and the regression line fits the observations perfectly. Normally, a higher value of r^2 indicates that the regression line provides a better fit to the data from which it was calculated. The coefficient of correlation, r, is simply the square root of r^2. The sign of r is the same as the sign of the regression coefficient b, and its range is from -1 to 1. The coefficient of correlation is a measure of the extent to which Y and X are related. A positive value of r indicates that, as the independent variable X increases,

Illustration 3-6 Measure of Variances

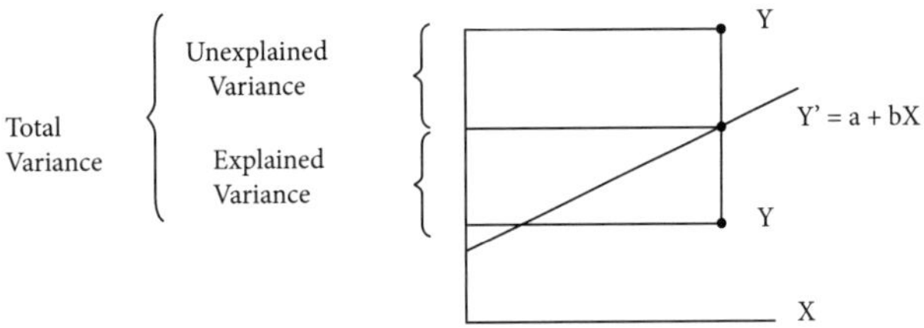

Y can be expected to increase. A negative r indicates the opposite relationship. When r = 0, there is no correlation between X and Y. When r = ± 1, the correlation is perfect.

Illustration 3-7 presents the calculation of variances, the coefficient of determination, and the coefficient of correlation for the example problem.

In the example, 95.14% of the variation in Y is explained by the variation in X. In this case, the regression line provides an excellent fit to the observed data. The value of r, 97.53%, indicates that there is a strong positive relationship between the total cost and units produced in the problem.

It should be mentioned that a high correlation between the dependent and independent variables does not necessarily imply a cause and effect relationship. A high correlation simply indicates that the two variables change in the same direction, but no conclusions about cause and effect should be drawn.

Assumptions Underlying Regression Analysis. Regression analysis is a useful tool for cost estimations if its underlying assumptions are satisfied and the relationships between dependent and independent variables persist over time. To make valid inferences from a set of observations about cost behavior, four assumptions must be satisfied:

1. The relationship between dependent and independent variables must be linear in the relevant range of observations.
2. The variance and the standard deviation of the error terms are constant, a condition referred to as "homoscedasticity." This condition indicates that there is a uniform scatter of observations around the regression line. For example, this assumption is satisfied in the first case but not in the second case in the following sets of observations.

Illustration 3-7 Calculation of Variances, r2, and r

Period	X	Y	Y' = 336.15 + 24.73(X)	$(Y - \bar{Y})^2$	$(Y - Y')^2$
1	40	1,300	1,325.35	191,406	643
2	60	1,800	1,819.95	3,906	398
3	70	2,000	2,067.25	68,906	4,523
4	50	1,600	1,572.65	18,906	748
5	30	1,000	1,078.05	543,906	6,092
6	60	1,900	1,819.95	26,406	6,408
7	70	2,100	2,067.25	131,406	1,073
8	80	2,300	2,314.55	316,406	212
9	60	2,000	1,819.95	68,906	32,418
10	70	1,950	2,067.25	45,156	13,748
11	40	1,400	1,325.35	113,906	5,573
12	50	1,500	1,572.65	56,406	5,278
Total		20,850		1,585,622	77,114

$$\bar{Y} = 20{,}850/12 = 1{,}737.50$$

$$r^2 = 1 - \frac{\sum (Y - Y')^2}{\sum (Y - \bar{Y})^2} = 1 - \frac{77{,}114}{1{,}585{,}622} = 95.14\%$$

$$r = \sqrt{0.9514} = 97.53\%$$

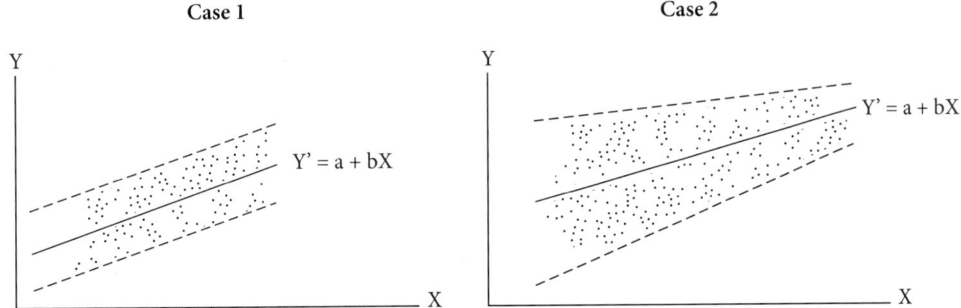

3. The error terms are independent of each other. This means that the error associated with the predicting equation for one observation is independent of the errors for all the other observations. If this condition is not satisfied, the problem of "serial correlation" is present. When serial correlation exists, the standard errors of the regression coefficients are underestimated.
4. The error terms are normally distributed. If this condition is not satisfied, the predicting equation will be influenced by extreme values.

Advantages and Weaknesses Regression analysis is an objective procedure and a useful tool for cost estimation. This method can be used to determine how well a predicting equation fits the observed data. a. It provides information about the expected variation between the actual costs and the estimated costs. Its major weakness is the possibility of inappropriate, use. Regression analysis may give misleading results if the necessary underlying assumptions about data are not satisfied.

Summary

This chapter has discussed several methods for estimating costs. When used properly, the techniques are useful accounting tools. They can be used to predict cost behavior patterns for planning, for control of operations, and for decision making.

The engineering method is a direct method of cost estimation. It is expensive and can be applied only to estimations of direct labor and direct material costs.

The historical cost approach is an indirect method of estimating future costs. Its usefulness relies upon certain data requirements and assumptions, and thus should be applied carefully. When used improperly, methods relying on historical costs may provide information that is misleading.

Appendix:

Additional Statistical Analysis

This appendix provides some additional statistical analyses for cost estimations based upon regression models.

Standard Error of the Estimate. The standard error of the estimate, S_e, is a measure of the dispersion of observed data around the regression line. It is similar to a standard deviation and can be used to make probability statements about cost predictions. The standard error of the estimate for a population may be estimated from a set of observations as follows:

$$S_e = \sqrt{\frac{\textit{Total Unexplained Variance}}{n - 2}} = \sqrt{\frac{\sum(\hat{Y} - Y)^2}{n - 2}}$$

where n is the number of observations. Two degrees of freedom are subtracted from n because two constants, a and b, are estimated on the basis of the original data. Another computational form for calculating the standard error of the estimate is:

$$S_e = \sqrt{\frac{\sum Y^2 - a\sum Y - b\sum XY}{n - 2}}$$

For our example problem, the standard error of the estimate is:

$$S_e = \sqrt{\frac{77{,}114}{12 - 2}} = \$87.82$$

If the four assumptions (linearity, independence, constant variance, and normality) underlying regression analysis are satisfied, the standard error of the estimate can be used to derive probability statements about the cost estimates. For example, approximately two-thirds of the observed data should fall within the range of Y' ± S_e. If X is 65, the total cost can be estimated to be between $1,943.60 + 87.82 and $1,943.60 – 87.82, with a confidence level of 2/3 = 66.67%. Similarly, 95% and 99.5% of the observed data should fall within the ranges of Y' ± 1.965 S_e and Y' ± 3 S_e, respectively.

Sampling Errors and Regression Coefficients. The b coefficient of the regression equation may be used as an estimate of the unit variable cost whenever there is a distinct relationship between a dependent variable Y and an independent variable X. If there is no distinct relationship between the dependent and independent variables, the slope of the regression line would be close to zero. In this case, no significant amount of variation would be explained by variation in X and the use of b as an estimate of variable cost would be inaccurate. Therefore, it is important to verify that the sample value b is significantly different from zero before the use of b as an estimate of variable cost.

The normal test for the significance of b is to test a null hypothesis that B, the true relationship between Y and X, is equal to zero. If the null hypothesis is rejected, the alternative hypothesis that B ≠ 0 will be accepted, one can conclude that there is a significant relationship between the dependent and independent variables. These hypotheses may be expressed as:

$$\text{Ho: } B = 0$$
$$\text{Ha: } B \neq 0$$

To test the hypothesis, tables of the student's t distribution can be used in the following way.

1. Calculate the standard error of the b regression coefficient, S_b.

$$S_b = \frac{S_e}{\sqrt{\Sigma(X-\bar{X})^2}} \text{ or } \frac{S_e}{\sqrt{\Sigma X^2 - \bar{X}\Sigma X}}$$

For our example, $S_b = \dfrac{87.82}{\sqrt{41{,}000 - 56.67(680)}} = 1.77$

2. Calculate the t-value of the regression coefficient.

The t-value is a measure of the number of standard errors between 0 and the regression coefficient. Mathematically,

$$t - value = \frac{b}{S_b}$$

A high t-value indicates a higher probability that B is not equal to 0, and that more confidence in the estimated cost is warranted. For the example problem,

$$t - value = \frac{24.73}{1.77} = 13.97$$

3. Determine the tabulated value of t.

A tabulated value of t is selected from a table of the student's t distribution with the specific degrees of freedom at a desired confidence level. Such a table is provided in Table 3-1. For example, if the desired confidence level in our example problem is 99%, the table value oft is 3.169 using 10 degrees of freedom and $t_{.005}$. Note that $t_{.005}$ instead of $t_{.01}$ is used here because the table is a one-tailed table.

4. Compare the calculated t-value from (2) with the tabulated value of t from (3) to determine whether the null hypothesis is true.

If the calculated t > the tabulated value t, reject H_0 and accept H_a.

For our example, since the calculated t, 13.97, is greater than the table value t, 3.169, the null hypothesis is rejected. The conclusion is that there is a significant relationship between Y and X. Consequently, b in this case may be used as an estimate of the unit variable cost.

The standard error of the regression coefficient and the tabulated value t may also be used to construct confidence intervals for the true B. These may be used to estimate a range of values for the true unit variable cost. For example, if the desired confidence level is 95%, the confidence interval of B would be equal to:

$b \pm t_{.025}S_b$
$= 24.73 \pm 2.228(1.77)$
$= 24.73 \pm 3.94.$

The t-value describes the sampling distribution of a deviation from a population value divided by the standard error. Probabilities indicated in the subordinate of t in the heading refer to a one-tailed area under the curve that lie beyond the point t. Degrees of freedom are listed in the first column.

For example, in the distribution of the means of sample size n = 12, df = n – 2 = 12 – 2; then .05 of the area under the curve falls in the two tails of the curve outside the interval t ± 2.228, which is taken from the $t_{.025}$ column of the table.

Table 3-1 Values of t

d.f.	$t_{.100}$	$t_{.050}$	$t_{.025}$	$t_{.010}$	$t_{.005}$
1	3.078	6.314	12.706	31.821	63.657
2	1.886	2.920	4.303	6.965	9.925
3	1.638	2.353	3.182	4.541	5.841
4	1.533	2.132	2.776	3.747	4.604
5	1.476	2.015	2.571	3.365	4.032
6	1.440	1.943	2.447	3.143	3.707
7	1.415	1.895	2.365	2.998	3.499
8	1.397	1.860	2.306	2.896	3.355
9	1.383	1.833	2.262	2.821	3.250
10	1.372	1.812	2.228	2.764	3.169
11	1.363	1.7%	2.201	2.718	3.106
12	1.356	1.782	2.179	2.681	3.055
13	1.350	1.771	2.160	2.650	3.012
14	1.345	1.761	2.145	2.624	2.977
15	1.341	1.753	2.131	2.602	2.947
16	1.337	1.746	2.120	2.583	2.921
17	1.333	1.740	2.110	2.567	2.898
18	1.330	1.734	2.101	2.552	2.878
19	1.328	1.729	2.093	2.539	2.861
20	1.325	1.725	2.086	2.528	2.845
21	1.323	1.721	2.080	2.518	2.831
22	1.321	1.717	2.074	2.508	2.819
23	1.319	1.714	2.069	2.500	2.807
24	1.318	1.711	2.064	2.492	2.797
25	1.316	1.708	2.060	2.485	2.787
26	1.315	1.706	2.056	2.479	2.779
27	1.314	1.703	2.052	2.473	2.771
28	1.313	1.701	2.048	2.467	2.763
29	1.311	1.699	2.045	2.462	2.756
inf.	1.282	1.645	1.960	2.326	2.576

Source: The data of this table were extracted from Table III of Fisher and Yates, *Statistical Tables for Biological Agricultural and Medical Research,* with permission of the publishers Oliver & Boyd Ltd., Edinburgh and London, © 1974, p. 46.

If all the regression assumptions are satisfied, we are 95% certain that the true variable cost is between \$20.79 and \$28.67. In the same manner, at the desired confidence level of 99%, the confidence interval is:

$$24.73 \pm 3.169(1.77)$$
$$= 24.73 \pm 5.61$$

Multiple Regression Analysis

Multiple regression analysis is an extension of simple regression which involves using two or more independent variables. Multiple regression in some instances may be used to substantially improve the accuracy of predictions of a cost. It is particularly useful in cost estimation when a firm produces two or more products, or when factors other than volume affect costs. The general equation of a multiple linear regression model is:

$$Y' = a + b_1 X_1 + b_2 X_2 + \ldots + b_n X_n$$

where

Y' is the dependent variable which is to be estimated;

$X_1, X_2, \ldots X_n$ are the independent variables on which the estimation is to be based;

$a, b_1, b_2, \ldots b_n$ are the regression coefficients; each coefficient measures the change in Y' due to per unit change in the independent variable while holding the other independent variables constant.

For example, the total monthly production cost of a department which produces two products may be more accurately predicted by the following multiple regression equation than by a simple regression equation of total units produced.

Y' = \$200 + \$20 (number of Model A produced) + \$30 (number of Model B produced).

In estimating of the regression coefficients, multiple regression is based on the same theory as in simple regression analysis. Of course, multiple regression analysis involves more computations because of the increase in number of independent variables. Computer programs are available that make the use of multiple regression feasible. A standard multiple regression computer program will provide the following data:

1. Regression coefficients; i.e., $a, b_1, b_2, \ldots b_n$
2. Standard error of regression coefficients; i.e., $S_a, S_{b1}, S_{b2}, \ldots S_{bn}$
3. Calculated t-value for each independent variable
4. Coefficient of determination, r^2
5. Standard error of the estimate, S_e.

Dummy variables may also be useful in multiple regression analysis for including the influence of unusual factors such as seasons of the year, weather, the direction of change in production, or quality of internal control. A dummy variable takes on a value of 1 or 0 depending upon whether the special condition exists.

In multiple regression analysis some of the independent variables may not be independent; they may be highly correlated with each other. This problem, called *multicollinearity,* can be detected by testing the correlation between the independent variables. Multicollinearity causes the regression coefficients to be unreliable as predictors of unit costs. For example, in the regression equation of

$$Y' = \$200 + \$20(X_1) + \$30(X_2)$$

the regression coefficients of \$20 and \$30 may not be meaningful estimates of the unit variable cost of each product if the problem of multicollinearity exists. However, the resulting regression equation may still provide useful estimates of total cost if the past relationships of production among the different products are maintained.

Key Definitions

Account classification method	An accounting method that can be used to determine cost behavior patterns by accountants' professional judgment of fixed costs and variable costs.
Coefficient of correlation	A measure of the relationship between a dependent variable and an independent variable. It is equal to the square root of the coefficient of determination.
Coefficient of determination	A measure of the percent of the total variance that is caused by variation in the independent variable.
High-Low method	An accounting method of determining cost behavior patterns based on the highest level of activity and its related cost and the lowest level of activity and its related cost.
Method of least squares	A statistical approach used to determine cost behavior patterns by selecting the trend line that best fits the observed costs.
Regression analysis	A statistical measure of the relationship between a dependent variable and one or more independent variables. When one independent variable is considered, the analysis is called "simple regression analysis." When more than one independent variable is studied, the analysis is called "multiple regression analysis."
Scattergraph method	A statistical method used to determine cost behavior patterns. It requires the plotting of cost and activity observations on a graph. The accountant's judgment is used to determine a line that best depicts the relationship between cost and activity.
Standard error of the estimate	A measure of the dispersion of observed data around the regression line. It is similar to a standard deviation and can be used to make probability statements about cost predictions.

Questions

3-1 What are the major purposes of analyzing cost behavior patterns?

3-2 What is an "activity base" in cost estimation? Give three examples of activity bases.

3-3 What steps are necessary before reliable cost estimates can be obtained?

3-4 Discuss the advantages and disadvantages of the account classification method in cost estimation.

3-5 Discuss the high-low method for determining cost behavior patterns.

3-6 What basic assumptions are made with the high-low method in analyzing cost behavior patterns?

3-7 What is regression analysis? Give the general form of a regression line.

3-8 What is the major difference between simple regression and multiple regression analysis?

3-9 What is the coefficient of determination?

3-10 What is the coefficient of correlation?

3-11 What does the standard error of the estimate measure?

3-12 What basic assumptions are made in regression analysis?

3-13 What are the major advantages and disadvantages of regression analysis?

Problems

3-14 *Terminology*

Match each of the following lettered terms on the left with the appropriate numbered definition on the right.

a. Coefficient of correlation	1. Used to make probability statements about cost predictions
b. Coefficient of determination	2. Determines cost behavior based on high and low activity levels
c. Dependent variable (example)	3. Measure of the variation in the dependent variable caused by changes in the independent variable(s)
d. High-Low method	4. Electricity costs
e. Independent variable (example)	5. Method that requires the plotting of cost activity observations on a graph
f. Regression analysis	6. Machine hours
g. Scattergraph method	7. Used to compute the relationship between a dependent variable and one or more independent variables
h. Standard error of the estimate	8. Measure of the relationship between a dependent variable and an independent variable

3-15 *Determining Mixed Costs*

The water for the Richmond Company costs $.05 for every unit used. There is a base charge of $10 per month. Determine the water bill for each of the following months:

	Units Used
January	2,000
February	2,200
March	2,500

3-16 *Scattergraph*

The cost records of Do-Well Hospital show the following costs of X-rays at various levels of activity:

Month	Total Costs	X-Rays Taken
1	$24,000	4,200
2	26,000	4,800
3	25,000	4,500
4	30,000	6,000
5	28,000	5,000
6	22,000	4,000

Required:

(1) Prepare a scattergraph by plotting the above date on a graph.
(2) Estimate the monthly fixed cost and the variable cost per X-ray taken.

3-17 *Analysis of Accounts*

The cost accountant of the production department of Bell Company has divided the production department's overhead costs for January into the fixed and variable costs shown below. (The department worked 2,000 machine hours in January.)

Fixed Costs		Variable Costs	
Rent	$2,000	Supplies	$2,000
Property taxes	1,000	Indirect labor	1,000
Insurance	1,000	Electricity	2,000
Depreciation	5,000		
Supervision	4,000		

Required:

Determine the overhead cost function using the account classification method.

3-18 *Application of the High-Low Method*

Given the following maintenance costs, determine their fixed and variable components using the high-low method.

Period	Cost	Hours Worked
1	$21,000	10,000
2	25,000	15,000
3	33,000	16,000
4	27,000	14,000

3-19 *Interpretation of Regression Coefficient*

The cost accountant of the Smart Company has applied regression analysis to a study of repair and maintenance costs in a plant. The resulting estimating equation for repair and maintenance costs based on the observed data in the past 12 months is:

$$Y = \$15,000 - .5(X)$$

where X = number of machine hours worked.

Required:

What is the most likely explanation of the negative regression coefficient?

3-20 *High-Low Cost Estimation*

The Portland Company wants to estimate the utility costs for the months of May and June. Some relevant information is listed below:

Month	Utility Cost	Machine Hours Worked
January	$1,400	1,000
February	1,500	1,050
March	1,600	1,120
April	1,700	1,300

Estimated units to be produced:

May	1,100 units
June	1,150 units

Each unit requires 1.1 machine hours.

Required:

Estimate the utility costs for the months of May and June using the high-low method.

3-21 *High-Low Cost Estimation*

The Stone Company has observed that its utility cost is $5,000 when operating at a level of 20,000 machine hours per period. The utility cost drops to $4,000 when the operating level drops to 15,000 machine hours.

Required:

Estimate the utility cost for an operating level of 18,000 machine hours.

3-22 *High-Low Method (Spreadsheet)*

The Franklin Furniture Co. builds its products in a highly automated facility, and has decided to predict future utility costs by using machine hours. The company has gathered the following data from the prior six months:

Month	*Machine Hours*	*Utility Costs*
January	3,000	$355
February	8,000	740
March	5,700	600
April	9,000	915
May	7,000	650
June	3,500	340

Required:

(a) Using a computer spreadsheet program, enter the above data and write a formula to predict future utility costs using the high-low method. Enter the cell addresses for the high and low points in the formula, not the values in the cells. Can you use the spreadsheet program to help identify the high and low points?

(b) Use the program to predict utility costs for July if 6,000 machine hours are anticipated.

3-23 *Estimating Variable Costs: Algebra Approach*

Total production costs for Gallop, Inc., are budgeted at $230,000 for 50,000 units of budgeted output and at $280,000 for 60,000 units of budgeted output. Because of the need for additional facilities, budgeted fixed costs for 60,000 units are 25% more than budgeted fixed costs for 50,000 units. How much is Gallop's budgeted variable cost per unit of output?

(*AICPA adapted*)

3-24 *Cost Analysis Decision*

William Company owns and operates a nationwide chain of movie theaters. The 500 properties in the William chain vary from low volume, small town, single-screen theaters to high volume, big city, multi-screen theaters.

The management is considering installing machines that will make popcorn on the premises. These machines would allow the theaters to sell popcorn that would be freshly popped daily rather than the pre-popped corn that is currently purchased in large bags. This proposed feature would be properly advertised and is intended to increase patronage at the company's theaters.

The machines can be purchased in several different sizes. The annual rental costs and the operating costs vary with the size of the machines. The machine capacities and costs are shown below.

	Popper Model		
	Economy	Regular	Super
Annual capacity..................	50,000 boxes	120,000 boxes	300,000 boxes
Costs:			
Annual machine rental......	$8,000	$11,000	$20,000
Popcorn cost per box.........	.13	.13	.13
Other costs per box...........	.22	.14	.05
Cost of each box................	.08	.08	.08

Required:

(a) Calculate the volume level in boxes at which the Economy Popper and Regular Popper would earn the same profit (loss).

(b) The management can estimate the number of boxes to be sold at each of its theaters. Present a decision rule that would enable William's management to select the most profitable machine without having to make a separate cost calculation for each theater.

(c) Could the management use the average number of boxes sold per seat for the entire chain and the capacity of each theater to develop this decision rule? Explain your answer.

(IMA adapted)

3-25 *Multiple Regression*

Regression analysis is a procedure used to measure the relationship of one variable with one or more other variables. Regression provides a rational statement rather than a causal statement with regard to the relationship. The basic formula for a regression equation is:

$$Yi = \alpha + \beta_1 X_{i1} + \beta_2 X_{i2} + E_i$$

For a regression equation to provide meaningful information, it should comply with the basic criteria of goodness of fit and specification analysis. Specification analysis is determined by examining the population relationships for: (1) linearity within a relevant range, (2) constant variance (homoscedasticity), (3) independence of observations (serial correlation), (4) normality, and (5) multicollinearity.

Required:

(a) Explain what is meant by the phrase "regression provides a rational statement rather than a causal statement."

(b) Explain the meaning of each of the following symbols which appear in the basic formula for a regression equation.

1. Y_i
2. α
3. β_1
4. X_{i1}
5. E_i

(c) Identify the statistical factors which are used to test a regression equation for goodness of fit and, for each item identified, indicate whether a high or low value describes a "good" fit.

(d) Explain what each of the following terms means with respect to regression analysis.
1. Linearity within a relevant range.
2. Constant variance (homoscedasticity).
3. Serial correlation.
4. Normality.
5. Multicollinearity.

(*IMA adapted*)

3-26 *High-Low Cost Estimation and Simple Regression Analysis*

The Blacksburg Company is separating materials handling cost into fixed and variable components. The following data have been collected over a five-month period (all amounts are in thousands):

Month	Direct Labor Hours	Cost of Materials Issued	Materials Handling Costs
1	4	$7	$1.60
2	5	5	1.70
3	6	4	1.80
4	7	8	1.90
5	8	6	2.00

Required:

(1) Determine the fixed and variable materials handling cost by the high-low method using direct labor hours as the measure of volume.

(2) Determine the fixed and variable materials handling cost by the method of least squares using direct labor hours as the measure of volume.

(3) Repeat (2) using cost of materials issued as the measure of volume.

(4) Which of the two measures of volume in (2) and (3) seems preferable? Why?

3-27 *High-Low Cost Estimation and Simple Regression Analysis*

Assume we have the following observations relating to overhead costs and direct labor hours for Department A of the ABC Company.

Direct Labor Hours	Overhead Costs
15	40
20	50
14	35
13	30
18	44
15	36
12	31
16	41
18	42
19	45

Required:

(1) Determine the budgeted overhead costs for Department A in a month when there are 13 direct labor hours if the high-low method of estimating cost behavior patterns is used.
(2) Using regression analysis determine what the budgeted overhead cost should be in a month when Department A should work 13 direct labor hours.
(3) Does the regression line in (2) explain the data well? Why?
(4) What is the range within which 95 percent of the observations should lie?

3-28 *Regression Coefficients and Significance of Independent Variables*

Assume that the following regression has been computed for your department's monthly overhead expense from data observed in the past 12 months.

$$Y = 1{,}000 + 10X_1 + 20X_2 + 30X_3$$
$$\quad (200) \quad (2) \quad (5) \quad (8)$$

$r^2 = 92\%$

$S_e = 400$

The numbers in parentheses are the standard errors of the regression coefficients.

Required:

(1) Assess the probability that the "true" coefficient of X_2 is between 15 and 25.
(2) Test whether the presence of each independent variable contributes significantly toward explanation of the changes in the dependent variable (at 99% confidence level).

3-29 *Multiple Regression Analysis*

Assume that the following regression equation has been computed for your department's monthly overhead expense from the data observed in the past 10 months.

$$Y = 120 + 23.5X_1 + 42X_2$$

where

X_1 = direct labor hours per month

X_2 = number of orders processed per month

standard error of estimate (S_e) = 60

standard deviation of monthly direct labor hours = $\sqrt{\dfrac{\Sigma(X_1 - \overline{X}_1)^2}{n-1}} = 8$

standard deviation of monthly number of orders processed = $\sqrt{\dfrac{\Sigma(X_2 - \overline{X}_2)^2}{n-1}} = 5$

Required:

(1) Calculate the standard error of the regression coefficient for X_1 and X_2.
(2) Assess the probability that the true coefficient of X_1 is between 20 and 31.
(3) If the total variance of monthly overhead expense over the past ten months is $100,000, calculate the coefficient of correlation, r.
(4) Estimate the probability that the overhead expense will be between $304 and $484 for a month where $X_1 = 4$ and $X_2 = 5$. Assume that the distribution of the overhead expense is normal.

(5) Test whether the presence of each independent variable contributes significantly toward explanation of the changes in the dependent variable (at 99% confidence level).

3-30 *Multiple Regression Analysis*
A regression equation for two independent variables and one department variable has the following form:

$$C = 20 + 4X_1 + 2X_2$$

Where
C = weekly cost
X_1 = direct labor hours per week
X_2 = number of orders processed per week
$S_e = 5$
standard deviation of weekly direct labor hours = $\sqrt{\dfrac{\Sigma(X_1 - \overline{X}_1)^2}{10 - 1}} = \sqrt{0.8} = .8944$

standard deviation of weekly number of orders processed =

$$\sqrt{\dfrac{\Sigma(X_2 - \overline{X}_2)^2}{10 - 1}} = \sqrt{0.5} = .7071$$

Required:
(1) Explain the meaning of the numbers 20, 4, and 2 in the regression equation.
(2) Assuming normality, estimate the probability that the cost of the activity will lie between 41 and 56 if $X_1 = 4$ and $X_2 = 5$.
(3) Calculate the standard error of the regression coefficient for X_1 and X_2.
(4) If the total variance of weekly cost for the activity is 1,000, calculate the coefficient of correlation, r.

3-31 *Coefficient of Determination and the Standard Error of the Estimate*
The ABC Company produces two products, known as A and B. The following predictions have been made for the coming month:

	Product	
	A	B
Selling price per unit	$60	$50
Direct material cost per unit of production	10	12
Direct labor hours per unit of production	3	1.5
Machine hours per unit of production:		
Type 1 machines	0.2	0.5
Type 2 machines	0.3	0.1
Total sales in units	9,000	22,000
Total production in units	10,000	20,000
Direct labor cost per hour	$8.00	

No predictions have yet been made for overhead and for selling and administrative costs, but the company intends to base these predictions on 24 months of observations of the following:

Overhead: .... (Y)
Selling and administrative costs .... (C)
Direct labor hours .... (X_1)
Type 1 machine hours.......................... (X_2)
Type 2 machine hours.......................... (X_3)
Sales of product A in dollars................ (X_4)
Sales of product B in dollars .... (X_5)

A computer program has been used to analyze the observed data; a partial result of this analysis is given below:

<u>For Overhead</u>

Prediction equation I: $Y = \$\,10{,}000 + 4X_1$
(500) (1)

$\Sigma(Y - \overline{Y})^2 = 400{,}000$

$\Sigma(Y - Y')^2 = 100{,}000$

Prediction equation II: $Y = \$\,9{,}000 + 13X_2 + 20X_3$
(360) (3.25) (4)

$\Sigma(Y - \overline{Y})^2 = 400{,}000$

$\Sigma(Y - Y')^2 = 60{,}000$

For Selling and Administrative Costs

Prediction equation: $C = \$4{,}100 + 0.08X_4 + 0.06X_5$
(410) (0.025) (0.02)

$\Sigma(C - \overline{C})^2 = 200{,}000$

$\Sigma(C'' - \overline{C})^2 = 160{,}000$

The numbers in parentheses are the standard errors of the regression coefficients.

Required:

(1) Calculate the coefficient of determination (r^2) and the standard error of the estimate (S_e) for each prediction equation.

(2) Predict the cost range of the total overhead and the total selling and administrative costs for the coming month (assume the desired confidence level is 95%). Select one prediction equation for the overhead cost estimation and state why you selected the equation.

3-32 *Assumptions and Applications of Linear Regression Analysis*

The controller of the Connecticut Electronics Company believes that the identification of the variable and fixed components of the firm's costs will enable the firm to make better planning and control decisions. Among the costs the controller is concerned about is the behavior of indirect supplies expense. He believes there is some correlation between the machine hours worked and the amount of indirect supplies used.

A member of the controller's staff has suggested that a simple linear regression model be used to determine the cost behavior of the indirect supplies. The regression equation shown below was developed from 40 pairs of observations using the least squares method of regression. The regression equation and related measures are as follows:

$$S = \$200 + \$4H$$

where:
S = Total monthly costs of indirect supplies
H = Machine hours per month
Standard error of estimate: $S_e = 100$
Coefficient of correlation: $r = .87$

Required:

(a) When a simple linear regression model is used to make inferences about a population relationship from sample data, what assumptions must be made before the inferences can be accepted as valid?

(b) Assume the assumptions identified in Requirement A are satisfied for the indirect supplies expense of Connecticut Electronics Company.

   (1) Explain the meaning of "200" and "4" in the regression equation S = $200 + $4H.

   (2) Calculate the estimated cost of indirect supplies if 900 machine hours are to be used during a month.

   (3) In addition to the estimate for the cost of indirect supplies, the controller would like the range of values for the estimate if a 95 percent confidence interval is specified. He would use this range to judge whether the estimated costs indicated by the regression analysis was good enough for planning purposes. Calculate, for 900 machine hours, the range of the estimate for the cost of indirect supplies with a 95 percent confidence interval.

(c) Explain briefly what the

   (1) coefficient of correlation measures.

   (2) value of the coefficient of correlation (r = .87) indicates in this case if Connecticut Electronics Company wishes to predict the total cost of indirect supplies on the basis of estimated machine hours.

(IMA adapted)

3-33 *Reliability of Prediction Equation*

The Johnstar Co. makes a very expensive chemical product. The costs average about $1,000 per pound and the material sells for $2,500 per pound. The material is very dangerous, therefore, it is made each day to fill the customer orders for the day. Failure to deliver the quantity required results in a shutdown for the customers and high cost penalty for Johnstar (plus customer ill will).

Predicting the final weight of a batch of the chemical being processed has been a serious problem. This is critical because of the serious cost of failure to meet customer needs.

A consultant recommended that the batches be weighed one-half way through the six hour processing period. He proposed that linear regression be used to predict the final weight from the mid-point weight.

If the prediction indicated that too little of the chemical would be available, then a new batch could be started and still delivered in time to satisfy customers needs for the day. Included in the report of a study made by the consultant during a oneweek period were the following items:

Observation No.	Weight 3 hrs.	Final Weight	Observation No.	Weight 3 hrs.	Final Weight
1	55	90	11	60	80
2	45	75	12	35	60
3	40	80	13	35	80
4	60	80	14	55	60
5	40	45	15	35	75
6	60	80	16	50	90
7	50	80	17	30	60
8	55	95	18	60	105
9	50	100	19	50	60
10	35	75	20	20	30

Data from the regression analysis:	
Coefficient of determination	0.4126
Coefficient of correlation	0.6424
Coefficients of the regression equation	
Constant	+28.6
Independent variable	+ 1.008
Standard error of the estimate	14.2
Standard error of the regression	
Coefficient for the independent variable	0.2796
The t-statistic for a 95% confidence interval (18 degrees of freedom)	2.101

Required:

(a) Using the results of the regression analysis by the consultant, calculate the estimate of today's first batch which weighs 42 lbs. at the end of 3 hours processing time.

(b) Customer orders for today total 68 pounds. The nature of the process is such that the smallest batch that can be started will weigh at least 20 pounds at the end of six hours. Using only the data from the regression analysis, would you start another batch? (Remember that today's first batch weighed 42 pounds at the end of 3 hours.)

(c) Is the relationship between the variables such that this regression analysis provides an adequate prediction model for the Johnstar Co.? Explain your answer.

(*IMA adapted*)

3-34 *Regression Analysis*

The Lockit Company manufactures door knobs for residential homes and apartments. Lockit is considering the use of simple and multiple linear regression analysis to forecast annual sales because previous forecasts have been inaccurate. The sales forecast will be used to initiate the budgeting process and to identify better the underlying process that generates sales.

Larry Husky, the controller of Lockit, has considered many possible independent variables and equations to predict sales and has narrowed his choices to four equations. Husky used annual observations from 20 prior years to estimate each of the four equations.

Following is a definition of the variables used in the four equations and a statistical summary of these equations:

S_t = Forecast sales (in dollars) for Lockit in time period t.
S_{t-1} = Actual sales (in dollars) for Lockit in time period t – 1.
G_t = Forecast United States gross national product in time period t.
G_{t-1} = Actual United States gross national product in time period t 1.
N_{t-1} = Lockit's net income in time period t – 1.

Statistical Summary of Four Equations

Equation	Dependent Variable	Independent Variable(s)	Coefficients: Dependent Variable (Intercept)	Coefficients: Independent Variable (Rate)	Standard Error of the Estimate	Coefficient of Correlation	t-Value
1	S_t	S_{t-1}	+ $ 500,000	+ $ 1.10	$500,000	+.97	5.50
2	S_t	G_t	+ $1,000,000	+ $ .00001	$510,000	+.95 10.00	
3	S_t	G_{t-1}	+ $ 900,000	+ $ .000012	$520,000	+'90	5.00
	S_t		+ $ 600,000		$490,000	+.98	
		N_{t-1}		+ $ 10.00			4.00
4		G_t		+ $ .000002			1.50
		G_{t-1}		+ $ .000003			3.00

Required:

(a) Write equations 2 and 4 in the form y = a + bx.
(b) If actual sales are $1,500,000 in 20X1, what would be the forecast sales for Lockit in 20X2?
(c) Explain the meaning and significance of the coefficient of correlation.
(d) Why might Larry Husky prefer equation 3 to equation 2?
(e) Explain the advantages and disadvantages of using equation 4 to forecast annual sales.

(IMA adapted)

1. *To understand the relationships between cost, volume, and profit.*
2. *To examine the effect of changes in cost, volume, and price on profit.*
3. *To understand the assumptions and limitations of cost-volume-profit analysis.*
4. *To study some modifications and extensions of*

4

Cost-Volume-Profit Analysis

One of the important phases of management planning is profit planning. Profit is a function of many factors; among the major ones are selling price, costs, and volume of sales. Cost-Volume-Profit (C-V-P) analysis provides a tool for studying the effects of selling price, costs, and volume on profit. The analysis provides not only information or profit planning but also information for management decision-making. For example, the analysis is useful in choice of product lines, pricing of products, make-or-buy decisions, marketing strategy, and accepting or rejecting special orders. In this chapter, we shall first discuss traditional cost-volume-profit analysis. Then the implicit assumptions of traditional cost-volume-profit analysis will be examined. Finally, traditional C-V-P analysis will be extended by relaxing some of these assumptions to broaden its applications.

Traditional Cost-Volume-Profit Analysis

C-V-P analysis is based upon knowledge of a firm's revenue and cost behavior patterns. Cost behavior describes the manner in which costs respond to changes in volume. In C-V-P analysis, a cost must be classified as either fixed or variable. Semivariable (or mixed) costs must be resolved into fixed and variable components before C-V-P analysis can be applied. Analysis of cost behavior patterns and methods for resolving semivariable costs have been discussed in Chapter Three.

The Breakeven Point

Because it can be used to find a breakeven point, C-V-P analysis is sometimes referred to as breakeven analysis. The *breakeven point* is the level of activity at which a firm's total revenue equals its total expenses. In other words, it is the point of zero profits. A level of activity below the breakeven point results in a loss, whereas a level of activity above the breakeven point results in a profit.

The breakeven point of a firm's operation may be determined by one of three techniques-the equation approach, the contribution margin approach, and the graphic approach.

Equation Approach

The equation approach is based on the formula behind the accounting income statement. The income statement is a mathematical model used by accountants to show the results of operations of a business over a period of time. In general, the model follows the following basic form:

Sales revenue – Variable costs – Fixed costs = Profit before taxes

or

Sales revenue = Variable costs + Fixed costs + Profit before taxes.

At the breakeven point, there is no profit or loss. Therefore, breakeven sales = variable costs + fixed costs = total costs.

Let

P = unit selling price
V = unit variable manufacturing and nonmanufacturing costs
FC = total fixed manufacturing and nonmanufacturing costs
Q_{be} = breakeven point in units

Using these symbols, the equation for the breakeven point can be developed from the following basic equation:

Total revenues = Total costs.

That is,

$$P * Q_{be} = V ‘ Q_{be} + FC. \qquad (1)$$

Given P, V, and FC, the breakeven point in units can be obtained by solving the above equation for Q_{be}. The breakeven point in dollars can be obtained by multiplying unit selling price (P) by breakeven quantity, Q_{be}. For purposes of illustration, the following budgeted income statement for The Lone Star Company will be used in this chapter.

In this example, The Lone Star Company's breakeven point in units can be computed by using equation (1) as follows:

$$\$5\ (Q_{be}) = \$3\ (Q_{be}) + \$50{,}000$$

The Lone Star Company
Condensed Budgeted Income Statement
For the Year Ended, 20X1

Sales (40,000 units @a \$5)		\$200,000
Costs:		
Variable (40,000 units @ \$3)	\$120,000	
Fixed	50,000	170,000
Income before income taxes		\$30,000

Solving for Q_{be},

$$Q_{be} = 25{,}000 \text{ units.}$$

The breakeven point in dollars would be:

$$P \bullet Q_{be} = \$5\ (25{,}000) = \$125{,}000.$$

CONTRIBUTION MARGIN APPROACH

Another method that can be used to calculate the breakeven point is the contribution margin approach. The contribution margin is the excess of sales revenue over variable cost. Under the contribution margin approach, the breakeven point in units is equal to the total fixed costs divided by the contribution margin per unit. That is,

$$Q_{be} = \frac{\textit{Total Fixed Costs}}{\textit{Contribution Margin Per Unit}} = \frac{FC}{P - V} \qquad (2)$$

This formula can be derived simply by rearranging the basic breakeven equation (1). Recall that the basic breakeven equation is expressed as:

$$P \bullet Q_{be} = V . Q_{be} + FC$$

or

$$(P - V) \bullet Q_{be} = FC$$

Thus,

$$Q_{be} = \frac{FC}{P - V}$$

The breakeven point in dollars can be determined by multiplying Q_{be} by unit selling price, or from the following formula:

$$\textit{Breakeven po int in dollars} = \frac{FC}{\textit{Contribution Margin Ratio}} \qquad (3)$$

This formula is derived from multiplying P on both sides of equation (2).

$$P \bullet Qbe = P \bullet$$

$$\frac{FC}{P - V} = \frac{FC}{\frac{P - V}{P}} = \frac{FC}{1 - \frac{V}{P}} = \frac{FC}{1 - VCR} = \frac{FC}{CMR}$$

where VCR is variable cost ratio and CMR is contribution margin ratio. The contribution margin ratio measures the percentage of each dollar of sales revenue that adds to net income. The relationship between variable cost ratio and contribution margin ratio can be explained as follows:

Unit contribution margin (CM) is equal to unit selling price (P) minus unit variable cost (V).

$$CM = P - V,$$

or

$$CM + V = P.$$

Dividing both sides by P,

$$\frac{CM}{P} + \frac{V}{P} = 1$$

$$CMR + VCR = 1$$

Therefore, the contribution margin ratio is the complement of the variable cost ratio. The contribution margin ratio is a useful guide to management in the formulation of general company policy. When this ratio is high, it is usually best to seek a strong sales promotion program because a relatively small increase in sales volume would generate a large increase in profits. On the other hand, when the ratio is low, the impact of volume changes on profit is relatively small. In such a situation, a cost-reduction program may be the best policy. The two basic formulas to determine the breakeven point in units and in dollars are summarized in the following:

$$\text{Breakeven point in units, } Q_{be} = \frac{FC}{P - V}$$

$$\text{Breakeven point in dollars} = \frac{FC}{1 - \frac{V}{P}}$$

Applying these formulas for the breakeven point in units and in dollars to the Lone Star example gives the following results:

$$Q_{be} = \frac{FC}{P - V} = \frac{\$50,000}{\$5 - \$3} = 25,000 \textit{ units}$$

Breakeven point in dollars = \$5 (25,000) = \$125,000.

$$\text{Or, } \frac{\$50,000}{1 - \frac{3}{5}} = \$125,000$$

Graphic Approach

Given variable cost per unit, total fixed cost, and unit selling price, C-V-P analysis and the breakeven point can be presented in a chart. Such a chart is usually referred to as a breakeven chart. A breakeven chart can be constructed in the following manner:

1. Sales volume in units is plotted along the horizontal line, the X axis; costs and revenues are plotted on the vertical line, the Y axis.

2. A fixed cost line is drawn parallel to the X axis from the point on the Y axis representing the total fixed costs.
3. A total cost line is drawn starting at the fixed cost point on the Y axis. This line has a slope which is equal to the unit variable cost.
4. The sales revenue line is drawn from zero (the origin), and has a slope equal to the unit selling price.
5. The intersection of the total cost line and the sales revenue line determines the breakeven point, which can be read on the X axis in terms of units and on the Y axis in terms of sales dollars.

Illustration 4-1 presents the breakeven chart for The Lone Star Company. In this example, the total cost line intersects the sales revenue line at $125,000 of sales revenue or 25,000 units. The breakeven point is determined at this intersection point. The breakeven chart discloses not only the sales volume required to break even but also the profit or loss that may be expected at different sales volumes. The expected profit or loss at different sales volumes can be read from the lined areas in the chart. The lined area to the right of the breakeven point is the profit area; the lined area to the left of the breakeven point is the loss area.

The breakeven chart in Illustration 4-1 shows that the fixed cost line is drawn first, parallel to the X axis. Such a breakeven chart emphasizes that fixed costs are unchanged for various levels of activity. However, an alternate breakeven chart in which the variable cost line is drawn first and fixed costs are plotted above the variable cost line is preferred by many accountants. A breakeven chart constructed in such a way emphasizes the contribution margin concept. Illustration 4-2 presents this alternate breakeven chart.

In Illustration 4-2, the difference between the total variable cost and the sales revenue represents the contribution margin. When the total contribution margin is less than fixed costs, there is a loss which is represented by the lined area to the left of the breakeven point. When the total contribution margin is greater than fixed costs, there is a profit which is represented by the lined area to the right of the breakeven point. At the breakeven point, the total contribution margin is just enough to recover fixed costs.

Illustration 4-1 Breakeven Chart

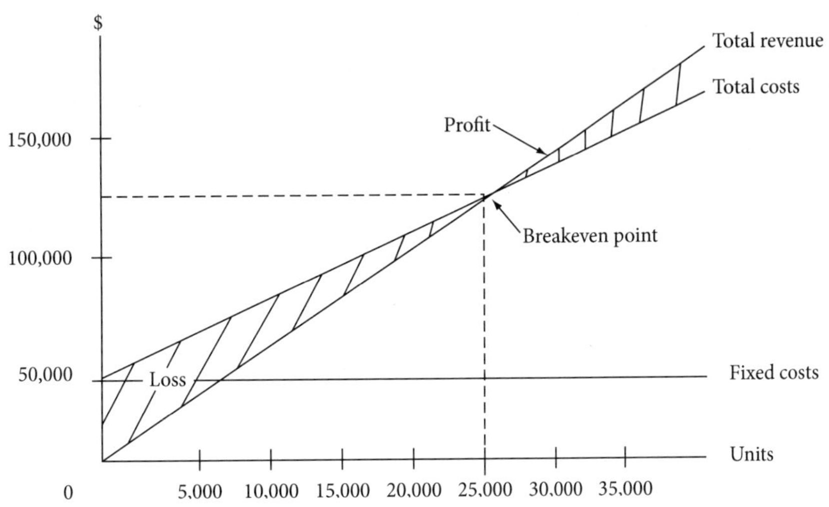

Illustration 4-2 An Alternate Breakeven Chart

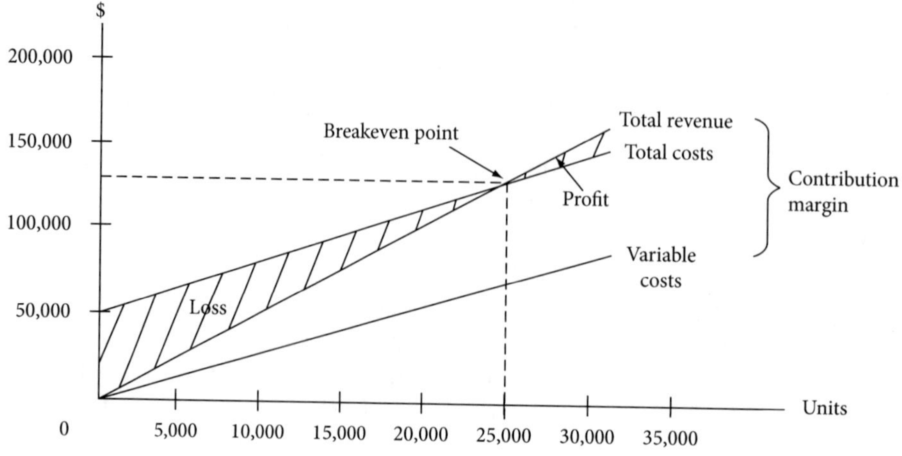

Sales Volume Needed for a Desired Profit

Generally, managers are interested not only in breakeven points but also in sales volume needed for a desired profit. The formulas and breakeven charts developed in the previous section can be expanded to provide such information for management. For example, suppose the management of The Lone Star Company wishes to achieve a profit of $10,000 before income taxes in the coming year. The management wants to know how many units must be sold during the coming year to achieve this desired profit.

According to the equation method, the basic equation for the income statement model is:

Sales revenue = Variable cost + Fixed costs + Profit before taxes

If we let X = number of units to be sold to achieve the desired profit of $10,000 before taxes, then

$$5 \bullet X = 3 \bullet X + 50{,}000 + 10{,}000$$
$$2X = 60{,}000$$
$$X = 30{,}000 \text{ units.}$$

Also, using the contribution margin approach, we can expand the breakeven formulas to include a profit goal in determining the desired sales volume. Including the profit goal, the formulas for the necessary sales volume become:

$$\textit{The Necessary Sales in Units} = \frac{FC + \textit{Desired Profit Before Taxes}}{P - V} \qquad (2.1)$$

and

$$\textit{The Necessary Sales in Dollars} = \frac{FC + \textit{Desired Profit Before Taxes}}{\textit{Contribution Margin Ratio}} \qquad (3.1)$$

For example, using equation (2.1), the number of units to be sold to achieve the desired profit of $10,000 before taxes can be determined as:

$$X = \frac{50,000 + 10,000}{5 - 3} = 30,000\ units.$$

The following budgeted income statement is prepared to show that sales of 30,000 units would result in a profit of $10,000 before taxes.

The Lone Star Company
Budgeted Income Statement
For Sales of 30,000 Units

Sales ($5 x 30,000)		$150,000
Costs:		
Variable ($3 x 30,000) =	$90,000	
Fixed	50,000	140,000
Income before income taxes		$10,000

The needed sales volume of 30,000 units (or $150,000) can also be found from the breakeven chart in Illustrations 4-1 and 4-2. On the charts, the difference between sales revenue and total costs at sales volume of 30,000 units represents a profit of $10,000.

Income tax effects can also be incorporated into the analysis. If a tax rate of t is expected, the profit before taxes will be equal to the profit after taxes divided by (1-t). Therefore, including taxes,

$$The\ Necessary\ Sales\ in\ Units = \frac{FC + \ Desired\ Profit\ After\ Taxes/(1 - \ ,t)}{P - \ V} \quad (2.2)$$

$$The\ Necessary\ Sales\ in\ Dollars = \frac{FC + \ Desired\ Profit\ After\ Taxes/(1 - \ t)}{Contribution\ Margin\ Ratio} \quad (3.2)$$

For example, if a tax rate of 40% is assumed and the company desired an after tax profit of $36,000, the necessary sales in units can be determined as:

$$X = \frac{50,000 + 36,000/(1 - .4)}{5 - 3} = 55,000\ units$$

The following budgeted income statement is prepared to show that sales of 55,000 units by The Lone Star Company would result in a profit of $36,000 after taxes.

The Lone Star Company
Budgeted Income Statement
For Sales of 55,000 Units

Sales ($5 x 55,000)		$275,000
Costs:		
Variable ($3 x 55,000) =	$165,000	
Fixed	50,000	215,000
Income before income taxes		60,000
Less: Income Taxes (40%)		24,000
Net Income		$36,000

An alternative way of expressing a desired profit is as a percent of sales. The formulas and breakeven charts developed in the previous section can be expanded to provide this information as well. For example, suppose the management of The Lone Star Company wishes to achieve a profit of 10 percent of sales before income taxes in the coming year. The management wants to know how many units must be sold during the coming year to achieve this desired profit.

According to the equation method, the basic equation for the income statement model is:

Sales revenue = Variable cost + Fixed costs + Profit before taxes

If we let X = number of units to be sold to achieve the desired profit of 10 percent of sales before taxes, then

$$5 \bullet X = 3 \bullet X + 50{,}000 + .10 \bullet 5$$
$$1.5X = 50{,}000$$
$$X = 33{,}333 \text{ units.}$$

Also, using the contribution margin approach, we can expand the breakeven formulas to include a profit goal in determining the desired sales volume. Including the profit goal, the formulas for the necessary sales volume become:

$$\textit{The Necessary Sales} = \frac{\textit{FC in Units}}{P - V - (\textit{Desired Profit Before Taxes} : P)} \qquad (2.3)$$

and

$$\textit{The Necessary Sales in Dollars} = \frac{\textit{FC}}{\textit{Contribution Margin Ratio} - \textit{Desired Profit Before Taxes}} \qquad (3.3)$$

For example, using equation (2.3), the number of units to be sold to achieve the desired profit of 10 percent of sales before taxes can be determined as:

$$X = \frac{50{,}000}{5 - 3 - (.1 \times 5)} = 33{,}333 \textit{ units.}$$

Using equation (3.3), the necessary dollars of sales to achieve the desired profit of 10 percent of sales before taxes can be determined as:

$$X = \frac{50{,}000}{1 - \frac{3}{5} - .1} = \$166{,}666$$

The following budgeted income statement is prepared to show that sales of 33,333 units would result in a profit of 10 percent of sales before taxes.

The Lone Star Company
Budgeted Income Statement
For Sales of 33,333 Units

Sales ($5 x 33,333)		$166,665
Costs:		
Variable ($3 x 33,333) =	$99,999	
Fixed	50,000	149,999
Income before income taxes		$16,666

The needed sales volume of 33,333 units (or $166,665) can also be found from the breakeven chart in Illustrations 4-1 and 4-2. On the charts, the difference between sales revenue and total costs at sales volume of 33,333 units represents a profit of $16,666.

Income tax effects can also be incorporated into the analysis. For example, if a tax rate (t) of 40% is assumed, the profit before taxes necessary to earn a profit after taxes of 10 percent of sales will equal the desired after-tax profit divided by (1-t). In the above equations, the necessary profit before taxes will become (.10) / (1 – t) = .1667, or 16.67% of sales.

Margin of Safety

The margin of safety is the difference (dollars or units) between the breakeven point and budgeted sales. Margin of safety may also be expressed as a percentage:

$$\textit{Margin of Safety} = \frac{\textit{Budgeted Sales - Breakeven Point}}{\textit{Budgeted Sales}} \qquad (4)$$

The margin of safety shows managers how much sales could fall without resulting in a loss. For example, in The Lone Star Company problem, the budgeted sale for the coming year is 40,000 units (or $200,000) and the breakeven point is 25,000 units (or $125,000). The margin of safety is thus 15,000 units (or $75,000) or 15,000/40,000 = 37.5% (or $75,000/$200,000 = 37.5%). This means that the company could absorb a 37.5% decline in budgeted sales without resulting in a loss. Generally, a high margin of safety indicates a relatively safe operating position.

What-If Analysis: The Effects of Changes in Cost, Volume, and Price on the Breakeven Point and Budgeted Profits

As stated at the beginning of the chapter, profit is a function of many factors. Changes in the factors underlying profit may cause the breakeven point and budgeted profits to change. C-V-P analysis is a useful tool to help managers in examining the effects of certain possible changes in the underlying factors on the breakeven point and budgeted profits. For purposes of illustration, the following six independent cases will be considered for The Lone Star Company. Each case represents a change from the original budgeted data on variable cost, selling price, sales volume, and/or fixed costs.

Case 1 Variable cost increases 10 percent.

An increase of 10 percent in variable cost would increase variable cost to $3.30 per unit. In other words, it would reduce the contribution margin from $2 to $1.70 per unit. Based on the new data, the breakeven point becomes:

$$Q_{be} = \frac{\$50,000}{\$1.70} = 29,412\ units,$$

or

$5 (29,412) = $147,060.

The budgeted profit at budgeted sales of 40,000 units becomes:

$5 (40,000) – $50,000 – $3.3 (40,000)
= $18,000.

Therefore, the effect of the 10% increase in variable cost will increase the breakeven point from 25,000 units to 29,412 units and decrease the budgeted profit from $30,000 to $18,000.

Case 2 Selling price is increased by 10 percent.

An increase of 10 percent in selling price would increase the contribution margin from $2 to $2.50 per unit. Based on the new data, the breakeven point becomes:

$$Q_{be} = \frac{\$50,000}{\$2.5} = 20,000\ units,$$

or

$5.50 (20,000) = $110,000.

The budgeted profit at budgeted sales of 40,000 units would be:

$5.50 (40,000) – $50,000 – $3 (40,000)
= $50,000.

Therefore, the effect of a 10% increase in selling price will decrease the breakeven point from 25,000 units to 20,000 units and increase the budgeted profit from $30,000 to $50,000.

Case 3 Budgeted volume of sales decreases 10 percent.

Since selling price, variable cost, and fixed cost are not changed, the breakeven point will remain the same as before, 25,000 units. However, the budgeted profit would change because of the decrease in budgeted volume of sales from 40,000 units to 36,000 units. Based on the new data, the budgeted profit becomes:

$5 (36,000) – $50,000 – $3 (36,000)
= $22,000.

Case 4 Fixed cost decreases $10,000.

If the fixed cost decreases $10,000, total fixed cost will decrease from $50,000 to $40,000. The new breakeven point would be:

$$Q_{be} = \frac{\$40,000}{\$5 - \$3} = 20,000\ units,$$

or

$5 (20,000) = $100,000.

The new budgeted profit at budgeted sales of 40,000 units will become:

$5 (40,000) – $40,000 – $3 (40,000)
= $40,000.

Case 5 Selling price is decreased 5 percent and variable cost decreases 5 percent.

A decrease of 5 percent in selling price and variable cost will result in a new contribution margin of $5 (1 – .05) – $3 (1 – .05) = $1.90 per unit. Based on the new contribution, the breakeven point becomes:

$$Q_{be} = \frac{\$50,000}{\$1.90} = 26,316\ units,$$

or

$4.75 (26,316) = $125,000.

The new budgeted profit will be:

$4.75 (40,000) – $50,000 – $2.85 (40,000)
= $26,000.

Case 6 Selling price is increased by 10 percent, variable cost increases 10 percent, and fixed cost decreases $5,000.

An increase of 10 percent in selling price and variable cost will result in a new contribution margin of $5.50 – $3.30 = $2.20 per unit. In addition, if the fixed cost decreases $5,000, the new total fixed cost will be $45,000. Based on the new data, the breakeven point becomes:

$$Q_{be} = \frac{\$45,000}{\$2.20} = 20,454\ units,$$

or

$5.50 (20,454) = $112,500.

The budgeted profit at budgeted sales of 40,000 units will be:

$5.50 (40,000) – $45,000 – $3.30 (40,000)
= $43,000.

Assumptions and Limitations of Traditional Cost-Volume-Profit Analysis

Traditional C-V-P analysis is based on some assumptions concerning the behavior of sales revenue, costs, and volume. Careful consideration of these assumptions will aid in understanding C-V-P analysis and its applications. The following assumptions underlie traditional C-V-P analysis:

1. Linear cost and revenue behavior-variable costs are assumed to be proportional to volume and fixed costs are assumed to remain constant within the relevant range. Selling prices are assumed to be unchanged. The assumption of linear revenue and cost functions permits the use of straight lines to represent revenue and cost functions in a breakeven chart. This assumption implies that efficiency and productivity of workers do not change in the period under consideration.
2. Constant inventory level-Traditional C-V-P analysis assumes either no inventory or no significant changes in the beginning and ending inventory levels. That is, inventory remains constant or is zero. This assumption implies that sales volume is equal to production volume.
3. Single product-The analysis assumes that there is only one product under consideration. In a case with multiple products, the sales mix must be assumed to remain constant. This will be discussed in a later section.
4. Deterministic model-Traditional C-V-P analysis assumes a single estimate of each model parameter. Thus it provides a deterministic solution. Risk and uncertainty associated with estimates of the parameter are not considered.

The business world is not static; it is dynamic. Few business situations satisfy the above assumptions, and recognition of them is necessary to avoid misapplication of the method. However, C-V-P analysis need not adhere rigidly to the assumptions discussed above. The analysis may be modified by relaxing some of the assumptions to make it more consistent with actual operating situations. In the following sections and the appendix to this chapter, some extensions of traditional C-V-P analysis will be discussed.

Cost-Volume-Profit Analysis with Nonlinear Cost and Revenue Functions

Traditional C-V-P analysis assumes linear cost and revenue functions. In reality the cost functions are more likely to be curvilinear, because of what is known in economic theory as the law of diminishing returns. The revenue functions would be linear only in a highly competitive industry, where demand for a firm's products is perfectly elastic. For firms not in a highly competitive industry, the revenue functions would be curvilinear because of inelastic demand for the products. The following example with curvilinear revenue and cost functions will be used to illustrate nonlinear C-V-P analysis.

Assume a firm has total revenue (TR) and total cost (TC) functions as follows: (X represents the units of output)

$$TR = 62X - 2X^2$$

$$TC = \frac{X^3}{3} - 2X^2 + 31X + \frac{308}{3}$$

These two functions are plotted in Illustration 4-3.

Illustration 4-3 Nonlinear Revenue and Cost Functions

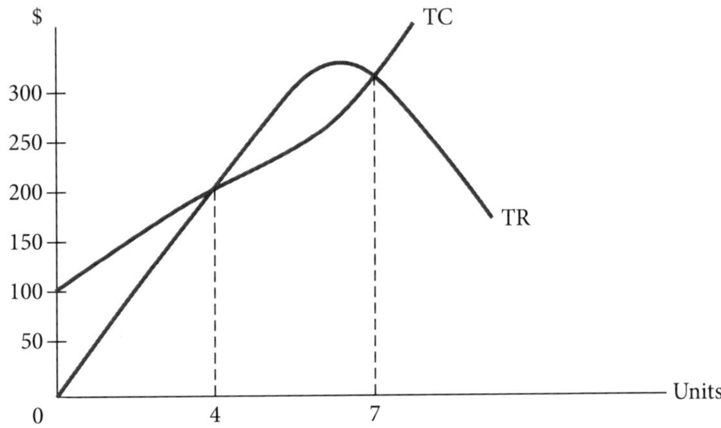

The breakeven point is the level of output at which TR = TC. In Illustration 4-3, we see that there are two breakeven points in the example. These two breakeven points can be obtained by solving the following equation for X:

TR = TC

that is, $$62X - 2X^2 = \frac{X^3}{3} - 2X^2 + 31X + \frac{308}{3}$$

or $186X - 6X^2 = X^3 - 6X^2 + 93X + 308$

$X^3 - 93X + 308 = 0$
$(X-4)(X-7)(X+11) = 0$
$X = 4, 7$, and -11.

Therefore, the breakeven points are 4 and 7 units (negative production is not possible).

It is interesting to note that this analysis can be extended to determine the output level that results in maximum profit. In the short-run, in order to maximize a firm's profits, management should expand its output to a level where marginal revenue (MR) equals marginal cost (MC) of a product. The output that maximizes profit can be found by the following two methods:

Method 1: The Marginal Cost and Revenue Approach

MR represents the rate of change in total revenue with respect to a change in volume. Therefore, the MR function can be found by differentiating the total revenue function with respect to the output. That is:

$$MR = \frac{d(TR)}{d(X)} = 62 - 4X.$$

Since MC represents the rate of change in total costs with respect to a change in volume, the MC function can be found by differentiating the total cost function with respect to the output. That is:

$$MC = \frac{d(TC)}{d(X)} = X2 - 4X + 31.$$

By setting MR = MC and solving for X, the output that results in maximum profit is determined as

$$\begin{aligned} MR &= MC \\ 62 - 4X &= X^2 - 4X + 31 \\ X &= 5.57. \end{aligned}$$

Method 2: Differentiating the Profit Function

Profit (π) is determined by total revenue minus total cost. Thus, the profit function may be expressed as:

$$\begin{aligned} \pi &= TR - TC \\ &= (62X - 2X^2) - (\frac{X^3}{3} - 2X^2 + 31X + \frac{308}{3}) \\ &= 31X - \frac{X^3}{3} - \frac{308}{3} \end{aligned}$$

Since the slope of a function is zero at its maximum, the output that maximizes profit can be found by the following three steps:

a. differentiating the profit function with respect to X,
b. setting the derivative equal to zero,
c. solving the equation resulting from step b for X.

That is: X = 5.57.

$$\frac{d(\pi)}{d(X)} = 31 - X^2 = 0$$

$$X = 5.57$$

Therefore, the firm should produce and sell 5.57 units to maximize profit. The profit at this level of output can be determined as follows:

$$\begin{aligned} \pi &= TR - TC \\ &= 31X - \frac{X^3}{3} - \frac{308}{3} \\ &= 31(5.57) - \frac{5.57^3}{3} - \frac{308}{3} \\ &= 12.4. \end{aligned}$$

Multi-Product C-V-P Analysis

The discussion to this point has been limited to a single product situation. The analysis can be extended to multiple products if the sales mix is known. For purposes of illustration, consider the following problem with a sales mix of 3 units of Product A and 1 unit of Product B:

Product	*Unit Contribution Margin*	*Sales Mix*
A	$1	3 units
B	$2	1 unit

Total fixed costs $100,000

If we consider the sales mix of 3 units of A and 1 unit of B as a package, the breakeven point can be determined as follows:

The contribution margin per package would be ($1) (3) + ($2) (1) = $5.

The breakeven point in packages would be $\frac{\$100,000}{\$5} = 20,000$ packages.

The breakeven point in units of Product A is 3 X 20,000 = 60,000 units.

The breakeven point in units of Product B is 1 X 20,000 = 20,000 units.

It should be noted that any change in the sales mix would change the C-V-P relationship. Therefore, in calculating breakeven point for a multi-product situation, it is necessary to assume a constant sales mix. Resource allocation among the various products is an important managerial decision in a multiproduct firm. When making product mix decisions, management must take into consideration the efficient allocation of scarce resources among the alternative products. If an additional unit of one product is produced, the firm will incur an opportunity cost from the decrease in quantities of other products. Linear programming is a useful mathematical tool that can be used to determine the product mix which maximizes the total contribution margin given a set of limited resources. This topic is discussed in a later chapter.

Summary

Profit planning is one of the most important management functions. Cost-volume-profit analysis provides a useful tool for examining the effect of selling price, costs, and volume on profit. In this chapter, we discussed traditional C-V-P analysis with its assumptions and limitations. We also discussed some modifications of traditional C-V-P analysis to make the analysis more consistent with reality and to broaden its area of application.

Key Definitions

Breakeven point	The level of activity at which total revenue equals total costs.
Contribution margin	The difference between sales price and variable costs. It may be expressed as a total, a ratio, or on a per-unit basis.
Contribution margin approach	An approach used to analyze the relationship between cost, volume, and profit using the contribution margin.
Contribution margin ratio	A ratio stating the amount which each dollar of sales adds to income.
Equation approach	An approach to cost-volume-profit analysis which establishes a basic relationship between sale revenues, variable costs, fixed costs, and desired profit.
Graphic approach	An approach to cost-volume-profit analysis which utilizes a graphic presentation of the relationship between volume, variable costs, fixed costs, and profit.
Margin of safety	The difference (dollars or units) between the breakeven point and budgeted sales.

Appendix

C-V-P Analysis Under Conditions of Uncertainty

Traditional C-V-P analysis assumes single estimates of unit variable cost, fixed cost, unit selling price, and volume. It does not consider risk and uncertainty associated with estimates, and ignoring these factors in the operations of business may severely limit the usefulness of traditional C-V-P analysis.

If any variable that is used in the determination of profit is subject to uncertainty, managers should analyze the potential effect of this uncertainty. In this appendix, a stochastic analytical method will be introduced to compute the expected profit and its related standard deviation. A procedure for estimating the probability of attaining a given level of profitability (including breakeven) will be discussed and illustrated.

First, let us assume that volume (Q) is a normally distributed random variable, with mean E(Q) and standard deviation a_Q. Assume also that the other model parameters (selling price, variable cost, and fixed cost) are known constants. Since a linear combination of normally distributed random variables is itself normally distributed, the resulting profit (π) is also normally distributed. In this case, the expected profit is

$$E(\pi) = (P - V) \bullet E(Q) - F \quad (5)$$

and the standard deviation for the profit function is given by:

$$\sigma_\pi = (P - V)\,\sigma_Q. \quad (6)$$

As an example, assume that the Belk Company has annual fixed costs of $100,000 and variable costs of $400 per unit of its product B. Management has set the unit selling price at $500, but annual demand is uncertain. Management expects annual sales to be 1,200 units with a standard deviation of 100 units.

Applying equations (5) and (6), we can estimate the expected profit and the related standard deviation as follows:

$$E(\pi) = (P - V) \bullet E(Q) - F$$
$$= (\$500 - \$400) \bullet (1{,}200) - \$100{,}000$$
$$= \$20{,}000$$

$$\sigma_\pi = (P - V)\,\sigma_Q.$$
$$= (\$500 - \$400) \bullet (100)$$
$$= \$10{,}000.$$

Given this information on the resulting profit, we can compute the probability of at least breaking even or the probability of achieving any given level of profitability.

To find the probability of at least breaking even, we first calculate the number of standard deviations between the expected profit and zero profit:

$$\frac{\$0 - \$20{,}000}{\$10{,}000} = -2$$

Referring to Table 4-1 (a normal probability distribution table), we can find the probability of at least breaking even:

$$\text{Prob.}(\pi \geq 0) = \text{Prob.}(Z \geq -2)$$
$$= 1 - .02275$$
$$= 97.725\%.$$

The probability distribution of profits and the probability of at least breaking even are shown in Illustration 4-4.

To find the probability of attaining a profit of $30,000 or more, again we first calculate the number of standard deviations between the expected profit and $30,000:

$$\frac{\$30{,}000 - \$20{,}000}{\$10{,}000} = 1$$

Illustration 4-4 A Probability Distribution of Profits

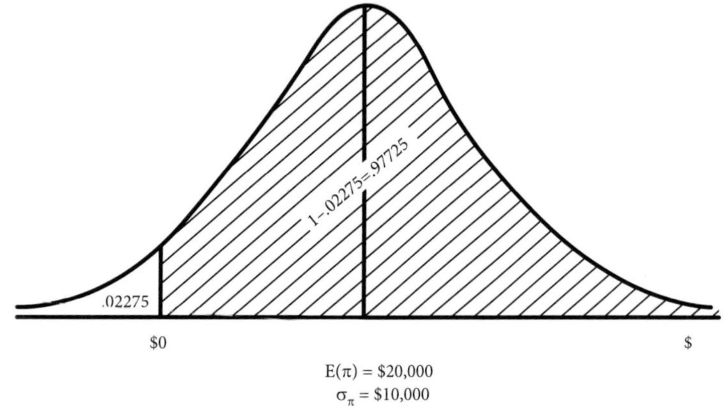

Using Table 4-1, we find

$$\text{Prob. } (\pi \geq 30{,}000) = \text{Prob. } (Z > 1)$$
$$= .15866$$
$$= 15.866\%.$$

The shaded area in Illustration 4-5 represents the probability of attaining a profit of $30,000 or more.

The above analysis is useful when a single variable is assumed to be normally distributed. When a number of variables are subject to uncertainty, the analysis becomes more complex.

Consider the following example where a firm has the following probabilistic estimates of variable cost, fixed cost, selling price, and volume:

Model Variable		*Expected Value*		*Standard Deviation*	
Unit variable cost	(V)	E(V) =	$20	σ_V =	$2
Fixed cost	(F)	E(F) =	$100,000	σ_F =	$5,000
Unit selling price	(P)	E(P) =	$30	σ_P =	$3
Volume	(Q)	E(Q) =	25,000 units	σ_Q =	1,000 units

For the sake of simplicity, the variables are assumed to be independent and normally distributed. In this case, the expected profit, $E(\pi)$, and the related standard deviation, σ_π can be calculated as follows:

$$E(\pi) = [E(P) - E(V)] \bullet E(Q) - E(F)$$
$$= (\$30 - \$20)(25{,}000) - \$100{,}000$$
$$= \$150{,}000$$

$$\textit{Cost of Units Completed} = \textit{Total Cost Per Equivalent Unit} \times \textit{Number of Units Completed}$$

Illustration 4-5 A Probability Distribution of Profits

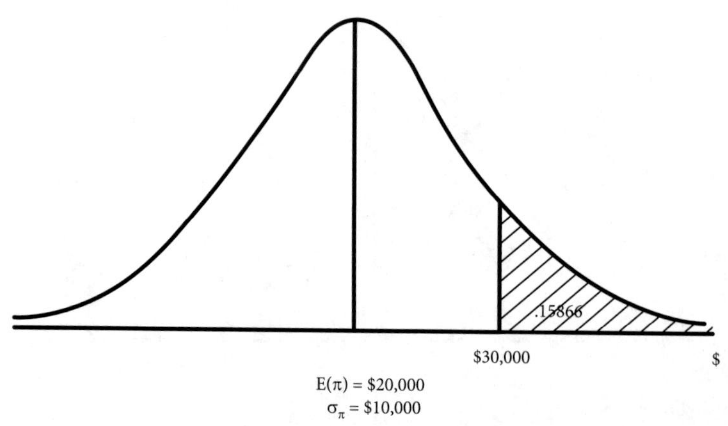

The expected profit is $150,000 and the related standard deviation is $95,724. If the resulting profit is known to be normally distributed, probabilistic statements of any desired profit range can be derived from use of a normal distribution table. The following table gives some examples:

Profit Range	*Probability*
(1) Profit at least $100,000	69.85%
(2) Profit greater than $300,000	5.82%
(3) Profit between $50,000 and $250,000	70.98%
(4) Profit greater than $0	94.18%

If the distribution of the resulting profit is not known, Tchebycheff's theorem may be used to calculate probabilistic statements of desired profit ranges.[1] It should be noted that our discussion is limited to a case where the model variables are independent and normally distributed. For a case where the model variables are not independent and not normally distributed, a simulation approach may be used to derive probabilistic statements of desired profit ranges. Since the subject of simulation is beyond the scope of this text, it is not discussed here.[2]

Questions

4-1 What can cause profit to change?

4-2 What is a breakeven point? How can a breakeven point be calculated?

4-3 How can a breakeven chart be used by managers as a planning device?

4-4 Define "contribution margin." Why is it important to managers in profit planning?

4-5 Define "margin of safety." How is it determined?

4-6 Why is the cost-volume-profit relationship important to managers?

4-7 Discuss the effects of the following changes on the breakeven point and budgeted profit: (Consider each case independently and assume all other factors remain constant.)

(a) a decrease in variable cost

(b) an increase in fixed cost

(c) an increase in selling prices

1 Buzby, S.L., "Extending the Applicability of Probabilistic Management Planning and Control Method," *The Accounting Review* (January 1974) pp. 42-49.

2 Students interested in such an approach are referred to the following article: "Model Sampling: A Stochastic C-V-P Analysis," by Mawsen Liao, *The Accounting Review* (October 1974), pp. 780-790.

Table 4-1 Areas Under the Normal Curve

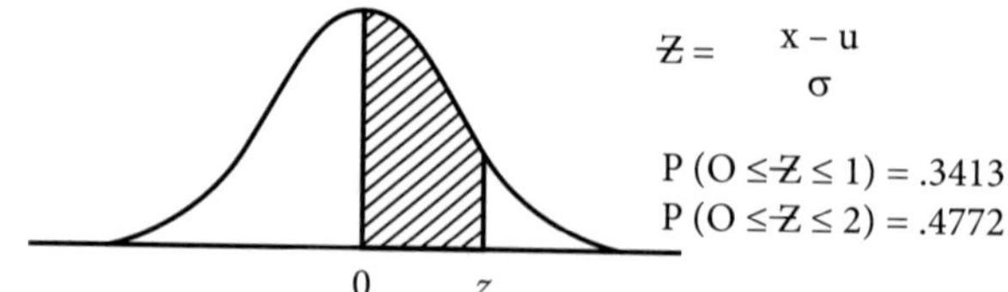

z	.00	.01	.02	.03	.04	.05	.06	.07	.08	.09
0.0	.0000	.0040	.0080	.0120	.0160	.0199	.0239	.0279	.0319	.0359
0.1	.0398	.0438	.0478	.0517	.0557	.0596	.0636	.0675	.0714	.0753
0.2	.0793	.0832	.0871	.0910	.0948	.0987	.1026	.1064	.1103	.1141
0.3	.1179	.1217	.1255	.1293	.1331	.1368	.1406	.1443	.1480	.1517
0.4	.1554	.1591	.1628	.1664	.1700	.1736	.1772	.1808	.1844	.1879
0.5	.1915	.1950	.1985	.2019	.2054	.2088	.2123	.2157	.2190	.2224
0.6	.2257	.2291	.2324	.2357	.2389	.2422	.2454	.2486	.2517	.2549
0.7	.2580	.2611	.2642	.2673	.2704	.2734	.2764	.2794	.2823	.2852
0.8	.2881	.2910	.2939	.2967	.2995	.3023	.3051	.3078	.3106	.3133
0.9	.3159	.3186	.3212	.3238	.3264	.3289	.3315	.3340	.3365	.3389
1.0	.3413	.3438	.3461	.3485	.3508	.3531	.3554	.3577	.3599	.3621
1.1	.3643	.3665	.3686	.3708	.3729	.3749	.3770	.3790	.3810	.3830
1.2	.3849	.3869	.3888	.3907	.3925	.3944	.3962	.3980	.3997	.4015
1.3	.4032	.4049	.4066	.4082	.4099	.4115	.4131	.4147	.4162	.4177
1.4	.4192	.4207	.4222	.4236	.4251	.4265	.4279	.4292	.4306	.4319
1.5	.4332	.4345	.4357	.4370	.4382	.4394	.4406	.4418	.4429	.4441
1.6	.4452	.4463	.4474	.4484	.4495	.4505	.4515	.4525	.4535	.4545
1.7	.4554	.4564	.4573	.4582	.4591	.4599	.4608	.4616	.4625	,4633
1.8	.4641	.4649	.4656	.4664	.4671	.4678	.4686	.4693	.4699	.4706
1.9	.4713	.4719	.4726	.4732	.4738	.4744	.4750	.4756	.4761	.4767
2.0	.4772	.4778	.4783	.4788	.4793	.4798	.4803	.4808	.4812	.4817
2.1	.4821	.4826	.4830	.4834	.4838	.4842	.4846	.4850	.4854	.4857
2.2	.4861	.4864	.4868	.4871	.4875	.4878	.4881	.4884	.4887	.4890
2.3	.4893	.4896	.4898	.4901	.4904	.4906	.4909	.4911	.4913	.4916
2.4	.4918	.4920	.4922	.4925	.4927	.4929	.4931	.4932	.4934	.4936
2.5	.4938	.4940	.4941	.4943	.4945	.4946	.4948	.4949	.4951	.4952
2.6	.4953	.4955	.4956	.4957	.4959	.4960	.4961	.4962	.4963	.4964
2.7	.4965	.4966	.4967	.4968	.4969	.4970	.4971	.4972	.4973	.4974
2.8	.4974	.4975	.4976	.4977	.4977	.4978	.4979	.4979	.4980	.4981
2.9	.4981	.4982	.4982	.4982	.4984	.4984	.4985	.4985	.4986	.4986
3.0	.4987	.4987	.4987	.4988	.4988	.4989	.4989	.4989	.4990	.4990

(d) an increase in volume by 5% over the original budgeted volume

(e) an increase in the commission rate for sales people.

4-8 How can cost-volume-profit analysis be used in management planning and control?

4-9 What are the merits of having a high contribution margin ratio as opposed to a low contribution margin ratio?

4-10 Discuss the assumptions and weaknesses inherent in traditional cost volume-profit analysis.

4-11 A company increased the selling price for its product from $1.00 to $1.10 per unit when total fixed costs increased from $400,000 to $480,000 and variable cost per unit remained unchanged. How would these changes affect the breakeven point?

4-12 The contribution margin per unit is the difference between the selling price and the variable cost per unit, and the contribution margin ratio is the ratio of the contribution margin to the selling price per unit. If the selling price and the variable cost per unit both increase 10% and fixed costs do not change, what is the effect on the contribution margin per unit and the contribution margin ratio?

(a) Contribution margin per unit and the contribution margin ratio both remain unchanged.

(b) Contribution margin per unit and the contribution margin ratio both increase.

(c) Contribution margin per unit increases and the contribution margin ratio remains unchanged.

(d) Contribution margin per unit increases and the contribution margin ratio decreases.

(AICPA adapted)

PROBLEMS

4-13 *(Terminology) Match the following lettered terms on the left with the appropriate numbered definition on the right.*

a. Breakeven point	1. Contribution margin divided by sales
b. Contribution margin	2. Utilizes a graphic presentation of the relationship between volume, variable and fixed costs, and profit
c. Contribution margin ratio	3. Total cost equals total revenue
d. Equation approach	4. Difference between the breakeven point and budgeted sales

e. Graphic approach	5. Establishes a relationship between sales revenue, variable and fixed costs, and desired profit
f. Margin of safety	6. Total sales minus all variable costs

4-14 *A Breakeven Chart and Relevant Range*

A breakeven chart, as illustrated below, is a useful technique for showing relationships between costs, volume, and profits.

(1) Identify the numbered components of the breakeven chart.

(2) Discuss the significance of the concept of the "relevant range" to breakeven analysis.

(*AICPA adapted*)

4-15 *Breakeven Analysis*

Candice Company has decided to introduce a new product. The new product can be manufactured by either a capital intensive method or labor intensive method. The manufacturing method will not affect the quality of the product. The estimated manufacturing costs by the two methods are as follows.

	Capital Intensive		Labor Intensive	
Raw Materials		$5.00		$5.60
Direct Labor	.5DLH @ $12	$6.00	.8DLH @ $12	$7.20
Variable Overhead	.5DLH @ $6	$3.00	.8DLH @ $6	$4.80
Directly Traceable incremental fixed manufacturing costs	$2,440,000		$1,320,000	

Candice's market research department has recommended an introductory unit sales price of $30. The incremental selling expenses are estimated to be $500,000 annually plus $2 for each unit sold regardless of manufacturing method.

Required:

(a) Calculate the estimated breakeven point in annual unit sales of the new product if Candice Company uses the:

1. capital intensive manufacturing method.
2. labor intensive manufacturing method.

(b) Determine the annual unit sales volume at which Candice Company would be indifferent between the two manufacturing methods.

(*IMA adapted*)

4-16 *Fundamental Terms and Assumptions in C-V-P Analysis*

Cost-volume-earnings analysis (breakeven analysis) is used to determine and express the interrelationships of different volumes of activity (sales), costs, sales prices, and sales mix to earnings. More specifically, the analysis is concerned with what will be the effect on earnings of changes in sales volume, sales prices, sales mix, and costs.

Required:

a. Certain terms are fundamental to cost-volume-earnings analysis. Explain the meaning of each of the following terms:

1. Fixed costs.
2. Variable costs.
3. Relevant range.
4. Breakeven point.
5. Margin of safety.
6. Sales mix

b. Several assumptions are implicit in cost-volume-earnings analysis. What are these assumptions?

c. In a recent period Zero Company had the following experience:

Sales (10,000 units @ $200)	Fixed	Variable	$2,000,000
Costs:			
Direct material..................	$ ----	$ 200,000	
Direct labor.........................	----	400,000	
Factory overhead.............	160,000	600,000	
Administrative expenses	180,000	80,000	
Other expenses................	200,000	120,000	
Total costs..........................	$540,000	$1,400,000	1,940,000
Net income.....................			$ 60,000

Each item below is independent.

1. Calculate the breakeven point for Zero in terms of units and sales dollars. Show your calculations.
2. What sales volume would be required to generate a net income of $96,000? Show your calculations.
3. What is the breakeven point if management makes a decision, which increases fixed costs by $18,000? Show your calculations.

(AICPA adapted)

4-17 *Sales Needed for a Desired Profit*

Freedom, Inc., management had formed cost studies and projected the following annual cost based on 40,000 units of production and sales:

	Total Annual Cost	*Percent of Variable Portion of Total Annual Costs*
Direct Material..................	$400,000	100%
Direct Labor......................	360,000	75
Manufacturing Overhead	300,000	40
Selling, general and administrative...................	200,000	25

Required:

1. Compute Freedom's unit selling price that will yield a projected 10% profit on sales if sales are 40,000 units.
2. Assume that management selects a selling price of $30 per unit. Compute Freedom's dollar sales that will yield a projected 10% profit on sales assuming the above variable-fixed costs relationship are valid.

4-18 *Selling Price Desired Profit*

The Seahawk Company is planning to sell 200,000 units of Product B. The fixed costs are $400,000 and the variable costs are 60% of the selling price. In order to realize a profit of $100,000, what would the selling price per unit have to be?

(*AICPA adapted*)

4-19 *Additional Contribution Margin and Fixed Costs*

The following data apply to Frelm Corporation for a given period:

Total variable cost per unit.................... $3.50
Contribution margin/sales.................... 30%
Breakeven sales (present volume) $1,000,000

Required:

Frelm wants to sell an additional 50,000 units at the same selling price and contribution margin. By how much can fixed costs increase to generate a contribution margin equal to 10% of the sales value of the additional 50,000 units to be sold?

(*AICPA adapted*)

4-20 *Determination of Sales for a Given Profit*

Day Company is a medium-sized manufacturer of lamps. During 20X9 a new line called "Twilight" was made available to Day's customers. The breakeven point for sales of Twilight is $400,000 with a contribution margin of 40%.

Required:

Assuming that the operating profit for the Twilight line for 20X9 amounted to $200,000, determine the total sales for 20X9.

(*AICPA adapted*)

4-21 *Sales Needed for a Desired Profit*

Moon Company sells Product Q at $6 a unit. In 20X0 fixed costs are expected to be $200,000 and variable costs are estimated at $4 a unit. How many units of Product Q must Moon sell to generate operating income of $40,000?

(*AICPA adapted*)

4-22 *C-V-P Analysis with Step Fixed Costs*

Dallas Corporation wishes to market a new product for $1.50 a unit. Fixed costs to manufacture this product are $100,000 for less than 500,000 units and $150,000 for 500,000 or more units. The contribution margin is 20%. How many units must be sold to realize an income from this product of $100,000?

(*AICPA adapted*)

4-23 *Multi-Product C-V-P Analysis*

Taylor, Inc. produces only two products, Acdom and Belnom. These account for 60% and 40% of the total sales dollars of Taylor, respectively. Variable costs (as a percentage of sales dollars) are 60% for Acdom and 85% for Belnom. Total fixed costs are $150,000. There are no other costs.

Required:

(1) What is Taylor's breakeven point in sales dollars?

(2) Assuming that the total fixed costs of Taylor increase by 30%, what amount of sales dollars would be necessary to generate an income of $9,000?

(*AICPA adapted*)

4-24 *Breakeven Point and Operating Income*

You are given the following information:

Full Ton Company
Financial Projection for Product USA
For the Year Ended December 31, 20X2

Sales (100 units at $100 a unit		$10,000
Manufacturing cost of good sold		
Direct Labor	$1,500	
Direct Materials Used	1,400	
Variable Factory Overhead	1,000	
Fixed Factory Overhead	500	
Total Manufacturing cost of goods sold		4,400
Gross Profit		5,600
Selling Expenses:		
Variable	600	
Fixed	1,000	
Administrative Expenses:		
Variable	500	
Fixed	1,000	
Total selling and administrative expenses		3,100
Operating Income		$ 2,500

Required:

(1) How many units of Product USA would have to be sold to break even?
(2) What would the operating income be if sales increase by 25%?
(3) What would be the dollar sales at the breakeven point if fixed factory overhead increases by $1,700?

(*AICPA adapted*)

4-25 *Variable Cost Ratio and Profit*

The Equality Company is now breaking even at sales of $400,000. The company has a total fixed cost of *$150,000*. The company's budgeted sales for next period are $600,000. What profit can the company expect for the next period?

4-26 *Analysis of an Expansion Proposal*

The Enchantment Company is considering an expansion of its present facilities to meet an expected increase demand for its product. The company's current contribution margin ratio is 30 percent. The expanding proposal requires an increase of $50,000 in fixed costs. No changes in unit selling price and unit variable cost are expected for the coming year. The company is now breaking even at $300,000 of sales.

Required:

(1) Determine the breakeven point after expansion.
(2) If the additional facilities are provided, determine the expected profit for sales of $600,000 in the coming year.

4-27 *Breakeven Point, Budgeted Profit, and Additional Sales Promotion*

The Golden Company has experienced a steady growth in the past three years. The management of the company believes that an additional sales promotion program is necessary to maintain the company's present growth. The company's normal activity is 20,000 units per year. The following budgeted data have been prepared for the current year 20Xl:

Unit variable cost	$ 15
Fixed costs:	
Factory overhead	30,000
Marketing	40,000
Administrative	20,000
Unit selling price	30
Budgeted sales and production	20,000 units

Required: (Assume unit selling price and cost behaviors remain the same in 20X2)

(1) Calculate the breakeven point in units for 20Xl.

(2) Determine the additional sales in dollars so that income in 20X2 will equal 20X1's budgeted profit, if an additional $15,000 will be spent for the sales promotion in 20X2.

(3) Determine the maximum amount that can be spent on the additional sales promotion in 20X2 to generate an overall sales level of 30,000 units if a profit of $280,000 is desired.

4-28 *Multi-Product Breakeven Analysis*

Highland Manufacturing Company produces three products: A, B, and C. The unit selling price, unit variable cost, and total fixed costs are given below:

	A	B	C
Unit selling price	$10	$8	$6
Unit variable price	8	5	3
Total Fixed Costs	$1,000,000		

The management of the company wishes to determine what the sales mix of the three products should be. Currently two sales mixes are under consideration: (a) equal quantities of each product (2A – 2B – 2C), and (b) one-sixth of the units will be A, one-third will be B, and one-half will be C (1A – 2B – 3C).

Required:

Calculate breakeven points (in units) for each sales mix.

4-29 *Multi-Product C-V-P Analysis (Spreadsheet)*

White Tire Company produces tires for mountain bikes and for racing bikes. The two products sell in a ratio of nine mountain bike tires to seven racing bike tires. Fixed costs for 2007 were $160,000. The following data are also available for each tire:

Racing Bike Tire	*Mountain Bike Tire*	
Selling Price	$12.00	$10.75
Direct Material	3.50	4.10
Conversion Cost	1.50	1.45
Variable Selling and Admin. Expenses	.35	.28

Required:

Using a computer spreadsheet program, prepare a schedule which contains the above data and which calculates the following for a basket consisting of nine racing bike tires and seven mountain bike tires:

(a) The contribution margin.
(b) The contribution margin ratio.
(c) The breakeven point in number of baskets and units of each type of tire
The breakeven point in total sales dollars and sales dollars for each type of tire.

4-30 *Sales Needed for a Desired Profit*

The Pelican Corporation has a variable cost ratio of 60 percent of sales and total fixed costs of $1,000,000 per year. The corporation expects the same variable cost ratio and fixed costs for the coming year.

Required:

(1) Calculate the breakeven point for the coming year.
(2) What income can be expected from a budgeted sales of $2,800,000?
(3) Calculate the level of sales required to produce an income of $500,000 after income taxes (assume a 40% of income tax rate).
(4) If the current year's operating income was $200,000, calculate the necessary increase in sales revenue in the coming year for an operating income of $300,000.

4-31 *Acquisition Analysis*

The Evergreen Company is currently considering an acquisition of either Firm A or Firm B, each having the same acquisition price. Both Firms A and B manufacture electrical pencil sharpeners of identical quality. Firm A and Firm B's unit variable cost, total fixed costs, and capacity are given below:

	Firm A	*Firm B*
Unit variable cost	$ 10	$ 12
Total fixed costs per year	700,000	400,000
Capacity per month	20,000 units	20,000 units

The selling price for the pencil sharpeners is $15 per unit.

Required:

(1) Which firm should be acquired if the estimated demand for the product is
(a) 240,000 units per year, and
(b) 140,000 units per year?
(2) At what level of demand would the Evergreen Company be indifferent to the acquisition of Firm A or Firm B?

4-32 *A Breakeven Chart and Budgeted Income*

The Garden Company's production and operating data for a typical month are as follows:

Sales (units)		50,000
Beginning inventory		0
Ending inventory		0
Unit selling price	$	20
Unit production costs:		
Direct material	$	8
Direct labor	$	4
Variable overhead	$	2
Fixed overhead (at normal volume of 60,000 units)	$	2
Variable selling expenses		$20,000
Fixed selling expenses		$10,000
Fixed administrative expenses		$30,000

Required:

(1) Prepare a breakeven chart.

(2) Calculate sales in units required to produce an income of $150,000 before taxes.

(3) Determine the income for the company operating at normal capacity.

4-33 *Breakeven Point and Sales Needed for a Desired Profit*

The following condensed statement of operating income is for the Empire Company for a typical year's operation.

Statement of Operating Income for Any Normal Year

Sales (50,000 units @ $40)		$ 2,000,000
Costs of sales:		
Direct materials	$ 400,000	
Direct labor	500,000	
Factory overhead (40% fixed, 60% variable)	200,000	1,100,000
Gross profit		900,000
Selling and administrative expenses:	400,000	
Selling expenses (50% fixed, 50% variable)		
Administrative expenses (80% fixed, 20% variable)	300,000	700,000
Operating income		$ 200,000

Required:

(1) Calculate breakeven point in units.

(2) Determine number of units that must be sold to produce an income of $300,000 per year before income taxes.

(3) Determine number of units that must be sold to produce an after-tax income of $120,000 if the income tax rate is 40%.

(4) Determine the number of units that must be sold to break even if wages for indirect labor are increased by 10 percent in an unusual year. (Assume 20 percent of the variable factory overhead is payroll expenses.)

4-34 *Breakeven Point and Sales Needed for a Desired Profit*

The Pine Tree Company is currently operating at its maximum capacity. Its budgeted income statement at maximum capacity of 1,000,000 units per year is as follows:

The Pine Tree Company
Budgeted Income Statement
For Any Year Operating at Maximum Capacity

Sales (1,000,000 units @ $5)		$ 5,000,000
Cost of goods sold:		
Variable	2,500,000	
Fixed	1,000,000	3,500,000
Gross profit		1,500,000
Selling and administrative expenses:		
Variable	400,000	
Fixed	400,000	800,000
Operating income		$ 700,000

The company is considering an expansion of its facility because the company expects that sales could be increased to 1,200,000 units per year. The company's engineering studies indicate that the increased volume of 200,000 units could be obtained through an additional facility that would cost $250,000 of fixed factory cost a year. However, the variable production cost and variable selling and administrative expenses are expected to decrease by 5 percent.

Required:

(1) Calculate the breakeven points before and after expansion.

(2) What dollar sales volume must be obtained after expansion to make as much income as before expansion?

(3) Calculate sales volume in units after expansion to earn an income of $800,000 before income taxes.

4-35 *Breakeven Point and Sales Needed for a Desired Profit*

The Carey Company sold 100,000 units of its product at $20 per unit. Variable costs are $14 per unit (manufacturing costs of $11 and selling costs of $3). Fixed costs are incurred uniformly throughout the year and amount to $792,000 (manufacturing costs of $500,000 and selling costs of $292,000). There are no beginning or ending inventories.

Required:

Determine the following:

(1) The breakeven point for this product.

(2) The number of units that must be sold to earn an income of $60,000 for the year (before income taxes).

(3) The number of units that must be sold to earn an after-tax income of $90,000, assuming a tax rate of 40 percent.
(4) The breakeven point for this product after a 10 percent increase in wages and salaries (assuming labor costs are 50 percent of variable costs and 20 percent of fixed costs).

(*AICPA adapted*)

4-36 *Selling Price, Income Statement, and Breakeven Point*

A client has recently leased facilities for manufacturing a new product. Based on studies made by his staff, the following data have been made available to you:

Estimated annual sales	24,000 units
Estimated costs:	*Amount*
Material	$ 96,000
Direct labor	14,400
Overhead	24,000
Administrative expense	28,800
Total	$163,200

Selling expenses are expected to be 15 percent of sales, and profit is expected to amount to $1.02 per unit.

Required:

(1) Compute the selling price per unit.
(2) Project a profit and loss statement for the year.
(3) Compute a breakeven point expressed in dollars and in units, assuming that overhead and administrative expenses are fixed but that other costs are fully variable.

(*AICPA adapted*)

4-37 *Effects of Changes in Variable Cost and Fixed Cost on C-V-P Analysis*

The president of Beth Corporation, which manufactures tape decks and sells them to producers of sound reproduction systems, anticipates a 10% wage increase on January 1 of next year to the manufacturing employees (variable labor). He expects no other changes in costs. Overhead will not change as a result of the wage increase. The president has asked you to assist him in developing the information he needs to formulate a reasonable product strategy for next year.

You are satisfied from regression analysis that volume is the primary factor affecting costs and have separated the semi-variable costs into their fixed and variable segments by means of the least-squares criterion. You also observe that the beginning and ending inventories are never materially different.

Below are the current year data assembled for your analysis:

Current selling price per unit	$80.00
Variable cost per unit:	
Material	30.00
Labor	12.00
Overhead	6.00
Total	$48.00
Annual volume of sales	5,000 units
Fixed costs	$51,000

Required:

Provide the following information for the president using cost-volume-profit analysis:

(1) What increase in the selling price is necessary to cover the 10% wage increase and still maintain the current profit-volume-cost ratio?

(2) How many tape decks must be sold to maintain the current income if the sales price remains at $80.00 and the 10% wage increase goes into effect?

(3) The president believes that an additional $190,000 of machinery (to be depreciated at 10% annually) will increase present capacity (5,300 units) by 30%. If all tape decks produced can be sold at the present price and the wage increase goes into effect, how would the estimated income, before capacity is increased, compare with the estimated income afterwards? Prepare computations of estimated income before and after the expansion.

4-38 *Cash Flow Breakeven Analysis*

Mr. Calderone started a pizza restaurant in 20X0. For this purpose a building was rented for $400 per month. Two women were hired to work full time at the restaurant and six college students were hired to work thirty hours per week delivering pizza. An outside accountant was hired for tax and bookkeeping purposes. For this service, Mr. Calderone pays $300 per month. The necessary restaurant equipment and delivery cars were purchased with cash. Mr. Calderone has noticed that expenses for utilities and supplies have been rather constant.

Mr. Calderone increased his business between 20X0 and 20X3. Profits have more than doubled since 20X0. Mr. Calderone does not understand why his profits have increased faster than his volume.

A projected income statement for 20X4 has been prepared by the accountant and is shown below:

Calderone Company
Projected Income Statement
For the Year Ended December *31, 20X4*

Sales		$95,000
Cost of goods sold	$28,500	
Wages and fringe benefits of restaurant help	8,150	
Wages and fringe benefits of delivery helpers	17,300	
Rent	4,800	
Accounting services	3,600	
Depreciation of delivery equipment	5,000	
Depreciation of restaurant equipment	3,000	
Utilities	2,325	
Supplies (soap, floor wax, etc.)	1,200	73,875
Net income before taxes		$21,125
Income taxes		6,338
Net income		$14,787

Note: The average pizza sells for $2.50. Assume that Mr. Calderone pays 30% of his income in income taxes.

Required:

(1) What is the breakeven point in number of pizzas that must be sold?

(2) What is the cash flow breakeven point in number of pizzas that must be sold?

(3) If Mr. Calderone withdraws $4,800 for personal use, how much cash will be left from the 20X4 income-producing activities?

(4) Mr. Calderone would like an after-tax net income of $20,000. What volume must be reached in number of pizzas to obtain the desired income?

(5) Briefly explain to Mr. Calderone why his profits have increased at a faster rate than his sales.

(6) Briefly explain to Mr. Calderone why his cash flow for 20X4 will exceed his profits.

(IMA adapted)

4-39 *Effects of Selling Price and Fixed Costs on C-V-P Analysis*

R.A. Ro and Company, maker of quality handmade pipes, has experienced a steady growth in sales for the past five years. However, increased competition has led Mr. Ro, the president, to believe that an aggressive advertising campaign will be necessary next year to maintain the company's present growth.

To prepare for next year's advertising campaign, the company's accountant has prepared and presented Mr. Ro with the following data for the current year, 20X2:

Cost Schedule

Variable costs:	
Direct labor	$ 8.00/pipe
Direct materials	3.25/pipe
Variable overhead	2.50/pipe
Total variable costs	$ 13.75/pipe
Fixed costs: Manufacturing	$ 25,000
Selling	40,000
Administrative	70,000
Total fixed costs	$135,000
Selling price, per pipe	$25.00
Expected sales, 20X2 (20,000 units):	$500,000
Tax rate: 40%	

Mr. Ro has set the sales target for 20X3 at a level of $550,000 (or 22,000 pipes).

Required:

(a) What is the projected after-tax net income for 20X2?

(b) What is the breakeven point in units for 20X2?

(c) Mr. Ro believes an additional selling expense of $11,250 for advertising in 20X3, with all other costs remaining constant, will be necessary to attain the sales target. What will be the after-tax net income for 20X3 if the additional $11,250 is spent?

(d) What will be the breakeven point in dollar sales for 20X3 if the additional $11,250 is spent for advertising?

(e) If the additional $11,250 is spent for advertising in 20X3, what is the required sales level in dollar sales to equal 20X2's after-tax net income?

(f) At a sales level of 22,000 units, what is the maximum amount that can be spent on advertising if an after-tax net income of $60,000 is desired?

(IMA adapted)

4-40 *Breakeven Point and Sales Needed for a Desired Profit*

All-Day Candy Company is a wholesale distributor of candy. The company services grocery, convenience and drug stores in a large metropolitan area.

Small but steady growth in sales has been achieved by the All-Day Candy Company over the past few years while candy prices have been increasing. The company is formulating its plans for the coming fiscal year. Presented below are the data used to project the current year's after-tax net income of $110,400.

Average Selling Price	$4.00	per box
Average variable cost		
Cost of candy	$2.00	per box
Selling Expenses	0.40	per box
Total	$2.40	per box
Annual Fixed Costs		
Selling	$160,000	
Administrative	280,000	
Total	$440,000	

Expected annual sales volume (390,000 boxes) $1,560,000.

Tax rate 40%

Manufacturers of candy have announced that they will increase prices of their products an average of 15 percent in the coming year due to increases in raw material (sugar, cocoa, peanuts, etc.) and labor costs. All-Day Candy Company expects that all other costs will remain at the same rates or levels as the current year.

Required:

a. What is All-Day Candy Company's breakeven point in boxes of candy for the current year?

b. What selling price per box must All-Day Candy Company charge to cover the 15 percent increase in the cost of candy and still maintain the current contribution margin ratio?

c. What volume of sales in dollars must the All-Day Candy Company achieve in the coming year to maintain the same net income after taxes as projected for the current year if the selling price of candy remains at $4.00 per box and the cost of candy increase 15 percent?

(*IMA adapted*)

4-41 *Multi-Product C-V-P Analysis*

Hewtex Electronics manufactures two products-tape recorders and electronic calculators-and sells them nationally to wholesalers and retailers. The Hewtex management is very pleased with the company's performance for the current fiscal year. Projected sales through December 31, 20X0, indicate that 70,000 tape recorders and 140,000 electronic calculators will be sold this year. The projected earnings statement, which appears below, shows that Hewtex will exceed its earnings goal of 9 percent on sales after taxes.

The tape recorder business has been fairly stable the last few years, and the company does not intend to change the tape recorder price. However, the competition among manufacturers of electronic calculators has been increasing. Hewtex's calculators have been very popular with consumers. In order to sustain this interest in their calculators and to meet the price reductions expected from competitors, management has decided to reduce the wholesale price of its calculator from $22.50 to $20.00 per unit effective January 1, 20X1. At the same time the company plans to spend an additional $57,000 on advertising during fiscal year 20X1. As a consequence of these actions, management estimates that 80 percent of its total revenue will be derived from calculator sales as compared to 75 percent in 20X0. As in prior years, the sales mix is assumed to be the same at all volume levels.

Hewtex Electronics
Projected Earning Statement
For the Year Ended December 31, 20X0

	Tape Recorders		*Electronic Calculators*		
	Total Amount (000 omitted)	*Per Unit*	*Total Amount (000 omitted)*	*Per Unit*	*Total Amount (000 omitted)*
Sales	$ 1,050	$ 15.00	$ 3,150	$ 22.50	$ 4,200.00
Production costs:					
Materials	$ 280	$ 4.00	$ 630	$ 4.50	$ 910.00
Direct Labor	140	2.00	420	3.00	560.00
Variable Overhead	140	2.00	280	2.00	420.00
Fixed Overhead	70	1.00	210	1.50	280.00
Total Production Costs	$ 630	$ 9.00	$ 1,540	$ 11.00	$ 2,170.00
Gross Margin	$ 420	$ 6.00	$ 1,610	$ 11.50	$ 2,030.00
Fixed selling and administrative					1,040.00
Net Income before income tax					$ 990.00
Income Taxes (55%)					544.50
Net Income					$ 445.50

The total fixed overhead costs will not change in 20X1, nor will the variable overhead cost rates (applied on a direct labor hour basis). However, the cost of materials and direct labor is expected to change. The cost of solid state electronic components will be cheaper in 20X1. Hewtex estimates that material costs will drop 10 percent for the tape recorders and 20 percent for the calculators in 20X1. However, direct labor costs for both products will increase 10 percent in the coming year.

Required:

a. How many tape recorder and electronic calculator units did Hewtex Electronics have to sell in 20X0 to break even?
b. What volume of sales is required if Hewtex Electronics is to earn a profit in 20X1 equal to 9 percent on sales after taxes?
c. How many tape recorder and electronic calculator units will Hewtex have to sell in 20X1 to break even?

(IMA adapted)

4-42 *Uncertainty and C-V-P Analysis*

A company is evaluating the profitability of a proposed new product. The unit selling price, variable costs, and fixed costs of the new product are given as follows:

Selling price	$ 200
Variable costs	100
Fixed costs	150,000

The sales volume is subject to uncertainty. Management estimates the expected value of sales volume to be 2,000 units and the related standard deviation to be 200 units. Assume the normal distribution.

Required:

(1) Compute the expected profit and the standard deviation of the profit for the new product.
(2) Determine the probability of at least breaking even for the new product.
(3) Determine the probability of attaining a profit of less than $25,000.
(4) Determine the probability of making a profit between $40,000 and $60,000.

4-43 *Uncertainty and C-V-P Analysis*

The Roger Company is introducing a new product. The product has fixed costs of $200,000 and variable costs of $20 per unit. Management is attempting to choose the more desirable of two possible prices. The prices, expected sales volume, and the standard deviation of the sales volume are as follows:

Prices	$ 100	$ 120
Expected sales (units)	3,100	2,500
Standard deviation (units)	250	220

Assume that the use of the normal distribution is justified.

Required:

(1) For each possible price, calculate the probability of operating at a loss.
(2) For each possible price, calculate the probability of making at least $60,000 in profit.
(3) What price would you recommend for the new product? Why?

4-44 *Nonprofit C-V-P Analysis*

Melford Hospital operates a general hospital, but rents space and beds to separately owned entities rendering specialized services such as pediatrics and psychiatry. Melford charges each separate entity for common services such as patients' meals and laundry and for administrative services such as billings and collections. Space and bed rentals are fixed charges for the year, based on bed capacity rented to each entity.

Melford charged the following costs to pediatrics for the year ended June 30, 2009:

	Patient Days (Variable)	Bed Capacity (Fixed)
Dietary	$ 600,000	-
Janitorial	-	$ 70,000
Laundry	300,000	-
Laboratory	450,000	-
Pharmacy	350,000	-
Repairs and maintenance	-	30,000
General and administrative	-	1,300,000
Rent	-	1,500,000
Billings and collections	300,000	-
Totals	$2,000,000	$2,900,000

During the year ended June 30, 2009, pediatrics charged each patient an average of $300 per day, had a capacity of 60 beds, and had revenue of $6,000,000 for 365 days. In addition, pediatrics directly employed the following personnel:

	Annual Salaries
Supervising nurses	$25,000
Nurses	20,000
Aides	9,000

Melford has the following minimum departmental personnel requirements based on total annual patient days:

Annual Patient Days	Aides	Nurses	Supervising Nurses
Up to 21,900	20	10	4
21,901 to 26,000	26	13	4
26,001 to 29,200	30	15	4

These staffing levels represent full-time equivalents. Pediatrics always employs only the minimum number of required full-time equivalent personnel. Salaries of supervising nurses, nurses, and aides are therefore fixed within ranges of annual patient days. Pediatrics operated at 100% capacity on 90 days during the year ended June 30, 2009. It is estimated that during these 90 days the demand exceeded 20 patients more than capacity. Melford has an additional 20 beds available for rent for the year ending June 30, 2010. Such additional rental would increase pediatrics' fixed charges based on bed capacity.

Required:

(a) Calculate the minimum number of patient days required for pediatrics to break even for the year ending June 30, 2010, if the additional 20 beds are not rented. Patient demand is unknown, but assume that revenue per patient day, cost per patient day, cost per bed, and salary rates will remain the same as for the year ended June 30, 2010.

(b) Assume that patient demand, revenue per patient day, cost per patient day, cost per bed, and salary rates for the year ending June 30, 2010, remain the same as for the year ended June 30, 2009. Prepare a schedule of increase in revenue and increase in costs for the year ending June 30, 2010, in order to determine the net increase or decrease in earnings from the additional 20 beds if pediatrics rents this extra capacity from Melford.

(AICPA adapted)

1. *To distinguish the characteristics of a job order cost system from those of a process cost system.*
2. *To explain the basic concepts and procedures of job order costing systems.*
3. *To study how to journalize all manufacturing cost transactions involved in a job order cost system.*
4. *To introduce the concepts of a predetermined overhead rate and factory overhead application.*
5. *To illustrate alternative approaches for handling overapplied or underapplied overhead.*

5

Traditional Product Cost Systems: Job Order Cost Systems

Product costing is one of the major objectives of cost accounting. Determination of product cost is necessary not only for product cost control but also for income determination and the valuation of ending work-in-process and finished goods inventories. There are two basic product costing systems-job order costing and process costing systems. The two systems have the same basic objectives but differ in approach and procedures. A general comparison of the two systems in terms of their characteristics is presented in this chapter. In addition, this chapter outlines and explains job order costing systems. Process costing systems are discussed in Chapter Five.

Job Order Costing vs. Process Costing: A General Comparison

Job order costing is a product costing system which is useful for accumulating product costs of special order products or projects. Each job has a distinct beginning and end. Examples range from a single scoreboard for a football stadium to 1,000 living room sets made to a customer's unique specifications. All manufacturing costs associated with a job are assigned to the specific job order. Unit product cost is computed by dividing total manufacturing costs of a job by the number of units produced.

A process costing system, on the other hand, is applicable to production situations where a large volume of similar products are produced on a continuous basis. It is not clear when the last unit will

Item	*Job Order Costing System*	*Process Costing System*
1. Cost Accumulation	For specific jobs, orders, or products.	For production departments or processes.
2. Work-in-Process inventory account	One work-in-process account is maintained and is supported by a subsidiary ledger comprised of job order cost sheets.	Individual work-in-process account is maintained for each department or process to accumulate manufacturing costs.
3. Time period for production measurement	Production is not measured for a specific time period. Costs and production are measured for each job.	Production in each department or process is measured for specific time periods.
4. Product	A single product or a few like units.	Continuous or mass production of like units.
5. Industry	CPA firms, construction, furniture, machinery, printing and aircraft.	Chemicals, oil, cement, and bolts and nuts.

be produced. Examples include chemicals, bolts and nuts, paint, and soft drinks. In contrast to job order costing, manufacturing costs are accumulated by departments or processes rather than by job orders. Cost per unit is then computed by dividing total manufacturing costs in each department by the equivalent number of whole units produced during the period. The procedures to accomplish this will be described in detail in the next chapter.

The characteristics of each system and their differences will become more apparent as they are discussed. Major differences between the two systems are summarized in the following table.

The Basics of Job Order Costing Systems

Job order costing systems are designed to associate the production costs with specific jobs or orders of production. Under a job order costing system, product costs are accumulated for each job or order. The primary objective of a job order cost system is to charge correctly the three manufacturing cost elements to the individual job orders. Each job is given a job number. When materials, direct labor, and factory overhead costs connected with the job are incurred, they are recorded in the work-in-process ledger account and a subsidiary ledger. The subsidiary ledger contains documents referred to as *job cost sheets,* the basic records used by a job order cost system to accumulate product costs. An example of a job cost sheet is given in Illustration 5-1. A job cost sheet contains spaces to record individual manufacturing cost elements that are charged to a job. For every cost recorded in the work-in-process account, an entry for the same amount is recorded on the job cost sheet. Thus, the work-in-process account is a control account for the subsidiary record of job cost sheets. The total of the costs recorded on the job cost sheets should equal the balance in the Work-in-Process account.

Manufacturing costs related to a job order are recorded in the manner described above as the job moves through the various departments in the factory. When a job is completed, its job cost sheet is taken from the work in-process file and placed in the finished goods file, where it summarizes the total production costs for the job. The completed job cost sheets thus serve as

Illustration 5-1 Job Cost Sheet

Job No. ________________

Product ________________

Date started ________________ Date completed ________________

Department A					
Direct materials		Direct labor		Overhead	
Date	Amount	Date	Amount	Date	Amount

Department B					
Direct materials		Direct labor		Overhead	
Date	Amount	Date	Amount	Date	Amount

Summary of costs			
	Department A	Department B	Total
Direct materials			
Direct labor			
Factory overhead			
Total			

the subsidiary ledger for the finished goods account. A journal entry is then made to transfer the total costs of the job from Work-in-Process to Finished Goods.

The job order cost system is simple to implement but may be expensive to maintain. It may require a considerable amount of clerical time to set up and record the detailed information on the job cost sheets. However, the job order cost system fills the need of product costing in certain industries and in the manufacturing operation for certain products. Computerized accounting systems can also greatly increase the efficiency of clerical activities.

Basic Cost Elements and Procedures

According to the nature of the products or jobs involved, the external and internal data requirements, and management preferences, job order cost systems may vary widely. However, the general procedure described in the previous section and the basic cost elements are the same for all systems. The basic cost elements consist of raw materials, direct labor, and factory overhead. As discussed before, a job cost sheet is set up for each job order to accumulate these costs charged to the job.

Direct Materials

When direct materials are issued to begin production, a materials requisition form is completed to document this issue. An example of a materials requisition form is given in Illustration 5-2. The amount recorded on the requisition form serves as the basis for: (1) increasing the balance in work-in process, (2) charging costs to a particular job, and (3) reducing the raw materials inventory account. This amount is also shown in the direct materials column of the Job Cost Sheet.

Direct Labor

Work tickets are filled out by employees to indicate the time spent on each job. A work ticket is shown in Illustration 5-3. These tickets provide the basis for charging a job for direct labor costs. The charge on the work ticket is also shown in the direct labor column of the Job Cost Sheet.

Time cards or time sheets are usually also used as employee attendance records and as the basis for the calculation of payroll. The total amount due employees will usually exceed the direct-labor costs charged to jobs. This difference is the result of non-direct labor activities, idle time, overtime premiums, and other nonchargeable time. The difference is usually treated as an element of factory overhead as discussed in Chapter Two.

Factory Overhead

Factory overhead is one of the three major elements of manufacturing costs, and should be considered along with direct materials and direct labor in determining total production costs of a job order. However, it is very difficult, if not impossible, to relate factory overhead directly to specific jobs. Factory overhead includes items such as indirect materials (nails, glue, etc.), depreciation, rent, insurance, property taxes or foreman's salary, which cannot be directly related to individual jobs. Because of the lack of direct relationship between overhead and individual jobs, overhead is usually allocated and charged to jobs on some predetermined basis. Typically, factory overhead cost is estimated for a year of normal activity, and this budgeted overhead cost is then divided by the level of normal activity in direct labor hours, machine hours, units, or some other base to obtain a predetermined overhead rate. The formula for computing a predetermined overhead rate is:

Illustration 5-2 Materials Requisition Form

Job No. ____________ Date ____________

Department ____________ Authorized by ____________

Description	Quantity	Unit cost	Amount

Received by

Issued by

Illustration 5-3 Work Ticket

Job No. ____________	Date ____________
Employee Name ____________	Employee No. ____________
Operation ____________	Department ____________
Time started ____________	Time completed ____________
Hours ______ Rate ______	Charge ______

$$\textit{Predetermined Overhead Rate} = \frac{\textit{Budgeted Overhead}}{\textit{Normal Activity}}$$

Normal activity is the level of annual activity that will meet an average demand over several years. Other annual activity measures include theoretical capacity which assumes maximum efficiency, practical capacity which allows for unavoidable interruptions such as maintenance and holidays, and expected capacity which is based on anticipated demand for the next year.

The amount of overhead charged to a particular job is thus determined by multiplying the predetermined overhead rate by the number of direct labor hours used, the number of machine hours used, or the observed level of whatever base is selected. To illustrate, assume that the Johnson Company has estimated its total factory overhead costs for the year to be $840,000 and normal activity for the year to be 120,000 direct labor hours. Its predetermined overhead rate for the year would be $7.00 per direct labor hour:

$$\frac{840{,}000}{120{,}000 \textit{ direct labor hours}} = \$7.00 \,/\, \textit{direct labor hour}$$

If a particular job required 50 direct labor hours to complete, then the job would be charged $7(50) = $350 of factory overhead. This charge would be shown in the overhead column of the Job Cost Sheet.

The application of factory overhead in the above manner is designed to achieve two main objectives:

1. To determine total production costs of a job before the actual expenditures for overhead items are known. Actual overhead costs are normally not available before the end of a period. However, a job may be completed before the end of a period and cost data may be needed at the time of its completion. For this reason, most firms use the predetermined overhead rate approach to apply factory overhead to products.
2. To eliminate variations in the overhead rate from one month to the next that would result from using actual monthly overhead cost as the numerator or the actual monthly level of activity as the denominator. This is the theoretical basis for using a predetermined overhead rate.

The application of factory overhead to jobs results in a product cost consisting of actual direct material costs, actual direct labor, and applied factory overhead. This is sometimes referred to as the normal product cost or the output of a normal product costing system. In contrast, an actual product costing system would use the actual overhead cost and the actual level of activity to compute an overhead rate.

Below is a detailed example of a job order cost system for a manufacturing organization. Job order costing is also used in service organizations such as accounting and law firms, hospitals and advertising agencies. The example below also applies to a service organization, except some of the account titles would differ. For instance, Factory Overhead would be called Service Overhead, and Cost of Goods Sold would be renamed Cost of Services Billed. Also, service organizations often use less direct materials than manufacturers, or none at all.

The Flow of Costs and Accounting Entries in a Job Order Cost System

The general concept and costing procedures of a job order cost system have been introduced in the previous section. Accounting entries to record the flow of costs for a job order cost system are now discussed.

Purchase and Issue of Materials and Supplies

Purchases of materials and supplies are, charged to inventory accounts when they are purchased. For example, during the month of June, the Johnson Company purchased $50,000 of raw materials and $10,000 of supplies for use in production. The purchases are recorded with the entry:

1)	Raw Materials......................	50,000	
	Supplies	10,000	
	Accounts Payable.........		60,000

The balances of raw materials and supplies accounts at the end of a period are reported on the balance sheet in the inventory section. In some firms, a single materials inventory account is used to record both raw materials and supplies. In such a case, only one materials inventory account will be reported on the balance sheet.

The issue of direct materials to production is debited to the Work-in-Process account to record direct materials assigned to job orders. It is also shown in the direct materials column of the Job Cost Sheet. On the other hand, supplies (indirect materials) issued to production are debited to the Factory Overhead Control account. For example, assume during June the Johnson Company issued $40,000 of raw materials and $8,000 of supplies from the storeroom to production. Journal entries to record the issue of raw materials and supplies are given below:

2)	Work-in-Process	40,000	
	Raw Materials......................		40,000
	Factory Overhead Control	8,000	
	Supplies		8,000

It should be noted that supplies issued to production were not assignable directly to a specific job. They were charged to the Factory Overhead Control account. These costs will remain in the Factory Overhead Control account until the end of an accounting period. In the meantime, factory overhead is applied to production of specific jobs through the use of the predetermined overhead rate as discussed in the previous section. At the end of an accounting period, the total factory overhead incurred is compared with the total factory overhead applied to determine underapplied or overapplied overhead. This will be discussed later in this chapter.

Labor Cost

As work is performed in production departments, employee work tickets are prepared. Labor costs are assigned to a work ticket according to the various rates paid to the employees. The resulting total labor costs are classified as either direct labor costs or indirect labor costs. Direct labor costs are debited to Work-in-Process and are recorded on the Job Cost Sheets for the specific jobs. Indirect labor costs (equipment maintenance, security, etc.) are debited to Factory Overhead Control. As in the case of indirect materials, the indirect labor cost is a part of actual factory overhead which will remain in the Factory Overhead Control account until the end of the period. To illustrate the entry for labor costs, assume that total direct labor and indirect labor costs incurred in June in the Johnson Company were $60,000 and $10,000, respectively. The journal entry to record the payroll for the month of June would be:

		Debit	Credit
3)	Work-in-Process	60,000	
	Factory Overhead Control	10,000	
	Payroll Payable		70,000

Other Factory Overhead

As other factory overhead costs are incurred, they are also recorded in the Factory Overhead Control account. For example, assume that the Johnson Company incurred the following factory overhead other than indirect materials and indirect labor during the month of June:

Utilities	$10,000
Supervisors' salaries......	4,000
	$14,000

The journal entry to record the incurrence of these factory overhead costs would be:

		Debit	Credit
4)	Factory Overhead Control	14,000	
	Accounts Payable		10,000
	Wages Payable		4,000

In addition, assume that the Johnson Company has to recognize the following items in June:

Depreciation on Factory Assets.........................	$20,000
Insurance on Factory Assets That Expired.......	5,000
Property Taxes Accrued	15,000
	$40,000

The entry to record these items would be:

		Debit	Credit
5)	Factory Overhead Control	40,000	
	Accumulated Depreciation........		20,000
	Prepaid Insurance.......................		5,000
	Property Taxes Payable		15,000

It should be emphasized that the actual costs of supplies (indirect materials), indirect labor and other factory overhead, which total $72,000 in the above journal entries, has been charged to the Factory Overhead Control account and has not had any effect on the Work-in-Process account. The overhead cost that will be charged to Work-in-Process is the applied factory overhead based on the predetermined overhead rate. Application of factory overhead to specific jobs is described in the following section.

Application of Factory Overhead

Overhead costs are debited to Work-in-Process through the use of a predetermined overhead rate, a process referred to as the application of overhead. The amount of factory overhead applied to a specific job is based on the predetermined overhead rate multiplied by the observed quantity of an application base. This amount is also recorded in the overhead column of the Job Cost Sheet.

In our example, direct labor hours were used as the application base. The Johnson Company's predetermined overhead rate is $7 per direct labor hour. During the month of June, 10,000 direct labor hours were used by the company. Therefore, the Johnson Company would apply total overhead of $7(10,000) = $70,000 during June. The journal entry to record the application of overhead would be:

6)	Work-in-Process	70,000	
	Factory Overhead Applied		70,000

Notice that two factory overhead accounts are used to record overhead costs. The first account, Factory Overhead Control, is used to record actual overhead costs incurred. The second account, Factory Overhead Applied, is used to apply factory overhead to Work-in-Process. It should be mentioned that some firms use one overhead account, Factory Overhead Control, to record both actual overhead costs and applied overhead costs. In such a case, all actual overhead costs are recorded in the debit side of the Factory Overhead Control account and applied overhead costs are recorded in the credit side of the account.

Regardless of whether one or two overhead accounts are used, any difference between the total debited to Factory Overhead Control and the total credited to Factory Overhead Applied should be computed and treated properly at the end of an accounting period. In the above journal entries, the difference is a total of $72,000 debited to Factory Overhead Control versus $70,000 credited to Factory Overhead Applied. The treatment of this difference, called under- or overapplied factory overhead, will be described in a later section.

Cost of Finished Goods

As a job order is completed, the finished goods are transferred from the production departments to the finished goods warehouse. The production costs charged to the job are totaled and transferred from Work-in-Process to Finished Goods. Completion of a job results in a credit to Work-in-Process and a debit to Finished Goods. In the example, the Johnson Company has incurred the following costs in their production process during June:

Direct Materials	$ 40,000
Direct Labor	60,000
Factory Overhead Applied	70,000
	$170,000

These costs have also been recorded on the Job Cost Sheets for each job. If there were no beginning Work-in-Process inventory and a job costing $150,000 was completed during the month, the journal entry to record the transfer of the finished goods from Work-in-Process to Finished Goods would be:

		Debit	Credit
7)	Finished Goods...................	150,000	
	Work-in-Process..........		150,000

Dividing the $150,000 by the number of units in the job would give the cost per unit. In addition, the Job Cost Sheet for this completed job would be moved to the finished goods file as subsidiary ledger backup. The balance of $20,000 in Work-in-Process represents the cost of goods in the uncompleted jobs at the end of the month. This balance will appear as Work-in-Process Inventory under the inventory section of the balance sheet.

Cost of Goods Sold

As finished goods are delivered to customers, sales invoices are prepared and the journal entries to record sales and cost of goods sold are made. For example, assume that during the month of June the Johnson Company delivered $140,000 of finished goods to customers. These finished goods were sold at a total selling price of $200,000. The journal entries to record the sale would be:

		Debit	Credit
8)	Accounts Receivable...........	200,000	
	Sales		200,000
	Cost of Goods Sold.............	140,000	
	Finished Goods........		140,000

With the journal entries prepared above, the flow of costs through a job order costing system is completed. At this point, it is helpful to reexamine the costing procedures step by step. To assist in this activity, the accounts are shown below in T-account form, with the transaction amounts referenced to the related journal entries.

Raw Materials

Debit	Credit
(1) 50,000	40,000 (2)
10,000	

Work-in-Process

Debit	Credit
(2) 40,000	150,000 (7)
(3) 60,000	
(6) 70,000	
20,000	

Factory Overhead Control

Debit	Credit
(2) 8,000	
(3) 10,000	
(4) 14,000	
(5) 40,000	
72,000	

Supplies

Debit	Credit
(1) 10,000	8,000 (2)
20,000	

Accounts Payable

Debit	Credit
	60,000 (1)
	10,000 (4)
	70,000

Wages Payable

Debit	Credit
	70,000 (3)
	4,000 (4)
	74,000

Prepaid Insurance

Debit	Credit
	5,000 (5)
	5,000

Accumulated Depreciation

Debit	Credit
	20,000 (5)
	20,000

Property Taxes Payable

Debit	Credit
	15,000 (5)
	15,000

Accounts Receivable	
(8) 200,000	
200,000	

Factory Overhead Applied	
	70,000 (6)
	70,000

Finished Goods	
(7) 150,000	140,000 (8)
10,000	

Sales	
	200,000 (8)
	200,000

Cost of Goods Sold	
(8) 140,000	
140,000	

UNDERAPPLIED OR OVERAPPLIED FACTORY OVERHEAD

The use of two factory overhead accounts to record factory overhead costs has been described in the previous section. The Factory Overhead Control account is debited to record the actual overhead costs incurred during the period. The Factory Overhead Applied account is credited to record the application of overhead to each job. Since the predetermined overhead rate is based on budgeted overhead and budgeted volume, the total overhead applied may be more or less than the total actual overhead costs incurred during a period. The difference between the balances of the two factory overhead accounts is underapplied factory overhead or overapplied factory overhead. Factory overhead is underapplied when the total applied overhead is less than the total actual overhead incurred, and it is overapplied when the total applied overhead is greater.

TREATMENT OF OVERAPPLIED OR UNDERAPPLIED FACTORY OVERHEAD

Although the balances of the two factory overhead accounts at the end of a month may not coincide, the final year-end balances are expected to be approximately equal. At the end of an accounting period, the two accounts are closed to a third variance account to recognize any underapplied factory overhead or overapplied factory overhead for the period. Using a slightly different example, assume that the total actual overhead costs incurred during a year were $600,000 and the total overhead applied was $620,000. All year long the Factory Overhead Control account has been debited, and the Factory Overhead Applied account has been credited. The journal entry to close the two overhead balances would be:

Factory Overhead Applied........................	620,000	
Overapplied Factory Overhead..........		20,000
Factory Overhead Control..................		600,000

In practice, two approaches are generally used to dispose of this overapplied or underapplied balance at the end of the reporting period:

1. Adjust Cost of Goods Sold for the overapplied or underapplied factory overhead, or
2. Allocate overapplied or underapplied factory overhead among Work-in-Process, Finished Goods, and Cost of Goods Sold on the basis of: (a) ending balances in these accounts, or (b) total overhead applied in these accounts.

Most firms use the first approach because of its simplicity. The corresponding journal entry to close the Overapplied Factory Overhead account and adjust Cost of Goods Sold would be:

Overapplied Factory Overhead	20,000	
Cost of Goods Sold		20,000

Cost of Goods Sold is being credited because it is being reduced by the amount of overapplied overhead. If there is underapplied factory overhead, the journal entry would be a credit to Underapplied Factory Overhead and a debit to Cost of Goods Sold.

Although the first approach is simple and used more often in practice, the second approach is more accurate. The second approach allocates overapplied or underapplied factory overhead to the accounts to which it would have been assigned if there had been no difference between actual overhead and applied overhead. It involves more time and also introduces an allocation problem. The allocation of overapplied or underapplied factory overhead over Work-in-Process, Finished Goods, and Cost of Goods Sold may be made on the basis of either their ending balances or the amounts of factory overhead applied to each account. Illustration 5-4 is an example of this allocation process.

The closing journal entry to allocate the overapplied factory overhead among the three accounts would appear as follows:

On the basis of overhead applied in each account:

Overapplied Factory Overhead	20,000	
Work-in-Process		1,000
Finished Goods..		3,000
Cost of Goods Sold		16,000

On the basis of ending balances in each account:

Overapplied Factory Overhead	20,000	
Work-in-Process		400
Finished Goods..		1,600
Cost of Goods Sold		18,000

Work-in-Process, Finished Goods and Cost of Goods Sold are being credited because they are being reduced by the amount of overapplied overhead. If there is underapplied factory

Illustration 5-4 Analysis for Allocation of Overapplied Overhead

	Overhead applied		*Ending balances*		*Allocation of overapplied overhead*	
Account	*Amount*	*%*	*Amount*	*%*	*Based on overhead applied*	*Based on ending balances*
Work-in-process	$31,000	5	$40,000	2	$1,000	$400
Finished goods	93,000	15	160,000	8	3,000	1,600
Cost of goods sold	496,000	80	1,800,000	90	16,000	18,000
Total	$620,000	100%	$2,000,000	100%	$20,000	$20,000

overhead, the journal entry would be a credit to Underapplied Factory Overhead and a debit to these three accounts.

The use of overhead applied as the base for allocating overapplied or underapplied factory overhead is conceptually superior to the use of ending balances in each account. The use of ending balances as the base is theoretically sound only when the proportions of direct materials, direct labor, and overhead costs are constant among jobs. If this is not the case, the allocation based on ending balances would be theoretically incorrect.

Interim Financial Reporting of Overapplied or Underapplied Factory Overhead

The closing entry for overapplied or underapplied overhead is ordinarily made at the end of an accounting period. If interim financial statements are required during the accounting period, overapplied or underapplied factory overhead may be reported in the financial statements in one of two ways:

1. Report overapplied or underapplied factory overhead as an adjustment to cost of goods sold on the income statement. This method treats overapplied or underapplied overhead as if it were immediately chargeable to the current accounting period. Illustration 5-5 presents an example of this treatment.
2. Report overapplied or underapplied factory overhead as an adjustment to inventories on the balance sheet. This method treats overapplied or underapplied factory overhead as a cost that will apply to the remaining production of the year. Illustration 5-6 provides an example of this treatment.

Method two is a preferable approach because it recognizes that overapplied or underapplied factory overhead is expected to disappear at the end of the year. However, top-management preference would decide which of the two methods is to be used for interim reporting purposes. If factory overhead is underapplied, method two reports higher net income in interim reports because it reports more assets and less cost of goods sold than does the first method.

Summary

Two basic product costing systems are job-order costing and process costing. Each is useful for accumulating costs of production in different types of industries. In practice, the selection of the approach is dependent upon a firm's needs. This chapter has discussed the cost flows,

Illustration 5-5 Reporting Overapplied or Underapplied Factory Overhead on an Interim Income Statement (Partial Income Statement)

Sales		XXX
Cost of Goods Sold	XXX	
Add: Underapplied Factory Overhead		
(Or Less: Overapplied Factory Overhead)	XXX	XXX
Gross Profit		XXX

Illustration 5-6 Reporting Overapplied or Underapplied Factory Overhead on an Interim Balance Sheet (Partial Balance Sheet)

Assets

Current assets:		
Cash		XXX
Accounts receivable		XXX
Inventories	XXX	
Add: Underapplied factory overhead		
(Or less: overapplied factory overhead)	XXX	XXX
Other current assets		XXX
Total current assets		XXX

components, and procedures involved in a job order cost system. Process cost accounting will be discussed in Chapter Five.

Direct materials, direct labor, and factory overhead are the basic product cost components. Many firms apply factory overhead at predetermined rates. The product cost under such an approach consists of actual material costs, actual direct labor, and applied overhead. This product costing system is referred to as a normal product costing system. Since factory overhead is applied using a predetermined rate, it is necessary to accumulate actual overhead costs incurred in a control account. The difference between the total applied overhead and the actual overhead incurred represents overapplied or underapplied factory overhead. At the end of an accounting period, overapplied or underapplied factory overhead is determined and treated as an adjustment either to Cost of Goods Sold or to the three relevant accounts-Cost of Goods Sold, Finished Goods, and Work-inProcess.

Key Definitions

Actual costing system A system which computes product or service cost as the total of actual direct material cost, actual direct labor cost, and overhead applied using a rate based on actual overhead cost and the actual level of activity.

Expected capacity A level of activity which is based on anticipated demand for the next year.

Factory overhead applied account A ledger account which accumulates the factory overhead attached to individual jobs.

Factory overhead control account A ledger account which accumulates actual factory overhead costs.

Job order cost system A product costing system which is used to accumulate product costs for individual jobs or projects.

Job cost sheet	The basic record for the accumulation of product costs debited to a specific job. The job cost sheet serves as the subsidiary ledger for the job.
Normal activity	A level of annual activity that will meet average demand over several years (three to seven years).
Normal costing system	A system which computes product or service cost as the total of actual direct material cost, actual direct labor cost, and overhead applied using a predetermined rate based on budgeted overhead cost and the normal level of activity.
Overapplied factory overhead	The excess of overhead cost applied to products over the amount of actual factory overhead costs incurred during a period.
Practical capacity	A level of annual activity which allows for unavoidable interruptions such as maintenance and holidays.
Predetermined overhead rate	A rate used to apply factory overhead costs to production.
Theoretical capacity	A level of annual activity which assumes maximum efficiency.
Underapplied factory overhead	The excess of actual overhead costs incurred over the amount of overhead cost applied to a job during a period.

Questions

5-1 What are the major purposes of a product costing system?

5-2 Describe the basic difference between job order costing and process costing.

5-3 What types of firms would use job order cost systems?

5-4 Discuss the purpose of the job cost sheet in a job order costing system.

5-5 What is a predetermined overhead rate and how is it computed?

5-6 Explain why firms use predetermined overhead rates rather than actual overhead costs in charging overhead to production.

5-7 Distinguish between actual job order costing and normal job order costing.

5-8 Explain underapplied overhead and overapplied overhead.

5-9 Discuss two alternative dispositions of underapplied or overapplied overhead at the end of an accounting period.

5-10 Describe two accounting treatments of reporting overapplied or underapplied overhead on interim financial statements.

Problems

5-11 *Terminology*

Match each of the following lettered terms on the left with the appropriate numbered description on the right.

a. Factory overhead control account
b. Job order costing
c. Normal activity
d. Overapplied factory overhead
e. Predetermined overhead rate
f. Underapplied factory overhead

1. The level of annual activity that will meet average demand over several years
2. Excess of actual overhead costs over the amount of overhead costs applied
3. Rate used to apply factory overhead costs to production
4. Costing system that is useful for accumulating costs for special order products
5. Excess of overhead costs applied over the actual amount of overhead incurred
6. Account used to record the actual overhead costs

5-12 *Components of Ending Work-in-Process*

The Oxford Company uses a job order cost system and applies factory overhead to jobs on the basis of direct labor cost. During the month of July, the following activities took place in the work-in-process account:

Work-in-Process

Beginning	$15,000	To finished goods	$50,000
Direct materials	10,000		
Direct labor	30,000		
Overhead applied	15,000		

At the end of July, only one job (Job #15), was still in-process. This job has been charged with $2,000 of direct materials cost.

Required:

Determine the amount of direct labor cost incurred and overhead applied in the ending inventory of work-in-process on July 31.

5-13 *Journal Entries*

The following data relating to the operations of the Sony Company in January, 20X6:

(1) Direct materials, $20,000 were issued to production.

(2) Supplies used were $1,000 for production and $400 for general administrative purposes.

(3) Depreciation for the month was $10,000 of which 80 percent was for production and 20 percent was for marketing and general administration.

Required.

Prepare the necessary journal entries for the above data.

5-14 *Complete a Partial Job Cost Sheet*

The following data relate to the manufacturing activities of the Anna Company for June, 20X7:

Work-in-Process

Beginning	$ 0	To finished goods	$45,000
Direct materials	20,000		
Direct labor	20,000		
Overhead applied	10,000		
Ending	5,000		

The Anna Company uses a job order costing system and applies factory overhead to each job on the basis of direct labor cost. At the end of June, Job #606 was still in-process. Direct materials used in this job were $3,200.

Required:

Complete the following partial job cost sheet for Job #606 at the end of June, 20X7.

Job Cost Sheet—Job #606

Direct materials	$3,200
Direct labor	?
Overhead applied	?
Total cost as of June 30, 20X7	$5,000

5-15 *Journal Entries for a Job Order Cost System*

The Maple Company operates under a job order cost system. The company applies factory overhead to jobs on the basis of 50 percent of direct labor cost. The following transactions were completed for 20X5:

1. Direct materials purchased	$20,000
2. Direct materials issued to production	15,000
3. Supplies purchased	1,000
4. Supplies used	800
5. Utility used and paid on the factory	2,000
6. Wages paid (80% direct labor; 20% indirect labor)	40,000
7. Depreciation on machinery and equipment	5,000
8. Other factory overhead incurred	4,000

9. Work-in-process (Ending) 2,000
10. Cost of goods sold 20,000

The balances in the beginning inventory accounts were:

Direct materials	$ 1,000
Supplies	100
Work-in-process	2,000
Finished goods...............	5,000

Required:

(1) Prepare journal entries to record the above transactions. (Under- or overapplied overhead is closed to cost of goods sold).

(2) Prepare a statement of cost of goods manufactured for 20X5.

5-16 *Cost of Goods Manufactured*

The Jacob Manufacturing Company uses a normal job order cost system. The following accounting data are related to the firm's operations of 20X6:

Finished goods inventory, January I	$ 20,000
Finished goods inventory, December 31	17,000
Inventory work-in-process, January 1	6,000
Inventory work-in-process, December 31......	7,500
Direct materials used	115,000
Direct labor (20,000 hours)	100,000
Indirect labor...	36,000
Indirect materials...	18,000
Office supplies used	10,000
Rent of factory building...................................	24,000
Depreciation of sales equipment	5,000
Other manufacturing overhead	20,000

Predetermined overhead rate: $4.80 per direct labor hour.

Required:

(1) Prepare a statement of Cost of Goods Manufactured for the Jacob Manufacturing Company for 20X6. Use only the items necessary.

(2) Was manufacturing overhead overapplied or underapplied for 20X6? By how much?

5-17 *Journal Entries for a Job Order Cost System*

The following transactions occurred during the month of January, 20X5:

1. Raw materials costing $40,000 were purchased on account.
2. Raw materials of $30,000 were issued to production.
3. Direct labor amounting to $60,000 and indirect labor of $10,000 were paid.
4. Supplies worth $5,000 were issued.
5. The utility bills for the month, amounting to $3,000, were received but not paid.
6. Plant depreciation of $3,000 was recorded.
7. Manufacturing overhead was applied to production at a rate of 40% of direct labor costs.
8. Units completed and transferred to finished goods amounted to $100,000.
9. Sales amounted to $120,000. The mark-up was 50% based on cost.

Required

Prepare the journal entries for January, 20X5.

5-18 *Journal Entries for Manufacturing Overhead*

The Donna Manufacturing Company expects to produce 10,000 units in a normal year. Its budgeted factory overhead is $20,000. Actual production in 20X9 was 10,000 units. During the year, the company incurred the following manufacturing overhead expenses:

Indirect labor	$2,000
Indirect materials (supplies)	4,000
Depreciation-plant and equipment	3,000
Insurance-plant	2,000
Property taxes	3,000
Utilities	5,000

Required:

(1) Calculate the predetermined overhead rate.
(2) Prepare journal entries for manufacturing overhead.
(3) Close any under- or overapplied overhead to cost of goods sold.

5-19 *Computation of Under- or Overapplied Overhead*
The Pendley Company uses a normal job order cost system. Manufacturing overhead is applied at $2 per direct labor hour. The results of operation for the current period are:

Direct labor cost (100,000 hours @ $6.00)	$600,000
Indirect labor	50,000
Direct materials used	400,000
Indirect supplies used	40,000
Utilities used in factory	100,000
Miscellaneous overhead	20,000
Cost of goods sold	800,000
Finished goods (ending)	100,000

The company has no beginning inventory in work-in-process or finished goods.

Required:

(1) Determine the amount of under- or overapplied overhead for the period.
Compute the ending inventory in work-in-process.

5-20 *Computation of Under- or Overapplied Overhead (Spreadsheet)*
Jackie and Company applies overhead at a combined rate for fixed and variable overhead of 220 percent of direct labor cost. The following data was gathered for the final quarter of 2007:

Month	*Direct Labor Cost*	*Factory Overhead Control (Actual)*
October	$175,000	$390,500
November	223,000	493,000
December	189,000	413,000

Required:

Using a computer spreadsheet program, create a schedule containing the following six columns:

Month	Direct Labor Cost	Fact. Overhead Control	Fact. Overhead Applied	Variance	Over or Under

The first three columns should contain the data from the above table. In the factory overhead applied column, the amounts should be calculated using the overhead application rate. The variance column should show the difference between the factory overhead control and the factory overhead applied columns, and the word UNDER or OVER should be displayed in the last column based on whether factory overhead is under- or overapplied.

5-21 *Cost of Goods Manufactured and Sold*

The Hardback Plastics Corporation manufactures plastic parts for customers' orders and uses a normal job order cost system. Their accounting department collected the following cost data in connection with their production for the month of September 20X6:

Beginning inventories, September 1, 20X6	
Raw materials	$15,000
Work-in-process	16,500
Finished goods	52,000

Costs for September:	
Purchases of raw materials	$ 63,000
Raw materials placed in production	70,000
Direct labor costs (20,000 hours)	80,000
Actual manufacturing overhead costs:	
Indirect labor	16,000
Indirect materials and supplies	5,000
Factory insurance	1,000
Factory property taxes	1,500
Depreciation factory building and equipment	2,500
Other factory overhead costs	13,000
Predetermined overhead rate: $4.00 per direct labor hour	
Costs of work-in-process transferred to finished goods inventory	170,000
Finished goods inventory, September 30, 20X6	36,000
Selling expenses	65,000
Administrative expenses	52,000

Required:

(1) Compute inventory of raw materials, September 30, 20X6.

(2) Compute work-in-process on September 30, 20X6

(3) Determine cost of goods sold for September, 20X6. (Any under- or overapplied overhead is closed to cost of goods sold.)

5-22 *Computation of Work-in-Process Inventory*

The Allan Manufacturing Company uses a normal job order cost system. For 20X9 the company's predetermined overhead rate is $2.50 per direct labor hour. On January 1, the company's inventory balances were:

Raw materials	$ 50,000
Work-in-process	60,000
Finished goods	100,000

During the year, the following data were recorded:

Purchases of direct materials	$ 70,000
Issue of direct materials to production	80,000
Direct labor cost incurred (20,000 hours)	100,000
Manufacturing overhead cost incurred	40,000
Cost of goods manufactured	200,000
Finished goods inventory on December 31, 20X9	80,000

Required:

(1) Give journal entries to record the above transactions.

(2) Determine and close the underapplied or overapplied factory overhead for 20X9 to cost of goods sold.

(3) Determine the balance of work-in-process on December 31, 20X9.

5-23 *Computation of Ending Inventories and Allocation of Under- or Overapplied Overhead*

The Golden Company uses a normal job order costing system. The following transactions relate to an accounting period:

a. Beginning inventory of raw materials, $50,000.

b. Raw material purchases, $90,000.

c. Direct labor costs, $60,000.

d. Actual overhead costs, $48,000.

e. Overhead applied to production at $2.00 per direct labor hour. Direct labor hours for the period were 25,000.

f. Ending inventory of raw materials was $40,000. (None of the raw materials were used for indirect materials.)

g. Beginning inventory of work-in-process, $50,000.

h. Production orders that cost $120,000 were completed and sold for $200,000.

Required:

Determine the adjusted balances of the various inventory accounts (Direct materials, work-in-process, finished goods). Allocate the under- or overapplied overhead to work-in-process, finished goods, and cost of goods sold on the basis of their ending balances.

5-24 *Entries for a Job Order Cost System*

The Houston Company uses a job order cost system. The following relate to the year of 20X4:

1. Raw materials issued to production:

Job No. 101	$2,000
Job No.102	5,000
Job No. 103	6,000

2. Direct labor incurred:

Job No. 101	1,000 hours	$1,500
Job No. 102	2,000 hours	4,000
Job No. 103	3,000 hours	3,600

3. Factory overhead is applied to production on the basis of $2 per direct labor hour.
4. Total factory overhead incurred was $24,000.
5. Jobs No. 101 and No. 102 were completed during the year.
6. Job No. 101 was sold for $7,500.

Required:

a. Prepare the journal entries required to record the above information. (Allocate any over- or underapplied overhead to work-in-process, finished goods, and cost of goods sold based on their total overhead applied.
b. Determine the beginning inventory of work-in-process at January 1, 20X5.

5-25 *Multiple Overhead Application Rates*

BXM Design Company employs a job order costing system and uses predetermined overhead rates to apply overhead to jobs. Variable overhead is applied based on direct labor hours, and fixed overhead is applied based on machine hours. In December 2006, the company estimated the following data for 2007:

Direct Labor Hours	1,200
Machine Hours	1,700
Variable Overhead	$ 73,000
Fixed Overhead	$116,000

Required:

(a) Compute the predetermined variable and fixed overhead application rates that should be used for BXM Design Company in 2007.

(b) Job Number 96 was started and completed during August 2007. Work was performed in two departments, Casting and Finishing. The following data for Job Number 96 was gathered from the departments:

	Casting	*Finishing*
Direct Material	$6,200	$550
Direct Labor Rate per Hour	$ 20	$ 32
Direct Labor Hours	17	63
Machine Hours	85	35

Compute the total cost of Job Number 96.

5-26 *Disposing of Under- or Overapplied Overhead*

The ZYX Company uses a job order cost system. The company's predetermined overhead rate is $4 per direct labor hour. The company's records show the following data for the first year's operations:

Direct labor hours used	20,000
Direct labor cost incurred	$100,000
Factory overhead cost incurred	150,000
Raw materials inventory (ending)	20,000
Work-in-process inventory (ending)	40,000
Finished goods inventory (ending)	60,000
Cost of goods sold	200,000

Required:

(1) Determine the underapplied or overapplied overhead for the year.
(2) Prepare the appropriate journal entry to close the underapplied or overapplied overhead directly to cost of goods sold.
(3) Prepare the appropriate journal entry to dispose of the underapplied or overapplied overhead. Assume that the company allocates any underapplied or overapplied overhead to work-in-process, finished goods, and cost of goods sold on the basis of their ending balances.

5-27 *Reporting Underapplied or Overapplied Overhead*

The Bering Company uses a job order cost system. The company's overhead is applied on the basis of direct labor costs. On January 1, 20X9, the company's records show the following account balances:

Raw materials		$20,000
Work-in-process:		
Materials	$10,000	
Direct labor	20,000	
Applied overhead	10,000	40,000
Finished goods		40,000

During January, the following transactions were recorded:

Materials purchased	$ 50,000
Direct labor costs incurred	50,000
Actual overhead incurred	32,000
Cost of goods sold	160,000
Cost of goods completed	150,000

The ending balance of raw materials on January 31 was $10,000.

Required:

(1) Determine the ending inventory of finished goods on January 31.
(2) Determine the amount of the underapplied or overapplied overhead for January.
(3) Explain how the underapplied or overapplied overhead should be reported on January 31, 20X9 financial statements.

5-28 *Computation of Work-in-Process Inventory*

On June 30, 20X8, a flash flood damaged the warehouse and factory of Padway Corporation, completely destroying the work-in-process inventory. There was no damage to either the raw materials or finished goods inventories. A physical inventory taken after the flood revealed the following valuations:

Raw materials	$ 62,000
Work-in-process	0
Finished goods	119,000

The inventory on January 1, 20X8, consisted of the following:

Raw materials	$ 30,000
Work-in-process	100,000
Finished goods	140,000
	$ 270,000

A review of the books and records disclosed that the gross profit margin historically approximated 25% of sales. The sales for the first six months of 20X8 were $340,000. Raw material purchases were $115,000. Direct labor costs for this period were $80,000 and manufacturing overhead has historically been applied at 50⁰76 of direct labor.

Required:

Compute the value of the work-in-process inventory lost at June 30, 20X8. Show supporting computations in good form.

(*AICPA adapted*)

5-29 *Computation of Sales Price, Work-in-Process Inventory, and Finished Goods Inventory*

The Connie Company manufactures a single product using a job order cost system. It charges actual factory overhead to individual jobs at the end of each month in proportion to the direct labor hours required by each job during the month.

The May 1 inventories consist of the following:

Materials and supplies	$4,000
Work-in-process (Job #502)	400
Finished goods (Job #501)	3,000

Information relating to the jobs worked during May is given below:

Job	*Materials Used*	*Direct Labor Incurred*
#502	$ 500	30 hrs. @ $10 = $ 300
#503	2,000	100 hrs. @ $10 = $1,000
#504	1,000	70 hrs. @ $10 = $ 700

Other costs incurred during May:

Factory repairs and maintenance	$2,000
Factory heat, light, and power	3,000
Factory supplies	1,000
Depreciation-factory equipment	2,000
Total	$8,000

Job #501 was shipped to the customer on May 2. The mark-up was 20% based on cost. Job #502 and Job #503 were completed on May 20 and transferred to finished goods.

Required:

(1) Determine the sales price of Job #501.
(2) Compute the work-in-process as of May 31.
(3) Determine the finished goods inventory as of May 31.
(4) Discuss any weakness existing in the company's overhead accounting system.

5-30 *Comprehensive Job Cost Problem*

Targon, Inc. manufactures lawn equipment. A job order system is used because the products are manufactured according to the specific requirements of each customer. Targon employs a full absorption accounting method for cost accumulation. The balances in selected general ledger accounts for the eleven month period ended August 31, 2009, are presented below:

Stores inventory	$ 32,000
Work in process inventory	1,200,000
Finished goods inventory	2,785,000
Factory overhead control	2,260,000
Cost of goods sold	14,200,000

The work in process inventory consists of two jobs:

Job No.	*Units*	*Items*	*Accumulated Cost*
3005-5	50,000	Estate sprinklers	$ 700,000
3006-4	40,000	Economy sprinklers	500,000
			$1,200,000

The finished goods inventory consists of five items:

Items	*Quantity and Unit Cost*	*Accumulated Cost*
Estate sprinklers	5,000 units @ $22 each	$ 110,000
Deluxe sprinklers	115,000 units @ $17 each	1,955,000
Brass nozzles	10,000 gross @ $14 per gross	140,000
Rainmaker nozzles	5,000 gross @ $16 per gross	80,000
Connectors	100,000 gross @ $ 5 per gross	500,000
		$2,785,000

The factory cost budget prepared for the 2009–10 fiscal year is presented below. The company applies factory overhead on the basis of direct labor hours.

The activities during the first eleven months of the year were quite close to the budget. A total of 367,000 direct labor hours have been worked through August 31, 2010.

Factory Cost Annual Budget
For the Year Ending September 30, 2010

Direct materials	$ 3,800,000
Purchased parts	6,000,000
Direct labor (400,000 hours)	4,000,000
Overhead:	
Supplies	190,000
Indirect labor	700,000
Supervision	250,000
Depreciation	950,000
Utilities	200,000
Insurance	10,000
Property taxes	40,000
Miscellaneous	60,000
Total factory costs	$16,200,000

The September 2010 transactions are summarized below.

1. All direct materials, purchased parts, and supplies are charged to stores inventory. The September purchases were as follows:

Materials	$410,000
Purchased parts	285,000
Supplies	13,000

2. The direct materials, purchased parts, and supplies were requisitioned from stores inventory as shown in the table below.

	Purchased Parts	*Materials*	*Total Supplies*	*Requisitions*
3005-5	$110,000	$100,000	-	$210,000
3006-4	-	6,000	-	6,000
4001-3 (30,000 gross rainmaker nozzles)	-	181,000	-	181,000
4002-1 (10,000 deluxe sprinklers)	-	92,000	-	92,000
4003-5 (50,000 ring sprinklers)	163,000	-	-	163,000
Supplies	-	-	20,000	20,000
	$273,000	$379,000	$20,000	$672,000

3. The payroll summary for September is as follows:

	Hours	Cost
3005-5	6,000	$ 62,000
3006-4	2,500	26,000
4001-3	18,000	182,000
4002-1	500	5,000
4003-5	5,000	52,000
Indirect	8,000	60,000
Supervision	-	24,000
Sales and administration	-	120,000
		$531,000

4. Other factory costs incurred during September were:

Depreciation	$62,500
Utilities	15,000
Insurance	1,000
Property taxes	3,500
Miscellaneous	5,000
	$87,000

5. Jobs completed during September and the actual output were:

Job No.	Quantity	Items
3005-5	48,000 units	Estate sprinklers
3006-4	39,000 units	Economy sprinklers
4001-3	29,500 gross	Rainmaker nozzles
4003-5	49,000 units	Ring sprinkles

6. The following finished products were shipped to customers during September:

Items	Quantity
Estate sprinklers	16,000 units
Deluxe sprinklers	32,000 units
Economy sprinklers	20,000 units
Ring sprinklers	22,000 units
Brass nozzles	5,000 gross
Rainmaker nozzles	10,000 gross
Connectors	26,000 gross

Required:

(a)
1. Calculate the over- or underapplied overhead for the year ended September 30, 2010. Be sure to indicate whether the overhead is over- or underapplied.
2. What is the appropriate accounting treatment for this over- or underapplied overhead balance? Explain your answer.

(b) Calculate the dollar balance in the work in process inventory account as of September 30, 2010.

(c) Calculate the dollar balance in the finished goods inventory as of September 30, 2010, for the estate sprinklers using a FIFO basis.

1. *To explain the basic concepts and procedures of process cost systems.*
2. *To introduce the cost components utilized for product costing in process cost systems.*
3. *To explain how to account for work-in-process inventories in a process cost system.*
4. *To explain the assumptions and procedures in accounting for processing losses.*
5. *To explain how just-in-time systems differ from traditional manufacturing systems.*
6. *To discuss cost accounting procedures for just-in time systems.*
7. *To describe the effects of just-in-time systems on managerial planning and control decisions.*

6 Traditional Product Cost Systems: Process Cost Systems and Just-in-Time Systems

In Chapter Four, the two basic approaches to product costing were introduced-job order costing systems and process costing systems. Job order costing systems were explained in detail and the methods of accounting for factory overhead were discussed. In this chapter, process costing systems will be described. The alternative accounting assumptions which are available to account for the existence of work-in-process inventories and the methods of accounting for losses during processing will be discussed.

The Basics of Process Costing Systems

Process costing systems are frequently used by companies which are engaged in mass production of a large number of identical or similar products. In such a production environment, the units in production typically pass in continuous fashion through a series of manufacturing steps called operations or processes. Administratively, one or more of these processes may be grouped together to form a department. The cost accounting system is then designed to record the costs which are incurred in each department over an elapsed period of time. Accountants frequently refer to such a department as a *cost center.*

By recording the total cost incurred in a department and the number of units completed during a time period, the process costing system provides the cost accountant with the data needed to compute an average cost per unit in the department during a time period. These systems achieve the dual accounting objectives of accumulating costs both by department for control purposes, and by units of production for inventory valuation and income determination. As was stated in Chapter Four, process costing systems are commonly used in the chemical and oil industries, as well as in manufacturing industries which utilize assembly line production methods. They may also be used in service organizations for high volumes of similar activities such as vehicle maintenance, payroll and tax return processing, carpet cleaning, or package deliveries.

Process Costing Procedures

In practice, process costing systems require the creation of a subsidiary work-in-process account for each department or cost center. As work progresses during a reporting period, direct material and direct labor expenditures are recorded for each department in its subsidiary account. Production counts are also maintained of the number of partially completed units transferred into and out of each department during that period. At the end of the reporting period, summary entries are made reflecting the transfer of units in process and the addition of material, labor and factory overhead in each department.

Frequently organizations which use process costing systems contain many departments, and partially finished units are transferred in sequence from one to another. In each department, additional labor, factory overhead, and possibly material are added to the units in-process. This is reflected in the accounts by an increase in the Work-in-Process subsidiary account for that department. When partially completed units are transferred out to another department, this is reflected by a decrease in the Work-in-Process subsidiary account for the transferring department and an increase in the Work-in-Process account for the receiving department. In the receiving department, these *preceding department* or *transferred-in* costs are treated in the accounts as if they were costs of raw material for that department.

For example, suppose Smith Company has two departments, Department A and Department B. The manufacturing process for a certain product begins in Department A and partially completed units are then transferred to Department B where manufacture is completed. Two Work-in-Process subsidiary accounts are required. The following entry would reflect the initiation of production in Department A during a reporting period:

Work-in-Process, Department A	XXX	
Direct Materials		X
Direct Labor		X
Factory Overhead Applied		X

During this period Department A normally would complete its manufacturing process on some units, which would have been transferred to Department B. Likewise, Department B would add labor, factory overhead, and possibly materials to these units, completing some of them, and transferring the completed units to finished goods inventory. The following entries would reflect the work performed by Department B during the same reporting period:

Work-in-Process, Department B	YYY	
Work-in-Process, Department A		Y
Direct Materials		Y
Direct Labor		Y
Factory Overhead Applied		Y
Finished Goods Inventory	ZZZ	
Work-in-Process, Department B		ZZZ

A determination of the cost of goods transferred between departmental Work-in-Process accounts and to Finished Goods requires knowledge of the number of units transferred, knowledge of the number of units in process at the end of the reporting period, and that a cost flow assumption be made. Procedures for doing this will be described later in this chapter. In practice, many organizations will establish additional subsidiary accounts for each department in which the direct materials, direct labor, and factory overhead applied are recorded for that department. This provides a record of the costs incurred in each department, and a means for management to control these costs.

The recording of costs through the accounts in a process costing system follows the flow of the units through the manufacturing process. This recording procedure is summarized in Illustration 6-1.

Illustration 6-1 Flow of Manufacturing Costs (Process Cost System)

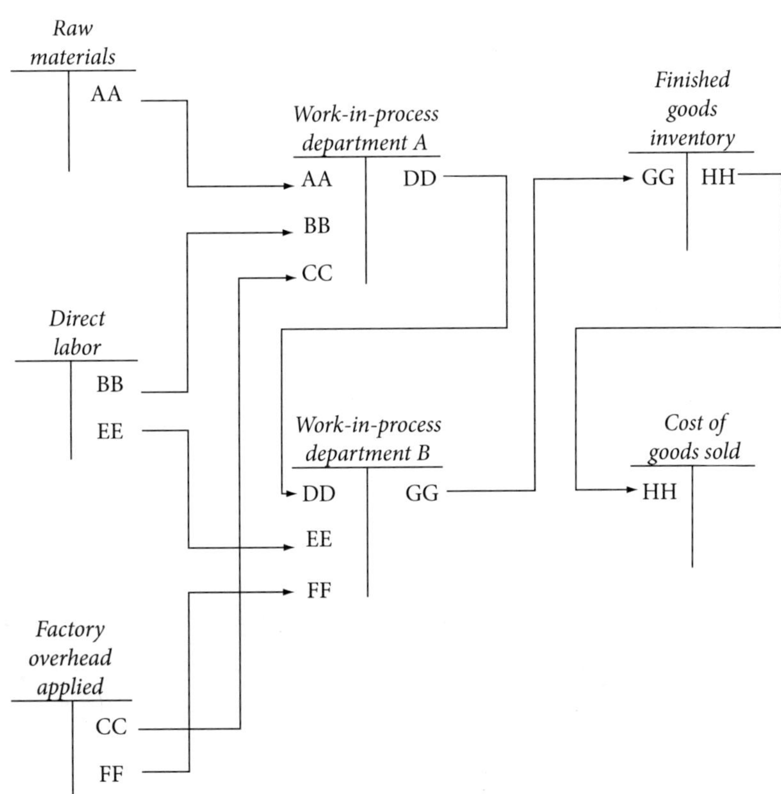

AA - cost of materials used in deaprtment A
BB - cost of direct labor used in department A
CC - cost of overhead applied in department A
DD - cost of units transferred from department A to department B
EE - cost of direct labor used in department B
FF - cost of overhead applied in department B
GG - cost of units transferred to finished goods
HH - cost of units sold

Accounting For Process Costs

In the previous section, the basic procedures followed in process costing systems were described. Costs and units produced are recorded by department or cost center rather than by job, as in a job order costing system. Costs are then transferred from departmental account to departmental account and ultimately into Finished Goods inventory, paralleling the actual physical flow of the units produced. In this section, these accounting procedures are described in more detail. Commonly accepted methods of estimating the costs of goods transferred are illustrated.

Cost Elements in Process Costing

As was stated in the previous chapter, the basic cost elements in any product costing system consist of raw materials, direct labor, and factory overhead. However, in a process costing system the materials, labor, and overhead costs attached to units in a preceding department are transferred to a receiving department's Work-in-Process subsidiary account when the units are transferred. In the receiving department, these are treated as a distinct cost component called transferred-in or preceding department costs. Also in Chapter 4 it was stated that overhead is applied to products based on an activity measure such as direct labor hours, machine hours, or units. In practice, measures of activity for applying factory overhead are frequently based on direct labor, and may be either direct labor hours or direct labor cost. When this is the case, accountants often combine the direct labor cost incurred in production with the factory overhead applied to it. This combination of direct labor and factory overhead may be referred to as *conversion costs.* The nature of the cost components added to units of production within a department in a process costing system is summarized in Illustration 6-2.

A Simple Process Cost System Without Work-in-Process Inventory

Conceptually, the cost of the units transferred from a preceding department to a receiving department, or to finished goods, is equal to the number of units transferred multiplied by the average cost per unit in the preceding department during the reporting period. (All departments except the first department of a manufacturing process have transferred-in costs. The discussion below is designed for an intermediate department rather than for the first department of a manufacturing process, in which the transferred-in cost does not exist.)

Illustration 6-2 Cost Components in a Process Costing System

Direct materials	-	Recorded costs of raw materials added to units in a production department.
Transferred-in costs	-	Costs of raw materials, direct labor, and applied overhead recorded in preceding departments in the production process.
Conversion costs	-	Recorded direct labor costs and factory overhead applied in a production department.

For a given department, the cost of goods transferred would be computed in the following manner:

$$Average\ Unit\ Cost = \frac{Direct\ Materials\ Cost + Transferred - In\ Cost + Conversion\ Cost}{Number\ of\ Units\ Manufactured}$$

Cost of Units Transferred = Average Unit Cost x Number of Units Transferred

In the simple (and unusual) situation where there are no units in process at the start or end of a period, the number of units manufactured is equal to the number of units transferred. Then the cost of the units transferred is equal to the total of the three cost components incurred in the department during the period. Consider the following example for a production department without inventory of work-in-process:

Units put into production	2,000
Units completed	2,000
Total Costs	$40,000

In this example, the unit cost is $40,000/2,000 = $20, and the cost of the units completed or transferred is $20 x 2,000 = $40,000, equal to the total costs incurred in the department.

Inventories of Work-in-Process

In an actual production environment, there will normally be beginning and ending work-in-process inventories in each department. In this case, the conceptual approach described previously must be modified. A portion of the direct materials, transferred-in costs, and conversion costs recorded in a department will be incurred to complete the units in process at the beginning of the period, and to begin the units still in process at the end of the period. The remaining costs will be incurred on the units which were started *and completed* during the period. In order to compute the average unit cost, the cost accountant must translate the number of partially completed units in process into an equivalent number of completed units. This quantity is frequently referred to as the number *of finished equivalent units* contained in the units in process.

Consider this example of a production department that has no beginning work-in-process inventory:

Beginning Inventory, in process	0
Units put into production	5,000
Total Units	5,000
Units Completed	4,000
Ending Inventory, in process	1,000
Total Units	5,000
Total Costs Incurred in the Period	$8,400

Assume that all costs (materials, labor, and overhead) are added uniformly as manufacturing progresses and that units in ending work-in-process are about 20% completed. In this case, equivalent units, unit cost, costs of units completed, and costs of ending work-in-process inventory can be determined as follows:

Units Completed	4,000
Equivalent Units of Ending Work-in-Process (1,000 x 20%)..	200
Total Equivalent Units Completed	4,200
Average Cost per Equivalent Unit ($8,400 / 4,200)	$ 2
Costs Applied to:	
Units Completed ($2 x 4,000)	$8,000
Ending Work-in-Process ($2 x 200)	400
Total Costs	$8,400

In this example, a unit still in process at the end of the period is only weighted at 20% of a finished unit, because the unit in process is only 20% complete. The total finished equivalent units of both the complete and the incomplete units are added together in calculating the unit cost of the work performed during the period.

Cost Components in Work-in-Process Inventories

Because direct materials and labor may be added to units at different stages in a production process, and because all transferred-in costs are present at the beginning of the process, the number of finished equivalent units contained in the in-process units may be different for each cost component. Accordingly, each must be considered separately in the determination of equivalent units and cost per equivalent unit.

In estimating the number of finished equivalent units for each cost component, the cost accountant may require the assistance of someone more knowledgeable in the manufacturing process. At the end of a reporting period, a shop foreperson or product engineer may physically observe the in process units in each department. This person then provides the cost accountant with estimates of percentage of completion in the units for both materials and conversion costs. The cost accountant can then estimate the finished equivalent units contained in the in-process units for a cost component using the following relationship:

$$\begin{matrix} \textit{Finished Equivalent Units} & & \textit{Estimated Percentage} & & \textit{Actual Number} \\ \textit{of In - Process Units for} & = & \textit{of Completion for} & \# & \textit{of In - Process} \\ \textit{Cost Component} & & \textit{Cost Component} & & \textit{Units} \end{matrix}$$

Sometimes materials are added at the beginning of processing in a department. In this case, each unit in-process will contain one finished equivalent unit of material. On the other hand, if materials are added at the end of a process, each unit in-process will contain zero finished equivalent units of material.

Determination of Cost per Equivalent Unit

After calculating the equivalent units for each cost component, the cost accountant can compute material cost per finished equivalent unit, a transferred-in cost per finished equivalent unit, and a conversion cost per finished equivalent unit. This is done by simply dividing the number of equivalent units into the corresponding costs. Summing these gives the unit cost per equivalent unit. The formulas for calculating the cost per finished equivalent unit are as follows:

$$\begin{matrix} \textit{Materials Cost Per} \\ \textit{Finished Equivalent Unit} \end{matrix} = \frac{\textit{Direct Materials Costs Incurred}}{\textit{Number of Finished Equivalent Units of Material}}$$

$$\frac{\text{Conversion Cost Per}}{\text{Finished Equivalent Unit}} = \frac{\text{Direct Labor Cost Incurred} + \text{Factory Overhead Applied}}{\text{Number of Finished Equivalent Units of Labor}}$$

$$\text{Transferred-In Cost Per Finished Equivalent Unit} = \frac{\text{Transferred-In Costs from Preceding Department}}{\text{Number of Finished Equivalent Units for Transferred-In Costs}}$$

$$\text{Cost Per Finished Equivalent Unit} = \text{Materials Cost Per Finished Equivalent Unit} + \text{Conversion Cost Per Finished Equivalent Unit} + \text{Transferred Cost Per Finished Equivalent Unit}$$

Determination of Cost of Ending Work-in-Process Inventory

The finished equivalent units of ending work-in-process are multiplied by the cost per equivalent unit to compute the cost of the ending work-in process inventory.

$$\text{Materials Cost in Ending Inventory} = \text{Materials Cost Per Finished Equivalent Unit} \; \# \; \text{Number of Finished Equivalent Units of Material in Ending Work-in-Process}$$

$$\text{Conversion Cost in Ending Inventory} = \text{Conversion Cost Per Finished Equivalent Unit} \; \# \; \text{Number of Finished Equivalent Units of Conversion in Ending Work-in-Process}$$

$$\text{Transferred-In Cost in Ending Inventory} = \text{Transferred-In Cost Per Finished Equivalent Unit} \; \# \; \text{Number of Ending Units-in-Process}$$

$$\text{Cost of Ending Work-in-Process Inventory} = \text{Materials Cost in Ending Inventory} + \text{Conversion Cost in Ending Inventory} + \text{Transferred-In Cost in Ending Inventory}$$

Note that the transferred-in cost in ending inventory is simply the cost per finished equivalent unit times the number of ending units in process. No computation of the finished equivalent units in ending work-in-process is necessary, since the ending units in process are already 100% complete as to transferred-in-costs.

The cost accountant must also determine the cost of the units transferred out of the department during the period. When there is no beginning inventory of work-in-process, the cost of units completed or transferred is determined as follows:

Cost of		*Total Cost*		*Number of*
Units	=	*Per*	×	*Units*
Completed		*Equivalent Unit*		*Completed*

If beginning work-in-process inventory exists, the product-costing procedure becomes more complicated. This will be described later in this chapter.

The Production Report

The procedure described in the previous section may be complicated and difficult if the calculations are not organized in a logical sequence in a production report. Production reports are an important element of a process cost system. They are used to summarize unit flows and cost data for each production department or process. They provide not only the source for summary journal entries at the end of a period but also a convenient format for presenting costs accumulated during the period. A typical production report contains five sections:

1. *Physical flow* of units. This section summarizes: (a) units to be accounted for, and (b) units accounted for. The following formulas should be used in completing this section:
   (a) Beginning Units In-Process + Units Started (or Transferred-In) = Total Units to be Accounted For
   (b) Total Units to be Accounted For—Ending Units In-Process—Beginning Units In-Process = Units Started and Completed
2. A computation of *finished equivalent units* for each cost component.
3. A determination of the *total costs* for each cost component that were incurred during the period.
4. A calculation of the *cost per equivalent unit* for each cost component. This entails dividing the resulting cost data of section (3) by the equivalent units calculated in (2).
5. *A cost reconciliation* and summary. This accounts for the costs of units completed plus the costs left in ending work-in-process inventory. The total costs accounted for in this section should equal the total costs to be accounted for from section 3. It is also the basis for summary journal entries.

A production report format such as the one just mentioned is not only useful for reporting purposes, but is also a convenient way to organize the calculations when they become more complex. An example of this type of production report is presented in Illustration 6-3 in which the five sections in the report have been identified. Note that separate columns are used for different cost components to account for equivalent units, total costs and average cost per equivalent unit. The total costs for units completed and the ending work-in-process inventory costs are summarized in section (5) of the production report.

Illustration 6-3 A Production Report

The Jayson company's production takes place in two departments: Assembly department and finishing department. The finishing department started operations of February 1, 19xx. Perior to that time, all assembled units were sold to other companies for finishing. After February 1, 19xx, all assembled units were transferred to the finishing department.

The finishing department had no beginning work-in-process inventory on February 1. During February, 2,000 assembled units were transferred in from the assembly department. Among them, 1,600 were completed and 400 units remained in work-in-process at the end of February. Because additional materials are added at the end of the finishing operation, no materials have been added to the units in ending work-in-process. However, the ending work-in-process inventory is 70% complete as to conversion.

Costs recorded for the finishing department in February include:

Transferred-in costs	$40,000
Materials	6,400
Direct labor	5,700
Overhead applied	3,800
	$55,900

The Jayson Company
Production report
Finishing department
February 19xx

	(1) Physical flow	*(2) Finished equivalent units*		
		Transferred-in	*Materials*	*Conversion*
Begining units in-process	0			
Units transferred-in	2,000			
Total	2,000			
Units completed:				
From beginning in-process	0	0	0	0
Started and completed	1,600	1,600	1,600	1,600
				(400 x .75)
Ending units in-process	400	400	0	300
Total	2,000	2,000	1,600	1,900

Costs

	Total	*Transferred-in*	*Materials*	*Conversion*
Beginning work-in-process	$ 0	$ 0	$ 0	$ 0
Incurred in current period	55,900	40,000	6,400	9,500
(3) To Accoount for	$55,900	$40,000	$6,400	$9,500
	(20 + 4 + 5)	(40,000/2,000)	(6,400/1,600)	(9,500/1,900)
(4) Per euqivalent unit	$ 29	$ 20	$ 4	$5
(5) Summary				
	(29 x 1,600)	(20 x 1,600)	(4 x 1,600)	(5 x 1,600)
(a) Costs of units completed	$ 46,400	$32,000	$6,400	$8,000
		(20 x 400)	(4 x 0)	(5 x 300)
(b) Ending work-in-process	9,500	8,000	0	1,500
Total accounted for	$55,900	$40,000	$6,400	$9,500

Cost Flow Assumptions

As has been described, a process costing system requires an estimate of the number of finished equivalent units which have absorbed the material, conversion, and transferred-in costs of the period. When beginning work-in-process inventories exist, the cost accountant must make an assumption about the flow of costs during the period. Two such cost flow assumptions have been widely accepted. They are the first-in-first-out method and the weighted average method. Under the first-in-first-out (or *FIFO)* method, production and costs during the current period are kept separate from those of the previous period; i.e., from beginning work-in-process. Under the weighted average method, beginning work-in-process and the current period's production and costs are combined in determining the number of equivalent units, total costs, and cost per equivalent unit. Each of these methods will now be discussed.

FIFO Method

In the FIFO method, the units in-process at the beginning of a reporting period, and the costs incurred on those units, are distinguished from those units started during the period. The assumption is made that the beginning units in-process are the first units completed and transferred out during the period, hence the description "first-in-first-out." The number of finished equivalent units for each cost component is computed from the work performed during the current period in the following fashion.

$$\begin{array}{c}\textit{Number of}\\ \textit{Finished Equivalent}\\ \textit{Units for}\\ \textit{Cost Component}\end{array} = \begin{array}{c}\textit{Finished Equivalent}\\ \textit{Units Added to}\\ \textit{Complete Beginning}\\ \textit{Work-in-Process}\end{array} + \begin{array}{c}\textit{Units Started}\\ \textit{and Completed}\\ \textit{During the}\\ \textit{Period}\end{array} + \begin{array}{c}\textit{Finished Equivalent}\\ \textit{Units Contained}\\ \textit{in Ending}\\ \textit{Work-in-Process}\end{array}$$

The numbers of finished equivalent units for the cost components are then used to compute the cost per finished equivalent unit as previously described. Because the finished equivalent units estimate the work actually performed during the current period, only the materials, conversion, and transferred-in costs of the *current* period are used in calculating the cost per equivalent unit. Under this method, the total cost of the units transferred out is the sum of three components: (a) the current period costs to complete the units started and finished during the period, (b) the previous period's cost, and (c) the current period costs to complete the units in beginning work-in-process. The formula for computing the total cost is shown below:

$$\begin{array}{c}\textit{Cost of}\\ \textit{Units}\\ \textit{Transferred}\end{array} = \underbrace{\left[\begin{array}{c}\textit{Cost per}\\ \textit{Equivalent}\\ \textit{Unit}\end{array} \times \begin{array}{c}\textit{Number of}\\ \textit{Units}\\ \textit{Started and}\\ \textit{Completed}\end{array}\right]}_{\text{Current period costs to complete the units started and finished during the period}} + \underbrace{\left[\begin{array}{c}\textit{Beginning}\\ \textit{Work-in}\\ \textit{Process}\end{array}\right]}_{\text{Previous period's cost}} + \underbrace{\left[\begin{array}{c}\textit{Cost per}\\ \textit{Finished}\\ \textit{Equivalent}\end{array} \times \begin{array}{c}\textit{Actual}\\ \textit{Work done}\\ \textit{on the}\\ \textit{Beginning}\\ \textit{Work-in}\\ \textit{Process}\\ \textit{During the}\\ \textit{Period}\end{array}\right]}_{\text{Current period costs to complete the units in beginning work in prcocess}}$$

The cost of the ending work-in-process inventory is determined from the current period's material, conversion, and transferred-in costs which have been absorbed by the units in the ending work-in-process. It is calculated by multiplying the cost per finished equivalent unit by the number of equivalent units in ending work-in-process for each cost component.

An example of the FIFO method is provided in Illustration 6-4. Several features of this Production Report should be emphasized. First, the units started and completed (4,700) equals the units to be accounted for (5,200) less the ending units in process (300) and the beginning units in process (200). Second, the finished equivalent units transferred out from beginning work-in-process for conversion (80) is the number of beginning units in process (200) times the work required to bring them from 60% complete to 100% (40% or .4). There are (0) finished equivalent units transferred out for materials because beginning work-in-process was already 100% complete as to materials. Third, the total costs of units completed ($39,678) consists of three parts: beginning inventory costs ($440 + $218 = $658), current costs to complete beginning work-in-process ($0 + $480 = $480), and the costs of units started and completed ($10,340 + $28,200 = $38,540).

The FIFO method is a conceptually superior approach to process costing because it clearly distinguishes between costs of successive reporting periods. Some cost accountants prefer it because it provides a logically defensible way of reporting the results of a continuous process on a periodic basis, and recognizes that production costs in successive periods may differ. However, the other approach, the weighted-average method, is more widely used in practice.

Weighted Average Method

The FIFO method distinguishes between the costs and the work performed in different reporting periods. On the other hand, the weighted average method combines the costs and production of the preceding and current periods when computing the cost per finished equivalent unit. This is accomplished in two steps. First, the work-in-process at the beginning of a reporting period is combined with the work required to bring it to 100% of completion. As a result, the number of finished equivalent units transferred out from beginning work-in-process equals the number of physical units transferred out. The equivalent units transferred out from beginning work-in-process are then added to the units started and completed during the period to obtain the total number of equivalent units transferred out. Next, these units are added to the number of finished equivalent units in ending inventory for each cost component to estimate the number of finished equivalent units of the period:

$$\begin{matrix} \textit{Number of Finished} & & \textit{Number of} & & \textit{Finished Equivalent} \\ \textit{Equivalent Units} & = & \textit{Units} & + & \textit{Units Contained in} \\ \textit{for Cos tComponent} & & \textit{Transferred out} & & \textit{Ending Work-in-Process} \end{matrix}$$

Secondly, the materials, conversion, and transferred-in costs of the beginning inventory are each added to materials, conversion, and transferred-in costs of the current period in determining the total cost for each cost component. The cost per finished equivalent unit of a cost component is thus determined by dividing the total cost of the component by the number of finished equivalent units of the component:

Illustration 6-4 FIFO Example Problem

On March 1, 19xx, the fabricating department of the Benson Company had a beginning work-in-processinventory of 200 units. They were 100% complete as to materials and 60% complete as to conversion. Costs related to these units were $440 for materials and $218 of conversion costs. During March, 5,000 units were started and 4,900 were completed. The March 31 work-in-processinventory of 300 units was 100% complete as to materials and 40% complete as to conversion. The fabricating department's March manufacturing costs include direct materials of $11,000, and direct labor of $19,600,and overhead applied of $9,800. Prepare a production report for the fabricating department for March assuming FIFO cost flow.

Benson Company
Production Report
Fabricating Department
March, 19xx

	(1) Physical Flow	*(2) Finished Equivalent Units*	
		Materials	*Conversion*
Beginning Units In-Process	200		
Units Started	5,000		
Total	5,200		
Units Transferred -out:			(200 x .4)
From Beginning In-Process	200	0	80
Started and Completed	4,700	4,700	4,700
			(300 x .4)
Ending Units In-Process	300	300	120
Total	5,200	5,000	4,900

	Costs		
	Total	*Materials*	*Conversion*
Work-In-Process, Beg.	$ 658		
Incurred in Current Period	40,400	$11,000	$29,400
(3) *To Account for*	$41,058		
	(2.20 + 6.00)	(11,000/5,000)	(29,400/4,900)
(4) *Per Equivalent Unit*	$ 8.20	$ 2.20	**$ 6.00**
(5) Summary			
(a) Costs of Units Completed:			
Beginning Inventory Costs	$ 658	$ 440	$ 218
		(2.20 x 0)	(6 x 80)
Current Costs on Beg. WIP	480	0	480
		(2.20 x 4,700)	(6 x 4,700)
Started and Completed	38,540	10,340	28,200
Transferred-Out	$39,678	$10,780	$28,898
		(2.20 x 300)	(6 x 120)
(b) Ending Work-in-Process	1,380	660	720
Total Accounted For	$41,058	$11,440	$29,618

$$\textit{Cost per Finished Equivalent Unit for Each Cost Component} = \frac{\textit{Beginning Work-in-Process Cost for Component} + \textit{Current Period Cost for Component}}{\textit{Number of Finished Equivalent Units for Cost Component}}$$

The overall cost per finished equivalent unit is equal to the sum of the cost per finished equivalent unit for each cost component. The cost of the units transferred out using the weighted-average method is then computed in the following way:

Cost of		*Overall Cost*		*Number of*
Units	=	*Per Equivalent*	×	*Units*
Transferred Out		*Unit*		*Transferred Out*

This is simpler than the comparable calculation under the FIFO method, in which the total costs of the units transferred out was the sum of three components (see Illustration 6-4).

The cost per equivalent unit of each component is used to compute the cost of ending Work-in-Process just as in the FIFO method. However, the average unit costs incorporate costs of both the preceding and current periods, "weighted" by the relative amounts of the costs (and number of units) in the two periods. Illustration 6-5 provides the production report for our example using the weighted average method instead of the FIFO method.

In theory, the weighted average method reflects less accurately the actual flow of costs in most environments where process costing systems are used. However, many cost accountants consider the calculations using this method to be less cumbersome, and prefer it for that reason.

Illustration 6-5 Weighted Average Solution to Example Problem

Benson Company
Production Report
Fabricating Department
March, 19xx

	(1) Physical Flow	*(2) Finished Equivalent Units*	
		Materials	*Conversion*
Beginning Units In-Process	200		
Units Started	5,000		
Total	5,200		
Units Transferred-out:			
From Beginning In-Process	200	200	200
Started and Completed	4,700	4,700	4,700
			(300 x .4)
Ending Units In-Process	300	300	120
Total	5,200	5,200	5,020

	Costs		
	Total	*Materials*	*Conversion*
Beginning Work-In-Process	$ 658	$ 440	$ 218
Incurred in Current Period	40,400	$11,000	$29,400
(3) *To Account for*	$41,058	111,440	$29,618
	(2.20 + 5.90)	(11,440/5,200)	(29,618/5,020)
(4) *Per Equivalent Unit*	$ 8.10	$ 2.20	$ 5.90
(5) Summary	(8.10 x 4,900)	(2.2 x 4,900)	(5.9 x 4,900)
(a) Costs of Units Completed	$39,690	$10,780	$28,910
		(2.2 x 300)	(5.9 x 120)
(b) Ending Work-in-Process	1,368	660	708
Total Accounted For	$41,058	$11,440	$29,618

The weighted average method is an acceptable alternative to the FIFO method whenever the difference between the methods, in cost of goods transferred and the costs of ending Work-in-Process inventory, are not material. A comparison of Illustrations 6-4 and 6-5 reveals no difference in the cost per equivalent unit for materials between the two methods ($2.20), whereas the cost per equivalent unit for conversion was a little lower under the weighted average method ($5.90 versus $6.00). The lower amount under the weighted average method was due to a lower conversion cost per equivalent unit in beginning inventory, thereby lowering the weighted average cost, than the cost per equivalent unit in the current period. In practice, a material difference may result if there are major fluctuations in labor or raw materials prices from one period to the next, or if the number of units in process at the end of a period is substantial relative to the number of units transferred. In most process costing systems this will not be the case.

As is evident from the previous discussion, the determination of product costs in process costing systems is fundamentally a process of averaging. The calculations are complicated somewhat by the presence of in-process units at the end of each reporting period, which require the cost accountant to make a cost flow assumption. Another complicating factor in practice is that frequently some of the units produced do not meet quality standards. The cost accountant must also consider the effects of processing losses in computing product costs.

Accounting for Processing Losses

Most manufacturing processes convert some of the raw material into products that are not salable as good units. These processing losses may take the form of waste, scrap, rework, or spoiled units. The cost accountant must determine the nature of the processing losses in order to choose the proper method of accounting for them. A summary of the characteristics of these four types of processing losses is provided in Illustration 6-6.

In general the preferred method of accounting for any type of processing loss depends on the nature of its source. A cost accountant attempts to determine if a loss is controllable or uncontrollable, and based on this distinction, selects an appropriate method of accounting for it.

Illustration 6-6 Types of Processing Losses

Waste	-	Material lost in the process which is unrecoverable and has no recovery value. Examples: smoke, dust, steam.
Scrap	-	Material left after a production process that is recoverable and can be sold for some minimal value. Examples: scrap metal, turnings, sawdust.
Rework	-	Finished units which do not meet quality standards, but with some additional work can be sold and used for their intended purpose. Example: factory "seconds."
Spoilage	-	Finished or partially finished units which cannot be reworked or used for their intended purpose; they may be discarded or sold for a minimal value. Example: printed materials (newspapers, magazines) which are illegible.

Industrial engineers normally expect to have some losses in any production process. Such losses, which are considered unavoidable, are inherent in the manufacturing process. The cost of these *uncontrollable* losses are considered by the accountant as a cost of the manufacturing process, and these costs are spread over the good units produced. The cost of waste, scrap, and rework are normally accounted for in this fashion, as well as certain types of spoilage. Examples of uncontrollable losses include sawdust resulting from the production of lumber or furniture, and evaporation from a cooking process.

Other losses are not inherent in the production process but are a result of human error. The cost of these *controllable* losses should not be considered a cost of the good units produced, but are recognized as a loss and recorded in a special loss account. As examples, controllable losses may result from employee negligence, improper machine adjustments or settings, or the use of a worker at an operation for which he or she is not qualified. In practice, certain types of spoilage are considered controllable losses.

Accounting for Waste, Scrap, and Rework

In accounting for waste, scrap, and rework, the cost accountant is concerned with both costs and revenues. The costs of waste and scrap are attached to the good units produced through the average unit cost calculations previously described in this chapter. Revenue from the sale of scrap is considered to be a recovery of factory overhead costs, and is thus also applied to the good units produced. The costs of rework are normally attached to all good units by a debit entry to the factory overhead control account. Typical entries reflecting these transactions may appear as follows:

Cash	XX	
Factory Overhead Control		XX
To record sale of scrap for month of March		
Factory Overhead Control	YYY	
Raw Materials		Y
Wages Payable		Y
Factory Overhead Applied		Y
To record costs of rework for month of March.		

Normally, revenue from the sale of reworked units is accounted for in the same fashion as the sale of good units, even though they may have been sold at a reduced price.

Accounting for Spoilage

Spoilage includes those units whose defects are such that they cannot be reworked and sold for their intended use. They may have some minimal sales value, and revenue from the sale of spoiled units is treated as revenue from the sale of scrap. In order to properly account for the costs of spoilage, the nature of its source must be determined.

As has been discussed, industrial engineers usually assume that some spoilage is inherent in the production process. Spoiled units may result whenever production is first begun while machines are being adjusted or a new production shift begins. Uncontrollable spoilage also may be produced near the end of processing a batch of raw material (such as a roll of newsprint or cloth), or when machine settings begin to exceed allowable tolerances as a result of wear.

For any process, industrial engineers can estimate with reasonable accuracy the percentage of spoiled units which should result from such uncontrollable factors. Spoilage within these limits, stated as a percentage of the number of units input to the production process, is considered to be *normal* spoilage. Its cost is considered to be a cost of the good units produced. Any units which exceed the predetermined normal spoilage rate are referred to as *abnormal* spoilage and are assumed to result from human error. The costs of abnormal spoilage is debited to a special loss account, such as "Loss from Abnormal Spoilage" and treated as a current period expense.

Significance of the Inspection Point

The cost accountant must estimate the cost of the spoiled units when computing the product costs for a reporting period. This is accomplished by including the number of finished equivalent units contained in both the normal and the abnormal spoilage in the determination of the cost per finished equivalent unit. Costs per finished equivalent unit for the period are then applied to the number of finished equivalent units in normal and abnormal spoilage to determine their costs.

In a production process, spoilage is normally discovered by inspection of the units. Inspection may occur anywhere in the process but will usually occur at the same point in the process. In estimating the finished equivalent units for spoilage, the cost accountant usually assumes that all spoilage occurs at the inspection point, and that the cost of spoilage consists only of the costs incurred in the process up to that point.

For example, if inspection occurs when all of the conversion is complete and 100 units were spoiled, then the spoilage contains 100 x 100% or 100 equivalent units for conversion. These 100 finished equivalent units are included in the number of finished equivalent units manufactured during the period in arriving at the conversion cost per finished equivalent unit. On the other hand, if inspection occurs before conversion is begun in a department, then no work has been performed on the spoiled units. The spoilage then contains 0 finished equivalent units for conversion, and the spoiled units are not included in computing the conversion cost per equivalent unit. If inspection occurs when conversion is 60% complete, then the spoilage contains 100 x 60% or 60 finished equivalent units for conversion.

Allocation of Normal Spoilage

The costs of normal spoilage during a reporting period are equal to the number of finished equivalent units in normal spoilage multiplied by the cost per equivalent unit. These costs are assumed to be a cost of producing good units, and are added to the cost of the good units produced. When ending work-in-process inventories exist, the costs of normal spoilage must be allocated between the good units transferred out and those remaining in the department at the end of the period. The method of allocation is chosen by the cost accountant based on judgment; two such methods are the *continuous method* and the *batch method.*

Continuous Method of Allocating Normal Spoilage

The continuous method is appropriate in certain situations where production is performed on an assembly line. It assumes that units are uniformly spread along the assembly line, and that they are passing in continuous fashion past the inspection point. At the end of a reporting period, some units have passed the inspection point and some have not. Since the units that have been inspected have had spoilage removed, some normal spoilage costs were incurred to produce them. The units that have not been inspected will have spoilage removed in the next reporting period. With the continuous method, normal spoilage costs are added to the ending inventory based only on the number of units that have been inspected. This is accomplished by allocating total normal spoilage costs between the units transferred out and the units in work-in-process that have passed the inspection point.

For example, assume a reporting period in which 970 good units have been transferred out and 50 units remain in ending work-in-process. The cost accountant has determined that the cost of normal spoilage is $2,000. Assume also that inspection occurs when conversion is 40% complete. In this case, 60% x 50 = 30 units have been inspected. Then with the continuous method, normal spoilage costs are allocated as follows:

To Ending Inventory: $\left(\frac{30}{970 + 30}\right) \times \$2,000 = \$60$

To Units Transferred Out: $\left(\frac{970}{970 + 30}\right) \times \$2,000 = \$1,940$

Had inspection been at the beginning of the process, $98[(1)] of normal spoilage costs would have been allocated to ending inventory, and $1,902[(2)] (= 97070 + 50 x 2,000) allocated to the units transferred out. With inspection at the end of the process, the entire $2,000 would be added to the costs of the units transferred.

(1) $\frac{50}{970 + 50} \times \$2,000 = \$98$

(2) $\frac{970}{970 + 50} \times \$2,000 = \$1,902$

Batch Method of Allocating Normal Spoilage

The batch method is more appropriate for production processes that do not utilize assembly lines. It assumes that all units in process at the end of a period are at the same stage of completion as the average unit. Thus the batch method requires an estimate of the stage of completion (stated as a %) of the average unit in ending work-in-process. This average stage of completion is then compared to the stage of completion at which inspection occurs to determine normal spoilage costs to be allocated to ending inventory.

When the average unit has passed the inspection point, the batch method assumes that *all* units have been inspected, and normal spoilage costs are allocated between units in ending work-in-process and units transferred out. Whenever the average unit has *not* passed the inspection point, it is assumed that *none* of the units have been inspected. Then costs of normal spoilage are added entirely to the costs of the good units transferred out.

In the previous example, assume that a production foreman estimates that ending inventory is 70% complete. Then the average unit has been inspected, because inspection occurs 40% through the process. Using the batch method, normal spoilage costs are allocated in the following way.

To Ending Inventory: $\left(\frac{50}{970 + 50}\right) \times \$2,000 = \$98$

To Units Transferred Out: $\left(\frac{970}{970 + 50}\right) \times \$2,000 = \$1,902$

Had the ending work-in-process been 30% completed, all normal spoilage costs would have been added to the cost of the units transferred out.

In practice, the continuous method is theoretically preferable in most situations where process costing is used. However, many cost accountants prefer the batch method because it is simpler, and because the differences between the two methods are normally not material.

Comprehensive Example

Illustration 6-7 presents a comprehensive process costing example that includes spoilage. In Illustrations 6-8 and 6-9 the production reports for this problem are presented using both the FIFO and the weighted average methods. Careful examination of these illustrations will reveal that the five step procedure in the production report described before requires the following modifications to account for spoilage.

Section 1: *Physical Flow*—units in normal and abnormal spoilage are distinguished in tracing the physical flow of units.

Section 2: *Computation of Equivalent Units*—compute equivalent units for normal spoilage and abnormal spoilage separately in the same way as for good units.

Section 3: *Summary of Total Costs to Account for*—the details contained in this section are the same as before.

Section 4: *Computation of Cost per Equivalent Unit*—the calculation procedure involved in this section is the same as before except that now the denominator includes the equivalent units contained in spoiled units.

Section 5: *Reconciliation and Summary of Costs*—compute the cost of normal spoilage and that of abnormal spoilage in the same way as the costs of good units and work-in-process. Allocate the cost of normal spoilage to the related good units as a product cost. The cost of abnormal spoilage is treated as a current period expense.

Accounting Entries

Once the cost of the units transferred, the cost of ending inventory, and the cost of abnormal spoilage have been determined, the cost accountant can make the journal entries reflecting the production of the reporting period. A general description of these entries was provided at the beginning of this chapter. In the comprehensive example, the following summary entry would reflect the production begun in Department B during the reporting period:

Work-in-Process, Department B	122,000	
Work-in-Process, Department A		76,000
Direct Materials		12,000
Direct Labor		17,000
Factory Overhead Applied		17,000

The journal entry reflecting the completion of production in Department B depends on the cost flow assumption made.

Illustration 6-7 Alphabet Manufacturing Company Comprehensive Example

Alphabet Manufacturing Company utilizes a process costing system. It recognizes two cost centers, Department A and Department B. Manufacturing on a certain product is initiated in Department A. When partially finished the units move into Department B, where they are completed and are transferred to the finished goods warehouse.

During the month of March, 2,400 partially completed units moved into Department B which had incurred $76,000 in costs in the preceding department. In Department B, materials costing $12,000 and direct labor of $17,000 were added, and applied overhead totaled $17,000. A total of 2,200 units were transferred to finished goods. The following was also observed in Department B:

Units In-Process (March 1), 500 units, 100% complete as to materials, 40% complete as to labor; materials costs $2,500, conversion costs $2,750, transferred-in costs $5,200;

Units In-Process (March 31), 600 units, 100% complete as to materials, 25% complete as to labor.

Overhead is applied on the basis of direct labor dollars. Inspection occurs in Department B at the end of the process, and normal spoilage of 3% of the units begun is anticipated.

Required: Using both the FIFO and Weighted Average methods, compute

1. Average unit cost;
2. Cost of units transferred to finished goods;
3. Cost of ending inventory in Department B;
4. Cost of abnormal spoilage.

Using the *FIFO* method, the cost accountant would record completed production as follows:

Finished Goods Inventory	106,733	
Loss from Abnormal Spoilage	1,450	
Work-in-Process, Department B		108,183

To record production completed in Department B for March

For the month of April, the cost of beginning inventory will be $24,267. Using the *weighted average* cost flow assumption the following entry would be made:

Finished Goods Inventory	109,056	
Loss from Abnormal Spoilage	1,344	
Work-in-Process, Department B		110,400

To record production completed in Department B for March

For the month of April, the cost of beginning inventory is $22,050.

The cost accountant would have carried out similar procedures to reflect the production in Department A during the same reporting period. In this case, a debit entry recording the completion of production in Department A would be made to the Work-in-Process subsidiary account for Department B. The amount of this debit would have been $76,000.

Illustration 6-8 Alphabet Manufacturing Company Production Report - Department B FIFO Method

	(1) Physical Flow	*(2) Finished Equivalent Units*		
		Transferred-In	*Materials*	*Conversion*
Beginning Units In-Process	500			
Units Transferred-In	2,400			
Total	2,900			
Units Transferred Out:				
From In-Process	500	0	0	(.6 x 500) 300
Started and Completed	1,700	1,700	1,700	1,700
Ending Units In-Process	600	600	600	(.25 x 600) 150
Spoilage (2900 -2800):				
Normal (3% x 2400)	72	72	72	(1 x 72) 72
Abnormal (100 -72)	28	28	28	(1 x 28) 28
Total	2,900	2,400	2,400	2,250
		Costs		
	Total	*Transferred-In*	*Materials*	*Conversion*
Beginning Work-In-Process	$ 10,450			
Current	122,000	$76,000	$12,000	$34,000
(3) *To Account for*	$132,450			
(4) *Per Finished Equivalent Unit*	51.7778	31.6667	5.00	15.1111
(5) Summary:				
(a) *Allocation of Normal Spoilage*				
To be Allocated	3,728	(31.6667 x 72) 2,280	(5 x 72) 360	(15.1111 x 72) 1,088
To Units Transferred:				
Weighting		100%	100%	100%
Amount	3,728	2,280	360	1,088
To Ending Inventory:				
Weighting		0%	0%	0%
Amount	0	0	0	0
(b) *Cost Reconciliation*				
Costs Transferred:				
Beginning Inventory Cost	10,450	5,200	2,500	2,750
Completed from Beg. Inv.	4,533	0	0	(15.1111 x 300) 4,533
Started and Completed	88,022	(31.6667 x 1700) 53,833	(5 x 1700) 8,500	(15.1111 x 1,700) 25,689
Normal Spoilage Allocated	3,728	2,280	360	1,088
Transferred Out	106,733	61,313	11,360	34,060
Ending Work-In-Process:				
Good Units	24,267	(31.6667 x 600) 19,000	(5 x 600) 3,000	(15.1111 x 150) 2,267
Normal Spoilage Allocated	0	0	0	0
Total	24,267	19,000	3,000	2,267
Abnormal Spoilage	1,450	(31.6667 x 28) 887	(5 x 28) 140	(15.1111 x 28) 423
Total Accounted for	$132,450			

Hybrid Cost Systems

Some companies manufacture a variety of products through a similar set of operations, but the direct materials used by each type of product are different. For example, two automobiles may be produced on the same assembly line, but the first has cloth seats and a basic audio system while the second has leather seats and an upgraded audio system. Or, two batches of men's jackets may be manufactured through the same process, but the first batch is made of cotton while the second is made of wool. In these situations, a hybrid cost system containing

Illustration 6-9 Alphabet Manufacturing Company Production Report - Department B Weighted Average Method

	(1) Physical Flow	*(2) Finished Equivalent Units*		
		Transferred-In	*Materials*	*Conversion*
Beginning Units In-Process	500			
Units Transferred-In	2,400			
Total	2,900			
Units Transferred Out	2,200	2,200	2,200	2,200
Ending Units In-Process	600	600	600	(.25 x 600) 150
Spoilage (2900 -2800):				
Normal (3% x 2400)	72	72	72	(1 x 72) 72
Abnormal (100 -72)	28	28	28	(1 x 28) 28
Total	2,900	2,900	2,900	2,450
	Costs			
	Total	*Transferred-In*	*Materials*	*Conversion*
Beginning Work-In-Process	$ 10,450	$ 5,200	$ 2,500	$ 2,750
Current	122,000	76,000	12,000	34,000
(3) *To Account for*	$132,450	81,200	14,500	36,750
(4) *Per Finished Equivalent Unit*	48.00	28.00	5.00	15.00
(5) Summary:				
(a) *Allocation of Normal Spoilage*				
To be Allocated	3,456	(28 x 72) 2,016	(5 x 72) 360	(15 x 72) 1,080
To Units Transferred:				
Weighting		100%	100%	100%
Amount	3,456	2,016	360	1,080
To Ending Inventory:				
Weighting		0%	0%	0%
Amount	0	0	0	0
(b) *Cost Reconciliation*				
Costs Transferred:				
Good Units	105,600	(28 x 2,200) 61,600	(5 x 2,200) 11,000	(15 x 2,200) 33,000
Normal Spoilage Allocated	3,456	2,016	360	1,080
Transferred Out	109,056	63,616	11,360	34,080
Ending Work-In-Process:				
Good Units	22,050	(28 x 600) 16,800	(5 x 600) 3,000	(15 x 150) 2,250
Normal Spoilage Allocated	0	0	0	0
Total	22,050	16,800	3,000	2,250
Abnormal Spoilage	1,344	(28 x 28) 784	(5 x 28) 140	(15 x 28) 420
Total Accounted for	$132,450			

features of both job and process cost systems will be utilized. Operation costing is another term frequently used to describe this type of system.

In a hybrid cost system, each unique production run (e.g., cotton jackets or wool jackets) is treated as a batch for the purpose of accumulating direct material costs. Consequently, as in a job cost system, the direct material cost per unit is different for each batch. But because each batch goes through a similar production process (cutting, stitching, etc.), the conversion costs per unit are assumed to be the same. The conversion costs per unit are based on the costs incurred over a period of time divided by the number of units (or equivalent units) produced, as in a process cost system. The amounts used to determine the conversion costs per unit may be actual, or they may be predetermined amounts from a budget prepared in advance. In the end, each batch contains a unique direct material cost per unit, but conversion costs per unit which are the same as any other batch manufactured through the same operations.

Just-in-Time Systems

The preceding sections have described traditional product costing systems, job order costing and process costing, and how information provided by those systems is useful for decision making and control. This section shall introduce an alternative to traditional systems that is useful in highly automated environments, namely just-in-time (JIT) systems. JIT systems represent a totally different approach to manufacturing than that for which traditional cost accounting systems were developed. For that reason, manufacturing companies that implement JIT have adopted different cost accounting practices. This section discusses how JIT production works and describes the cost accounting methods that are appropriate for them.

Distinctive Features of JIT Production

Accountants develop a cost accounting system based on the production environment in which it is used. Earlier in this chapter, you learned how to characterize traditional factories as either job shops or assembly lines. You studied how cost accountants use either job order costing or process costing depending on characteristics of the factory.

Similarly, when a company adopts JIT production methods, accountants must adapt the cost accounting system to them. For this reason, to understand JIT cost accounting you must first know how the production systems work. JIT factories have four characteristics that distinguish them from traditional ones.

1. Manufacturing Cells: A traditional factory contains departments that each represents either direct or indirect labor. Direct labor departments in turn contain work stations where highly specialized workers carry out specific production processes. In a JIT factory, the assembly line is composed of small production centers called "cells." Each cell contains all the machines necessary to apply a set of production processes to a product. Units in process travel from cell-to-cell within the factory, and additional production processes are applied in each cell. The factory itself is physically arranged to facilitate the flow of material from one cell to the next.

JIT cells differ from work stations in a traditional factory. In JIT, workers are permanently assigned to a cell where they are encouraged to learn all the processes performed there. They produce additional units only when required in order to satisfy demand from the cell immediately following it in the process. This often results in idle time for the cell, which workers use for training, for practicing machines setups, for repairs, or for identifying improvements in production methods.

2. Demand Pull Approach: In a traditional factory, workers obtain raw materials from a warehouse and begin the manufacturing process on them. At each work station, workers create work-in-process inventories which they move to the next work station and ultimately to a finished goods warehouse. In this environment, the factory uses inventories to anticipate customer demand and to allow work stations to progress at different rates.

The workers in a JIT factory produce products only when they are needed and only in the quantity required. When a customer requires products, the last cell in the process completes them from in-process units it has on hand. It then signals the preceding cell to prepare additional in-process units, which must then attain work-in-process from its preceding cell, and so on. For this reason, you hear a JIT production systems described as a "demand pull" system. Raw materials are only ordered when they are required by the first cell in the process. This approach minimizes the total investment in inventory.

3. Commitment to Total Quality: JIT places a greater emphasis on quality control than do traditional factories. In a traditional factory, a certain number of defective units are expected from any manufacturing operation. These are considered as normal spoilage and their costs are absorbed by the good units produced. Workers find defective units during inspections in the production process.

JIT production systems attempt to produce products that are totally free of defects. When a worker finds a defective unit in a cell, production work in the cell halts until the defect is corrected. This may require halting work on the entire assembly line. Managers consider producing quality products as more important than obtaining production volume or efficiency within cells. They refer to this as the concept of *total quality control.*

4. Decentralization of Supporting Services: JIT decentralizes supporting services such as warehousing, receiving, and shipping. A traditional factory has a warehouse where inventory is stored, a receiving department where transportation companies unload raw material, and a shipping department that prepares goods for delivery to customers.

JIT production facilities require quick access to materials, parts, and other services. It locates these services at the manufacturing cells where they are required. Workers who provide these services are assigned to manufacturing cells and work along side those involved in manufacturing. Workers within a cell also are responsible for obtaining material or in-process units from the preceding cell in the manufacturing process.

Just-in-Time Purchasing

Traditional factories seek to manage inventory levels in order to anticipate customer demand. They use the economic order quantity (EOQ) model, which is to be discussed in Chapter 14, to minimize the total costs of ordering and holding inventory. JIT factories, on the other hand, purchase materials only when needed to replenish those used in production. They take other steps to decrease ordering costs to insignificant levels. Thus, a JIT factory attempts to minimize the total costs of ordering and holding inventory without using EOQ's. Organizations implementing JIT make many substantial changes in their operations in order to reduce ordering and inventory carrying costs.

Supplier Relationships: JIT factories develop long-term relationships with suppliers of material. Before using a supplier, personnel from the JIT factory examine the material it produces and determine that it is of adequate quality. Then they sign long-term purchasing contracts for undetermined quantities at a specified price. Frequently, suppliers build factories or warehouses adjacent to the JIT factory. In this way, suppliers, rather than the JIT factory, maintain the raw material inventory.

Number of Suppliers: A traditional factory usually maintains several suppliers for each type of raw materials and shops among them for the best price. In contrast, a JIT factory usually identifies one supplier for each type of raw material. Their emphasis is on maintaining adequate quality and prompt delivery rather than on obtaining the lowest price. This allows them to rely on the supplier for prompt shipments rather than carrying raw material inventory.

Ordering Policies: A traditional factory determines when to order based on lead times and order quantities using EOQ's. A JIT factory usually orders each day only the quantity of material necessary for that day's production. These orders are usually placed by telephone or by computer rather than by mail, and are ordinarily much smaller than those specified by the EOQ model. Placing frequent small orders minimizes inventories, and doing so electronically decreases ordering costs.

Payment Policies: Traditional factories ordinarily pay for each shipment separately within thirty days after the shipment. JIT factories, which have a smaller number of steady suppliers, agree in the purchase contract to pay them for goods received at regular intervals. This may be weekly, biweekly, or monthly. This simplifies accounts payable procedures and decreases ordering costs.

JIT factories use these techniques to lower their total costs without using EOQs. The EOQ model is still appropriate and quite useful, however, for traditional factories and in merchandising companies such as retailers and wholesalers.

Illustration 6-10 summarizes the major differences between JIT and traditional manufacturing companies.

Traceability of Overhead Costs

The organization of a JIT factory enables the accounting system to trace many costs directly to products that, in a traditional factory, would be considered indirect costs. Each manufacturing cell has a set of workers and a set of processes assigned to it. Any costs of material, labor, supplies, and utilities incurred in a cell are directly traceable to that cell.

For example, the depreciation on equipment used at a cell is directly traceable to that cell. The accounting system can assign these depreciation costs to the units worked on in that cell. Workers in a cell are trained to set up the equipment for production, maintain the equipment, and to move materials from cell-to-cell. Thus maintenance, setups, materials handling, and supporting services costs that are indirect in a traditional factory can be assigned to specific cells in a JIT one.

Illustration 6-10 Key Differences Between JIT and Traditional Factories

Traditional Factory	JIT Factory
Push through system	Demand pull system
Inventories are desirable	Inventories are minimized
Organized by work station within departments	Organized by cell
Specialized labor	Interdisciplinary labor
Normal spoilage expected Centralized service activities	Total quality control
Many suppliers Buy materials based on cost	Decentralized service activities
Order using lead time and EOQ	Few long-term suppliers
Payments to suppliers based on delivery date	

Illustration 6-11 Traceability of Manufacturing Costs in JIT and Traditional Systems

Manufacturing Cost	*Traditional Manufacturing*	*JIT Manufacturing*
Direct materials	Direct	Direct
Direct labor	Direct	Direct
Machine setup	Indirect	Direct
Repairs and maintenance	Indirect	Direct
Power	Indirect	Direct
Equipment	Indirect	Direct
Indirect materials	Indirect	Direct
Materials handling	Indirect	Direct
Cell supervision	Indirect	Direct
Plant supervision	Indirect	Indirect
Building insurance	Indirect	Indirect
Building taxes	Indirect	Indirect
Building depreciation	Indirect	Indirect

Illustration 6-11 compares the traceability of some selected manufacturing costs in each type of production system.

Because JIT production systems convert many indirect manufacturing costs to direct ones, they reduce the required number of overhead cost pools and the amount of overhead that must be allocated to products. This improves the accuracy of the product costs recorded by a cost accounting system at a JIT factory.

Accounting for JIT Production Systems

Accountants characterize a traditional factory that produces many different products to order as a job shop. They use a job costing system to keep its cost records. If a traditional factory produces large quantities of one of a few products, accountants use a process costing system. Either type of factory can implement just-in-time production.

JIT and Job Order Costing

A factory using JIT production obtains raw material just-in-time for production and completes finished products just-in-time for use or sale. Materials arrive at a receiving area and immediately enter a cell for use in production. Upon completion, products are immediately shipped to the customer. The factory stores no material on its premises, and no production takes place until the receipt of a customer order. These practices eliminate the need for raw material and finished goods inventory accounts. Although units in-process exist in a JIT factory, their costs are relatively small. For this reason, most cost accountants do not track costs through a work-in process inventory account in a JIT system.

Routine Entries: Because a JIT accounting system does not use inventory accounts, its procedures are much simpler than in a traditional system. When material is received at the JIT factory, accountants debit its cost directly to cost of goods sold. Direct labor costs are treated as overhead with JIT, so accountants also debit them directly to cost of goods sold. This eliminates many of the journal entries that characterize a traditional cost accounting system.

Periodic Reporting: GAAP requires that the company using JIT disclose its inventory values in its balance sheet. To do so, accountants first calculate the cost of the inventories that exist at the end of a reporting period using standard material, labor, and overhead costs. They then post adjusting journal entries to reverse, or back out, the costs of these inventories from cost of goods sold. One approach is to debit these costs to accounts labeled as "raw and in-process

Illustration 6-12 Comparison of Cost Flows Traditional and JIT Costing Systems

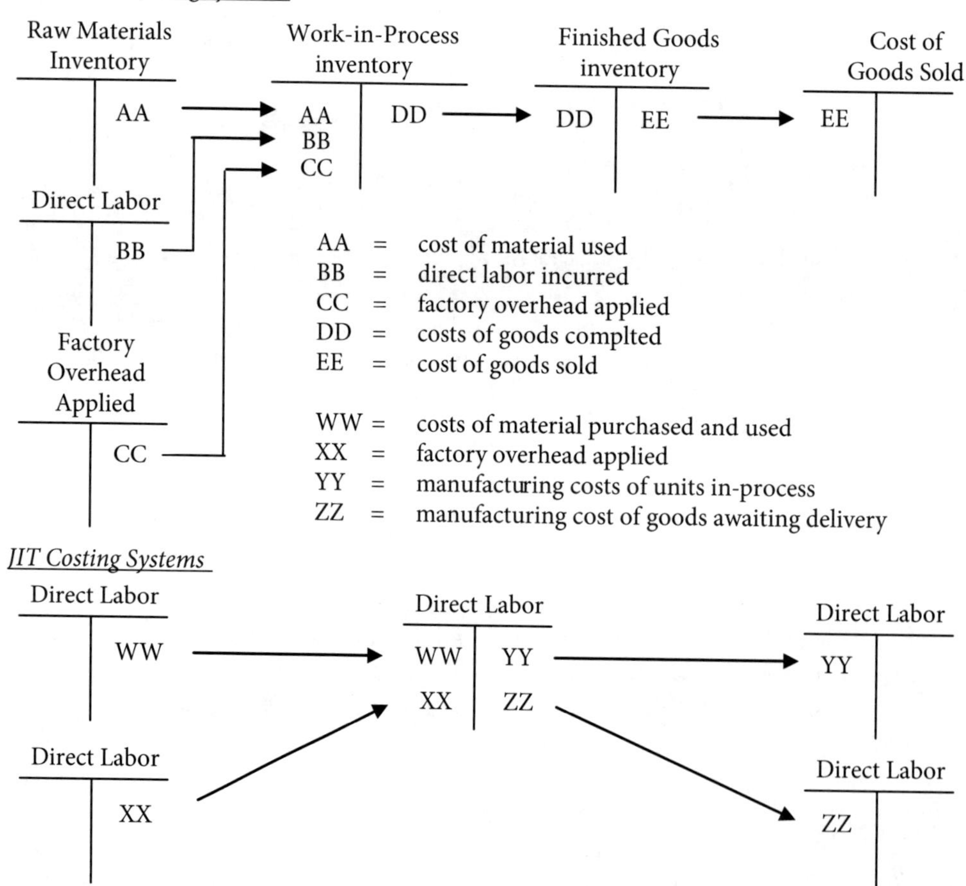

inventory" for production in-progress and "finished goods inventory" for units awaiting delivery. Illustration 6-12 compares the accounting procedures for a JIT system with those of a traditional one.

To illustrate these procedures, consider the following example. UCR Precision Instruments Inc. manufactures gas measurement meters in its JIT factory. In May, the company receives an order for 1,000 units of the Model M meter. Assume UCR incurs $15,000 in materials costs and applies a factory overhead of $10,000 to this order. For simplicity, also assume that production for this order is started and completed during the month of May. UCR's JIT accounting system uses the following entries to record the transactions.

1) To record materials purchased and used:
Cost of goods sold 15,000
Accounts payable 15,000

2) To record application of overhead:
Cost of goods sold 10,000
Factory overhead applied..... 10,000

As discussed above, the JIT accounting system charges all costs incurred during manufacture to cost of goods sold. If work on the order takes place during two successive reporting periods, then the accountant must make adjusting entries to record the ending inventory amounts.

For example, assume that in June UCR receives an order for 5,000 units of its Model N meter. The factory incurs $100,000 in materials costs and applies $100,000 of factory overhead to this order. During June, 2,000 units of the meter are completed and delivered. At the end of June, another 2,000 units of the product are still in-process. The cost accountant observes that the work on these units is 50 percent complete, but that 100 percent of the materials have been added. Additionally, on June 30 the factory has 1,000 units awaiting shipment. The following entries record these transactions.

1) To record material purchased and used:
Cost of Goods Sold 100,000
Accounts Payable..................... 100,000

2) To record the application of factory overhead:
Cost of Goods Sold...........................100,000
Factory Overhead Applied 100,000

3) To reverse ending inventory amounts from Cost of Goods Sold:
Raw and In-Process Inventory.......65,000
Finished Goods Inventory..............45,000
Cost of Goods Sold.................. 110,000

Illustration 6-13 shows how the debit entries in (3) above are calculated.

JIT and Process Costing

With a traditional process costing system, cost accountants divided a production department's total manufacturing costs by its total finished equivalent units of production to determine its unit cost. They then use this unit cost to calculate the costs of units in-process and of

Illustration 6-13 Calculation of Example Ending Inventory Amounts

Costs	*Units Finished and Delivered*		*Units Awaiting Delivery*		*Production In-Progress*	
Materials	2,000 / 5,000	x 100,000	1,000 / 5,000	x 100,000	2,000 / 5,000	x 100,000
	=	$40,000	=	$20,000	=	$40,000
Conversion	2,000 / 4,000	x 100,000	1,000 / 4,000	x 100,000	1,000 / 4,000	x 100,000
	=	$50,000	=	$25,000	=	$25,000
Total		$90,000		$45,000		$65,000

goods, completed. As described earlier in this text, the number of finished equivalent units of production differs from the number of units completed when beginning or ending inventories exist. Fortunately, calculating unit costs is much simpler in a JIT system.

Finished Equivalent Units: With a JIT system, where all work-in-process inventories are insignificant, beginning and ending inventories are assumed nonexistent. The number of finished equivalent units of work is approximately equal to the number of units completed. Therefore, cost accountants normally calculate the total cost per unit using the number of units completed. This greatly simplifies the time and cost required for data collection, analysis, and reporting.

Spoilage: Additionally, when a JIT factory successfully implements the objective of total quality control, the number of defective units and spoiled materials becomes minimal. This makes accounting for normal spoilage costs unnecessary. In most cases, cost accountants consider any spoilage as abnormal and controllable. They record its costs by debiting the account loss from abnormal spoilage.

Although companies using job order and process costing can implement a JIT system, most companies that implement JIT manufacturing use it with standard costing systems. This simplifies record keeping even further.

Summary

Process costing systems are useful in companies which are engaged in the mass production of many similar units. Product costs are determined by averaging the costs incurred during a reporting period over the number of units manufactured during the period. Because of the existence of units in process at the end of a period, and because spoilage may occur during the process, the number of units manufactured must be stated in terms of the number of finished units which would contain the same amounts of materials, labor, overhead as those actually incurred.

In process costing systems, the basic cost components are direct materials costs, conversion costs, and costs transferred in from a preceding department or process. An average unit cost is computed for each of these components, which when summed gives the overall average unit cost. This unit cost is then used to determine the cost of the units transferred out, either to another department or to finished goods inventory.

Material lost in a process may be in the form of waste, scrap, rework, or spoilage. If these losses are considered uncontrollable, they are allocated to the good units produced. If they are controllable, they are recognized as a loss from operations.

Hybrid cost systems incorporate features of job costing for direct materials and process costing for conversion costs. Many companies which have highly automated factories adopt just-in-time systems. Just-in-time systems convert many indirect costs to direct ones and trace them to individual production cells. Within a cell, the system identifies direct costs with the units worked on in that cell. Performance measurement in a just-in-time system relies on nonfinancial as well as financial measures.

Key Definitions

Abnormal spoilage Units spoiled in a production process which are considered avoidable and result from human error.

Conversion costs Direct labor costs and factory overhead when it is applied based on a measure of labor activity.

Cost centers A production department or process for which a subsidiary work-in-process account exists. Materials, labor, and overhead costs are applied to products through these subsidiary accounts.

First-in-First-out A cost flow assumption in which beginning units in-process, and their costs, are kept separate from units and costs of a current reporting period in computing an average unit cost.

Finished equivalent units The number of finished units which would have equivalent amounts of work as the units in-process.

Hybrid cost system A cost system which is similar to job costing for computing direct material cost per unit and process costing for computing conversion costs per unit.

Just-in-time manufacturing An approach to manufacturing that minimizes inventories by producing only to satisfy existing demand.

Manufacturing cell A manufacturing unit containing all the machines necessary to apply a set of production processes to a product.

Normal spoilage Units spoiled in a production process as a result of the inherent nature of the process. They are considered unavoidable.

Process cost system A product costing system in which costs are accumulated by cost center or department. Product costs are determined by averaging over an entire reporting period.

Raw and in-process inventory An inventory account used in JIT systems to record the costs associated with production in progress.

Total quality control A manufacturing standard that requires zero defects in a production process.

Transferred-in costs Manufacturing costs associated with those units transferred from a preceding department to a receiving department.

Weighted average A cost flow assumption in which units and costs of a current reporting period are combined with those in-process at the beginning of the period before computing an average unit cost

Questions

6-1 Under what conditions should process costing methods be used in assigning costs to products?

6-2 What is meant by the "finished equivalent units" for materials? For conversion?

6-3 Describe how the finished equivalent units for a period are used to calculate the cost of ending work-in-process inventories.

6-4 Describe the similarities and differences between transferred-in costs and raw materials costs.

6-5 Under what conditions would the use of conversion costs *not* be appropriate? How are unit product costs computed under these circumstances?

6-6 Distinguish between the underlying assumptions of the FIFO method and the weighted average method. When is such a cost flow assumption not necessary?

6-7 What are the differences in procedure when calculating unit product costs using the FIFO method and the weighted average method?

6-8 Distinguish between waste, scrap, and spoilage.

6-9 Describe the differences between normal spoilage and abnormal spoilage. How should the costs of each be reported?

6-10 What are the six steps in determining unit product costs in a process costing system?

6-11 In a process costing system, how is the unit product cost affected in a production cost report when materials are added in a department subsequent to the first department and the added materials result in additional units?

(*AICPA adapted*)

6-12 An error was made in estimating the percentage of completion of the current year's ending work-in-process inventory. The error resulted in assigning a lower percentage of completion to each component of the inventory than actually was the case. What is the effect of this error upon:

a. the total number of finished equivalent units?

b. the costs per finished equivalent unit?

c. the costs assigned to cost of goods completed for the year?

(*AICPA adapted*)

6-13 Describe how a JIT factory differs from a traditional factory.

6-14 Discuss how a manufacturing cell in a JIT factory differs from a production department in a traditional factory.

6-15 How does JIT manufacturing affect job order costing? process costing?

6-16 Why must factories that use JIT production have reliable suppliers?

6-17 What are the key features of JIT purchasing?

6-18 Explain why some overhead costs in a traditional factory become direct costs in a JIT factory.

6-19 In a traditional factory, worker idle time is considered a bad thing. In a JIT factory, this is not the case. Can you suggest why?

Problems

6-20 *Terminology*

Match each of the following lettered terms on the left with the appropriate numbered definition on the right.

a. Abnormal spoilage
b. First in first out
c. Normal spoilage

1. Costs are accumulated by cost center or department
2. Material that can be sold for

d. Process cost system
e. Rework
f. Scrap
g. Waste

minimal value
3. Spoilage that is unavoidable
4. Material lost in the process which has no value
5. Spoilage that is a result of human error
6. Products that do not meet quality standards
7. Cost flow assumption where beginning units-in-process are not considered

6-21 *Finished Equivalent Units*

The Felix Manufacturing Company uses a process cost system to account for the costs of its only product known as "Nino." Production begins in the fabrication department where units of raw material are molded into various connecting parts. After fabrication is complete, the units are transferred to the assembly department. There is no material added in the assembly department. After assembly is complete, the units are transferred to the packaging department where the units are packaged for shipment. At the completion of this process, the units are complete and they are transferred to the shipping department.

At year end, December 31, 2007, the following inventory of "Nino's" is on hand:

- No unused raw material or packing material.
- Fabrication department: 6,000 units, 25% complete as to raw material and 40% complete as to direct labor.
- Assembly department: 10,000 units, 75% complete as to direct labor.
- Packaging department: 3,000 units, 60% complete as to packing material and 75% complete as to direct labor.
- Shipping department: 8,000 units.

Prepare in proper form schedules showing the following at December 31, 2007:

(a) The number of equivalent units of raw material in all inventories.
(b) The number of equivalent units of fabrication department directs labor in all inventories.
(c) Number of equivalent units of packaging department material and direct labor in the packaging department inventory.

(AICPA adapted)

6-22 *Finished Equivalent Units—FIFO and Weighted Average*

On November 1, 20XX, Yankee Company had 20,000 units of work-in-process in Department No. 1 which was 100% complete as to material costs and 20% complete as to conversion costs. During November, 160,000 units were started in Department No. I and 170,000 units were completed and transferred to Department No. 2. The work-in-process on November 30 was 100% complete as to material costs and 40% complete as to conversion costs. Compute the finished equivalent units for materials and conversion using (a) the weighted average method, and (b) the FIFO method.

(AICPA adapted)

6-23 *Finished Equivalent Units—FIFO and Weighted Average*

Walton, Inc., had 8,000 units of work-in-process in Department A on October 1. These units were 60% complete as to conversion costs. Materials are added at the beginning of the process. During the month of October, 34,000 units were started and 36,000 were completed. Walton had 6,000 units of work-in-process on October 31, 80% complete as to conversion costs. Compute the finished equivalent units for materials and conversion assuming (a) the weighted average method, and (b) the FIFO method. *(AICPA adapted)*

6-24 *Cost per Equivalent Unit—Weighted Average Method*

On April 1, the Collins Company had 6,000 units of work-in-process in Department B, the second and last stage of their production cycle. The costs attached to these 6,000 units were $12,000 of costs transferred from Department A, $2,500 of material costs added in Department B, and $2,000 of conversion costs added in Department B. Materials are added at the beginning of the process in Department B. Conversion was 50% complete on April 1. During April, 14,000 units were transferred in from Department A at a cost of $27,000; material costs of $3,500 and conversion costs of $3,000 were added in Department B. On April 30, Department B had 5,000 units of work-in-process, 60% complete as to conversion costs. Using the weighted average method, compute the cost per equivalent unit in Department B for April.

6-25 *Cost per Equivalent Unit—FIFO and Weighted Average Methods (Spreadsheet)*

Beck Corporation makes wooden bed frames. The following data pertain to the company's costs in beginning work-in-process inventory at October 1st, 2006 and for the month of October:

	Beginning Work-in Process Inventory	*Current Period Costs*
Direct Materials	$7,400	$9,747
Direct Labor	1,665	2,100
Factory Overhead	1,000	1,560

Beck Corporation had 700 units in process on October 1st. These units were 70% complete as to material and 50% complete as to conversion. During the month of October the company started 400 units, and ended the month with 300 units in ending inventory. The units in ending inventory were 30% complete as to material and 20% complete as to conversion.

Required:

(a) Using a computer spreadsheet program, determine the units started and completed, the total equivalent units of production, and the cost per equivalent unit for direct materials, direct labor and factory overhead using the FIFO method. The schedule should resemble the FIFO production report presented in the chapter. Use formulas to perform all calculations on the above data, such as the determination of units started and completed, equivalent units, totals, and costs per equivalent unit.

(b) Repeat the above requirement using the weighted average method. The schedule should resemble the weighted average production report presented in the chapter.

(c) Explain any differences between the costs per equivalent unit computed using the FIFO method and those computed using the weighted average method .

6-26 Equivalent Unit Costs With Normal Spoilage—No Beginning Inventories
Read, Inc., instituted a new process in October. During the month, 10,000 units were started in Department A. Of the units started, 1,000 were lost due to unavoidable factors at the beginning of the process, 7,000 were transferred to Department B, and 2,000 remained in work-in-process at October 31. The ending work-in-process was 100% complete as to materials cost and 50% complete as to conversion costs. Materials costs of $27,000 and conversion costs of $40,000 were recorded in Department A during October. What was the cost per finished equivalent unit in Department A?

(AICPA adapted)

6-27 *Finished Equivalent Units With Normal Spoilage—Weighted Average Method*
Milton, Inc. had 8,000 units of work-in-process in Department M on March 1 which were 50% complete as to conversion costs. Materials are introduced at the beginning of the process. During March, 17,000 units were started, 18,000 units were completed and there were 2,000 units of normal spoilage. Milton had 5,000 units of work-in-process at March 31 which was 60% complete as to conversion costs. Under Milton's cost accounting system, spoiled units reduce the number of units over which total cost can be spread. Compute the finished equivalent units of production for materials and conversion using the weighted average method.

(AICPA adapted)

6-28 *Total Costs—Weighted Average Method*
Information for the month of May concerning Department A, the first stage of Wit Corporation's production cycle, is as follows:

	Materials Costs	Conversion Costs
Beginning Work-in-Process	$ 4,000	$ 3,000
Current Costs	20,000	16,000
Total Costs	$ 24,000	$ 19,000
Equivalent Units Based on Weighted Average Method	100,000	95,000
Average Unit Costs	$ .24	$ .20

During the month 90,000 units were completed. The ending work-in-process of 10,000 units is 50% complete as to conversion costs. Materials are added at the beginning of the process. Determine the total costs of (a) the goods completed, and (b) the ending work-in-process.

(AICPA adapted)

6-29 *Total Costs—Weighted Average Method*
Abacus Corp. manufactures Product A in a single production process. The following information was recorded for the year 20XX:

Beginning work-in-process inventory:
10,000 units, .20 complete as to conversion;
Materials costs $25,000;
Conversion costs $20,500.

Ending work-in-process inventory:
4,000 units, .50 complete as to conversion.

For the current year:
60,000 units started, 66,000 units completed and transferred to finished goods;
Materials costs recorded, $150,000;
Conversion costs recorded, $115,500.

Materials are added at the beginning of the process. Assuming Abacus uses the weighted average method, show:

(a) Total cost of goods completed;
(b) Total cost of ending work-in-process inventory;
(c) Entry to record transfer of completed units to finished goods.

6-30 *Total Costs—FIFO Method*
Repeat Problem 5-20 for Abacus Corp. using the FIFO method.

6-31 *Total Costs—Weighted Average Method*
Winnie International produces Product X in two departments. Material is added to the process at the beginning of Department 1. Additional material is added halfway through the process in Department 2. The following data is provided for Department 2 for June.

Units completed: 25,000 with current costs as follows: Transferred from Department 1, $216,000; materials, $252,000, and conversion, $228,000.

Ending inventory: 6,000 units which were 1/3 complete as to conversion.

During the month, 24,000 units were transferred from Department 1. The beginning units in process consisted of 7,000 units which were 60% complete as to conversion. The beginning inventory costs consisted of $32,000 of transferred-in costs, $48,000 of materials costs, and $42,000 of conversion costs. Using the weighted average method, compute:
(a) Total cost of Product X completed during June; and
(b) Total cost of ending work-in-process inventory at June 30.

6-32 *Total Costs—FIFO Method*
Repeat Problem 5-22 for Winnie International using the FIFO method, except that ending inventory was 30 percent complete as to conversion.

6-33 *Normal Spoilage—Weighted Average Method*
Spot Cola Bottling Co. manufactures a beverage which is sold in quart bottles. Its manufacturing process uses two departments, Blending and Bottling. The following data pertains to the Blending Department for the month of July.

Beginning inventory: 20,000 quarts, 75% complete as to conversion. Costs were $3,190 for materials, $1,080 for labor, and $2,160 for factory overhead.

Ending inventory: 22,000 quarts also 50% complete as to conversion.
Cost for July: $20,790 of materials, $5,988 of labor.
During the month of July, 100,000 quarts were started and 96,000 were completed. Normal spoilage is 3% of the production begun, and inspection occurs at the end of the blending process. Materials are added uniformly throughout the process. Factory overhead is applied to the product at the rate of 200% of direct labor dollars. If Spot Cola uses the weighted average method, show:
(a) Total cost of the product transferred to the Bottling Department in July;
(b) Total cost of ending inventory in the Blending Department;
(c) Entry to record transfer of work-in-process.

6-34 *Normal Spoilage—FIFO Method*
Repeat Problem 5-24 assuming Spot Cola Bottling Co. uses the FIFO method.

6-35 *Abnormal Spoilage—Weighted Average Method*
The Trinity River Corp. manufactures sporting goods. Production of the Model HQ baseball passes through two departments. Department A winds a fiber cord tightly around a hard rubber core. In Department B a horsehide cover is prepared and laced onto the balls received from Department A. Finished baseballs then move into another department for packaging. The following information is recorded in Department B for November:

Production completed:	10,700 units.
Production started:	10,000 units.
Costs:	$20,370 for materials, $44,440 for conversion, and $30,000 of costs transferred from Department A.
Spoilage:	300 units.

In Department B the balls are inspected immediately upon receipt from Department A. If accepted, additional materials are added at the beginning of the process. Normal spoilage is 2% of the units begun. Department B's work-in-process on November 1 consisted of 2,000 units which were 60% complete as to conversion. Work-in-process costs at November I were: materials, $3,030; conversion, $9,235, and transferred-in, $9,000. At November 30, 1,000 units were in-process, 60% complete as to conversion. Using the weighted average method, determine:

(a) Total cost of the Model HQ transferred out of Department B.
(b) Total cost of ending inventory in Department B.
(c) Cost of abnormal spoilage.
(d) Entry reflecting transfer of goods out of Department B.

6-36 *Abnormal Spoilage—FIFO Method*
Repeat Problem 5-26 for Trinity River Corp. using the FIFO method.

6-37 *Inspection During Process—Weighted Average Method*
Woodman Enterprises manufactures noodles which are packaged and sold to wholesale grocers. All ingredients are added at the beginning of the process, and inspection occurs halfway through it. During the month of May, 16,600 packages were started

and 14,500 packages were completed. Spoilage consisted of 1,500 packages, of which 1,000 was considered unavoidable. The following data were recorded for the month:

Beginning inventory: 2,400 units which were 40% complete as to conversion; $2,400 of materials costs and $7,358 of conversion costs were included.
Current costs: $16,600 of materials and $27,342 of conversion.
Ending inventory: 3,000 units which were 70% complete as to conversion.

Using the weighted average method, compute:
(a) Total cost of goods transferred.
(b) Total cost of ending inventory for May.
(c) Cost of abnormal spoilage.

6-38 *Inspection During Process—FIFO Method*
Complete Problem 5-28 for Woodman Enterprises using the FIFO method. Assume that the ending work-in-process inventories are 30% (rather than 70%) complete for conversion.

6-39 *Spoilage with Two Departments—No Beginning Inventories*
The Dexter Production Company manufactures a single product. Its operations are a continuing process carried on in two departments-machining and finishing. In the production process, materials are added to the product in each department *without increasing the number of units produced.*
For the month of June, 20X1, the company records indicated the following production statistics for each department:

	Machining Department	*Finishing Department*
Units in-process, June 1, 20X1	0	0
Units transferred from preceding department	0	60,000
Units started in production	80,000	0
Units completed and transferred out	60,000	50,000
Units in-process, June 30, 20X1*	20,000	8,000
Units spoiled in production	0	2,000

*Percent of completion of units in process at June 30, 20X1:		
Materials	100%	100%
Labor	50%	70%
Overhead	25%	70%

The units spoiled in production had no scrap value and were 50% complete as to material, labor, and overhead. The company's policy is to treat the cost of spoiled units in production as a separate element of cost *in the department in which the spoilage occurs.*

Cost records showed the following charges for the month of June:

	Machining Department	*Finishing Department*
Materials	$240,000	$ 88,500
Labor	140,000	141,500
Overhead	65,000	25,700

For both the machining and finishing departments, prepare in good form the following reports for the month of June:
(a) Quantity of production report.
(b) Cost of production report, using the following columnar headings:

Machining Department		*Finishing Department*	
Cost	per Unit	Cost	per Unit

Round all computations to the nearest cent.

(*AICPA adapted*)

6-40 *Spoilage with Three Departments—Weighted Average Method*

Ballinger Paper Products manufactures a high quality paper box. The box department applies two separate operations-cutting and folding. The paper is first cut and trimmed to the dimensions of a box form by one machine group. One square foot of paper is equivalent to four box forms. The trimmings from this process have no scrap value. Box forms are then creased and folded (i.e., completed) by a second machine group. Any partially processed boxes in the department are cut box forms that are ready for creasing and folding. These partly processed boxes are considered 50% complete as to labor and overhead. The materials department maintains an inventory of paper in sufficient quantities to permit continuous processing, and transfers to the box department are made as needed. Immediately after folding, all good boxes are transferred to the finished goods department.

During June, 20X1, the materials department purchased 1,210,000 square feet of unprocessed paper for $244,000. Conversion costs for the month were $226,000. A quantity equal to 30,000 boxes was spoiled during paper cutting, and 70,000 boxes were spoiled during folding. All spoilage has a zero salvage value, is considered normal and cannot be reprocessed. All spoilage loss is allocated between the completed units and partially processed boxes. Ballinger applies the weighted average cost method to all inventories. Inventory data for June are given below:

Inventory	*Physical Unit*	*June 30 Units on Hand*	*June 1 Units on Hand*	*Cost*
Materials Department:				
paper	square feet	200,000	390,000	$76,000
Box Department:				
boxes cut, not folded	number	300,000	800,000	55,000*
Finished Goods Department:				
completed boxes on hand	number	50,000	250,000	18,000

*Materials	$35,000
Conversion cost	20,000
	$55,000

Prepare the following for the month of June, 20X1:

(a) A report of cost of paper used for the Materials Department.

(b) A schedule showing the physical flow of units (including beginning and ending inventories) in the Materials Department, in the Box Department and in the Finished Goods Department.

(c) A schedule showing the computation of equivalent units produced for materials and conversion costs in the Box Department.

(d) A schedule showing the computation of unit costs for the Box Department.

(e) A report of inventory valuation and cost of completed units for the Box Department.

(f) A schedule showing the computation of unit costs for the Finished Goods Department.

(g) A report of inventory valuation and cost of units sold for the Finished Goods Department.

(*AICPA adapted*)

6-41 *Spoilage with Two Departments—FIFO Method*

Poole, Inc. produces a chemical compound by a unique chemical process which Poole has divided into two departments: A and B for accounting purposes. The process functions as follows:

1) The formula for the chemical compound requires one pound of Chemical X and one pound of Chemical Y. In the simplest sense, one pound of Chemical X is processed in Department A and transferred to Department B for further processing where_ one pound of Chemical Y is added when the process is 50% complete. When the processing is complete in Department B, the finished chemical compound is transferred to finished goods. The process is continuous, operating twenty-four hours a day.
2) Normal spoilage occurs in Department A. Five percent of Chemical X is lost in the first few seconds of processing.
3) No spoilage occurs in Department B.
4) In Department A conversion costs are incurred uniformly throughout the process and are allocated to good pounds produced because spoilage is normal.
5) In Department B conversion costs are allocated equally to each equivalent pound of output.

6) *Poole's unit of measure for work-in-process and finished-goods inventories is pounds.*
7) The following data are available for the month of October, 20X0:

	Department A	Department B
Work-in-process October 1	8,000 pounds	10,000 pounds
Stage of completion of beginning inventory (one batch per department)	3/4	3/10
Started or transferred in	50,000 pounds	
Transferred out	46,500 good pounds	?
Work-in-process, October 31	?	?
Stage of completion of ending inventory (one batch per department)	1/3	1/5
Total equivalent pounds of material added in Department B		44,500 pounds

Prepare schedules computing equivalent unspoiled pounds of production (materials and conversion costs) for Department A and for Department B for the month of October 20X0 using the first-in, first-out method for inventory costing.

(*AICPA adapted*)

6-42 *Finished Equivalent Units*

The Brown Company manufactures hair spray in a three-department process. The molding department produces the plastic bottles and caps in which the product is placed. The mixing department combines the raw materials for the hair spray and puts the mixture into bottles. In the packaging department, the product is boxed and sealed in cellophane.

A description of the departmental activities as well as the units associated with the work in process at the beginning of March 20X5 were as follows:

Molding Department: In the molding department, the plastic is added at the beginning of the process, overhead is uniformly incurred, and the only direct labor occurs at the end of the process. A worker trims the bottle and cap and places them on a conveyer for transport to the mixing department. The work in process at March 1 was 1,000 units estimated to be one-half complete.

Mixing Department: All the materials for the hair spray are combined in a large vat, thoroughly mixed, and pumped into the plastic bottles conveyed from the molding department. The overhead costs for the mixing department are uniformly incurred during the mixing process. Materials and direct labor are added at the beginning of the process. At the beginning of March, no work in process existed in the mixing department.

Packaging Department: The capped bottles are conveyed to the packaging department where they are automatically boxed. At the end of the process, the boxes are sealed in cellophane and a worker packs them in cases of 24 bottles each. The individual box is added at the beginning of the process and the cellophane, direct labor, and casing are added at the end of the process. Overhead is incurred uniformly. On March 1, 960 units were considered to be 40% complete.

Plastic for 100,000 bottles and caps was added into production in the month of March in the molding department. The work in process inventories at the end of March included: 2,000 units 80% complete in the molding department; 1,000 units 50% complete in the mixing department; and 640 units 25% complete in the packaging department.

The molding and mixing departments use weighted average process costing, while the packaging department uses first-in, first-out process costing.

Required:

Complete a finished equivalent unit schedule for March 20X5 for the three departments. Assume that Brown Co. calculates equivalent units for each identifiable input in each department, and that no spoilage occurs in any of the processes.

6-43 *Abnormal Spoilage*

APCO Company manufactures various lines of bicycles. Because of the high volume of each type of product, the company employs a process cost system using the weighted average method to determine unit costs. Bicycle parts are manufactured in the molding department. The parts are consolidated into a single bike unit in the molding department and transferred to the assembly department where they are partially assembled. After assembly the bicycle is sent to the packing department.

Cost per unit data for the 20-inch dirt bike has been completed through the molding department. Annual cost and production figures for the assembly department are presented in the schedules at the bottom of the page.

Defective bicycles are identified at an inspection point when the assembly labor process is 70% complete; all assembly material has been added at this point of the process. The normal rejection percentage for defective bicycles is 5% of the bicycles reaching the inspection point. Any defective bicycles over and above the 5% quota are considered as abnormal. All defective bikes are removed from the production process and destroyed.

Assembly Department Cost Data

	Transferred in from Molding Department	Assembly Material	Assembly Conversion Cost	Total Cost of Dirt Bike Through Assembly
Prior period costs	$ 82,200	$ 6,660	$ 11,930	$ 100,790
Current period costs	1,237,800	96,840	236,590	1,571,230
Total costs	$1,320,000	$103,500	$248,520	$1,672,020

Assembly Department Production Data

	Bicycles	Percent Complete Transferred In	Assembly Material	Assembly Conversion
Beginning inventory	3,000	100	100	80
Transferred in from molding during year	45,000	100	-	-
Transferred out to packing during year	40,000	100	100	100
Ending inventory	4,000	100	50	20

Required:

(a) Compute the number of defective bikes that are considered to be:
1. A normal amount of defective bikes.
2. An abnormal amount of defective bikes.

(b) Compute the equivalent units of production for the year for:
1. Bicycles transferred in from the molding department.
2. Bicycles produced with regard to assembly material.
3. Bicycles produced with regard to assembly conversion.

(c) Compute the cost per equivalent unit for the fully assembled dirt bike.

(d) Compute the amount of the total production cost of $1,672,020 that will be associated with the following items.
1. Normal defective units.
2. Abnormal defective units.
3. Good units completed in the assembly department.
4. Ending work in process inventory in the assembly department.

(e) Describe how the applicable dollar amounts for the following items would be presented in the financial statements.
1. Normal defective units.
2. Abnormal defective units.
3. Completed units transferred into the packing department.
4. Ending work in process inventory in the assembly department.

6-44 *Just-in-Time—Direct and Indirect Costs*

Classify each of the following costs from a JIT factory as a direct or indirect cost. Assume that each manufacturing cell produces a single product and is responsible for setups, repairs, maintenance, and inspections within the cell.

a. Plant depreciation
b. Machinery depreciation
c. Repairs and maintenance on machinery
d. Plant supervisory salaries
e. Cell supervisory salaries
f. Machine setup costs
g. Salaries of janitors and security guards
h. Direct labor
i. Raw materials
j. Tax and insurance on plant
k. Tax and insurance on machinery

l. Overtime premium for cell workers
m. Repair parts for machinery
n. Setups and inspection
o. Materials handling
p. Cafeteria services
q. Accounting and computing services
r. Electricity
s. Materials ordering and receiving costs
t. Finished goods packaging costs

6-45 *Just-in-Time and Product Costs*

Matrix Manufacturing Company recently changed its factory to JIT production. The following expenditures occurred during the month of April:

1. Raw materials purchased and used, $100,000.
2. Factory overhead incurred, $100,000. Of this amount, $40,000 was labor.
3 Ending inventories for April were $2,000 in raw and in-process inventory, and $8,000 in finished goods inventory.

Required:

Prepare journal entries recording the above transactions.

6-46 *Just-in-Time and Job Order Costing*

California Hi-Tech Inc. uses a just-in-time production system. The factory has received an order for 1,000 units of Model RS to be filled this month. For this order they purchased and used materials costing $20,000 and incurred other manufacturing costs of $46,000 (including $10,000 in labor costs). During the month, 800 units were completed and shipped. Ending inventories include 100 finished units and 100 units in-process, 20 percent complete as to conversion. Conversion costs were incurred evenly throughout the conversion process.

Required:

Prepare the necessary journal entries for recording the production activities concerning this order.

6-47 *Just-in-Time and Process Costing*

Klear-Tone Electronics Corp. is a producer of low-cost transistor radios using a JIT production system. They have incurred the following transactions for the month of September.

1. Raw materials purchased and used were $50,000.
2. $80,000 in factory overhead was applied to products.
3. Costs of ending finished goods inventory totaled $10,000.

Required:

Prepare journal entries recording the above transactions.

6-48 *Just-in-Time Systems*

The management at Megafilters Inc. has been discussing the possible implementation of a just-in-time (JIT) production system at its Illinois plant, where oil filters and air filters for heavy construction equipment and large, off-the-road vehicles are manufactured. The metal stamping department at the Illinois plant has already instituted a JIT system for controlling raw materials inventory, but the remainder of the plant is still discussing how to proceed with the implementation of this concept. Some of the other department managers have grown increasingly cautious about the JIT process after hearing about the problems that have arisen in the metal stamping department.

Robert Goertz, manager of the Illinois plant, is a strong proponent of the JIT production system, and recently made the following statement at a meeting of all departmental managers. "Just-in-time is often referred to as a management philosophy of doing business rather than a technique for improving efficiency on the plant floor. We will all have to make many changes in the way we think about our employees, our suppliers, and our customers if we are going to be successful in using just-in-time procedures. Rather than dwelling on some of the negative things you have heard from the metal stamping department, I want each of you to prepare a list of things we can do to make a smooth transition to the just-in-time philosophy of management for the rest of the plant."

Required:

(a) The just-in-time management philosophy emphasizes objectives for the general improvement of a production system. Describe several important objectives of this philosophy.

(b) Discuss several actions that Megafilters Inc. can take to ease the transition to a just-in-time production system at the Illinois plant.

(c) In order for the just-in-time production system to be successful, Megafilters, Inc. must establish appropriate relationships with its suppliers and employees. Describe each of these relationships.

(*ICMA adapted*)

1. *To identity the accounting problems created by the existence of joint products.*
2. *To discuss the various methods available for allocating joint manufacturing costs to joint products.*
3. *To discuss methods of accounting for by-products and scrap.*
4. *To study several methods available for allocating service department costs to production departments.*

7 Cost Allocation

In Chapters 5 and 6, we discussed product costing for production processes where all production inputs can be associated with a particular product or department. In many manufacturing processes, a certain amount of joint manufacturing cost is incurred to produce two or more products. An example of joint manufacturing cost is the cost of crude oil used by an oil refining company in its manufacturing process. The refining process may produce several products including different grades of gasoline, fuel oil, kerosene, tar, and other chemical products. The outputs from such a production process are called joint (or multiple) products. This type of situation presents the accounting problem of allocating joint manufacturing cost to the individual products for the purpose of product costing.

The joint cost allocation problem is also frequently found in allocating a service department's costs when the service department provides services to production departments and other service departments.

The purpose of this chapter is to present several widely used approaches for allocating joint costs to joint products or to departments. In addition, special attention is given to managerial decision-making regarding the further processing of joint products.

Main Products and By-Products

When two or more products are simultaneously produced from a single manufacturing process, the outputs are called *joint products.* They are not identifiable as individual products until a certain stage of production. This point at which joint products can be separately identified is known as the *split-off point.* All production costs incurred prior to the split-off point are called *joint manufacturing costs,* and those costs

Illustration 7-1 Joint Costs, Joint Products, and Split-off Point

Joint costs, joint products and split-off point

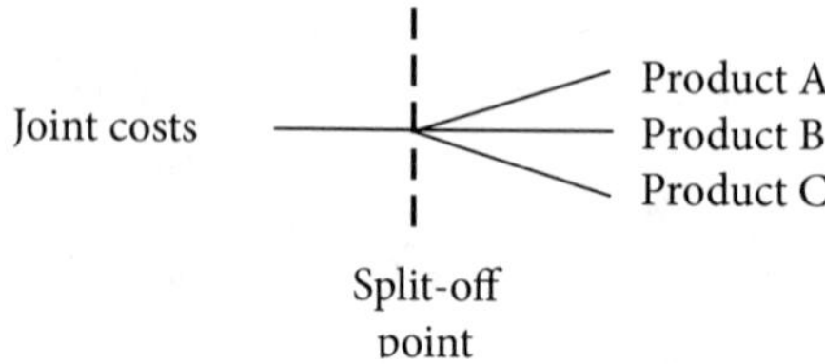

incurred after the split-off point are called *additional processing or separable costs.* Illustration 7-1 shows the relationship between joint costs, the split-off point, and joint products.

For purposes of accounting, joint products are usually classified as either main products or by-products. The distinction between main products and by-products is usually made based upon the total sales value of each product. A main product is a joint product that has a significant relative sales value when compared to the by-products. A by-product is a joint product that has a relatively small sales value.

Accounting for Joint Products

The accounting objective for joint products is to determine the unit cost of each joint product for inventory valuation and income determination. In order to achieve this objective the following two accounting procedures are necessary: (1) allocating joint manufacturing costs to each joint product and (2) identifying additional processing costs beyond the split-off point. If a product is sold at the split-off point without further processing, its unit cost includes only the allocated joint manufacturing costs. If a product is further processed after the split-off point, its unit cost will include the allocated joint manufacturing costs and the additional processing costs. In either case, allocation of joint manufacturing costs to each product is necessary.

Two basic methods used for allocating joint manufacturing costs are: (a) the physical measure approach and (b) the sales (or market) value approach. The latter approach is sometimes called the *net realizable value* method.

The Physical Measure Approach

The physical measure approach allocates joint costs to joint products on the basis of a physical measure that is common to all the products. Weight, volume, and feet are some measures that are commonly used. Under this approach, the common measure is summed and the joint costs are allocated according to each product's relative portion of the total physical measure. For example, assume the following data were accumulated for a manufacturing process for a month:

Costs Incurred	
Raw Materials	$2,000
Direct Labor	2,000
Factory Overhead	1,000
Total	5,000

Joint Products	
Product A	80 lbs.
Product B	20 lbs.
	100 lbs.

Illustration 7-2 Joint Cost Allocation Using Physical Volume

Product	*Volume*	*Allocation ratio*	*Joint cost allocation*	*Unit cost*
A	80 lbs.	80%	$4,000	$50/lb.
B	20 lbs.	20%	1,000	50/lb.
Total	100 lbs.		$5,000	

Illustration 7-2 shows the allocation of the joint manufacturing costs of $5,000 to joint products A and B using the number of pounds as the common measure.

As shown in the table, 80% of the joint production cost is allocated to product A and 20% of the joint production cost is allocated to product B. The joint costs allocated to products A and B are $4,000 (= 5,000 x 80%) and $1,000 (= 5,000 x 20%), respectively. It should be noted that the unit cost is the same in this case, *$50/lb.* This is the nature of the physical measure approach.

Journal entries relevant to the manufacturing process in the example are:

1. Raw materials issued to production

Work-in-process	2,000	
Materials inventory..................		2,000

2. Direct labor costs incurred

Work-in-process	2,000	
Wages payable		2,000

3. Factory overhead applied to production

Work-in-process	1,000	
Factory Overhead Applied		1,000

4. Joint costs allocated to products

Finished goods—Product A	4,000	
Finished goods—Product B	1,000	
Work-in-process		5,000

The physical measure approach is simple and easy to apply. However, the approach does not consider the revenue producing ability of each joint product. When selling prices differ markedly between joint products, this method may produce a large profit for one product and a large loss for another. To illustrate this problem, assume that selling prices for product A and product B are $30/lb. and $280/lb., respectively. Illustration 7-3 shows product line income statements assuming no beginning and ending finished goods inventories.

The income statements show an unreasonable profit for product B and an unreasonable loss for product A. This is sometimes a major disadvantage of allocating joint production costs based on physical measures. Product A has a selling price of $30 per pound, but the allocated joint cost is $50 per pound. On the other hand, product B has a selling price of $280 per pound and the allocated joint cost is also *$50* per pound. Therefore, this approach does not provide a reasonable unit cost in relation to the market value of the products. It is satisfactory only when

Illustration 7-3 Product-line Income Statements (Joint Costs Allocated by the Physical Measure Approach)

	Product A	*Product B*	*Total*
Sales	$2,400	$5,600	$8,000
Cost of golds sold	4,000	1,000	5,000
Gross Margin	($1,600)	$4,600	$3,000
Gorss Margin on Sales	(66.67%)	82.14%	37.5%

there is a close relationship between the physical measure and the market value of the joint products.

The Sales Value Approach

The sales value approach is based on the assumption that it costs more to produce a product with a higher sales value than a product with a lower sales value. Under this approach, joint manufacturing costs are allocated to joint products on the basis of their relative sales values at the split-off point. For example, Illustration 7-4 shows the allocation of the joint manufacturing costs of $5,000 in the previous example to products A and B using the sales value approach.

In this example, 30% of the joint costs are allocated to product A and the remaining 70% is assigned to product B. Although this approach recognizes the revenue-producing ability of each product and avoids the major disadvantage of the physical measure approach, it is not without its drawbacks. A major criticism of the sales value approach is that the resulting percentage of gross margin on sales is the same for all products. Illustration 7-5 shows the equality of the percentage of gross margin on sales in the example problem.

The market price of a joint product at split-off is not always available. In such cases, an approximate market value must be determined so that the joint cost can be reasonably allocated. The market value of a joint product at the split-off point can be approximated by its net realizable value, which is commonly defined as the predicted ultimate sales value less expected additional costs of completion and disposal. Illustration 7-6 demonstrates an example using the

Illustration 7-4 Joint Cost Allocation Using Sales Value

Product	*Production*	*Sellin Price at Split-off*	*Sales Value*	*Allocation Ratio*	*Joint Cost Allocation*
A	80 lbs.	$ 30/lb.	$2,400	30%	$1,500
B	20 lbs.	280/lb.	5,600	70%	3,500
Total			$8,000		$5,000

Illustration 7-5 Product-Line Income Statements (Joint Costs Allocated by the Sales Value Approach)

	Product A	*Product B*	*Total*
Sales	$2,400	$5,600	$8,000
Cost of golds sold	1,500	3,500	5,000
Gross Margin	$ 900	$2,100	$3,000
Gorss Margin on Sales	37.5%	37.5%	37.5%

Illustration 7-6 Joint Cost Allocation Using the Net Realizable Value Approach

Product	*Production*	*Selling Price*	*Total Sales Value*	*Additional Processing Cost*	*Net Realizable Value*	*Allocation Ratio*	*Joint Costs Allocation*
A	80 lbs.	$ 40*	$3,200	$400	$2,800	1/3	$1,667
B	20 lbs.	280**	5,600	0	5,600	2/3	3,333
Total					$8,400		$5,000

net realizable value as a basis for joint cost allocation. It uses the same data as before, except that there is no market price available for product A at the split-off point. As a result, product A needs to be further processed before being sold for $40 per pound. The total additional processing costs are estimated to be $400.

It should be noted that further processing costs for a product are a part of the total manufacturing costs of the product. Therefore, in the determination of the total production costs, the further processing cost should be included. Total production costs of products A and B in the example are:

Product	*Production*	*Allocated joint Costs*	*Further Processing Costs*	*Total Production Costs*
A	80 lbs.	51,667	$400	$2,067
B	20 lbs.	3,333	0	3,333
Total		$5,000	$400	$5,400

The discussion so far has assumed that some joint products are main products, and that there is no by-product. Accounting for by-products is discussed in the following section.

ACCOUNTING FOR BY-PRODUCTS

By-products are multiple products that have relatively small sales values in comparison to those of main products. The distinction between byproducts and scrap is often not clear. Generally by-products have a relatively larger sales value than scrap and sometimes may need further processing after the split-off point. Basically, there are two general methods of accounting for by-products:

Method 1: By-products produced are assigned an inventory cost equal to their estimated net realizable value. This estimated net realizable value is treated as a reduction of joint manufacturing costs.

Method 2: By-products are assigned no inventory cost. When byproducts are sold, the net revenue is treated in one of the following ways:

a. a reduction in cost of main products sold.
b. other income.
c. a reduction in cost of main products produced.
d. additional sales revenue.

By-Products Are Assigned Inventory Cost

Under this method, the net realizable value of by-products produced is treated as a reduction in the production cost of main products. By-products are assigned an inventory cost equal to the net realizable value, which is defined as sales value less estimated processing, marketing and administrative costs.

To illustrate this method, assume that main products X and Y are manufactured in a production department that also produces by-product Z. Other relevant data are given below:

1. Joint production costs (Materials, Labor, and Factory overhead) $5,000
2. Production and sales during the period:

	Main Products		
	X	*Y*	*By-Product Z*
Units Produced	100	100	50
Units sold	80	90	40
Ending Inventory (Units)	20	10	10
Sales price per unit	$40	$60	$ 5

3. Additional processing and disposal costs to by-product Z are estimated to be $2 per unit.

By-product Z's net realizable value is $4 – 2 = $2 per unit. The total net realizable value of by-product Z produced, $2 *(50)* = $100, is recorded as by-product inventory and deducted from the production costs of the main products. Necessary journal entries for by-product Z are given below:

1. Record by-product inventory at the net realizable value
   By-product inventory.........100
   Work in process 100
2. Debit additional costs to the by-product inventory account (including additional processing and disposal costs)
   By-product inventory.........100
   Various Accounts......... 100
3. Record sales of by-product (40 units @ $4)
   Cash......................................160
   By-product inventory.. 160

In this case, the net production cost of the main products is equal to $5,000 – 100 = $4,900. This net production cost of main products may be allocated between main products X and Y based on either the physical measure method or the relative sales value method. The relative sales value method is used here for illustration. In this case, the resulting joint cost allocation, total costs, unit cost, and ending inventory of each product are:

Product	*Allocated Joint Costs*	*Additional Cost*	*Total Costs*	*Unit Cost*	*Ending Inventory Units*	*Ending Inventory $*
X	$1,960 *	$ 0	$1,960	$19.60	20	392
Y	2,940**	0	2,940	29.40	10	294
Z	100	100	200	4.00	10	40
Total	$5,000	$100	$5,100			

* $4,900 x (4,000/10,000)
** $4,900 x (6,000/10,000)

Illustration 7-7 provides the income statement of each main product line and the production department for the period.

The inventory ledger account for each product in the example appears as follows:

Product X		Product Y		Product Z	
1,960		2,940		100	
	1,568		2,646	100	160
392		294		40	

No Inventory Costs Assigned to By-Products

This approach assigns no inventory cost to by-products as they are produced. The only record may be a memorandum entry to show the physical volume of by-products produced. Net revenue from by-products sold is treated in one of four ways: (a) a reduction in cost of main products sold, (b) other income, (c) a reduction in cost of main products produced, (d) additional sales revenue. Net revenue is defined as gross sales revenue less additional costs (i.e., further processing costs and marketing costs) incurred. In the example problem, the net revenues from product Z during the period are ($4 – $2)(40) = $80.

When net revenue from by-products sold is treated as a reduction in cost of the main products sold, as other income, or as additional sales revenue, allocated joint costs and ending inventory in the above example are as follows:

Product	*Total Sales Value*	*Allocation Ratio*	*Allocated Joint Costs*	*Units Produced*	*Unit Cost*	*Units in Ending Inventory*	*Ending Inventory*
X	$ 4,000	40%	$ 2,000	100	$20	20	$400
Y	6,000	60%	3,000	100	30	10	300
	$10,000	100%	$5,000				$700

If net revenue from by-products sold is considered to be a reduction in the cost of the main products produced, the joint costs to be allocated in the example problem are $5,000 – $80 =

Illustration 7-7 Income Statement (By-Product Inventories are Assigned)

	Product X	*Product Y*	*Total*
Sales	$3,200	$5,400	$8,600
Cost of Goods Sold	1,568*	2,646**	4,214
Gross Margin	1,632	2,754	4,386
Selling and Administrative Expenses (Assumed)			2,000
Income Before Income Taxes			$2,386

*$19.60(80) = $1,568
**$29.40(90) = $2,646

$4,920. Then the allocated joint costs and ending inventories may be calculated in the following way.

Product	Total Sales Value	Allocation Ratio	Allocated Joint Costs	Units Produced	Unit Cost	Units in Ending Inventory	Ending Inventory
X	$ 4,000	40%	$ 1,968	100	$19.68	20	$393.60
Y	6,000	60%	2,952	100	29.52	10	295.20
	$10,000	100%	$4,420				$688.80

Note that the above unit costs and ending inventories of main products X and Y are different from those determined by Method 1 where by-products are assigned inventory cost. Illustration 7-8 provides the income statement of the production process to show the four ways of recognizing the net revenue of by-product Z sold during the period.

Additional Processing Decisions

Frequently managers must decide whether a joint product should be sold at the split-off point or processed further. In making this decision, incremental analysis, which compares the incremental revenues and incremental costs of further processing, is useful. Incremental revenue is defined as the revenue available after further processing less the revenue available at the split-off point. The incremental cost is equal to the additional processing cost and the additional selling and administrative expenses. The further processing alternative is justified if the incremental revenue is greater than the incremental cost. It should be noted that costs incurred before the split-off point are not relevant in this managerial decision. Whether a joint product should be processed further is not affected by the amount of joint costs allocated to the joint product. The following example illustrates this point.

Illustration 7-8 Income Statement (By-Product Inventories Are Not Assigned)

	(a) Reduction in Cost of Main Products Sold	(b) Other Income	(c) Reduction in Cost of Main Products Produced	(d) Additional Sales Revenue
Sales (Main Products X and Y)	$8,600	$8,600	$8,600	$8,600
Net Revenue of By-Product				80
Total Sales Revenue	8,600	8,600	8,600	8,680
Cost of Goods Sold:				
Gross Production Costs	5,000	5,000	5,000	5,000
Less: Net Revenue of By-Product			80	
Net Production Costs	5,000	5,000	4,920	5,000
Ending Inventory of Main Products	700	700	688.80	700
Gross Cost of Goods Sold	4,300	4,300	4,231.20	4,300
Less: Net Revenue of By-Product	80			
Net Cost of Goods Sold	4,220	4,300	4,231.20	4,300
Gross Margin	4,380	4,300	4,368.80	4,380
Selling & Administrative Expense	2,000	2,000	2,000	2,000
Operating Income	2,380	2,300	2,368.80	2,380
Other Income:-Product				
Net Revenue of By-Product		80		
Income Before Taxes	$2,380	$2,380	$2,368.80	$2,380

Assume that a manufacturing process produces three joint products X-l, X-2, and X-3. The number of units of X-1 produced by the process is 100. Joint product X-l is salable for $10 per unit at the split-off point. In addition, the firm can further process X-1 and then sell it for $15 per unit. The additional processing cost is estimated to be $300. The selling and administrative expenses for product X-1 before and after further processing are the same. Should product X-1 be processed further?

The following is an analysis of incremental costs and revenues if product X-1 is processed further.

Incremental revenues ($1,500 – $1,000)	$500
Incremental costs`	300
Incremental profit	$200

The incremental profit of $200 is the amount by which the company would be better off by further processing joint product X-1. Therefore, the decision to process further is financially preferable. If additional processing costs were $600, the incremental profit would be a negative $100, and the company would prefer to sell product X-1 at the split-off point.

In order to illustrate that the joint cost allocation does not affect a further processing decision, consider the following two independent situations associated with the above example.

Situation [1]: The joint production costs allocated to joint product X-1 by the relative sales value method are $800.

Situation [2]: The joint production costs allocated to joint product X-t by the physical measure method are $400.

Different amounts of joint costs may be allocated to product X-1, depending on the choice of the allocation method. Comparative income statements for the alternatives of selling at split-off or processing further are presented in Illustration 7-9 for situation [1] and in Illustration 7-10 for situation [2].

A comparison of Illustrations 7-9 and 7-10 shows that incremental profits are the same in both situations although joint costs allocated to product X-l are different. The difference in joint cost allocation does not affect the further processing decision. The only relevant factors in the decision are incremental revenues and incremental costs of further processing.

Careful attention must be given to the determination of incremental costs. Incremental costs of further processing should include all additional costs of materials, direct labor, variable overhead, and fixed overhead required by additional processing. Common fixed overhead that will be incurred regardless of the decision should be excluded from the analysis. However, the opportunity cost associated with the existing facility available for further processing should not

Illustration 7-9 Comparative Income Statements for Product X-1 (Situation [1] - Joint Costs Allocated are $800)

	Alternative		
	Sell at Split-off	*Process Further*	*Incremental Analysis*
Sales revenues (at $10; $15)	$1,000	$1,500	$500
Joint cost allocation	(800)	(800)	0
Additional processing costs	0	(300)	(300)
Profit	$ 200	$ 400	$200

Illustration 7-10 Comparative Income Statements for Product X-1 (Situation [2] - Joint Costs Allocated are $400)

	Alternative		
	Sell at Split-off	*Process Further*	*Incremental Analysis*
Sales revenues (at $10; $15)	$1,000	$1,500	$500
Joint cost allocation	(400)	(400)	0
Additional processing costs	0	(300)	(300)
Profit	$ 600	$ 800	$200

be ignored. For example, if the company could rent the facility used for further processing to a customer for $100, the $100 rental should be included in the decision analysis. This opportunity cost is an incremental cost because if the company decides to process further, the rental will be foregone.

Allocation of Service Department Costs

Most organizations contain not only production cost centers that are directly involved in the manufacturing process, but also service cost centers as well. Such service departments may include factory administration, data processing, and repairs and maintenance, among others. In many cases, service departments provide supporting services to other service departments as well as to production departments. Although they do not participate directly in a production process, their services are necessary for efficient operation in the production departments. Thus the costs incurred by service departments should be included in the costs of the units manufactured by the production departments. This is accomplished by allocating service department costs to production departments.

In some companies the costs that are allocated may be the actual costs incurred during a reporting period. More commonly, budgeted service department costs will be allocated to production departments, and these allocated costs will be included in the budgeted factory overhead costs of the production departments. The resulting total costs are then used to compute departmental factory overhead rates in production departments. When factory overhead is applied to units in a producing department, a portion of each service department's costs are thus included in the unit cost.

The allocation should be based on some common denominator that best measures the services provided to the production departments and other service departments. Some service departments and the bases most commonly used for allocating their costs are given in the following table:

Service Departments	*Cost Allocation Bases*
Personal administration	Number of employees, labor hours
Repairs and maintenance	Machine hours, square footage
Storage and warehousing	Square footage, volume and value of materials
Data processing services	Computer time used, number of reports
Power plant	Usage, capacity of machines
Engineering	Direct labor hours, machine hours

Any one of three methods may be used in allocating service department costs to production departments: (1) the direct method, (2) the step method, and (3) the linear algebra method. These methods are discussed and illustrated through the use of the following example.

A company has two production departments (fabrication and assembly) and two service departments (general factory administration and factory maintenance). During an upcoming month, the following costs have been budgeted for each department. In the case of the production departments, these represent costs for factory overhead items such as supplies and supervision.

Department	*Budgeted Costs*
Fabrication	$6,000
Assembly	3,000
Factory Administration	1,400
Factory Maintenance	2,000

A summary of their relationships prior to the allocation of service department costs is as follows:

	% of Service Cosumed by				
Services Provided by	*Factory Administration*	*Factory Maintenance*	*Fabrication*	*Assembly*	*Total*
Factory Administration	10%	20%	30%	40%	100%
Factory Maintenance	10%	10%	40%	40%	100%

The numbers in the table represent the percent of the total services provided by a service department to each of the departments. The percentage is calculated from observed values of appropriate allocation bases for the service departments during a past month. *Reciprocal services* are said to exist because the factory administration department provides services to factory maintenance, while at the same time factory maintenance is providing services to factory administration. *Self-consumption* of services is also present, because each service department is providing services to itself. The relationships among the service and production departments can be graphically shown in Illustration 7-11.

The Direct Method

The direct method allocates each service department's costs directly to the production departments, and ignores the service provided by one service department to another. Using this

Illustration 7-11 Relationship Among Service and Production Departments

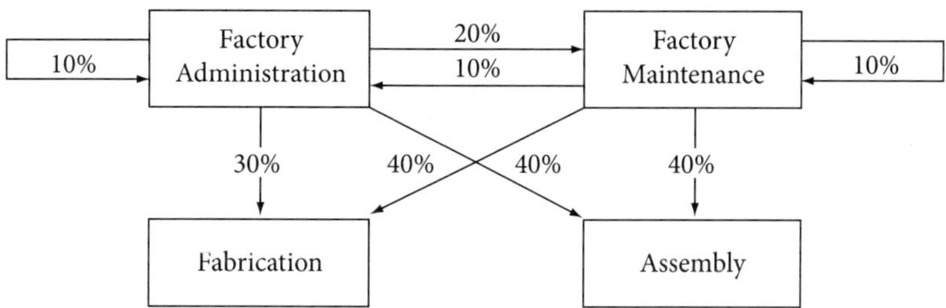

method, the service department costs in the example are allocated to the production departments as shown in Illustration 7-12. In this example, the total budgeted factory overhead costs would be $7,600 (= $1,600 + $6,000) in the fabrication department, and $4,800 (= $1,800 + $3,000) in assembly. Note that the allocation percentages used in Illustration 7-12 are different from the original percent-ages. The recalculated percentages are determined from the percentages of services provided only to the production departments. For example, 70% of the factory administration services is provided to the production departments; 30% to fabrication and 40% to assembly. Therefore, 30%/70% of the service costs should be allocated to the fabrication department and 40%/70% of the service costs should be allocated to the assembly department.

Simplicity and ease of calculation are the advantages of the direct method. However, this method does not consider services received from and provided to other service departments. It ignores both reciprocal services and self-consumption.

The Step Method

This approach is more complicated than the direct method because it requires a sequence of reallocations. Costs are allocated from each service department to the remaining departments in a predetermined sequence. The sequence is usually selected so that the department, which renders the most services to other service departments, has its costs allocated first. Once costs are allocated from a service department, none are allocated back in subsequent steps of the procedure. The process is complete when all service costs have been allocated to production departments, and no costs remain in any service department. Since a department is eliminated from subsequent allocations, this method gives only partial recognition to the reciprocal relationships among the service departments. Furthermore, self-consumption of services is ignored entirely.

In the illustrative problem, the factory administration department's costs are allocated first because it provides a greater quantity of its service to the other service department, factory maintenance. Allocation of factory administration costs and factory maintenance costs to the

Illustration 7-12 Service Department Cost Allocation (Direct Method)

	Production Departments				
Service Departments	*Fabrication*		*Assembly*		*Total*
	%	*Amount*	*%*	*Amount*	
Factory Administration	3/7	$ 600	4/7	$ 800	$1,400
Factory Maintenance	4/8	1,000	4/8	1,000	2,000
Total Allocated		$1,600		$1,800	$3,400

Illustration 7-13 Service Department Cost Allocation (Step Method)

	Service Department		*Production Department*	
	Factory Administration	*Factory Maintenance*	*Fabrication*	*Assembly*
Service Department Costs	$1,400	$2,000	0	0
Allocation of Factory Administration	(1,400)	311	467	622
		(2/9)	(3/9)	(4/9)
Allocation of Factory Maintenance		(2,311)	1,155.50	1,155.50
			(4/8)	(4/8)
Total Allocated	0	0	$1,622.50	$1,777.50

fabrication and assembly departments using the step method is shown in Illustration 7-13. Using the step method, total budgeted factory overhead costs become $7,622.50 for fabrication and $4,777.50 for assembly.

Note that factory administration costs are allocated first to the factory maintenance department and to the production departments. The resulting total of factory maintenance costs to be allocated to the production departments includes the share of factory administration costs allocated to factory maintenance: i.e., $2,000 + 311 = $2,311.00.

The step method gives a partial recognition to the reciprocal relationships among the service departments. However, the ultimate costs allocated to each department depend on the sequence followed, and in some situations the sequence may be arbitrary.

The Linear Algebra Method

The linear algebra method overcomes the disadvantages of the other approaches to service department cost allocation, because it recognizes both reciprocal services and self-consumption. Thus it is the only method that is theoretically correct. However, applying the linear algebra method in an actual business context requires knowledge of the mathematical rules governing matrix algebra. This has delayed its acceptance somewhat among practicing accountants. A simplified linear algebra approach to cost allocation is to solve a set of simultaneous equations, and this approach will now• be presented. A more formal mathematical formulation that is appropriate in complicated situations is presented in the Appendix to this chapter.

The linear algebra method requires the formulation of a set of linear equations, each representing the services provided and received by a service department. Thus one equation is developed for each of the service departments. For the example problem, let:

S_1 = Factory administration's costs after reciprocal allocation.
S_2 = Factory maintenance's costs after reciprocal allocation.

Then the costs after allocation can be obtained by solving the following set of simultaneous equations.

$$S_1 = 1{,}400 + .1S_1 + .1S_2 \qquad (1)$$
$$S_2 = 2{,}000 + .2S_1 + .1S_2 \qquad (2)$$

Equation (2) states that the budgeted costs of the factory maintenance department after reciprocal al1ocation will be $2,000 plus: (a) an amount allocated due to reciprocal services ($.2S_1$), and (b) an amount allocated due to self-consumption ($.1S_2$). Solving for S_1 and S_2 in equations (I) and (2) gives the total amount of costs for each service department, including self-consumption and reciprocal services.

In solving equations (1) and (2), we first rearrange the two equations as follows:

$$.9S_1 - 1S_2 = 1{,}400 \quad (3)$$
$$-.2S_1 + .9S_2 = 2{,}000 \quad (4)$$

From (3)

$$S_2 = 9S_1 - 14{,}000 \quad (5)$$

Substituting (5) in (4), we have

$$-.2S_1 + 8.1S_1 - 12{,}600 = 2{,}000$$
$$7.9S_1 = 14{,}600$$
$$S_1 = 1{,}848 \quad (6)$$

By substituting (6) in (5), we obtain

$$S_2 = 9\,(1{,}848) - 14{,}000$$
$$= 2{,}632 \quad (7)$$

The amounts S_1 and S_2 are the budgeted service department costs including self-consumption and reciprocal services. These costs must now be allocated to the production departments based on the services provided to them. Recall that 70% of factory administration's services are provided to the production departments. Then the net factory administration costs applicable to the production departments are $.7S_1 = .7 \times \$1{,}848 = \$1{,}294$. Of this amount, % are applicable to fabrication and % are applicable to assembly. Thus factory administration costs are allocated in the following way:

Factory administration costs:

allocated to fabrication	= 3/7 x $1,294 =	$ 355
allocated to assembly	= 4/7 x $1,294 =	739
		$1,294

Similarly, 80% of factory maintenance's services are provided to the production departments. Then $.8S_2 = .8 \times \$2{,}632 = \$2{,}106$.

Factory maintenance costs:

allocated to fabrication	= 1/2 x $2,106 =	$ 1,053
allocated to assembly	= 1/2 x $2,106 =	$ 1,053
		$ 2,106

The resulting service cost allocation to the production departments may be summarized as follows:

From	*To*				*Total*
	Fabrication		*Assembly*		
Factory Adminstration	$1,294 (3/7)	= 555	$1,294 (4/7)	- 739	$1,294
Factory Maintenance	2,106 (.50)	= 1,053	2,106 (.50)	-1,053	2,106
Total		$1,608		$1,792	$3,400

Using the linear algebra method, the budgeted factory overhead costs for the fabrication department includes $1,608 allocated from service departments, plus $6,000 in supplies, utilities, and other costs to be incurred in fabrication, for a total of $7,608. In the same way, total budgeted factory overhead for assembly would be $1,792 + $3,000 = $4,792.

This example illustrates conceptually how the linear algebra method accounts for self-consumption and reciprocal services. In practice, however, a medium-sized organization may have as many as 20 service departments. In such a situation, the effort in solving a set of 20 simultaneous equations becomes prohibitive. A more practical approach, which utilizes matrix algebra, is presented in the Appendix.

Summary

Joint cost allocation is important for purposes of product costing. In this chapter, we have discussed various techniques to allocate joint manufacturing costs to joint products and service department costs to production departments. The advantages and disadvantages of each method have also been discussed. No matter how sophisticated the allocation technique may be, cost allocations are of limited value in decision-making. Cost allocation is made for product-costing purposes alone.

Key Definitions

Additional processing costs	Production costs incurred after the split-off point in order to further process a joint product. Also called separable costs.
By-product	A joint product that has a relatively small sales value.
Incremental analysis	A comparison of the incremental revenues and incremental costs between two alternatives.
Joint manufacturing costs	All production costs incurred prior to the split-off point.
Joint products	Multiple products that are produced simultaneously from a single manufacturing process.
Main product	A joint product which has a significant relative sales value when compared to the by-products.
Net realizable value	The estimated sales value less expected costs of completion and disposal.
Reciprocal services	The services provided by service departments to each other.
Self-consumption	Services provided by a department to itself.
Split-off point	The point in a manufacturing process at which joint products can be separately identified.

Appendix

Matrix Methods in Service Cost Allocation

Two approaches to the allocation of service department costs are described in this section. The first expresses in matrix notation the procedures described in the chapter for solving simultaneous equations. The second is a less procedural formulation based on the theory of Markov chains.

Matrix Approach to Solving Simultaneous Equations

Two equations for service department costs after reciprocal allocation were derived in the chapter. They were:

$$S_1 = 1{,}400 + .1S_1 + .1S_2$$
$$S_2 = 2{,}000 + .2S_1 + .1S_2$$

In matrix notation, these can be written as

$$\mathbf{S = B + AS} \tag{8}$$

Where

$$S = \begin{pmatrix} S_1 \\ S_2 \end{pmatrix} \quad b = \begin{pmatrix} 1{,}400 \\ 2{,}000 \end{pmatrix} \quad A = \begin{pmatrix} .1 & .1 \\ .2 & .1 \end{pmatrix}$$

Equation (8) can be solved for S.

$$\begin{aligned} S - AS &= b \\ (I - A)S &= b \\ (I - A)^{-1}(I - A) &= (I - A)^{-1}b \\ S &= (I - A)^{-1}b \end{aligned} \tag{9}$$

Thus the values of S1 and S2 can be found by forming the matrix (I – A), taking its inverse, and post multiplying it by B. For the example,

$$I - A = \begin{pmatrix} 1 & 0 \\ 0 & 1 \end{pmatrix} - \begin{pmatrix} .1 & .1 \\ .2 & .1 \end{pmatrix} = \begin{pmatrix} .9 & -.1 \\ -.2 & .9 \end{pmatrix}$$

$$(I - A)^{-1} = \begin{pmatrix} 1.139 & .127 \\ .253 & 1.139 \end{pmatrix}$$

$$S = \begin{pmatrix} S_1 \\ S_2 \end{pmatrix} = \begin{pmatrix} 1.139 & .127 \\ .253 & 1.139 \end{pmatrix} \bullet \begin{pmatrix} 1{,}400 \\ 2{,}000 \end{pmatrix} = \begin{pmatrix} 1{,}848 \\ 2{,}632 \end{pmatrix}$$

Service department costs allocated to the production departments can be found using the relationship

$$C = P \bullet S.$$

Here P is the matrix of allocation percentages from the service departments to the production departments. The vector C contains the costs allocated to production departments, and in the example is of the form:

$$C = \begin{pmatrix} C_F \\ C_A \end{pmatrix}$$

Where subscripts F and A refer to the fabrication and assembly departments. Matrix P is formed as follows:

		To	
		Fabrication	*Assembly*
From	Factory administration	.3	.4
	Factory maintenance	.4	.4

Then

$$P = \begin{pmatrix} .3 & .4 \\ .4 & .4 \end{pmatrix}$$

$$C = P \cdot S = \begin{pmatrix} .3 & .4 \\ .4 & .4 \end{pmatrix} \begin{pmatrix} 1{,}848 \\ 2{,}632 \end{pmatrix} = \begin{pmatrix} 1{,}608 \\ 1{,}792 \end{pmatrix}$$

Thus CF – $1,608 represents the service department costs allocated to the fabrication department. Likewise CA = $1,792 are costs allocated to assembly.

Markov Chain Approach to Service Cost Allocation

A different approach to service department cost allocation is presented in this section. It recognizes that service costs can be allocated to production departments by a series of iterations. In each iteration, additional costs are allocated from service departments until all costs are assigned to the production departments. In practice this may require many iterations; however, the theory of Markov chains can be applied to shorten the procedure.

Form an allocation matrix M which shows the percentage of costs to be allocated from every department to every other department. In the example, there are two production departments and two service departments. Then M is formed as follows:

		To			
		Fabrication	*Assembly*	*Factory Administration*	*Factory Maintenance*
From	Fabrication	1	0	0	0
	Assembly	0	1	0	0
	Factory Administration	.3	.4	.1	.2
	Factory Maintenance	.4	.4	.1	.1

Then in the example

$$M = \begin{pmatrix} 1 & 0 & 0 & 0 \\ 0 & 1 & 0 & 0 \\ .3 & .4 & .1 & .2 \\ .4 & .4 & .1 & .1 \end{pmatrix}$$

Note that in this matrix, all costs of a production department (fabrication and assembly) will be reallocated to the same production department. None of the production costs will be allocate to service departments.

Next form a row vector C0 containing the costs of each department before allocation. In the example, it is of the form:

$$C_0 = (C_F \quad C_A \quad C_{FA} \quad C_{FM})$$
$$= (6{,}000 \quad 3{,}000 \quad 1{,}400 \quad 2{,}000)$$

By multiplying C0.M, Some costs will be allocated from the service departments to the producing departments. Note also that this procedure provides for self-consumption and for reciprocal services. This first iteration produces a new cost vector C1.

$$C1 = C0 \cdot M$$

$$= (6{,}000 \quad 3{,}000 \quad 1{,}400 \quad 2{,}000) \begin{pmatrix} 1 & 0 & 0 & 0 \\ 0 & 1 & 0 & 0 \\ .3 & .4 & .1 & .2 \\ .4 & .4 & .1 & .1 \end{pmatrix}$$

$$= (7{,}220 \quad 4{,}360 \quad 340 \quad 480).$$

In the second iteration, postmultiply C1 by M in order to produce C2:

$$C_2 = C_1 \bullet M$$
$$= (7{,}514 \quad 4{,}688 \quad 82 \quad 116).$$

Similarly, we can continue the same procedure in subsequent iterations.

$$C_3 = C_2 \bullet M$$
$$= (7{,}585 \quad 4{,}767 \quad 19.8 \quad 28)$$

•

•

•

$$C_6 = C_5 \bullet M$$
$$= (7{,}607.2 \quad 4{,}792.0 \quad .3 \quad .4)$$

After six iterations, $7,607 are budgeted for the fabrication department, of which $1,607 were allocated from service departments. The assembly department has budgeted costs of $4,792, with $1,1,792 being the allocated portion.

This iterative process can be avoided by partitioning M in the following way.

$$M = \left(\begin{array}{cc|cc} 1 & 0 & 0 & 0 \\ 0 & 1 & 0 & 0 \\ \hline .3 & .4 & .1 & .2 \\ .5 & .4 & .1 & .1 \end{array}\right) = \left(\begin{array}{c|c} \mathbf{I} & \mathbf{O} \\ \hline \mathbf{R} & \mathbf{Q} \end{array}\right)$$

Then a new allocation matrix N can be formed representing the cost transfers after an infinite number of iterations.

$$N = \begin{pmatrix} I & 0 \\ (I-Q)^{-1}R & 0 \end{pmatrix}$$

The cost vector C after an infinite number of iterations can be found from the relationship:

$$C = C_0 \bullet N$$

In the example problem,

$$R = \begin{pmatrix} .3 & .4 \\ .4 & .4 \end{pmatrix} \qquad Q = \begin{pmatrix} .1 & .2 \\ .1 & .1 \end{pmatrix}$$

Then

$$I - Q = \begin{pmatrix} 1 & 0 \\ 0 & 1 \end{pmatrix} - \begin{pmatrix} .1 & .2 \\ .1 & .1 \end{pmatrix} - \begin{pmatrix} .9 & -.2 \\ -.1 & .9 \end{pmatrix}$$

$$(I-Q)^{-1}R = \begin{pmatrix} 1.139 & .253 \\ .127 & 1.139 \end{pmatrix} \begin{pmatrix} .3 & .4 \\ .4 & .4 \end{pmatrix}$$

$$= \begin{pmatrix} .443 & .557 \\ .494 & .506 \end{pmatrix}$$

So the matrix N can be found

$$N = \begin{pmatrix} 1 & 0 & 0 & 0 \\ 0 & 1 & 0 & 0 \\ .443 & .557 & 0 & 0 \\ .494 & .506 & 0 & 0 \end{pmatrix}$$

Then the final cost vector is

$$C = C_0 \bullet N$$

$$= (6{,}000 \quad 3{,}000 \quad 1{,}400 \quad 2{,}000)\begin{pmatrix} 1 & 0 & 0 & 0 \\ 0 & 1 & 0 & 0 \\ .443 & .557 & 0 & 0 \\ .494 & .506 & 0 & 0 \end{pmatrix}$$

$$= (7{,}608 \quad 4{,}792 \quad 0 \quad 0).$$

Although this approach is much simpler to implement than any of the others relying on linear algebra, its derivation is beyond the scope of this text.

Questions

7-1 Define joint products, main products, and by-products.

7-2 Distinguish between the manufacturing costs incurred before and after the split-off point.

7-3 What methods can be used for allocating joint manufacturing costs?

7-4 What method can be used in determining whether a joint product should be sold at split-off or processed further?

7-5 Discuss the advantages and disadvantages of the physical measure method and the relative sales value method in the allocation of joint manufacturing costs.

7-6 What two general methods are used in accounting for by-products?

7-7 What is the purpose of allocating joint manufacturing costs to joint products?

7-8 Describe three approaches for allocating the costs of service departments to production departments.

7-9 What is the purpose of allocating service department costs to production departments?

7-10 Under the step method, which service department's costs should be allocated first?

7-11 Discuss the advantages and disadvantages of the direct method, the step method and the linear algebra method in the allocation of service department costs to production departments

Problems

7-12 (*Terminology*) Match the following numbered terms on the left with the appropriate lettered definition on the right.

1. By-product	a. Joint product that has relatively high sales value
2. Joint cost	b. Point at which joint products can be separately identified
3. Joint product	c. Additional processing costs
4. Main product	d. Multiple products produced from a single manufacturing process
5. Net realizable value	e. Estimated sales value less expected costs of completion
6. Separable costs	f. Product with small sales value
7. Split-off point	g. A cost that will not change regardless of further processing

7-13 *Joint Product Inventories*

Products A and B are joint products. The joint manufacturing costs of A and B were $10,000. The production and unit selling price of A and B are as follows:

Product	*Production*	*Unit Selling Price*	*Ending Inventory*
A	10,000 units	$4.00	1.000 units
B	40,000 units	1.50	2,000 units

Required:

Determine cost of ending inventory for Products A and B using:

(1) The physical measure method

(2) The relative sales value method.

7-14 *Joint Cost Allocation*

The Oilers Company produces two joint products: A and B. During the current period, $16,000 of joint costs were incurred to produce 100 units of A and 50 units of B. Product A can be sold at split-off for $150 per unit. Product B needs additional processing and then can be sold for $200 per unit. The total additional processing cost for B is $5,000.

Required:

Allocate the joint manufacturing cost to Product A and Product B based on their relative sales values at split-off.

7-15 *Joint Cost Allocation with Additional Processing Costs*

The CMA Manufacturing Company produces three products: C, M, and A in its manufacturing process. After split-off, these products are further processed separately. Additional information is as follows:

Total manufacturing costs incurred before the split-off point was $15,000.

Products	Units Produced	Additional Processing Cost	Unit Selling Price
C	100	$1,000	$100
M	100	3,000	120
A	200	7,000	80

Required:

Using the relative sales values at split-off, determine the joint cost allocated to each product.

7-16 *Joint Cost Allocation*

Vreeland, Inc. manufactures Products X, Y, and Z from a joint process. Joint product costs were $60,000. Additional information is as follows:

Required:

			Sales Values and Additional Costs if Processed Further	
Product	*Units Produced*	*Sales Value at Split-off*	*Sales Values*	*Additional Costs*
X	6,000	$40,000	$55,000	$ 9,000
Y	4,000	35,000	45,000	7,000
Z	2,000	25,000	30,000	5,000

(1) Assuming that joint product costs are allocated using the physical measures (units produced) approach, what were the total production costs for Product X?

(2) Assuming that joint product costs are allocated based on relative sales values at split-off, what were the total production costs for Product Y?

(*AICPA adapted*)

7-17 *Estimation of Sales Value at Split-off*

Stellar Corporation manufactures Products R and S from a joint process. Additional information is as follows:

	Product		
	R	*S*	*Total*
Units produced	4,000	6,000	10,000
Joints costs allocation	$36,000	$ 54,000	$ 90,000
Sales value at split-off	?	?	?
Additional costs if processed further	$ 3,000	$ 26,000	$ 29,000
Sales value if processed further	$63,000	$126,000	$189,000
Additional margin if processed further	$12,000	?	$ 40,000

Required:

Assuming that joint costs are allocated on the basis of relative sales values at split-off, what was the sales value at split-off for Product S?

(*AICPA adapted*)

7-18 *Accounting for By-Product and Joint Cost Allocation*

Superior Company manufactures Products A and B from a joint process which also yields a by-product, X. Superior accounts for the revenues from its by-product sales as a deduction from the cost of goods sold of its main products.

Additional information is as follows:

	Products			
	A	*B*	*X*	*Total*
Units produced	15,000	9,000	6,000	30,000
Joint costs	?	?	?	264,000
Sales value at split-off	$290,000	$150,000	$10,000	$450,000

Assuming that joint product costs are allocated using their relative sales values at split-off, what was the joint cost allocated to Product B?

(*AICPA adapted*)

7-19 *Simple Joint Cost Allocation*

Helen Corp. manufactures Products W, X, Y, and Z from a joint process. Additional information is as follows:

			If Processed Further	
Producer	*Units Produced*	*Sales Value at Split-off*	*Additioanl Costs*	*Sales Value*
W	6,000	$ 80,000	$ 7,500	$ 90,000
X	5,000	60,000	6,000	70,000
Y	4,000	40,000	4,000	50,000
Z	3,000	20,000	2,500	30,000

Required:

Assuming that total joint costs of $160,000 were allocated using relative sales values at split-off, what were the joint costs allocated to each product?

(*AICPA adapted*)

7-20 *Determining Joint Costs*

Kyle Company manufactures Products S and T from a joint process. The sales value at split-off was $50,000 for 6,000 units of Product S and $25,000 for 2,000 units of Product T. Assuming that the portion of the total joint costs properly allocated to Product S using the relative sales values at split-off was $30,000, what were the total joint costs?

(*AICPA adapted*)

7-21 *Joint Cost Allocation*

A company uses a single process to produce three joint products, E, M, and H. Raw materials in the amount of 100,000 gallons are processed in each batch to yield 40,000 gallons of E, 30,000 gallons of M, and 20,000 gallons of H. The joint costs of processing a batch of raw materials are:

Materials (100,000 gallons)	$60,000
Conversion Costs	75,000

After split-off, product E can be sold for $1.50 per gallon. Products M and H must be processed further before they can be sold. The separate processing costs are $1.50 per gallon for product M and $2.00 per gallon for product H. Product M can then be sold for $3.00 per gallon and product H for $4.25 per gallon.

During March, the company processed 100,000 gallons of raw materials. There were no inventories of finished product on hand on March 1. March sales were 30,000 gallons of E, 28,000 gallons of M, and 16,000 gallons of H.

The company uses the net realizable value method for allocating joint costs.

Required:

(a) Prepare a schedule showing the allocation of the $135,000 joint cost between products E, M, and H. Clearly label your answer.

(b) Prepare a statement of gross margin for products E, M, and H for March.

(c) Product E can be processed further into product Super E by additional processing which costs $14,000. 35,000 gallons of Super E can be produced per batch of 100,000 gallons of raw materials. Super E can be sold for $2.00 per gallon. Will the company be better off by producing and selling Super E rather than product E? Show computations to support your answer.

(*IIA adapted*)

7-22 *Accounting for By-Product*

Lares Confectioners, Inc., makes a candy bar called Rey, which sells for $.50 per pound. The manufacturing process also yields a product known as Nagu. Without further processing, Nagu sells for $.10 per pound. With further processing, Nagu sells for $.30 per pound. During the month of April, total joint manufacturing costs up to the point of separation consisted of the following charges to work in process:

Raw Materials	$150,000
Direct Labor	120,000
Factory Overhead	30,000

Production for the month aggregated 394,000 pounds of Rey and 30,000 pounds of Nagu. To complete Nagu during the month of April and obtain a selling price of $.30 per pound, further processing of Nagu during April would entail the following additional costs:

Raw Materials	$2,000
Direct Labor	1,500
Factory Overhead	500

Required:

Prepare the April journal entries for Nagu, if Nagu is:

(a) Transferred as a by-product at sales value to the warehouse without further processing, with a corresponding reduction of Rey's manufacturing costs.

(b) Further processed as a by-product and transferred to the warehouse at net realizable value, with a corresponding reduction of Rey's manufacturing costs.
(c) Further processed and transferred to finished goods, with joint costs being allocated between Rey and Nagu based on relative sales value at the split-off point.

(AICPA adapted)

7-23 *Joint Cost Allocation*

Forward, Inc. manufactures Products P, Q, and R from a joint process. Additional information is as follows:

	Product			
	P	*Q*	*R*	*Total*
Units produced	4,000	2,000	1,000	7,000
Joint costs	$36,000	?	?	$ 60,000
Sales value at split-off	?	?	$15,000	$100,000
Additional costs if processed further	$7,000	$ 5,000	$ 3,000	$ 15,000
Sales value if processed further	$70,000	$30,000	$20,000	$120,000

Required:

(1) Determine the joint costs allocated to Products Q and R assuming that joint costs are allocated based on relative sales values at split-off.
(2) Determine the sales value at split-off for Product P assuming that joint costs are allocated using the sales value method.

(AICPA adapted)

7-24 *Joint Cost Allocation for a Service Organization (Spreadsheet)*

Reliable Transit, Inc. operates a taxi and courier company. The company offers three services: Taxi, Airport Shuttle, and Courier Delivery. The drivers perform all three services based on demand, which varies from day to day. For February 2005, joint costs including labor, fuel, depreciation, etc. were $575,000. All three services also incur their own separate costs. The revenues and separate costs of each service for February 2005 are the following:

	Taxi	*Airport Shuttle*	*Courier Services*
Revenues	$500,400	$750,600	$225,000
Separate Costs	35,150	15,800	61,000

Required:

(a) Using a computer spreadsheet program, prepare a schedule which allocates the joint costs of Reliable Transit, Inc. based on the revenues of each service, and again based on the net realizable values of each service.
(b) If you were the manager of Courier Services, which approach for allocating joint costs would you prefer? What justification would you give for using this approach?

7-25 *Joint Cost Allocation and Ending Inventory*

A manufacturing process produces three products: A, B and C. The joint products can be sold at split-off or processed further. The total joint manufacturing costs are $100,000. Other relevant data are as follows:

Joint Product	*Units Produced*	*Selling Price at Split-off*	*Total Additional Processing Cost*	*Selling Price After Further Processing*
A	2,000	$ 5/unit	$ 1,000	$6/unit
B	3,000	2/unit	3,000	4/unit
C	5,000	1.8	2000	

Required:

(1) Allocate the joint manufacturing costs using (a) the physical measure method and (b) the sales value method.

(2) If all three joint products are processed further and their ending inventories in units are: A – 100, B – 200, and C – 300, determine the values of ending inventories based on answers obtained in (1).

7-26 *Accounting for By-Product*

The Hobbs Company produces three joint products: A, B, and C. Product C is treated as a by-product. Joint manufacturing costs, $40,050, are allocated to main products on the basis of their net realizable values. Product C is recorded at the net realizable value at the time of production. The following data relate to January: (after split-off, all three products are further processed separately).

Product	*Production*	*Additional Processing Cost*	*Unit Selling Price*
A	500	$1,000	$20
B	1,000	1,000	40
C	100	50	1

Required:

(I) Determine the joint cost allocated to each product.

(2) Prepare the necessary journal entries for January.

7-27 *Further Processing Decisions*

The Bama Company produced three joint products at a joint manufacturing cost of $100,000. The joint products can be sold at split-off or further processed independently as follows:

Product	*Production*	*Sales Value at Split-off*	*Sales After Further Processing*	*Additional Processing Cost*
A	1,000	$50,000	$ 80,000	$20,000
B	2,000	80,000	100,000	20,000
C	3,000	60,000	70,000	20,000

Required:

(1) Which product(s) should be processed further and which should be sold at split-off?

(2) Comment on the following statement: The approach that is useful for allocating joint cost should be used for making decisions regarding whether or not a joint product should be processed after split-off.

7-28 *Determining Ending Inventories and Further Processing Decision*
The ABC Company manufactures three products: A, B and C. The company's monthly capacity is 20,000 machine hours. In the current month, the total cost of producing 1,000 units of A, 2,000 units of B, and 2,000 units of C was $22,000. Selling prices per unit of the three products at split-off are: A, $18; B, $6; C, $1.15. Products A and B are considered as main products; Product C is a by-product. Net realizable value of the by-product after deducting 15 cents per unit for disposal cost is treated as a reduction in joint manufacturing costs. Ending inventories include 100 units of A, 200 units of B, 500 units of C.

Required:

(1) Compute ending inventories of A and B on the basis of relative sales value at split-off.
(2) Repeat (1) using physical units as the basis.
(3) Suppose Product A can be further processed and then sold for a net selling price of $21 per unit, and the necessary additional processing cost is $2,000. Should Product A be further processed? Why?
(4) Assume that Products A and B can be further processed and then sold for net selling prices of $21 and $9 per unit, respectively. It is estimated that the additional costs of processing A or B is $1 per unit. Suppose that the company has idle machine capacity of 2,500 hours to further process Products A and B, and that the machine hours required to further process each unit of A and B are 2 and 1, respectively. Should the company further process A and/or B? If yes, how many?

7-29 *Accounting for By-Product*
Products A, B and C are manufactured from a single process. During a period, the material and conversion cost totaled $60,000. Production (in pounds) was as follows: Product A, 2,000; Product B, 4,000; Product C, 4,000. Sales for the period were:

Product A — 1,000 lbs. @ $2.00 = $2,000
Product B — 3,000 lbs. @ 15.00 = 45,000
Product C — 2,000 lbs. @ 20.00 = 40,000

Required:

Assuming no beginning inventories, determine ending inventories for each product under each of the following assumptions:

(1) Product A is a by-product and Products B and C are main products; the net realizable value of the by-product produced is treated as a reduction in joint manufacturing costs; joint costs are allocated by the sales value method.
(2) Repeat requirement (1) except that the net revenue of the by-product sold is treated as a reduction in the cost of main products sold.

7-30 *Accounting for By-Products and Income Statement*

The New England Chemical Company produces three joint products: A, B, and C. Product C is treated as a by-product. The following data is obtained from the company's records of 20X1:

	Main Products		*By Product*
	A	B	C
Production (units)	10,000	20,000	1,000
Sales (units)	8,000	15,000	800
Unit selling price	$10.00	$20.00	$.50
Further processing cost			10/unit
Selling and administrative expenses	$50,000		10/unit

Total joint manufacturing cost was $300,000

Required:

Prepare income statements using the two basic methods of accounting for by-products. (Use the relative sales values approach for allocating joint costs to main products).

7-31 *Allocation of Service Department Costs*

The AB Company produces two products, A and B, in two separate departments. In addition, the company has two service departments (X and Y) providing service to the production departments in manufacturing Products A and B. An analysis of the service provided by Departments X and Y in a period is as follows:

	To				
From	X	Y	A	B	*Total Services Provided (Units)*
X	0	20	50	30	100
Y	50	0	100	50	200

Service costs to be allocated are:

Department	*Amount*
X	$ 2,000
Y	10,000

Required:

Determine the allocation of service costs to Production Departments A and B using:

(1) The Direct Method

(2) The Step Method (allocate Service Department Y's costs first)

(3) The Linear Algebra Method

7-32 *Allocation of Service Department Cost with Self-Consumption*

A manufacturer's plant has two production departments and two service departments. Data regarding costs and allocation percentages are given as follows:

	To			
	Service Departments		*Production Departments*	
From	*S-1*	*S-2*	*P-1*	*P-2*
S–1	10%	10%	60%	20%
S–2	20%	20%	20%	40%

Service costs to be allocated are:

Department	*Amount*
S–1	$3,000
S–2	1.000

Required:

Allocate the service department costs to production departments by using:

(1) The Direct Method

(2) The Step Method (allocate S-2's costs first).

(3) The Linear Algebra Method.

7-33 *Allocation of Service Department Costs*

The Howell Company uses the following as basis for allocating service department costs to production departments.

Service Department	*Base*
Store room	Number of requisitions
Factory Administration	Number of employees
Repair and Maintenance	Number of service requests

Relevant data fox a period are:

Department	*Requisitions*	*Employees*	*Service Requiests*	*Costs to be Allocated*
Store Room	10	20	5	$10,000
Factory Administration	10	10	5	5,000
Repair and Maintenance	20	10	5	5,000
Production - Dept. A	30	40	30	
Productioin - Dept. B	30	20	40	

Required:

Allocate the service department costs to the production departments using the following methods:

(1) The Direct Method

(2) The Step Method (according to the following sequence: Store Room, Factory Administration, and Repair and Maintenance)

7-34 *Service Cost Allocations*

A plant operates its own steam-generation facility under the administration of the utilities department. The other service departments are janitorial and personnel. The assembly department manufactures the plant's output, and the packaging department prepares the product for shipping. Plant management is comparing different methods of allocating service department costs. The following are annual data for the departments. Power costs are allocated per thousand cubic feet (MCF), janitorial per square foot, and personnel per employee.

	Department				
	Utilities	*Janitorial*	*Personnel*	*Assembly*	*Packaging*
MCF Steam	—	4,000	6,000	50,000	40,000
Square feet	10,000	—	5,000	100,000	50,000
Employees	30	20	—	120	80
Departmental costs before allocation (in thousands)	$900	$300	$386	$5,000	$4,000
Equivalent units produced				10,000	9,000

Required:

(a) 1. Prepare a schedule showing total assembly department and total packaging department costs in thousands after allocation if the direct method of service department cost allocation is used.

2. What are the characteristics of the direct method of allocation?

(b) The company is considering the step method to allocate service department costs. Total service department costs before allocation are used in determining the sequence of allocation with those departments having the highest costs allocated first.

1. Prepare a schedule showing the cost per equivalent unit produced in the assembly department and in the packaging department, after allocation of service department costs.

2. What are the characteristics of the step method of allocation?

(*IIA adapted*)

7-35 *Allocation of Service Department Costs: Matrix Algebra*

A manufacturer's plant has two service departments (designated below as S_1 and S_2) and three production departments (designated below as P_1, P_2 and P_3) and wishes to allocate all factory overhead to production departments. A primary distribution of overhead to all departments has already been made and is indicated below. The company makes the secondary distribution of overhead from service departments to production departments on a reciprocal basis, recognizing the fact that services of one service department are utilized by another. Data regarding costs and allocation percentages are as follows:

	Service Department Overhead Cost Allocation Percentages to be Allocated to Departments				
Service Department	S_1	S_2	P_1	P_2	P_3
S_1	0%	10%	20%	40%	30%
S_2	20%	0	50%	10%	20%
		Primary Overhead to be Allocated			
	$98,000	$117,600	$1,400,000	$2,100,000	$640,000

Matrix algebra is to be used in the secondary allocation process. The amount of overhead to be allocated to the service departments you express in two simultaneous equation as:

S_1 = \$ 98,000 + .20S_2 or S_1 – .20S_2 = \$ 98,000
S_2 = \$117,600 + .10S_1 or S_2 – 10S_1 = \$117,600

Required:

(1) The system of simultaneous equations above may be stated in matrix form as

a.

$$\overset{A}{\begin{pmatrix} 1 & -.20 \\ -.10 & 1 \end{pmatrix}} \overset{S}{\begin{pmatrix} S_1 \\ S_2 \end{pmatrix}} = \overset{b}{\begin{pmatrix} \$\,98{,}000 \\ \$117{,}600 \end{pmatrix}}$$

b.

$$\overset{A}{\begin{pmatrix} 1 & \$\,98{,}000 & 1 \\ -.20 & \$117{,}600 & -.10 \end{pmatrix}} \overset{S}{\begin{pmatrix} S_1 \\ S_2 \end{pmatrix}} = \overset{b}{\begin{pmatrix} \$\,98{,}000 \\ \$117{,}600 \end{pmatrix}}$$

c.

$$\overset{A}{\begin{pmatrix} 1 & S_1 & 1 \\ -.20 & S_2 & -.10 \end{pmatrix}} \overset{S}{\begin{pmatrix} S_1 \\ S_2 \end{pmatrix}} = \overset{b}{\begin{pmatrix} \$\,98{,}000 \\ \$117{,}600 \end{pmatrix}}$$

d.

$$\overset{A}{\begin{pmatrix} 1 & 1 & S_1 \\ -.20 & -.10 & S_2 \end{pmatrix}} \overset{S}{\begin{pmatrix} S_1 \\ S_2 \end{pmatrix}} = \overset{b}{\begin{pmatrix} \$\,98{,}000 \\ \$117{,}600 \end{pmatrix}}$$

(2) For the correct matrix A in item (I), there exists a unique inverse matrix A^{-1}. Multiplication of the matrix A^{-1} by the matrix A will produce

a. The matrix A'.
b. Another inverse matrix.
c. The correct solution to the system.
d. An identity matrix.

(3) Without prejudice to your previous answers, assume that the correct matrix form in item (1) was:

$$\overset{A}{\begin{pmatrix} 1 & -.20 \\ -.10 & 1 \end{pmatrix}} \overset{S}{\begin{pmatrix} S_1 \\ S_2 \end{pmatrix}} = \overset{b}{\begin{pmatrix} \$\,98{,}000 \\ \$117{,}600 \end{pmatrix}}$$

Then the correct inverse matrix A^{-1} is:

a. $\begin{pmatrix} \frac{1}{.98} & \frac{.20}{.98} \\ \frac{.10}{.98} & \frac{1}{.98} \end{pmatrix}$

b. $\begin{pmatrix} \frac{1}{.98} & \frac{1}{.98} \\ \frac{.20}{.98} & \frac{.10}{.98} \end{pmatrix}$

c. $\begin{pmatrix} \frac{1}{.30} & \frac{.20}{.30} \\ \frac{.10}{.30} & \frac{1}{.30} \end{pmatrix}$

d. $\begin{pmatrix} \frac{1}{.98} & -\frac{1}{.98} \\ -\frac{.20}{.98} & \frac{.10}{.98} \end{pmatrix}$

(4) The total amount of overhead allocated to department S, after receiving the allocation from department S_2 is

a. $141,779.
b. $124,000.
c. $121,520.
d. $117,600.

(5) The total amount of overhead allocated to department ~2 after receiving the allocation from department S_1 is

a. $392,000.
b. $220,000.
c. $130,000.
d. $127,400.

(6) Without prejudice to your previous answers, assume that the answer to item (4) is $100,000 and to item *(5)* is $150,000; then the total amount of overhead allocated to production department P, would be

a. $1,508,104.
b. $1,495,000.
c. $1,489,800.
d. $ 108,104.

(*AICPA adapted*)

7-36 *Departmental Factory Overhead Rates*

MumsDay Corporation manufactures a complete line of fiberglass attache cases and suitcases. MumsDay has three manufacturing departments: molding, component, and assembly; and two service departments: power and maintenance.

The sides of the cases are manufactured in the molding department. The frames, hinges, locks, etc., are manufactured in the component department. The cases are completed in the assembly department. Varying amounts of materials, time, and effort are required for each of the various cases. The power department and maintenance department provide services to the three manufacturing departments.

MumsDay has always used a plant-wide overhead rate. Direct labor hours are used to assign the overhead to its product. The pre-determined rate is calculated by dividing the company's total estimated overhead by the total estimated direct labor hours to be worked in the three manufacturing departments.

Whit Portlock, manager of cost accounting, has recommended that MumsDay use departmental overhead rates. The planned operating costs and expected levels of activity for the coming year have been developed by Portlock and are presented by department in the schedules (000 omitted) below.

	Manufacturing Depatments		
	Molding	*Component*	*Assembly*
Departmental activity measures			
Direct labor hours	500	2,000	1,500
Machine hours	875	125	0
Departmental costs:			
Raw materials	$12,400	$30,000	$ 1,250
Direct labor	3,500	20,000	12,000
Variable overhead	3,500	10,000	16,500
Fixed overhead	17.500	6,200	6,100
Total departmental costs	$36,900	$66,200	$35,850
Use of service departments:			
Maintenance			
Estimated usage in labor hours for coming year	90	25	10
Power (in kilowatt hours)			
Estimated usage for coming year	360	320	120
Maximum allotted capacity	500	350	150

Required:

(a) Calculate the plant-wide overhead rate for MumsDay Corporation for the coming year using the same method as used In the past.

(b) Whit Portlock has been asked to develop departmental overhead rates for comparison with the plant-wide rate. The following steps are to be followed in developing the departmental rates.

1. The maintenance department costs should be allocated to the three manufacturing departments using the direct method.
2. The power department costs should be allocated to the three manufacturing departments using the dual method (i.e., the fixed costs allocated according to long-term capacity and the variable costs according to planned usage.
3. Calculate departmental overhead rates for the three manufacturing departments usingamachinehourbaseforthemoldingdepartmentandadirectlaborhourbaseforthe component and assembly departments.

(c) Should MumsDay Corporation use a plant-wide rate or departmental rates to assign overhead to its products? Explain your answer.

1. *To compare traditional costing and activity based costing.*
2. *To describe how an activity based product costing system provides more accurate product costs.*
3. *To identify and explain cost distortions.*
4. *To describe activity-based management and its relationship to activity-based costing.*

8 Activity Based Costing Systems and Activity Based Management

Previous chapters have described traditional product costing systems, and how information provided by those systems is useful for decision making and control. Traditional cost accounting systems, which most commonly allocate factory overhead to products based on direct labor, may be useful in those manufacturing companies where labor costs are a significant portion of total product costs.

Many modern manufacturing companies, however, have created highly automated production facilities. They have replaced human labor in manufacturing with robots and computer-controlled machines. In many such organizations, direct labor now constitutes less than 10 percent of total product costs. These costs are replaced by the overhead costs associated with machine acquisition, machine operation, machine maintenance, and the indirect labor of the skilled technicians who maintain them. Traditional cost accounting systems are inadequate in such an environment because they allocate overhead costs using measures that no longer accurately represent production activity.

This chapter describes activity based costing as an alternative to traditional systems that are useful in highly automated environments. Activity based costing allocates overhead costs to a product based on a more meaningful and more accurate activity measure.

Traditional Costing

Traditional systems use a single overhead cost pool and a single volume based cost driver to allocate overhead costs to products.

This chapter is adapted from *Management Accounting Concepts and Techniques*, (c) 2006 by Dr. Dennis Caplan, and is used by permission.

A **cost pool** is a group of overhead costs whose variations can be explained by a single cost driver. Under traditional costing, the cost pool is all overhead costs combined.

A **cost driver** is an activity measure that explains the occurrence of overhead costs. Many companies will use a cost driver such as machine hours or direct labor hours to allocate overhead under the traditional method.

The overhead rate under a traditional product costing system is computed using the following three steps:

1. Identify **overhead costs.**
2. Select the **cost allocation base** for assigning overhead costs to the cost object.
3. Compute the **overhead rate** per unit for allocating overhead to the cost object by dividing total overhead costs by the total quantity of the allocation base.

Once the overhead rate is determined, overhead is allocated to each product using the allocation base of each product.

Traditional Costing Example

Consider the following example of a Candy Company, a highly automated facility that manufactures two products: Milk Chocolate and Dark Chocolate candy bars. Assume that the company uses direct labor hours as the allocation base for overhead under traditional costing. The company incurs the following overhead costs for the month.

Supervisor salaries	$170,000
Maintenance	80,000
Depreciation	180,000
Rent	120,000
Total Overhead costs	$550,000
Total direct labor hours	22,000

Operational data for the month is as follows:

	Milk Chocolate	Dark Chocolate	Total
Units produced	800,000	500,000	1,300,000
Direct labor hours	12,000	10,000	22,000
Average direct labor rate per hour	$10	$10	
Total direct labor cost	$220,000	$180,000	400,000
Direct labor cost per unit	$0.28	$0.36	
Direct materials cost per unit	$0.60	$0.80	
Total direct materials cost	$120,000	$64,000	184,000

Under a traditional costing system in this example, overhead costs are pooled together and then allocated to each product based on direct labor hours. Specifically, the overhead rate under traditional costing is calculated by dividing the total overhead costs by direct labor hours:

Total overhead costs	$550,000
Quantity of allocation base (direct labor hours)	22,000
Overhead rate per direct labor hour	$25.00

Overhead costs are allocated to each product using traditional costing by multiplying the overhead rate determined above by the quantity of the allocation base, in this case direct labor hours, of each product:

	Milk Chocolate	Dark Chocolate	Total
Overhead rate per direct labor hour	$25.00	$25.00	$25.00
Quantity of allocation base (direct labor hours)	12,000	10,000	22,000
Overhead costs allocated by product	$300,000	$250,000	550,000
Units produced	800,000	500,000	1,300,000
Average cost per unit	$0.38	$0.50	

Thus, the total product cost to manufacture each product, including direct materials, direct labor and allocated overhead, is as follows:

	Milk Chocolate	Dark Chocolate
Direct Materials	$0.60	$0.80
Direct Labor	$0.28	$0.36
Overhead	$0.38	$0.50
Total product costs per unit	$1.25	$1.66

If the dark chocolate product manager asks why her product incurs more overhead costs on a per-unit basis than milk chocolate, even though milk chocolate production is greater, the answer is that her product uses more direct labor per unit, which perhaps is not a very satisfying explanation from her perspective.

Problems with Traditional Costing

The traditional approach normally assumes that overhead consumption is highly related to the volume of production. Accordingly, traditional systems allocate factory overhead costs to products on the basis of direct labor hours, direct labor costs, machine hours, or units produced. These are volume-based measures.

However, in highly automated factories, many components of factory overhead are caused by factors other than production volume. As examples, factory setup costs are related to the number of different products produced, and inspection costs are related to the number of inspections. Neither is affected by the quantity produced or by the direct labor and machine hours required to produce them. If there are many such non-volume related factory overhead costs, allocating factory overhead based on volume based measures may lead to severe cost distortions in the product costs reported by a traditional costing system.

Traditional systems are simple and typically use a single overhead cost pool and a single volume based cost driver to allocate overhead costs to products. In contrast, activity based systems use several overhead cost pools and several cost drivers but can be much more complex. However, activity based costing can improve the accuracy of the product costs reported by the cost accounting system.

Activity Based Costing

Activity based costing (ABC) refines the procedures under traditional costing by partitioning large heterogeneous cost pools into multiple smaller, homogeneous cost pools. ABC then attempts to select, as the cost allocation base for each overhead cost pool, a cost driver that best captures the ***cause and effect relationship*** between the cost object and the incurrence of overhead costs.

ABC focuses on activities. A key assumption in activity-based costing is that overhead costs are caused by a variety of activities, and that different products utilize these activities in a non-homogeneous fashion. Usually, costing the activity is an intermediate step in the allocation of overhead costs to products, in order to obtain more accurate product cost information. Sometimes, however, the activity itself is the cost object of interest. For example, managers at Levi Strauss & Co. might want to know how much the company spends to acquire denim fabric, as input in a sourcing decision. The "activity" of acquiring fabric incurs costs associated with negotiating prices with suppliers, issuing purchase orders, receiving fabric, inspecting fabric, and processing payments and returns.

Cost Hierarchy

In ABC, cost pools are often established for each level in a hierarchy of costs. For manufacturing firms, the following **cost hierarchy** is commonly identified:

> **Unit-level costs:** For any given product, these costs change in a more-or-less linear fashion with the number of units produced. For example, fabric and thread are unit-level costs for an apparel manufacturer: if the company wants to double production, it will need twice as much fabric and thread.
>
> **Batch-level costs:** These costs change in a more-or-less linear fashion with the number of batches run. Machine setup costs are often batch-level costs. The time required to prepare a machine to run one batch of product is usually independent of the number of units in the batch: the same time is required to prepare the machine to run a batch of 100 units as a batch of 50 units. Hence, batch-level costs do not necessarily vary in a linear fashion with the number of units produced.
>
> **Product-level costs:** These costs are usually fixed and direct with respect to a given product. An example is the salary of a product manager with responsibility for only one product. The product manager's salary is a fixed cost to the company for a wide range of production volume levels. However, if the company drops the product entirely, the product manager is no longer needed.
>
> **Facility-level costs:** These costs are usually fixed and direct with respect to the facility. An example is property taxes on the facility, or the salaries of front office personnel such as the receptionist and office manager.

ACTIVITY BASED COSTING PROCEDURES

It is important to note that direct materials costs and direct labor costs will be the same for each product whether using traditional costing or activity based costing. Overhead is allocated to each product using activity rates. The amount allocated to overhead will be different under activity based costing than it would be under traditional costing.

The steps to completing an activity based allocation of overhead costs by product are:

1. Identify all of the major activities performed.
2. Establish an activity cost pool for each activity. (This is the stage one allocation which will be discussed further later in the chapter.)
3. Choose cost driver and compute the activity cost rate for each cost pool by dividing the total overhead costs recorded in each cost pool by the total quantity of the cost driver incurred.
4. Allocate the activity costs to products using the activity cost rate by multiplying the activity cost rate for each cost pool by the quantity of the cost driver used in the production of each product. (This is the stage two allocation which will be discussed further later in the chapter.)

ACTIVITY BASED COSTING EXAMPLE

Consider the Candy Company example again using activity based costing. Now let's assume that the company has two cost pools and two cost drivers. Supervisor salaries represents one cost pool, allocated on the basis of direct labor hours. A second factory cost pool combines maintenance, depreciation and rent and allocates these costs on the basis of square feet of factory space utilized.

Supervisor Salary Cost Pool	
Supervisor salaries	$170,000
Factory Cost Pool	
Maintenance	$80,000
Depreciation	180,000
Rent	120,000
Total factory cost pool	$380,000
Total Overhead costs	$550,000
Total direct labor hours	22,000

Remember that the factory manufactures two candy bars: Milk Chocolate and Dark Chocolate. Operational data with additional information on square feet for the month is as follows:

	Milk Chocolate	Dark Chocolate	Total
Units produced	800,000	500,000	1,300,000
Direct labor hours	12,000	10,000	22,000
Average direct labor rate per hour	$10	$10	
Total direct labor cost	$220,000	$180,000	400,000
Direct labor cost per unit	$0.28	$0.36	
Direct materials cost per unit	$0.60	$0.80	
Total direct materials cost	$120,000	$64,000	184,000
Square feet of factory space utilized	34,000	16,000	50,000

Each cost pool will be allocated based on the most meaningful activity under activity based costing. In this example, supervisor salaries are allocated based upon direct labor hours. The costs included in the factory cost pool are allocated based on square feet of factory space utilized.

The activity rate for supervisor salaries is $7.73, computed by dividing the total supervisor salary cost of $170,000 by total direct labor hours of 22,000. The activity rate for the pooled factory costs is $7.60, computed by dividing the total factory pooled costs of $380,000 by total square feet of utilized space of 50,000 square feet.

Activity rate for supervisor salaries:	
Total supervisor salaries cost	$170,000
Total direct labor hours	22,000
Activity rate per direct labor hour	$7.73

Activity rate for pooled factory costs	
Maintenance	$80,000
Depreciation	180,000
Rent	120,000
Total factory cost pool	$380,000
Total square feet of factory space	50,000
Activity rate per square foot of space	$7.60

The final step in activity based costing is to assign overhead costs to each product. For each cost pool, allocate the costs to each product according to the quantity of activity used by each product. For supervisor salaries, the overhead cost total of $170,000 will be allocated to each product based on the number of direct labor hours per product. Milk Chocolate has 12,000 direct labor hours and Dark Chocolate has 10,000 direct labor hours. For the factory cost pool, the overhead cost total of $380,000 will be allocated to each product based on the number of direct labor hours per product.

Supervisor Salaries Allocation	Milk Chocolate	Dark Chocolate	Total
Direct labor hours by product	12,000	10,000	22,000
Activity rate for supervisor salaries	$7.73	$7.73	
Supervisor salaries allocated to each product	$92,727.27	$77,272.73	$170,000.00

Factory Cost Allocation	Milk Chocolate	Dark Chocolate	Total
Square feet of factory space utilized by product	34,000	16,000	50,000
Activity rate per square foot of space	$7.60	$7.60	
Factory costs allocated to each product	$258,400.00	$121,600.00	$380,000.00

Total supervisor salaries remains the same at $170,000 but $92,727.27 and $77,272.73 is allocated to Milk Chocolate and Dark Chocolate, respectively. Total factory costs remain the same at $380,000 with $258,400 and $121,600 allocated to Milk Chocolate and Dark Chocolate, respectively. These allocations are substantially different than the allocations determined using traditional costing because activity based costing better captures relative consumption of resources by various products.

To determine the total product cost, combine the costs allocated from each cost pool to each product.

	Milk Chocolate	Dark Chocolate	Total
Supervisor salaries	$92,727.27	$77,272.73	$170,000.00
Pooled factory costs*	258,400	121,600	380,000
Total overhead costs allocated to each product	$351,127	$198,873	$550,000
Units produced	800,000	500,000	1,300,000
Average overhead cost per unit	$0.44	$0.40	

*includes all maintenance, depreciation and rent

Total product costs under activity based costing also include direct materials cost and direct labor costs in addition to overhead costs. The product cost per unit is calculated the same way as under traditional costing, except that the overhead cost per unit will differ.

Total product costs per unit under ABC	Milk Chocolate	Dark Chocolate
Direct Materials	$0.60	$0.80
Direct Labor	$0.28	$0.36
Overhead	$0.44	$0.40
Total product costs per unit	$1.31	$1.56

Comparing Traditional and ABC

Direct materials cost and the direct labor cost are the same under both traditional and activity based costing. The total overhead cost in this example is also the same, but the amount of overhead costs allocated to each product differ under each method as follows:

Total overhead cost difference	Milk Chocolate	Dark Chocolate	Total
Traditional	$300,000	$250,000	$550,000
ABC	$351,127	$198,873	$550,000
Overcosted/(Undercosted)	($51,127.27)	$51,127.27	$0

The above calculations indicate a significant cost distortion. In this example, Milk chocolate is undercosted by $51,127 and Dark Chocolate is overcosted by $51,127. This result demonstrates that the rate used under traditional costing did not allocate enough overhead costs to Milk Chocolate and allocated too much overhead cost to Dark Chocolate. Activity based costing provides a more accurate measure of cost due to the more detailed cost pools and activity rates.

Activity Based Management

Ultimately, it is important to know the most accurate product cost per unit for planning and budgetary purposes and for pricing the products accordingly. A product that is overcosted under traditional costing may be priced too high while a product that is undercosted using traditional costing may be priced too low. In the Candy Company example, Milk Chocolate is undercosted by $0.06 and Dark Chocolate is overcosted by $0.10. Depending on the number of units sold, this cost distortion can have a significant effect on each product's profit margin.

Per unit cost difference	Milk Chocolate	Dark Chocolate
Traditional	$1.25	$1.66
ABC	$1.31	$1.56
Overcosted/(Undercosted)	($0.06)	$0.10

Such cost distortions can produce poor decisions when managers use the allocated cost information for special decisions and for performance evaluations. In situations where a product is overcosted, pricing may be too high resulting in lost sales due to lower demand. Where a product is undercosted, pricing may be too low resulting in lower profits. For this reason, in production environments with significant factory overhead costs, an activity-based system is a better approach. Activity based management utilizes activity based costing concepts to improve the efficiency and effectiveness of operations.

Further, when considering product mix decisions, managers should be aware of cost distortions. In the above example, if using traditional costing and deciding to spend more time and resources to support additional production of the Milk Chocolate bar, a manager may have supported the less profitable product when considering ABC the costs are higher. The manager may have made the opposite decision to support Dark Chocolate if ABC was used.

Activity based management includes minimizing any cost distortions and pricing a product appropriately so that profits are maximized. Further, information on value added versus non-value added activities obtained during the activity identification process is subsequently used to remove non-value added activities. Value added activities are those activities perceived by the customer to have value, such as production costs. Non-value added activities are those activities for which there is no perceived value, such as storage cost and inspection costs. By eliminating the non-value added activities, such as inspection, operating efficiency as well as profit margin are improved.

ABC Two-Stage Allocation

Many companies find that gathering the data necessary to determine the cost pools is time consuming. The allocation process under activity based costing can become complex and require a two stage allocation process. In the first stage, costs are allocated to cost pools. In the second stage, costs from stage one are allocated to each product.

Consider Apparel Factory that uses forklifts in only two departments:

- The first department is Receiving, where large rolls of fabric are unloaded from semi-trailers and moved into storage, and later moved from storage to the cutting room.

- The second department is Shipping, where cartons of finished pants are staged and then loaded onto semi-trailers for shipment to the warehouse.

Costs associated with operating these forklifts consist of the following:

Forklift costs:	
Operator salaries	$ 80,000
Maintenance	8,000
Depreciation expense	7,500
Other	2,500
Total forklift costs	$ 98,000
All other overhead	1,400,000
Total overhead for the factory	$1,498,000

The factory operates two production lines. One line is for jeans, which are made from denim fabric. The other production line is for casual slacks, which are made from a cotton twill fabric. Operational data for the month is as follows:

	Jeans	Casual Slacks	Total
Units produced	420,000	200,000	620,000
Direct labor hours	70,000	40,000	110,000
Rolls of fabric	1,750	640	2,390
Cartons shipped	52,500	20,000	72,500

The factory ships product to the company's warehouse, not directly to customers. Hence, to facilitate stocking at the warehouse, each carton is packed with jeans or casual slacks, but not both. An examination of the information in the above table reveals that a carton holds more slacks than jeans, and that fewer pants are cut from a roll of denim fabric than from a roll of cotton twill. These operational statistics are driven by the fact that denim is a heavier-weight fabric than cotton twill, and hence, it is bulkier. The data also indicate that more direct labor minutes are required for a pair of slacks than for a pair of jeans, which reflects greater automation on the jeans production line.

Traditional Costing

Under a traditional costing system, forklift costs are pooled with all other overhead costs for the factory (electricity, property taxes, front office salaries, etc.), and then allocated to product based on direct labor hours (sewing operator time) for each product.

Overhead rate under traditional costing:

Total overhead costs	$1,498,000
Quantity of allocation base (direct labor hours)	÷ 110,000
Overhead rate per direct labor hour	$13.62

of which the following is due to forklift costs:

Forklift overhead	$98,000
Quantity of allocation base (direct labor hours)	÷ 110,000
Overhead rate for forklift costs per direct labor hour	$0.8909

Forklift overhead applied to product using traditional costing:

	Jeans	Slacks
Overhead rate	$0.8909	$0.8909
Quantity of allocation base (direct labor hours)	× 70,000	× 40,000
Forklift costs allocated	$62,364	$35,636
Units produced	420,000	200,000
Approximate cost per unit	$0.15	$0.18

Note that all forklift overhead is allocated: $62,364 + $35,636 = $98,000.

If the casual slacks product manager asks why her product incurs more forklift costs on a per-unit basis than jeans, even though casual slacks use a lighter-weight fabric, the answer is that her product uses more direct labor per unit, which perhaps is not a very satisfying explanation from her perspective.

Activity-Based Costing

An ABC system might first allocate forklift costs into two cost pools: one for the Receiving Department and one for the Shipping Department. Then costs from each of these two departments would be allocated to the two product lines.

ABC First-Stage Allocation

The first-stage allocation might use an estimate of the amount of time the forklifts spend in each department. A one-time study indicates that forklifts spend approximately 70% of their time in the Shipping Department and 30% of their time in the Receiving Department. An additional benefit of ABC is that if this information were collected periodically, the managers of these two departments might be more willing to share the forklifts with each other, since the reported costs of each department would then depend on the time the forklifts spend in each department. In any case, the 70/30 allocation results in the following first-stage allocation:

30% of $98,000 = $29,400 is allocated to the Receiving Department
70% of $98,000 = $68,600 is allocated to the Shipping Department

ABC Second-Stage Allocation

	Receiving	Shipping
Total costs	$29,400	$68,600
Quantity of allocation base	÷ 2,390 rolls	÷ 72,500 cartons
Overhead rate	$12.30 per roll	$0.946 per carton
Allocation to Jeans		
Overhead rate	$12.30 per roll	$0.946 per carton
Quantity of allocation base	x 1,750 rolls	x 52,500 cartons
	$21,525	$49,665
Allocation to Slacks		
Overhead rate	$12.30 per roll	$0.946 per carton
Quantity of allocation base	x 640 rolls	x 20,000 cartons
	$7,872	$18,920

Total forklift costs allocated to each product:

	Jeans	Slacks	Total
From Receiving	$21,525	$ 7,872	$29,397
From Shipping	49,665	18,920	68,585
Total	$71,190	$26,792	$97,982
Units produced	420,000	200,000	
Approximate cost per unit	$0.17	$0.13	

The $18 difference between total costs allocated of $97,982 and the original cost of $98,000 is due to rounding.

The first-stage allocation allows the second-stage to allocate forklift costs to product using rolls of fabric as the allocation base in Receiving, and cartons of pants as the allocation base in Shipping. Since there are no rolls of fabric in the shipping department, and no cartons in the Receiving Department, without the first stage allocation, there would be no obvious choice of an allocation base that would capture the cause-and-effect relationship between the costs of operating the forklifts, and the utilization of forklift resources by each product in the two departments.

The traditional costing method allocates more forklift costs to slacks than to jeans on a per-unit basis because casual slacks require more sewing effort. ABC allocates more forklift costs to jeans than to casual slacks, on a per-unit basis, which is intuitive because denim is a heavier-weight fabric than cotton twill.

Cost Hierarchy with First- and Second-Stage Allocations

One reason why ABC provides more accurate product cost information is that traditional costing systems frequently allocate all overhead, including batch-level, product-level, and facility-level overhead, using an allocation base that is appropriate only for unit-level costs. The better information obtained from explicitly incorporating the cost hierarchy is illustrated in the following example.

MILWOOD MILLS:

Milwood Mills makes decorative woodcut prints for sale to restaurants. Its Billings, Montana factory makes two of the company's more popular designs: *Bull and Matador* and *Dogs Playing Poker*. Following is selected information for a typical month:

	Bull	*Dogs*	*Total*
Number of woodcuts produced	500	1,500	2,000
Direct materials costs	$2,500	$3,300	$5,800
Direct labor costs	$1,400	$1,600	$3,000
Number of batches	10	30	40
Total overhead			$42,000
Batch setup costs (included in total overhead)			$12,000

The traditional costing system allocates all overhead based on number of units produced. This method allocates overhead of $21 ($42,000 ÷ 2,000 units) to each *Bull and Matador* woodcut and to each *Dogs Playing Poker* woodcut, of which $6 ($12,000 ÷ 2,000 units) represents batch setup costs.

The manager of the *Bull and Matador* production line develops a technique for doubling the batch size on her line without incurring any additional costs. Hence, she can now make 500 woodcuts per month using only 5 setups. She thinks this should cut her batch setup costs in half. She reasons as follows:

What "drives" batch setup costs? It is the number of batches. The cost per batch is $300. ($300 per batch x 40 batches = $12,000, which agrees to the monthly information provided above.) Using the new batch size, the batch setup cost is still $300, but instead of spreading this $300 over 50 units, the $300 will be spread over 100 units, lowering my per-unit batch setup cost from $6 to $3, and lowering my total unit cost by $3.

However, the following month, after implementation of the manager's increased batch size, reported costs are as follows: Total overhead drops by $1,500, which represents the cost savings from eliminating five batch setups for the *Bull and Matador* production line. Hence, total overhead drops from $42,000 to $40,500. The traditional costing system allocates this $40,500 to 2,000 units as $20.25 per unit. This new overhead rate represents a savings of $0.75 per unit for every woodcut: every *Bull and Matador* woodcut, and every *Dogs Playing Poker* woodcut. The manager of the *Bull and Matador* production line is disappointed. Her reported costs did not decrease by as much as she had anticipated, because most of the benefit from the reduction in batch setups has been allocated to the *Dogs Playing Poker* production line.

An ABC system that explicitly recognizes the cost hierarchy would correct this problem. Under the old production process, ABC would have allocated costs as follows: The cost pool for batch setup costs was previously $12,000, which would have been allocated to the two product lines based on the number of batches run by each line:

Overhead rate = total batch setup costs ÷ total number of batches
= $12,000 ÷ 40 batches = $300 per batch

Batch setup costs of $300 per batch
x 10 batches = $3,000 would have been allocated to *Bull*,
x 30 batches = $9,000would have been allocated to *Dogs*.

In a second-stage allocation, the $3,000 allocated to the *Bull and Matador* production line would have been allocated to 500 units for a cost of $6 per woodcut. This allocation is the same as under the traditional costing system only because the batch size of 50 woodcuts per batch was originally the same on both production lines.

After the batch size is increased for *Bull and Matador*, production information is as follows:

	Bull	*Dogs*	*Total*
Number of woodcuts produced	500	1,500	2,000
Direct materials costs	\$2,500	\$3,300	\$5,800
Direct labor costs	\$1,400	\$1,600	\$3,000
Number of batches	5	30	35
Total overhead			\$40,500
Batch setup costs (included in total overhead)			\$10,500

Now ABC would allocate costs as follows:
In the first stage: \$10,500 ÷ 35 batches = \$300 per batch (same as before).

\$300 per batch x 5 batches = \$1,500 to *Bull and Matador* (50% less than before),
\$300 per batch x 30 batches = \$9,000 to *Dogs Playing Poker* (same as before).

In the second stage, the \$1,500 is allocated to the 500 *Bull and Matador* woodcuts, for \$3 per woodcut. This \$3 per woodcut reflects the cost savings originally anticipated by the manager of the *Bull and Matador* production line. The cost per woodcut for *Dogs Playing Poker* remains unchanged (\$9,000 ÷ 1,500 units = \$6), which is appropriate because nothing has changed on the *Dogs Playing Poker* production line.

ABC in the Service Sector

ABC is as important to companies in the merchandising and service sectors as to manufacturing companies. In fact, although the origination of ABC is generally ascribed to manufacturing companies in the 1980s, by then hospitals were already allocating overhead costs to departments and then to patient services using methods similar to ABC. Hospitals were required to implement relatively sophisticated allocation processes in order to comply with Medicare reimbursement rules. After its inception in the 1960s, Medicare established detailed rules regarding how overhead costs should be grouped into cost pools, and the choice of appropriate allocation bases for allocating overhead costs to departments and then to patients. Within these rules, hospitals were able to maximize revenues by shifting costs from areas such as pediatrics, labor and delivery, and maternity (which have low rates of Medicare utilization) to the intensive care unit, the critical care unit, and surgery (which have higher rates of Medicare utilization). Other non-manufacturing industries that have benefited from ABC include financial services firms and retailers.

ABC Implementation Issues

The successful implementation of ABC usually requires participation by managers from non-accounting functions, such as production and marketing. Because ABC focuses on activities, and activities often cut across departments and functional areas, implementing ABC can improve lines of communication and cooperation within the company. On the other hand, more accurate cost allocation does not, by itself, reduce costs. The initial move from a traditional costing system to ABC usually shifts overhead costs from some products to other products, with some managers "winning" and some "losing." Some companies have found that hiring an outside consulting firm to assist with the ABC adoption facilitates obtaining "buy-in" by managers and employees throughout the company. Perhaps partly for this reason, ABC implementation has become an important consulting product for many consulting firms.

Although ABC should provide the company more accurate information, it is not a panacea; some companies that invested time and money implementing ABC did not obtain the benefits they expected. Some of these companies have reverted to simpler, more traditional costing systems.

Summary

This chapter describes activity based costing and traditional cost accounting methods. Activity based costing requires that activities be matched with appropriate cost drivers. Under activity based costing, overhead costs are grouped into activity cost pools for which an activity cost rate is determined. The cost driver is an activity measure that causes the cost to occur, such as machine hours or production runs. Activity based costing then allocates overhead costs to products based on the identified quantity of the cost driver for each pool. Many companies that have highly automated factories adopt activity based costing because it provides more accurate computations of actual product costs. Consequently, activity based costing can offer significant advantages for managerial planning, decision making, and control.

Activity based management utilizes activity based costing concepts to improve the efficiency and effectiveness of operations. Activity based management includes minimizing any cost distortions and pricing a product appropriately so that profits are maximized. Further, information on value added versus non-value added activities obtained during the activity identification process is subsequently used to eliminate non-value added activities.

Key Definitions

Activity based costing	A product costing system which traces costs to activities and then traces costs from activities to products.
Batch-level costs	These costs change in a more-or-less linear fashion with the number of batches run.

Cost driver An activity measure that explains the occurrence of overhead costs.

Cost hierarchy

Cost pool A group of cost categories whose variations can be explained by a single cost driver.

Facility-level costs These costs are usually fixed and direct with respect to the facility

Product-level costs These costs are usually fixed and direct with respect to a given product.

Unit-level costs For any given product, these costs change in a more-or-less linear fashion with the number of units produced.

Questions

8-1. What is the major problem with using a volume based costing system for product costing in highly automated factories?

8-2. What are some examples of non-production volume related overhead costs?

8-3. Describe how activity based product costing procedures differ from volume based ones.

8-4. What is an overhead cost pool?

8-5. How can a product's cost be overstated with a volume based costing approach? How can it be understated?

8-6. Identify problems with traditional costing. In what sectors of business is activity based costing most appropriate? In what sectors of business is activity based costing not always appropriate?

Problems

8-7 Colorado Airlines is operating at capacity on its Denver-to-New York route, offering three flights each day on this route, using Boeing 737's, each with a capacity of 135 passengers. Airline management wants to determine the least expensive way to increase daily capacity from 405 passengers to 540 passengers. One possibility is to add one more Boeing 737 per day. The other possibility is to replace the current equipment with Boeing 757's, which hold 180 passengers each. In either case, management believes the planes will continue to operate at capacity.

To ascertain the least expensive way to increase passenger capacity on the Denver-to-New York route, management has asked you to determine what "drives" the airline's operating costs.

Required:

Consider the following cost drivers:
a. Number of flights per day
b. Number of miles flown per day
c. Number of passengers served per day
d. Number of passenger miles (miles flown per day multiplied by number of passengers)

For each of the following costs, identify the most appropriate cost driver from the above list.

1. Passenger meals
2. Airplane fuel
3. Ground personnel who refuel the plane, and mechanics on the ground
4. Ground personnel who serve passengers at the ticket counter and at the gate.
5. Cockpit crew salaries
6. Flight attendant salaries
7. Economic depreciation of the airplane (i.e., without regard to the depreciation method chosen for accounting purposes, choose the cost driver that best captures the wear and tear on the equipment, and determines the economic life of the plane).
8. Personnel who handle baggage

8-8 You are the Chief Financial Officer of a large New York hospital that has decided to implement activity-based costing. Which of the following would you choose as the allocation base for allocating the costs of the Linen and Laundry Department to the four patient wards that utilize linen and laundry services, if your objective is to generate the most accurate cost information possible? The four wards are: (1) surgery, (2) adolescent care, (3) maternity and nursery, and (4) pediatric care.

(A) Patient occupancy rates (i.e., patient days) in each ward.
(B) The number of washing machines in the Laundry and Linen Department
(C) The number of Medicare patients in each ward.
(D) The number of patient admissions to each ward.

8-9 In which of the following situations are the techniques of activity-based costing most likely to lead to improved production or marketing decisions.
(I) The All-Direct Company, which incurs significant direct costs, but no overhead costs, to manufacture its extensive and ever-changing product line.
(II) The One-Size-Fits-All Hat Company, which makes a single product that is sold to many different kinds of retailers, in varying volumes, through various marketing channels, in many different geographic regions.
(III) The Iowa Wind Turbine Electric Cooperative, which has direct costs and fixed overhead, but no variable overhead.

(A) (I) and (II), but not (III)

(B) (I) and (III), but not (II)
(C) (I) only
(D) (II) only

8-10 For a generic manufacturing facility (i.e., without being told what the factory makes):

A) Give two examples of overhead expenses for which direct labor hours is a more appropriate allocation base than machine time.
B) Give two examples of overhead expenses for which machine time is a more appropriate allocation base than direct labor hours.

8-11 The Santa Cruz Candy Company makes five types of candies in its sole factory, including chocolate truffles and chocolate mints. Truffles are hand-dipped, so making truffles is labor intensive, and furthermore, only the most experienced (and highest paid) employees can make truffles. Production of mints is highly automated: they don't require much labor, but the machine operators are also highly skilled and highly paid. The manager of truffles production (Candy Lowenski) and the manager of mints production (Coco Hernandez) are discussing their preferences for how factory overhead should be allocated to their products. The three choices are direct labor dollars, direct labor hours, and machine hours. Of course, each manager would like to report the highest profits possible from her product line.

Required:

In one, two or three (no more than three) complete sentences (each sentence must have a verb and a period, among other grammatical components), predict what position each manager will take with respect to her preferred allocation base, and explain your reasoning.

8-12 The Braintree Furniture Company manufactures two lines of furniture: an upscale, handcrafted line called Richleau, which is produced in small quantities; and a mass-produced, inexpensive line called Particleboard. Both lines are made in the same factory. Richleau is very labor intensive relative to Particleboard. Braintree just switched from a traditional costing method that allocated overhead based on direct labor hours to an activity-based costing system. Under activity-based costing, the amount of overhead allocated to Richleau will be

(A) higher than under the traditional costing method.
(B) lower than under the traditional costing method.
(C) either higher or lower than under the traditional costing method, depending on the underlying economics of the business.
(D) lower than under traditional costing, as long as activity-based costing is implemented in a way that provides more accurate cost information.

8-13 The not-for-profit health clinic Shots-Я-Us provides various types of vaccinations and other shots, especially flu shots, to the public for free or for a nominal fee. The clinic is funded by several local governmental agencies as well as by a number of charitable organizations. Since different donors wish to fund different types of shots, the clinic determines the full cost of each type of shot, by adding overhead to the direct costs, and then provides this information to current and prospective donors.

Following are actual and budgeted costs for Shots-Я-Us for 2010:

	Actual	Budgeted
Number of patient visits	5,000	4,000
Number of shots administered	6,000	4,500
Fixed overhead: salaries, rent for the facility, insurance, depreciation.	$94,000	$110,000
Variable overhead: nursing staff hourly wages, utilities, disposable supplies.	$66,000	$40,500
Cost of hypodermics (a direct cost)	$1,000	$750
Cost of medications (a direct cost)	$30,000	$20,000

Which of the following is probably not a significant cost driver for variable overhead, and hence, would probably be a poor choice as the cost allocation base for allocating variable overhead?

(A) The number of shots administered
(B) The dollar value of the medication administered
(C) The number of patient visits
(D) The amount of nursing staff time spent administering each type of shot

8-14 Pink Ink, Inc. has two products and two overhead cost pools:

	Product A	Product B	In Total
Units produced	200	50	
Direct Costs (per unit):			
Materials	$10	$20	
Labor (paid $20 per hour)	$20	$40	
Materials Handling cost pool			$24,000
Everything Else cost pool			$76,000

Required:

A) Using direct labor hours as the allocation base, what is the overhead rate for Materials Handling overhead?
B) What is the total cost to make each unit of Product B, if all overhead is allocated based on units produced?
C) How much Everything Else overhead would be applied to each unit of product A, if this cost pool is allocated to product using direct materials dollars as the allocation base?

8-15 Following is information about Aztech Industries:

	Model A	Model B	Model C	Total
Units produced	300	500	200	1,000
Direct materials (per unit)	$50	$75	$100	
Direct labor (per unit)	$20	$50	$40	
Cost driver information:				
number of parts (per unit)	20	42	30	
direct labor hours (per unit)	3	4.60	4	
square feet (in total for all units)	400	600	1,000	
Overhead costs:				
Labor Support				$22,000
Materials Support				$33,000
Facility Cost				$90,000
Total overhead				$145,000

Use activity-based costing to calculate the total cost for each Model C heater. Allocate Labor Support using direct labor hours, Materials Support using number of parts, and Facility Cost using square feet.

8-16 The Crouse Travel Company applies overhead to its international camping tours using activity-based costing. Following is information about the three overhead cost pools:

	Total Costs	Allocation Base	Total Quantity of the Allocation Base Incurred
Administration	$200,000	Number of tours	40
Operations	600,000	Tourist travel days*	6,000
Marketing	180,000	Number of tourists	600

* For any given tour, the number of tourist travel days is the number of tourists multiplied by the number of days in the tour. For example, 10 tourists on a seven-day tour would constitute 70 tourist travel days.

Required:

A) Calculate the overhead rates.

B) Five of the 40 tours were 10-day trips to Patagonia. These tours averaged 12 tourists per trip. How much overhead would be applied to these five Patagonia tours?

8-17 The 601 Blue Jean Company has decided to allocate the cost of its Warehouse and Distribution Center to its customers using activity-based costing, in order to better assess profitability by customer. The warehouse manager determines that the only costs that are economically feasible to trace directly to the customer are outbound freight costs. The manager then decides that the following overhead cost pools should be allocated to customers using the following cost drivers:

Overhead Cost Pool	Cost Driver (Allocation Base)
Order Processing Department	Number of individual orders processed for that customer
Order Filling Department	Number of line items on all pull-tickets for that customer
Quality Control Department	Number of cartons shipped to that customer
Shipping Department	Number of cartons shipped to that customer

Following are relevant data for each overhead cost pool:

Order Processing Department	
Total costs for this department	$3,000,000
Total number of orders processed	200,000
Order Filling Department	
Total costs for this department	$4,000,000
Total number of line-items on all pull tickets	4,000,000
Quality Control Department	
Total costs for this department	$500,000
Total number of cartons shipped	2,000,000
Shipping Department	
Total costs for this department	$7,500,000
Total number of cartons shipped	2,000,000

Following is information pertaining to two customers:

7-9-11 Stores:	
Sales revenue for the year	$2,400,000
Number of orders	500
Number of pull ticket line-items	100,000
Number of cartons	50,000
Outbound freight costs	$75,000
Men's Large and Big Stores:	
Sales revenue for the year	$1,500,000
Number of orders	250
Number of pull ticket line-items	20,000
Number of cartons	40,000
Outbound freight costs	$56,000

Required:

A) Compute the overhead rates for each of the four overhead cost pools.
B) Calculate the amount of overhead that would be applied to 7-9-11 Stores
C) Calculate the amount of overhead that would be applied to Men's Large & Big Stores
D) Explain (in one or two sentences) or show (by calculation) how your answers to Parts (B) and (C) would change if the company combined Quality Control and Shipping into one overhead cost pool, and allocated overhead for this cost pool to customers based on the number of cartons shipped to that customer.

1. *To describe the role of budgets in the process of profit planning.*
2. *To discuss five purposes of budgeting.*
3. *To describe and illustrate a formal procedure for developing a master budget.*
4. *To discuss and illustrate the major components of a master budget.*

9

Profit Planning and the Master Budget

Previous chapters have described some uses of cost accounting data for the planning of operations. Another effective tool for planning is the budget, which provides a summary of projected revenues and expenses over some time period in the future. A budget is a document which provides a quantitative statement of a plan of action, and can be used for predicting resource requirements and for measuring how effectively the plan of action is implemented.

Budgets are created as a result of the process of profit planning. This refers to the process whereby an organization's profit and growth objectives are established by its management, and the means of attaining these objectives are developed. Profit planning attempts to translate overall corporate objectives into individual goals for all parts of the organization. Successful organizations recognize the necessity for careful and inclusive profits plans, and may devote substantial time and managerial resources to the process.

Adequate profit planning encompasses a period of time far in excess of the traditional reporting cycle used in accounting. Many companies develop long range profit plans which may cover five, ten or twenty years into the future. Such plans are of course highly speculative and normally only outline major expansions and expenditures for capital equipment. Within their context short range profit plans can be developed in much more detail, which accurately reflect anticipated conditions for the immediate future. When developed to coincide with the annual accounting reporting cycle, such a plan is often referred to as a master budget. The development and use of master budgets will be described in this chapter.

Budgets for Short-Range Planning

Budgets provide month-to-month guidance to the managers of a company in achieving the corporate objectives established in a long range profit plan. A well-designed budgeting system provides this guidance by serving five broad purposes.

Purposes of Budget Systems

Budgets aid managers in achieving corporate goals when they serve the following purposes: (1) communications, (2) coordination, (3) resource planning, (4) motivation, and (5) control. Budgets are developed within the framework of a long-term corporate profit plan, and are a means of communicating to individual managers the actions or performance level desired in order to follow the plan. In fulfilling the role as a communications device, the budget shows a manager not only what is considered acceptable performance but also how the manager's actions contribute to the achievement of overall corporate objectives. When combined with an appropriate system of performance reporting, budgets also communicate the extent to which individual efforts have been successful.

Coordination between all subunits and managers in an organization is necessary for overall objectives to be achieved. When a company-wide profit plan is decomposed into departmental budgets, each manager is working toward a common set of goals. Frequently the success of one department in achieving its goals will be dependent on the performance of others. Without the direction provided by the budget, each department may pursue its own goals to the detriment of the organization as a whole. A budget thus aids in maintaining goal congruence between the organization and all of its parts.

The communication and coordination purposes are closely related to the use of budgets as a tool in resource planning. In the budget, corporate goals are translated into planned activity levels for the upcoming year. These planned activity levels can be used to estimate the resources of materials, manpower, and cash that will be necessary in order to achieve the objectives. Budgets provide the capability of anticipating these needs and preventing possible difficulties in satisfying them before difficulties occur. In order to fulfill this resource planning function, a budget must coordinate the activities of all the departments of an organization and communicate the expected activity levels to all operating managers.

A properly designed budget system can additionally be used for motivation and control. The budget is frequently used to state goals for individual managers in the organization in terms of revenue and cost- targets. With proper reward and recognition when these targets are attained, the budget can motivate managers to increase revenues and to decrease costs. This type of budgeting structure can be coupled with a system of performance reporting for individual managers. Actual costs and revenues are compared with those budgeted in these performance reports, providing feedback to each manager concerning the adequacy of his or her performance during a reporting period. When combined with a system of performance reporting, budgets aid in providing control of managers' activities. Effective budget systems for motivation and control are difficult to develop, and will be discussed in detail in Chapter seventeen.

Types of Budgets for Planning

Different organizations have developed various types of planning budgets, depending on the preferences of management and on how the budgets are used. Differences exist in the time period into the future covered by the budget, and in the extent of disaggregation of company totals to produce lower level budgets.

The most common approach is to develop an annual budget encompassing the financial reporting period. The annual budget is developed prior to the start of the period and expresses expected activity, revenues, and costs for the entire period. These are then broken down and reported by month or quarter so that during the year, company progress in achieving annual objectives can be monitored. At any time during the year, the annual budget reports actual and budgeted activity up to that time, along with budgeted costs and revenues until the end of the reporting period.

A different approach is the continuous budget, which always reports budgeted revenues and costs for one year into the future. Each month, the previous month is deleted from the budget, and projections are added for an additional one eleven months later. Advocates of continuous budgeting feel that it directs the attention of managers further into the future, and discourages decisions which, although beneficial in the current accounting period, might have detrimental effects in a future period. Continuous budgets require constant updating and are usually adopted by companies which have a permanent staff of budgetary accountants. Because of its increased cost, the continuous budget is used by fewer companies than the annual budget.

A master budget summarizes expected revenues and costs for an entire company. This budget is normally composed of separate budgets for each of the functional areas of the business, such as sales, manufacturing, or research and development. These functional area budgets may be further composed of budgets for major activities within an area, such as direct labor or selling. The contents of all lower level budgets are coordinated with the projected activities of the functional level and of the organization as a whole. When budgets are additionally used for motivation and control, they are also developed at the departmental level. The content of the master budget is then summarized to reflect the effect of expected operations on the financial position of the company. Financial budgets used for this purpose include projections of cash flow, net income, and of the assets, liabilities and equity of the company at the end of the budgetary period. The distinction between these various types of budgets is summarized in Illustration 9-1.

The process of developing a master budget that is useful for planning resource requirements is a major one, and requires a commitment of time and effort from all segments of an organization. Cost accountants are usually involved in summarizing the inputs to the budget from other operating areas and stating them in terms of their financial impact. A formal method of developing a company budget in a large organization will now be described. In smaller companies, the process will be less formalized, but the same basic procedures are followed.

The Budget Development Process

If a budget is to achieve effectively all of its purposes, each manager in the organization who can influence revenues or costs should be involved in its development. An operating manager is more familiar with the activities and limitations in an operating area than anyone else, and is frequently better able to assess the impact of overall corporate objectives in the area. A large company may in addition maintain a permanent staff of budgetary accountants supervised by a budget director, whose responsibility is to compile the budget and to coordinate the activities in its development. In smaller companies these functions may be performed by a budget director alone, or by a controller who assumes the duties of a budget director. Although the structure of

Illustration 9-1 Types of Budgets Contrasted

Categorized by Time Period Covered:

A. Annual Budget – coincides with the accounting reporting period.
B. Continuous Budget – covers one full year into the future.

Categorized by Level or Disaggregation:

A. Sales Budget
   1. Selling Expense Budget
   2. Promotion and Advertising Budget

B. Manufacturing Budget
   1. Direct Labor Budget
   2. Direct Materials Budget
   3. Factory Overhead Budget

C. Purchases Budget

D. Financial Budgets
   1. Cash Budget
   2. Budgeted Income Statement
   3. Budgeted Balance Sheet

the budget organization may vary from company to company, someone in the company must be assigned these responsibilities.

A formal budgeting process may be described as consisting of two phases, a preplanning phase and a preparation phase. Preplanning for the budget involves the company president and the corporate planning staff. The preparation phase is accomplished by the budget director with the aid of operating managers and the approval of the president.

Budget Preplanning

Preplanning for the annual budget is necessary in order to coordinate it with long range corporate objectives. The long range planning horizon should encompass at least the next five years and normally covers many more. Long range corporate plans may identify potential new products or services, new markets for existing products, or new channels of distribution. They are developed in a large organization by a staff of one or more corporate planners under the direction of the president. Such plans also typically will describe how resources will be provided to implement these suggested changes over the planning horizon.

During the last half of the year preceding the budget year, the president and planning staff will begin to translate long range plans into more detailed ones for the coming budgetary period. This process will include an analysis of possible profit objectives for the year, of the degree of success in attaining previous objectives, and of the economic, political, and competitive environment in which the company will operate. The president must decide if the company has been achieving a sufficient level of profitability, and if not, what level can reasonably be expected.

The preplanning phase culminates in a report from the president to the corporate vice presidents and functional division heads which is sometimes referred to as a budget planning report. This report provides a statement of objectives and policies which will guide the development of the budget. It may include sales and production goals for the next year and stipulate policies relating to inventory levels, customer service, and staffing. The actual preparation of the master budget is then ready to begin.

Budget Preparation

The budget preparation phase is initiated when the budget planning report is received by managers of the functional areas of the organization. Each operating manager then prepares an operating plan for the next year, and submits it to the budget director. The operating plan summarizes the activities of a functional area necessary to achieve overall company objectives subject to the policies stated in the president's budget planning report. For example, a sales vice president may provide sales projections by product or product line for each quarter during the upcoming year, along with proposed advertising campaigns and other promotional activities. A manufacturing vice president may produce a master production schedule by plant or product line for each month in the year, including a statement of desired inventory levels. Other functional heads will produce similar operating plans disclosing anticipated activities under their responsibilities. For managers of clerical activities such as the treasurer or controller, an operating plan may include a manning table. The manning table summarizes the positions required and may state desired salary levels for employees in these positions.

The budget director collects these operating plans and assigns monetary values to the activities projected in them. This information is summarized into budgets for each functional area, and consolidated to provide pro forma (budgeted) financial statements. These statements project the effect on the company's financial position of the operating plans, and predict whether or not company profit objectives will be met. These budget summaries are submitted to the president along with any comments and recommendations that the budget director feels appropriate.

The president, after reviewing the budget proposal, may return it to managers of the functional areas with suggestions for changes in their operating plans. When these changes are made, the budget director then incorporates them into the budget proposal and resubmits it to the president. This cycle may be repeated several times until the result is satisfactory to all concerned. The budget preparation phase ends with the approval by the president of the budget proposal.

During the budget development process, the budget director analyzes the operating plans, develops cost projections, and serves as a catalyst in the creation of the budget. Although the director may make recommendations to the president and devise possible alternatives to the operating plans, he or she does not make decisions, approve the plans, or develop them for the functional managers. As any employee in a staff position, the budget director serves in an advisory capacity. The steps in the development of a master budget are depicted in Illustration 9-2.

The Master Budget—An Example

Illustration 9-1 and 9-2 have indicated the major operating and financial budgets included in a company's master budget. Budgets are developed for each of the functional areas of the company, including sales, manufacturing, purchasing, and administration. To aid in planning

Illustration 9-2 Developing the Master Budget

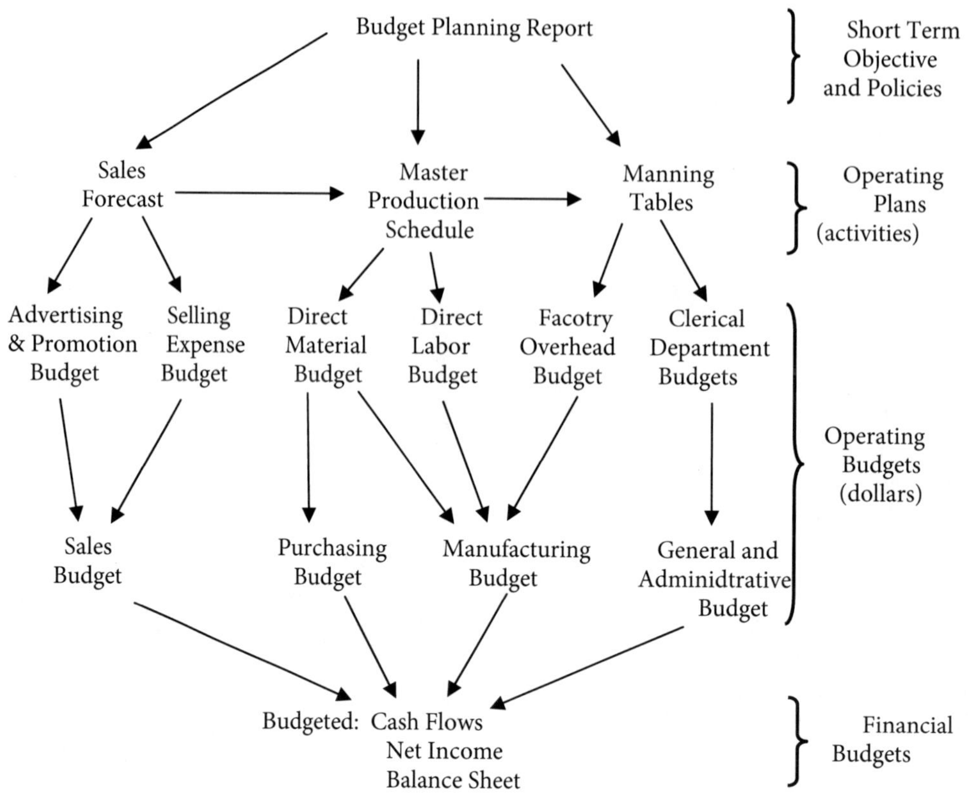

Budget Planning Report — Short Term Objective and Policies

Sales Forecast → Master Production Schedule → Manning Tables — Operating Plans (activities)

Advertising & Promotion Budget; Selling Expense Budget; Direct Material Budget; Direct Labor Budget; Facotry Overhead Budget; Clerical Department Budgets

Sales Budget; Purchasing Budget; Manufacturing Budget; General and Adminidtrative Budget — Operating Budgets (dollars)

Budgeted: Cash Flows, Net Income, Balance Sheet — Financial Budgets

the operations of each area, these major operating budgets may be supplemented by other minor operating budgets governing specific activities within the area. All the budgets are interrelated, with the contents of any one of them being dependent upon the activities projected in one or more of the others. These relationships will now be illustrated with a comprehensive example of a master budget. The necessary data for the comprehensive example are presented in Illustration 9-3.

Preparing the Sales Budget

The starting point for the entire budgeting process is the sales forecast. Sales projections in units are prepared for each product or major product line. These provide a basis for predicting activity levels and estimating revenues and costs.

Three approaches are commonly used for developing sales forecasts: statistical models, market research surveys, and sales personnel estimates. A sophisticated but very effective approach utilizes a statistical multiple regression model. A linear relationship is developed, using the method of least squares, between sales volume of a product abd other economic factors affecting sales volume. As long as the relationship described by the statistical model remains unchanged, the model can be used to predict future sales. Market research surveys use statistical sampling methods to arrive at estimates of sales volume. Aless complex and more common approach in smaller companies relies on estimates of volume from sales persons. Operating sales people are asked to project their sales in the upcoming year, and these are aggregated by sales region and by product line to develop overall sales projections for the company.

Once a sales forecast is created, the sales branch of the company can develop its marketing plan, which describes sales goals in units, and the advertising, promotional, and selling activities necessary to achieve these goals. The budget director summarizes these activities in an advertising and promotion budget and a selling expenses budget. Collectively these budgets, together with budgeted sales in units and dollars, constitute the sales budget.

Illustratiuon 9-4 contains an example of a sales budget for Highlight Corporation which includes budgeted selling expenses. Because Highlight uses no advertising, an advertising and promotion budget is not required.

Highlight Corporation is a small, highly automated manufacturer of electric light bulbs. The products are packaged in cases of 1,000 bulbs for sale to wholesale distribution outlets. Three types of raw materials are required for production in the quantities stated below.

Preparing the Manufacturing Budget

The operating plan for the manufacturing branch of a company consists of the master production schedule, which projects over the budgetary period how much will be produced and when it will be produced. Production quantities are normally set in order to balance the costs of carrying inventory with the costs of acquiring it; methods of achieving this balance were described in the previous chapter. Production is scheduled in order to maintain adequate finished goods inventory levels consistent with inventory and delivery policies set by top management. The following relationship can be used to determine the required production during a budgetary period.

Illustration 9-3 Comprehensive Example - Master Budget Highlight Corporation

Highlight Corporation is a small, highly automated manufacturer of electric light bulbs. The products are packaged in cases of 1,000 bulbs for sale to wholesale distribution outlets. Three types of raw materials are required for production in the quantities stated below.

Raw materials per case (1,000 bulbs):
glass .... 250 sq. ft. at $.40 per sq. ft.
tungsten .... 500 ft. at $.20 per ft.
aluminum .... 20 sq. ft. at $2.00 per sq. ft.

The selling price is $550.00 per case. The assembly process can produce at the rate of 1.5 cases per hour, and requires 8 workers who are paid $10 per hour. In addition, the following indirect labor is used:

one supervisor ($2,000 per month);
one inspector ($500 per month);
two packing clerks ($500 per month each); two shipping clerks
($500 per month each).

During a typical month the following factory overhead costs are incurred:

indirect materials..........$1,500 plus $1 per case,
electricity ....$1,000 plus $2 per case,
repairs and maintenance..........$1,100 plus $.50 per case,
water $300,
insurance $300,
property taxes..........$300,
depreciation ....$2,000.

Monthly selling costs include salaries of $4,000, supplies of $500, and travel costs of $1,000. Sales persons are paid a $5 commission on each case sold.

Monthly administrative costs include the president's salary of $3,500, the accountant's salary of $1,500, supplies $200, electricity $100, telephone $100, and depreciation on office equipment of $1,100. Three clerks are employed at a salary of $500 each.

The following information is provided as of January 1, 20XX.

Sales forecasts for 20xx: January	200 cases
February	180 cases
March	190 cases
April	180 cases
May	190 cases

Raw materials inventories:

glass	60,000 sq. ft.
tungsten	100,000 ft.
aluminum	5,000 sq. ft.

Company inventory policies:

1. Sufficient raw materials should be on hand at the end of each month to satisfy the next month's production.
2. Finished goods inventories at the end of each month should equal 20% of the next month's expected sales.

Company sales policy: Goods are shipped when produced, and customers pay the selling price, with no discount, within 30 days.

Company purchasing policy: All bills for purchases on account are paid for 30 days after receipt. Raw materials are readily available and can be received within one day of order. Materials can be purchased only in lots of 1,000 units.

Company advertising policy: No advertising is used.

The following states the financial position of the company as of January 1, 20XX.

Highlight Corporation
Balance Sheet as of 1/1/20XX

Current Assets:		
Cash	$ 14,000	
Accounts Receivable	60,000	
Raw Materials	54,000	
Finished Goods (40 cases)	14,000	$142,000
Fixed Assets:		
Land	$ 26,000	
Building and Equipment	400,000	
Accumulated Depreciation	(68,000)	358,000
Total Assets		$500,000
Current Liabilities:		
Accounts Payable*	$ 60,000	
Income Tax Payable	10,000	$ 70,000
Long -Term Bank Loan		50,000
Stockholders' Equit y:		
Common Stock	$250,000	
Retained Earnings	130,000	380,000
Total Liabilities and Stockholders Equity		$500,000
*Accounts payable are for the following:		
Raw Materials	$ 50,000	
Factory Expenses	6,000	
Selling Expenses	2,000	
Administrative Expenses	2,000	

Illustration 9-4 Example of a Sales Budget

Highlight Corporation Sales Budget First Quarter, 20XX			
	Jan.	Feb.	Mar.
Sales Forecast (cases)	200	180	190
Sales Revenues (@$550)	$110,000	$99,000	$104,500
Selling Expenses:	4,000	4,000	4,000
Commissions ($5 x sales)	1,000	900	950
Supplies	500	500	500
Travel	1,000	1,000	1,000
Total	$ 6,500	$ 6,400	$ 6,450

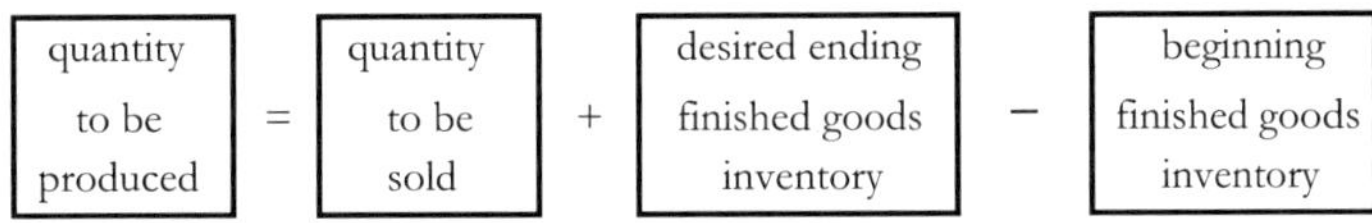

Thus, the master production schedule is developed based on sales forecasts and the inventory policy specified in the budget planning report. An example of a master production schedule for Highlight Corporation is contained in Illustration 9-5. From the master production schedule, the budget director can prepare three budgets which are components of the manufacturing budget. The budget project expenditures for these items over the upcoming budgetary period. A direct materials budget can be prepared from the production schedule if the amount of material required per unit is known. When this data is not available, historical ratios such as the material required to the number of units produced, or to the number of production hours used, can be employed. A direct labor budget is a projection of manpower requirements in hours and dollars for the planned production levels. It may also be determined from historical records of the amount of labor time per unit. The factory overhead budget projects expenditures for indirect materials, indirect labor, and other indirect manufacturing costs. It is developed from manning tables for indirect labor, and from an analysis of the behavior of other indirect costs in past periods.

Illustration 9-5 Example of a Master Production Schedule

Highlight Corporation Master Production Schedule First Quarter, 20XX			
	Jan	Feb	Mar
Sales Forecast (cases)	200	180	190
Plus Desired Ending Inventory	36	38	36
Quantity Needed	236	218	226
Less Beginning Inventory	(40)	(36)	(38)
Required Production	196	182	188

Direct materials, direct labor, and factory overhead budgets have been prepared for Highlight Corporation and are presented in Illustrations 9-6, 9-7 and 9-8. In the factory overhead budget, the variable and fixed behavior characteristics of indirect material, electricity, and repair and maintenance costs were considered in projecting expenditures for these items.

Preparing the Purchases Budget

A purchases budget is frequently prepared as a guide to the purchasing department, which is responsible for obtaining raw materials for production. The purchases budget projects the quantity of raw materials needed and the time these quantities should be ordered.

Purchasing decisions are affected by the quantity of production scheduled, the inventory policies set by top management, and the expected availability and delivery times for each type of raw material used. In many companies, purchasing decisions can have a major impact on cash flows because raw materials purchases may be substantial in amount and are paid for promptly. In addition, an adequate supply of raw materials is necessary for production to

Illustration 9-6 Example of a Direct Materials Budget

Highlight Corporation
Direct Materials Budget
First Quarter, 20XX

	Jan	Feb	Mar
Scheduled Production (Cases)	196	182	188
Component Materials			
Glass:			
Quantities (250 sq. ft. per case)	49,000	45,500	47,000
Costs ($.40persq.ft.)	$19,600	$18,200	$18,800
Tungsten:			
Quantities (500 ft. per case)	98,000	91,000	94,000
Costs ($.20perft.)	$19,600	$18,200	$18,800
Aluminum:			
Quantities (20 sq. ft. per case)	3,920	3,640	3,760
Costs ($2.00 per sq. ft.)	$ 7,840	$ 7,280	$ 7,520
Total Materials Cost	$47,040	$43,680	$45,120
Materials Cost Per Unit	$ 240	$ 240	$ 240

Illustration 9-7 Example of a Direct Labor Budget

Highlight Corporation
Direct Labor Budget
First Quarter, 20XX

Scheduled Production (cases)	196	182	188
Production Hours Required (1 1/2 cases per machine hour)	130 2/3	121 1/3	125 1/3
Hourly Production Costs (8 workers @ $10 per hour)	x 80	x 80	x 80
Total Direct Labor Costs	$10,454	$ 9,707	$10,027
Labor Costs Per Unit	$53.33	$53.33	$53.55

Illustration 9-8 Example of a Factory Overhead Budget

Highlight Corporation
Factory Overhead Budget
First Quarter, 20XX

	Jan	Feb	Mar
Scheduled Production (Cases)	196	182	188
Indirect Labor:			
Supervision (1 @ $2,000/mo.)	$ 2,000	2,000	2,000
Inspection (1 @ $500/mo.)	500	500	500
Packing (2 @ $500/mo.)	1,000	1,000	1,000
Shipping (2 @ $500/mo.)	1,000	1,000	1,000
Total Indirect Labor	4,500	4,500	4,500
	(1,500 + 1 x 196)	(1,500 + 1 x 182)	(1,500 + 1 x 188)
Indirect Material	1,696	1,682	1,688
	(1,000 + 2 x 196)	(1,000 + 2 x 182)	(1,000 + 2 x 188)
Electricity	1,392	1,364	1,376
Water	300	300	300
	(1,100 + .5 x 196)	(1,100 + .5 x 182)	(1,100 + .5 x 188)
Repairs and Maintenance	1,198	1,191	1,194
Insurance	300	300	300
Property Taxes	300	300	300
Depreciation	2,000	2,000	2,000
Total Factory Overhead	$11,686	$11,637	$11,658
Factory Overhead Per Unit	$59.62	$63.94	$62.01

continue. Because an entire plant can be shut down due to lack of a single raw material, a purchasing budget is an important component of the master budget.

The purchases budget can be developed from the data obtained for the direct materials budget. The quantities of each material to be purchased can be computed as follows:

$$\begin{matrix} minimum \\ quantity\ to\ be \\ purchased \end{matrix} = \begin{matrix} quantity \\ required\ for \\ production \end{matrix} + \begin{matrix} desired \\ ending \\ inventory \end{matrix} - \begin{matrix} beginning \\ inventory \end{matrix}$$

The timing of a purchase must be far enough in advance of the scheduled production so that the materials will arrive prior to the start of production. Purchase quantities may be adjusted upward to reflect minimum order quantities and to balance the costs of carrying raw materials inventory with the costs of ordering it. Methods of accomplishing the latter objective have been described in the previous chapter.

Illustration 9-9 contains a purchases budget for Highlight Corporation based on the required quantities from the direct materials budget. In this example, the desired ending inventories for March equal the raw materials requirements for April, based on April's scheduled production of 180 units. Highlight purchases materials in minimum lots of 1,000; consequently the purchase quantities sometimes exceed the minimum required for production. The ending inventory quantity in each month results from actual quantities purchased and is equal to the beginning inventory quantities of the next month. For example, the beginning inventory of glass for February is calculated as follows:

Illustration 9-9 Example of a Purchases Budget

Highlight Corporation
Purchases Budget
First Quarter, 20XX

	Jan.	Feb.	Mar.
Production Requirements:			
Glass (sq. ft.)	49,000	45,500	47,000
Tungsten (ft.)	98,000	91,000	94,000
Aluminum (sq. ft.)	3,920	3,640	3,760
Plus Desired Ending Inventory:			
Glass	45,500	47,000	45,000
Tungsten	91,000	94,000	90,000
Aluminum	3,640	3,760	3,600
Less Beginning Inventory:			
Glass	60,000	46,000	47,500
Tungsten	100,000	91,000	94,000
Aluminum	5,000	4,080	4,440
Minimum Requirements:			
Glass	34,500	46,500	44,500
Tungsten	89,000	94,000	90,000
Aluminum	2,560	3,320	2,920
Purchase Quantities:			
Glass (sq. ft.)	35,000	47,000	45,000
Tungsten (ft.)	89,000	94,000	90,000
Aluminum (sq. ft.)	3,000	4,000	3,000
Purchase Amounts:			
Glass (@ $.40 per sq. ft.)	$ 14,000	$18,800	$18,000
Tungsten (@ $.20 per ft.)	17,800	18,800	18,000
Aluminum (@ $2 per sq. ft.)	6,000	8,000	6,000
Amount of Total Purchases	$ 37,800	$45,600	$42,000
Amount of Ending Inventory:			
Glass (@ $.40 per sq. ft.)	$ 18,400	$19,000	$18,200
Tungsten (@ $.20 per ft.)	18,200	18,800	18,000
Aluminum (@ $2 per sq. ft.)	8,160	8,880	7,360
Total	$ 44,760	$46,680	$43,560

Beginning inventory (Jan.)	60,000	sq. ft.
Plus purchases (Jan.)	35,000	
	95,000	
Less production (Jan.)	(49,000)	
Beginning inventory (Feb.)	46,000	sq. ft.

PREPARING THE GENERAL AND ADMINISTRATIVE EXPENSE BUDGET

General and administrative expenses are primarily personnel-related costs. They include salaries and wages of clerical personnel and the costs of supplies, equipment and buildings used by those personnel. As a result, they can most directly be related to personnel staffing levels rather than levels of production. In most organizations, general and administrative expenses are not significant relative to the costs of producing goods or services. Yet general and administrative expense budgets are useful in preventing any gradual increase in administrative costs, which over an extended period of time may result in their becoming substantial.

An operating plan in clerical departments normally states the anticipated level of operations in those departments. From this, a manning table is created which states the positions needed in order to accomplish the expected workload. The budget director then develops the general and administrative expense budget by estimating salary levels for these positions, and the associated supplies, building, and equipment costs. Frequently, these cost projections will rely on past costs incurred in the same clerical department.

A general and administrative expense budget for Highlight Corporation is shown in Illustration 9-10.

Preparing Financial Budgets

Operating budgets have been described and illustrated which are used by operating managers in planning resource requirements for material and labor. The information, from these budgets can be used to develop other budgets which are used in planning for an additional resource, corporate cash, and in projecting the effect of planned operations on company profits. These financial budgets will now be described.

The cash budget developed by the budget director summarizes the projected cash inflows and outflows resulting from planned operations during a budgetary period. It is used by the corporate treasurer to anticipate cash shortages or excesses resulting from fluctuations in production levels. Projected cash shortages may signal the need for short-term bank financing, while projected excesses allow the treasurer to plan for short-term investments of cash in securities such as commercial paper or treasury bills. Projected shortages over an extended period of time may indicate the need for major changes in operating plans, such as a decrease in operating levels or an increase in product prices. A cash budget can be developed from the information contained in the operating budgets. The purchase of materials and supplies and the payment of wages and salaries represent cash outflows; cash inflows principally arise from the collection of accounts receivable. The cash budget normally summarizes these and other cash transactions and discloses beginning and ending cash balances for each budgetary period.

Illustration 9-10 Example of a General and Administrative Expense Budget

Highlight Corporation
General and Administrative Expense Budget
First Quarter, 20XX

	Jan.	Feb.	Mar.
Executive Salaries:			
President	$3,500	$3,500	$3,500
Accountant	1,500	1,500	1,500
Clerical Salaries:			
(3 clerks @ $500)	1,500	1,500	1,500
Supplies	200	200	200
Electricity	100	100	100
Telephone	100	100	100
Depreciation	1,100	1,100	1,100
Total	$8,000	$8,000	$8,000

A cash budget for Highlight Corporation, developed from the information in Illustrations 9-3 through 9-10, is presented in Illustration 9-11. The schedule of cash outflows reflects that payments for payroll expenses are made during the month the expenses are incurred, while payments for other expenditures are made during the succeeding month. Also in this example, payments for all sales are received in the month following production. This cash budget indicates that a short-term bank loan may be necessary during the month of January, but that sufficient cash should be generated during the following two months to repay the loan.

Top management is always interested in the effects of a proposed operating plan on company profits. This information is provided in the pro forma financial statements developed by the budget director. A budgeted income statement shows what net income would be if the proposed operating plan were adopted, and is produced from the operating budgets. To aid in its creation, the budget director will also develop a schedule of budgeted ending finished goods inventories and a schedule of budgeted cost of goods sold. These schedules are presented for Highlight Corporation in Illustrations 9-12 and 9-13. A budgeted income statement based on the preceding data is contained in Illustration 9-14. This example shows how a company can encounter cash flow difficulties even during periods of profitable operations. Even though net income is highest during the month of January, a shortage of cash during that month is expected. This is a result of the higher-than-average production activity during that month. The importance to profit planning of preparing both a cash budget and a budgeted income statement is thus demonstrated.

Illustration 9-11 Example of a Cash Budget

Highlight Corporation
Cash Budget
First Quarter, 20XX

	Jan	Feb	Mar
Beginning cash balance	$ 14,000	$(12,454)	$ 27,053
Cash Inflows:			
Receipts from sales on account (1)	60,000	110,000	99,000
Cash available	74,000	97,546	126,053
Cash Outflows:			
Materials purchases (2)	50,000	37,800	45,600
Payroll Expenses:			
Direct labor (3)	10,454	9,707	10,027
Indirect labor (4)	4,500	4,500	4,500
Selling (5)	5,000	4,900	4,950
General and Administrative (6)	6,500	6,5 00	6,500
Other Expenses:			
Factory overhead (7)	6,000	5,186	5,137
Selling (8)	2,000	1,500	1,500
General and Administrative (9)	2,000	400	400
Total cash outflows	86,454	70,493	78,614
Ending cash balance	$(12,454)	$ 27,053	$ 47,439

Sources of Data:
(1) balance sheet of 1/l/XXand sales budget
(2) balance sheet of 1/1/XXand purchases budget
(3) direct labor budget
(4) factory overhead budget
(5) selling expenses in sales budget
(6) general and administrative expense budget
(7) balance sheet of 1/l/XXand factory overhead budget
(8) balance sheet of 1/1/XXand sales budget
(9) balance sheet of 1/1/XXand general and administrative budget

Illustration 9-12 Example of Budgeted Ending Inventory

Highlight Corporation
Schedule of Ending Finished Goods Inventory
First Quarter, 20XX

	Jan	Feb	Mar
Cases in Inventory	36	38	36
Direct Materials Costs:			
(@ $240 per case)	$ 8,640	$ 9,120	$ 8,640
Direct Labor Costs:			
(@ $53.33 per case)	1,920	2,027	1,920
Factory Overhead Costs:			
(@ $59.62 per case)	2,146		
(@ $63.94 per case)		2,430	
(@ $62.01 per case)			2,232
Total	$12,706	$13,577	$12,792

Illustration 9-13 Example of Budgeted Cost of Goods Sold

Highlight Corporation
Schedule of Budgeted Cost of Goods Sold
First Quarter, 20XX

	Jan	Feb	Mar
Beginning Finished Goods Inventory (1)	$14,000	$12,706	$13,577
Plus Costs Incurred:			
Direct Materials (2)	47,040	43,680	45,120
Direct Labor (3)	10,454	9,707	10,027
Factory Overhead (4)	11,686	11,637	11,658
Goods Available for Sale	83,180	77,730	80,382
Less Ending Finished Goods Inventory (5)	12,706	13,577	12,792
Cost of Goods Sold	$ 70,474	$ 64,153	$ 67,590

Sources of Data:
(1) balance sheet of 1/1/xx and schedule of ending inventory
(2) direct materials budget
(3) direct labor budget
(4) factory overhead budget
(5) schedule of ending inventory

Illustration 9-14 Example of Budgeted Income Statement

Highlight Corporation
Budgeted Income Statement
First Quarter, 20XX

	Jan	Feb	Mar
Sales Revenue	$110,000	$ 99,000	$104,500
Cost of Goods Sold	(70,474)	(64,153)	(67,590)
Gross Profit	39,526	34,847	36,910
Less:			
General and Administrative Expense	(8,000)	(8,000)	(8,000)
Selling Expense	(6,500)	(6,400)	(6,450)
Operating Income	$ 25,026	$20,447	$ 22,460
Less:			
Estimated Income Tax (40%)	(10,010)	(8,179)	(8,984)
Net Income	$ 15,016	$12,268	$ 13,476

Illustration 9-15 Example of Budgeted Balance Sheet

Highlight Corporation
Budgeted Comparative Balance Sheets
First Quarter, 20XX

	End of Month		
	Jan	Feb	Mar
Current Assets:			
Cash (1)	$(12,454)	$ 27 ,053	$ 47,439
Accounts Receivable (2)	110,000	99,000	104,500
Raw Materials (3)	44,760	46,680	43,560
Finished Goods (4)	12,706	13,577	12,792
Total	155,012	186,310	208,291
Fixed Assets:			
Land	26,000	26,000	26,000
Building and Equipment	400,000	400,000	400,000
Accumulated Depreciation (5)	(71,100)	(74,200)	(77,300)
Total	354,900	351,800	348,700
Total Assets	$509,912	$538,110	$556,991
Current Liabilities:			
For Direct Material (6)	$ 37,800	$ 45,600	$ 42,000
For Factory Overhead (7)	5,186	5,137	5,158
For Selling Expense (8)	1,500	1,500	1,500
For General and Administrative Expense (9)	400	400	400
Income Tax Payable (10)	20,010	28,189	37,173
Total	64,896	80,826	86,231
Long -Term Bank Loan	50,000	50,000	50,000
Stockholders' Equity:			
Common Stock	250,000	250,000	250,000
Retained Earnings (11)	145,016	157.284	170,760
Total Liabilities and Stockholders' Equity	$509,912	$538,110	$556,991

Sources of Data:
(1) Cash budget
(2) Sales budget
(3) Purchases budget
(4) Schedule of budgeted finished goods inventory
(5) Balance sheetof 1/1/XX, factory overhead and general and administrative budgets
(6) Purchases budget
(7) Factory overhead budget
(8) Sales budget
(9) General and administrative expense budget
(10) Balance sheet of 1/1/XXand budgeted income statement
(11) Budgeted income statement

Top management is also concerned with the effect of a proposed operating plan on the financial position of the company. This information is provided by the budgeted balance sheet for the end of the budgetary reporting period. This component of the master budget is produced by the budget director from the data contained in the operating and other financial budgets. An example of a budgeted balance sheet for the example problem is presented in Illustration 9-15.

Other Planning Budgets

Many organizations, because of their structure or of the nature of their businesses, may develop types of planning budgets other than the basic ones described here. Budgets are especially useful in controlling programmed costs, which represent periodic expenditures subject to management's discretion. Examples of programmed costs include research and development costs and public relations expenses, and budgets are commonly developed for these expenditures. Another frequently used budget is the capital expenditures budget, which provides detail on projected cash outlays for capital equipment over a planning horizon. Expenditures for capital equipment may be substantial and should be coordinated with the long-term corporate plan. Methods of budgeting for capital expenditures will be described in a later chapter.

Summary

This chapter has described how budgets can be used for purposes of communication, coordination, and planning resource requirements. Such budgets represent short-term profit plans, and must be developed within the framework of long-range corporate objectives and policies. A formal procedure for developing a master budget has been described and illustrated with a comprehensive example problem. The major components of the master budget have been discussed and illustrated. They include the sales budget, the manufacturing budget, the purchases budget, and the general and administrative expense budget.

Key Definitions

Annual budget A master budget which covers the annual accounting reporting period. It may also provide summaries by quarter or by month.

Budget A document which provides a quantitative statement of a plan of action.

Budget planning report A statement of corporate policies and short-term objectives produced by the company president. It marks the beginning of the budget preparation phase.

Continuous budget A type of master budget which always covers a period one year into the future. It is updated on a monthly basis.

Master budget A budget which is used for communication, coordination, and planning resource requirements. It includes a budget for each of the functional areas of the organization.

Operating plan A description of projected activities during a budgetary period. When stated in terms of its financial impact, it becomes an operating budget.

Profit planning The process in which a company's profit and growth objectives are established, and the means of attaining these objectives are developed.

Questions

9-1 Briefly describe how budgets can be used for

communication,

coordination, and

resource planning.

9-2 Distinguish between an annual budget and a continuous budget.

9-3 How can cost-volume-profit analysis be used in profit planning?

9-4 What is the function of a budget director?

9-5 What is contained in a budget planning report?

9-6 What is a manning table?

9-7 How can statistical regression analysis be used in developing a sales forecast?

9-8 What potential problems exist in allowing individual sales persons to develop their own sales forecasts?

9-9 What is the objective of a general and administrative expenses budget?

9-10 Why is the cash budget important for planning?

9-11 Why are pro forma financial statements produced as part of the budgeting process?

Problems

9-12 *Budgeted Cash Disbursements*

Terry Company is preparing its cash budget for the month of April. The following information is available concerning its inventories:

Inventories at beginning of April	$ 90,000
Estimated purchases for April	440,000
Estimated cost of goods sold for April	450,000

Estimated payments in April for purchases in March 75,000
Estimated payments in April for purchases prior to March 20,000
Estimated payments in April for purchases in April.....................75%

What are the estimated cash disbursements for inventories in April?

(AICPA adapted)

9-13 *Budgeted Cash Receipts*

Varsity Co. is preparing its cash budget for the month of May. The following information on accounts receivable collections is available from Varsity's past collection experience:

Current month's sales 12%
Prior month's sales 75%
Sales two months prior to current month 6%
Sales three months prior to current month.... 4%
Cash discounts taken 2%
Doubtful accounts 1%
Credit sales are as follows:

May—estimated $100,000
April 90,000
March 80,000
February 95,000

What are the estimated collections of accounts receivable for May?

(AICPA adapted)

9-14 *Budgeted Production*

Arpo Products, Inc. has developed the following sales forecast for its most popular product, Product X, covering the months of April through July.

Sales Forecast—Product X	
April	20,000 units
May	22,000 units
June	24,000 units
July	25,000 units

Arpo's inventory policy specifies that the inventory on hand at the beginning of each month should equal one-half of that month's projected sales.
Given this information, develop a master production schedule for Arpo for April, May and June.

9-15 *Budgeted Cash Receipts*

The Fresh Company is preparing its cash budget for the month of May.
The following information is available concerning its accounts receivable:

Estimated credit sales for May..$200,000
Actual credit sales for April...$150,000

Estimated collections in May for credit sales in May	20%
Estimated collections in May for credit sales in April	70%
Estimated collections in May for credit sales prior to April	$ 12,000
Estimated write-offs in May for uncollectible credit sales	$ 8,000
Estimated provision for bad debts in May for credit sales in May	$ 7,000

Compute the estimated cash receipts from accounts receivable collections in May.

9-16 *Budgeted Cash Receipts and Disbursements*

Patsy Corp., has estimated its activity for December 20X6. Selected data from these estimated amounts are as follows:

Sales	$350,000
Gross profit (based on sales)	30%
Increase in trade accounts receivable during month	$ 10,000
Change in accounts payable during month	$ 0
Increase in inventory during month	$ 5,000

Variable selling, general and administrative expenses (S,G&A) includes a charge for uncollectible accounts of 1% of sales.
Total S,G&A is $35,500 per month plus 15% of sales.
Depreciation expense of $20,000 per month is included in fixed S,G&A.
On the basis of the above data, determine:

(a) the estimated cash receipts from operations for December,
(b) the estimated cash disbursements from operations for December.

(AICPA adapted)

9-17 *Budgeted Cash Balance*

Smith Corporation had the following transactions in 20X6, their first year of operations:

Sales (90% collected in 20X6)	$1,500,000
Bad debt write-offs	60,000
Disbursements for costs and expenses	1,200,000
Disbursements for income taxes	90,000
Purchases of fixed assets	400,000
Depreciation on fixed assets	80,000
Proceeds from issuance of common stock	500,000
Proceeds from short-term borrowings	100,000
Payments on short-term borrowings	50,000

What is the estimated cash balance at December 31, 20X6?

(AICPA adapted)

9-18 *Budgeted Cash Increase*

Davis Company has budgeted its activity for April. Selected data from estimated amounts are as follows:

Net income	$120,000
Increase in gross amount of trade accounts receivable during month	35,000
Decrease in accounts payable during month	25,000

Depreciation expense	65,000
Provision for income taxes	80,000
Provision for doubtful accounts receivable	45,000

On the basis of the above data, compute the amount of the cash increase for the month.

(AICPA adapted)

9-19 *Budgeted Merchandise Purchases*

The Zel Company, a wholesaler, budgeted the following sales for the indicated months:

	June	July	August
Sales on account	$1,500,000	$1,600,000	$1,700,000
Cash sales	200,000	210,000	220,000
	$1,700,000	$1,810,000	$1,920,000

All merchandise is marked up to sell at its invoice cost plus 25%. Merchandise inventories at the beginning of each month are at 30% of that month's projected cost of goods sold. Determine the dollar amount of budgeted merchandise purchases for June and July.

(AICPA adapted)

9-20 *Budgeted Cash Collections, Net Income, Accounts Payable*

The January 31, 20X6, balance sheet of Shelpat Corporation follows:

Cash	$ 8,000
Accounts receivable (net of allowance for uncollectible accounts of $2,000)	38,000
Inventory	16,000
Property, plant and equipment (net of allowance for accumulated depreciation of $60,000)	40,000
	$ 102,000
Accounts payable	$ 82,500
Common stock	50,000
Retained earnings (deficit)	(30,500)
	$ 102,000

Additional information:

Sales are budgeted as follows:

February	$ 110,000
March	$ 120,000

Collections are expected to be 60% in the month of sale, 38% the next month, and 2% uncollectible. The gross margin is 25% of sales. Purchases each month are 75% of the next month's projected sales. The purchases are paid in full the following month. Other expenses for each month, paid in cash, are expected to be $16,500. Depreciation each month is $5,000.

For February, 20X6, compute:

(a) budgeted cash collections,

(b) the pro forma income or loss before taxes,

(c) the projected ending balance of accounts payable.

(AICPA adapted)

9-21 *Selling Expense Budget*

Miraclean Corp. produces an industrial cleaning compound which is sold nationally at a price of $10 per one gallon container. The marketing division is subdivided into sales regions each headed by a sales manager, whose salary is $60,000 per year. Each region is in turn composed of sales districts, managed by a district director. A director is paid a salary of $2,000 per month plus a commission of $.10 per gallon on the sales of the district. Each district has one or more sales persons who are each paid $1,000 per month and $.20 per gallon sold. The following sales forecast has been developed for Region 2 for September.

District A	
Salesperson X	7,500 gal.
Salesperson Y	10,000 gal.
District B	
Salesperson P	8,000 gal.
Salesperson Q	12,000 gal.
Salesperson R	10,000 gal.
District C	
Salesperson S	14,000 gal.

Each district office has a bookkeeper who is paid $1,000 per month. Other expenses at a district office normally total $6,000 per month plus $2,000/mo. for each sales person serviced at the office. Regional office expenses are $10,000 per month. Prepare a selling expense budget for Region 2 in good form, showing budgeted revenues and costs by district.

9-22 *Budgeted Labor, Materials, and Purchases*

Worldwide Fabricating Co. manufactures small parts from steel. Based on a sales forecast, the following production schedule has been established for its two products during four months of 20XX.

Master Production Schedule (Units)

	July	August	September	October
Model 101	10,000	8,000	10,000	12,000
Model 102	5,600	6,000	5,400	5,900

Each product is made from the same raw material, Type 4000 steel. Delivery time for the steel is such that it must be ordered one month in advance, in quantities which are multiples of 10,000 lbs. Each product also passes through two operations, a lathe and a grinder. Historically the following costs have been incurred for one unit of each product.

Model 10—2 lbs. Type 4000 at $.50 per lb.
$^1/_2$ hour on lathe,
$^1/_4$ hour on grinder.

Model 102—4 lbs. Type 4000 at $.50 per lb.,
1 hour on lathe,

$^1/_4$ hour on grinder.

The beginning inventory of Type 4000 steel is 42,400 lbs. The lathe requires one operator who is paid $10 per hour. The grinder uses one operator at $5 per hour. One operator is required for every 750 machine-hours worked during a month. Develop the following for Worldwide for July, August and September.

(a) Direct materials budget,

(b) Purchases budget,

(c) Direct labor budget, including proposed staffing levels for the lathe and grinder departments.

9-23 *Budgeted Cash Receipts and Disbursements*

The Dilly Company marks up all merchandise at 25% of gross purchase price. All purchases are made on account with terms of 1/10, net/60. Purchase discounts, which are recorded as miscellaneous income, are always taken. Normally, 60% of each month's purchases are paid for in the month of purchase while the other 40% are paid during the first 10 days of the first month after purchase. Inventories of merchandise at the end of each month are kept at 30% of the next month's projected cost of goods sold. Terms for sales on account are 2/10, net/30. Cash sales are not subject to discount. Fifty percent of each month's sales on account are collected during the month of sale, 45% are collected in the succeeding month, and the remainders are usually uncollectible. Seventy percent of the collections in the month of sale are subject to discount while 10% of the collections in the succeeding month are subject to discount.

Projected sales data for selected months follow:

	Sales on Account-Gross	Cash Sales
December	$1,900,000	$400,000
January	1,500,000	250,000
February	1,700,000	350,000
March	1,600,000	300,000

Prepare a schedule of budgeted cash receipts and disbursements for the months of January and February.

(AICPA adapted)

9-24 *Cash Budget*

The Patton Corporation has gone through a period of rapid expansion to reach its present size of seven divisions. The expansion program has placed strains on its cash resources. Therefore, the need for better cash planning at the corporate level has become very important.

At the present time each division is responsible for the collection of receivables and the disbursements for all operating expenses and approved capital projects. The corporation does exercise control over division activities and has attempted to coordinate the cash needs of the divisions and the corporation. However, it has not yet developed effective division cash reports from which it can determine the needs and availability of cash in the next budgetary year. As a result of inadequate information, the corporation permitted some divisions to make expenditures for goods and services which need not have been made or which could have been postponed until a later time while other divisions had to delay expenditures which should have had a greater priority. The 20X6 cash receipts and disbursements plan prepared by the Western Division for submission to the corporate office is presented below. The following additional information was used by the Western Division to develop the cash receipts and disbursements budget.

1. Receipts-Miscellaneous receipts are estimated proceeds from the sales of unneeded equipment.
2. Sales-Travel and entertainment represents the costs required to produce the sales volume projected for the year. The other sales costs consist of $50,000 for training new sales personnel, $25,000 for attendance by sales personnel at association meetings (not sales shows), and $125,000 for sales management salaries.
3. Administration-The personnel costs include $50,000 for salary and department operating costs, $20,000 for training new personnel and $40,000 for management training courses for current employees. The general management costs include salaries and office costs for the division management, $310,000, plus $10,000 for officials' travel to Patton Corporation meetings and $30,000 for industry and association conferences.
4. Capital expenditures-Planned expenditures for capital items during 20X6 are as follows:

Capital programs approved by the corporation:

Items ordered for delivery in 20X6	$300,000
Items to be ordered in 20 X 6 for delivery in 20 X 6	700,000
New programs to be submitted to corporation during 20 X 6	240,000

Western Division

Budgeted Cash Receipts and Disbursements For the Year Ended December *31, 20X6* (000 omitted)

Receipts:	
Collections on account	$9,320
Miscellaneous	36
	$9,356
Disbursements:	
Production	
Raw materials	2,240
Labor and fringe benefits	2,076
Overhead	2,100
Sales	
Commissions	395
Travel and entertainment	600
Other	200
Administrative	
Accounting	80
Personnel	110
General management	350
Capital expenditures	1,240
	$9,391
Excess of receipts over (under) disbursements	$ (35)

Required:

Present a revised budgeted cash receipts and disbursement statement for the Western Division. Design the format of the revised statement to include adequate detail so as to improve the ability of the corporation to judge the urgency of the cash needs. Such a statement would be submitted by all divisions to provide the basis for overall corporation cash planning.

(*IMA adapted*)

9-25 Purchases and Cash Budget

Tomlinson Retail seeks your assistance to develop cash and other budget information for May, June, and July 20X6. At April 30, 20 X 6, the company had cash of $5,500, accounts receivable of $437,000, inventories of $309,400 and accounts payable of $133,055.

The budget is to be based on the following assumptions:

I. Sales

a. Each month's sales are billed on the last day of the month.

b. Customers are allowed a 3% discount if payment is made within ten days after the billing date. Receivables are booked gross.

c. 60% of the billings are collected within the discount period, 25% are collected by the end of the month, 9% are collected by the end of the second month, and 6% prove uncollectible.

II. Purchases

a. 54% of all purchases of material and selling, general, and administrative expenses are paid in the month purchased and the remainder in the following month.

b. Each month's units of ending inventory are equal to 130% of the next month's units of sales.

c. The cost of each unit of inventory is $20.

d. Selling, general, and administrative expenses of which $2,000 is depreciation, are equal to 15% of the current month's sales.

Actual and projected sales are as follows:

20X6	Dollars	Units
March	$354,000	11,800
April	363,000	12,100
May	357,000	11,900
June	342,000	11,400
July	360,000	12,000
August	366,000	12,200

Develop the following for the months of May, June, and July:

(a) Purchases budget in units and dollars,

(b) Schedule of budgeted cash disbursements,

(c) Schedule of budgeted cash receipts.

(*AICPA adapted*)

9-26 *Cash Budget*

The Barker Corporation manufactures and distributes wooden baseball bats. The unit sales volume for the past two months and the estimate for the next four months is:

October (actual)	70,000	January (estimated)	90,000
November (actual)	50,000	February (estimated)	90,000
December (estimated)	50,000	March (estimated)	120,000

The bats are sold for $3 each. All sales are made on account. One-half of the accounts are collected in the month of the sale, 40% are collected in the month following the sale, and the remaining 10% in the second month following the sale. Customers who pay in the month of the sale receive a 2% cash discount. The production schedule for the six-month period beginning with October is:

October (actual)	90,000	January (estimated)	90,000
November (actual)	90,000	February (estimated)	100,000
December (estimated)	90,000	March (estimated)	100,000

Since wooden blocks from which bats are made are purchased a year in advance in order to be aged, Barker pays $60,000 a month for raw materials. Workers can produce 7.5 bats per hour. Normal monthly output is 75,000 bats. Employees are paid $4.00 per hour for regular time and time and one-half for overtime. All hours over the normal monthly output of 75,000 bats are overtime hours.

Other manufacturing costs include variable overhead of $.30 per unit and annual fixed overhead of $280,000. Depreciation charges totaling $40,000 are included among the fixed overhead. Selling expenses include variable costs of $.20 per unit and annual fixed costs of $60,000. Fixed administrative costs are $120,000 annually. All fixed costs are incurred uniformly throughout the year.

The controller has accumulated the following additional information:

1. The balances of selected accounts as of November 30, 20X6, are as follows:

Cash	$12,000
Marketable securities (cost and market are the same)	40,000
Accounts receivable	96,000
Prepaid expenses	4,800
Account payable (arising from raw material purchase)	300,000
Accrued vacation pay	9,500
Equipment note payable	102,000
Accrued income taxes payable	50,000

Interest to be received from the company's temporary investments is estimated at $500 for December.

Prepaid expenses of $3,600 will expire during December, and the balance of the prepaid account is estimated at $4,200 for the end of December.

Barker purchased new machinery in 20X6 as part of a plant modernization program. The machinery was financed by a 24-month note of $144,000. The terms call for equal principal payments over the next 24 months with interest paid at the rate of one percent per month on the unpaid balance at the first of the month. The first payment was made May 1, 20X6.

Old equipment, which has a book value of $8,000, is to be sold during December for $7,500.

Each month the company accrues $1,700 for vacation pay by charging vacation pay expense and crediting accrued vacation pay. The plant closes for two weeks in June when all plant employees take a vacation.

Quarterly dividends of $.20 per share will be paid on December 15 to stockholders of record. Barker Corporation has authorized 10,000 shares. The company has issued 7,500 shares, and 500 of these are classified as treasury stock.

The quarterly income taxes payment of $50,000 is due on December 15, 20X6.

Required:

Prepare a schedule which forecasts the cash position at December 31, 20X6.

(*IMA adapted*)

9-27 *Sales and Production Budgets*

The Scarborough Corporation manufactures and sells two products: Thingone and Thingtwo. In July 20X7, Scarborough's budget department gathered the following data in order to project sales and budget requirements for 20X8.

20X8 Projected Sales:

Product	Units	Price
Thingone	60,000	$ 70
Thingtwo	40,000	$100

20X8 Inventories—in units:

Expected	Desired	
Product	January 1, 20X8	December 31, 20X8
Thingone	20,000	25,000
Thingtwo	8,000	9,000

In order to produce one unit of Thingone and Thingtwo, the following raw materials are used:

		Amounts used per unit	
Raw Materials	Units	Thingone	Thingtwo
A	lbs.	4	5
B	lbs.	2	3
C	each		1

Projected data for 20X8 with respect to raw materials are as follows:

Raw Materials	Anticipated Purchase Price	Expected Inventories January 1, 20X8	Desired Inventories December 31, 20X8
A	$8	32,000 lbs.	36,000 lbs.
B	$5	29,000 lbs.	32,000 lbs.
C	$3	6,000 each	7,000 each

Projected direct labor requirements for 20X8 and rates are as follows:

Product	Hours per unit	Rate per hour
Thingone	2	$3
Thingtwo	3	$4

Overhead is applied at the rate of $2 per direct labor hour.

Based upon the above projections and budget requirements for 20X8 for Thingone and Thingtwo, prepare the following budgets for 20X8:

Sales budget (in dollars).
Production budget (in units).
Raw materials purchase budget (in quantities).
Raw materials purchase budget (in dollars).
Direct labor budget (in dollars).
Budgeted finished goods inventory at December 31, 20X8 (in dollars).

(AICPA adapted)

9-28 *Production Budgets*

The Wyoming Division of Reid Corporation produces an intricate component part used in Reid's major product line. The division manager has been concerned recently by a lack of coordination between purchasing and production personnel and believes that a monthly budgeting system would be better than the present system.

Wyoming's division manager has decided to develop budget information for the third quarter of the current year as a trial before the budget system is implemented for an entire fiscal year. In response to the division manager's request for data which could be used to develop budget information, the division controller accumulated the following data.

Sales

Sales through June 30, 20X6, the first six months of the current year, are 24,000 units. Actual sales in units for May and June and estimated unit sales for the next four months are detailed as follows:

May(actual).. 4,000
June (actual) 4,000
July (estimated)................................. 5,000
August (estimated) 6,000
September (estimated)...................... 7,000
October (estimated) 7,000

Wyoming Division expects to sell 60,000 units during the year ending December 31, 20X6.

Direct Material

Data regarding the materials used in the component are shown in the schedule below. The desired monthly ending inventory for all direct materials is to have sufficient materials on hand to produce the next month's estimated sales.

Direct Materials	Units of Direct Materials Finished Component	Cost per Unit	Inventory Level 6/30/20X6
#101	6	$2.40	35,000 units
#211	4	3.60	30,000 units
#242	2	1.20	14,000 units

Direct Labor

Each component must pass through three different processes to be completed. Data regarding the direct labor is presented below.

Process	Direct Labor Hours per Finished Component	Cost per Direct Labor Hour
Forming	0.80	$8.00
Assembly	2.00	5.50
Finishing	0.25	6.00

Factory Overhead

The division produced 27,000 components during this six-month period through June 30, 20X6. The actual variable overhead costs incurred during this six-month period are shown below. The division controller believes the variable overhead costs will be incurred at the same rate during the last six months of 20X6.

Supplies	$ 59,400
Electricity	27,000
Indirect labor	54,000
Other	8,100
Total variable overhead	$148,500

The fixed overhead costs incurred during the first six months of 20X6 amounted to $93,500. Fixed overhead costs are budgeted for the full year as follows:

Supervision	$ 60,000
Taxes	7,200
Depreciation	86,400
Other	32,400
Total fixed overhead	$186,000

Finished Goods Inventory

The desired monthly ending inventory in units of completed components is 80% of the next month's estimated sales. There are 5,000 finished units in the inventory on June 30, 20X6.

Required:

a. Prepare a production budget in units for the Wyoming Division for the third quarter ending September 30, 20X6.

b. Without prejudice to your answer in requirement (a), assume the Wyoming Division plans to produce 18,000 units during the third quarter ending September 30, 20X6, and 60,000 units for the year ending December 31, 20X6.

1. Prepare a direct materials purchase budget in units and dollars for third quarter ending September 30, 20X6.
2. Prepare a direct labor budget in hours and dollars for the third quarter ending September 30, 20X6.
3. Prepare a factory overhead budget for the six-month period ending December 31, 20X6.

c. Assume Wyoming Division actually produced 38,000 components during the six-month period of July 1–December 31, 20X6, and incurred variable overhead of $203,300 and fixed overhead of $95,000. Evaluate Wyoming Division's performance for the last six months of 20X6 with respect to its control of factory overhead costs. Show and explain briefly any supporting calculations used in your evaluation.

(IMA adapted)

9-29 *Profit Planning*

Arment Co. has sales in the range of $25 to 30 million, has one manufacturing plant, employs 700 people, including 15 national account salesmen and 80 traveling sales representatives. The home office and plant is in Philadelphia, and the product is distributed east of the Mississippi River. The product is a line of pumps and related fittings used at construction sites, in homes, and in processing plants. The company has total assets equal to 80% of sales. Its capitalization is: accruals and current liabilities 30%, long-term debt 15%, and shareholders' equity 55%. In the last two years sales have increased 7% each year, and income after tax has amounted to 5% of sales.

Required:

(a) Strategic decisions by top management on a number of important topics serve as a basis for the annual profit plan. What are these topics, and why are they important.

(b) What specific procedures will be followed each year in developing the annual profit plan?

(IMA adapted)

9-30 *Budgeted Revenues-Nonprofit Organization*

The administrator of Wright Hospital has presented you with a number of service projections for the year ending June 30, 20X6. Estimated room requirements for inpatients by type of service are:

Type of Patients	Total Patients Expected	Average Number of Days in Hospitals: Regular	Medicare	Percent of Regular Patients Selecting Types of Service: Private	Semiprivate	Ward
Medical	2,100	7	17	10%	60%	30%
Surgical	2,400	10	15	15	75	10

Of the patients served by the hospital 10% are expected to be Medicare patients, all of whom are expected to select semi-private rooms. Both the number and proportion of Medicare patients have increased over the past five years. Daily rentals per patient are: $40 for a private room, $35 for a semi-private room and $25 for a ward.

Operating room charges are based on man-minutes (number of minutes the operating room is in use multiplied by number of personnel assisting in the operation). The per man-minute charges are $.13 for inpatients and $.22 for outpatients. Studies for the current year show that operations on inpatients are divided as follows:

Type of Operation	Number of Operations	Average Number of Minutes per Operation	Average Number of Personnel Required
A	800	30	4
B	700	45	5
C	300	90	6
D	200	120	8
	2,000		

The same proportion of inpatient operations is expected for the next fiscal year and 180 outpatients are expected to use the operating room. Outpatient operations average 20 minutes and require the assistance of three persons.

The budget for the year ending June 30, 20X6, by departments, is:

General services:	
Maintenance of plant	$ 50,000
Operation of plant	27,500
Administration	97,500
All others	192,000
Revenue producing services:	
Operating room	68,440
All others	700,000
	$1,135,440

Prepare schedules showing the computation of:

a. The number of patient days (number of patients multiplied by average stay in hospital) expected by type of patients and service.

b. The total number of person-minutes expected for operating room services for inpatients and outpatients. For inpatients show the breakdown of total operating room person-minutes by type of operation.

c. Expected gross revenue from routine services.

d. Expected gross revenue from operation room services.

(AICPA adapted)

9-31 *Cash Budget*

Prime Time Court Club (PTCC) has been in business for five years. The club has experienced cash flow problems each year, especially in the summer when court use is quite low and new membership sales are insignificant. Temporary loans have been obtained from the local bank to cover the summer shortages. Additional permanent capital has also been invested by the owners.

The owners and the bank have decided some action needs to be taken at this time to improve PTCC's net cash flow position. They would like to review a quarterly cash budget based upon a revised fee structure that hopefully would increase club revenues. The purpose of the cash budget would be to better anticipate both the timing and amounts of the probable cash flow of the club and to determine if the club can survive. John Harper, club manager, recommended that the membership dues be increased and that the hourly court time fees be replaced with a monthly charge for unlimited court use. He believes that this plan will increase membership and that the cash flow and timing problem should be reduced. The proposed fee schedule, which is consistent with rates at other clubs, is presented below. In his opinion, the proportions of the different membership categories should not change, but the total number of members will increase by 10%. Court use will also increase an estimated 20% as a result of this new program. The pattern of use throughout the year is not expected to change.
The present fee structure, the distribution among membership categories, and the projected 20X6 operating data including membership status, court usage, and estimated operating costs are presented below. The projected operating data presented in the table were based on the present fee structure before Harper's proposed fee schedule was recommended.

Proposed Fee Schedule

Membership Category	Annual Membership Fees	Monthly Court Charges
Individual	$75	$10
Youth	45	8
Family	150	18

Present Fee Structure

Annual membership dues	
Individual	$ 45
Youth	30
Family	100
Court time fees	
Prime	$10 per hour
Regular	6 per hour
Membership Distribution	
Individual	50%
Youth	20
Family	30
	100%

Projected Operating Data

Quarter	Membership Renewal or New Memberships	Court Time in Hours Prime	Regular	Costs Fixed Costs*	Variable Costs
1	600	5,500	6,000	$ 56,500	$ 57,500
2	200	2,000	4,000	56,500	30,000
3	200	1,000	2,000	56,500	15,000
4	600	5,500	6,000	56,500	57,500
	1,600			$226,000	$160,000

* Includes a quarterly depreciation charge of $12,500.

Required:

(a) Construct a quarterly cash budget for one year for PTCC assuming the new fee structure is adopted and John Harper's estimates of increases in membership and court use occur. Assume the transition from the old to the new fee structure is immediate and complete when preparing the budget.

(b) Will John Harper's proposal solve the summer cash shortfall problem? Explain your answer.

(c) Will John Harper's proposal support a conclusion that the club can become profitable and survive in the long-run? Explain your answer.

(*IMA adapted*)

9-32 *Production Schedule*

Calen Co. manufactures and sells three products. The three products are manufactured in a factory consisting of four departments. Both labor and machine times are applied to the products as they pass through each applicable department. The nature of the machine processing and labor skills required in each department is such that neither machines nor labor can be switched from one department to another.

Calen's management is attempting to plan its production schedule for the next several months. The planning is complicated by the fact that there are labor shortages in the community and some machines will be down several months for repairs.

The following information regarding available machine and labor time by department and the machine hours and direct labor hours required per unit of product has been accumulated to aid in the decision. These data should be valid for at least the next six months.

	Department			
	1	2	3	4
Monthly Capacity Availability				
Normal machine capacity in machine hours	3,500	3,500	3,000	3,500
Capacity of machine being repaired in machine hours	(500)	(400)	(300)	(200)
Available machine capacity in machine hours	3,000	3,100	2,700	3,300
Labor capacity in direct labor hours	4,000	4,500	3,500	3,000
Available labor in direct labor hours	3,700	4,500	2,750	2,600

Labor and Machine Specifications per Unit of Product

Product	Labor and Machine Time				
401	Direct labor hours	2	3	3	1
	Machine hours	1	1	2	2
403	Direct labor hours	1	2		2
	Machine hours	I	1	-	2
405	Direct labor hours	2	2	2	1
	Machine hours	2	2	1	1

The sales department believes that the monthly demand for the next six months will be as follows:

Product	Monthly Sales Volume in Units
401	500
403	400
405	1,000

Inventory levels are at satisfactory levels and need not be increased or decreased during the next six months. The unit price and cost data that will be valid for the next six months are presented below:

	Product		
	401	403	405
Unit Costs:			
Direct material	$ 7	$ 13	$ 17
Direct labor............			
Department 1	12	6	12
Department 2	21	14	14
Department 3	24	-	16
Department 4	9	18	9
Variable overhead	27	20	25
Fixed overhead	15	10	32
Variable selling	3	2	4
Unit selling price....	$196	$123	$167

Required:

(a) Calculate the monthly requirement for machine hours and direct labor hours for the production of products 401, 403, and 405 to determine if the monthly sales demand for the three products can be met by the factory.

(b) What monthly production schedule should Calen Co. select in order to maximize its dollar profits? Explain how you selected this production schedule, and present a schedule of the contribution to profit that would be generated by your production schedule.

(c) Identify the alternatives Calen Co. might consider so it can supply its customers with the entire product they demand.

(*IMA adapted*)

1. *To identify the major advantages offered by standard costing systems.*
2. *To discuss the approaches and methods used in developing cost standards.*
3. *To describe how variance analysis can provide information for the control of operations.*
4. *To describe how materials and labor costs are recorded and summarized in standard costing systems.*
5. *To discuss modern costing systems such as Kaizen and target costing.*

10

Standard Costs and Control

In the previous chapter a type of accounting system was described which provides information useful for the control of operations. A responsibility accounting system provides performance reports at each managerial level in the organization. These reports disclose, for each manager, the difference between actual costs and revenues and those budgeted during a reporting period. The manager can then be held responsible for this variance.

Traditionally, responsibility accounting systems are most successful in achieving their objectives when used in conjunction with a system of standard costs. Traditional standard costing systems have gained wide acceptance because they provide meaningful performance measures and make it easier for management to isolate responsibility for variances. In this chapter, the use of traditional standard costs in controlling materials and labor costs will be first described. After that, other cost control systems (such as Benchmarking, Kaizer Costing, and target costing) will also be discussed. The subsequent chapters contain discussions of the use of standards to control overhead costs, and how variances can be further utilized to achieve the control objective.

Objectives of Standard Costs

Previous chapters have discussed two types of cost accounting systems and the organizational environments in which they are typically implemented. These types, job order costing systems and process costing systems, both were described as ways of recording and summarizing actual, or *historical* costs. Many organizations find it is preferable for planning and control purposes to record in the accounts a type of *predetermined* cost, called standard costs. These predetermined costs represent costs which management feels should have been incurred for the work which was performed. They can be compared to the actual costs incurred and the source of any variances can be explained.

Shortcomings of Historical Costs

A cost accounting system must provide information on the actual costs incurred for purposes of income determination and external reporting. Actual costs are summarized and reported in the financial statements as a historical record of costs and income. For purposes of planning and controlling operations, historical costs are deficient in several respects.

First of all, historical costs do not provide an effective basis against which performance can be evaluated. Some organizations attempt to measure managerial performance by comparing current costs or revenues with those of previous periods. Although this practice does provide an indication of trends over time, it tends to disguise inefficiencies which exist in the operations of previous periods. In addition, there may be valid reasons other than poor managerial performance why costs increase or revenues decrease. If the performance evaluation system is to be an effective motivator, managers should not be held responsible for factors which are beyond their control.

Related to this deficiency is the difficulty of using historical costs for budgeting. Factors which affected costs and revenues in past periods may no longer be present during a current budgetary period. Thus, a budget based on past experience which incorporates those factors will not be an accurate predictor of current costs and revenues for planning purposes. Predetermined costs, which state what costs should be under current circumstances, are superior for use in developing budgets.

Costs accounting systems which record historical costs do not provide evidence of excessive expenditures until the end of a reporting period. As a result, managers are not aware of the problems creating the expenditures until they have already occurred, when it may be too late to correct them. Using a standard cost system, the existence of excessive expenditures is disclosed when the costs are recorded and problems may be investigated promptly. The method of accomplishing this disclosure will be described later in this chapter. Predetermined costs are contrasted with historical costs in Illustration 10-1.

Approaches to Setting Standards

Cost standards are a form of predetermined cost which provides unit cost objectives for materials, labor and factory overhead. The method of arriving at the standards reflects the philosophy of management regarding how the cost standards should be used. Three basic approaches to setting standards include the basic standard, the ideal standard, and the currently attainable standard. Each approach will result in different standard costs for the same unit of product or service, and performance reports based on each should be interpreted differently.

The *basic* standard, sometimes referred to as the past performance standard, is one which is seldom changed. It is used as a point of reference to which future costs can be compared, and is useful as an indicator of trends. Basic standards are developed during a base period, which frequently is the time period that the standard cost system is first placed in operation. In subsequent reporting periods variances reflect the differences between the actual costs incurred and what those costs would have been during the base period. In many industries production methods or materials may change, rendering basic standards obsolete and making them ineffective both for budgeting and for performance reporting. When a basic standard is revised to reflect such changes, it ceases to be a valid indicator of trends.

The *ideal* or perfection standard is sometimes advocated by top management because it reflects what costs would be if the organization were operating at maximum efficiency. Its advocates feel that standards should provide goals that are difficult to achieve in order to obtain maximum effort from employees. Variances produced by a standard cost system utilizing this approach represent the extent to which actual operations differ from the ideal of perfect efficiency, and decreased variances are assumed to indicate better performance. In practice an organization seldom operates at maximum efficiency. Consequently the ideal standard does not provide an effective basis for budgeting, and employees may be reluctant to work to achieve cost objectives which can never be attained.

The *currently attainable* standard overcomes some of the disadvantages of the other two approaches. It represents the costs that management feels should be incurred under expected efficient operating conditions. Standards set using this approach provide for less than ideal operations, including allowances for normal spoilage, routine machine breakdowns, and employee idle time. When standards are attainable, employees are more likely to accept them as personal goals and to accept as fair the performance reports based on them. Costs utilizing currently attainable standards provide reasonable estimates for budgeting and for product costing in external reporting. Because this type of standard provides major advantages over the other approaches, it is the one that is most frequently used. Use of the currently attainable standard will be assumed in the remaining discussions in this text.

Using Standard Costs

Standard costing systems differ from historical costing systems in that predetermined, rather than actual, costs are recorded in the accounts. They represent a modification to the basic

Illustration 10-1 Comparison of Historical and Predetermined Costs

	Historical Costs	Predetermined Costs
When are they computed?	After the costs have been Incurred	Prior to the time the costs are incurred
Usefulness for budgeting?	Questionable, since factors affecting past costs may change or no longer exist	Useful, since they reflect costs that management feels should be incurred under expected operating condi tions
Usefulness for performance evaluation?	Questionable, since they hide inefficiencies and may reflect factors be yond a manager's control	May be useful, when they reflect controllable costs at a managerial level of responsibility
Usefulness for external reporting?	Required under generally accepted accounting principles (GAAP)	Adjust standard cost account balances to approximate results when historical costs are used

cost accounting systems discussed earlier in the text. Cost standards can be used in conjunction with job order costing, resulting in *a standard job order costing* system. Such a system would be used in any production environment where costs are accumulated by jobs, but would provide additional information useful for planning and control. Similarly a different type of organization might employ *a standard process costing* system, in which predetermined costs are accumulated by cost centers. Some characteristics which distinguish the types of cost accounting systems discussed thus far are summarized in Illustration 10-2.

Developing Standards

Cost standards are set by a coordinated effort between cost accountants and other employees of an organization. The function of the cost accountant is to apply costs to physical standards which have been determined by others.

The physical standards for a unit of product include specifications of how a task should be performed, the skill levels required of the workers who perform it, and the types and quantities of raw material which should be used. Typically organizations employ product engineers who design the products and determine the types, amounts, and grades of materials required. The designed quantities of material are increased by a small percentage (usually determined from past experience) to allow for normal spoilage in manufacture, in order to arrive at a standard quantity of material for each unit of output. Industrial engineers are frequently employed to determine the steps involved in a manufacturing process, and the skill levels and amount of time required for each step.

These time estimates are increased by a small percentage (again determined from experience) to allow for machine breakdowns and idle time, in order to arrive at standard production times for a unit of product.

The cost accountant is utilized to translate the physical standards into cost standards. Standard prices for raw materials may be established after consultation with purchasing agents and by reference to current market prices. Standard labor rates are established for each manufacturing operation from current or anticipated pay rates for the skill levels required. Standard materials prices and labor rates can be applied to the standard material and labor quantities to compute the standard prime cost per unit of product. The unit standard cost also includes a portion of overhead costs attached at a standard overhead rate. The determination of these rates will be discussed in the next chapter. A predetermination

Illustration 10-2 Types of Cost Accounting Systems Compared

Job Order Actual Costing
- costs are determined after they are incurred
- costs are recorded by job or batch

Job Order Standard Costing
- costs are determined before they are incurred
- costs are recorded by job or batch

Process Actual Costing
- costs are determined after they are incurred
- costs are recorded by cost center

Process Standard Costing
- costs are determined before they are incurred
- costs are recorded by cost center

of costs to this level of detail is necessary if the cost accounting system is to provide the information needed for planning and control. The distinction between physical and cost standards is presented in Illustration 10-3.

Standard Costs in Planning

Cost standards, when properly determined, accurately predict unit product costs. As a result, they provide a sounder basis for budgeting than methods which utilize historical costs. As is described in a previous chapter, the process of developing a master budget begins with a forecast of future sales volume. Sales forecasts then are used to predict production volume in units. Accurate cost predictions in budgetary plans can be obtained from multiplying unit standard costs by the anticipated production volume in units. Such budgets reflect only expected activity in the current budgetary period. Any factors affecting costs in prior periods that are not present in the current period will not be incorporated in the budget, as would be the case if historical costs were used.

As is discussed in the chapter on responsibility accounting, frequently organizations develop budgets not only for the organization as a whole but for individual responsibility centers as well. When standard costs are used in conjunction with such a budgetary system, the cost accounting system becomes an effective aid to management in the control of operations.

Standard Costs in Control

A system for managerial control provides cost and revenue targets for managers and then evaluates each manager's performance based on how closely these targets were attained. In a standard costing system, cost targets are the budgeted costs based on the predetermined cost standards. When the standards are perceived by managers as attainable, the budgetary targets may become effective motivators for improved managerial performance.

Illustration 10-3 Physical Standards and Cost Standards

Physical Standards and Cost Standards

Fine Fair Food Products, Inc., manufactures specialty candies on a seasonal basis. During the winter, chocolate eggs are produced for sale during the Easter season. These are sold by the carton, which consists of 160 4-ounce eggs. The following standards have been established.

Physical standards (one carton)

1 quart milk (32 oz.)
8 pounds cocoa (128 oz.)
32 pounds sugar (512 oz.)
5 minutes production time using semiskilled labor

Cost standards

milk -$2.00 per gallon
cocoa -$1.00 per pound
sugar -$.40 per pound
semiskilled labor - $9.00 per hour

Standard cost of one carton

Materials:		
milk (1/4 x $2.00)	.50	
cocoa (8 x $1.00)	8.00	
sugar (32 x $.40)	12.80	$21.30
Labor ($9.00 x 5/60)		.75
Standard prime cost per carton		$22.05

Budgetary systems utilizing standard costs provide prompt feedback to a manager regarding his or her performance. During each budgetary period, the actual costs incurred are compared to the budgeted costs, disclosing a variance. This variance is then analyzed to determine its source. An individual manager can be held responsible for that portion of the variance which he or she is able to influence.

Variances are normally described as being either favorable or unfavorable. *A favorable* variance is one in which actual costs were less than those budgeted. Conversely, an *unfavorable* variance occurs when actual costs are greater than those budgeted. These terms should not be interpreted as being descriptive of the performance of the manager who is responsible for the variance. An unfavorable variance is not always an indicator of poor performance; similarly a large favorable variance may result when a manager fails to carry out responsibilities adequately. This point will be illustrated later in the chapter. In general, a large variance may be interpreted as evidence of a possible problem which should be investigated. The nature of the variance, whether favorable or unfavorable, provides a clue as to the nature of the problem. Other information can be obtained by analyzing the variance in order to explain its source.

Analyzing Material and Labor Variances

A variance is the difference between actual costs and those budgeted during a reporting period. In higher level responsibility centers, such as that of a plant manager, it is possible to hold the manager in charge responsible for all controllable variances reported at that level.

If the manager is to be expected to show improved performance in later reporting periods, he or she should be provided with information isolating sources of these variances. At the cost center level, such as individual departments within a plant, a manager can be held responsible for that portion of the total variance for which the manager controls the source. In general a cost variance can arise from two sources: (1) the price paid for the input (material, labor, overhead) differs from that anticipated when the standards were set, or (2) the quantity of inputs used differs from those incorporated into the standard. The cost accountant can determine the amount of the cost variance arising from these two sources, called the price variance and the quantity variance, respectively. Methods for doing this will now be illustrated for inputs of labor and material; analysis of overhead variances will be discussed in the next chapter.

Price Variances

A price variance is defined as favorable if the actual price paid for the input is less than that called for by the standard. The price variance for labor is frequently called the *labor rate variance,* because the price paid for labor is normally stated in terms of an hourly pay rate. It may be computed from the following relationship:

Labor Rate Variance = Actual Hours Used x *[Actual Hourly Rate - Standard Hourly Rate]*

In this equation, the standard hourly rate is the pay rate which, according to the standards, should be paid for the work which was performed.

The existence of a labor rate variance may indicate the utilization of workers at a higher or lower skill level than that called for by the standard. This may occur, for example, when workers normally assigned to an operation are ill or on vacation, or when workers are overqualified or under-qualified for work they are performing. A high favorable labor rate variance may be an indicator of potential quality deficiencies in the products manufactured, or of potential machine maintenance problems resulting from the use of an unskilled operator. A high unfavorable labor rate variance may result from the inefficient use of the available workforce. This variance can be controlled most directly by the supervisor responsible for assigning jobs to workers; although in many cases upon investigation it may be found to be unavoidable.

A materials price variance results when the price paid for raw material differs from the standard. If the actual price is less than the standard, the variance is favorable; otherwise, it is unfavorable.

$$\begin{matrix} \textit{Material} \\ \textit{Price} \\ \textit{Variance} \end{matrix} = \underset{\left\{\begin{matrix} \textit{Consumed} \\ \textit{or} \\ \textit{Purchased} \end{matrix}\right\}}{\begin{matrix} \textit{Actual} \\ \textit{Quantity} \end{matrix}} \times \left(\begin{matrix} \textit{Actual} \\ \textit{Unit} \\ \textit{Price} \end{matrix} - \begin{matrix} \textit{Standard} \\ \textit{Unit} \\ \textit{Price} \end{matrix}\right)$$

The materials price variance is computed in either of two ways, depending on the nature of the standard cost system. Some companies carry raw materials inventory at their actual costs. When this is the case, the price variance is computed when the materials are issued for production, and the actual quantity is the quantity that is consumed. Others carry raw materials at standard cost, and the variance is computed when the materials are received. In this case, the actual quantity is the quantity that is purchased.

The material price variance is normally considered to be the responsibility of a purchasing agent, who is the person that exerts the greatest influence over the prices paid for materials. A large favorable variance may indicate that the purchasing agent is aggressively seeking lower priced supplies, or it may result from the purchase of materials of inferior quality. A large unfavorable variance may occur when the purchasing agent is inattentive to his or her duties, or when materials prices are rising rapidly. Again, the existence of a large price variance signifies a potential problem which may or may not be avoidable.

Quantity Variances

A quantity variance explains the amount of the total variance attributable to the efficient or inefficient use of an input, and is thus sometimes referred to as an efficiency variance. It measures the difference between the cost of the actual inputs used and the cost of the inputs which, according to the standards, should have been used for the output which was achieved. This latter quantity is referred to as the *standard costs allowed* for the output attained, and is equal to the *standard inputs allowed* (based on the physical standard) multiplied by the standard price for the input. For labor inputs,

$$\begin{matrix} \textit{Number of} \\ \textit{Units} \\ \textit{Produced} \end{matrix} \; \# \; \begin{matrix} \textit{Standard} \\ \textit{Labor Hours} \\ \textit{Per Unit} \end{matrix} = \begin{matrix} \textit{Standard} \\ \textit{LaborCosts} \\ \textit{Allowed} \end{matrix}$$

$$\begin{matrix} \textit{Standard} & & \textit{Standard} & & \textit{Standard} \\ \textit{Hourly} & \# & \textit{Labor Hours} & = & \textit{Labor Cost} \\ \textit{Rate} & & \textit{Allowed} & & \textit{Allowed} \end{matrix}$$

The quantity variance for labor, usually called the *labor usage variance*, can be computed from the following relationship:

$$\begin{matrix} \textit{Labor Usage} \\ \textit{Variance} \end{matrix} = \begin{matrix} \textit{Standard Hourly} \\ \textit{Rate} \end{matrix} \text{ x } \left[\begin{matrix} \textit{Actual Labor} \\ \textit{Hours} \end{matrix} - \begin{matrix} \textit{Standard Hours Allowed} \\ \textit{for Output Attained} \end{matrix} \right]$$

If the actual hours used are less than the hours which according to the standard should have been used, the variance is favorable.

The labor usage variance is attributable to the productivity of the workers involved in the process, and its responsibility is usually fixed on a production supervisor or foreman. A favorable labor usage variance may signify that employees have been working efficiently, or it may be an indicator of poor quality workmanship. An unfavorable variance may result from the use of inefficient or unqualified workers or from poor supervision. Any significant favorable or unfavorable labor usage variance provides evidence of a potential problem which merits investigation.

The material quantity variance is computed similarly from the standard inputs of material allowed. Depending on the type of material, it may be described variously as the standard pounds allowed, standard gallons allowed, or standard liters allowed.

$$\begin{matrix} \textit{Material Quantity} \\ \textit{Variance} \end{matrix} = \begin{matrix} \textit{Standard Price} \\ \textit{Per Unit Input} \end{matrix} \text{ x } \left[\begin{matrix} \textit{Actual Quantity} \\ \textit{Used} \end{matrix} - \begin{matrix} \textit{Standard Quantity Allowed} \\ \textit{for Output Attained} \end{matrix} \right]$$

A favorable variance exists whenever the actual quantity used is less than the standard quantity of inputs allowed for the number of outputs produced.

An excessive favorable material quantity variance can provide evidence of efficient use of material or of the possibility of poor quality products. An unfavorable one may be explained by inefficiency in production, or by excessive waste due to unqualified or inattentive workers. Normally a production foreman would be held responsible for the material quantity variance.

The analysis of standard cost variances for labor and materials provide information for control because they aid in pinpointing responsibility for deviations from the budget. Additionally they alert management to potential problems before they become serious in their consequences. Only after an excessive variance has been investigated can responsibility for it be explained adequately. Methods of determining when a variance is excessive will be described in a later chapter. Examples of the computation of labor and material variances are shown in Illustration 10-4 and 10-5.

Analysis of the Quantity Variance: Mix and Yield Variances

A quantity variance is recorded whenever the actual quantity of inputs used differs from the quantity called for by the standard, for the number of outputs produced. In practice,

Illustration 10-4 Labor Variances Illustrative Problem

During the month of February, Fine Fair Food Products worked a total of 160 production hours. The 5 workers utilized in the manufacture of chocolate eggs were paid $9.15 per hour. A total of 10,080 cartons were produced. The labor standards for this product (see Illustration 10-3) specify a standard production time of 5 minutes per carton at a standard hourly rate of $9.00.

(1) Labor Usage (Efficiency) Variance:

Standard Hours Allowed =
Number of Units Produced x Standard Hours per Unit

- 10,080 cartons x 1/12 hour/per carton
- 840 standard labor hours

Labor Usage (Efficiency) Variance = Standard Hourly Rate x [Actual Labor Hours - Standard Hours Allowed]

- 9.00 x ((5)(160) - (10,080)(1/12)]
- 9.00 x (800-840)
- $360 F.

(2) Labor Rate Variance:

Labor Rate Variance =
Actual Hours Worked x [Actual Hourly Rate – Standard Hourly Rate]

- (5)(160) x (9.15 -9.00)
- $120 U.

Note: F indicates a favorable variance.
U indicates an unfavorable variance.

Illustration 10-5 Materials Variances Illustrative Problem

During February, 10,080 cartons of chocolate eggs were produced. Fine Fair purchased 80,000 pounds of cocoa at a cost of $.98 per pound. The physical standards (see Illustration 12-3) specify 8 pounds of cocoa per carton at a standard cost of $1.00 per pound. A total of 81,000 pounds were used in production. The materials variances for cocoa are computed as follows:

(1) Materials Quantity (Usage) Variance:

Standard Pounds Allowed =
Number Units of Produced x Standard Pounds Per Unit

= 10,080 x 8
= 80,640 pounds of cocoa.

Materials Quantity Variance =
Standard Price Per Pound x [Actual Pounds Used – Standard Pounds Allowed]

= 1.00 x [81,000-(10,080)(8)]
= 1.00 x (81,000-80,640)
= $360 U.

(2) Materials Price Variance:

If Fine Fair carries raw materials inventory at actual:

Materials Price Variance =
Actual Pounds Consumed x [Actual Unit Price – Standard Unit Price]

= 81,000 x (.98 -1.00)
= $1,620 F.

If Fine Fair carries raw materials inventory at *standard:*

Materials Price Variance = Actual Pounds Purchased x [Actual Unit Price – Standard Unit Price]
= 80,000 x (.98 -1.00)

products are frequently manufactured from more than one type of raw material. Physical standards specify that the different materials are to be combined in a standard proportion to produce a unit of output. If the ingredients are combined in any other proportion, the cost and quantities of the finished product will change as a result. This change will be reflected in the materials quantity variance, and companies frequently find it useful to analyze this variance in terms of two additional variances, a mix variance and a yield variance.

Further analysis of the quantity variance is valuable for planning and control in industries such as chemicals and food processing. Mix and yield variances show the amount of the total variance arising from the use of a nonstandard combination of ingredients. In such processes, it may be possible to decrease the quantity of a more expensive ingredient and increase the quantity of a less expensive one and still produce a usable product. Such a substitution may produce a more favorable materials quantity variance with an associated decrease in product quality. In such industries, monitoring mix and yield variances is beneficial for purposes of quality control.

Quantity Variance for Multiple Ingredients

When the materials quantity variance is computed for a single ingredient, it was found by multiplying the standard unit cost of the ingredient by the difference between the actual quantity and the standard quantity. When multiple ingredients are required, each will have a different standard cost and the materials quantity variance is the sum of the quantity variances for each ingredient. For example, if there are n ingredients, then

$$\begin{matrix}\textit{Materials}\\\textit{Quantity}\\\textit{Variance}\end{matrix} = \sum_{i=1}^{n}\left\{\begin{matrix}\textit{Standard}\\\textit{Cost of}\\\textit{Input } i\end{matrix} \times \left(\begin{matrix}\textit{Actual}\\\textit{Quantity}\\\textit{of}\\\textit{Input } i\end{matrix} - \begin{matrix}\textit{Standard Quantity}\\\textit{of Input } i\\\textit{Allowed for}\\\textit{Output}\\\textit{Attained}\end{matrix}\right)\right\}$$

This quantity variance can arise from two sources, and the amounts from each source are called the mix variance and the yield variance.

Materials Mix Variance

A materials mix variance is created when the different ingredients are not added in the same proportion as that called for by the standard. For example, physical standards may specify that a product be composed of 40% Material A and 60% Material B. If the materials have different standard prices and the mix is changed to 30% Material A and 70% Material B, then the cost of a unit of output will be different from the standard cost. The mix variance explains that portion of the materials quantity variance which arises, as the mix changes, from the change in the cost of an average unit of input. When there are n ingredients, the mix variance may be computed as follows:

$$\text{Materials Mix Variance} = \sum_{i=1}^{n}\left\{\text{Standard Cost of Input } i \times \left(\text{Actual Quantity of Input } i - \text{Standard Quantity of Input } i \text{ for Actual Total Inputs}\right)\right\}$$

In this equation, the "standard quantity of input i for actual total inputs" is the amount of input i which would have been required if the standard mix had been used:

$$\text{Standard Quantity of Input } i \text{ for Actual Total Input} = \left(\text{Actual Total Inputs}\right) \times \left(\text{\% of Input } i \text{ in the Standard Mix}\right)$$

The mix variance is defined as favorable if the cost of the actual quantities used is less than the cost of the quantities based on the standard mix. An example demonstrating the calculations of a mix variance is contained in Illustration 10-6.

Materials Yield Variance

In some manufacturing processes a change in the mix of ingredients not only alters the average cost of the input but also changes the quantity of the units produced as well. For example in food processing, lower cost meat containing more fat than the standard can be substituted for leaner meat. But after cooking some of the fat is lost as grease, yielding a lower quantity of the final product. When physical standards are set in such situations, a standard yield is specified for the standard mix of ingredients. When the actual yield attained differs from the standard yield which is expected for the standard mix, the cost of the change in yield is described as *a yield variance.* The yield variance explains that portion of the quantity variance not attributable to the change in the average unit price of the input. If a product is composed of n materials, the materials yield variance is computed from the following relationship:

$$\text{Materials Yield Variance} = \sum_{i=1}^{n}\left\{\text{Standard Cost of Input } i \times \left(\text{Standard Quantity of Input } i \text{ for Actual Total Inputs} - \text{Standard Quantity of Input } i \text{ Allowed for Output Attained}\right)\right\}$$

Thus it measures the difference between the cost of the standard inputs of each ingredient for the output attained and the cost of the actual inputs had they been at the standard mix. The materials yield variance is favorable whenever the cost of actual inputs (at standard mix) is less than the cost of standard inputs. Illustration 10-6 demonstrates the calculation of materials mix and yield variances and the difficulties encountered when inputs are measured in different units.

Recording Materials and Labor Variances

Standard costing systems provide information for planning and control by allowing analysis of the variances between budgeted costs and those incurred during a budgetary reporting period. By analyzing the total variances, their sources can be isolated, potential problems may be disclosed, and responsibility for them can be assigned. The superiority of standard costing systems over historical ones for these purposes is achieved in part because the variances are computed as production activity occurs. The method by which this is typically done will now be described.

In addition to the major inventory accounts that are utilized in historical costing systems, standard costing systems employ four accounts for the materials and labor variances. Thus, a standard costing system will typically contain the following accounts:

1. Raw Materials Inventory,
2. Work-in-Process inventory,
3. Finished Goods Inventory,
4. Labor Rate Variance,
5. Labor Usage Variance,
6. Materials Price Variance,
7. Materials Quantity Variance.

The disposition of the balances in these accounts for income determination will be discussed in Chapter 11.

Flow of Labor Cost

As labor is expended in the manufacturing process, work is recorded on *time tickets.* On a daily or weekly basis, the Work-in-Process Inventory account is debited from the time tickets for the standard labor costs of the work performed. Any labor rate or usage variances are computed and their amounts entered in the corresponding account. An unfavorable variance results in a debit entry to the variance account; a favorable variance creates a credit entry. A typical journal entry might be:

Work-in-Process Inventory........................	XX	
Labor Rate Variance....................................	X	
Labor Usage Variance..................................	X	
Wages Payable.......................................		XXXX.

To record expenditure of labor.

As units are completed, their costs (including material, labor, and factory overhead) are transferred from Work-in-Process Inventory to Finished Goods Inventory at standard cost with the following entry:

Finished Goods Inventory	YY	
Work-in-Process Inventory		YY

To record the completion of units.

Illustration 10-6 Mix and Yield Variances Illustrative Problem

Fine Fair Products manufactured 10,080 cartons of 4 oz. chocolate eggs during the month of February. The following standards have been established (see Illustration 10-3) for one carton of 160 eggs:

	Physical Standard	*Standard Mix*	*Cost Standard*
Milk	1/4 gal. (32 oz.)	5%	$2.00/gal.
Cocoa	8 lb. (128 oz.)	19%	1.00/lb.
Sugar	32 lb. (512 oz.)	76%	.40/lb.

The month's production utilized 81,000 pounds of cocoa, 340,000 pounds of sugar, and 2,600 gallons of milk. Some weight is lost during the process as a result of evaporation. The quantity, mix, and yield variances are computed as follows:

$$\sum_{i=1}^{3}\left\{\begin{matrix}\text{Standard}\\\text{Cost of}\\\text{Input I}\end{matrix} \times \left(\begin{matrix}\text{Actual}\\\text{Quantity}\\\text{of Input}\\\text{i Used}\end{matrix} - \begin{matrix}\text{Standard}\\\text{Quantity of}\\\text{input i Allowed}\\\text{for Output Attained}\end{matrix}\right)\right\}$$

= $2.00 [2,600-(1/4)(10,080)] (milk)
+ $1.00[81,000-(8)(10,080)] (cocoa)
+ $ .40[340,000-(32)(10,080)] (sugar)
= ($5,200 - $5,040) (milk)
+ ($81,000 - $80,640) (cocoa)
+ ($136,000 - $129,024) (sugar)
= $222,200 - $214,704 (total)
= $7,496 U.

There are 128 ounces in a gallon, and 16 ounces in a pound. So measured in ounces, the actual inputs were 1,296,000 ounces of cocoa, 5,440,000 ounces of sugar, and 332,800 ounces of milk. Actual total inputs were then 7,068,800 ounces of all ingredients.

Materials Mix Variance

$$\overset{3}{\underset{i=1}{c}}\left\{\begin{matrix}\text{Standard}\\\text{Cost of}\\\text{Input i}\end{matrix} \times \left(\begin{matrix}\text{Actual}\\\text{Quantity}\\\text{of Input}\\\text{i Used}\end{matrix} - \begin{matrix}\text{Standard}\\\text{Quantity of}\\\text{Input i for}\\\text{Actual Total Inputs}\end{matrix}\right)\right\}$$

= $2.00 [2,600 - (7,068,800)(.05)/128] (milk)
+ $1.00 [81,000 - (7,068,800)(.19)/16] (cocoa)
+ $ .40 [340,000 - (7,068,800)(.76)/16] (sugar)
= $222.200 - $223.771.70 (total)

Materials Yield Variance

$$\sum_{i=1}^{3}\left\{\begin{matrix}\text{Standard}\\\text{Cost of}\\\text{Input i}\end{matrix} \times \left(\begin{matrix}\text{Standard}\\\text{Quantity of}\\\text{Input i for}\\\text{Actual Total}\\\text{Inputs}\end{matrix} - \begin{matrix}\text{Standard}\\\text{Quantity of}\\\text{Input i}\\\text{Allowed for}\\\text{Output Attained}\end{matrix}\right)\right\}$$

= $2.00 [(7,068,800)(.05)/128 - (10,080)(1/4)] (milk)
+ $1.00 [(7,068,800)(.19)/16 - (10,080)(8)] (cocoa)
+ $ .40 [(7,068,800)(.76)/16 - (10,080)(32)] (sugar)
= ($5,522.50 - $5,040) (milk)
+ ($83,942 - $80,640) (cocoa)
+ ($134,307.20 - $129,024) (sugar)
= $223,771.70 - $214,704 (total)
= $9,067.70 U.

A cost flow assumption need not be made as with a historical costing system. Finally when the units are sold, the following entry is made, again at the standard cost:

Cost of Goods Sold................................	ZZ	
Finished Goods Inventory..........		ZZ

To record the sale of units.

Such a system clearly simplifies the clerical procedures in accounting for the cost of goods manufactured. The flow of labor costs in a standard costing system is summarized in Illustration 10-7. The disposition of the balances in the variance accounts at year-end will be discussed in the next chapter. The flow of materials costs in standard costing system may differ, depending on the nature of the system. Some systems record raw materials inventory at the standard cost, while others record them at the actual invoice cost. These methods will now be compared.

Raw Materials Inventory Carried at Standard Cost

When Raw Materials Inventory is carried at the standard cost, the materials price variance is computed when the materials are received. The Raw Materials Inventory account is debited by an amount equal to the standard price per unit multiplied by the quantity received. An unfavorable price variance produces a debit entry in the Materials Price Variance account; a favorable variance results in a credit entry. A typical entry would appear as follows:

Raw Materials Inventory......................	WW	
Materials Price Variance.......................	W	
Accounts Payable.........................		WWW

To record purchase of materials.

Illustration 10-7 Flow of Labor Costs Standard Costing Systems

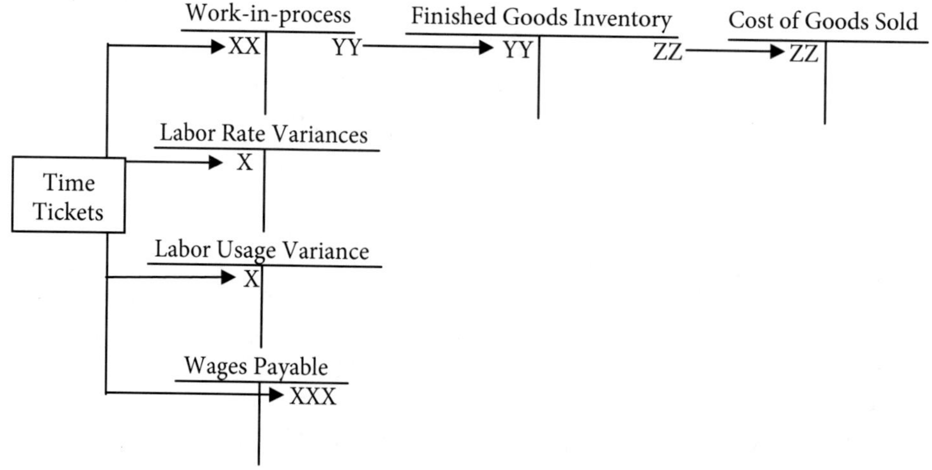

Raw materials are typically issued for production using *a material requisition,* which specifies the number of units to be manufactured. The quantity of material issued is determined from physical material standards, and the issue is recorded in the accounts at standard:

Work-in-Process Inventory................ XX
  Raw Materials Inventory............ XX

To record the issue of material.

If additional material beyond the standard is required, the worker completes an *excess material requisition.* From it an unfavorable material quantity variance is calculated and the following entry made:

Material Quantity Variance................X
  Raw Materials Inventory............ X

To record issue of excess material.

If, on the other hand, material is left over after the process is complete, the worker completes *a material return slip* and returns the material to inventory. The favorable material quantity variance is calculated and the following entry is made:

Raw Material Inventory.......................Y
  Material Quantity Variance....... YY

To record return of material.

Then as units are completed and sold, costs are transferred at standard cost as has been described. Carrying Raw Materials Inventory at standard cost is the preferable method for purposes of control. The materials price variance is computed early in the accounting process, and any potential problems evidenced by it can be corrected promptly. However, in industries where raw materials costs fluctuate markedly, management may prefer to carry Raw Materials Inventory at its actual purchase cost.

Raw Materials Inventory Carried at Actual Purchase Cost

When Raw Materials Inventory is carried at the *actual* cost, the materials price variance is computed later in the manufacturing cycle. In this case, the purchase of material is recorded at invoice cost:

Raw Materials Inventory.....................WW
  Accounts Payable........................ WW

To record purchase of material.

When materials are issued for production, the materials price variance is calculated from the standard unit materials cost and the actual quantity issued. Work-in-Process is debited at standard and Raw Materials Inventory is credited for the actual cost of material issued:

Work-in-Process Inventory................	XX	
Material Price Variance........................	XX	
Raw Materials Inventory............		XXX

To record issue of material.

If additional material is issued or if material is returned to Raw Materials Inventory, entries are required in both materials variance accounts:

Material Quantity Variance................	X	
Material Price Variance........................	X	
Raw Materials Inventory............		XX

To record issue of additional material.

Raw Materials Inventory......................	XX	
Material Quantity Variance.......		X
Material Price Variance.............		X

To record return of material to inventory.

The transfer of goods from Work-in-Process is done at standard costs.

The flow of materials cost in a standard costing system is summarized in Illustration 10-9. A comprehensive problem demonstrating these accounting entries is stated in Illustration 10-10 and its solution is presented in Illustration 10-11.

Graphical Approach to Variance Analysis

The preceding discussion has described methods of analyzing standard cost variances using equations. Computationally these are frequently convenient to use. However, many cost accountants prefer a graphical approach to variance analysis. The graphical approach clearly illustrates how, in any specific situation, the variances explain the difference between actual costs incurred and those allowed by the standards. A general description of the graphical approach is presented in Illustration 10-12. It is applied to the example problem in Illustration 10-13.

Disadvantages of Standard Costing

We have discussed so far in this chapter how traditional standard cost systems can be used to help managers plan and control the cost of operations. While a standard cost system has several advantages (analyzing cost variances, practicing management by exception, facilitating product costing, and evaluating performance), it has its disadvantages and weaknesses. Typical criticisms of standard costing in modern competitive manufacturing environment are:

1. Standard cost systems assume and rely on a stable production technology and competitive environment. They provide management a stable target product cost for the currently existing technology and manufacturing environment. But, necessary and frequent adjustments for products in a highly competitive business environment may reduce the usefulness of this stable standard cost.
2. Cost variances are calculated periodically and thus may arrive too late to be useful.
3. The focus of cost variances in standard cost systems may emphasize too much on cost management and cost minimization and not enough on leading successful factors such as product quality, customer satisfaction, internal process efficiency, and organizational learning and growth.

As a result, modern manufacturing firms have been making changes in their use of standard costing systems by frequent and timely reviews of cost standards and redesign operational activity, strategy, and control systems. Modern activity-based costing (ABC) and balanced scorecard (BSC) control systems are discussed in other chapters in this book. Below let's discuss two specific techniques to manage (1) the current production costs in the manufacturing process and (2) the costs of new products to improve competitiveness.

Kaizen Costing

"Kaizen" means continuous improvement and "Kaizen Costing" means continuous improvement in cost reduction. Modern business conditions require that firms produce and deliver the products customers want in quality, on-time delivery, and at the lowest possible cost. This means that, in order to compete successfully, a modern firm must continually strive for incremental improvements of existing products and processes.

Therefore, the focus of Kaizen costing is continuous process improvement and cost reduction. Activity analysis is a critical element of Kaizen costing for process improvement and cost reduction. It can be used to accomplish process improvement and cost reduction in a number of ways. For example, non-value-added activities in a process may be first identified to improve their efficiencies and eventually to eliminate the unnecessary activities. Necessary value-added activities may also be further improved for their efficiencies by reducing the time and resources required by the activities.

A systematic approach to provide continuous improvement is the Plan-Do-Check-Act (PDCA) cycle. The basic elements of the PDCA cycle are summarized in Illustration 10-8. At the "Plan" phase, the amount of an attainable improvement in cost reduction is planned for the coming period. This represents the Kaizen cost reduction standard. In the "Do" phase, actions are taken to implement the planned cost reduction. In the "Check" phase, the actual results are collected and compared with the kaizen cost reduction standard to provide a measure of the improvement attained. Finally, at the "Act" phase, search for additional improvement opportunities and set a new Kaizen standard for the next period's performance. In summary, Kaizen costing is concerned with continuous improvement in reducing the costs of existing products and processes by developing improvement standards based on prior improvements. Thus, Kaizen cost reduction is accomplished through a repetitive use of the PDCA cycle.

Target Costing

Although cost-based pricing is often used to determine the price for a product that has already been developed and ready for production and distribution. But, for a highly competitive

Illustration 10-8 Kaizen Cost Reduction Cycle

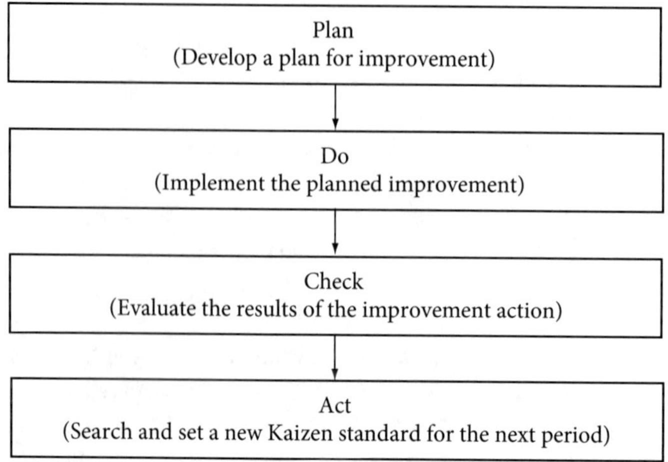

business environment, many firms may have less control on price than they would like to have. In such a market condition, the supply and demand actually determine the price and management needs to consider the anticipated price and develop a product that can be produced and sold profitably at the price. This is called target costing which is also referred to as the price-driven costing method. Thus, target costing is a method of determining the allowable manufacturing cost of a new product based on the anticipated price that buyers are willing to pay. Target costing has significant implications for new product development and production cost control and reduction. Let's discuss below why and how firms use target costing.

The target costing approach addresses two important management concerns of competitive market and production cost control and reduction. In a competitive market environment, the anticipated market price should be considered in determining whether and how a new product should be developed and produced. Target costing is a method of determining the maximum cost allowed for a new product. Since a firm must recover the costs and make a profit from a new product. The target cost is determined first from the anticipated price and then used to design the product so that the target cost can be attained. This is different from the cost-based pricing approach where the product is developed first and costs are calculated to determine the price by adding the desired profit.

The target cost for a product is computed by deducting the desired profit from the anticipated selling price given in the market. That is,

$$\text{Target Cost} = \text{Anticipated Selling Price} - \text{Desired Profit}$$

The target cost is then used to develop the new product so that it can be produced for no more than the target cost. If the product cannot be produced within the target cost, the design of the product will be modified or scratched.

To provide an example of target costing, let's assume that a company is considering to enter the rapidly growing market for golf drivers. After a marketing study on the features and prices of current drivers on the market, management believes that a price of $400 would be needed to capture a desired market share. If the company's desired profit is $100 per unit, the target cost to produce and sell each driver is computed as follows:

Target Cost = \$400 – \$100 = \$300

This target cost can be further broken down into target cost for manufacturing, marketing, distribution, and service. With the target manufacturing cost, the product development team is responsible for designing the product within the allowable cost.

Illustration 10-9 Flow of Material Costs Standard Costing Systems

Raw Materials Inventory Carried at Standard Cost:

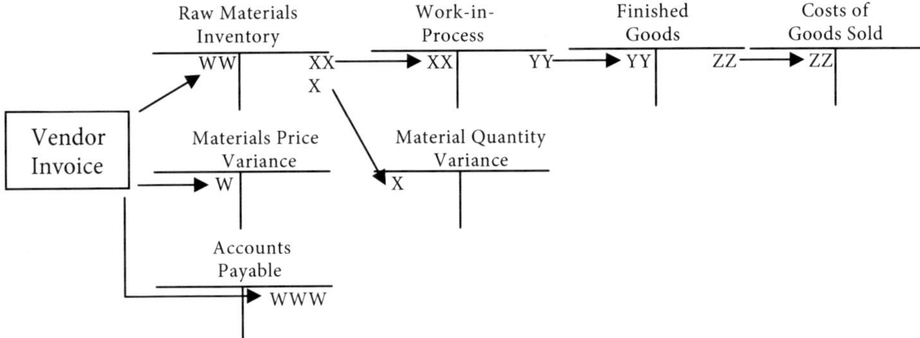

Raw Materials Inventory Carried at Actual Cost:

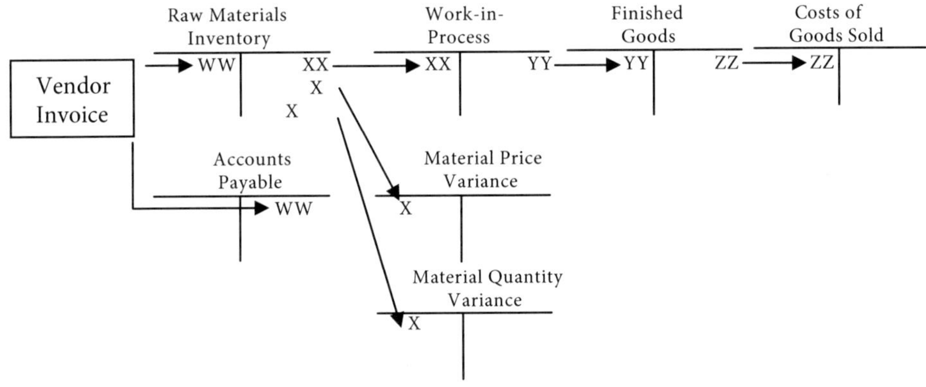

Illustration 10-10 Comprehensive Problem

Mini Machine Shop uses standard costs in its job order costing system. During April, Job No. 215 was filled for 200 units of Product A. This product is machined entirely from 1 inch steel bars. Job No. 215 required 420 hours of labor at an hourly rate of \$4.75. A total of 2,200 pounds of steel was purchased for the job at a cost of \$.45 per pound. Of this amount, 2,060 pounds were used. The standards for one unit of Product A are:

Material, 10 pounds @ \$.50	\$ 5.00
Labor, 2 hours @ \$5.00	10.00

Show journal entries for Job No. 215 reflecting:

1. Recording labor costs;
2. Recording purchase and issue of material if Raw Materials Inventory is carried at actual costs;
3. Recording purchase and issue of material if Raw Materials Inventory is carried at standard cost.

Illustration 10-11 Solution to Comprehensive Problem

The variances are computed as follows:

Labor rate variance = 420 hours ($4.75-$5.00)
=$105F.

Labor usage variance = $5.00 [420 hours-(200 units)(2 firs./unit)]
=$100U.

Materials quantity variance = $.50 [2,060 lbs.-(200 units)(10lbs./unit)]
=$30U.

If Raw Materials Inventory is carried at actual cost,
Materials price variance = 2,060 lbs. ($.45-$.50)
= $103 F.

If Raw Materials Inventory is carried at standard cost,
Materials price variance = 2,200 lbs. ($.45-$.50)
= $110 F.

Entry recording labor expenditure:

	Debit	Credit
Work-in-Process	(200x2x5) 2,000	
Labor Usage Variance	100	
Labor Rate Variance		105
Wages Payable		(420x4.75) 1,995

To record labor for Job No. 215. 2.

If Raw Materials Inventory is carried at actual cost:

	Debit	Credit
Raw Materials Inventory	(2,200 x .45) 990	
Accounts Payable		(2,200 x .45) 990

To record purchase of material Job No. 215.

	Debit	Credit
Work-in-Process	(200X10X.50) 1,000	
Materials Quantity Variance	30	
Materials Price Variance		103
Raw Materials Inventory		(2,060 x .45) 927

To record issue of material, Job No. 215.

If Raw Materials Inventory is carried at standard cost:

	Debit	Credit
Raw Materials Inventory	(2,200 x .50) 1,100	
Accounts Payable		(2,200 x .45) 990
Material Price Variance		110

To record purchase of material Job No. 215.

	Debit	Credit
Work-in-Process	(200 x 10 x.50) 1,000	
Materials Quantity Variance	30	
Raw Materials Inventory		(2,060 x .50) 1,030

To record issue of material Job No. 215.

Illustration 10-12 Graphical Approach to Variance Analysis

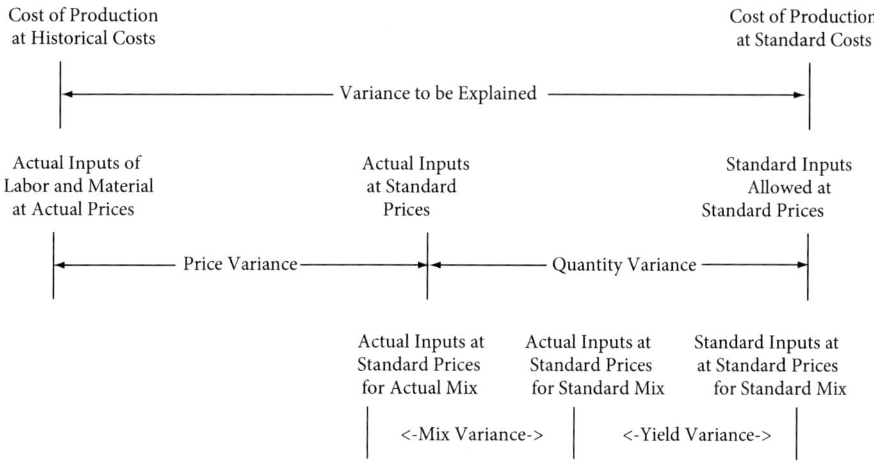

Illustration 10-13 Graphical Approach to Mini Machine Example

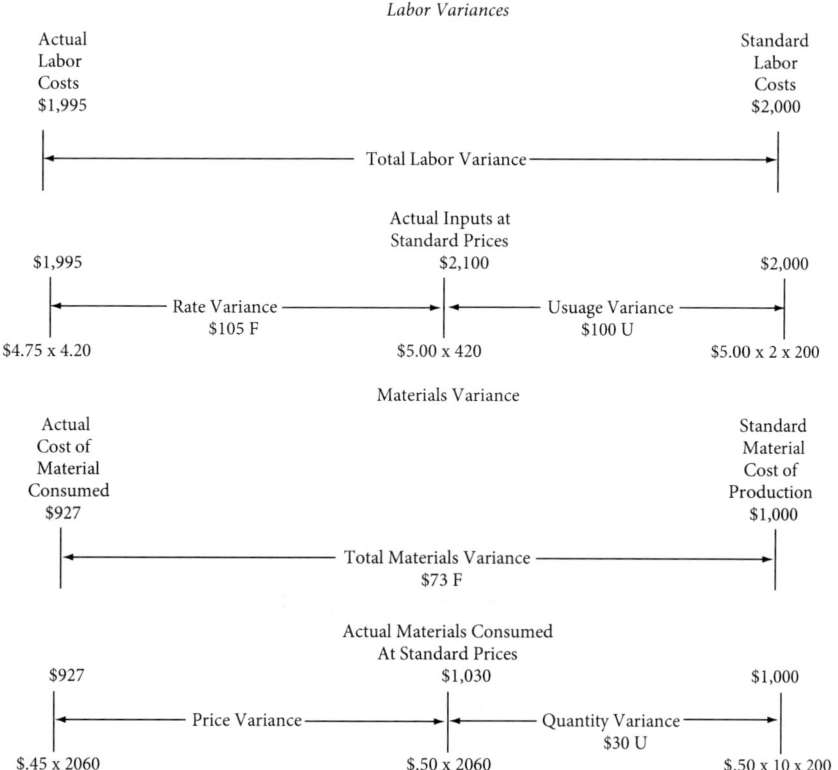

Summary

This chapter has described standard costing systems, a method of cost accounting which provides information for the objectives of product costing, planning, and control. Such systems rely on the development of physical standards for products manufactured to which carefully predetermined costs are applied. Standard costs aid in management control by allowing the analysis of variances, which are the differences between actual costs and those budgeted for a reporting period. An approach to variance analysis has been described, and has been illustrated graphically. This approach aids management in explaining the source of the variance, pinpointing potential problem areas, and assigning responsibility for the variance. The flow of materials and labor costs in a standard costing system has been described. The chapter also discussed two specific cost management techniques to manage (1) the current production costs in the manufacturing process and (2) the costs of new products to improve competitiveness. Kaizen costing provides continuous process improvement and current cost reduction. Target costing is a method of determining the allowable manufacturing cost of a new product based on the anticipated price that buyers are willing to pay. It has significant implications for new product development and production cost control and reduction.

Key Definitions

Currently attainable standard	Physical and cost standards which reflect expected efficient operating conditions. Historical cost Actual costs which are computed after they have been incurred.
Mix variance	A component of the quantity variance, which arises from the change in the cost of an average unit of input as the mix of the ingredients changes.
Physical standard	The quantities of materials and labor which management feels should be used to produce one unit of output.
Price variance	A component of the cost variance, which is due to the actual price of an input differing from the standard price.
Quantity variance	A component of the cost variance, which is due to the quantity of an input used differing from that specified in the physical standard.
Standard cost	A predetermined cost for a unit of product, determined from its physical standards.
Standard inputs allowed	The quantity of labor or materials which, according to physical standards, should be used to produce the number of outputs actually attained.

Variance The difference between actual costs incurred and the costs budgeted for the actual output attained.

Yield variance A component of the quantity variance, which arises when the actual quantity of output differs from that called for by the standard due to a change in a mix of ingredients.

Questions

10-1 What are the advantages of standard costs over historical costs for planning and control?

10-2 Distinguish between three approaches to setting standards. Which approach is preferable for control?

10-3 Describe the role of the cost accountant in the process of setting material and labor standards.

10-4 How do standard costs aid in assigning responsibility for variances disclosed in a responsibility accounting system?

10-5 What is meant by "standard hours allowed?" How is it used?

10-6 Who in an organization may be held responsible for a labor rate variance? A materials price variance?

10-7 Who in an organization may be held responsible for a labor usage variance? A materials quantity variance?

10-8 What is the significance of mix and yield variances for purposes of control?

10-9 Why is a cost flow assumption for work-in-process inventories (weighted average or FIFO) not required in a standard costing system?

10-10 What are two ways of recording raw materials inventory costs in a standard costing system? Which method is preferable for purposes of control? Why?

10-11 Excessive direct labor wages resulting from overtime premiums will be disclosed in what type of variance?

(*AICPA adapted*)

10-12 What is the significance of a debit balance in a labor efficiency variance account?

(*AICPA adapted*)

Problems

10-13 *Labor Variances*

Information on Westcott Company's direct labor costs is as follows:

Standard direct labor rate..$3.75
Actual direct labor rate $3.50
Standard direct labor hours...10,000
Actual direct labor hours...11,120.

Compute:

(a) Labor usage variance
(b) Labor rate variance.

(*AICPA adapted*)

10-14 *Materials Variances*

Matt Company uses a standard cost system. Information for raw materials for Product RBI for the month of October is as follows:

Standard unit price...$1.60
Actual purchase price per unit..$1.55
Actual quantity *purchased* ....2,000 units
Actual quantity used...1,900 units
Standard quantity allowed for actual production..................1,800 units

Calculate the following:

(a) Material quantity variance,
(b) Material price variance, assuming raw materials inventories are carried at standard cost,
(c) Material price variance, assuming raw materials inventories are carried at actual cost.

10-15 *Materials Variances*

Home Company manufactures tables with vinyl tops. The standard material cost for the vinyl user per Type-R table is $7.80 based on six square feet of vinyl at a cost of $1.30 per square foot. A production run of 1,000 tables in January 20XX resulted in usage of 6,400 square feet of vinyl at a cost of $1.20 per square foot, a total cost of $7,680. Raw materials are carried at actual cost.

Compute:

(a) Materials quantity variance,
(b) Materials price variance.

(*AICPA adapted*)

10-16 *Labor Variances*

Lion Company's direct labor costs for the month of January 20XX were as follows:

Actual direct labor hours	20,000
Standard hours allowed	21,000
Labor rate variance, unfavorable	$ 3,000
Total payroll	$126,000

Compute the labor usage (efficiency) variance.

(*AICPA adapted*)

10-17 *Material Variances*

Information on Kennedy Company's direct material costs is as follows:

Standard unit price	$3.60
Actual quantity purchased	1,600
Standard quantity allowed for actual production	1,450
Materials price variance, favorable	$240

Compute the actual purchase price per unit.

10-18 *Labor Variances*

Lab Corp. uses a standard cost system. Direct labor information for Product CER for the month of October is as follows:

Standard rate	$6.00 per hour
Actual rate paid	$6.10 per hour
Standard hours allowed for actual production	1,500
Labor usage variance, unfavorable	$600

Compute the labor rate variance.

(*AICPA adapted*)

10-19 *Labor Variances*

Data on Goodman Company's direct labor costs is given below:

Standard hours allowed	30,000
Actual direct labor hours	29,000
Labor usage variance, favorable	$ 4,000
Labor rate variance, favorable	$ 5,800
Total payroll	$110,200

Calculate the:

(a) Standard direct labor rate.

(b) Actual direct labor rate.

(*AICPA adapted*)

10-20 *Materials Variances with Multiple Ingredients*

Miraclean Corp. produces a chemical cleaner which is sold in one-gallon containers. It is manufactured from two ingredients, Material X and Material Y. The materials standards for one gallon of Miraclean are as follows:

Material X—3/4 gal. @ $2.00/gal	$1.50
Material Y—1/4 gal. @ $6.00/ gal	1.50
	$3.00

During November 60,000 gallons of Miraclean were produced, requiring 46,000 gallons of Material X and 17,000 gallons of Material Y. The Material X cost $2.10 per gallon, and the Material Y was purchased for $6.40 per gallon.

Compute:

(a) Total material price variance.
(b) Total material quantity variance.

10-21 *Working Backward from Variances*

On May 1, 20XX, Bovar Company began the manufacture of a new mechanical device known as "Dandy." The company installed a standard cost system in accounting for manufacturing costs. The standard costs for a unit of "Dandy" are as follows:

Raw materials	6 lbs. @ $1 per lb.	$ 6.00
Direct labor	1 hour @ $4 per hour	4.00
Overhead	75% of direct labor costs	3.00
		$13.00

The following data were obtained from Bovar's records for the month of May:

	Units
Actual production of "Dandy	4,000
Units sold of "Dandy"	2,500

	Debit	Credit
Sales		$50,000
Purchases (26,000 pounds)	$27,300	
Material price variance	1,300	
Material quantity variance	1,000	
Direct labor rate variance	760	
Direct labor efficiency variance		800

The amount shown above for material price variance is applicable to raw material purchased during May.

Compute each of the following items for Bovar for the month of May. Show computations in good form.

(a) Standard quantity of raw materials allowed (in pounds).
(b) Actual quantity of raw materials used (in pounds).
(c) Standard hours allowed.
(d) Actual hours worked.
(e) Actual direct labor rate.

10-22 *Mix Variance*

Sure-Gro Company is a manufacturer of fertilizer which is sold in 40 lb. bags. Its major product, Sure-Gro I, is composed of three active chemicals and an inert filler (which has no nutritive value) in the following proportions:

Chemical 1: 8%
Chemical 2: 8%
Chemical 3: 8%
Inert filler: 76%.

The standard prices paid for these ingredients are: Chemical 1:$1.00 per lb.; Chemical 2: $.50 per lb.; Chemical 3: $.40 per lb., and filler: $.05 per lb. During August, 10,000 bags of Sure-Gro I were produced. The following quantities of each ingredient were used:

Chemical 1: 28,000 lbs.
Chemical 2: 32,000 lbs.
Chemical 3: 36,000 lbs.
Inert filler: 304,000 lbs.

Determine the materials mix variance

10-23 *Yield Variance*

Wurstenheimer Company is a small manufacturer of specialty meat products which utilizes a standard cost system. The following standards have been developed for one pound of smoked German sausage.

Pork (.9 lb. @ $2.00)	$ 1.800
Cereal (.15 lb. @ $.50)	.075
Spices (.15 lb. @ $6.00)	.900
	$2.775

The ingredients are blended, cooked, and smoked, utilizing a traditional family process before being packaged. During June, little Johnny Wurstenheimer was home from college and supervised the process while his parents were on vacation. During the month 1,000 pounds of German sausage were produced using the following ingredients:

Pork	1,200 lbs.
Cereal	200 lbs.
Spices	200 lbs.
Total	1,600 lbs.

Upon returning from vacation, Johnny's parents concluded that the sausage, although very tasty, had been overcooked. Johnny, an accounting student, was asked to determine the effect on net income of his mistake. You can help Johnny in his predicament by computing:

(a) the standard mix of ingredients,
(b) the standard quantity of each ingredient allowed for the output attained, and
(c) the materials yield variance for Wurstenheimer Company for June.

10-24 *Analyzing the Materials Quantity Variance*

Alternative Energies, Inc., a subsidiary of a large oil company, manufactures and distributes gasohol. Gasoline is purchased from the parent company at a cost $1.00 per gallon and blended with pure alcohol, which is purchased on the open market. The standard mix is 80% gasoline and 20% alcohol, and some of the resulting mixture is normally lost due to evaporation. The standard price paid for alcohol is $1.25 per gallon.

During the month of March, 75,000 gallons of gasohol were produced. The process utilized 59,000 gallons of gasoline and 17,000 gallons of alcohol. Determine the materials quantity variance. What information can you provide to Alternative's management to explain its source?

10-25 *Approaches to Setting Standards*

The Alton Company is going to expand its punch press department. It is about to purchase three new punch presses from Equipment Manufacturers, Inc. Equipment Manufacturers' engineers report that their mechanical studies indicate that for Alton's intended use, the output rate for one press should be 1,000 pieces per hour. Alton has very similar presses now in operation. At the present time, production from these presses averages 600 pieces per hour.

A study of the Alton experience shows the average is derived from the following individual outputs.

Worker	*Daily Output*
L. Jones	750
J. Green	750
R. Smith	600
H. Brown	500
R. Alters	550
G. Hoag	450
Total	3,600
Average	600

Alton management also plans to institute a standard cost accounting system in the very near future. The company engineers are supporting a standard based upon 1,000 pieces per hour, the accounting department is arguing for 750 pieces per hour and the department foreman is arguing for 600 pieces per hour.

(a) What arguments would each proponent be likely to use to support his case?
(b) Which alternative best reconciles the needs of cost control and the motivation of improved performance? Explain why you made that choice.

10-26 *Cost Standards and Budgeting*

The Molding Department of the Western Corp. produces molded brass belt buckles for later use in assembling leather belts. The buckles are produced in two sizes, small and large.

	Small	*Large*
Material (brass)	4 oz.	8 oz.
Labor	6 min.	6 min.

Brass is purchased under a long-term contract at $.64 per pound. Current labor contracts call for wages of $10.00 per hour in the molding operation. Factory overhead is fixed at $8,000 per month and is considered uncontrollable at the departmental level.

(a) Compute the standard prime costs of

(1) a small buckle,

(2) a large buckle.

(b) Develop a budget for the Molding Department for the month of July assuming expected production is 12,000 small buckles and 8,000 large ones.

(c) Sales forecasts have been inaccurate during past months, often by as much as 25%. Develop a budget which projects costs for the month at

(1) 25% below the expected production level,

(2) 25% above the expected production level.

10-27 *Flow of Standard Costs*

Tolbert Manufacturing Company uses a standard cost system in accounting for the cost of production of its only product, Product A. The standards for the production of one unit of Product A are as follows:

Direct materials: i0 feet of item 1 at $.75 per foot and 3 feet of item 2 at $1.00 per foot.
Direct labor: 4 hours at $3.50 per hour.

There was no inventory on hand at July 1, 20X0. Following is a summary of costs and related data for the production of Product A during the year ended June 30, 20X1.

100,000 feet of item 1 were purchased at $.78 per foot.
30,000 feet of item 2 were purchased at $.90 per foot.
8,000 units of Product A were produced which required 78,000 feet of item 1, 26,000 feet of item *2* and 31,000 hours of direct labor at $3.60 per hour.
6,000 units of Product A were sold.

At June 30, 20X1, there are 22,000 feet of item 1, 4,000 feet of item 2, and 2,000 completed units of Product A on hand. All purchases and transfers are "charged in" at standard. The beginning balances in all variance accounts is zero.

(a) From the above data, show entries recording the following:

(1) Purchase of raw material,
(2) Issue of raw material for production,
(3) Direct labor costs.

(b) Compute the ending balance in the following accounts:
(1) Raw materials inventory,
(2) Materials quantity variance,
(3) Materials price variance.

(*AICPA adapted*)

10-28 *Interpreting Mix and Yield Variances*

Hideaway Distillery manufactures a pleasant-tasting beverage known in its local vicinity as Georgia Mountain Nectar. Because its production facilities must be moved from time to time, its productive capacity is of necessity limited. The following standards have been established for one batch (100 quarts) of GMN:

Chopped corn (19 lbs. @ $.30)..............	$ 5.70
Sugar (80 lbs. @ $.80..............................	64.00
Yeast (1 lb. @ $3.00	3.00
Water (40 gals..	0
	$72.70

Plant locations are normally chosen so that water is readily obtainable free of charge. The ingredients are mixed and allowed to develop for 3–4 days. The resulting mixture is then processed using Hideaway's custom-built distilling equipment. After an aging period of approximately one week, GMN is sold through the usual distribution channels in one-quart jars.

Although normally known for the quality of its product, Hideaway has recently been receiving complaints from customers about the mellowness of GMN. To investigate the complaint, management recorded the following data for the month of August (which is a peak sales period).

quantity of production: 1,600 quarts.
requiring 335 lbs. of corn, at $.32 per lb.
1,050 lbs. of sugar, at $1.05 per lb.
15 lbs. of yeast, at $2.80 per lb.,
640 gallons of water, no cost.

(a) You are to aid management in finding the source of its quality problem by computing:
 (1) materials price variance
 (2) materials quantity variance
 (3) materials mix variance
 (4) materials yield variance

(b) What can you suggest as a source of the decrease in quality of Georgia Mountain Nectar?

10-29 *Standards and Job Order Costing*

Finley Foundry Corp. manufactures iron castings to order for other manufacturing companies. A standard costing system is used in which raw materials inventories are carried at actual costs. The following standards have been established for one part, the $3_{1/2}$" bushing.

Materials, 3 lb. @ $.50............................	$1.50
Labor, 1/3 hr. $6.00..................................	2.00
Standard prime unit cost	$3.50

During a recent month Job. No. 120 was completed which consisted of 600 such bushings. A total of 1,950 pounds of iron were used, which had been purchased at a cost of $.48 per pound. Job. No. 120 required 4 workers a total of 55 hours each to complete. They were each paid $6.10 per hour. Factory overhead is allocated to products at a rate of 150% of *actual* direct labor cost.

Show the following:
(a) The actual (historical) unit cost for Job No. 120,
(b) All materials and labor variances for Job No. 120,
(c) Entries recording:
- (1) issue of material,
- (2) direct labor,
- (3) application of overhead,
- (4) transfer of Job No. 120 to finished goods inventory.

10-30 *Standards and Process Costing*

Wearight Shoe Corp. utilizes a standard process cost system in the manufacture of heavy duty work shoes. The production process is carried out in two processes. In the cutting department, leather is cut into pieces and transferred into the assembly department. There the pieces are glued, sewed, and tacked together and transferred to finished goods. The standard cost of the pieces for a pair of shoes are $8.00 when transferred from cutting. All materials added in assembly are indirect and considered part of factory overhead. In assembly, the standard labor for a pair of shoes is ‘/4 hour at a standard labor rate of $16.00 per hour.
The following has been recorded in the assembly department for April:

Pairs completed:	3,100.
Labor:	880 hours, $13,860 actual costs.
Beginning inventory:	80 pairs, .5 complete.
Ending inventory:	125 pairs, .8 complete.
Factory overhead applied:	$12,640, of which $12,240 is applicable to units completed and $400 is applicable to ending work-in-process inventory.

From the above data, determine:
(a) Cost of units transferred from the cutting department,
(b) Cost of units completed in the assembly department,
(c) Labor variances in the assembly department,
(d) Entries recording for the assembly department,
(1) transfer-in of units in process,
(2) direct labor,
(3) application of factory overhead,
(4) transfer-out of finished units.
(e) Cost of ending work-in-process inventory in the assembly department.

10-31 *Usefulness of the Yield Variance*

Steel Slitting Company divides 24” widths of rolled sheet steel into 2” and 4” widths. The 24” widths are delivered to Steel Slitting Company by its customers and the new widths are picked up by the customers after slitting. The cut widths plus scrap loss (caused by starting and ending rolls of steel or jams on the slitters) cannot cost the customers more than acquiring the correct widths direct from steel mills. Therefore, Steel Slitting Company uses tight standard costs to stay competitive.

If bought directly from steel mills, steel would cost customers the following:

Size	*Gauge*	*Cost per Ton*
24"	14	$125
24"	12	120
2"	14	136
2"	12	130
4"	12	130

Steel Slitting Company price for slitting a ton of input steel from customers is:

Size	*Gauge*	*Customer Price per Ton, Slit*
2"	14	$8.00
2"	12	7.00
4"	12	6.00

Standard and actual slitting costs per input ton for October are as follows:

	Standard Cost per Ton-2"	*Actual Cost per Ton-2"*	*Standard Cost per Ton-4"*	*Actual Cost per Ton 4"*
Direct labor....................	$3.00	$3.10	$2.50	$2.60
Variable overhead.........	2.80	3.00	2.00	2.10
Nonvariable overhead..	1.00	1.00	1.00	1.00
	$6.80	$7.10	$5.50	$5.70
Customer scrap loss-percent of input tons (absorbed by customer)	1%	2%	1%	3%

Standard cost per ton is based on width of strips regardless of gauge.

Budgeted and actual sales for the month of October are as follows:

Size	*Gauge*	*Budgeted*	*Actual*
2"	14	500 input tons	300 input tons
2"	12	400 input tons	400 input tons
4"	12	100 input tons	300 input tons

(a) Steel Slitting Company does not own the material, nor absorb any yield loss. Can a materials yield variance be calculated? If so, how would you calculate it? Would it be useful to Steel Slitting management? Explain.

(b) Could the company's customers have done better if they had purchased steel strips directly from steel mills? Explain your answer with appropriate numbers.

(IMA adapted)

10-32 *Variances with Multiple Raw Materials*

The Bayou Manufacturing Corporation produces only one product, Bevo, and accounts for the production of Bevo using a standard cost system.

Following are the standards for the production of one unit of Bevo: 3 units of item A @ $1.00 per unit; 1 unit of item B @ $.50 per unit; 4 units of item C @ $.30 per unit; and 20 minutes of direct labor @ $4.50 per hour. Separate variance accounts are maintained for each type of raw material and for direct labor. Raw material purchases are recorded initially at standard. Manufacturing overhead is applied at $9.00 per actual direct labor hour and is not related to the standard cost system. There was no over applied or under applied manufacturing overhead at December 31, 20X0.

The various inventories at December 31, 20X0, were priced as follows:

	Raw Material		
	Number of	Unit	
Item	Units	Cost	Amount
A	15,000	$1.10	$16,500
B	4,000	.52	2,080
C	20,000	.32	6,400
			$24,980

Work-in-Process

9,000 units of Bevo which were 100% complete as to items A and B, 50% complete as to item C, and 30% complete as to labor. The composition and valuation of the inventory follows:

Item	Amount
A	$28,600
B	4,940
C	6,240
Direct labor	6,175
	45,955
Overhead	11,700
	$57,655

Finished Goods

4,800 units of Bevo composed and valued as follows:

Item	Amount
A	$15,180
B	2,704
C	6,368
Direct labor	8,540
	32,792
Overhead	16,200
	$48,992

Following is a schedule of raw materials purchased and direct labor incurred for the year ended December 31, 20X1. Unit cost of each item of raw material and direct labor cost per hour remained constant throughout the year.

	Purchases		
Item	Number of Units or Hours	Unit Cost	Amount
A	290,000	$1.15	$333,500
B	101,000	.55	55,550
C	367,000	.35	128,450
Direct labor	34,100	4.60	156,860

During the year ended December 31, 20X1. Bayou sold 90,000 units of Bevo and had ending physical inventories as follows:

Raw Materials

Item	Number of Units
A	28,300
B	2,100
C	28,900

<u>Work-in-Process</u>

7,500 units of Bevo which were 100% complete as to items A and B. 50% complete as to item C, and 20% complete as to labor as follows:

<u>Item</u>	Number of Units or Hours
A	22,900
B	8,300
C	15,800
Direct labor	800

Finished Goods
5,100 units of Bevo, as follows:

Item	Number of <u>Units or Hours</u>
A	15,600
B	6,300
C	21,700
Direct labor	2,050

There was no overapplied or underapplied manufacturing overhead at December 31, 20X1.

Required:

Answer each of the following questions. Supporting computations should be prepared in good form.

(a) What was the total debit or credit to the three material price variance accounts for items A, B, and C for the year ended December 31, 20X1?
(b) What was the total debit or credit to the three material quantity variance accounts for items A, B, and C for the year ended December 31, 20X1?
(c) What was the total debit or credit to the direct labor rate variance account for the year ended December 31, 20X1?
(d) What was the total debit or credit to the direct labor efficiency variance account for the year ended December 31, 20X1?

(*AICPA adapted*)

10-33 *Mix and Yield Variances*

Energy Products Company produces a gasoline additive, *Gas Gain*. This product increases engine efficiency and improves gasoline mileage by creating a more complete burn in the combustion process.

Careful controls are required during the production process to ensure that the proper mix of input chemicals is achieved and that evaporation is controlled. If the controls are not effective, there can be loss of output and efficiency.

The standard cost of producing a 500-liter batch of *Gas Gain is* $135. The standard materials mix and related standard cost of each chemical used in a 500-liter batch are as follows:

Chemical	Standard Input Quantity in Liters	Standard Cost per Liter	Total Cost
Echol	200	$.200	$ 40.00
Protex	100	.425	42.50
Benz	250	.150	37.50
CT-40	50	.300	15.00
	600		$135.00

The quantities of chemicals purchased and used during the current production period are shown in the schedule below. A total of 140 batches of *Gas Gain* were manufactured during the current production period. Energy Products determines its cost and chemical usage variations at the end of each production period.

Chemical	Quantity Purchased	Total Purchase Price	Quantity Used
Echol	25,000 liters	$ 5,365	26,600 liters
Protex	13,000 liters	6,240	12,880 liters
Benz	40,000 liters	5,840	37,800 liters
CT-40	7,500 liters	2,220	7,140 liters
total	85,500 liters	$19,665	84,420 liters

Required:

(a) Calculate the purchase price variances by chemical for Energy Products Company.

(b) Calculate the total material quantity variance related to *Gas Gain* for Energy Products Company and then analyze this total usage variance into the following two components:
(1) Total mix variance.
(2) Total yield variance.

(*IMA adapted*)

10-34 *Analyzing Materials Variances*

Maidwell Company manufactures washers and dryers on a single assembly line in its main factory. The market has deteriorated over the last five years and competition has made cost control very important. Management has been concerned about the materials cost of both washers and dryers. There have been no model changes in the past two years and economic conditions have allowed the company to negotiate price reductions in many key parts.

Maidwell uses a standard cost system in accounting for materials. Purchases are charged to inventory at a standard price with purchase discounts considered an administrative cost reduction. Production is charged at the standard price of the materials used.

Thus, the price variance is isolated at time of purchase as the difference between gross contract price and standard price multiplied by the quantity purchased. When a substitute part is used in production rather than the regular part, a price variance equal to the difference in the standard prices of the materials is recognized at the time of substitution in the production process. The quantity variance is the actual quantity used compared to the standard quantity allowed with the difference multiplied by the standard price.

The materials variances for several of the parts Maidwell uses are unfavorable. Part No. 4121 is one of the items that has an unfavorable variance. Maidwell knows that some of these parts will be defective and fail. The failure is discovered during production. The normal defective rate is 5% of normal input. The original contract price of this part was $.285 per unit; thus, Maidwell set the standard unit price at $.285. The unit contract purchase price of Part No. 4121 was increased $.04 to $.325 from the original $.285 due to a parts specification change. Maidwell chose not to change the standard, but treat the increase in price as a price variance. In addition, the contract terms were changed from n/30 to 4/10, n/30 as a consequence of negotiations resulting from changes in the economy.

Data regarding the usage of Part No. 4121 during December is as follows:

• Purchases of Part No. 4121.	150,000 units
• Unit price paid for purchases of Part No. 4121.	$.325
• Requisitions of Part No. 4121 from stores for use in products.	134,000 units
• Substitution of Part No. 5125 for Part No. 4121 to use obsolete stock (standard unit price of Part No. 5125 is $.35).	24,000 units
• Units of Part No. 4121 and its substitute (Part No. 5125) identified as being defective.	9,665 units

- Standard allowed usage (including normal defective units) of Part No. 4121 and its substitute based upon output for the month. 153,300 units

Maidwell's material variances related to Part No. 4121 for December were reported as follows:

Price variance	$7,560.00 U
Quantity variance	1,339.50 U
Total material variances for Part No. 4121	$8,899.50 U

Bob Speck, the purchasing director, claims the unfavorable price variance is misleading. Speck says that his department has worked hard to obtain price concessions and purchase discounts from suppliers. In addition, Speck has indicated that engineering changes have been made in several parts increasing their price even though the part identification has not changed. These price increases are not his department's responsibility. Speck declares that the price variance simply no longer measures the purchasing department's performance.

Jim Buddle, the manufacturing manager, thinks that responsibility for the quantity variance should be shared. Buddle states that manufacturing cannot control quality arising from less expensive parts, substitutions of material to use up otherwise obsolete stock, or engineering changes that increased the quantity of materials used.

The accounting manager, Mike Kohl, has suggested that the computation of variances be changed to identify variations from standard with the causes and functional areas responsible for the variances. The following system of materials variances and the method of computation for each was recommended by Kohl.

Variance	Method of Calculation
Economics Variance	Quantity purchased times the changes made after setting standards that were the result of negotiations based on changes in the general economy.
Engineering Change Variance	Quantity purchased times change in price due to part specifications changes.
Purchase price Variance	Quantity purchased times change in contract price due to changes other than parts specifications or the general economy.
Substitutions Variance	Quantity substituted times the difference in standard price between parts substituted.
Excess usage Variance	Standard price times the difference between the standard quantity allowed for production minus actual parts used (reduced for abnormal scrap).

Abnormal failure Rate Variance	Abnormal scrap times standard price.

Required:

(a) Discuss the appropriateness of Maidwell Company's current method of variance analysis for materials and indicate whether the claims of Bob Speck and Jim Buddle are valid.

(b) Compute the materials variances for Part No. 4121 for December using the system recommended by Mike Kohl.

(c) Indicate who would be responsible for each of the variances in Mike Kohl's system of variance analysis for materials.

(*IMA adapted*)

1. *To distinguish between a flexible budget and a static budget.*
2. *To describe how flexible budgets are developed.*
3. *To discuss the use of flexible budgets for purposes of planning and control.*
4. *To describe the commonly used methods of analyzing factory overhead variances in standard costing systems.*
5. *To discuss the proper disposition of standard cost variances for purposes of income determination.*
6. *To discuss the nature and sources of cost variances.*
7. *To understand how statistical control charts may be used to isolate random variances from nonrandom variances.*
8. *To understand how cost-benefit analysis may be used in assessing the significance of variances for further investigation and correction.*

11 Flexible Budgets, Overhead Control, and Variance Investigation Decisions

The previous chapter described the use of standard costing systems for controlling materials and labor costs. Differences between actual costs incurred and those which, according to the standards, should have been incurred were analyzed in terms of price and quantity variances. The variances can be disclosed on performance reports and managers can be held responsible for them.

Standard costing systems also utilize standards for the control of factory overhead costs. Because of the nature of these indirect costs, it is more difficult to predict their behavior and to assign responsibility for them. This is usually accomplished using a more complex type of budgeting and performance reporting system called the *flexible budget.* Information provided by a flexible budgeting system discloses *a factory overhead variance,* which is the difference between budgeted factory overhead costs and those actually incurred during a budgetary reporting period. This factory overhead variance can then be analyzed in order to explain its source and to aid in assigning responsibility. The first part of this chapter describes methods of analyzing this variance utilizing factory overhead cost standards, and incorporating them into a flexible budget for planning and control.

It should be noted that a reported variance indicates only the existence of a deviation of the actual cost from the budget. It does not indicate the cause of the variance and the remedial action. Variances may be due to random or nonrandom causes. Random variances call for no investigation or corrective action because random variation cannot be eliminated. Nonrandom variances, on the other hand, may require investigations of the cause and corrective actions if they are significant. This is an example of the implementation of *management by exception.* Management by exception signifies that management concentrates its attention on the area where a significant exception has occurred. Therefore, in the second part of the charter, a logical approach to the variance investigation decision is first presented to isolate nonrandom variances from random variances, and then to determine whether or not costs justify an investigation of the nonrandom variances.

Using the Flexible Budget

Chapter 9 describes the process of developing a master budget which is useful for the planning of operations. The master budget is sometimes referred to as *a static budget* because it assumes that a single activity or production level will be attained during the budgetary period. The sales, production, purchases and cash budgets are developed from this static level of activity, which usually reflects an estimate of the anticipated or most likely production level. Such estimates are seldom very precise; many factors can cause actual activity to differ substantially from that anticipated when the budget is developed. These factors include strikes, physical catastrophes, general economic conditions, and the actions of competitors. Because many such factors are not controllable by managers, a master budget does not provide a valid basis for evaluating managerial performance in controlling costs.

Flexible budgets are developed in order to overcome these disadvantages. A flexible budget provides an estimate of costs at several different possible levels of activity, usually the most likely one and at levels above and below that considered most likely. Thus, flexible budgets provide estimates of a range of costs within which actual costs are likely to occur, and is valuable for planning purposes. The information used to develop a flexible budget can be used to provide performance reports reflecting what costs should have been at the production level attained, for purposes of management control. Flexible budgets are especially useful for the control of factory overhead costs because they recognize cost behavior patterns.

Developing the Flexible Budget

The use of flexible budgets for planning and control of overhead costs requires that overhead items be classified by their behavior patterns. Direct material and direct labor are always considered to be variable costs, but the classification of factory overhead costs is more difficult. Some costs, such as leases or depreciation on factory equipment, may remain relatively constant over a budgetary period and thus may be treated as fixed costs. Others, such as certain types of indirect materials, may be purely variable. However, most factory overhead costs are not clearly in either category and should be treated as mixed costs. In developing a flexible budgeting system, the cost accountant must analyze each overhead cost account individually in order to determine its fixed and variable components.

This analysis begins with the choice of a suitable activity measure to which each variable cost or variable cost component can be related. Different activity measures may be chosen for different overhead costs; however, flexible budgeting procedures are greatly simplified if the same measure can be used for all costs. Frequently used activity measures include the number of units produced, the standard direct labor hours allowed, or the number of machine hours utilized. The measure chosen should either represent production volume or be significantly affected only by volume. Activity measures such as direct labor costs are affected by labor rates as well, and should only be used when labor rates remain relatively stable over the budgetary period.

Once an activity measure is chosen, the cost behavior relationship between the activity measure and each factory overhead cost is determined. Several methods for doing this were described in Chapter 3. They include the high-low method, the engineering approach, and statistical regression analysis. Any such method can be used to determine, for each factory overhead cost account, its fixed and variable cost components. These can then be used in budgeting to predict what costs will be incurred at a given level of the activity measure.

Once the fixed and variable cost components have been calculated for each factory overhead item, the flexible budget formula can be determined. This budget formula expresses total factory overhead cost as a function of the activity measure, and is in the general form:

$$TC = a + bX.$$

where

TC = total budgeted factory overhead cost;

b = variable overhead cost per unit of activity, which equals the sum of all the variable overhead cost components per unit of activity;

a = fixed overhead costs, which equals the sum of all the fixed cost components;

X = the quantity of the activity measure.

An example of the development of a flexible budget formula is given in Illustration 11-1.

Flexible Budgets in Planning

The cost behavior patterns expressed in the budget formula can be used for planning purposes by incorporating them into a flexible budget. This budget shows the factory overhead costs which are expected at several different possible production volumes during the budgetary period. These production volumes may represent the most likely one (also used in the static budget) and volumes at some quantity above and below the most likely volume. Or they may represent the minimum expected, most likely, and maximum expected production volumes.

An example of a flexible budget for planning, using the budget formula developed in Illustration 11-1, is shown in Illustration 11-2. Similar budgets could be prepared for other departments in the same company, and combined to form overhead budgets at higher level responsibility centers.

Flexible Budgets in Control

Although flexible budgets are useful for planning purposes, their primary advantage over static budgets is in their information content for management control. Just as the budget formula can be used to compute budgeted costs at various anticipated production volumes, it can also be used to compute what budgeted costs should have been at the actual volume attained during a budgetary period. At the end of a budgetary period, the budgeted costs at actual volume can be incorporated into a performance report, which discloses the effectiveness of a manager in controlling overhead costs. An example of a performance report based on the flexible budget formula of Illustration 11-1 is shown in Illustration 11-3.

Had a flexible budgeting system not been employed, the budgeted costs disclosed in the performance report of Illustration 11-3 would have been based on the static budget's anticipated

Illustration 11-1 Cost Components and the Flexible Budget Formula

The Machining Department of ABC Company incurs four types of factory overhead costs. Using regression analysis, the fixed and variable components of each cost have been computed and are shown in the table below. The budget formulas for each type of cost and for the department in total are computed. The activity measure (X) is the number of units produced.

Factory Overhead Cost	Behavior	Variable Component (per unit)	Fixed Component (per month)	Budget Formula
Supplies	variable	.30	0	.30X
Utilities	mixed	.10	500	500 + .10X
Supervision	fixed	0	2,000	2,000
Maintenance	mixed	.05	100	100 + .05X
Total	mixed	.45	2,600	2,600 + .45X

Machining Department overhead budget formula:

TC = 2,600 + .45X.

volume of 4,000 units. In this situation, the variance between budgeted and actual costs would have been due in part to the lower production volume (3,800 units) actually attained during the month. This decrease in volume may have been beyond the control of the manager; thus, the variance would not have been an appropriate measure of managerial performance. On the flexible budget performance report, budgeted costs are based on the activity measure actually attained.

Thus, the amount of the variance due to volume differences is eliminated. The resulting variances are better indicators of performance, and the reporting system is superior for purposes of control.

When standard costs are used in conjunction with a flexible budgeting system, the fixed and variable components of the budget equation are frequently adopted as factory overhead cost standards. The factory overhead variance disclosed on the performance report can then be further analyzed to explain its source, much as direct material and direct labor variances are analyzed. Several different methods of analyzing the factory overhead variance are in use; three of the most common methods will be described in the remainder of the chapter.

Variance Analysis for Overhead Control

In the previous chapter, the development and use of standard costs for materials and labor were described. The standard cost for a unit of product includes not only a standard material and labor cost but also a standard factory overhead cost as well. When actual overhead costs differ from those called for by the standard during a reporting period, a factory overhead variance is created. Factory overhead variances, both at the departmental level and at a company-wide level, can be analyzed and responsibility for them assigned.

Illustration 11-2 Flexible Budgets for Planning

Normal activity for the Machining Department of ABC Company during the month of April is 4,000 units. However, production can vary up to 10% in either direction depending on sales. The following budget has been developed for use in planning the month's expenditures.

Machining Department
Factory Overhead Budget
April, 20XX

		Expected Activity (Units)		
	Formula	3,600	4,000	4,400
Supplies	.30X	$1,080	$1,200	$1,320
Utilities	500+.10X	860	900	940
Supervision	2,000	2,000	2,000	2,000
Maintenance	100+.05x	280	300	320
Total		$4,220	$4,400	$4,580

Illustration 11-3 Performance Report Based on the Flexible Budget Formula

During the month of April, Machining Department of ABC Company produced 3,800 units. Normal volume for the month was 4,000 units. The following performance report is produced for use in evaluating the supervisor's control of overhead costs.

Machining Department
Performance Report - Factory Overhead
April, 20XX

	Formula (X in units)	Budgeted Costs	Actual Costs	Variance
Supplies	.30X	$1,140	$1,200	$ 60U
Utilities	500+.10X	880	980	100U
Supervision	2,000	2,000	2,000	-
Maintenance	100+.05X	290	250	40F
Total		$4,310	$4,430	$120U
Units scheduled			4,000	
Units produced			3,800	

Recording Standard Cost Overhead Variances

Chapter 5 discusses the method of applying factory overhead costs to products in historical costing systems. This is accomplished through a predetermined overhead rate, which is computed from the total budgeted overhead and an estimate of normal activity for one year. Costs which have been attached to units of product are recorded in a Factory Overhead Applied account; actual expenditures for overhead items are recorded in a Factory Overhead Control account. At the end of a period, the two accounts are closed and an underapplied or overapplied balance is recorded. The under- or overapplied overhead is most commonly closed to the Cost of Goods Sold account at the end of a year.

In standard costing systems similar procedures are followed. However, the predetermined overhead rate consists of two components, a fixed rate and a variable rate. The fixed overhead rate is computed as follows:

$$\frac{\text{Standard Fixed}}{\text{Overhead Rate}} = \frac{\text{Budgeted Fixed Overhead}}{\text{Normal Activity}}$$

The variable overhead rate is obtained from the flexible budget formula. Whenever the same activity measure is used for both rates:

$$\text{Standard Overhead Rate} = \text{Standard Variable Overhead Rate} + \text{Standard Fixed Overhead Rate}$$

Factory overhead costs are also attached to products in a slightly different fashion. In historical costing systems, the predetermined overhead rate is multiplied by the actual direct labor hours, machine hours, or some other base to compute the factory overhead applied. In a standard costing system the standard rate is multiplied by the amount of the base which, according to the physical standard, should have been used to achieve the actual output:

$$\text{Factory Overhead Applied} = \text{Standard Overhead Rate} \times \text{Standard Inputs Allowed for the Outputs Attained}$$

In most systems, the "standard inputs allowed" are the standard direct labor hours allowed for the outputs actually attained. Since standard cost systems also establish a standard amount of direct labor per unit produced, the standard overhead rate can be expressed either in dollars per unit or in dollars per standard hour allowed.

Some organizations develop departmental overhead rates which may differ from one department to the next. When this is the case, the standard variable overhead rate and the standard fixed overhead rate are the components of the budget formula used for flexible budgeting within a department. Other organizations choose to adopt a company-wide overhead rate in which the same rate is used in all departments within the company. In this situation flexible budgeting can still be used, but within a department the standard overhead rates are not equal to the components of the budget formula for that department.

At the end of an accounting period, an underapplied or overapplied factory overhead balance may be created in standard costing systems just as in historical ones. However, the use of fixed and variable rates allows the cost accountant to analyze this balance in order to determine its source. The underapplied or overapplied balance is called the total *factory overhead variance.* When departmental overhead rates are used, the factory overhead variance to be analyzed includes that variance disclosed on the performance report of Illustration 11-3. When company-wide rates are used, the total variance is that for the entire organization. Different methods of analyzing the total factory overhead variance are in use. They include the *Two-Variance Method,* the *Three-Variance Method,* and the *Four-Variance Method.* The Two-Variance Method and the Three-Variance Method are also referred to as the two-way combined overhead variance analysis and the three-way combined overhead variance analysis, respectively. The Four-Variance Method analyzes fixed overhead and variable overhead variances separately.

Two-Variance Method

The Two-Variance Method of analysis recognizes two possible sources for the total factory overhead variance. A portion of it, called the *volume variance,* arises whenever the actual volume of production during a reporting period differs from the normal activity used in computing the standard overhead rate. When flexible budgeting is used, it is the difference between the fixed overhead costs which were applied and those which were budgeted for the period. It may be computed as follows:

$$\text{Volume Variance} = \text{Standard Fixed Overhead Rate} \times \left[\text{Normal Activity} - \text{Standard Inputs Allowed for Output Attained} \right]$$

When the normal activity is stated in direct labor hours, the standard inputs allowed are measured in standard hours allowed. If the normal activity is in units, then the standard activity allowed is the number of units produced. The volume variance is favorable whenever the normal activity is less than the standard activity allowed, and is unfavorable otherwise. If the standard activity allowed is equal to the normal activity, there is no volume variance.

A second portion of the total factory overhead variance is the *budget variance*, sometimes called the *controllable variance* because it is more readily controllable at the departmental level. The budget variance is the difference between actual factory overhead costs and those which are justifiable with a flexible budget. It may be computed using the following relationship:

$$\text{Budget Variance} = \text{Actual Factory Overhead} - \left[\text{Budgeted Fixed Overhead} + \text{Standard Variable Overhead Rate} \times \text{Standard Inputs Allow for Output Attained} \right]$$

If actual overhead costs exceed those budgeted, the budget variance is unfavorable.

The budget variance is disclosed on a performance report produced by a flexible budgeting system, such as that shown for the Machining Department in Illustration 11-3. The relationship between the budget and volume variances is expressed graphically in Illustration 11-4. An example problem demonstrating the calculation of these variances is contained in Illustration 11-5.

The Two-Variance Method provides useful information for managerial control because it distinguishes two portions of the total overhead variance. The volume variance arises because actual production volume differs from normal activity, and is seldom controllable at the operating manager level. For performance evaluation, a manager should not be held responsible for it. However, operating managers who incur factory overhead costs are able to influence the budget variance. Consequently it will frequently be disclosed on performance reports such as Illustration 11-3.

Even though the Two-Variance Method isolates that part of the factory overhead variance due to volume differences, the method still does not isolate other sources. As a result, many cost accountants prefer a more detailed method of variance analysis.

Illustration 11-4 Two-Variance Method

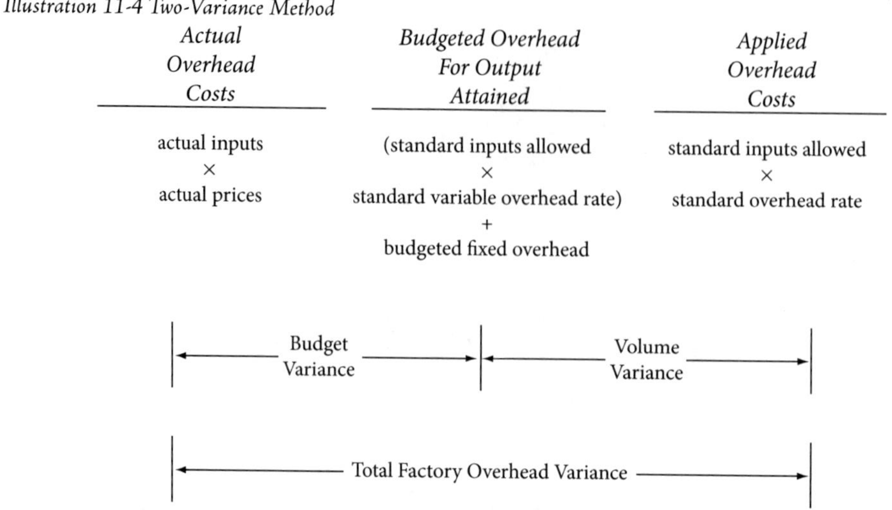

Three-Variance Method

The Three-Variance Method isolates three sources for the total factory overhead variance. *A volume variance is* computed just as in the Two Variance Method. Two additional variances, the efficiency variance and the spending variance, are computed which explain the source of the budget variance discussed previously. The factory overhead *efficiency variance* explains the amount of the total overhead variance which results from production efficiency or inefficiency. The efficiency variance may be computed from the following relationship:

$$\text{Efficiency Variance} = \text{Standard Variable Overhead Rate} \times \left(\text{Actual Inputs Used} - \text{Standard Inputs Allowed for Output Attained} \right)$$

The magnitude of the efficiency variance is directly related to the amount by which the actual inputs used differ from the inputs which, according to standards, should have been used. Whenever the actual inputs are less than the standard inputs allowed, the resulting variance is favorable.

The factory overhead *spending variance* isolates the amount of the budget variance which cannot be traced to production efficiency. It represents the difference between actual overhead costs and those costs expected for the actual inputs used. The overhead spending variance may be computed as follows:

$$\text{OVERHEAD SPENDING VARIANCE} = \text{ACTUAL FACTORY OVERHEAD} - \left[\text{BUDGETED FIXED OVERHEAD} + \left(\text{STANDARD VARIABLE OVERHEAD RATE} \right) \left(\text{ACTUAL INPUTS USED} \right) \right]$$

The spending variance is favorable whenever the actual costs are less than those which would be expected based on the standards. This variance may reflect excessive spending for

Illustration 11-5 Two-Variance Method Example Problem

The following information applies to the Maching Department for the month of April:

Standard Variable Overhead Rate	$ .45 per unit
Standard Fixed Overhead Rate	$ .65 per unit
Actual Factory Overhead Costs	$ 4,430
Actual Production	3,800 units
Normal Activity	4,000 units
Budgeted Fixed Overhead	$ 2,600 per month.

The standard overhead rate is ($.45 + $.65) = $1.10 per unit.

The total factory overhead variance is:

Actual Costs	$ 4,430
Costs Applied (3,800 x $1.10)	4,180
Total Overhead Variance	$ 250 U.

Using the Two-Variance Method to explain this total overhead variance, we obtain the following variances:

Volume Variance	=	$.65 per unit x (4,000 units – 3,800 units)
	=	$130 U.
Budget Variance	=	$4,430 – [$2,600 + ($.45 per unit) (3.800 units)]
	=	4,430 – 4,310
	=	$ 120 U.

Graphically:

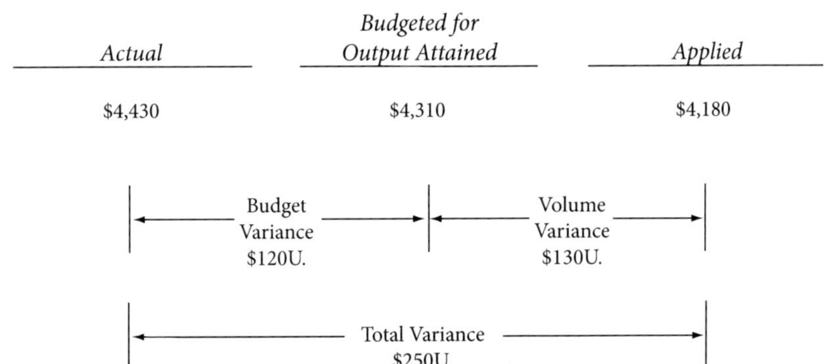

overhead items. However, it may also result from a number of other sources, including price changes for indirect materials, inefficient use of indirect materials or indirect labor, or from errors in the budget estimates. An excessive spending variance, like the materials and labor variances discussed in the previous chapter, is an indicator of a potential problem which may merit investigation. A graphical approach to factory overhead variance analysis using the Three-Variance Method is shown in Illustration 11-6. Note that the sum of the spending and efficiency variances always equals the budget variance of the Two-Variance Method.

The Three-Variance Method has the advantage of isolating that portion of the overhead variance resulting from production efficiency or inefficiency. A production foreman can then be held responsible for controlling this variance. Many flexible budgeting systems produce periodic performance reports which disclose the spending and efficiency variances instead of the budget

Illustration 11-6 Three-Variance Method

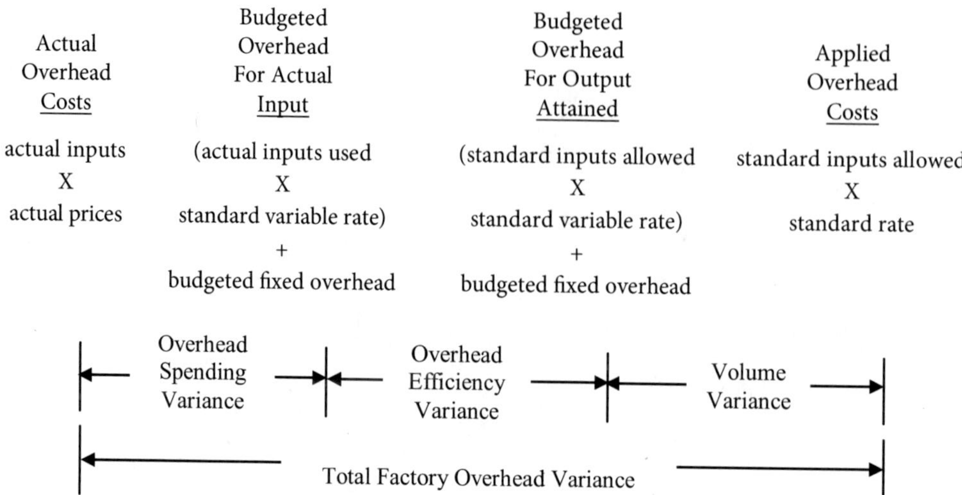

variance. An example problem using the Three-Variance Method is presented in Illustration 11-7. A typical performance report based on this example is contained in Illustration 11-8.

Four-Variance Method

Two commonly used methods of analyzing the factory overhead variance have been discussed. Another approach, the Four-Variance Method, is sometimes preferred because it clearly distinguishes between variable overhead variances and fixed overhead variances. Using this method, the variances that are computed are:

- Variable Overhead Efficiency Variance
- Variable Overhead Spending Variance
- Fixed Overhead Budget Variance
- Volume Variance.

The *volume variance is* calculated in the same way as the volume variances using the other two methods of analysis. The *variable overhead efficiency variance* is the same as the overhead efficiency variance of the Three-Variance Method. The *variable overhead spending variance* and the *fixed overhead budget variance* are obtained by decomposing the spending variance into its variable and fixed components. They may be calculated using the following relationships:

$$\begin{matrix}\textit{Variable Overhead} \\ \textit{Spending Variance}\end{matrix} = \begin{matrix}\textit{Actual Variable} \\ \textit{Factory Overhead}\end{matrix} \text{ X } \left(\begin{matrix}\textit{Standard Variable} \\ \textit{Overhead Rate}\end{matrix} - \begin{matrix}\textit{Actual Inputs} \\ \textit{Used}\end{matrix}\right)$$

$$\begin{matrix}\textit{Fixed} \\ \textit{Overhead} \\ \textit{Budget} \\ \textit{Variance}\end{matrix} = \begin{matrix}\textit{Actual} \\ \textit{Fixed} \\ \textit{Factory} \\ \textit{Overhead}\end{matrix} - \begin{matrix}\textit{Budgeted} \\ \textit{Fixed} \\ \textit{Factory} \\ \textit{Rate}\end{matrix}$$

Illustration 11-7 Three-Variance Method Example Problem

The following information is recorded for the Machining Department for the month of May:

Standard Variable Overhead Rate .... $ .45 per unit
Standard Fixed Overhead Rate .... $ .65 per unit
Actual Factory Overhead Costs $5,200
Actual Production ....4,100 units
Normal Activity..4,000 units

Budgeted Fixed Overhead .... $2,600 per month.

Physical standards call for 5 direct labor hours per unit produced. During May 21,000 direct labor hours were required.

The standard overhead rates per standard direct labor hour are:

Variable rate:	$.45 per unit/5 hrs. per unit = $.09
Fixed Rate:	$.65 per unit/5 hrs. per unit = $.13
Standard Overhead Rate:	$.22 per standard direct labor hour.

The total factory overhead variance is:

Actual Costs..$5,200
Costs Applied (4,100 x 5 x $.22) 4,510
Total Overhead Variance..$ 690U

Using the Three-Variance Method to explain this variance:

Volume Variance	= $.13 per hr.X [(4,000 units x 5 hrs. per unit) - (4,100 units x 5 hrs. per unit)]
	= $.13 (20,000- 20,500)
	= $65F.
Efficiency Variance	= $.09 per hr.X [21,000 hrs. - (4,100 units) (5 hrs. per unit)]
	= $.09 (21,000- 20,500)
	= $45U.
Spending Variance	= $5,200 - [$2,600+ ($.09 per hr.) (21,000 hrs.)]
	= $5,200 - 4,490
	= $710U.

Graphically:

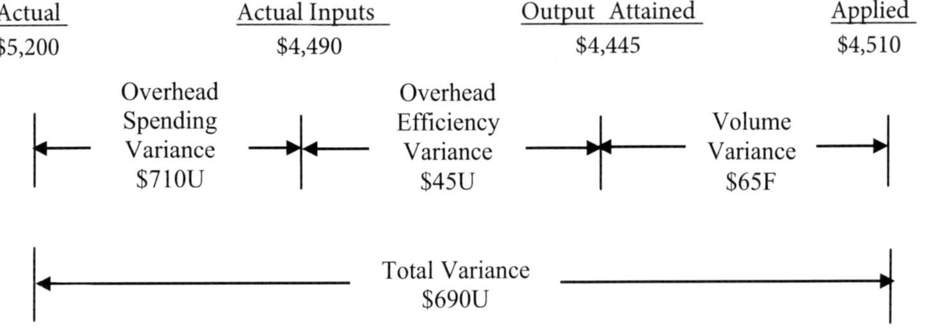

*Illustration 11-8 Three-Variance Method Performance Report**

Machining Department
Performance Report -Factory Overhead
May, 20XX

	Formula (X in hours)	Budget for Actual Inputs	Budget for Output Attained	Actual Costs	Variances Spending	Efficiency
Supplies	.06X	$1,260	$1,230	$1,600	$340U	$30U
Utilities	500 + .02X	920	910	900	20F	10U
Supervision	2,000	2,000	2,000	2,000		
Maintenance	100 + .01X	310	305	700	390U	5U
Total		$4,490	$4,445	$5,200	$710U	$45U

Units scheduled: 4,000
Units produced : 4,100
*The volume variance of $65F is not shown on the performance report because it is not under the Machining Department manager's control.

Choice of the Four-Variance Method of analysis in a standard costing system requires the use of four factory overhead accounts rather than two, as required by the other methods. The four accounts are:

- Variable Factory Overhead Control
- Fixed Factory Overhead Control
- Variable Factory Overhead Applied
- Fixed Factory Overhead Applied.

Factory overhead expense items must be separated into their fixed and variable parts. When an overhead expenditure is made, Variable Factory Overhead Control is debited for the variable portion and the Fixed Factory Overhead Control account is debited for the fixed portion. Accounts Payable (or some other account) is credited for the sum of the two amounts. As work progresses, the variable and fixed overhead rates are used to make credit entries to the factory overhead applied accounts. At the end of a budgetary reporting period, the four variances can be calculated.

This type of standard costing system is more difficult to implement. However, many accountants believe that the additional information provided by the method makes the additional clerical effort worthwhile. Control is improved because the variable spending variance, which is subject to the control of an operating manager on a daily basis, has been isolated. The fixed portion (the fixed budget variance) is ordinarily not subject to the manager's control except on a long-term basis. A graphical interpretation of the Four-Variance Method is contained in Illustration 11-9. An example problem using this method is presented in Illustration 11-10.

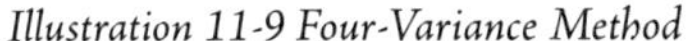

Illustration 11-9 Four-Variance Method

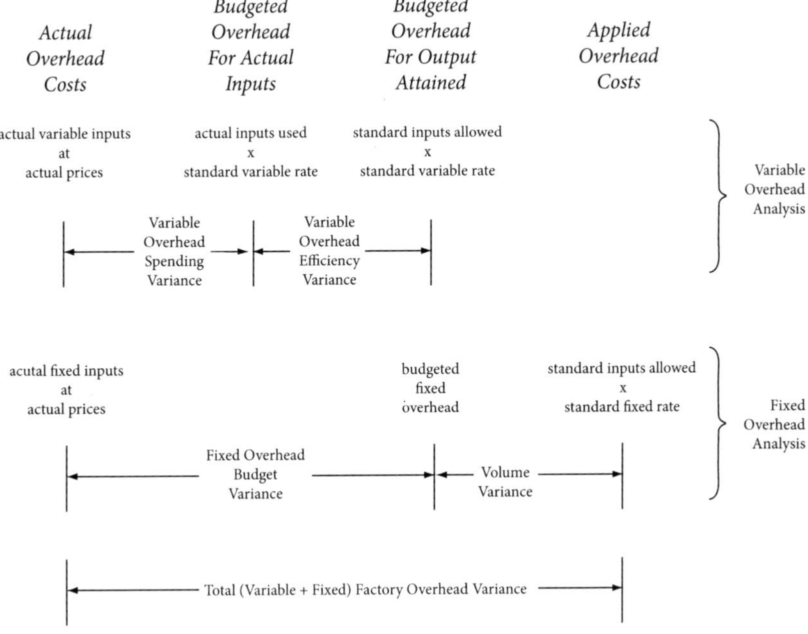

Disposition of Standard Cost Variances

This chapter has discussed the use of standard cost factory overhead variances for purposes of control. But as was pointed out in the previous chapter, standard costing systems must achieve a second objective which is associated with product costing and income determination. The disposition of standard cost variances for the periodic reporting of net income will now be discussed.

As has been described, standard costing systems utilize four variance accounts for materials and labor, and either two or four variance accounts for factory overhead. Some systems may in addition utilize an account for each factory overhead variance. These accounts are summarized in Illustration 11-11. At the end of a reporting period, the balances in these accounts must either be closed to another account or disclosed on the income statement or balance sheet. The treatment of underapplied or overapplied factory overhead was described in Chapter 5. Similar treatment is utilized for all the standard cost accounts, depending on the reporting period.

Disposition at Interim Periods

Many organizations produce financial statements at quarterly or monthly intervals. For such interim reports, the variance accounts are usually not closed. In practice, their balances are reflected in the financial statements as adjustments either to Cost of Goods Sold or to the Inventory accounts. Such treatments are demonstrated in Illustrations 11-12 and 11-13.

Disposition at Year-End

For income reporting at the end of a year, the variance accounts are closed to other accounts. The proper method of closing depends on the approach used in setting the standards.

Illustration 11-10 Four-Variance Method Example Problem

The following applied to the Machining Department for the month of May:

Standard Variable Overhead Rate	$ .09 per hour
Standard Fixed Overhead Rate	.13 per hour
Budgeted Fixed Overhead Costs	$ 2,600
Actual Fixed Overhead Costs	$ 2,700
Actual Variable Overhead Costs	$ 2,500
Actual Production	4,100 units
Normal Activity	4,000 units
Actual Direct Labor Hours	21,000
Standard Hours Allowed for Actual Production	20,500

Using the Four-Variance Methid:

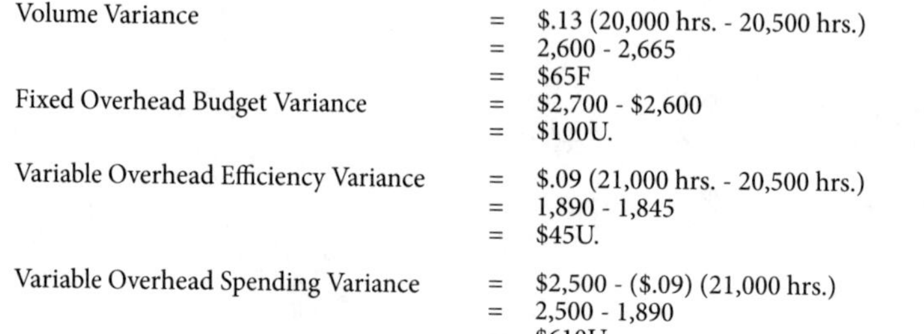

Volume Variance = $.13 (20,000 hrs. - 20,500 hrs.)
= 2,600 - 2,665
= $65F

Fixed Overhead Budget Variance = $2,700 - $2,600
= $100U.

Variable Overhead Efficiency Variance = $.09 (21,000 hrs. - 20,500 hrs.)
= 1,890 - 1,845
= $45U.

Variable Overhead Spending Variance = $2,500 - ($.09) (21,000 hrs.)
= 2,500 - 1,890
= $610U.

Graphically:

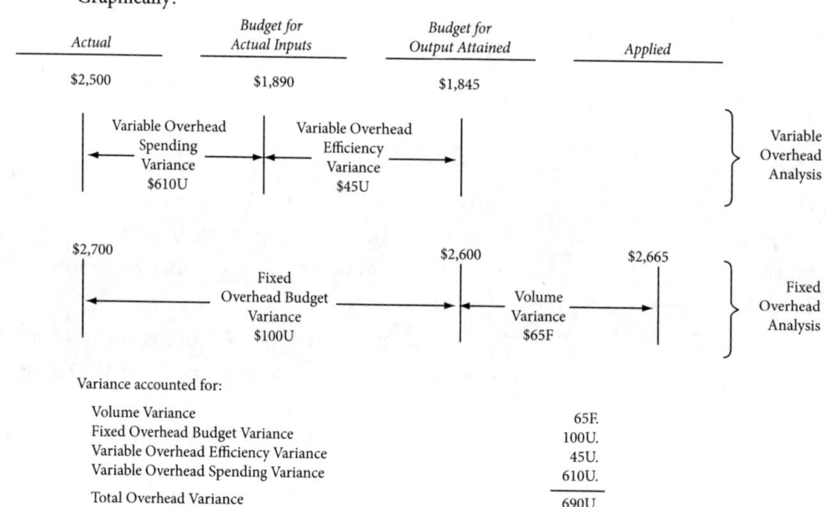

Variance accounted for:

Volume Variance	65F.
Fixed Overhead Budget Variance	100U.
Variable Overhead Efficiency Variance	45U.
Variable Overhead Spending Variance	610U.
Total Overhead Variance	690U.

When *currently attainable* standards have been adopted by management, the variances reflect the achievement of either efficient or inefficient operations. In such a situation, the preferable treatment is to close the variance accounts to Cost of Goods Sold. The efficiencies or inefficiencies of the current period will directly affect the net income of the current period. This is the most frequently used method of disposition at year-end.

Illustration 11-11 Variance Accounts in Standard Costing System

ACCOUNTS THAT ARE ALWAYS USED:

- Material Price Variance
- Materials Quantity (Usage, Efficiency) Variance
- Labor Rate (Price) Variance
- Labor Quantity (Usage, Efficiency) Variance
- Factory Overhead Control
- Factory Overhead Applied
- Overapplied/Underapplied Factory Overhead

ACCOUNTS THAT MAY BE USED (depending on the system):

- Variable Factory Overhead Control
- Fixed Factory Overhead Control
- Variable Factory Overhead Applied
- Fixed Factory Overhead Applied
- Volume Variance
- Overhead Budget Variance
- Overhead Spending Variance
- Overhead Efficiency Variance
- Variable Overhead Spending Variance
- Fixed Overhead Budget Variance

Illustration 11-12 Interim Reporting of Standard Cost Variances

Sales		XXX
Cost of Goods Sold (at Standard)	XXX	
Add: Unfavorable Variances		
(Or Less: Favorable Variances)	XXX	XXX
Gross Profit		XXX

Illustration 11-13 Interim Reporting of Standard Cost Variances Adjustment to Inventories (Partial Balance Sheet)

Assets

Current Assets:		
Cash		XXX
Accounts Receivable		XXX
Inventories (at Standard)	XXX	
Add: Unfavorable Variances		
(Or Less: Favorable Variances)	XXX	XXX
Other Current Assets		XXX
Total Current Assets		XXX

For example, assume that the following variances are in the accounts at year-end.

Material Price Variance	$ 2,000 U
Material Quantity Variance	8,000 U
Labor Rate Variance	2,000 F
Labor Usage Variance	5,000 U
Underapplied Factory Overhead	7,000 U
Net Variance	$20,000 U

Recall that unfavorable variances are represented by debit balances, and favorable variances produce a credit balance. Then the following entry would close the balances in the variance accounts to Cost of Goods Sold.

Cost of Goods Sold..........................	20,000	
Labor Rate Variance..........................	2,000	
Material Price Variance.................		2,000
Material Quantity Variance...........		8,000
Labor Usage Variance....................		5,000
Underapplied Factory Overhead...		7,000

Sometimes management will choose to use standards which are either *ideal* or *basic* standards. In this case the standards are not attainable, and the variances represent amounts by which inventories are in theory misstated. The proper treatment is to prorate the variances among Cost of Goods Sold, Work-in-Process, and Finished Goods Inventory accounts based on their ending balances.

Illustration 11-14 demonstrates the method of proration for the $20,000 net unfavorable variance in the above example. The required closing entry would be as follows:

Work-in-Process	400	
Finished Goods................................	1,600	
Cost of Goods Sold..........................	18,000	
Labor Rate Variance.........................	2,000	
Material Price Variance.................		2,000
Material Quantity Variance..........		8,000
Labor Usage Variance....................		5,000
Underapplied Factory Overhead...		7,000

As was described in Chapter 10, some systems record raw materials inventories at standard cost. Theoretically, a portion of the materials price variance should be prorated between Raw Materials, Work-in-Process, Finished Goods, and Cost of Goods Sold in such systems. This allocation should be based on the raw materials costs recorded in each of the accounts. Similarly, any underapplied or overapplied factory overhead should be prorated based on the factory overhead applied in the accounts. In practice, however, few cost accountants consider

Illustration 11-14 Year-End Proration of Standard Cost Variances

	Ending Balances		*Variances*					
			Materials Price	*Materials Quantity*	*Labor Rate*	*Labor Usage*	*Underapplied Factory Overhead*	*Prorated*
Account	*Amount*	*%*	*($2,000 U)*	*($8,000 U)*	*($2,000 F)*	*($5,000 U)*	*($7,000 U)*	*Amount*
Work-in-Process	$ 40,000	2	40 U	160 U	40 F	100 U	140 U	$ 400
Finished Goods	160,000	8	160 U	640 U	160 F	400 U	560 U	1,600
Cost of Goods Sold	1,800,000	90	1,800 U	7,200 U	1,800 F	4,500 U	6,300 U	18,000
	$2,000,000	100						$20,000

the increased accuracy of these methods worthy of their added complexity. Any differences between these methods and the one of Illustration 11-14 are normally considered immaterial.

The Decision to Investigate Cost Variances

In variance investigation analysis, cost accountants are concerned with two questions: (1) whether a variance is due to random variations or to nonrandom ones; and (2) whether a nonrandom variance requires further investigation and corrective action. This section discusses a variety of causes of variances and methods for distinguishing random variances from nonrandom variances. A cost-benefit approach for determining whether or not a variance is significant enough for further investigation is described.

Sources of Variances

Conceptually, variances may be classified as one of five types: implementation, prediction, measurement, model and random. These are distinguished in the following ways:

1. An *implementation* variance is caused by a failure to achieve a specific obtainable standard. For example, careless handling of materials or machinery would cause the usage of a greater quantity of material than the budget allowed.
2. *A prediction* variance is a variance caused by a mistake in predicting a parameter value in a model. For example, a mistake in predicting the price of materials would cause a material price variance.
3. A *measurement* variance results from an error in measuring the actual cost of operating a process. For example, incorrect classification, counting, or recording inventory would produce a material quantity variance.
4. *A model* variance is a deviation due to an incorrect model used in the process or analysis. For example, working with incorrect standards or changed conditions would cause materials and labor quantity variances.
5. A *random* variance is a chance variation without an assignable cause.

Illustration 11-15 Variance Classification

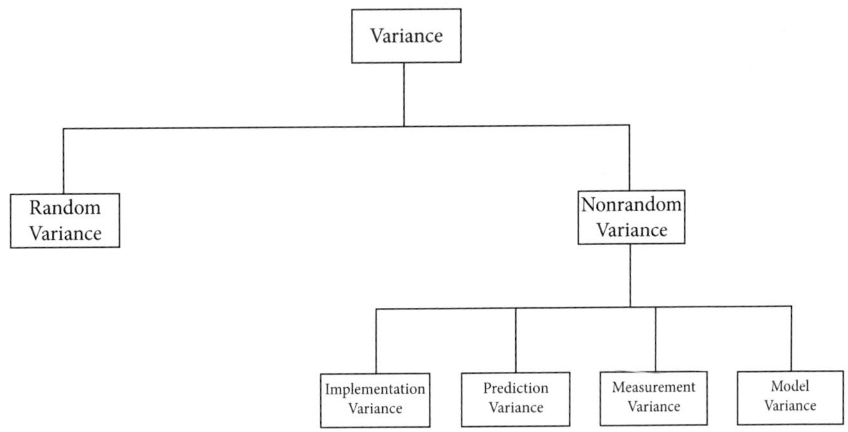

Illustration 11-15 shows the classification of variances into random and nonrandom variances and a further division of nonrandom variances into implementation, prediction, measurement, and model variances.

The distinction of variances into five types will enhance management's ability to deal with the reported variances. It should be noted, however, that some of the causes may not be easy to isolate. Furthermore, some of the variances may not be independent. Cost accountants must be aware of these possibilities and select a logical approach to the investigation.

Random variances are due to chance occurrences, have no assignable cause and require no investigation or corrective action. Nonrandom variances, on the other hand, may be caused by one or more of the four assignable causes. Nonrandom variances may or may not require investigation and correction. In the determination of whether nonrandom variances should be investigated, economic considerations must be evaluated. An investigation and corrective action is warranted only when the expected benefits exceed the cost of investigation and correction. A logical approach to the investigation of variances will first separate random variances from nonrandom variances, and then will determine whether or not to investigate the nonrandom variances. Statistical quality control techniques are available for separating random and nonrandom variances. One of these techniques, the control chart, will be described in the following section. An approach that measures the cost and benefit relationship in investigating and correcting variances will be discussed in a later part of this chapter.

Statistical Quality Control Charts

As stated in the previous section, in deciding whether or not to investigate variances, cost accountants should first distinguish random variances from nonrandom variances. The statistical quality control chart has proven to be useful for this purpose. It provides a systematic means for isolating random variances (due to chance variations) from nonrandom variances (due to assignable variations). The control chart is based on the concept that a standard is best described by a band or range of acceptability, rather than by single point. In this sense, any variation falling within the acceptable range is considered to be due to random causes and, because it is unavoidable, is not of concern to management.

On the other hand, any variation falling outside the acceptable range is considered to have a controllable source and thus should be a concern of management. Accountants should realize that the quality control chart simply provides a signal of an exceptional condition. It does not indicate the cause of a nonrandom variance nor does it prescribe any action to be taken.

Statistical control charts are developed by first taking sample observations from a process when it is in normal operation, or "in control." If labor usage variances are to be investigated, the observations will be of production times for a process. If materials quantity variances are of concern, the observations may be of material quantities used in a process. These observations are then used to determine statistically a band of acceptability for the item to be analyzed, such as production time or material quantity. This band or range of acceptability is plotted in the form of a control chart. Then in later periods sample observations of the item are taken, and the result of the sample plotted on the control chart. If the sample observation falls outside of the acceptable band, the process is considered "out of control" and any resulting variance is assumed to be due to an assignable cause. If the sample observation falls within the band, the process is assumed to be "in control" and the associated variance is considered unavoidable.

In practice, two types of control charts, the X chart and the R chart, are usually used. The X chart shows variations in the average value of the sample observations. The R chart, on the other hand, shows the variations in ranges of the samples. The control chart for range (the R chart) should be used in conjunction with the control chart for the mean (the X chart) because in some cases the sample means may be within the control limits but the ranges may be unusually large, indicating a variance which merits investigation.

Development of Control Charts

Steps involved in developing control charts are described as follows:

Step 1: Selection of samples—draw a desired number of samples from the process when the process is assumed to be in control, each with a subsample of usually four or five observations of the item to be measured.

Step 2: Calculation of means—calculate the mean (X) for each subsample and the grand mean (X) for all the subsample means.

Step 3: Determination of the range (R) for each subsample—the range for a subsample is the difference between the highest observation and the lowest observation in the subsample.

Step 4: Calculation of the mean for all the ranges (K).

Step 5: Determination of the upper and the lower control limits for the X chart; depending upon the desired confidence level, the control limits may be determined as X ± zo. o is the standard deviation of the population of the item to be measured which can be estimated from the samples. The value for z can be obtained from a normal distribution table given a desired confidence level. For example, the control limits will be in the interval X ± 1 a for a confidence level of 68.27%, in the interval X ± 2 a for a confidence level of 95.45%, and in the interval X ±

Table 11-1 Table of Factors for 3-Sigma Control Limits*

Number of Observations in Subgroup n	*Factor for X Chart* A_2	*Factors for R Chart* *Lower Control Limit* D_3	*Upper Control Limit* D_4
2	1.88	0	3.27
3	1.02	0	2.57
4	0.73	0	2.28
5	0.58	0	2.11
6	0.48	0	2.00
7	0.42	0.08	1.92
8	0.37	0.14	1.86
9	0.34	0.18	1.82
10	0.31	0.22	1.78

$$\text{Upper control limit for } \bar{X} = \bar{\bar{X}} + A_2\bar{R}$$
$$\text{Lower control limit for } \bar{X} = \bar{\bar{X}} - A_2\bar{R}$$
$$\text{Upper control limit for R} = D_4\bar{R}$$
$$\text{Lower control limit for R} = D_3\bar{R}$$

* Abridge from Eugene L. Grant and Richard S. Leavenworth, *Statistical Quality Control*, 4th ed. (New York: Mc Graw-Hill Book Company, 1972), Table C, p. 645. Reproduced by permission of the publisher.

3 a for a confidence level of 99.73%. In addition, statistical tables are available for setting control limits without calculating a when X, R, and the sample size are known. The table to be used for ± 3 is given in Table 11-1. Using the table, the control limits are computed as follows:

Upper control limit = X + A_2R
Lower control limit = X – A_2R

Step 6: Where A_2 is a statistical factor which can be obtained from Table 11-1.

Determination of the upper and the lower control limits for the R chart—the range control limits in the R chart are computed as follows:

Upper control limit = RxD_4
Lower control limit = R x D_3

Again, D_4 and D_3 are statistical factors which can be obtained from Table 11-1.

Step 7: Plotting samples-plot the mean and the range of each subsample on the X chart and the R chart. All the subsample means and ranges are expected to be within the control limits because the samples are taken from a process assumed to be in control. Any subsample mean or range falling outside the control limits is presumed to represent unusual operating conditions. Accordingly, it is excluded from the data when the control limits are developed.

During later periods of time, as samples are taken they are plotted on the control chart. Samples falling within the range are considered acceptable. Samples falling outside the acceptable band are indicators of a variance which should be a concern of management.

An Example

The manager of a golf cart assembly department wishes to develop a statistical control chart for use in determining when to investigate a labor usage variance in the department. During the past week, ten samples, each containing four observations of the assembly time spent on a golf cart, were randomly taken from the process when it is considered to be in control. The results of the samples are summarized in Illustration 11-16.

Upper control limit for X = X + A_2R Lower control limit for X = X – A_2R
Upper control limit for R = D_4R Lower control limit for R = D_3R

* Abridged from Eugene L. Grant and Richard S. Leavenworth, *Statistical Quality Control,* 4th ed.

(New York: McGraw-Hill Book Company, 1972, Table C, p. 645. Reproduced by permission of the publisher.)

Since Table 11-1 will be used for setting the control limits, it is necessary to calculate the mean (X) and range (R) of each sample, the grand arithmetic mean (X) of all samples, and the average range (R) of samples. These calculations are included in Illustration 11-16. Using the calculated X and R , the equations given in steps 5 and 6, and the statistical factors obtained from Table 11-1, the control limits can be set as follows:

For the X Chart:
Control limits = X ± A_2R

Illustration 11-16 Observations of Golf Cart Assembly Time

Sample	Observation (in minutes) 1	2	3	4	Average ($\bar{X}$)	Range (R)
1	21	20	28	23	23	8
2	28	22	25	21	24	7
3	30	26	24	24	26	6
4	28	25	23	24	25	2
5	26	22	27	29	26	7
6	27	26	27	28	27	2
7	23	21	20	24	22	4
8	29	23	28	24	26	6
9	27	28	21	24	25	7
10	27	24	25	28	26	4
				Totals	250	56

$$\bar{\bar{X}} = \frac{250}{10} = 25$$

$$\bar{\bar{R}} = \frac{56}{10} = 5.6$$

Upper control limit (UCL_X) = 25 + .73 (5.6) = 29.09
Lower control limit (LCL_X) = 25 – .73 (5.6) = 20.91

For the R Chart:
Upper control limit (UCL_R) = D_a R = 2.28 (5.6) = 12.77
Lower control limit (LCL_R) = D_3 R = 0 (5.6) = 0

The X chart and the R chart are shown in Illustrations 11-17 and 11-18, respectively.

In Illustrations 11-17 and 11-18, no observation is found outside the control limits. Therefore, the variations in the samples of the golf cart assembly time appear to be random variations and no samples represent unusual operating conditions. These control charts can be used to monitor the assembly process by plotting samples observed in later periods. For example, if a sample mean of 30 minutes was observed for a period, the manager would be concerned about the labor usage variance.

As indicated previously, the control chart is useful in separating nonrandom variances from random variances. However, it does not indicate what is wrong in the process or system. Furthermore, it does not indicate whether an investigation and corrective action are economically justified. How can management decide whether to investigate and to take a corrective action? A form of cost-benefit analysis, which will be discussed in the following section, provides an approach to determine the appropriate action.

Illustration 11-17 Control Count for X

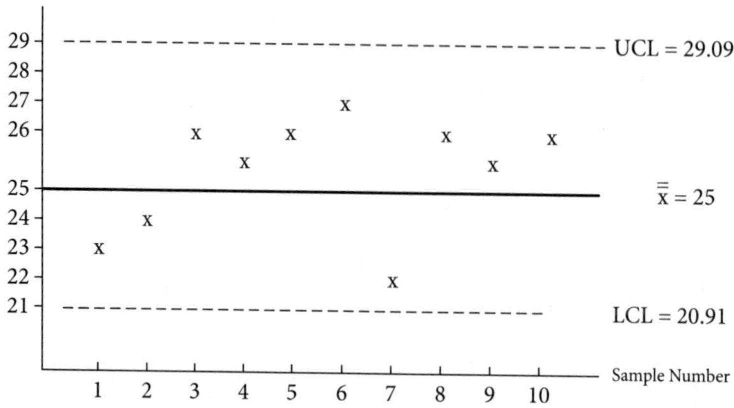

Illustration 11-18 Control Chart for R

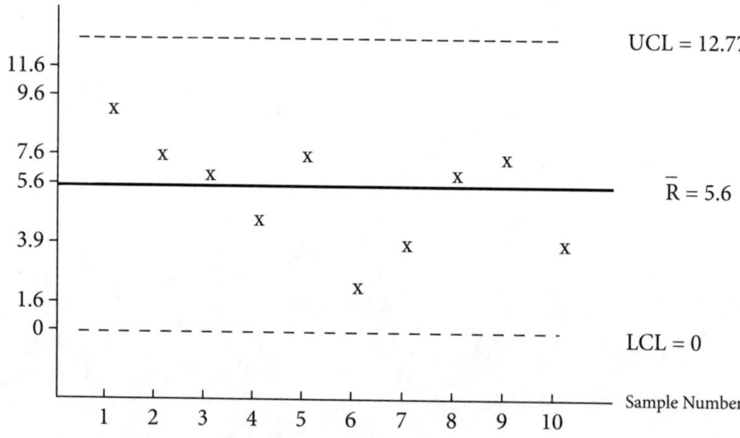

A Cost-Benefit Approach

In deciding whether to investigate a variance, a manager must recognize the cost and benefit implications of the decision. The expected costs of investigation and correction must be compared with the expected benefit before a decision is made to investigate. If the expected benefit does not exceed the expected costs, an investigative action should not be taken. On the other hand, when the expected benefit exceeds the expected costs, some further action may be warranted.

The Cost-Benefit Table

The information required for the cost-benefit analysis includes:

I = Cost of investigation
C = Cost of correction

Illustration 11-19 General Form of the Cost-Benefit Table

	States	
Action	In Control (P_1)	Out of Control (P_2)
Investigate (A_1)	I	I + C
Do Not Investigate (A_2)	0	B

B = Benefits expected from the remedial action when the process is out of control
P_1 = Probability of process in control
P_2 = Probability of process out of control

Illustration 11-19 provides the general form of a cost-benefit table that summarizes the costs and benefits of all possible outcomes. Each element in the table represents the estimated cost associated with a particular action under a particular state. For example, if the state of the process is in control and an investigation is made, the cost of investigation, I, would be incurred. Another example, if the state of the process is out of control and a do-not investigate action is taken, the cost would be B which represents the expected benefits lost from no investigation and correction.

The Decision Rule

In applying this cost-benefit approach, managers should compare the expected costs to determine the appropriate action to be taken. The general decision rule is to investigate if the expected cost of investigation is less than the expected cost of not investigating. Whenever the expected cost of investigation is greater than the expected cost of not investigating, further action is not justified. In other words, the decision rule is to select the action with the lowest expected cost.

The expected cost of each action can be obtained by summing the conditional value associated with each state under the action. The conditional value is determined by multiplying the individual cost element in the table by its probability of occurrence. Mathematically, the expected cost of each action can be determined as follows:

$$\text{Expected cost of } A_1 = IP_t + (I+C)(P_2) = I + CP_2 \quad (1)$$

$$\text{Expected cost of } A_2 = OP_1 + BP_{2\,=}BP2 \quad (2)$$

An Example

The manager of a golf cart assembly department has assessed that the probability of the assembly process being out of control is 20%. The cost to investigate the process is estimated to be \$4,000. If the process is discovered to be out of control, its cost of correction is \$2,000. The manager has estimated that the present value of cost savings resulting from investigating and correcting the out-of-control situation is \$21,000. The manager is trying to decide whether to investigate.

Illustration 11-20 General Form of the Cost-Benefit Table

	States	
Action	In Control (P1=.80)	Out of Control (P2=.20)
Investigate (A_1)	I = $40,000	I + C = $6,000
Do Not Investigate (A_2)	0	B = $21,000

Expected Cost of A_1 = $4,000 (.80) + $6,000(.20)
= $4,400.
Expected Cost of A_2 = $0(.80) + $21,000(.2)
= $4,200.

Illustration 11-20 summarizes the above information in a cost-benefit table. Applying the decision rule, the appropriate action is not to investigate, because its expected cost of $4,200 is less than the alternative action's expected cost of $4,400.

In the analysis of whether or not to investigate a process, the estimates of the elements in the cost-benefit table are critical. A different estimate of an element may result in a different optimal action. For example, if the assessment of probabilities of the states in Illustration 11-20 is P_1 = .70 and P_2 = .30, the optimal action would be to investigate the process because the cost of investigation ($4,000 x .70 + 6,000 x .3 = $4,600) is less than the cost of not investigating ($21,000 x .3 = $6,300). Therefore, it may be useful to know the probability of each state at which cost considerations are the same between the alternative actions. At this point of probability the two actions are indifferent. An *indifference point* thus provides a benchmark to measure the maximum deviation of the estimate of an element that would not change the optimal action. Indifference analysis is discussed in the next section.

Indifference Analysis

Referring to Equations (1) and (2), investigative action should be taken if the expected cost obtained from Equation (1) is less than the one obtained from Equation (2). That is, one should investigate if $I + CP_2 < BP_2$, and not investigate if $I + CP_2 > BP_2$. When $I + CP_2 = BP_2$, a manager is indifferent to a choice between the two actions. Indifference analysis can be performed based on these equations to provide additional information.

The indifference point can be determined by solving the equation, $I + CP_2 = BP_2$, for P_2. It is

$$\textit{Indifference } P_2 = \frac{I}{B - C} \qquad (3)$$

or alternatively,

$$\textit{Indifference } P_1 = I - \frac{I}{B - C} \qquad (4)$$

For the example problem in Illustration 11-6, the indifference point can be determined as follows:

$$\textit{Indifference } P_2 = \frac{I}{B - C} = \frac{4{,}000}{21{,}000 - 2{,}000} = 21.05\%$$

or

$$Indifference\ P_1 = \frac{I}{B - C} = I - \frac{4,000}{21,000 - 2,000} = 78.95\%$$

The indifference point serves as a threshold, and can be compared with the manager's assessment of probability to determine the appropriate action. For example, if the manager's subjective assessment of probability of out of control is less than the indifference P_2, the investigation decision should not be taken. On the other hand, if it is greater than the indifference P_2, the investigate action should be taken. For the example problem in Illustration 11-6, the optimal action is not to investigate because the subjective probability of out of control (20%) is less than the indifference P_2 (21.05%). In the alternative example, however, the investigate action should be taken because the subjective probability of out of control (30%) is greater than the indifference P_2 (21.05%).

A similar type of indifference analysis can also be performed to determine the minimum benefits necessary to warrant an investigation. The minimum benefits (minimum B) necessary to justify an investigation can be determined as follows:

$$Minimum\ B = \frac{I + CP_2}{P_2} \qquad (5)$$

This minimum B can be compared with the manager's expected benefits to determine the appropriate action. If the expected benefits are greater than the minimum B, then investigative action is justified. For the illustrative problem, the minimum B is equal to:

$$\frac{\$4,000 + 2,000\,(.20)}{.20} = \$22,000$$

Since the expected benefits ($21,000) are less than the minimum B ($22,000), the appropriate action is not to investigate.

Similarly, the basic equation $1 + CP_2 = BP_2$ can be used to determine the maximum investigation cost (maximum I) and the maximum correction cost (maximum C) that management would be willing to pay in a variance investigation decision. The equations used to calculate the maximum I and maximum C allowed are given below:

$$\text{Maximum } I = (B\text{-}C)P_2 \qquad (6)$$

$$Minimum\ C = B - \frac{I}{P_2} \qquad (7)$$

The use of Equations (6) and (7) provides the maximum I and maximum C for which an investigation is warranted. Whenever the cost of investigation and cost of correction are greater than their maximum values allowed, investigations and corrections are not justified. For the illustrative problem, the maximum I and maximum C are:

$$Maximum\ I = (B\text{-}C)P_2 = (\$21,000 - 2,000)(.20) = \$3,800$$

$$Minimum\ C = B - \frac{I}{P_2} = \$21,000 - (\$4,000/.2) = \$1,000$$

Assumptions

Although this cost-benefit approach appears to be relatively simple, there are several implicit assumptions in it. The user of the approach must be aware of these assumptions because some of them may limit its applicability. The underlying assumptions are:

1. The estimate of I, C, and B can be determined with reasonable accuracy.
2. An investigation always reveals the cause of an out-of-control situation which can and will be immediately corrected.
3. If the situation is not investigated, then the process will remain out of control until the next cost observation period.

Summary

This chapter has described the use of cost standards for the control of factory overhead. By recognizing the behavior patterns of overhead costs, flexible budgets can be developed and used for planning. The budget formula can then be used in the preparation of performance reports, and the sources of variances from budgeted costs can be isolated. Three methods of analyzing the factory overhead variance have been described and each has been illustrated graphically. Finally, the alternative methods of treating standard cost variances for income determination were discussed.

Therefore, in the second part of the charter, a logical approach to the variance investigation decision is first presented to isolate nonrandom variances from random variances, and then to determine whether or not costs justify an investigation of the nonrandom variances.

This chapter has discussed four sources of nonrandom variances and described the statistical control chart approach to isolate random and nonrandom variances. Control charts simply isolate nonrandom variances from random ones; they do not indicate the nature of a problem or how to correct it. The cost-benefit approach (also referred to as the decision theory approach) discussed in this chapter can be used to evaluate whether or not investigation of a nonrandom variance is justified.

Key Definitions

Activity measure — A measure that varies directly with production volume, which can be used to predict the behavior of factory overhead costs.

Budget formula — An equation which expresses a factory overhead cost in terms of its fixed and variable components and of an activity measure.

Budget (controllable) variance — An amount representing the difference between actual overhead costs and the costs which, according to the standards, should have been incurred for the output attained.

Cost-benefit approach	A decision theory approach which measures cost and benefit relationships in investigating and correcting variances. According to this method, the decision rule is to select the action with the lowest expected cost.
Factory overhead variance	In a standard costing system, the amount of the underapplied or overapplied factory overhead at the end of a reporting period.
Fixed overhead budget variance	The portion of the overhead spending variance which occurs when actual fixed overhead differs from the budgeted fixed overhead.
Flexible budget	A budget which recognizes the behavior patterns of overhead costs. It can be used to estimate costs at several different production volumes.
Implementation variance	A variance caused by a failure achieve a specific obtainable standard.
Indifference analysis	As used in the cost-benefit approach, indifference analysis provides a threshold representing the maximum deviation of the estimate of a probability that would not change the resulting action.
Management by exception	A management concept which requires management's concentration in the area where a significant exception has occurred.
Measurement variance	A variance caused by an error in measuring the actual cost of operating a process.
Model variance	A variance due to an incorrect model being used in the process or analysis.
Nonrandom variance	A variance due to some assignable cause(s). A nonrandom variance may require an investigation of its cause and corrective action if the expected benefits of the investigation exceeds its costs.
Overhead efficiency variance	That portion of the total factory overhead variance which arises due to production efficiency or inefficiency. Also called the variable overhead efficiency variance.
Overhead spending variance	That portion of an overhead budget variance which is not due to production efficiency or inefficiency.

Prediction variance	A variance caused by a mistake in predicting a parameter's value in a model.
Standard fixed overhead rate	A predetermined cost, used to apply fixed factory overhead to units produced and to analyze the factory overhead variance. It is usually determined by dividing budgeted fixed overhead by the normal activity.
Random variance	A variance due to non-assignable causes. A random variance requires no investigation of its cause and corrective action.
R chart	A control chart for range, which shows the variations in range in a set of samples.
Standard variable overhead rate	A predetermined cost, used to apply variable factory overhead to units produced and to analyze the factory overhead variance.
Static budget	A budget which provides cost estimates at a single, most likely production volume.
Statistical control charts	Control charts are constructed from samples of the items to be measured. They are used to isolate nonrandom variances from random variances.
Variable overhead spending 'variance	The portion of the overhead spending variance which occurs when actual variable overhead differs from the budgeted variable overhead for the number of hours worked.
Volume variance	A portion of the factory overhead variance, which occurs because the actual volume of production differs from the normal-activity used in computing the standard overhead rate.
X chart	A control chart for the mean, which shows variations in the average values in a set of samples.

Questions

11-1 Why is the control of factory overhead costs a particularly useful application for flexible budgets?

11-2 What are the assumptions underlying the flexible budget formula? Are these assumptions always valid when flexible budgets are used?

11-3 Describe the advantages of flexible budgets over static budgets for planning.

11-4 Describe the advantages of flexible budgets over static budgets for control.

11-5 What are the advantages of departmental factory overhead rates? the disadvantages?

11-6 At what level in an organization is a factory overhead volume variance controllable? Who should be held responsible for it?

11-7 Intuitively, what is the significance of the factory overhead budget variance? Why is it sometimes called the controllable variance?

11-8 How may the factory overhead efficiency variance be interpreted? Is it useful for control?

11-9 What are the sources of the factory overhead spending variance?

11-10 Describe the methods for disposing of standard cost variances at year-end. When is each method appropriate?

11-11 Distinguish between random and nonrandom variances or deviations.

11-12 Describe four possible sources of nonrandom variances or deviations.

11-13 Do you agree with the following statement: "When a process has a favorable variance, it requires no investigation"?

11-14 If a cost variance is not investigated, will the variance continue in the future?

11-15 Describe how control charts are set up and used in cost control.

11-16 Explain why both the X chart and the R chart are needed in the use of control charts for cost control.

11-17 What is the advantage and the disadvantage of using the control chart approach in cost control?

11-18 Describe how the cost-benefit approach can be used in determining whether or not to investigate a variance.

11-19 If a cost variance is investigated, will the cause of the variance always be found?

11-20 When would an out-of-control process be allowed to continue?

11-21 What are the major assumptions underlying the cost-benefit approach to the variance investigation decision?

Problems

11-22 *Cost Behavior*

The following relationships pertain to a year's budgeted activity for Smythe Company:

Direct labor hours	300,000	400,000
Total costs	$129,000	$154,000

What are the budgeted fixed costs for the year?

(*AICPA adapted*)

11-23 *Total Overhead Variance*

Information on Fire Company's overhead costs is as follows:

Actual variable overhead	$73,000
Actual fixed overhead	$17,000
Standard hours allowed for actual production	32,000
Standard variable overhead rate per direct labor hour	$2.50
Standard fixed overhead rate per direct labor hour	$0.50

What is the total overhead variance?

(*AICPA adapted*)

11-24 *Total Overhead Variance*

Air, Inc. uses a standard cost system. Overhead cost information for Product CO for the month of October is as follows:

Total actual overhead incurred	$12,600
Fixed overhead budgeted	$ 3,300
Total standard overhead rate per direct labor hour	$4.00
Variable overhead rate per direct labor hour	$3.00
Standard hours allowed for actual production	3,500

What is the overall (or net) overhead variance?

(*AICPA adapted*)

11-25 *Total Overhead Variance*

Information on Overhead Company's overhead costs is as follows:

Standard applied overhead	$80,000
Budgeted overhead based on standard direct labor hours allowed	$84,000
Budgeted overhead based on actual direct labor hours allowed	$83,000
Actual overhead	$86,000

What is the total overhead variance?

(*AICPA adapted*)

11-26 *Budget Formula*

Adams Corporation has developed the following flexible budget formula for annual indirect labor cost:

Total cost = \$4,800 + \$0.50 per machine hour.

Operating budgets for the current month are based upon 20,000 hours of planned machine time. What are the budgeted indirect labor costs?

(*AICPA adapted*)

11-27 *Budget Variance*

Alden Company has a standard costing and flexible budgeting system and uses a two-way analysis of overhead variances. Selected data for the month of February's production activity is as follows:

Budgeted fixed factory overhead costs	\$ 64,000
Actual factory overhead incurred	\$ 230,000
Variable factory overhead rate per direct labor hour	\$5
Standard direct labor hours	\$ 32,000
Actual direct labor hours	\$ 33,000

What is the budget (controllable) variance?

(*AICPA adapted*)

11-28 *Spending and Efficiency Variances*

The following information is available from the Tyro Company

Actual factory overhead	\$15,000
Fixed overhead expenses, actual	\$ 7,200
Fixed overhead expenses, budgeted	\$ 7,000
Actual hours	3,500
Standard hours	3,800
Variable overhead rate per direct labor hour	\$ 2.50

Assuming that Tyro uses a three-way analysis of overhead variances, what is:
(a) overhead spending variance,
(b) overhead efficiency variance.

(AICPA adapted)

11-29 *Three Methods for Overhead Variance Analysis*
The data below relate to the month of April 20X1 for Marilyn, Inc., which uses a standard cost system:

Actual total direct labor	$43,400
Actual hours used	14,000
Standard hours allowed for good output	15,000
Direct labor rate variance-debit	$ 1,400
Actual total overhead	$32,000
Budgeted fixed costs	$ 9,000
"Normal" activity in hours	12,000
Total overhead application rate per standard direct labor hour:	$2.25
Actual fixed costs	$10,000

(a) Determine the total overhead variance for Marilyn, Inc. for April.
(b) Analyze the total overhead variance using:
(1) Two Variance Method
(2) Three Variance Method
(3) Four Variance Method.

(AICPA adapted)

11-30 *Working Backward from Variances*
Beth Company's budgeted fixed factory overhead costs are $50,000 per month plus a variable factory overhead rate of $4 per direct labor hour. The standard direct labor hours allowed for October production were 18,000. An analysis of the factory overhead indicates that, in October, Beth had an unfavorable budget (controllable) variance of $1,000 and a favorable volume variance of $500. Beth uses a two-way analysis of overhead variances.

Determine:
(1) Actual factory overhead incurred in October,
(2) Applied factory overhead in October.

11-31 *Working Backward from Variances*
The following information relates to a given department of Herman Company for the fourth quarter of 20X0.

Actual total overhead (fixed plus variable)	$178,500
Budget formula	$110,000 plus $.50 per hour
Total overhead application rate	$1.50 per hour
Spending variance	$8,000 unfavorable
Volume variance	$5,000 favorable

The total overhead variance is divided into three variances: spending, efficiency, and volume.

From the above information, compute:

(a) The actual hours worked in the department during the quarter;

(b) The standard hours allowed for the good outputs produced.

(*AICPA adapted*)

11-32 *Flexible Budget for Planning*

AB Company utilizes a standard cost system. The following static budget has been developed for Department X for April, when expected production is 4,000 units.

Direct material	$ 8,000
Direct labor	9,200
Factory overhead:	
Indirect material	1,000
Indirect labor	800
Utilities	400
Depreciation	6,400
Total	$25,800

Analysis has shown that of these costs, the following amounts are fixed and are incurred on a monthly basis regardless of the level of production: In direct labor $600, utilities $200 and depreciation $6,400. From the above data, prepare a flexible budget for Department X showing projected costs when production is

(a) 3,500 units

(b) 4,000 units

(c) 4,500 units

11-33 *Analysis of Overhead Variances*

Strayer Company, which uses a fully integrated standard cost system, had budgeted the following sales and costs for 20X5:

Unit Sales	20,000
Sales	$200,000
Total production costs at standard cost	130,000
Gross Margin	70,000
Beginning inventories	none
Ending inventories	none

At the end of 20X5 Strayer Company reported production and sales of 19,200 units. Total factory overhead incurred was exactly equal to budgeted factory overhead for 20X5 and there was underapplied total factory overhead of $2,000 at December 31, 20X5. Factory overhead is applied to the work-in-process inventory on the basis of standard direct labor hours allowed for units produced. Also, there was favorable direct labor efficiency variance, but no direct labor rate variance and no raw material variances for 20X5.

Explain why factory overhead was underapplied by $2,000, and being as specific as the data permit, indicate which overhead variances may have been affected. Strayer uses a three variance method of analyzing the total factory overhead variance; the three variances are (1) spending variance, (2) efficiency variance, and (3) volume variance.

(*AICPA adapted*)

11-34 *Flexible Budget Performance Report*

Julia Jones, cost accountant for Clanton Corp., has developed the following budgetary information for the Production Department's monthly overhead expense. X represents the monthly production in units.

Cost Category	*Formula*	
Supervision (uncontrollable)	$2,000	
Indirect materials (controllable)		$.25X
Indirect labor (controllable)	7,000	+.5X
Electricity (controllable)	200	+ .05X
Water (controllable)	100	+ .02X
Repairs (variable is controllable, fixed is uncontrollable)	4,000	+ .10X
Depreciation (uncontrollable)	8,000	

During the month of February, 20,000 units were produced. The following costs were incurred: Supervision $2,000, Indirect materials $4,900, Indirect labor $18,400, Electricity $1,500, Repairs $5,600, Water $400, and Depreciation $8,000. Prepare a flexible budget overhead performance report for the manager of the Production Department, in good form.

11-35 *Four-Variance Method*

The Organet Stamping Company manufactures a variety of products made of plastic and aluminum components. During the winter months substantially all of the production capacity is devoted to the production of lawn sprinklers for the following spring and summer season. Other products are manufactured during the remainder of the year. Because a variety of products are manufactured throughout the year, factory volume is measured by production labor hours rather than units of product.

Production and sales volume have grown steadily for the past several years as can be seen from the following schedule of standard production labor content of annual output:

20X5	32,000 hours
20X4	30,000 hours
20X3	27,000 hours
20X2	28,000 hours
20X1	26,000 hours

The company has developed standard costs for its several products. Standard costs for each year are set in the preceding October. The standard cost of a sprinkler for 20X5 was $2.50, computed as follows:

Direct materials		
Aluminum	0.2 lbs. @ $0.40 per lb.	$0.08
Plastic	1.0 lbs. @ $0.38 per lb.	0.38
Production labor	0.3 hrs. @ $4.00 per hr.	1.20
Overhead (calculated using 30,000 production labor hours as normal capacity)		
Variable	0.3 hrs. @ $1.60 per hr.	0.48
Fixed	0.3 hrs. @ $1.20 per hr.	0.36
Total		$2.50

During February 20X5, 8,500 good sprinklers were manufactured. The following costs were incurred and charged to production:

Materials requisitioned for production		
Aluminum	1,900 lbs. @ $0.40 per lb.	$ 760
Plastic		
Regular grade	6,000 lbs. @ $0.38 per lb.	2,280
Low grade	3,500 lbs. @ $0.38 per lb.	1,330
Production labor		
Straight time	2,300 hrs. @ $4.00 per hr.	9,200
Overtime	400 hrs. @ $6.00 per hr.	2,400
Overhead		
Variable		5,200
Fixed		3,100
Costs charged to production		$24,270

From the above data, compute:
(a) Fixed overhead budget variance,
(b) Variable overhead spending variance.

11-36 *Standard Cost Variances*

Melody Corporation is a manufacturing company that produces a single product known as "Jupiter." Melody uses the first-in, first-out (FIFO) process costing method for both financial statement and internal management reporting.

In analyzing production results, standard costs are used, whereas actual costs are used for financial statement reporting. The standards, which are based upon equivalent units of production, are as follows:

Raw material per unit	1 lb. @ $10 per lb.
Direct labor per unit	2 hrs. @ $4 per hr.
Factory overhead per unit	2 hrs. @ $1.25 per hr.

Budgeted factory overhead for standard hours allowed for April production is $30,000. Costs applicable to April production are as follows:

	Actual Cost	*Standard Cost*
Raw material used (11,000 pounds)	$121,000	$100,000
Direct labor (25,000 hours actually worked)	105,575	82,400
Factory overhead	31,930	25,750

Prepare a schedule analyzing for April production the following variances as either favorable or unfavorable:

(a) Total materials.
(b) Materials price.
(c) Materials usage.
(d) Total labor.
(e) Labor rate.
(f) Labor efficiency.
(g) Total factory overhead.
(h) Factory overhead volume.
(i) Factory overhead budget.

Show supporting computations in good form.

(*AICPA adapted*)

11-37 *Flexible Budget for Control*

The Melcher Co. produces farm equipment at several plants. The business is seasonal and cyclical in nature. The company has attempted to use budgeting for planning and controlling activities, but the variable nature of the business has caused some company officials to be skeptical about the usefulness of budgeting to the company. The accountant for the Adrian plant has been using a system he calls "flexible budgeting" to help his plant management control operations.

The company president asks him to explain what the term means, how he applies the system at the Adrian plant and how it can be applied to the company as a whole. The accountant presents the following data as part of his explanation:

Budget data for 20X1		
Normal monthly capacity of the plant in		
Direct labor hours		10,000 hours
Material costs	6 lbs. @ $1.50	$9.00 per unit
Labor costs	2 hours @ $3.00	$6.00 per unit

Overhead estimate at normal monthly capacity	
Variable (controllable):	
Indirect labor	$ 6,650
Indirect materials	600
Repairs	750
Total variable	$ 8,000
Fixed (uncontrollable):	
Depreciation	3,250
Supervision	3,000
Total fixed	$ 6,250
Total fixed and variable	$14,250

Planned units for January 20X1	4,000
Planned units for February 20X1	6,000
Actual data for January 20X1	
Hours worked	8,400
Units produced	3,800
Costs incurred:	
Material (24,000 lbs.)	$36,000
Direct labor	25,200
Indirect labor	6,000
Indirect materials	600
Repairs	1,800
Depreciation	3,250
Supervision	3,000
Total	$75,850

Required:

(a) Prepare a budget for January.

(b) Prepare a report for January comparing actual and budgeted costs for the actual activity for the month.

11-38 *Methods of Overhead Variance Analysis*

The Groomer Company manufactures two products, Florimene and Glyoxide, used in the plastics industry. The company uses a flexible budget in its standard cost system to develop variances. Selected data follow:

	Florimene	Glyoxide
Data on Standard Costs:		
Raw material per unit	3 lbs. @ $1.00 per lb.	4 lbs. @ $1.10 per lb.
Direct labor per unit	5 hrs. @ $2.00 per hr.	6 hrs. @ $2.50 per hr.
Variable factory overhead per unit	$3.20 per direct labor hour	$3.50 per direct labor hr.
Fixed factory overhead per month	$20,700	$26,520
Normal Activity per month	5,750 direct labor hrs.	7,800 direct labor hrs.
Units produced in September:	1,000	1,200
Raw material	3,100 lbs. @ $0.90 per lb.	4,700 lbs. @ $1.15 per lb.
Direct labor	4,900 hrs. @ $1.95 per hr.	7,400 hrs. @ $2.55 per hr.

Variable factory overhead ...	$16,170	$25,234
Fixed factory overhead	$20,930	$26,400

Determine the following factory overhead variances for each product.

(a) Total overhead variance.
(b) Volume variance.
(c) Budget variance.
(d) Efficiency variance.
(e) Spending variance.
(f) Variable spending variance.
(g) Fixed budget variance.

(AICPA adapted)

11-39 *Proration of Standard Cost Variances*

The Butrico Manufacturing Corporation uses a standard cost system which records raw materials at actual cost, records materials price variance at the time that raw materials are issued to work-in-process, and prorates all variances at year-end. Variances associated with direct materials are prorated based on the direct material balances in the appropriate accounts, and variances associated with direct labor and manufacturing overhead are prorated based on the direct labor balances in the appropriate accounts. The following information is available for Butrico for the year ended December 31, 20X5.

Raw materials inventory at December 31, 20X5	$ 65,000
Finished goods inventory at December 31, 20X5:	
Direct material	87,000
Direct labor...	130,500
Applied manufacturing overhead..	104,400
Cost of goods sold for the year ended December 31, 20X5:	
Direct material	348,000
Direct labor...	739,500
Applied manufacturing overhead..	591,600
Direct material price variance (unfavorable)	10,000
Direct material usage variance (favorable).....................................	15,000
Direct labor rate variance (unfavorable)	20,000
Direct labor efficiency variance (favorable)	5,000
Manufacturing overhead incurred	690,000

There were no beginning inventories and no ending work-in-process inventory. Manufacturing overhead is applied at 80% of standard direct labor.

(a) Determine the ending balances of raw materials inventory, finished goods inventory, and cost of goods sold after proration.
(b) How would the proration procedures have differed if:
(1) Raw materials inventories had been carried at standard costs?
(2) There had been an ending balance in the work-in-process inventory account?
(3) There had been beginning balances in these accounts?

(AICPA adapted)

11-40 *Overhead Cost Behavior and Flexible Budgets*

Department A is one of 15 departments in the plant and is involved in the production of all of the six products manufactured. The department is highly mechanized and as a result its output is measured in direct machine hours. Variable (flexible) budgets are utilized throughout the factory in planning and controlling costs, but here the focus is upon the application of variable budgets only in Department A. The following data covering a time span of approximately six months were taken from the various budgets, accounting records and performance reports (only representative items and amounts are utilized here):

On March 15, 20X5, the following variable budget was approved for the department; it will be used throughout the 20X6 fiscal year which begins July 1, 20X5. This variable budget was developed through the cooperative efforts of the department manager, his supervisor and certain staff members from the budget department.

20X6 Variable Budget—Department A

Controllable Costs	*Fixed Amount per Month*	*Variable Rate per Direct Machine*
Employee salaries	$ 9,000	
Indirect wages	18,000	$.07
Indirect materials		.09
Other costs	6,000	.03
	$33,000	$.19

On May 5, 20X5, the annual sales plan and the production budget were completed. In order to continue preparation of the annual profit plan (which was detailed by month) the production budget was translated to planned activity for each of the factory departments. The planned activity for Department A was:

	For the 12 months ending June 30, 20X6				
	Year	*July*	*Aug.*	*Sept.*	*Etc.*
Planned output in direct machine hours	325,000	22,000	25,000	29,000	249,000

On August 31, 20X5, the manager of Department A was informed that his planned output for September had been revised to 34,000 direct machine hours. He expressed some doubt as to whether this volume could be attained.

At the end of September 20X5 the accounting records provided the following actual data for the month for the department:

Actual output in direct machine hours	33,000
Actual controllable costs incurred:	
Employee salaries	$ 9,300
Indirect wages	20,500
Indirect materials	2,850
Other costs	7,510
	$40,160

Required:

The requirements relate primarily to the potential users of the variable budget for the period March through September 20X5.

(a) What activity base is utilized as a measure of volume in the budget for this department? How should one determine the range of the activity base to which the variable rates per direct machine hour are relevant? Explain.

(b) The high-low point method was utilized in developing this variable budget. Using indirect wage costs as an example, illustrate and explain how this method would be applied in determining the fixed and variable components of indirect wage costs for this department. Assume that the high-low budget values for indirect wages are $19,400 at 20,000 direct machine hours and $20,100 at 30,000 direct machine hours.

(c) Explain and illustrate how the variable budget should be utilized:

(1) In budgeting costs when the annual sales plan and production budget are completed (about May 5, 20X5 or shortly thereafter).

(2) In budgeting a cost revision based upon a revised production budget (about August 31, 20X5 or shortly thereafter).

(3) In preparing a cost performance report for September 20X5.

(*AICPA adapted*)

11-41 *Comprehensive Standard Job Order Cost Problem*

The Justin Company has recently installed a standard cost system to simplify its factory bookkeeping and to aid in cost control. The company makes standard items for inventory, but because of the many products in its line, each is manufactured periodically under a production order. Prior to the installation of the system, job order cost sheets were maintained for each production order.

Since the introduction of the standard costs system, however, they have not been kept.

The fabricating department is managed by a general supervisor who has overall responsibility for scheduling, performance and cost control. The department consists of four machine/work centers. Each work center is manned by a four-person work group or team and the centers are aided by a 12-person support group.

Departmental practice is to assign a job to one team and expect the team to perform most of the work necessary to complete the job, including acquisition of materials and supplies from the stores department and machining and assembling. This has been practical and satisfactory in the past and is readily accepted by the employees.

Information regarding production cost standards, products produced, and actual costs for the fabricating department in March is presented below.

Unit Standard Costs

	Part		
	A7A	C6D	C7A
Material	$2.00	$3.00	$1.50
Direct labor	1.50	2.00	1.00
Overhead (per direct labor dollar)*:			
Variable	3.00	4.00	2.00
Fixed	.75	1.00	.50
	$7.25	$10.00	$5.00

* The departmental standard overhead rates are applied to the products as a percentage of direct labor dollars. The labor base was chosen because nearly all of the variable overhead costs are caused by labor activity. The departmental overhead rates were calculated at the beginning of the year as follows.

	Variable (Including Indirect Labor)	*Fixed*
Estimated annual cost	$360,000	$ 90,000
Estimated annual department direct labor dollars	$180,000	$180,000
Overhead rate	200%	50%

Analysis of the Fabricating Department Account for March

Charges		
Materials		
Job No. 307-11	$5,200	
Job No. 307-12	2,900	
Job No. 307-14	9,400	$17,500
Labor charges		
Job No. 307-11	$4,000	
Job No. 307-12	2,100	
Job No. 307-14	6,200	
Indirect labor	12,200	24,500
Variable overhead costs (e.g., supplies, electricity, etc.)		18,800
Fixed overhead costs (e.g. supervisor's salary, depreciation, property tax and insurance, etc.)		7,000
Total charges to department for March		$67,800
Credits		
Completed Jobs		
Job No. 307-11		
2,000 units part A7A @ 7.25	$14,500	
Job No. 307-12		
1,000 units part C6D @ 10.00	10,000	
Job No. 307-14		
6,000 units part C7A @ 5.00	30,000	$54,500
Variances transferred to the factory variance account		
Materials[1]	$1,500	
Direct labor2	1,300	
Variable overhead	9,000	
Fixed overhead	1,500	13,300
Total credits		$67,800

[1] Material price variances are isolated at acquisition and charged to the Stores Department.
[2] All direct labor was paid at the standard wage rate during March.

(a) Justin Company assumes that its efforts to control costs in the fabricating department would be aided if variances were calculated by jobs. Management intends to add this analysis next month. Calculate all the variances by job that might contribute to cost control under this assumption.

(b) Do you agree with the company's plan to initiate the calculation of job variances in addition to the currently calculated departmental variances? Explain you answer.

(*IMA adapted*)

11-42 *Comprehensive Standard Process Cost Problem*

The Bronson Company manufactures a fuel additive which has a stable selling price of $40 per drum. Since losing a government contract, the company has been producing and selling 80,000 drums per month, 50% of normal capacity. Management expects to increase production to 140,000 drums in the coming fiscal year.

In connection with your examination of the financial statements of the Bronson Company for the year ended September 30, 20X4, you have been asked to review some computations made by Bronson's cost accountant. Your working papers disclose the following about the company's operations:

1. Standard costs per drum of product manufactured:

Materials:	
8 gallons of miracle mix ...	$16
1 empty drum	1
	$17
Direct labor-1 hour	$ 5
Factory overhead	$ 6

2. Costs and expenses during September 20X5

Miracle mix:
500,000 gallons purchased at cost of $950,000; 650,000 gallons used

Empty drums:
94,000 purchased at cost of $94,000; 80,000 used

Direct labor:
82,000 hours worked at cost of $414,100

Factory overhead:

Depreciation of building and machinery (fixed)..	$210,000
Supervision and indirect labor (semi-variable)....	460,000
Other factory overhead (variable)	98,000
	$768,000

3. Other factory overhead was the only actual overhead cost which varied from the overhead budget for the September level of production; actual other factory overhead was $98,000 and the budgeted amount was $90,000.

4. At normal capacity of 160,000 drums per month, supervision and indirect labor costs are expected to be $570,000. All cost functions are linear.

5. None of the September 20X4 cost variances are expected to occur proportionally in future months. For the next fiscal year, the cost standards department expects the same standard usage of materials and direct labor hours. The average prices expected are: $2.10 per gallon of miracle mix, $1 per empty drum and $5.70 per direct labor hour. The current flexible budget of factory overhead costs is considered applicable to future periods without revision.

6. The company uses the two variance method of accounting for overhead.

(a) Prepare a schedule computing the following variances for September 20X9: 1. materials price variance, 2. materials usage variance, 3. labor rate variances, 4. labor usage (efficiency) variance, 5. controllable (budget or spending) overhead variance, 6. volume (capacity) overhead variance. Indicate whether variances were favorable or unfavorable.

(b) Prepare a schedule of the actual manufacturing cost per drum of product expected at production of 140,000 drums per month-using the following cost categories: materials, direct labor, fixed factory overhead, and variable factory overhead.

(AICPA adapted)

11-43 *Flexible Budget*

Wielson Company employs flexible budgeting techniques to evaluate the performance of several of its activities. The selling expense flexible budgets for three representative monthly activity levels are shown below.

Representative Monthly Flexible Budgets
for Selling Expenses

Activity measures:			
Unit sales volume	400,000	425,000	450,000
Dollar sales volume	$10,000,000	$10,625,000	$11,250,000
Number of orders	4,000	4,250	4,500
Number of salespersons	75	75	75
Monthly expenses:			
Advertising and promotion	$ 1,200,000	$ 1,200,000	$ 1,200,000
Administrative salaries	57,000	57,000	57,000
Sales salaries	75,000	75,000	75,000
Sales commissions	200,000	212,500	225,000
Salesperson travel	170,000	175,000	180,000
Sales office expense	490,000	498,750	507,500
Shipping expense	675,000	712,500	750,000
Total selling expenses	$ 2,867,000	$ 2,930,750	$ 2,994,500

The following assumptions were used to develop the selling expense flexible budgets.

- The average size of Wielson's sales force during the year was planned to be 75 people.
- Salespersons are paid a monthly salary plus commission on gross dollar sales.
- The travel costs are best characterized as a step variable cost. The fixed portion is related to the number of salespersons while the variable portion tends to fluctuate with gross dollar sales.
- Sales office expense is a mixed cost with the variable portion related to the number of orders processed.

- Shipping expense is a mixed cost with the variable portion related to the number of units sold.

A sales force of 80 persons generated a total of 4,300 orders resulting in a sales volume of 420,000 units during November. The gross dollar sales amounted to $10.9 million. The selling expenses incurred for November were as follows:

Advertising and promotion	$1,350,000
Administrative salaries	57,000
Sales salaries	80,000
Sales commissions	218,000
Salesperson travel	185,000
Sales office expense	497,200
Shipping expense	730,000
Total	$3,117,200

Required:

(a) Explain why flexible budgeting is a useful management tool.

(b) Explain why the selling expense flexible budgets presented above would not be appropriate for evaluating Wielson Company's November selling expenses, and indicate how the flexible budget would have to be revised.

(c) Prepare a selling expense report for November that Wielson Company can use to evaluate its control over selling expenses. The report should have a line for each selling expense item showing the appropriate budgeted amount, the actual selling expense, and the monthly dollar variation.

11-44 *Interpreting Variances*

The controller of a company which manufactures home-permanent kits has just received the following final production reports and cost figures for the month of May:

Standard Product Costs	
Direct materials (4 ounces @a $.50/ounce)	$2.00
Direct labor (10 workers of an hour @ $7.50/hour)	75
Variable overhead* (0.1 x $15)	1.50
Fixed overhead**	1.00
Total standard cost	$5.25

*Applied on the basis of direct labor hours.

**Based on normal activity of 120,000 direct labor hours per year and $1,200,000 of estimated fixed overhead costs for the year.

Production Costs for 90,000 Units

	Quantity	*Actual Cost*
Direct materials	405,000 ounces	$190,350
Direct labor	10,000 hours	71,500
Variable overhead		160,000
Fixed overhead		150,000

As early as the first week of May, the foremen were complaining about foul-ups and giving excuses for what they considered would be poor performances this month. Such excuses included:

(1) "I had to reassign my bottler who makes $8.00 per hour to a job that usually costs $6.50 per hour."
(2) "The bottling machine was broken again for an hour today."
(3) "How can I expect to utilize economies of scale when production has been so sporadic—ten hours one day and six the next?"
(4) "The materials we used gummed up the injection nozzle twice today."
(5) "The sales department again failed to calculate demand, and I had to bring in two days' supply of raw materials by air freight until we could get some by train."

Required:

(a) Compute the material price and quantity variances, labor rate and efficiency variances, variable overhead spending and efficiency variances, and fixed overhead budget and volume variances for the month of May.
(b) Evaluate each of the five excuses presented by the foremen.
(c) Using the variances computed in Part (a) and the analysis in Part (b), suggest the likely cause(s) of the problem and implied action(s).

(*IIA adapted*)

11-45 Disposition of Variances

The Kalman Co., a subsidiary of the Camper Corporation, submits interim financial statements. Camper combines these statements with similar statements from other subsidiaries to prepare its quarterly statements. The following data are taken from the records and accounts of the Kalman Co.

Sales forecasts for the year are:

Quarter	*Stove Units*	*Percent*
First	450,000	30%
Second	600,000	40
Third	150,000	10
Fourth	300,000	20
	1,500,000	100%

Sales have been achieved as forecast in the first and second quarters of the current year.

- Management is considering increasing the selling price of a stove from $30 to $34. However, management is concerned that this increase may reduce the already low sales volume forecasts for the third and fourth quarters.
- The production schedule calls for 1,500,000 stoves this year. The manufacturing facilities can produce 1,720,000 units per year or 430,000 units per quarter during regular hours. The quarterly production schedule shown below was developed to meet the seasonal sales demand and is being followed as planned.

Quarter	Scheduled Production (in units)	Percent
1	465,000	31%
2	450,000	30
3	225,000	15
4	360,000	24
	1,500,000	100%

The standard manufacturing cost of a stove unit, as established at the beginning of the current year, is as shown below. This standard cost does not incorporate any charges for overtime.

Material	$ 4
Labor	9
Variable overhead	2
Fixed overhead	3
Standard cost per stove	$18

- A significant and permanent price increase in the cost of raw material resulted in a material price variance of $270,000 for the materials used in the second quarter.
- There was a $120,000 unfavorable direct labor variance in the second quarter due in part to overtime pay to meet the heavy production schedule. An overtime premium equal to .5 times the standard labor rate is paid whenever production requires working beyond regular hours. The remaining amount of the labor variance during the quarter occurred as a result of unexpected inefficiencies.
- The second quarter unfavorable variable overhead variance of $36,000 was entirely related to the excess direct labor costs.
- Total fixed overhead expected to be incurred and budgeted for the year is $4,500,000. Through the first two quarters, $2,745,000 of fixed overhead has been absorbed into the production process. Of this amount, $1,350,000 was absorbed in the second quarter. The high production activity resulted in a total fixed overhead volume variance of $495,000 for the first two quarters.
- Selling expenses are 1001o of sales and are expected to total $4,500,000 for the year.
- Administrative expenses are $6,000,000 annually and are incurred uniformly throughout the period.
- Inventory balances as of the end of the second quarter are as follows:

Raw material—at actual cost complete	$400,000
Work in process 50%—at standard cost	72,000
Finished goods—at standard cost	900,000

The stove product line is expected to earn $7,500,000 before taxes this year. The estimated state and federal income tax expenses for the year are $4,500,000.

Any unplanned variances which are significant and permanent in nature are prorated to the applicable accounts during the quarter in which they are incurred.

Required:

Prepare the second quarter interim income statement for the Kalman subsidiary of Camper Corporation.

(*IMA adapted*)

11-46 *Statistical-Control Limits*

Assume X = 100; R = 10; and the number of observations in each sample is 5.

Required.

Determine the 3-sigma control limits for the X chart and the R chart. (Use the 3-sigma control limit table)

11-47 *Using the Standard Error of the Sample Means to Calculate Control Limits*

In order to establish 2-sigma control limits on the time it takes to complete an operation, a manager took random samples of four operator's performance every hour for five consecutive hours. The manager found that the overall average time of the operation is 30 minutes and the standard deviation of time is 3 minutes.

Required:

Determine the upper and lower control limits for the X chart.

11-48 *Interpreting an X Chart*

Mr. Blue has been hired as a consultant by the Reds Company to establish statistical quality control for their production process. Mr. Blue has drawn fifteen samples with four observations in each sample for purposes of setting up control charts. Mr. Blue developed the following X chart for the observed data:

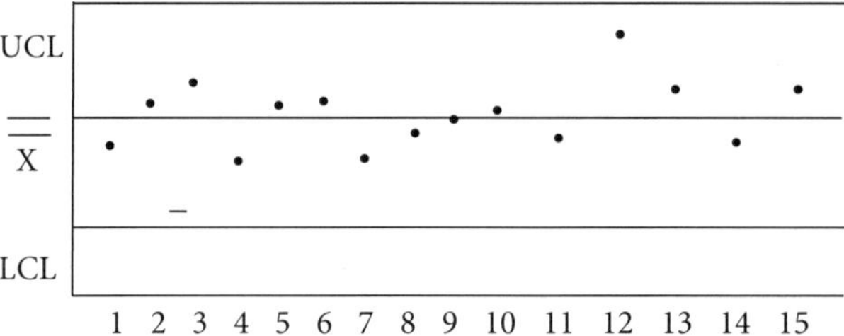

Required:

Discuss the usefulness of the X chart developed by Mr. Blue.

11-49 *Developing X and R Charts*

The manager of the Ace Motel wants to establish statistical control on the time it takes a maid to make up a room. The manager took random samples of 4 maids' performance every day for seven consecutive days. The results of the sample are as follow:

Day	Sample Times (in minutes)
1	22, 16, 20, 28
2	20, 18, 22, 24
3	30, 20, 26, 22
4	24, 28, 30, 20
5	18, 28, 22, 28

6	27, 23, 22, 28
7	18, 28, 20, 24

Required:

Construct the control charts and plot the samples. (Use the 3-sigma control limit table.)

11-50 *Decision to Investigate a Process*

Given the current period's operating results, the Show-Me Company has estimated that the probability of its process being in a controlled situation is 90% and the probability of an out-of-control situation is 10%. The cost of investigation is estimated to be \$8,000. The cost of correction if the process is out-of-control is \$2,000. The total excess operating costs if an out-of-control situation is not corrected are \$40,000.

Required:

Determine whether or not the company should investigate the process.

11-51 *Decision to Investigate a Variance*

Given a \$1,000 unfavorable labor efficiency variance for the month of May, the manager of the manufacturing department has estimated that the probability of his process being in control is 85% and the probability of an out-of-control situation is 15%. The cost of investigation is estimated to be \$5,000 and the cost of correcting an out-of-control situationis about \$6,000. The estimated present value of cost savings associated with correcting the process is \$50,000 if the process is dicovered to be out-of-control.

Required:

Determine whether or not the company should investigate the process.

11-52 *Determing the Critical Probability*

For each of the following independent cases, find the probability of the process being in control, at which a manager would be indifferent to investigating the source of the variance.

Case	Cost of Investigation	Cost of Correction	Present Value of Cost Savings
1	\$100	\$ 50	\$200
2	50	100	400
3	200	50	250
4	100	50	100

11-53 *Decision to Investigate and Indifference Point*

Assume that an investigation of a process would cost approximately \$500. If the process is out-of-control, the cost of correcting the condition would be \$1,000. The present value of cost savings over the planning period is estimated to be \$5,000.

Required:

(1) If the probability of the process being out-of-control is 50%, should the process be investigated?

(2) What maximum probability is necessary for the process to be in control in order to warrant an investigation of the process?

11-54 *Determing the Necessary Cost Savings for Investigation*
Assume that the cost of investigation is $2,000 and the cost of correction is $500 for positive and negative variances. The manager is always indifferent about conducting an investigation when there is a probability of 90% that the process is in control.

Required:

Estimate the present value of cost savings assoicated with the correctingthe process.

11-55 *Determing Expected Costs of Investigation and No Investigation*
The manager of the Delta Company is always indifferent about conducting an investigation when there is a probability of 80% that the process is in control. The manager estimated that the cost to investigate is $4,000 and the cost to correct the process if an out-of-control situation is discovered is $2,000. For the current period, the probability that the process is out-of-control is assessed to be 85%.

Required:

(1) Estimate the present value of the cost savings (B) associated with correcting the process.
(2) Determine the expected costs of investigation for the current period.
(3) Determine the expected costs of no investigation for the current period.

11-56 *Determing the Value of Additional Information*
Assume the probability that a process is in control is 80%. The cost of investigation is $100. The cost of correction is $500. The present value of cost savings over the planning period is $1,200.

Required:

Determine the maximum amount that a firm would pay for additional information concerning the true state of the process.

11-57 *Cost Payoff Tables and Probabilities*
The accountant and production manager of the Merrick Company have agreed that the following values are applicable in the investigation of a certain process:

Cost of investigation	$ 400
Cost of remedy action, if process is out of order	1,600
Anticipated savings	5,000

Required:

Assuming that the subjective probability that the process may be out of control is .10, determine whether or not an investigation of the process is justified.
Compute that calculated minimum probability for the process to be out of control at which one would be indifferent as to whether or not to investigate the process.

(IMA adapted)

1. *To describe three alternative assumptions regarding the determination of product costs, absorption costing, variable costing and throughput costing.*
2. *To explain the choice of an activity level used in computing the predetermined factory overhead rate.*
3. *To illustrate the effects of alternative product costing assumptions on reported income.*
4. *To understand the advantages of variable costing for purposes of planning, decision-making and control.*

12 Variable Costing

Previous chapters have described different methods of determining product costs for purposes of inventory valuation and income determination. These methods recorded either standard costs or actual historical costs utilizing either a job order costing system or a process costing system. An underlying assumption behind each of these methods was that the costs of a product consisted of three major components, namely direct materials, direct labor and factory overhead. Under such an assumption, a portion of fixed factory overhead costs are absorbed by each unit of products manufactured; as a result, these costing systems are commonly referred to as *absorption costing* or *full costing.* Since absorption costing is the required method under GAAP for external reporting, it is also referred to as *conventional costing.*

For purposes of planning, decision-making and control, many cost accountants find absorption costing deficient. An alternative approach to product costing, called *variable costing,* has been advocated by them for these internal reporting objectives. With variable costing, only the variable manufacturing costs are inventoried. Since inventoried costs under variable costing are composed of primarily direct costs such as direct material and direct labor costs, variable costing is also referred to as *direct costing.* However, we must be clear that variable costs are not necessarily direct costs and direct costs are not always variable costs. For instance, variable factory overhead costs are indirect costs, but direct labor costs tend to be fixed.

More recently, cost accountants have argued that managers have little flexibility adjusting the capacity of committed production resources except that of direct materials and thus have proposed another approach to production costing, called *throughput costing or super-variable costing.* With throughput costing, only the direct material costs are inventoried and all other costs are treated as expenses of the period in which they are incurred.

In this chapter, the implications and problems associated with absorption costing will first be described in greater detail. Then variable costing and throughput costing methods will be described. The differences between these three costing methods are discussed at the end of this chapter.

Absorpton Costing

All accounting systems produce a measure of reported income by attempting to match revenues with the costs that produced them. For this purpose, costs are classified as either product costs or period costs. Product costs are inventoried and matched against revenues when the products are sold; period costs are matched against revenues during the period in which they are incurred.

Since all manufacturing costs are product costs under absorption costing, a portion of factory overhead costs, both fixed and variable, were attached to each unit of products manufactured using a predetermined overhead rate and were matched against revenues as part of cost of goods sold. Other costs not directly associated with the manufacturing process, such as selling and administrative expenses, are considered to be period costs excluded from the calculation of product costs.

In costing systems discussed in Chapters 5 and 6, the predetermined overhead rate is computed by dividing a measure of the normal activity level for a budgetary period into the budgeted factory overhead. The choice of the activity level used directly affects the portion of fixed costs attached to the products and thus affects the recorded cost of goods sold. It also affects the amount of the factory overhead that is underapplied or overapplied at the end of a reporting period, which has been called the total factory overhead variance.

Activity Level and the Overhead Variance

During any reporting period, factory overhead is applied to products based on some measures of the activity level for the period. In a historical costing system, the overhead rate is multiplied by the actual direct labor hours or some other actual measures to arrive at applied factory overhead. In a standard costing system, factory overhead applied is computed as the product of the predetermined overhead rate and the standard hours allowed for the output actually attained. In either case, actual factory overhead at the end of a period may differ from that applied, resulting in a factory overhead variance. In Chapter 11, we have described methods for analyzing such a variance when standard costs are used.

The magnitude of the factory overhead variance depends on the predetermined overhead rate, which in turn depends on the activity level assumed in computing the predetermined overhead rate. Thus, whenever the actual activity level consumed differs significantly from that assumed by the overhead rate, a large overhead variance will result because a significant amount of fixed factory overhead has been underapplied or overapplied. In a standard costing system, the volume variance measures the factory overhead variance arising from this source. This relationship is summarized for both historical and standard costing systems in Illustration 12-1.

In the chapter on standard costing, it was stated that many accountants regard the volume variance as uncontrollable. It should now be clear why this is the case; the difference between

Illustration 12-1 Effect of Budgeted Activity Level on Factory Overhead Variance

Standard Cost System		*Historical Cost System*	
Applied Factory Overhead	Budgeted Factory Overhead	Applied Factory Overhead	Actual Factory Overhead
Overhead Rate X Standard Hours Allowed for Actual Output	Budgeted Fixed Costs + (Variable Rate X Standard Hours Allowed)	Overhead Rate X Actual Hours	Costs Recorded
Volume Variance		Factory Overhead Variance	

$$\text{Overhead Rate} = \frac{\text{Budgeted Factory Overhead}}{\text{Budgeted Standard Hours}} \qquad \text{Overhead Rate} = \frac{\text{Budgeted Factory Overhead}}{\text{Budgeted Overhead}}$$

actual activity level and the budgeted activity level used in determining the overhead rate is frequently beyond the control of individual managers in the organization. This difference may be due to such factors as competition, critical material shortages or general economic conditions. The volume variance is nevertheless subject to further interpretation; its significance depends on the nature of the activity level used in calculating the predetermined overhead rate.

Choice of the Activity Level

Just as accountants have varying philosophies regarding the setting of physical standards, there are likewise different opinions on what level of activity should be chosen for purposes of establishing an overhead application rate. In previous chapters, it was stated that an activity level equivalent to the normal activity capacity is chosen. Although this is a common method, other levels in activity capacity are frequently used as well. In practice, there are four capacity concepts which may be used.

The activity level may be set equal to the maximum capacity, or *ideal capacity,* of the production facilities of the organization. This is the activity level which would be attained if the plant operated at peak efficiency on a continuous basis. There are no allowances for machine breakdowns, strikes, decreased demand for products, or production errors of any kind. Because such a situation is realistically unattainable, the factory overhead applied will always be less than that occurred, and in a standard costing system an unfavorable volume variance will result. In this case, the magnitude of the volume variance provides a measure of the extent to which actual production is less than the ideal capacity. The volume variance thus becomes a measure of the cost of unused capacity.

An alternative approach, using an activity level equal to the *practical capacity* of the production facilities, recognizes that workers and equipment do not operate at peak efficiency for an extended period of time. Practical capacity is the activity level at which production could be maintained indefinitely, and contains allowances for machine breakdowns, preventive maintenance, and holidays and vacation periods. When this activity level is used, the volume variance results from the fact that sales volume did not permit operation at this desired level. Thus, the magnitude of the volume variance is to some extent controllable by the sales branch of the organization.

The use of *normal capacity* in setting the overhead rate has already been discussed in a previous chapter. Normal activity capacity is an annual volume of production which would satisfy consumer demand for production over a planning cycle of several years. It allows for idleness of production facilities due to lack of sales in certain years, assuming that this lack of sales will be made up during other years in the cycle. It is frequently used by organizations which have a relatively stable demand for their products. When normal activity capacity is used, favorable and unfavorable volume variances can be expected to offset each other over the years of the planning cycle. The volume variance is a result of factors related to the general business cycle and is usually considered uncontrollable

A final approach sets the overhead rate as an extension of the process of developing an annual budget. The rate may be computed using *expected annual capacity,* which represents the anticipated production level and capacity utilization for the upcoming year. When this approach is used, the overhead rates are revised each year and provide a better basis for controlling overhead costs at the cost center level. The magnitude of the volume variance represents the amount of the total overhead variance which arises because the actual production level differed from that budgeted.

Absorption costing requires the choice of an activity capacity level in order to determine an overhead rate. The common approaches of doing this are summarized in Illustration 12-2. With absorption costing, both fixed and variable factory overhead costs are inventoried. When actual activity level differs from the one chosen, the fixed overhead costs applied will differ from those incurred, producing a volume variance and a misstatement of inventory values. In direct costing, where only variable costs are inventoried, no volume variance exists.

Variable Costing

Variable costing is advocated by many accountants for performance evaluation of managers because it avoids the allocation of fixed factory overhead costs to units of products manufactured. With variable costing, only those manufacturing costs which vary in proportion to the volume of production are considered as product costs. These include direct material costs, direct labor

Illustration12-2 Overhead Rate Activity Capacity Levels in Absorption Costing

Activity Capacity Level	*Distinguishing Assumptions*	*Interpretation of the Volume Variance*
Ideal Capacity	Operation at peak efficiency on a continuous basis	Cost of idle capacity due to all factors
Practical Capacity	Operation at sustainable efficiency, production not limited by sales demand	Cost of idle capacity due to lack of sales
Normal Capacity	Operation at a level to satisfy sales demand over several years	Due to cyclical fluctuations and uncontrollable
Expected Annual Capacity	Operation at a level to satisfy sales demand in a single year	Fixed overhead underapplied or overapplied due to deviation from budgeted sales

costs, and the costs of variable factory overhead which are applied using a predetermined variable overhead rate. Fixed factory overhead costs are assumed to be a cost of being in business, of providing the ability to produce, rather than a cost of production. As a result, they are considered to be associated with periods of time rather than with products. That is, fixed factory overhead costs in variable costing are classified as period costs and are matched against revenues in the period in which they are incurred; they are not included in the valuation of inventories and costs of goods sold for purposes of income determination. Variable costing utilizes a different form of the income statement and may produce different measures of reported income.

The Variable Costing Income Statement

Variable costing produces, for internal reporting purposes, an income statement based on the *contribution approach* to income determination. Whereas the traditional income statement aggregates and discloses costs only by functional classification, using the contribution approach costs are grouped first by their behavior patterns and then by functional classifications within each behavior pattern. The traditional income statement used in absorption costing discloses cost of goods sold (which includes fixed manufacturing costs) and gross profit or gross margin. With the contribution approach, total variable costs are subtracted from sales revenue to disclose the *contribution toward fixed costs and profits.* This amount is frequently referred to as the *contribution margin,* or simply the *contribution.* Total fixed costs are then subtracted from contribution to arrive at the direct costing measure of reported income. These two forms of the income statement are contrasted in Illustration 12-3.

On the variable costing income statement, the variable manufacturing costs are those of the goods sold, not of the goods manufactured during the reporting period. The variable manufacturing cost of goods sold may be computed on a variable manufacturing cost statement similar to that used in absorption costing. Such a statement is shown in Illustration 12-4.

Effect of the Costing Method on Net Income

Under absorption costing a portion of fixed manufacturing costs are included in inventory values, while under variable costing they are not. Therefore, the two methods may produce

Illustration 12-3Absorption Costing and Variable Costing Income Statements Compared

Absorption Costing Income Statement

Sales		XXX
Less: Cost of Goods Sold		
Beginning Finished Goods Inventory	XX	
Plus: Cost of Goods Manufactured	XX	
Manufacturing Costs to Account for	XX	
Less: Ending Finished Goods Inventory	(XX)	XXX
Gross Profit		XXX
Less:		
Selling Expenses	XX	
Administrative Expenses	XX	XXX
Operating Income		XX
Other Income and Expense		XX
Net Income		XX

Variable Costing Income Statement

Sales		XXX
Less: Variable Costs		
Variable Manufacturing Costs	XX	
Variable Selling Costs	XX	
Variable Administrative Costs	XX	XXX
Contribution		XX
Less:		
Fixed Manufacturing Expenses	XX	
Fixed Selling Expenses	XX	
Fixed Administrative Expenses	XX	XX
Operating Income		XX
Other Income and Expense		XX
Net Income		XX

Illustration 12-4 Variable Manufacturing Cost Statement Variable Costing

During the month of July, RiversideCorporation incurred direct material costs of $200 and direct labor costs of $400. Variable factory overhead applied to the products totaled $200. The beginning finished goods inventory included $150 in variable manufacturing costs. Ending finished goods inventory was $100.

Riverside Corporation
Variable Manufacturing Cost Statement
July, 20xx

Finished Goods Inventory, July 1		$150
Plus: Variable Manufacturing Costs		
Direct Material	200	
Direct Labor	400	
Variable Factory Overhead	200	800
Variable Manufacturing Costs to Account for		950
Less: Finished Goods Inventory, July 31		100
Variable Manufacturing Cost of Goods Sold		$850

different measures of reported income. In general, the two methods will give different levels of income for any reporting period in which the quantity of the ending inventory differs from that at the beginning of the period.

During periods when inventory quantities *increase,* a portion of the fixed manufacturing costs of the period are applied to the increase in inventory under absorption costing. These fixed costs are then matched against revenues in a later period when the additional units are sold. With a variable costing, the fixed costs are considered period costs and deducted from revenues during the current period. Consequently, variable costing will report a lower net income than that computed using absorption costing.

Conversely, when inventory quantities *decrease,* the quantity of the beginning inventory is greater than the quantity of the ending inventory. Using absorption costing, a portion of fixed costs applied during a prior period to the decrease in inventory are matched against revenues in the current reporting period. With variable costing, these fixed costs were matched with revenues during the prior period. Thus, a variable costing system will report a higher net income than an absorption costing system during the current period. In reporting periods during which unit sold equals unit manufactured, beginning and ending inventory quantities will be the same and the two methods report identical net income.

An example demonstrating the effect of these two alternative costing methods on net income is contained in Illustration 12-5.

Variable Costing in Practice

Variable costing differs from absorption costing because of its underlying assumptions regarding product costs and period costs. Fixed manufacturing costs are considered as product costs by absorption costing and as period costs with direct costing. Either assumption can be made in the other types of cost accounting systems which have been discussed.

For example, variable costing can be used in job order costing systems or process costing systems. If used with job order costing, only variable factory overhead is applied to each job or batch of units. If used with process costing, only the variable factory overhead will be included in the conversion costs used to compute a cost per equivalent unit. In either case, fixed factory overhead items are not treated as product costs.

Illustration 12-5 Reconciliation of Net Incomes Absorption Costing and Variable Costing

During the month of August, Riverside Corporation incurred the following costs while producing 400 units of its product.

	Tdta	*Per Unit*
Direct Material	$200	$ .50
Direct Labor	400	1.00
Variable Factory Overhead Applied and Incurred	200	.50
Fixed Factory Overhead Applied and Incurred	100	.25

Sales for the month were 300 units at $5.00 each. Fixed selling costs were $200 and fixed administrative costs totaled $100.

Using Absorption Costing

Unit Product Cost: $2.25

Computation of net income:		
Sales (300 x $5)		$1,500
Cost of Goods Sold (300 x $2.25)		675
Gross Profit		825
Less:		
Selling Expenses	200	
Administrative Expenses	100	300
Income		$525

Using Variable Costing

Unit Product Cost: $2.00

Computation of net income:		
Sales (300 x $5)		$1,500
Variable Cost of Goods Sold (300 x $2)		600
Contribution		900
Less: Fixed Cost		
Manufacturing	100	
Selling	200	
Administrative	100	400
Income		$ 500
Difference in reported net incomes:		
Absorption costing	$525	
Variable Costing	500	
Difference		$ 25
Difference accounted for as follows:		
Increase in Inventory (400 - 300)	100 units	
Fixed factory overhead applied to each unit	$.25	
Fixed factory overhead applied to increase in inventory		$ 25

Variable costing can also be used in conjunction with standard costing systems. In such a situation, the standard cost of a unit of product includes standard direct material costs, standard direct labor costs and standard variable factory overhead. Because no fixed factory overhead is applied to products, no volume variance is produced in a standard direct costing system. The other standard cost variances are computed and are treated as adjustments to the variable cost of goods sold in arriving at net income. An example income statement using standard variable costing is provided in Illustrations 12-6 and 12-7.

Variable costing is not allowed under generally accepted accounting principles for purposes of external reporting, nor is it an acceptable method of inventory valuation under the U.S. tax code for determining taxable income. As a result, many organizations maintain dual accounting systems utilizing absorption costing for external reporting purposes and direct costing for internal reporting objectives. This requires some extra clerical effort and accounting expertise even with recent advances in the information technology; yet many organizations feel that the advantages offered by variable costing for internal reporting make the additional costs of such a dual system worthwhile.

Advantages of Variable Costing

Many cost accountants feel that variable costing offers a number of advantages over absorption costing for purposes of internal reporting. Some of these are as follows:

Illustration 12-6 Comprehensive Example Variable Costing

Dallas International is a large, highly diversified manufacturing corporation which utilizes a variable costing system for internal reporting. Its Widget Division employs a standard process costing system in accounting for its production costs. Factory overhead is applied to widgets based on standard direct labor hours allowed. Other standards for a widget are:

Direct Material.........2 lb. @ \$3 / lb. = \$6.00
Direct Labor............5 hr. @ \$6 / hr. = \$3.00

The following data is provided for the month of April, 20xx:

Beginning Finishing Goods Inventory................10,000 units
Sales (at a unit price of \$15)... ....35,000 units
Production completed...................................32,000 units
Budgeted activity..15,000 hours
Budgeted Variable factory Overhead................\$30,000
Budgeted Fixed factory Overhead....................\$90,000
Variable Selling Cost ....\$1 per unit
Fixed Costs incurred:
Selling..\$30,000
Administrative.....................................\$10,000
Manufacturing..................... ....\$90,000
Standard Cost Variances recorded:
Materials Quantity Variance...................... ..\$1,000 unfavorable
Labor Usage Variance..............................2,000 unfavorable
Material Price Variance.............................1,000 favorable

Required:

1. Compute standard variable cost per unit.
2. Compute variable cost goods sold at standard.
3. Compute cost of ending finished goods inventory.
4. Prepare an income statement.

Illustration 12-7 Solution to Comprehensive Example

1. Variable Factory Overhead Rate = $30,000/15,000 hours = $2.00 per standard hour

Standard Variable Unit Cost:	
Direct Material	$ 6.00
Direct Labor	3.00
Variable Factory Overhead ($2/hr. X .5 hr.)	1.00
	$10.00 per unit

2. Variable Cost of Goods Sold:

Variable Manufacturing Costs ($10 x 35,000)	$350,000
Variable Selling Costs ($1 x 35,000)	35,000
	$385,000

3. Cost of Ending Finished Goods Inventory:

Beginning balance (10,000 units @ $10)	$100,000
Plus units completed (32,000 units @ $10)	320,000
Less units sold (35,000 units @ $10)	(350,000)
	$ 70,000

4.

Widget Division
Income Statement
April, 20xx

Sales Revenue (35,000 x $15)		$525,000
Variable Standard Cost of Goods Sold:		
Manufacturing	350,000	
Selling	35,000	385,000
Contribution (at Standard)		140,000
Variances from Standard:		
Material Quantity Variance (unfavorable)....	1,000	
Labor Usage Variance (unfavorable)	2,000	
Material Price Variance (favorable)	(1,000)	2,000
Contribution (at Actual)		138,000
Fixed Costs:		
Manufacturing	90,000	
Selling	30,000	
Administrative	10,000	130,000
Net Income		$ 8,000

1. Variable costing recognizes the behavior patterns of the costs of being in business. All costs recorded by such a system are classified as either a fixed cost, a variable cost, or a mixed cost with fixed and variable components. Costs produced by the system are thus useful for making decisions utilizing cost-volume-profit analysis, which has been described in an earlier chapter. The recognition of cost behavior patterns also facilitates the development of flexible budgets for controlling factory overhead costs, as has been

discussed. And as will be covered in the next chapter, the recognition of cost behavior is useful for making certain types of non-routine managerial decisions which require knowledge of the marginal costs of production for different products.

2. Variable costing isolates the effects of fixed costs on reported income. In a capital intensive industry, fixed manufacturing costs may constitute a major proportion of all costs. With absorption costing, these costs are not aggregated on the income statement or on internal performance reports, but are hidden as a part of inventories, cost of goods sold, and overhead or volume variances. In variable costing fixed manufacturing costs are disclosed in a single amount, making them more controllable and their magnitude more apparent. Many managers are astonished at the amount of their fixed manufacturing costs when provided with such disclosure.
3. Variable costing avoids the allocation of fixed costs which is required by absorption costing. Such allocations are made based on the judgment of a managerial accountant which may sometimes appear arbitrary. For example, the choice of an activity capacity level in determining a factory overhead rate, as discussed earlier in this chapter, is a matter of preference. However, the choice may have a significant effect on product costs and productions and pricing decisions based on product costs. Such allocations may be disfunctional or counterproductive if used for performance evaluation, and misleading or incorrect if used improperly.
4. Variable costing motivates managers to produce for sales, not for inventories since profits always vary directly with sales revenues; when sales increase in a reporting period, profits will increase. Conversely, when sales revenues decrease, profits will decrease. With absorption costing, changes in profit levels are subject not only to changes in sales but also to major inventory buildups or depletions as well. It is difficult to explain to the uninitiated how sales can decrease dramatically in a period when higher profits are reported. Such may be the case in absorption costing if there has been a significant increase in inventory levels during the period. This is particularly true when managers' bonus is based on reported operating income since they will have the incentive to build up excess inventories to increase operating income by increasing production volume.

Because of its advantages, variable costing is achieving increased acceptance for purposes of planning, decision making and control. A comprehensive example of an application of variable costing is provided in Illustration 12-6; its solution is presented in Illustration 12-7.

Throughput Costing

Many cost accountants have argued that managers have little control over the costs of committed production resources except that of direct materials. For instance, labor costs tend to be fixed due to the prevalent use of long-term contract in practice. Workers are no longer paid on a piece rate basis. Instead, they are compensated on a weekly, monthly, annually or even multi-year contract basis. Since managers have little flexibility adjusting labor resources capacity once committed, labor resources become less controllable especially in the short term duration. To reflect the fact that managers have limited flexibility adjusting capacities of committed resources and to eliminate managers' incentive to spread the costs of committed production resources by increasing production volume when their performance measurement is based on reported operating income of absorption costing or variable costing, cost accountants have advocated an alternative approach to product costing, called *throughput costing*. *Throughput costing*, also referred to as *super-variable costing*, treats all costs except direct material costs as period costs regardless of how many units of products manufactured in the reporting period. Throughput costing differs from *variable costing* in the treatment of direct labor costs and variable factory overhead. Variable costing inventories direct labor costs and variable factory overhead. In contrast, these costs under throughput costing are excluded from the calculation of product costs and considered as expenses of the period in which they are incurred. Thus, only direct material costs are included as product costs and all other costs are reported as period costs under throughput costing. The remaining sales amount after direct material costs have been deducted is called throughput contribution.

Illustration 12-8 demonstrates throughput costing income statement using the same data for variable costing income statement as in Illustration 12-6 discussed earlier. Note that net income reported in Illustration 12-8 under throughput costing is greater than that reported in Illustration 12-7 under variable costing because units sold are more than units manufactured in April. That is, with variable costing a portion of direct labor costs and variable factory overhead applied during a prior period to the decrease in inventory are matched against revenues in the current reporting period. However, these variable conversion costs were matched with revenues during the prior period under throughput costing. As a result, throughput costing reports a higher net income than variable costing during the current period.

Summary

Three alternative methods of determining product costs have been described, absorption costing, variable costing and throughput costing. With absorption costing, a portion of all manufacturing costs are included in unit inventory values. Both variable and fixed factory overhead are attached to products using a predetermined overhead rate. Computation of this overhead rate requires the choice of an appropriate activity level. Common methods of selecting this activity level have been described. In variable costing, only the variable manufacturing costs

Illustration12-8 Throughput Costing Income Statement

Widget Division
Income Statement
April, 20xx

Sales Revenue (35,00 x $15)		$525,000
Variable Standard Material Costs (35,000 x $6)		210,000
Throughput Contribution (at Standard)		$315,000
Variances from Standard:		
Material Quantity Variance (unfavorable)	1,000	
Material Price Variance (favorable)	(1,000)	0
Throughput Contribution (at Actual)		$315,000
Other Costs:		
Direct Labor Costs (32,000 x $3)	96,000	
Manufacuturing Overhead ($90,000+$30,000)	120,000	
Selling Costs (35,000 x $1 + $30,000)	65,000	
Adminstrative Costs	10,000	
Labor Usage Variance (unfavorable)	2,000	293,000
Net Income		$ 22,000

Illustration 12-9 Types of Cost Accounting Systems Compared

Job Order Costing	Process Costing
Actual Absorption Costing	Actual Absorption Costing
— costs are determined after they are incurred	— costs are determined after they are incurred
— costs are recorded by job or batch	— costs are recorded by cost center
— costs include all manufacturing costs	— costs include all manufacturing costs
Actual Variable Costing	Actual Variable Costing
— costs are determined after they are incurred	— costs are determined after they are incurred
— costs are recorded by job or batch	— costs are recorded by cost center
—costs include only variable manufacturing costs	— costs include only variable manufacturing costs
Actual Throughput Costing	Actual Throughput Costing
— costs are determined after they are incurred	— costs are determined after they are incurred
— costs are recorded by job or batch	— costs are recorded by cost center
— costs include all direct material costs	— costs include only direct material costs
Standard Absorption Costing	Standard Absorption Costing
— costs are determined before they are incurred	— costs are determined before they are incurred
— costs are recorded by job or batch	— costs are recorded by cost center
— costs include all manufacturing costs	— costs include all manufacturing costs
Standard Variable Costing	Standard Variable Costing
— costs are determined before they are incurred	— costs are determined before they are incurred
— costs are recorded by job or batch	— costs are recorded by cost center
— costs include only variable manufacturing costs	— costs include only variable manufacturing costs
Standard Throughput Costing	Standard Throughput Costing
— costs are determined before they are incurred	— costs are determined before they are incurred
— costs are recorded by job or batch	— costs are recorded by cost center
— costs include only direct material costs	— costs include only direct material costs

are included in inventory values, which may cause a reported net income different from the one reported with absorption costing. Some of the advantages provided by variable costing for internal reporting have been enumerated. In throughput costing, only direct material costs are included as products costs and all other costs are considered as expenses of the period in which they are incurred.

From the discussion in this chapter, it is clear that a wide variety of cost accounting systems exist, depending the method of recording costs, the times that they are determined, and the nature of the product costs assumed. This variety of cost accounting systems is shown in Illustration 12-9.

KEY DEFINITIONS

Absorption costing	A method of product costing in which all manufacturing costs, both variable and fixed, are included in inventory values. Also referred to as full costing or conventional costing.
Budgeted activity level	A measure of production activity which, when divided into budgeted factory overhead costs, gives the predetermined factory overhead rate.
Contribution	The difference between sales revenue and total variable costs. Also called the contribution margin, or the contribution to fixed costs and profits.
Contribution approach	An approach to determining and reporting net income which discloses the contribution of sales revenues toward the recovery of fixed costs and profits.
Expected annual capacity	An approach to setting the budgeted activity level, which assumes that production will be at the level to satisfy sales demand during a single, upcoming year.
Ideal capacity	An approach to setting the budgeted activity level, which assumes that production will be at its maximum possible level. This requires operations at peak efficiency on a continuous basis.
Normal capacity	An approach to setting the budgeted activity level, which assumes that production will be at a level to satisfy sales demand over a planning cycle of several years.
Practical capacity	An approach to setting the budgeted activity level, which assumes that production will be at a level of efficiency sustainable over an extended period, but will not be limited by sales demand.
Throughput costing	A method of product costing in which only direct material costs are included in inventory values. Also referred to as supervariable costing.
Variable costing	A method of product costing in which only variable manufacturing costs are included in inventory values. Also referred to as direct costing.

Questions

12-1 Identify four activity capacity concepts that are used in determining a fixed factory overhead application rate, and for each describe the interpretation of the volume variance.

12-2 With variable costing, what is the *contribution?* Does it have a more descriptive name?

12-3 What advantages over absorption costing does variable costing offer for internal reporting?

12-4 In a standard absorption costing system, how is the fixed factory overhead rate determined? The variable factory overhead rate?

12-5 Describe the differences in the income statement presentation between absorption costing and variable costing.

12-6 How do net incomes reported under absorption costing and variable costing compare when: (a) Inventory quantities *increase* during the reporting period? Why? (b) Inventory quantities *decrease* during the reporting period? Why?

12-7 Identify the costs which are considered as product costs under (a) absorption costing, and (b) variable costing. Explain the rationale for any differences.

12-8 Cost accounting systems may exist in many different forms. What are the factors which distinguish between the different types of cost accounting systems?

12-9 Why is absorption costing sometimes called *full costing* system? Why is variable costing system sometimes called *direct costing* system? Are direct costs always varaible costs?

12-10 The use of normal activity capacity as the activity level in computing fixed overhead rates has been practiced by some major corporations in the automobile and steel industries. Why might the use of normal activity capacity be appropriate for these companies?

12-11 What reasons can you suggest that variable costing is not acceptable for purposes of external reporting?

12-12 How does throughput costing differ from absorption costing and variable costing?

Problems

12-13 Product Costs

The following standards have been developed for the product of Gimlet Corp.

Direct material: .... 2 lbs. @ $3.20 per lb.,
Direct labor: .... .3 hrs. @ $12 per hr.,
Variable overhead: .... $4 per direct labor hour,
Fixed overhead: .... $1 per unit.

Required:.

(a) Calculate inventoriable unit cost under absorption costing.
(b) Calculate inventoriable unit cost under variable costing.

12-14 Fixed Overhead Rate and the Activity Level

Diamond Company manufactures a single product: Product A, at its western plant. The corporate planning staff has projected the following annual sales and production plan for Product A over the company's five year planning horizon:

20X1	20,000 units
20X2	16,500 units
20X3	15,500 units
20X4	17,600 units
20X5	19,400 units

Maximum production capacity at the western plant is 70,000 direct labor hours. However, due to plant shutdowns for repair, holidays, vacations, and other factors, the greatest attainable production capacity level is 56,000 direct labor hours. Production standards call for 2.5 hours of direct labor for each unit of Product A. During the upcoming year (20X1), the budgeted fixed factory overhead at the western plant is $350,000.

Required:

Compute the standard fixed overhead application rate for 20X1 assuming Diamond uses as its activity level:
(a) Ideal capacity.
(b) Practical capacity.
(c) Normal capacity.
(d) Expected annual capacity.

12-15 Variable Manufacturing Cost of Goods Sold

During September the Brewer Corporation recorded direct materials costs of $18,000. A total of 5,000 direct labor hours were expended at an average rate of $6.00 per hour. Variable factory overhead is applied at the rate of $2.00 per direct labor hour, and the fixed overhead rate is $3.50 per hour. Finished goods inventory under direct costing was as follows:

Sept. 1	$4,500
Sept. 30	$6,000

Required:

From the above data, compute the variable manufacturing cost of goods sold.

12-16 *Variable Costing Income Statement*

Midway Manufacturing Company produces a single product and utilizes a direct costing system, based on historical costs, for internal reporting purposes. During 20X1, 200,000 units were sold at a price of $30 each. Variable manufacturing costs of each unit sold were $11.75 each, and the fixed manufacturing costs totaled $1,200,000. Midway incurred fixed selling costs, primarily for advertising and sales management, of $250,000. A commission of 10% on sales is paid to sales persons, and distribution costs averaging $2.00 per unit were incurred.

Required:

Prepare, in good form, a variable costing income statement for Midway for the year 20X1.

12-17 *Absorption Costing, Variable Costing, and Throughput Costing*

JV Company began its operations on January 1, 20X1, and produces a single product that sells for $7.00 per unit. Standard capacity is 100,000 units per year. 100,000 units were produced and 80,000 units were sold in 20X1.

Manufacturing costs and selling and administrative expenses were as follows:

	Fixed Costs	*Variable Costs*
Raw materials	-	$1.50 per unit produced
Direct labor	-	1.00 per unit produced
Factory overhead	$150,000	.50 per unit produced
Selling and administrative.	$ 80,000	.50 per unit sold

There were no variances from the standard variable costs. Any under- or overapplied overhead is written off directly at year-end as an adjustment to cost of goods sold.

Required:

Compute net income under absorption costing.
Compute net income under variable costing.
Compute net income under throughput costing.

12-18 *Difference in Inventory Values*

Fleet, Inc. manufactured 700 units of Product A, a new product, in 20X1. Product A's variable and fixed manufacturing costs per unit were $6.00 and $2.00, respectively. The inventory of Product A on December 31, 20X1 consisted of 100 units. There was no inventory of Product A on January 1, 20X1.

Required:

What would be the change in the dollar amount of inventory on December 31, 20X1 if the variable costing method was used instead of the absorption costing method?

(*AICPA adapted*)

12-19 *Absorption Costing Income from Variable Costing Income*

A company had income of $50,000 using variable costing for a given period. Beginning and ending inventories for that period were 13,000 units and 18,000 units, respectively.

Required:

Ignoring income taxes, if the fixed overhead application rate was $2.00 per unit, what was the income using absorption costing?

(AICPA adapted)

12-20 *Costing Methods and Inventory Valuation*

The following information is available for Keller Corporation's new product line:

Selling price per unit	$ 15
Variable manufacturing costs per unit of production	$ 8
Total annual fixed manufacturing costs	$25,000
Variable administrative costs per unit of production	$ 3
Total annual fixed selling and administrative expenses	$15,000

There was no inventory at the beginning of the year. During the year 12,500 units were produced and 10,000 units were sold.

Required:

(a)Determine the cost of ending inventory, assuming Keller uses variable costing,
(b)Determine the cost of ending inventory, assuming Keller uses absorption costing.

(AICPA adapted)

12-21 *Standard Job Order Direct Costing*

Sarah Manufacturing Co. is a producer of men's slacks in a variety of styles, colors, and price ranges, which uses a standard direct costing system for internal reporting. During October Job *#423* was completed which consisted of *20* dozen slacks in Style X. Job *#423* utilized *760* sq. yds. of cloth which had been purchased at a cost of $5 per yard. A total of *226* direct labor hours were required, at a wage rate of $8.50 per hour. Total factory overhead incurred during October was $118,600.The following standards have been established for one pair of slacks in Style X:

Direct materials: .... 3 sq. yds. @ $5 per sq. yd.,
Direct labor: .... I hr. @ $10 per hr.,
Variable factory overhead:................................ $5 per pair.

Sarah carries raw materials inventories at actual cost. The selling price of one pair of slacks of Style X is $40. Distribution costs for a pair of slacks average $0.50 each; all other selling costs apply to all product lines and are considered fixed. Fixed manufacturing costs for the month were $80,000 and budgeted activity was *9,600* direct labor hours.

Required:

(a) Determine the standard unit cost of one pair of Style X slacks for internal reporting purposes.

(b) Compute all materials and labor variances.

(c) Prepare in good form a report showing the contribution to fixed costs and profits by Job #423.

(d) Comment on the effect of factory overhead costs on your answer to (c).

12-22 *Choice of the Activity Level*

Maypool Corporation is the major consumer appliance manufacturer in a country that experiences no inflation. The company produces a variety of large appliances for the home such as stoves, refrigerators, washers and dryers. Each fall its executive committee meets and develops operating plans for the next three years and a budget for the upcoming year. Standard absorption costing methods are used, and factory overhead rates are developed in the fall for the next year based on the year's projected sales. Sales and other economic factors indicate that the country is in a recession which is expected to last about five years.

The president, while considering the budget for 20X3, has become concerned about observed trends in decreasing sales volume and increasing product costs. The actual sales of the model 200 dryer for 20X1 and 20X2, and projected sales for 20X3–X5 are as follows:

Year	Sales and Production
20X1	10,000 units (actual)
20X2	8,000 units (actual)
20X3	6,000 units (projected)
20X4	7,000 units (projected)
20X5	9,000 units (projected)

Maypool could raise prices to maintain its profitability, but the president is concerned that this action would depress sales even further. Fixed factory overhead for the dryer will remain constant at $500,000 over this five year period. Variable manufacturing costs are $200 per unit and are not expected to change.

Required:

(a) Compute the standard absorption cost per unit for each year from 20X1 through 20X5.

(b) What problems can you foresee with using these unit costs for making decisions regarding cost control and product prices?

(c) As a management accountant and advisor to the president, what recommendations can you make?

12-23 *Costing Methods and the Flexible Budget*

The following annual flexible budget has been prepared for use in making decisions relating to Product X.

	100,000 Units	150,000 Units	200,000 Units
Sales volume........................	$800,000	$1,200,000	$1,600,000
Manufacturing costs:	300,000	450,000	600,000
Variable................................	200,000	200,000	200,000
Fixed	500,000	650,000	800,000
Selling and other expenses:	200,000	300,000	400,000
Variable...............................	160,000	160,000	160,000
Fixed	360,000	460,000	560,000
Income (or loss)................	$(60,000)	$ 90,000	$ 240,000

The 200,000 unit budget has been adopted and will be used for allocating fixed manufacturing costs to units of Product X; at the end of the first six months the following information is available:

	Units
Production completed	120,000
Sales	60,000

All fixed costs are budgeted and incurred uniformly throughout the year and all costs incurred coincide with the budget. Overapplied and underapplied overhead balances treated as adjustments to cost of goods sold at year-end.

Required:

(a) Compute the amount of the overapplied or underapplied fixed factory costs under absorption costing during the first six months.

(b) Determine the reported net income (or loss) for the first six months under

(1) absorption costing

(2) direct costing

(c) How can the difference in reported income between the two methods be explained?

(AICPA adapted)

12-24 *Throughput Costing*

Blaine Company produces and sells a single product, called X. The following data are available for the year ended December 31, 20X1:

Sales (90,000 units x $120)..............	$1,080,000
Normal capacity................................	100,000 units
Manufacturing costs:	
Direct material..............................	$25 per unit
Direct labor....................................	$20 per unit
Variable overhead..........................	$10 per unit
Fixed overhead.............................	$5 per unit
Selling and administrative costs:	
Variable selling.............................	$3 per unit
Variable administrative................	$2 per unit
Fixed selling and administrative	$300,000 per year

Required:

(1) Determine the cost per unit if variable costing is used.
(2) Determine the cost per unit if throughput costing is used.
(3) Determine the total throughput contribution.

12-25 *Relationship of Income and Sales*

On August 5, 20X2, Jack Jackson, controller for Wixson Company, arrived at his office to find the company president in a rage. "These income statements you've prepared for June and July are ridiculous," the president said. "Sales and expenses for the two months were identical, yet you claim that we moved from a profit of $15,000 in June to a loss of $1,000 in July. Now I'm not an accountant, but I know better than to believe that. I expect a satisfactory explanation before you go home today." Somewhat sheepishly, Jack began to review the company's financial data for the previous two months. Sales of Wixson's single product each month had indeed been identical: 10,000 units in June and 10,000 units in July. The *standard* costs of the product were as follows:

Direct material	$ 6
Direct labor	$ 8
Variable factory overhead	$ 2
Fixed factory overhead	$ 4
	$20

The selling price was $30 per unit, and selling and administrative expenses (all fixed) were $90,000 each month. Normal activity was 10,000 units per month. Unfavorable materials, labor, and variable overhead variances totaled $3,000 in each month, and there were no fixed budget variances. Inventory levels were as follows: June 1—1,000 units; June 30—3,000 units; and July 31—1,000 units.

Required:

In order to aid Jack in this situation, complete the following:
(a) Compute the volume variance for June and for July.
(b) Present comparative income statements for the months of June and July using absorption costing.
(c) Explain why net income changed as it did over the two month period.
(d) Present comparative income statements using variable costing.

12-26 *Net Income Under Variable Costing and Absorption Costing*

Management of Bicent Company uses the following unit costs for the one product it manufactures:

	Projected Cost per Unit
Direct material (all variable)	$30.00
Direct labor (all variable)	$19.00
Manufacturing overhead:	

Variable cost	$ 6.00
Fixed cost (based on 10,000 units per month)	$ 5.00
Selling, general and administrative:	
Variable cost	$ 4.00
Fixed cost (based on 10,000 units per month)	$ 2.80

The projected selling price is $80 per unit. The fixed costs remain fixed within the relevant range of 4,000 to 16,000 units of production.
Management has also projected the following data for the month of June 20X1.

	Units
Beginning inventory	2,000
Production	9,000
Available	11,000
Sales	7,500
Ending inventory	3,500

Required:

Prepare projected income statements for June 20X1 for management purposes under each of the following product costing methods:
(a) Absorption costing with all variances charged to cost of goods sold each month.
(b) Variable costing.
Supporting schedules calculating inventoriable production costs per unit should be presented in good form. Ignore income taxes.

(AICPA adapted)

12-27 Direct Costing and C-V-P Analysis

The following data relate to a year's budgeted activity for Patsy Corporation, a single product company:

	Units
Beginning inventory	30,000
Production	120,000
Available	150,000
Sales	110,000
Ending inventory	40,000
	Per Unit
Selling price	$5.00
Variable manufacturing costs	$1.00
Variable selling costs	$2.00
Fixed manufacturing costs (based on 100,000 units)	$ .25
Fixed selling costs (based on 100,000 units)	$ .65

Required:

Total fixed costs remain unchanged within the relevant range of 25,000 units. Total capacity is 160,000 units.

(a) What is the projected net income for Patsy Corporation for the year under direct (variable) costing?

(b) If all the variances are charged to cost of goods sold, what is the projected net income for Patsy Corporation for the year under absorption costing?

(c) What is the projected annual breakeven sales in units?

(d) Patsy has received a special order for 10,000 units to be sold in an unrelated market. What price per unit should be charged on this order to increase Patsy's net income by $5,000?

(e) Given the above data for Patsy Corporation, assume the selling price increases by 20%; variable manufacturing costs increase by 10%; variable selling costs remain the same; and total fixed costs increase to $104,400. How many units must then be sold to generate a profit equal to 10% of the contribution margin?

(AICPA adapted)

12-28 Costing Methods and Management Decisions

Playtime, Inc. is a nationwide manufacturer of leisure products. In September of 20X2, the manager of the Men's Swimwear Division is considering the division's production schedule for the fourth quarter. The manager is being considered for a promotion to corporate headquarters, and would like to show a healthy profit for the year in the division. However, a substantial federal income tax cut will occur in 20X3, and a prudent policy would be to defer as much income as possible into that year. The following data is provided for each quarter in 20X2:

	1st	2nd	3rd	4th
Production (units)........	52,000	60,000	55,000	?
Sales (units)..................	50,000	60,000	60,000	40,000(est.)
Beginning inventory...	12,500	15,000	15,000	10,000
Ending inventory........	15,000	15,000	10,000	?

The standard variable cost is $1.50 per unit. Fixed factory overhead, budgeted at $220,000 per year, is allocated to units based on a normal activity of 55,000 units per quarter. Fixed selling and administrative expenses are budgeted at $60,000 per year. In the past, the division has followed the policy of setting production levels so that the inventory at the beginning of a quarter is equal to 1/4 of the quarter's sales. Practical capacity is 75,000 units; to maintain a stable work force production is never set at less than 30,000 units in a quarter. Projected sales for the first quarter of 20X3 are 50,000 units. No materials, labor or variable overhead variances from standard are expected for the year. The selling price is $3.00 per unit, and absorption costing methods are used.

Required:

(a) If the previous inventory policy is followed, what production level would be set for the fourth quarter? What would be the resulting net income for 20X2?
(b) What production level for the fourth quarter would maximize net income? What would net income for the year be?
(c) What production level would defer income into the next year when tax rates will be lower? What would be the net income?
(d) For the three production levels above, determine the net income if variable costing methods were used.

12-29 Standard Process Direct Costing

Norwood Corporation is considering changing its method of inventory valuation from absorption costing to direct costing and engaged you to determine the effect of the proposed change on the 20X0 financial statements.

The corporation manufactures Gink which is sold for $20 per unit. Marsh is added before processing starts and labor and overhead are added evenly during the manufacturing process. Production capacity is budgeted at 110,000 units of Gink annually. The standard costs per unit of Gink are:

Marsh, 2 pounds	$3.00
Labor	$6.00
Variable manufacturing overhead	$1.00
Fixed manufacturing overhead	$1.10

A process cost system is used employing standard costs. Variances from standard costs are now charged or credited to cost of goods sold. If direct costing were adopted, only variances resulting from variable costs would be charged or credited to cost of goods sold.

Inventory data for 20X0 follow:

	Units	
	January 1	December 31
Marsh (pounds)	50,000	40,000
Work-in-process		
(2/5) Processed	10,000	
(1/3) Processed		15,000
Finished goods	20,000	12,000

During 20X0, 220,000 pounds of Marsh were purchased and 230,000 pounds were transferred to work-in-process. Also, 110,000 units of Gink were transferred to finished goods. Actual fixed manufacturing overhead during the year was $121,000. There were no variances between standard variable costs and actual variable costs during the year.

Required:

(a) Prepare schedules which present the computation of:
   (1) Equivalent units of production for material, labor, and overhead.

(2) Number of units sold.
(3) Standard unit costs under direct costing and absorption costing.
(4) Amount, if any, of over- or underapplied fixed manufacturing overhead.

(b) Prepare a comparative statement of cost of goods sold using standard direct costing and standard absorption costing.

(AICPA adapted)

12-30 *Costing Methods and Profit Performance*

Sun Company, a wholly owned subsidiary of Guardian, Inc., produces and sells three main product lines. The company employs a standard cost accounting system for record-keeping purposes.

At the beginning of 20X1, the president of Sun Company presented the budget to the parent company and accepted a commitment to contribute $15,800 to Guardian's consolidated profit in 20X1. The president has been confident that the year's profit would exceed budget target, since the monthly sales reports have shown that sales for the year will exceed budget by 10%. The president is both disturbed and confused when the controller presents an adjusted forecast as of November 30, 20X1, indicating that profit will be 11% under budget. The two forecasts are as the follows:

Sun Company

Forecasts of Operating Results

	Forecasts as of	
	Jan. 1, 20X1	Nov. 30,20X1
Sales	$268,000	$294,800
Cost of sales at standard	212,000 *	$233,200
Gross margin at standard	$ 56,000	$ 61,600
Over or (under) absorbed fixed manufacturing overhead	0	(6,000)
Actual gross margin	$ 56,000	$ 55,600
Selling expenses	$ 13,400	$ 14,740
Administrative expenses	$ 26,800	$ 26,800
Total operating expenses	$ 40,200	$ 41,540
Earnings before tax	$ 15,800	$ 14,060

*Includes fixed manufacturing overhead of $30,000.

There have been no sales price changes or product mix shifts since the forecast of January 1, 20X1. The only cost variance on the income statement is the underabsorbed manufacturing overhead. This arose because the company produced only 16,000 standard machine hours (budgeted machine hours were 20,000) during 20X1 as a result of a shortage of raw materials while its principal supplier was closed by a strike. Fortunately, Sun Company's inventory of finished goods was large enough to fill all sales orders received.

Required:

(a) Analyze and explain why the profit declined in spite of increased sales and good control over cost

(b) What plan, if any, could Sun Company adopt during December to improve their reported profit at year-end? Explain your answer.

(c) Illustrate and explain how Sun Company could adopt an alternative internal cost reporting procedure that would avoid the confusing effect of the present procedure.

(IMA adapted)

12-31 *Costing Methods and Standard Costs*

Milner Manufacturing Company uses a job order costing system and standard costs. It manufactures one product whose standard cost is as follows:

Materials	20 yds. @ \$.90 per yd.	\$18.00
Direct labor	4 hrs. @ \$6.00 per hr.	\$24.00
Total factory overhead	Applied at 5/6 of direct labor (the ratio of variable costs to fixed costs is 3 to 1)	\$20
Variable selling, general, and administrative expenses		\$12.00
Fixed, selling, general, and administrative expenses		\$ 7.00
Total unit cost		\$81.00

The standards are set based on "normal" activity of 2,400 direct labor hours. Actual activity for the month of October 20X0 was as follows:

Materials purchased	18,000 yds. @ \$.92 per yd.	\$16,560
Materials used	9,500 yds.	
Direct labor	2,100 hrs. @ \$6.10 per hr.	12,810
Total factory overhead	500 units actually produced	11,100

Required:

(a) Based on the standard costs, compute the inventoriable unit cost for internal reporting purposes under direct (variable) costing.

(b) Based on the standard costs, a certain selling price per unit and number of units will yield an operating profit of \$5,200. Increasing this selling price by 4% will increase the operating profit to \$6,800. All costs and the number of units remain unchanged. Compute the selling price per unit and the number of units to yield an operating profit of \$5,200.

(c) Compute the variable factory overhead rate per direct labor hour and the total fixed factory overhead based on "normal" activity capacity.

(d) Prepare a schedule computing the following variances for the month of October 20X0:

(1) Materials price variance.
(2) Materials usage variance.
(3) Labor rate variance.
(4) Labor usage (efficiency) variance.
(5) Controllable (budget or spending) overhead variance.
(6) Volume (capacity) overhead variance.

Indicate whether each variance is favorable or unfavorable.

(AICPA adapted)

12-32 *Direct Costing for Annual Reporting*

The S.T. Shire Company uses direct costing for internal management purposes and absorption costing for external reporting purposes. Thus, at the end of each year financial information must be converted from direct costing to absorption costing in order to satisfy external requirements.

At the end of 20X0, it was anticipated that sales would rise 20% the next year. Therefore, production was increased from 20,000 units to 24,000 units to meet this expected demand. However, economic conditions kept the sales level at 20,000 units for both years.

The following data pertain to 20X0 and 20X1.

	20X0	*20X1*
Selling price per unit	$ 30	$ 30
Sales (units)	20,000	20,000
Beginning inventory (units)	2,000	2,000
Production (units)	20,000	24,000
Ending inventory (units)	2,000	6,000
Unfavorable labor, materials, and variable overhead variances (total)	$ 5,000	$4,000

Standard Variable Costs per Unit for 20X0 and 20X1:

Labor	$ 7.50
Materials	$ 4.50
Variable overhead	$ 3.00
	$15.00

Annual Fixed Costs for 20X0 and 20X1
(Budgeted and Actual)

Production	$ 90,000
Selling and administrative	100,000
	$190,000

The overhead rate under absorption costing is based upon practical plant capacity which is 30,000 units per year. All variances and under- or over absorbed overhead are taken to cost of goods sold. All taxes are to be ignored.

Required:

(a) Present the income statement based on direct costing for 20X1.

(b) Present the income statement based on absorption costing for 20X1.

(c) Explain the difference, if any, in the net income figures. Give the entry necessary to adjust the book figures to the financial statement figure, if one is necessary.

(d) The company finds it worthwhile to develop its internal financial data on a direct cost basis. What advantages and disadvantages are attributed to direct costing for internal purposes?

(e) There are many who believe that direct costing is appropriate for external reporting and there are many who oppose its use for external reporting. What arguments for and against the use of direct costing are advanced for its use in external reporting? (*IMA adapted*)

12-33 *Data Accumulation—Contribution Approach*

Forward Corporation is a progressive and fast-growing company. The company's executive committee consists of the president and the four vice presidents who report to the president-marketing, manufacturing, finance, and systems.

The company has ordered a new computer for use in processing its financial information. Because the computer acquisition required a substantial investment, the president wants to make certain that the computer is employed effectively.

The new computer will enable Forward to revise its financial information system so that the several departments will get more useful information. This should be helpful especially in marketing because its personnel are distributed widely throughout the country.

The marketing department is organized into nine territories and 25 sales offices. The vice president of marketing wants the monthly reports to reflect those items for which the department is responsible and can control. The marketing department also wants information which identifies the most profitable products; this information is used to establish a discount policy which will enable the company to meet competition effectively. Monthly reports showing performance by territory and sales office also would be useful.

The vice president of finance has recommended that the accounting system be revised so that reports would be prepared on a contribution margin basis. Further, only those cost items which are controlled by the respective departments would appear on their reports. The monthly report for the manufacturing department would compare actual production costs with a budget containing the standard costs for the actual volume of production. The marketing department would be provided with the standard variable manufacturing cost for each product so it could calculate the variable contribution margin of each product. The monthly reports to the marketing department would reflect the variable contribution approach; the reports would present the net contribution of the department calculated by deducting standard variable manufacturing costs and marketing expenses (both variable and fixed)from sales.

A portion of Forward Corporation's chart of accounts is shown below.

Account Number	*Description*
2000	Sales
2500	Cost of sales
3000	Manufacturing
4000	Engineering expenses
5000	Marketing expenses
6000	Administrative expenses

The company wants to retain the basic structure of the chart of accounts to minimize the number of changes in the system. However, the numbering system will have to be expanded in order to provide the additional information that is desired.

Required:

The coding structure now in effect must be modified to satisfy the needs of Forward Corporation's management. Using the marketing areas as the example, devise an account number coding system which will permit the preparation of the contribution reports for the marketing department. In the presentation of the account number coding system.

(1) Add additional accounts to the chart of accounts as needed.

(2) Provide flexibility in the coding structure so that it would not have to be revised completely should Forward Corporation expand or restructure its sales area.

(3) Explain and justify the coding structure presented.

(IMA adapted)

12-34 *Variable Costing Income Statement*

BBG Corporation is a manufacturer of a synthetic element. Gary Voss, President of the company, has been eager to get the operating results for the just completed fiscal year. He was surprised when the income statement revealed that income before taxes has dropped to $885,000 from $900,000 even though sales volume had increased 100,000 kg. This drop in net income had occurred even though Voss had implemented the following changes during the past 12 months to improve the profitability of the company.

- In response to a 10% increase in production costs, the sales price of the company's product was increased by 12%. This action took place on December 1, 20X1.
- The managements of the selling and administrative departments were given strict instructions to spend no more in fiscal 20X2 than in fiscal 20X1.
- BBG's accounting department prepared and distributed to top management the comparative income statements presented below. The accounting staff also prepared related financial information to assist management in evaluating the company's performance. BBG uses the FIFO inventory method for finished goods.

BBG Corporation

Statement of Operating Income

For the Years Ended November 30, 20X1 and 20X2

($000 omitted)

	20X1	*20X2*
Sales revenue	$9,000	$11,200
Cost of goods sold	$7,200	$ 8,320
Manufacturing volume variance	(600)	495
Adjusted cost of goods sold	$6,600	$ 8,815
Gross margin	$2,400	$ 2,385
Selling and administrative expenses	1,500	1,500
Income before taxes	$ 900	$ 885

BBG Corporation

Selected Operating and Financial Data

for 20X1 and 20X2

	20X1	*20X2*
Sales price	$ 10/kg.	$11.20/kg.
Material cost	$1.50/kg.	$ 1.65/kg.
Direct labor cost	$2.50/kg.	$ 2.75/kg.
Variable overhead cost	$1.00/kg.	$ 1.10/kg.
Fixed overhead cost	$3.00/kg.	$ 3.30/kg.
Total fixed overhead costs	$3,000,000	$3,300,000
Selling and administrative (all fixed)	$1,500,000	$1,500,000
Sales volume	900,000 kg.	1,000,000 kg.
Beginning inventory	300,000 kg.	600,000 kg

Required:

(a) Explain to Gary Voss why BBG Corporation's net income decreased in the current fiscal year despite the sales price and sales volume increases.

(b) A member of BBG's accounting department has suggested that the company adopt variable (direct) costing for internal reporting purposes.

1. Prepare an operating income statement through income before taxes for the year ended November 30, 20X2, for BBG Corporation using the variable costing method.
2. Present a numerical reconciliation of the difference in income before taxes using the absorption costing method as currently employed by BBG and the variable costing method as proposed.

(c) Identify and discuss the advantages and disadvantages of using the variable costing method for internal reporting purposes.

(IMA adapted)

12-35 *Performance Report*

Caprice Company manufactures and sells two products—a small portable office file cabinet that it has made for over 15 years and a home/travel file introduced recently. The files are made in Caprice's only manufacturing plant. Budgeted variable production costs per unit of product are as follows:

	Office File	*Home/Travel File*
Sheet metal	$ 3.5	-
Plastic		$3.75
Direct labor (@ $8 per DLH)	4.00	2.00
Variable manufacturing overhead (@ $9 per DLH)	4.50	2.25
	$12.00	$8.00

Variable manufacturing overhead costs vary with direct labor hours. The annual fixed manufacturing overhead costs are budgeted at $120,000. A total of 50% of these costs are directly traceable to the office file department and 22% of the costs are traceable to the home/travel file department. The remaining 28% of the costs are not traceable to either department.

Caprice employs two full-time salespersons—Pam Price and Robert Flint. Each salesperson receives an annual salary of $14,000 plus a sales commission of 10% of his/her total gross sales. Travel and entertainment expense is budgeted at $22,000 annually for each salesperson. Price is expected to sell 60% of the budgeted unit sales for each file and Flint the remaining 40%. Caprice's remaining selling and administrative expenses include fixed administrative costs of $80,000 that cannot be traced to either file plus the following traceable selling expenses.

	Office File	*Home/Travel File*
Packaging expenses per unit................	$ 2.00	$ 1.50
Promotion...	$30,000	$40,000

Data regarding Caprice's budgeted and actual sales for the fiscal year ended May 31, 20XX, are presented below. There were no changes in the beginning and ending balances of either finished goods or work in process inventories.

	Office File	*Home/Travel File*
Budgeted sales volume in units	15,000	15,000
Budgeted and actual unit sales price..	$29.50	$19.50
Actual unit sales:		
Pam Price	10,000	9,500
Robert Flint	5,000	10,500
Total units	15,000	20,000

Data regarding Caprice's operating expenses for the year ended May 31, 20XX, follow:

- There were no increases or decreases in raw materials inventory for either sheet metal or plastic and there were no usage variances. However, sheet metal prices were 6% above budget and plastic prices were 4% below budget.
- The actual direct labor hours worked and costs incurred were as follows:

	Hours	*Amount*
Office file	7,500	$ 57,000
Home/travel file	6,000	45,600
	13,500	$102,600

Fixed manufacturing overhead costs attributable to the office file department were $8,000 above the budget. All other fixed manufacturing overhead costs were incurred at the same amounts as budgeted, and all variable manufacturing overhead costs were incurred at the budgeted hourly rates.

All selling and administrative expenses were incurred at budgeted rates or amounts except the following items.

Non-traceable administrative expenses..........		$ 34,000
Promotion:		
Office files	$32,000	
Home/travel files..........	58,000	90,000
Travel and entertainment:		
Pam Price..........	$24,000	
Robert Flint	28,000	52,000
		$176,000

Required:

(a) Prepare a performance report for the year ended May 31, 20XX, that would be useful in evaluating the performance of Robert Flint.

(b) Discuss the effects of Robert Flint's sales mix on Caprice Company's.

1. Manufacturing operations.
2. Profits.

12-36 *Throughput Costing, Variable Costing and Absorption Costing*

The following data relates to year 20XX for Plano Manufacturing Company:

Units produced	2,000
Units sold	1,800
Selling price	$200/per unit
Direct material costs...	$80,000
Direct labor costs.........	$26,000
Variable overhead........	$18,000
Variable selling costs...	$6,000
Fixed overhead............	$40,000
Fixed selling costs.......	$60,000

Required:

(a) Calculate cost of goods sold under throughput costing, variable costing, and absorption costing.

(b) Calculate ending inventory under throughput costing, variable costing, and absorption costing.

(c) Calculate operating income under throughput costing, variable costing, and absorption costing.

1. *To describe the role of the cost accountant in making special managerial decisions.*
2. *To discuss the contribution approach to special managerial decisions.*
3. *To discuss the relevant cost approach to special managerial decisions.*
4. *To provide examples of common special managerial decisions and illustrate the approaches to solving them.*
5. *To discuss product mix problems under constrained resources.*
6. *To discuss the theory of constraints.*

13 Approaches to Special Managerial Decisions

Previous chapters have described the use of cost accounting data for two broad purposes. The first of these recognizes that information on product costs is necessary for the external reporting of inventory and net income. Methods of historical costing have been described which serve this objective. A second purpose of cost accounting data is for internal reporting. Standard and variable costing systems serve this objective by providing information that is useful for budgeting, benchmarking, motivation, and performance evaluation. This chapter describes how cost accounting data is used for a third broad purpose-that of making special managerial decisions.

Decisions of this type, sometimes called *project planning decisions,* are characterized by their non-routine nature. Whereas decisions concerning budgeting or performance evaluation are typically made annually or monthly, project planning decisions are not encountered on a regular basis. Managers frequently face decisions of this type but each such decision may differ significantly from previous ones. The time period affected by project planning decisions may be short-term, covering a few weeks or months, or may have long-term effects over a period of many years. Examples of the former include the decision to accept or reject a special order, the decision to make or buy materials required in the manufacture of a product, the decision to determine the optimal product mix under constrained resources, or the decision to maximize operating income when faced with some bottleneck operations. Examples of the later include decisions to add or delete a product, production facilities, or a segment of a business, and decisions to replace capital equipment. Many of the costs which are relevant for such special decisions may not be appropriate for the other two purposes of cost data; similarly, costs recognized for periodic internal and external reporting may not be relevant for making project planning decisions. As a supplier of cost data to management, the cost accountant must be able to appraise intelligently the propriety of the data used in making these decisions.

A Systematic Approach to Special Decisions

An appropriate use of cost accounting data in project planning decisions requires that the decisions be approached in a systematic manner. Such an approach utilizes an evaluation of each decision alternative in five steps based on both quantitative and qualitative factors, and is summarized in Illustration 13-1.

This systematic approach recognizes that a decision alternative which is taken is not always the one that has the most favorable effect on profits. Qualitative factors that may impact on a decision include the effects on society of the decision, its legal implications, or the reliability and accuracy of the data used in the quantitative evaluation. Frequently a decision-maker will pursue a course of action because of these considerations even though more profitable alternatives are available.

The cost accountant is most heavily involved in this process during its second step, the quantitative evaluation of the available alternatives. This requires the use of cost and revenue data, the area in which cost accountants have special expertise. Their knowledge of cost concepts and cost behavior can be employed to ensure that management with decision-making responsibility will utilize only the data which is relevant to the decision being made. Cost accountants also may be involved in the choice of an alternative, the third step, because of their abilities to communicate and interpret the results of the analysis.

Different approaches can be used for the quantitative evaluation of decision alternatives. The contribution approach attempts to determine each alternative's contribution to the recovery of fixed costs and the generation of profit. The relevant cost approach attempts to compare only these costs and benefits that differ across the decision alternatives. Each will now be discussed.

Illustration 13-1 Steps in Project Planning Decisions

Step 1: Identify Alternatives

Specify each alternative which is available to the decision maker. Frequently one alternative will be to take some actions, while another alternative will be to do nothing.

Step 2: Evaluate Each Alternative in Quantitative Terms

Compute the effects on costs, revenues, profits, or contribution of each alternative.

Step 3: Choose Best Alternative Based on Quantitative Factors

This will be the alternative requiring the least cost, or producing the greatest profit or contribution, or having the greatest net benefit.

Step 4: Evaluate Best Alternative Based on Qualitative Factors

The decision which appears best may be impractical or undesirable due to factors which cannot be easily measured and stated in numbers.

Step 5: Make the Decision

This is based on both quantitative and qualitative considerations.

Contribution Approach to Special Decisions

As was described in the previous chapter, variable costing utilizes the contribution approach to income determination. This approach, because it recognizes cost behavior patterns, can be readily adapted to the quantitative evaluation of alternatives in making project planning decisions. The contribution approach aids in a choice between alternatives because it can be used to predict the effect on net income of a decision. Using this approach, a variable costing income statement is prepared for each alternative. The alternative which produces the greatest net income is the one which is preferable based on the quantitative evaluation.

An Example—The Special Order Decision

To illustrate the method of the contribution approach, an example problem is provided in Illustration 13-2. This problem concerns a common type of special decision faced by management whether or not to manufacture a special order of products for sale at a reduced price. The solution to the example problem is contained in Illustration 13-3.

This example demonstrates the difficulty in using absorption costing data in making project planning decisions. Based on absorption costing methods, the product cost was $5.60 per unit. One might erroneously conclude that selling the special order at a price of $5.00 per unit would result in a loss of $.60 per unit, and would reject the order. However, analysis using the contribution approach shows that, even though the special order is sold at less than absorption cost, it would make a contribution to fixed costs and profits of $30,000. Thus, the special order would have a positive effect on profits of $30,000, and should be accepted. This does not mean that the absorption unit cost is incorrect, but rather that its use is inappropriate in this case. Although absorption costing is appropriate for income determination in external reporting, the contribution approach is superior for making this type of special decisions.

Illustration 13-2 Contribution Approach to the Special Order Decision Example Problem

Red Giant Packing Company produces cans of mixed vegetables for sale to wholesale grocers. These are sold by the carton at a normal price of $6.00 per carton. The maximum capacity of the company is 70,000 cartons per month. Normal activity for Red Giant is 56,000 cartons per month; however, during July the company expects to sell 60,000 cartons. Budgeted monthly fixed costs are: manufacturing, $201,600; and selling and administrative, $50,000. The unit variable product cost of a carton is $2.00. There is no variable selling and administrative expenses.

Red Giant has the opportunity to produce during July a special order of 10,000 cartons. These will be sold to a grocery chain which will market them under a private label. The chain is willing to pay $5.00 per carton for the product.

Required:

I. Compute the cost per carton

(a)Using absorption costing

(b)Using variablecosting

2. What is the effect onnet income if the special order is accepted?

Illustration 13-3 Contribution Approach to the Special Order Decision Solution to Example Problem

1. Cost per carton:

(a) Absorption costing

Fixed Factory Overhead Rate = $201,600/56,000 = $3.60

Unit variable product cost	$2.00
Unit fixed product cost	3.60
Unit product cost	$5.60

(b) Variable costing

Unit product cost = variable product cost = $2.00

2. The alternatives are:

Alternative (1) - accept the special order

Alternative (2) - reject the special order

	Variable Costing Net Income		
	(1) *Accept*	*(2)* *Reject*	*Difference* *(1) - (2)*
	(60,000 x $6 + 10,000 x $5)	*(60,000 x $6)*	
Sales revenue	$410,000	$360,000	$50,000
Less:			
	(70,000 x $2)	*(60.000 x $2)*	
Variable costs	(140,000)	(120,000)	(20,000)
Contribution	270,000	240,000	30,000
Less Fixed Costs:			
Manufacturing	(201,600)	(201,600)	-
Selling and administrative	(50,000)	(50,000)	-
Net Income (Loss)	$18,400	$(11,600)	$30,000

An Example—The Make or Buy Decision

In the example of Illustration 13-3, the fixed costs were identical under each alternative and had no impact on the decision. In many situations, different alternatives may have associated with them different fixed costs that may affect the decision. This is shown in the example problem of Illustration 13-4. In this problem management is faced with another common special decision, whether make or buy a subassembly required for the manufacture of a finished product. A solution to this problem using the contribution approach is provided in Illustration 13-5.

This example demonstrates that fixed costs, as well as variable costs, may affect a project planning decision. In this example, an increase in fixed costs more than offset any savings in variable costs obtained by manufacturing the subassembly rather than purchasing it externally. Use of the contribution approach made this change in costs evident. Had an absorption costing measure of net income been computed, the relationship between fixed and variable costs would have been less apparent because fixed costs would have been included in product costs.

Advantages of the Contribution Approach

As the previous examples have illustrated, the contribution approach to income determination offers several advantages over an absorption costing approach for making project planning decisions.

Illustration 13-4 Contribution Approach to the Make or Buy Decision Example Problem

Forest Manufacturing Company is a producer of gasoline powered chainsaws. In the past, Forest has purchased small gasoline engines from a supplier and mounted them on its own frame, completing assembly in its own factory. The company is now considering the manufacture of its own gasoline engines.

Currently variable costs are $60 per unit. If Forest makes its own engines, variable costs will decrease to $50 per unit; however, fixed manufacturing costs will increase from the current $300,000 per year to $500,000 per year. Currently the budgeted sales are 15,600 units per year at a price of $100. Budgeted fixed selling and administrative costs are $100,000 per year.

Required:

Using the contribution approach, determine if Forest should make or buy the gasoline engines.

Illustration 13-5 Contribution Approach to the Make or Buy Decision Solution to Example Problem

The alternatives are:

Alternative (1) - Make the engines

Alternative (2) - Buy the engines

	Variable Costing Net Income		
	(1) *Make*	*(2)* *Buy*	*Difference* *(1) - (2)*
Sales revenue	1,560,000	1,560,000	-
Less:	(15,600 x $50)	(15,600 x $60)	
Variable costs	780,000	936,000	(156,000)
Contribution	780,000	624,000	156,000
Less Fixed Costs:			
Manufacturing	(500,000)	(300,000)	200,000
Selling and administrative	(100,000)	(100,000)	-
Net Income	180,000	224,000	(44,000)

Conclusion: If Alternative (1) is chosen, net income will decrease by $44,000 per year.

1. The contribution approach recognizes the behavior patterns of costs. This more detailed information frequently makes the evaluation of alternatives easier by allowing the use of such techniques as cost-volume-profit analysis.
2. Many special decisions are concerned with short-term product pricing strategies. Variable costs provide a guide to the minimum acceptable prices in such situations. An objection frequently offered to the contribution approach is that prices set based on unit variable costs may be too low to assure long-term profitability. This assertion is valid when variable costs are the only factors considered in setting prices; however, this is seldom the case. Unit absorption costs and the actions of competitors are frequently considered as well. Additionally, unit absorption costs may be deficient for setting prices if an inappropriate activity level is used in determining the fixed overhead rates.
3. The contribution approach isolates fixed costs, which when considered in total may affect the choice of a decision alternative. Using an absorption costing approach, fixed manufacturing costs are allocated to products which make their magnitudes and effects difficult to

determine. In making special decisions based on the profitability of a product or segment of a business, for example, it may be impossible to isolate all fixed costs associated with a single product or segment. These *common costs* may be incurred for the benefit of all products or segments. With the contribution approach, common costs may be isolated and excluded from the analysis. Under absorption costing, where common costs are allocated to products, these costs may affect the decision even though the decision will have no bearing on the incurrence of the costs. This advantage of the contribution approach is illustrated by the example problem of Illustration 13-6. The solution to this example problem is provided in Illustration 13-7.

4. A related advantage of the contribution approach is that it avoids the allocation of fixed costs. The method of such allocations frequently is only incidentally related to the occurrence of the costs, and is based on judgment which may differ from accountant to accountant. In some instances, it may be completely arbitrary. In absorption costing, allocation methods are utilized extensively in the choice of depreciation methods, selection of an activity for allocating factory overhead, and the allocation of joint costs to joint products. Although appropriate for external reporting, these allocation methods should have no bearing on the choice of alternatives in making special decisions.

The contribution approach offers a number of advantages over traditional absorption costing methods in making special decisions. However, in certain situations even this approach may be deficient. The contribution approach only recognizes accounting costs, which are represented by future or past expenditures. In many project planning situations, implied costs may be of economic importance even though they do not represent an expenditure. These costs are considered in the relevant cost approach to special decisions.

Illustration 13-6 Contribution Approach to the Product Profitability Decision Example Problem

The Widget Division of Apex International currently manufactures widgets in only one size. Management is considering the introduction of a new product, a large size widget. If this is done, an additional $50,000 per year in fixed manufacturing costs will be incurred in producing the new product. Currently $40,000 per year of fixed manufacturing costs isrequired in the production of smaller widgets. Additionally, the following common costs will be incurred for *both* products: Fixed manufacturing $100,000, fixed selling $30,000, and fixed administrative $10,000. For the small widget, the standard variable cost is $10 per unit and the selling price is $15. Expected annual sales is 30,000 units. For the large widget, the standard variable cost will be $18, with a selling price of $27, and expected annual sales of 10,000 units.

Required:

1. Using the absorption costing approach, determine the profit attributable to (1) the small widget, and (2) the large widget, if common costs are allocated to products:

(a) equally,

(b) based on the percentage of total sales revenue.

What decision should be made?

2. Using the contribution approach, determine the contribution of each product. What decision should be made?

Illustration 13-7 Contribution Approach to the Product Profitability Decision Solution to Example Problem

1. Absorption costing approach

(a) Common costs allocated equally:

	Small Widget	Large Widget
Fixed factory overhead rate	($40,000+$50,000)/30,000	($50,000+$50,000)/10,000
	= $3/unit	= $10/unit
Unit costs	$10+$3 = $13	$18+$10 = $28
Sales revenue	30,000 x $15 = $450,000	10,000 x $27 = $270,000
Cost of good sold	30,000 x $13 = $390,000	10,000 x $28 = $280,000
Gross profit	$60,000	($10,000)
Selling and administrative	0.5 x $40,000 = $20,000	0.5 x $40,000 = $20,000
Prof it (loss)	$4,000	($30,000)

(b) Common costs allocated based on sales revenue:

	Small Widget	Large Widget
% of sales revenue	62.50%	37.50%
Fixed factory overhead rate	$3.42/unit*	$8.75/unit**
Unit costs	$10+$3.42 = $13.42	$18+$8.75 = $26.75
Sales revenue	30,000 x $13.42 = $402,600	10,000 x $26.75 = $267,500
Cost of good sold	30,000 x $13 = $390,000	10,000 x $28 = $280,000
Gross profit	$47,400	$2,500
Selling and administrative	0.625 x $40,000 = $25,000	0.375 x $40,000 = $15,000
Prof it (loss)	$22,400	($12,500)

* [40,000 + .625x100,000]/30,000; ** [50,000 + .375x100,000]/10,000

The appropriate decision is unclear. Based on absorption costing methods, the new product will produce a loss. However, it may produce a positive gross profit, depending on the method of allocating common costs.

2.Contribution approach (common costs are not allocated)

	Small Widget	Large Widget
	(30,000 x $15)	(10,000 x $27)
Sales revenue	$450,000	$270,000
	(30,000 x $10)	(10,000 x $18)
Variable cost of goods sold	300,000	180,000
Contribution	150,000	90,000
Fixed costs due to product	40,000	50,000
Contribution to common fixed costs and profits	110,000	40,000

The new product should be introduced because it contributes to the recovery of common fixed costs and profits.

RELEVANT COST APPROACH TO SPECIAL DECISIONS

The contribution approach demonstrates the effect on net income of the decision alternatives which are available. In the preceding example problems, a decision alternative was chosen not because of the net income under the alternative, but rather because of the *difference* in incomes between the available alternatives. This difference in incomes arose because of differences in revenues and costs between the alternatives. Consequently each decision situation could have been analyzed by considering only the revenues and costs which differed, rather than all revenues and costs. This is frequently described as the relevant cost approach to special decisions.

The *relevant cost approach* recognizes that the only costs (and revenues) which are relevant to any decision are those which differ among the decision alternatives. Costs which differ across different alternatives have been described as the *incremental costs,* the *differential costs,* or sometimes the *marginal costs* associated with the decision. These may include not only accounting costs, but also other costs which are implied but will not be evidenced by expenditures. Incremental costs may be of many types; some of the terms used to describe them will now be discussed.

Costs Which May Be Incremental

Many of the costs which will be incremental to a decision are the type of cost recorded by accounting systems, and are referred to as *outlay costs,* or sometimes as *out-of-pocket costs.* They are costs created by an expenditure, or outlay, of funds. Most project planning decisions will have one or more outlay costs that are incremental; for example, in the special order decision of Illustration 13-2 the variable cost of the units in the special order was an outlay cost.

Other costs may not require an expenditure but still may constitute a very real cost in an economic sense. A decision alternative may have associated with it an *opportunity cost,* which is a benefit not received as a result of the selection of another alternative. In Illustration 13-3 the special order, if accepted, would generate added income of $30,000.

This additional income would constitute an opportunity cost of not accepting the order. Opportunity costs are examples of *imputed costs* or *implied costs,* because they do not represent cash outlays.

A similar concept is that of the *avoidable cost.* A cost which is an incremental outlay cost under one alternative may be avoidable under another; thus, it is an economic benefit received because of a cost not incurred. In Illustration 13-5, an added $200,000 in fixed manufacturing costs would be incurred if the company decided to make the subassembly in house. This represents an avoidable cost under the buy alternative.

Costs Which Are Not Incremental

Just as some types of costs may be expected to be relevant to a special decision, other types of costs will never be incremental. A cost representing an expenditure previously incurred as a result of a past decision and can't be changed by future decisions is referred to as *a sunk cost.* The existence of sunk costs has no bearing on future decisions because they will not change, no matter which alternative is chosen. Examples of sunk costs include the cost of obsolete inventory and the cost of machinery purchased in the past.

Any type of *allocated costs* is also not an incremental cost. Allocated costs vary as a result of the chosen allocation method and not as a result of the decision alternative chosen. Illustration 13-7 demonstrates the fallacy of attempting to make a project planning decision based on allocated costs. One common type of allocated costs is the portion of *joint costs* allocated to joint products. The discussion in Chapter Seven describes the methods of making this allocation for external reporting purposes, and shows that such methods are not appropriate for special decisions. A similar non-incremental cost is *depreciation.* Defined as an allocation of the cost of equipment over the life of the equipment, depreciation is in fact an allocation of a sunk cost.

Although a sunk cost itself has no bearing on a special decision, the effect of income tax laws may produce an incremental benefit associated with a sunk cost. For example, although the cost of obsolete inventory is never incremental, the sale of obsolete inventory at a loss may produce a deduction for purposes of computing income tax. The *tax savings* associated with the sale is therefore an incremental benefit. The existence of depreciation as a tax deductible expense, or of a loss on the sale of a fixed asset, may produce similar incremental tax benefits. The factor relevant to the decision is the effect of income tax on the decision, and not the sunk cost producing the tax effect.

Using the Relevant Cost Approach

In addition to its ability to recognize non-accounting costs, the relevant cost approach offers the advantage of simplicity over the contribution approach. Decision alternatives are evaluated two at a time, by identifying the quantitative benefits and costs of the first alternative that are not present with the second. Quantitative benefits may include incremental revenues, incremental cost savings, or avoidable costs. Quantitative costs may include incremental outlay costs, incremental opportunity costs, or other imputed costs which are incremental. Total incremental costs are subtracted from total incremental benefits to compute the *net incremental benefit* (or net incremental cost, if costs are greater) of the first alternative over the second.

The relevant cost approach frequently requires less data than using the contribution approach in evaluating the same decision alternatives. This can be a significant advantage if the data is very imprecise or is not readily available. However, if more than two alternatives are to be compared, the relevant cost approach must be used several times for each pair of alternatives. With the contribution approach, all alternatives can be compared simultaneously.

Application of the Relevant Cost Approach

The use of the relevant cost approach to project planning decisions will now be illustrated with several example problems. These problems represent common decision making situations in which the approach is useful, and will provide examples of some of the cost concepts discussed in this chapter.

The Special Order Decision

The contribution approach to the special order decision was demonstrated in Illustrations 13-6 and 13-7. That example and other similar situations can be analyzed using the relevant cost approach. Consider the following example.

Big Apple Amalgamated manufactures wooden boxes from low grade lumber which are used in packing and shipping fruit. Each unit must pass through two departments: the Cutting Department and the Assembly Department. Products are sold by the gross, and the normal selling price is $10 per gross. In the Cutting Department, where maximum capacity is 10,000 gross per month, variable costs of $3 per gross are incurred. In Assembly, variable costs are $4 per gross and capacity is 15,000 gross. Overtime work is possible, but results in a 50% increase in variable costs. A fruit packer in another region, Sour Lemon Ltd., has offered to purchase 1,000 gross during the month of February at $7.50 each.

1. If expected sales (excluding the special order) for February are 8,000 gross, should the special order be accepted?

2. Should the order be accepted if expected sales are 10,000 gross?

This example illustrates the effect of capacity limitations on a special order decision. The solution, presented in Illustration 13-8, shows that accepting the special order is beneficial as long as sufficient excess capacity in the Cutting Department exists for meeting it. When capacity is limited, profit is improved by declining the special order and selling all available units to regular customers at a higher price.

The Make or Buy Decision

Capacity limitations may also affect the choice of alternatives in the make or buy decision. This point is demonstrated in the following example problem, which is analyzed in Illustration 13-9.

Austin Corp. manufactures Part X for use in its production process. The standard manufacturing costs per 100 units of Part X are as follows:

Direct Material	$ 5.00
Direct Labor	$20.00
Variable Overhead	$ 8.00
Fixed Overhead	$12.00
	$45.00

Illustration 13-8 Relevant Cost Approach to the Special Order Decision Solution to Big Apple Problem

The alternatives are:

1. Accept the special order
2. Decline the special order

(1) Expected sales of 8,000 gross

Incremental benefits of Alternative 1:			
Revenues	1,000 x $7.50 =		$7,500
Incremental costs of Alternative 1:			
Cutting Department	1,000 x $3.00 =	$3,000	
Assembly Department	1,000 x $4.00 =	4,000	7,000
Net incremental benefit to Alternative 1:			$500

(2) Expected sales of 10,000 gross*

Incremental benefits of Alternative 1:			
Revenues	1,000 x $7.50 =		$7,500
Incremental costs of Alternative 1 (includes overtime):			
Cutting Department	1,000 x $3.00 x 1.5 =	4,500	
Assembly Department	1,000 x $4.00 =	4,000	8,500
Net incremental cost to Alternative 1: (benefit to Alternative 2)			$1,000

*Note: Cutting Department capacity is a limiting resource. The special order cannot be filled without working overtime in that department.

Illustration 13-9 Relevant Cost Approach to the Make or Buy Decision Solution to Austin Corp. Problem

The alternatives are:

1. Purchase Part X from Sam
2. Manufacture the parts

Increme ntal benefits of Alternative 1:		
Savings on Part Y	$1,000	
Variable costs of Part X:		
Direct Material (10,000100) x 5	500	
Direct Labor (10,000/100) x 20	2,000	
Variable Overhead (10,000 / 100) x 8	800	$4,300
Incremental costs of Alternative 1:		
Purchase cost of Part X (10,000/ 100) x 40		4,000
Net incremental benefit to Alternative 1:		$ 300

Sam Corp. has offered to sell 10,000 units of X to Austin for $40 per 100 units. If Austin purchases the parts, the released facilities can be used in the manufacture of Part Y at a total savings of $1,000. Should Austin buy the parts from the outside supplier, or continue to manufacture them?

In this example, the purchase alternative was a favorable one because Austin Corp. had another use for the facilities made available by not manufacturing the 10,000 units of Part X. If these facilities would have remained idle, quantitative evaluation shows that the parts should be manufactured. Fixed factory overhead costs are not relevant to the decision, because the $12 per 100 units of fixed overhead is an allocation of a sunk cost. These would be incurred regardless of the decision made. Direct material, direct labor, and variable overhead are avoidable costs under the buy alternative, and the purchase price of Part X is an outlay cost.

The Decision to Replace Equipment

Another common project planning decision concerns the purchase of new equipment. Frequently technological changes will result in the development of new machinery which will provide advantages over existing production methods. Organizations must consider the purchase of new equipment to replace existing equipment which is still in use. The following examples illustrates such a situation, and the effect of income taxes on the decision. Its solution is presented in Illustration 13-10.

An organization purchased a piece of research equipment, an alpha machine, 5 years ago for $100,000. The alpha machine has a useful life of 10 years and is depreciated on a straight-line basis. A new model has been developed, which due to better technology can increase productivity at a savings of $25,000 per year. The new model has a 5 year useful life and will cost $100,000, also to be depreciated on a straight-line basis. The old alpha machine has no resale value. Determine if the new model should be purchased if (1) the organization is a university (which is tax exempt), and (2) the organization is a corporation with a 40% effective tax rate.

Purchase of the new model would be advisable for the university but not for the corporation. A tax exempt organization can evaluate such a proposal on its own merits, but one subject to income tax must consider the tax effects of the decision. In the case of the corporation, the $25,000 per year savings would increase income by that amount. Only 60% (=100% – 40%) of that amount would be retained after income tax. Since depreciation is a tax deductible expense, the annual depreciation on the new model would shield earnings from tax at the rate of 40% of

Illustration 13-10 Relevant Cost Approach to the Decision to Replace Equipment Solution to the Alpha Machine Problem*

The alternatives are:

1. Replace the alpha machine with a new model
2. Keep the alpha machine

(1) Organization is a university		
Incremental benefits of Alternative 1:		
Annual savings (5 x 25,000):		$125,000
Incremental costs of Alternative 1:		
Purchase cost of new model:		$100,000
Net incremental benefit to Alternative 1		$25,000
(2) Organization is a corporation		
Incremental benefits of Alternative 1:		
Annual savings after tax (5 x 25,000 x .6):	$75,000	
Tax savings on loss from disposal of alpha (50,000 x .4)	$20,000	
Tax effect of depreciation on new model (5 x 20,000 x .4):	$40,000	$135,000
Incremental costs of Alternative 1:		
Purchase cost of new model	$100,000	
Tax effect of depreciation on alpha (5 x 10,000 x .4):	$20,000	$120,000
Net incremental benefit to Alternative I (cost to Alternative 2)		$15,000

*Note: The time value of money is ignored in this chapter. A consideration of the time value of money in capital expenditure decisions is discussed in Chapter 16.

the amount of the depreciation. The purchase price of the old alpha machine is a sunk cost and has no bearing on the decision.

The Decision to Add or Eliminate Facilities

Managers frequently encounter the decision of whether or not to add or eliminate facilities, such as a plant, a department, or a segment of the business. The application of the relevant cost approach to such a decision is considered in the following example.

International Industries, Inc., is a decentralized conglomerate consisting of three divisions. Top management has become concerned about the ability of Division C to contribute to the profitability of the company, and is considering either selling it or closing it completely. The following income statements reflect the performance of the three divisions for the year 20XX.

	Division A	*Division B*	*Division C*
Revenue..	$500,000	$500,000	$500,000
Variable Cost of Goods Sold....................	(300,000)	(200,000)	(300,000)
Divisional Contribution...........................	200,000	300,000	200,000
Fixed Costs of Division............................	(100,000)	(175,000)	(175,000)
Contribution to Common Costs.............	100,000	125,000	25,000
Common Costs Allocated to Division....			
from Corporate Office.............................	(50,000)	(50,000)	(50,000)
Income..	$ 50,000	$ 75,000	$(25,000)

(1) Based only on the above information, should Division C be closed? (2) A buyer is willing to purchase Division C for $600,000. Assuming the same revenue and expense levels will continue for the next 10 years, should the division be sold?

The solution to this example problem is presented in Illustration 13-11. The division should not be closed because it contributes to the recovery of the common costs incurred by the corporate office. However, sale of the division should be considered further. The cash to be received from the sale exceeds the potential earnings of Division C for the next 10 years. The $600,000 sales price is an opportunity cost associated with alternative 2, retaining the division. The common costs allocated to Division C will be incurred regardless of whether the division is retained, closed, or sold. These allocated costs are therefore not relevant to the decision.

The last part of this example, and the previous example, described decisions affecting an extended period of time. In such decisions, benefits to be received in the present are much more valuable than benefits to be received at some point in the future. This fact, known as the *time value of money* was not considered in the analysis. Methods for calculating the time value of money will be described in Chapter 16.

Illustration 13-11 Relevant Cost Approach to the Decision to Eliminate Facilities Solution to the International Industries Problem

(1) Should Division C be closed?		
The alternatives are:		
1. Close the division		
2. Retain the division		
Incremental benefits of Alternative 1:		
Savings in variable costs	300,000	
Savings in fixed costs	175,000	$475,000
Revenue not received		500000
Net incremental cost per year of Alternative 1		$25,000
(2) Should Division C be sold?		
2. Retain the division		
3. Sell the division		
Incremental benefits of Alternative 2:		$5,000,000
Revenue received (10 x 500,000)		
Incremental costs of Alternative 2:		
Variable costs (10 x 300,000)	3,000,000	
Fixed costs (10 x 175,000)	1,750,000	
Loss of cash from sale	600,000	5,350,000
Net incremental cost per year of Alternative 2:		$350,000

Product Mix Problems Under Constrained Resources

Now we extend the discussion on contribution approach to product mix decisions under resource constraints. When there is no constraint in production resources, managers use the contribution margin per unit of product as a critical criterion to determine whether to produce a product or not. A thumb of rule is that any products with positive contribution margin should be produced to maximize the operating profit. When there is a constraint in resources, however, the contribution margin per unit of constrained resources should be used to determine the optimal product mix. The firm will incur an opportunity cost from the decease in quantities of other products if an additional unit of one product is produced when resources are constrained. Thus, the efficient allocation of scarce resources among the alternative products should be based on the contribution margin per unit of constrained resources, not on the contribution margin per unit of product.

Single-Resource Constraint

For purpose of illustration, consider Tustin Company that has three departments: machining, assembly, and finishing. The company manufactures and sells two products, A and B, with unlimited demand in the market. The company has 900 hours of finishing time available in a planning period. The finishing hours requirement for production of a unit of Products A and B and their unit contribution margins are given in the following table:

Product	*Finishing Time*	*Contribution Margin*
A	6 hours	$10
B	20	12

The production of the two products is constrained by the availability of finishing time. To determine the optimal product mix of the two products, the management at Tustin Company has to calculate the contribution margin per unit of constrained resources. Based on the above information, the contribution margin per hour of finishing time is $1.67 (=$10/6) and $0.60 (=$12/20) for Products A and B, respectively. Since the contribution margin per finishing hour of Product A is greater than that of Product B, all the available 900 hours of finishing time should be devoted to the production of Product A. Therefore, the optimal production mix for Tustin Company is to produce 150 (900/6) units of Product A and zero unit of Product B.

Multiple-Resources Constraints

While the contribution margin per unit of constrained resources is good for use in the determination of the optimal product mix under single rescource constraint, an alternative method called linear programming is widely employed to determine the optimal product mix decisions when there are two or more constraints in resources. Linear programming is a mathematical tool that permits a solution to the problem of maximization or minimization of a linear objective function subject to certain linear constraints. Linear programming models are widely used in various business problem situations. In this section we shall discuss their accounting implications and examine how they are applied in the determination of a product mix. The product mix problem and a linear programming formulation will be first described with the example of Tustin Company. The graphic method for solving the problem is then discussed.

A Linear Programming Formulation for a Product Mix Problem

Assume further that Tustin Company expects to confront with two additional constraints in its production resources: 900 hours of machine time and 900 hours of assembly time available. The resource requirement for production of a unit of Products A and B and their unit contribution margins are given in the following table:

Product	*Machine Time*	*Assembly Time*	*Finishing Time*	*Contribution Margin*
A	10 hours	9 hours	6 hours	$10
B	10	15	20	12

The problem that management faces is to determine the optimal product mix of the two products. The number of units of the two products (A and B) to be produced are the decision variables, and the capacities of the three manufacturing processes (machining, assembly, and finishing) are the limited resources. If profit maximization is the objective, the objective can be formulated into the following expression:

Objective function: Z = 10A + 12B
Where **Z** = the total contribution margin
A = the number of units of Product A to be produced
B = the number of units of Product B to be produced

The production of the two products is constrained by the availability of the scarce resources; i.e., machine time, assembly time, and finishing time. The resource requirements in production and the resource constraints can be expressed as:

$10A + 10B \leq 900$
$9A + 15B \leq 900$
$6A + 20B \leq 900$

These three constraint equations state that the total consumption of each scarce resource must be equal to or less than the total available time in each department. Since negative production of each product is not possible, constraints requiring A and B to be positive are necessary. This will eliminate negative solutions of A and B from consideration. Therefore, we can formulate our example of Tustin Company as a linear programming problem in the following way:

Maximize:	Z = 10A + 12B	Objective function
Subject to:	10A + 10 B ≤ 900	Machining constraint
	9A + 15B 9 ≤ 00	Assembly constraint

$6A + 20B \leq 900$ Finishing constraint

and

A and B are non-negative.

The above linear programming problem can be solved by the graphic method and the simplex method. While the simplex method is more general and more powerful, an understanding of the graphic method will provide a foundation for better understanding the concepts and rationale of the simplex algorithm. Since the simplex method is beyond the scope of the discussion of this book, interested readers should refer to any introductory textbooks in management science/operations research.

The Graphic Method

The first step in solving a linear programming problem employing the graphic method is to construct a graph. Illustration 13-12 presents an example of the graphic solution. The number of units of Product A is represented by values on the vertical axis, while the number of units of Product B is represented by values on the horizontal axis. The non-negativity constraints, $A \geq 0$ and $B \geq 0$, restrict the feasible values of A and B to the first quadrant of the AB plane shown on the graph. All values of A and B are either positive or zero.

The next step is to plot the constraints on the graph. For example, consider the constraint equationfor the machine time:

$$10A + 10\,B \leq 900$$

This constraint equation can be plotted on the graph by connecting the points where the quation intersects the vertical and horizontal axis. Substituting $A = 0$ into the equation and solving for B, we obtain $B = 90$. Likewise, $A = 90$, if $B = 0$. These two points can be connected by a straight line. This line represents all the possible combinations of the number of units of Products A and B that use exactly 900 hours of machine time. Points below the line represent the combinations of numbers of units of Products A and B that require less than 900 hours of machine time. The assembly constraint and the finishing constraint can be plotted in a similar way on the graph as shown. The shaded area in the graph represents the feasible region. Any point in the region represents a combination of the number of units of Products A and B that satisfy simultaneously the non-negativity, the machining, the assembly, and the finishing constraints.

The final step is to find a point in the feasible region area that maximizes the total contribution margin. There are two approaches to find the optimal point: the corner points approach and the iso-profit line approach.

The Corner Points Approach

The optimum solution to the problem is represented by one of the corner points of the feasible region. This point can be found by computing the contribution margin at each corner point. In our illustration, evaluating the corner points O, W, X, Y, and Z of the feasible region with respect to the total contribution margin, we find:

Illustration 13-12 Graphic Solution

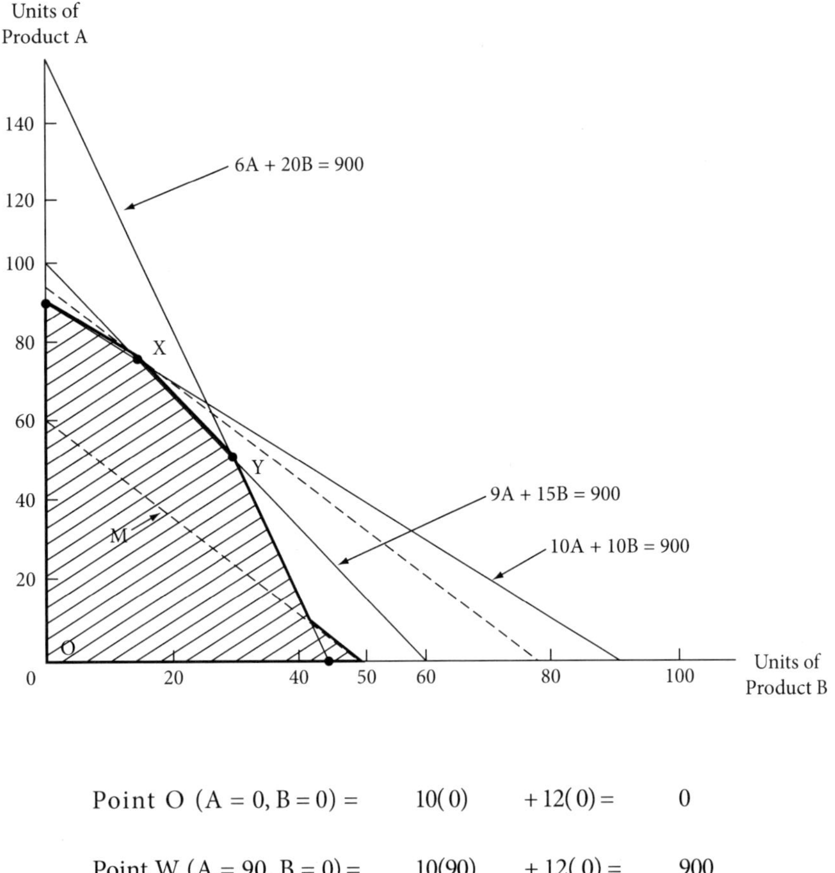

Point O (A = 0, B = 0) =	10(0)	+ 12(0) =	0
Point W (A = 90, B = 0) =	10(90)	+ 12(0) =	900
Point X (A = 75, B = 15)[1] =	10(75)	+ 12(15) =	930
Point Y (A = 50, B = 30) =	10(50)	+ 12(30) =	860
Point Z (A = 0, B = 40) =	10(0)	+ 12(40) =	480

The point that provides the most contribution margin is Point X, with a contribution margin of $930. Therefore, the optimal solution to the problem is to produce 75 units of Product A and 15 units of Product B with a resulting total contribution margin of $930.

1 Point X represents A=75 and B=15 which are determined by solving the following two simultaneous equations for A and B:

$$10A + 10B = 900$$
$$9A + 15B = 900$$

The Iso-Profit Line Approach

Another way to find the optimal solution to the problem is the iso-profit line approach. An iso-profit line is the locus of all points that yield a particular total contribution margin. For example, line M in Illustration 13-12 is an iso-profit line which represents all combinations of A and B that yield a total contribution margin of $600. Our objective is to find a combination of A and B in the feasible region that belongs to the iso-profit line with the highest contribution margin. In order to achieve this objective, we could continue to construct these iso-profit lines for higher and higher profits as long as the iso-profit lines stay within the feasible region. It should be noted that we would have to stop when an iso-profit line is tangent to a corner point or a boundary line of the feasible solution area. When this occurs, we have found the optimal solution for the problem. In our example, there is an infinite number of iso-profit lines within the feasible region. However, we can see that in the illustration the furthest iso-profit line from the origin that is still within the feasible region is the one tangent to Point X. Therefore, this point determines the optimal solution. The coordinates of Point X can be read directly from the graph at A=75 and B=15. This means that the firm should produce 75 units of Product A and 15 units of Product B and that the associated contribution margin is $930.

Although the graphic method provides useful insights into the structure of the problem, it can only solve problems with three or less decision variables. This limitation is due to the fact that we are not able to draw more than three dimensions in a graph. A more general and powerful approach for solving linear programming problems, as mentioned earlier, is the simplex method. In practice, managerial accountants use computer package that employ simplex method to solve the linear programming models.

Assumptions Underlying the Linear Programming Model

Three basic assumptions underlying the linear programming model are:

1. Linearity—The total of each resource used and the total contribution margin is directly proportional to the number of units produced of each product. In other words, the mathematical model can be formulated in terms of linear relations.
2. Deterministic—Estimates of contribution margins, coefficients, and scarce resources are stated with certainty. They are known parameters.
3. Proportionality—Solutions in fractional units are permissible. Integer solutions are available if integer programming is applied.

It should be noted that few real-life situations satisfy these assumptions. In some cases, they may hold only approximately. The user of the model should make sure that the underlying assumptions hold well enough to permit useful application of the linear programming approach. If the underlying assumptions are not valid, some advanced mathematical programming approaches may be used to solve the problem.

Theory of Constraints

Like situations of constrained resources discussed earlier, it is not uncommon for firms to face bottlenecks in operations. Bottlenecks interrupt productive process, build up excess inventory, and cause the delay of product delivery. When encountered with bottlenecks, one approach available to management to solving bottlenecks is the application of the theory of constraints (TOC). TOC is a tool that helps identify and eliminate bottlenecks to improve the firm's production efficiency and operating income.

In general, there are four steps involved in the application of TOC as described below:

1. Identify bottlenecks: Almost all production resources/facilities have bottlenecks to some extent. A bottleneck is the constraint that limits the capacity or throughput of the production. Management needs to identify possible bottlenecks.
2. Calculate throughput contribution: The objective of TOC is to increase throughput for the identified bottleneck. It is necessary to figure out the throughput contribution of each product. As was described in the previous chapter, throughput contribution is the sales amount after the direct material costs have been deducted. The use of throughput contribution under the bottleneck is in spirit similar to that of contribution margin per unit of constrained resources discussed in the previous section.
3. Maximize throughput contribution: Except direct material costs, all other costs are considered fixed in the short run. That is, maximizing a firm's throughput contribution under the bottleneck is equivalent to maximizing its operating profit. Management has to manage the bottleneck effectively by producing only the products that maximize the total throughput contribution.
4. Take actions to eliminate bottlenecks: In the short run, bottlenecks can be eliminated by adding capacity or outsourcing the production process. Adding capacity in house has the advantage of quality assurance while outsourcing has the advantage of low costs. Management must tradeoff between the quality and the cost to make appropriate decisions.

Consider Richardson Company which manufactures and sells two different types of machine tools, MT#1 and MT#2. The production process involves 2 operations: Fabrication and Installation. The resources requirements for production of a unit of MT#1 and MT#2 and their unit throughput contribution are given in the following table:

Product	*Fabrication Time*	*Installation Time*	*Throughput Contribution*
MT#1	1 hours	2 hours	$20
MT#2	1 hours	1 hours	$15

The market demand for each of the two products is 5,000 units per month. The monthly capacity for fabrication and installation time is 10,000 hours each. Clearly, installation is the bottleneck for production. Throughput contribution per unit of installation hour is $10 (=$20/2) and $15 (=$15/1) for MT#1 and MT#2, respectively. For the given bottleneck, Richardson Company should use 5,000 hours of installation time to produce 5,000 units of MT#2 and then use the remaining 5,000 hours to produce 2,500 (=5,000/2) units of MT#1 in order to maximize the total throughput contribution.

Now, suppose that management at Richardson Company is considering the following two viable options to solve the bottleneck:

- Option A: Add 5,000 hour of installation time per month by asking installation workers to work during the weekend. This option shall incur additional monthly costs of $20,000.
- Option B: Outsource the production of 2,500 units of MT#1 to an outside contractor. The outside contractor will charge $10 for each unit of MT#1 installed.

What option should Richardson Company choose? Based on the above information, the incremental throughput contribution of option A is $30,000 (=2,500 x $20 – $20,000) and the incremental throughput contribution of option B is $25,000 (=2,500 x ($20-$10)). Therefore, Richardson Company should choose option A. Additionally, producing MT#1 in house under option A would not have the concern of quality issue.

The above example illustrates the application of TOC when there exists only one bottleneck. Under such a situation, total throughput contribution can be maximized by producing products with highest throughput contribution per unit of constrained resources. However, when there are multiple bottlenecks as those discussed earlier under multiple resources constraints, the application of TOC involves the use of linear programming to determine what products to produce in order to maximize the total throughput contribution.

Summary

Managers of organizations must frequently make decisions which are unique to a special situation and are not repetitive. In these situations, the data used in the quantitative evaluation of decision alternatives is provided by the cost accounting system. Cost accountants participate in the decision making process by communicating this data to managers and by advising them in its interpretation.

Two approaches have been described for evaluating alternatives in making special decisions. The contribution approach utilizes the direct costing method of income determination, and offers several advantages over absorption costing methods for this purpose. The relevant cost approach considers only those costs which differ among the decision alternatives, and may include certain types of non-accounting costs. Several example applications of each of these approaches have been provided.

Contribution approach can be applied to product mix decision. Product mix problems with a single scarce resource can be solved by comparing the contribution margins of the limiting factors. However, with more than one scarce resource, the product mix decision cannot be made by simply comparing the contribution margin of each product. In this case, consideration must be given to interactive effects between products. Linear programming is widely used for the analysis of such a problem. Linear programming is a powerful mathematical tool that permits determination of the optimal product mix under certain linear resource constraints. This chapter has introduced the linear programming formulation to product mix problems and has illustrated graphical method. This chapter has also introduced the theory of constraints which is a tool available to management to resolving the problem of bottlenecks in operations.

Key Definitions

Avoidable costs	A type of incremental cost which will be incurred under one decision alternative but will be avoided with another alternative.
Common costs	Costs which are incurred for the benefit of several products, departments, or divisions, and are not attributable to any one of them.
Contribution approach	An approach to analyzing project planning decisions by computing the effect of a decision on direct costing net income.
Incremental cost	A cost or benefit which differs among decision alternatives. Incremental costs are relevant to project planning decisions.
Iso-profit line	A line which is the locus of all points that yields a particular total contribution margin.
Linear programming	A mathematical tool that provides a solution to the problem of maximization or minimization of a linear objective function subject to certain linear constraints.
Net incremental benefit	The difference in amount between incremental benefits and incremental costs.
Opportunity cost	The amount of a benefit not received due to the choice of a decision alternative.
Outlay cost	A cost represented by an expenditure of funds. Outlay costs are recorded by an accounting system.
Project planning decisions	Decisions encountered by managers which arenonrepetitive and nonroutine in their nature.
Relevant cost approach	An approach to analyzing a project planning decision by considering only the costs which are incremental to the decision.
Sunk cost	A cost which was fixed by a past decision and cannot be changed regardless of decisions made in the future

Questions

13-1 What characteristics distinguish project planning decisions from other types of managerial decisions? What are some examples of project planning decisions?

13-2 Give some examples of decision making situations in which qualitative factors may affect management's choice of alternatives.

13-3 What is the role of the cost accountant in making project planning decisions?

13-4 Describe the advantages of the contribution approach over absorption costing methods in evaluating decision alternatives.

13-5 In what situations might the use of the relevant cost approach to project planning decisions be preferred over the contribution approach?

13-6 How can limitations on production capacity affect the choice of alternatives in (a) a special order decision, and (b) a make or buy decision?

13-7 What types of costs may be relevant to a project planning decision even though they will never be recorded in the accounts?

13-8 What is a "sunk cost?" When is such a cost relevant to a project planning decision?

13-9 Is depreciation on equipment ever an incremental cost? Should the amount of depreciation ever affect the choice between alternatives in a project planning decision?

13-10 Some project planning decisions involve incremental cash flows over an extended period of time. What modifications should be made to the relevant cost approach in such situations?

13-11 What is linear programming?

13-12 Evaluate the following statement: "A firm should always attempt to maximize production and sale of the product with the highest contribution margin."

13-13 Why is a linear programming model useful in solving the product mix problem?

13-14 Distinguish between the corner points approach and the iso-profit line approach for finding the optimal solution in a linear programming problem.

13-15 Why are fixed costs not incorporated in linear programming models? How should fixed costs be treated in evaluating the profitability of the optimal solution?

13-16 Identify the basic assumptions underlying any linear programming model.

13-17 What is the theory of constraints?

Problems

13-18 *Cost Terms and Definitions*

Valley Plumbing Co. has 500 rusted plumbing fixtures that are carried in inventory at a purchase cost of $3,000. If the fixtures are reworked for $1,000, they can be sold for $4,000. Alternatively, they can be sold for salvage for $1,500.

Required:

(a) For this decision making situation, identify any
(1) opportunity costs
(2) sunk costs.
(3) Outlay cost,
(4) Avoidable cost.
(b) What qualitative considerations may affect the decision?

13-19 *Disposition of Obsolete Inventory*

The Lantern Corporation has 1,000 obsolete lanterns that are carried in inventory at a manufacturing cost of $20,000. If the lanterns are re-machined for $5,000, they could be sold for $9,000. If the lanterns are scrapped, they could be sold for $1,000. Which alternative is more desirable and what is the net incremental benefit to that alternative?

(*AICPA adapted*)

13-20 *Special Order Decision*

Marathon Manufacturing, which produces running shoes, has enough idle capacity available to accept a special order of 1,000 pairs of shoes at $24 per pair. The following data has been obtained from their budget for the current year.

	Per Unit	*Total*
Sales	$37.50	$3,750,000
Variable manufacturing costs	(18.75)	(1,875,000)
Fixed manufacturing costs	(5.25)	(525,000)
Gross profit	13.50	1,350,000
Variable selling expenses	(5.40)	(540,000)
Fixed selling expenses	(4.35)	(435,000)
Operating income	$ 3.75	$ 375,000

No additional selling expenses will be incurred due to the-special order.

Required:

If the special order is accepted, what will be the effect on operating income?

13-21 *Special Order Decision*

Relay Corporation manufactures batons. Relay can manufacture 300,000 batons a year at a variable cost of $750,000 and a fixed cost of $450,000. Based on Relay's predictions, 240,000 batons will be sold at the regular price of $5.00 each. In addition, a special order was placed for 60,000 batons to be sold at a 40% discount off the regular price.

Required:

By what amount would income before income taxes be increased or decreased as a result of the special order?

(*AICPA adapted*)

13-22 *Make or Buy Decision*

American Motor Company annually manufactures 100,000 units of its Part No. 42356, a bearing, for use in the production of its automobiles. The following costs will be incurred for this part in the current year:

Direct materials	$ 200,000
Direct labor	550,000
Variable factory overhead.....	450,000
Fixed factory overhead.........	700,000
	$1,900,000

Smaller Manufacturing Co. has offered to sell American 50,000 bearings at a cost of $18 per unit. If the offer is accepted, American can terminate its lease on certain existing facilities at an annual savings of $150,000. In addition, $4 per unit of the fixed overhead utilized for manufacture of the bearing would be eliminated.

Required:

Using the relevant cost approach, determine if American should make or buy the bearings.

(b) What qualitative factor(s) may affect the decision?

13-23 *Cost Savings from External Purchase*

The Reno Company manufactures Part No. 498 for use in its production cycle. The cost per unit for 20,000 units of Part No. 498 is as follows:

Direct materials.......................	$ 6
Direct labor.............................	30
Variable overhead...................	12
Fixed overhead applied..........	16
	$64

The Tray Company has offered to sell 20,000 units of Part No. 498 to Reno for $60 per unit. Reno will make the decision to buy the part from Tray if it produces a net incremental benefit of

$25,000 for Reno. If Reno accepts Tray's offer, $9 per unit of the fixed overhead applied would be totally eliminated. Furthermore, Reno has determined that the released facilities could be used to save relevant costs in the manufacture of Part No. 575.

Required.

How much savings must be attained in the production of Part No. 575 in order to produce a net incremental benefit of $25,000?

(*AICPA adapted*)

13-24 Make or Buy Decision with Limited Capacity

Standard costs and other data for two component parts used by Griffon Electronics are presented below:

	Part A4	*Part B5*
Direct material	$0.40	$ 8.00
Direct labor	1.00	4.70
Factory overhead	4.00	2.00
Unit standard cost	$5.40	$ 14.70
Units needed per year	6,000	8,000
Machine hours per unit	4	2
Unit cost if purchased	$5.00	$ 15.00

In past years, Griffon has manufactured all of its required components; however, in 20X1 only 30,000 hours of otherwise idle machine time can be devoted to the production of components. Accordingly, some of the parts must be purchased from outside suppliers. In producing parts, factory overhead is applied at $1.00 per standard machine hour. Fixed capacity costs, which will not be affected by any make-buy decision, represent 60%of the applied overhead. The 30,000 hours of available machine time are to be utilized such that Griffon realizes maximum potential cost savings on Products A4 and B5.

Required:

(a) What are the relevant unit costs for making this decision?

(b) How should machine time be allocated to the products?

(*AICPA adapted*)

13-25 Decision to Replace Equipment

Maxwell Company has an opportunity to acquire a new machine to replace one of its present machines. The new machine would cost $90,000, have a five-year life, and no estimated salvage value. Variable operating costs would be $100,000 per year.

The present machine has a book value of $50,000 and a remaining life of five years. Its disposal value now is $5,000, but it would be zero after five years. Variable operating costs would be $125,000 per year.

Required:

Ignore the time value of money and income taxes. Considering the five years in total, what would be the difference in profit before income taxes by acquiring the new machine as opposed to retaining the present one?

(*AICPA adapted*)

13-26 *Tax Considerations in Equipment Replacement*

Joe Carolina is considering the purchase of a new car. His current vehicle is a 9 year old Mercedes which has a resale value of $3,500 and has a remaining life of approximately 3 years. Joe has looked at a luxurious 20X2 Newmobile which sells for $10,000 and will have a salvage value of $2,000 at the end of 3 years. Joe expects to drive 12,000 miles a year over this period. His Mercedes gets 12 miles per gallon of premium gas, which sells for $1.50 per gallon. Although in reasonable condition, the Mercedes is expected to incur $500 in maintenance costs next year, and this will increase by 10% in each of the following years. The Newmobile will get 24 miles per gallon of unleaded gasoline, that sells for $1.30 per gallon, and will be maintenance free.

Required:

(a) Assume Joe is a wealthy college student. His car will represent a personal expense with no income tax impact. Based on quantitative considerations and ignoring the time value of money, should Joe purchase the Newmobile?

(b) Assume Joe is a salesman with an effective income tax rate of 30%. His car is used exclusively for business purposes; thus, it must be capitalized and related expenses are tax deductible. The Mercedes is fully depreciated and has no book value for tax purposes. Ignoring the time value of money, should Joe purchase the Newmobile?

(c) What qualitative considerations might affect Joe's decision?

13-27 *Contribution Approach to Production Decisions*

The officers of Bradshaw Company are reviewing the profitability of the company's four products and the potential effect of several proposals for varying the product mix. An excerpt from the income statement and other data follow:

	Totals	*Product P*	*Product Q*	*Product R*	*Product S*
Sales	$62,600	$10,000	$18,000	$12,600	$22,000
Cost of goods sold	$44,274	$ 4,750	$ 7,056	$13,968	$18,500
Gross profit	$18,326	$ 5,250	$10,944	($1,368)	$ 3,500
Operating expenses	$12,012	$ 1,990	$ 2,976	$ 2,826	$ 4,220
Income before income taxes	$ 6,314	$ 3,260	$ 7,968	($ 4,194)	($ 720)
Units sold		1,000	1,200	1,800	2,000
Sales price per unit		$10.00	$15.00	$ 7.00	$11.00
Variable manufacturing costs per unit		$ 2.50	$ 3.00	$ 6.50	$ 6.00
Variable selling expenses per unit		$ 1.17	$ 1.25	$ 1.00	$ 1.20

Required:

Each of the following proposals is to be considered independently of the other proposals. Consider only the product changes stated in each proposal; the activity of other products remains stable. Ignore income taxes.

(a) If Product R is discontinued, what will be the effect on net income?

(b) If Product R is discontinued and a resulting loss of customers causes a decrease of 200 units in sales of Q, what will be the total effect on net income?

(c) If the sales price of R is increased to $8 with a decrease in the number of units sold to 1,500, what will be the affect on net income?

(d) The plant in which R is produced can be utilized to produce a new product, T. The total variable costs and expenses per unit of T are $8.05, and 1,600 units can be sold at $9.50 each. If T is introduced and R is discontinued, what will be the effect on net income?

(e) Part of the plant in which P is produced can easily be adapted to the production of S, but changes in quantities may make changes in sales prices advisable. If production of P is reduced to 500 units (to be sold at $12 each) and production of S is increased to 2,500 units (to be sold at $10.50 each), what is the effect on net income?

(f) Production of P can be doubled by adding a second shift, but higher wages must be paid, increasing variable manufacturing costs to $3.50 for each of the additional units. If the 1,000 additional units of P can be sold at $10 each, what is the effect on net income?

(AICPA adapted)

13-28 *Contribution Approach to Pricing Decisions*

E. Berg and Sons build custom made pleasure boats which range in price from $10,000 to $250,000. For the past 30 years, Mr. Berg, Sr. has determined the selling price of each boat by estimating the costs of material, labor, a prorated portion of overhead, and adding 20% to these estimated costs.

For example, a recent price quotation was determined as follows:

Direct materials.........	$ 5,000
Direct labor...............	8,000
Overhead	2,000
	$15,000
Plus 20%.....................	3,000
Selling price..............	$18,000

The overhead figure was determined by estimating total overhead costs for the year and allocating them at 25% of direct labor.

If a customer rejected the price and business was slack, Mr. Berg, Sr. would often be willing to reduce his markup to as little as 5% over estimated costs. Thus, average markup for the year is estimated at 15%.

Mr. Ed Berg, Jr. has just completed a course on pricing and believes the firm could use some of the techniques discussed in the course. The course emphasized the contribution margin approach to pricing and Mr. Berg, Jr. feels such an approach would be helpful in determining the selling prices of their custom made pleasure boats.

Total overhead which includes selling and administrative expenses for the year has been estimated at $150,000 of which $90,000 is fixed and the remainder is variable in direct proportion to direct labor.

Required:

(a) Assume the customer in the example rejected the $18,000 quotation and also rejected a $15,750 quotation (5% markup) during a slack period. The customer countered with a $15,000 offer.

(1) What is the difference in net income for the year between accepting or rejecting the customer's offer?

(2) What is the minimum selling price Mr. Berg, Jr. could have quoted without reducing or increasing net income?

(b) What advantages does the contribution margin approach to pricing have over the approach used by Mr. Berg, Sr.?

(c) What pitfalls are there, if any, to contribution margin pricing?

(*IMA adapted*)

13-29 *Decision to Make or Buy*

The Vernom Corporation, which produces and sells to wholesalers a highly successful line of summer lotions and insect repellents, has decided to diversify in order to stabilize sales throughout the year. A natural area for the company to consider is the production of winter lotions and creams to prevent dry and chapped skin.

After considerable research, a winter products line has been developed. However, because of the conservative nature of the company management, Vernom's president has decided to introduce only one of the new products for this coming winter. If the product is a success, further expansion in future years will be initiated.

The product selected (called Chap-off) is a lip balm that will be sold in a lipstick-type tube. The product will be sold to wholesalers in boxes of 24 tubes for $8.00 per box. Because of available capacity, no additional fixed charges will be incurred to produce the product. However, a $100,000 fixed charge will be absorbed by the product to allocate a fair share of the company's present fixed costs to the new product.

Using the estimated sales and production of 100,000 boxes of Chap-off as the standard volume, the accounting department has developed the following costs:

Direct labor.................	$2.00/box
Direct material	3.00/box
Total overhead............	1.50/box
Total	$6.50/box

Vernom has approached a cosmetics manufacturer to discuss the possibility of purchasing the tubes for Chap-off. The purchase price of the empty tubes from the cosmetics manufacturer would be $.90 per 24 tubes. If the Vernom Corporation accepts the purchase proposal, it is estimated that direct labor and variable overhead costs would be reduced by 10 percent and direct material costs would be reduced by 20 percent.

Required:

(a) Should the Vernom Corporation make or buy the tubes? Show calculations to support your answer.

(b) What would be the maximum purchase price acceptable to the Vernom Corporation for the tubes? Support you answer with an appropriate explanation.

(c) Instead of sales of 100,000 boxes, revised estimates show sales volume at 125,000 boxes. At this new volume additional equipment, at an annual rental of $10,000, must be acquired to manufacture the tubes. However, this incremental cost would be the only additional fixed cost required even if sales increased to 300,000 boxes. (The 300,000 level is the goal for the third year of production.) Under these circumstances should the Vernom Corporation make or buy the tubes? Show calculations to support your answer.

(d) The company has the option of making and buying at the same time. What would be your answer to part (c) if this alternative was considered? Show calculations to support your answer.

(e) What nonquantifiable factors should the Vernom Corporation consider in determining whether they should make or buy the lipstick tubes?

(*IMA adapted*)

13-30 *Decision to Add or Delete Facilities*

You have been engaged to assist the management of the Arcadia Corporation in arriving at certain decisions. Arcadia has its home office in Ohio and leases factory buildings in Texas, Montana and Maine, all of which produce the same product. The management of Arcadia has provided you with a projection of operations for 20X2, the forthcoming year, as follows:

	Total	*Texas*	*Montana*	*Maine*
Sales	$4,400,000	$2,200,000	$1,400,000	$800,000
Fixed costs:				
Factory	1,100,000	560,000	280,000	260,000
Administration	350,000	210,000	110,000	30,000
Variable costs	1,450,000	665,000	425,000	360,000
Allocated home office costs	500,000	225,000	175,000	100,000
Total	3,400,000	1,660,000	990,000	750,000
Net profit from operations	$1,000,000	$ 540,000	$ 410,000	$ 50,000

The sales price per unit is $25

Due to the marginal results of operations of the factory in Maine, Arcadia has decided to cease operations and sell that factory's machinery and equipment by the end of 20X1. Arcadia expects that the proceeds from the sale of these assets would be greater than their book value and would cover all termination costs.

Arcadia, however, would like to continue serving its customers in that area if it is economically feasible and is considering one of the following three alternatives:

(1) Expand the operations of the Montana factory by using space presently idle. This move would result in the following changes in that factory's operations:

	Increase over Factory's Current Operations
Sales	50%
Fixed costs:	
Factory	20%
Administration	10%

(1) Under this proposal, variable cost would be $8 per unit sold.

(2) Enter into a long-term contract with a competitor who will serve that area's customers. This competitor would pay Arcadia a royalty of $4 per unit based upon an estimate of 30,000 units being sold.

(3) Close the Maine factory and not expand the operations of the Montana factory.

Required:

In order to assist the management of Arcadia Corporation in determining which alternative is more economically feasible, prepare a schedule computing Arcadia's estimated net profit from total operations that would result from each of the following methods:

(a) Expansion of the Montana factory.

(b) Negotiation of long-term contract on a royalty basis.

(c) Shutdown of Maine operations with no expansion at other locations.

Note: Total home office costs of $500,000 will remain the same under each situation.

(AICPA adapted)

13-31 *Interpreting Cost Information*

Nubo Manufacturing, Inc. is presently operating at 50% of practical capacity producing about 50,000 units annually of a patented electronic component. Nubo recently received an offer from a company in Yokohama, Japan, to purchase 30,000 components at $6.00 per unit, FOB Nubo's plant. Nubo has not previously sold components in Japan. Budgeted production costs for 50,000 and 80,000 units of output follow:

Units	50,000	80,000
Costs:		
Direct material	$ 75,000	$120,000
Direct labor	$ 75,000	$120,000
Factory overhead	$200,000	$260,000
Total costs	$350,000	$500,000
Cost per unit	$7.00	$6.25

The sales manager thinks the order should be accepted, even if it results in a loss of $1.00 per unit, because he feels the sales may build up future markets. The production manager does not wish to have the order accepted primarily because the order would show a loss of $.25 per unit when computed on the new average unit cost. The treasurer has made a quick computation indicating that accepting the order will actually increase gross margin.

Required:

(a) Explain what apparently caused the drop in cost from $7.00 per unit to $6.25 per unit when budgeted production increased from 50,000 to 80,000 units. Show supporting computations.

(b) (1) Explain whether (either or both) the production manager or the treasurer is correct in his reasoning.

(2) Explain why the conclusions of the production manager and the treasurer differ.

(c) Explain why each of the following may affect the decision to accept or reject the special order.

(1) The likelihood of repeat special sales and/or all sales to be made at $6.00 per unit.

(2) Whether the sales are made to customers operating in two separate, isolated markets or whether the sales are made to customers competing in the same market.

(*AICPA adapted*)

13-32 *Decision to Expand Production*

Valbec Company manufactures and distributes toy doll houses. The toy industry is a seasonal business. Therefore, a large portion of Valbec's sales occur in the late summer and fall.

The projected sales in units for 20X8 are shown in the schedule below. With a sales price of $10 per unit, the total sales revenue for 20X8 is projected at $1.2 million. Valbec scheduled its production in the past so that finished goods inventory at the end of each month, exclusive of a safety stock of 4,000 doll houses, would equal the next month's sales. One-half hour of direct labor time is required to produce each doll house under normal operating conditions. Using the production schedule followed in the past, the total direct labor hours by month that would be required to meet the 20X8 sales estimate are also shown in the schedule following:

Valbec Company

Projected Sales and Planned Production
For the Year Ending December *31, 20X8*

	Projected Sales (in units)	Direct Labor hours required*
January	8,000	4,000
February	8,000	4,000
March	8,000	4,000
April	8,000	4,000
May	8,000	5,000
June	10,000	6,000
July	12,000	6,000
August	12,000	6,500
September	13,000	6,500
October	13,000	6,000
November	12,000	4,000
December	8,000	4,000**
Total	120,000 units	60,000 hours

*This schedule does not incorporate any additional direct labor hours resulting from inefficiences.

**Sales for January, *20X9* are projected at *8,000* units.

The production schedule followed in the past requires the scheduling of overtime hours for any production over 8,000 units (4,000 direct labor hours) in one month. While the use of overtime is feasible, the Valbec management has decided that it should consider two other possible alternatives: (1) hire temporary help from an agency during the peak months, or (2) expand its labor force and adopt a level production schedule. The use of a second shift was not considered because management believed the community would not support this alternative.

Factory employees are paid $6.00 per hour for regular time; the fringe benefits average 20% of regular pay. For hours worked in excess of 4,000 hours per month, employees receive time and one-half; however, fringe benefits only average 10% on these additional wages. Past experience has shown that when overtime is required, labor inefficiencies do occur during overtime at the rate of 5% of overtime hours; this 5% inefficiency was not included in the direct labor hour estimates presented in the schedule.

Rather than pay overtime to its regular labor force, Valbec could hire temporary employees when production exceeds 8,000 units per month. The temporary workers can be hired through an agency at the same labor rate of $6.00 per hour, but there would be no fringe benefit costs. Management estimates that the temporary workers would require 25% more ore time than the regular employees to produce the doll houses.

If Valbec goes to a level production schedule, the labor force would be expanded. However, no overtime would be required. The same labor rate of $6.00 per hour and fringe benefit rate of 20% would apply.

The manufacturing facilities have the capacity to produce 18,000 doll houses per month. On-site storage facilities for completed units are adequate. The estimated annual cost of carrying inventory is $1 per unit. Valbec is subject to a 40% income tax rate.

Required:

(a) Prepare an analysis which compares the costs associated with each of Valbec Company's three alternatives:

(1) chedule overtime hours.

(2) Hire temporary workers.

(3) Expand labor force and schedule level production.

(b) Identify and discuss briefly the non-cost factors and the factors which are difficult to cost that Valbec Company should consider in conjunction with the cost analysis prepared in requirement A before a final decision is made relative to the three alternatives.

(*IMA adapted*)

13-33 Decision to Add a Department

The management of Bay Company is considering a proposal to install a third production department within its existing factory building. With the company's present production setup, raw material is passed through Department I to produce Materials A and B in equal proportions. Material A is then passed through Department II to yield Product C. Material B is presently being sold "as is" at a price of $20.25 per pound. Product C has a selling price of $100 per pound.

The per pound standard costs currently being used by the Bay Company are as follows:

	Department I	Department II	
	Materials A&B	Product C	Material B
Prior department costs	-	$53.03	$13.47
Direct material	$20.00	-	-
Direct labor	7.00	12.00	-
Variable overhead	3.00	5.00	-
Fixed overhead:	-	-	-
Attributable	2.25	2.25	-
Allocated (2/3, 1/3)	1.00	1.00	
	$33.25	$73.28	$13.47

These standard costs were developed by using an estimated production volume of 200,000 pounds of raw material as the standard volume. The company assigns Department I costs to Materials A and B in proportion to their net sales values at the point of separation, computed by deducting subsequent standard production costs from sales prices. The $300,000 of common fixed overhead costs are allocated to the two producing departments on the basis of the space used by the departments.

The proposed Department III would be used to process Material B into Product D. It is expected that any quantity of Product D can be sold for $30 per pound. Standard costs per pound under this proposal were developed by using 200,000 pounds of raw material as the standard volume and are as follows:

	Department I Materials A&B	Department II Product C	Department III Product D
Prior department costs.....	-	$52.80	$13.20
Direct material..................	$20.00		-
Direct labor.......................	7.00	12.00	5.50
Variable overhead.............	3.00	5.00	2.00
Fixed overhead:.................			
Attributable	2.25	2.25	1.75
Allocated (1/2, 1/4, 1/4)...	.75	.75	.75
	$33.00	$72.80	$23.20

Required:

(a) If (1) sales and production levels are expected to remain constant in the foreseeable future, and (2) there are no foreseeable alternative uses for the available factory space, should the Bay Company install Department III and thereby produce Product D? Show calculations to support your answer.

(b) Instead of constant sales and production levels, suppose that under the present production setup $1,000,000 additions to the factory building must be made every 10 years to accommodate growth. Suppose also that proper maintenance gives these factory additions an infinite life and that all such maintenance costs are included in the standard costs which are set forth in the text of the problem. How would the analysis that you performed in Part A be changed if the installation of Department III shortened the interval at which the $1,000,000 factory additions are made from 10 years to 6 years? Be as specific as possible in your answer.

(*IMA adapted*)

13-34 *Relevant Costs to Special Order Decision*

George Jackson operates a small machine shop. He manufactures one standard product available from many other similar businesses and he also manufactures products to customer order. His accountant prepared the annual income statement shown below:

	Custom Sales	Standard Sales	Total
Sales	$50,000	$25,000	$75,000
Material	$10,000	$ 8,000	$18,000
Labor	20,000	9,000	29,000
Depreciation ..	6,300	3,600	9,900
Power	700	400	1,100
Rent	6,000	1,000	7,000
Heat and light	600	100	700
Other................	400	900	1,300
Total Expenses.	$44,000	$23,000	$67,000
Net Income.....	$ 6,000	$ 2,000	$ 8,000

The depreciation charges are for machines used in the respective product lines. The power charge is apportioned on the estimate of power consumed. The rent is for the building space which has been leased for 10 years at $7,000 per year. The rent, and heat and light are apportioned to the product lines based on amount of floor space occupied. All other costs are current expenses identified with the product line causing them.

A valued custom parts customer has asked Mr. Jackson if he would manufacture 5,000 special units for him. Mr. Jackson is working at capacity and would have to give up some other business in order to take this business. He can't renege on custom orders already agreed to but he could reduce the output of his standard product by about one-half for one year while producing the specially requested custom part. The customer is willing to pay $7.00 for each part. The material cost will be about $2.00 per unit and the labor will be $3.60 per unit. Mr. Jackson will have to spend $2,000 for a special device which will be discarded when the job is done.

Required.

(a)Calculate and present the following costs related to the 5,000 unit custom order:

(1) The incremental cost of the order;

(2) The full cost of the order;

(3) The opportunity cost of taking the order;

(4) The sunk cost related to the order.

(b) Should Mr. Jackson take the order? Explain your answer.

(IMA adapted)

13-35 *Special Order Decision*

The Keylo Co. manufactures a line of plastic products that are sold through hardware stores. The company sales have declined slightly for the past two years leaving them with idle plants and equipment.

A Keylo engineer met a former college classmate while attending a recent convention of machinery builders. The classmate is employed by the Paddington Co. which is also in the plastic products business. During the course of their conversation it became evident that Keylo might be able to make a particular product for Paddington with the currently unused equipment and space. The following requirements were specified by Paddington for the new product:

1. Paddington needs 80,000 units per year for the next three years.
2. The product is to be built to Paddington specifications.
3. Keylo is not to enter into the independent production of the product during the three year contract.
4. Paddington would provide Keylo, without charge, a special machine to finish the product. The machine becomes the property of the Keylo at the end of the three year period.

Although Keylo is not operating at capacity, the company generated a profit last year as is shown in the income statement presented as follows:

Keylo Co.
Income Statement
For the Fiscal Year Ended October 31, 20X2
(000 omitted)

	Dollar Amount	*Percent*
Sales	$1,500	100%
Cost of goods sold:		
Material	$ 200	13%
Direct labor	400	27
Overhead[1]	390	26
Cost of goods sold	$ 990	66%
Manufacturing margin before unapplied overhead	$ 510	34%
Unapplied manufacturing overhead[2]	10	1
Manufacturing margin	$ 500	33%
Operating expenses:		
Sales commissions	$ 60	4%
Sales administration	30	2
General administration	110	7
Total operating expenses	$ 200	13%
Net income before income taxes	$ 300	20%
Income taxes (40%)	120	8
Net income	$ 180	12%

[1] Schedule of manufacturing overhead

Variable:	
Indirect labor	$100
Supplies	40
Power	120
Fixed costs applied:	
Administration	60
Depreciation	70
	$390

[2] Schedule of unapplied manufacturing overhead (due to idle capacity)

Depreciation	$ 10

The Keylo engineering, production, and accounting departments agreed upon the following facts if the contracts were accepted.

1. Manufacturing
   a. The present idle capacity would be fully used.
   b. One additional supervisor would be required; the annual salary would be $15,000 at the present rates.
   c. The annual requirements for material and labor would increase by 10% at current prices.
   d. The power and supply requirements would increase 10% at current prices due to the reactivation of idle machines.
   e. The machine provided by Paddington would increase the annual power and supply costs by $10,000 and $4,000, respectively, at current prices.
   f. The Paddington machine would have no value to Keylo at the end of the contract.

2. Sales:
   a. A sales commission of $10,000 would be paid to the sales persons arranging the contract.
   b. No additional sales administrative costs would be incurred.

3. General administration: No additional general administrative costs would be incurred.

4. Other information
   a. Estimated cost increases due to inflation for the entire three year period are shown below:

Material	5%
Labor	10%
Power	20%
Depreciation	0
Sales commissions	0
Income taxes	0
All other items	10%

   b. Inventory balances which have remained stable for the past three years will not be increased
   c. or decreased by the production of the new product.

Required:

(a) Calculate the total price needed for the three year order (240,000 units) if the company wants to make 10% after taxes on the sales price of this order.
(b) Calculate the total price for the three year order (240,000 units) if this order were to contribute nothing to net income after taxes.
(c) Would the answer you calculated in (b) above contribute to existing fixed costs? Explain your answer.

(IMA adapted)

13-36 *Best Utilization of Facilities*

Marshall Manufacturing, Inc. has produced two products, Z and P, at its Richmond plant for several years. On March 31, 20X2, P was dropped from the product line. Marshall manufactures and sells 50,000 units of Z annually, and this is not expected to change. Unit material and direct labor costs are $12 and $7, respectively.

The Richmond plant is in a leased building; the lease expires June 30, 20X6. Annual rent is $75,000. The lease provides Marshall the right of sublet; all non-removable leasehold improvements revert to the lessor. At the end of the lease, Marshall intends to close the plant and scrap all equipment.

P has been produced on two assembly lines which occupy 25% of the plant. The assembly lines will have a book value of $135,000 and a remaining useful life of seven years as of June 30, 20X2. This is the only portion of the plant available for alternative uses.

Marshall uses one unit of D to produce one unit of Z. D is purchased under a contract requiring a minimum annual purchase of 5,000 units. The contract expires June 30, 20X6. A list of D unit costs follows:

Alternatives are available for using the space previously used to manufacture P. Some may be used in combination. All can be implemented by June 30, 20X2. Should no action be taken, the plant is expected to operate profitably, and manufacturing overhead is not expected to differ materially from past years when P was manufactured.

Following are the alternatives:

1. Sell the two P assembly lines for $70,000. The purchaser will buy only if he can acquire the equipment from both lines. The purchaser will pay all removed and transportation costs.
2. Sublet the floor space for an annual rental of $12,100. The lease will require that the equipment be removed (cost nominal) and leasehold improvements costings $38,000 be installed. Indirect costs are expected to increase $3,500 annually as a result of the sublease.
3. Convert one or both P assembly lines to produce D at a cost $45,500 for each line. The converted lines will have a remaining useful life of 10 years. Each modified line can produce any number of units of D up to a maximum of 37,000 units at a unit direct material and direct labor cost sof $.10 and $.25, respectively. Annual manufacturing overhead is expected to increase from $550,000 to $562,000 if one line is converted and to $566,000 if both lines are conveted.

Required:

Prepare a schedule to analyze the best utilization of the following alternatives for the four years ended June 30, 20X6. Ignore income taxes and the time value of money.

1. Continue to purchase D; sell equipment; rent space.
2. Continue to purchase D; sell equipment.
3. Produce D on two assembly lines; purchase D as needed.
4. Produce D on one assembly line; purchase D as needed.

Set up your workpaper allowing one column for the evaluation of each alternative. The columns should be numbered 1, 2, 3, and 4.

(AICPA adapted)

13-37 Eliminate a Product Line

A typewriter manufacturer is considering dropping its manual typewriter product line due to consistent losses from this model over the past three years. The recent poor performance of this product (known as Model A) is reflected below:

	20X6	20X7	20X8
Sales (average price $100/unit)	$14,600,000	$14,400,000	$14,200,000
Variable costs:			
Direct materials ($40/unit)	$ 5,840,000	$ 5,760,000	$ 5,680,000
Direct labor ($20/unit)	2,920,000	2,880,000	2,840,000
Variable manufacturing ($10/unit)	1,460,000	1,440,000	1,420,000
Other variable costs ($5/unit)	730,000	720,000	710,000
Total variable costs	$10,950,000	$10,800,000	$10,650,000
Selling expenses (10% of sales)	1,460,000	1,440,000	1,420,000
Total variable and selling expenses	$12,410,000	$12,240,000	$12,070,000
Contribution margin	$ 2,190,000	$ 2,160,000	$ 2,130,000
Fixed costs:			
Avoidable	$ 2,022,000	$ 1,997,000	$ 1,972,000
Unavoidable (3% of sales)	438,000	432,000	426,000
Total	$ 2,460,000	$ 2,429,000	$ 2,398,000
Operating loss	$ (270,000)	$ (269,000)	$ (268,000)

The decreasing trends in sales and avoidable fixed costs are expected to continue in 20X9. Both the cost of direct materials and direct labor are expected to increase by 5% in 20X9 unless a new attachment for the production equipment, estimated to have a two-year life, is purchased for $150,000. The new attachment would replace another attachment purchased only two years ago at a cost of $200,000 which was expected to have a fouryear life at the time of its purchase. If the new attachment is purchased, the cost of labor and materials would not increase in 20X9.

Required.

(a) Assuming the new attachment is *not* purchased for the current equipment, should the company continue to manufacture and sell Model A typewriters? Explain your answer clearly by labeling all supporting calculations.

(b) Should the new attachment to the current equipment be purchased?
Explain your answer clearly, labeling all supporting calculations.

(c) What effect, if any, would the capacity made available by discontinuing Model A production have on your decision on whether to purchase the new attachment?

(d) What qualitative factors could affect your responses in (a) and (b)?

(AICPA adapted)

13-38 *Corner Points Analysis*

Solve for the values of A and B that maximize the total contribution margin expressed as:

Z=2A+5B

Subject to:

$2A+B \leq 5200$

$4A + 5B \leq 500$

$A, B \geq 0$

Required:

Use the corner points approach.

13-39 *Iso-Profit Line Analysis*

Solve for the values of X and Y that maximize the total contribution margin expressed as:

$Z = 5X + 10Y$

Subject to:

$X + Y \leq 400$

$2X + 5Y \leq 1{,}000$

$4X + 2Y \leq 1{,}200$

$X,Y \geq 0$

Required:

Use the iso-profit line approach.

13-40 *Formulation and Graphic Analysis*

The Brown Company produces two products: X and Y. The unit contribution margins are $8 and $5 for X and Y, respectively. Production information is given below:

	Requirements		
Inputs	*X*	*Y*	*Capacity*
Machine hours	4	5	1,000
Labor hours	10	6	1,800
Materials	8	4	1,600

Required:

1. Formulate the objective function and the constraints necessary to determine the optimal product mix.
2. Determine the optimal solution using the graphic approach.

13-41 *Graphic Analysis*

The Four-Season Corporation manufactures two products: H and C. Product H requires two units of materials and 4 direct labor hours. Product C requires four units of materials and two direct labor hours. The unit contribution margins are $6 and $4 for H and C, respectively. There are 100 direct labor hours and 80 units of materials available.

Required.

1. Formulate the objective function and the constraints necessary to determine the optimal product mix.
2. Use the graphic method to determine the optimal product mix.

13-42 *Graphic Analysis*

The cost accountant of the Stangren Corporation, your client, wants your opinion of a technique suggested to him by a young accounting graduate he employed as a cost analyst. The following information was furnished you for the corporation's two products, trinkets and gadgets:

a.

Exhibit A

Daily Capacities in Units

	Cutting Department	*Finishing Department*	*Sales Price per Unit*	*Variable Cost per Unit*
Trinkets	*400*	*240*	$50	$30
Or				
Gadgets	200	320	$70	$40

b. The daily capacities of each department represent the maximum production for either trinkets or gadgets. However, any combination of trinkets and gadgets can be produced as long as the maximum capacity of the department is not exceeded. For example, two trinkets can be produced in the cutting department for each gadget not produced and three trinkets can be produced in the finishing department for every four gadgets not produced.

c. Material shortages prohibit the production of more than 180 gadgets per day.

d. Exhibit B is a graphic expression of simultaneous linear equations developed from the production information above.

Exhibit B

Graph of Production Relationships

Required:

a. For what kinds of decisions are contribution margin data (revenue in excess of variables cost) useful?

b. Comparing the information in Exhibit A with the graph in Exhibit B, identify and list the graphic location (coordinate) of the

1. cutting department's capacity.
2. production limitation for gadgets because of the materials shortage.
3. area of feasible (possible) production combinations.

c. 1. Compute the contribution margin per unit for trinkets and gadgets.

2. Compute the total contribution margin of each of the points of intersections of lines bounding the feasible (possible) production area.
3. Identify the best production alternative.

(*AICPA adapted*)

13-43 *Formulating Linear Programming Models: Use of Multiple Regression Data*

The Tripro Company produces and sells three products hereafter referred to as Products A, B, and C. The company is currently changing its shortrange planning approach in an attempt to incorporate some of the newer planning techniques. The controller and some of his staff have been conferring with a consultant on the feasibility of using a linear programming model for determining the optimum product mix.

Information for short-range planning has been developed in the same format as in prior years. This information includes expected sales prices and expected direct labor and material costs for each product. In addition, variable and fixed overhead costs were assumed to be the same for each product because approximately equal quantities of the products were produced and sold.

Price and Cost Information (Per Unit)

	A	B	C
Selling price	$25.00	$30.00	$40.00
Direct labor	7.50	10.00	12.50
Direct materials	9.00	6.00	10.50
Variable overhead	6.00	6.00	6.00
Fixed overhead	6.00	6.00	6.00

All three products use the same type of direct material which costs $1.50 per pound of material. Direct labor is paid at the rate of $5.00 per direct labor hour. There are 2,000 direct labor hours and 20,000 pounds of direct materials available in a month.

Required:

(a) Formulate and label the linear programming objective function and constraint functions necessary to maximize Tripro's contribution margin. Use Q_A, Q_B, Q_c to represent units of the three products.

(b) What underlying assumptions must be satisfied to justify the use of linear programming?

(c) The consultant, upon reviewing the data presented and the linear programming functions developed, performed further analysis of overhead costs. He used a multiple linear regression model to analyze the overhead cost behavior. The regression model incorporated observations from the past 48 months of total overhead costs and the direct labor hours for each product. The following equation was the result:

$$Y = \$5{,}000 + 2X_A + 4X_B + 3X_C$$

where

Y = monthly total overhead in dollars

X_A = monthly direct labor hours for Product A

X_B = monthly direct labor hours for Product B

X_C = monthly direct labor hours for Product C

The total regression has been determined to be statistically significant as has each of the individual regression coefficients.

Reformulate the objective function for Tripro Company using the results of this analysis.

(IMA adapted)

13-44 *Linear Programming Problem*

The controller of the Rustler Company attended a seminar on linear programming and feels that some of the concepts may be useful in planning operations for the coming year. The Rustler Company produces two models (Standard and Deluxe) of its basic product. The company can sell as many of each unit as it can produce.

The controller has prepared the following estimates of prices and costs (per unit) for the coming year.

	Standard	*Deluxe*
Selling price	$112.00	$152.00
Direct material A	$ 54.00	$108.00
Direct material B	$ 18.75	$ 18.75
Direct labor	$ 18.00	$ 9.00
Variable overhead	$ 6.25	$ 6.25

Direct material A cost $9 per kilogram and the company can purchase up to 60,000 kilograms from its supplier. Direct material B is in short supply and Rustler Company can only acquire 90,000 liters at a price of $1.25 per liter. Direct labor is paid $4.50 an hour and the capacity of the factory is 20,000 direct labor hours.

Required:

Set up in algebraic form the linear programming equations relevant to this problem.

(IMA adapted)

13-45 *Equipment Replacement Decision with Tax Considerations*

The Beta Corporation manufactures office equipment and distributes its products through wholesale distributors.

Beta Corporation recently learned of a patent on the production of a semi-automatic paper collator that can be obtained at a cost of $60,000 cash. The semi-automatic model is vastly superior to the manual model that the corporation now produces. At a cost of $40,000, present equipment could be modified to accomodate the production of the new semiautomatic model. Such modifications would not affect the remaining useful life of four years or the salvage value of $10,000 that the equipment now has. Variable costs, however, would increase by one dollar per unit. Fixed costs, other than relevant amortization charges, would not be affected. If the equipment is modified, the manual model cannot be produced.

The current income statement relative to the manual collator appears as follows:

Sales (100,000 units @ $4).....................		$400,000
Variable costs...	$180,000	
Fixed costs**................................	$120,000	
Total costs..		$300,000
Net income before income taxes...		$100,000
Income taxes (40%)............................		$ 40,000
Net income after income taxes......		$60,000

**All fixed costs are directly allocable to the production of the manual collator and include depreciation on equipment of $20,000, calculated on the straight-line basis with a useful life of ten years.

Market research has disclosed three important findings relative to the new semi-automatic model. First, a particular competitor will certainly purchase the patent if Beta Corporation does not. If this were to happen, Beta Corporation's sales of the manual collator would fall to 70,000 units per year. Second, if no increase in the selling price is made, Beta Corporation could sell approximately 190,000 units per year of the semi-automatic model. Third, because of the advances being made in this area, the patent will be completely worthless at the end of four years.

Because of the uncertainty of the current situation, the raw materials inventory has been almost completely exhausted. Regardless of the decision reached, substantial and immediate inventory replenishment will be required. The engineering department estimates that if the new model is to be produced, the average monthly raw materials inventory will be $20,000. If the old model is continued, the inventory balance will average $12,000 per month.

Required:

(a) Prepare a schedule which shows the incremental after tax cash flows for the comparison of the two alternatives. Assume that the corporation will use the sum of the year's digits method for depreciating the costs of modifying the equipment.

(b) What concerns would you have about using the information, as given in the problem, to reach a decision in this case?

(IMA adapted)

1. *To discuss inventory costs that influence the inventory order quantity decision.*
2. *To understand and apply the economic order quantity model.*
3. *To understand various assumptions of the economic order quantity model and discuss some extensions of it.*
4. *To discuss the difficulty of inventory cost estimation and the insensitivity of the economic order quantity model.*

14

Inventory Management

Inventories are normally held to enable a firm to respond quickly to customers' orders and to provide security against future materials shortages or price increases. In many firms, inventory is one of the assets which requires a large investment of funds. One question that managers face in inventory management (including inventory planning and control) is: How much inventory should be held? If inventory is insufficient, a production process may be disrupted and sales may be lost. On the other hand if the inventory level is too high, unnecessary inventory carrying costs and risk of obsolescence are incurred. Inventory should be held at the optimum level which minimizes the total cost of inventory. The purposes of this chapter are (1) to discuss inventory costs; i.e., the costs that would affect inventory planning decisions, (2) to examine some of the inventory planning and control models, and (3) to discuss the difficulty of inventory cost estimation and the insensitivity of inventory control models.

Inventory Costs

In analyzing inventory management problems, managers deal with the costs associated with inventories. Costs associated with inventories are usually grouped into two categories: inventory acquisition costs and inventory management costs. The former category consists of the cost paid to suppliers and freight-in costs while the later one includes three types of costs, namely inventory ordering costs, inventory carrying costs, and stockout costs.

Inventory Ordering Costs

Ordering costs are those associated with the acquisition of inventory, and include the costs of placing and receiving an order. The costs of placing and receiving orders may include the following items:

1. the costs of filing and receiving the requisitions,
2. the costs of processing the purchase orders,
3. the costs of inspecting the order and placing it in storage,
4. the costs of checking the vouchers and paying the bills.

Inventory Carrying Costs

Carrying costs are those costs associated with holding the inventory. Some of the typical carrying costs are:

1. Capital cost—Inventories require investment of funds. Funds tied up in inventories are not available for other uses. The opportunity cost of money invested in inventory is the capital cost of carrying it, and is determined by the alternative use to which the funds could be invested. For example, if the firm has an alternative use for the funds that would earn 10 percent, then its cost of capital is 10 percent.
2. Storage costs—Costs of renting, lighting, and heating the space in which inventory is kept.
3. Spoilage and shortage costs—Costs of obsolescence and deterioration of inventory. The costs represent a reduction in the firm's assets. Therefore, the costs of spoilage and shortage are a part of the cost of carrying inventories.
4. Insurance and taxes—Since inventories represent a significant investment of a firm's funds, conservative managers usually have some insurance protection on them. The cost of this insurance is a cost of carrying inventories. The same is true for inventory taxes that exist in some states. The costs of insurance and taxes are usually based on the value of inventory held.

Stockout Costs

Stockout costs are those costs associated with not holding sufficient inventories. Factors contributing to stockout costs include lost sales, loss of goodwill, and the additional selling and administrative efforts required to process backorders.

The purpose of inventory management is to maintain the investment in inventory which will minimize total inventory costs. There are two key inventory decisions in inventory management: how *much to order* and *when to order.* The optimal number of units to be ordered is usually referred to as the economic order quantity (EOQ). The appropriate time to place a new order is usually determined by the reorder point. The following discussion concentrates on how managers can determine how many units of a given item should be purchased for stock at a given time. *When to order* will be discussed in a later section.

The Basic Economic Order Quantity Model

The basic economic order quantity (EOQ) model, first developed in the 1920's, computes the order quantity that minimizes the total of ordering costs and carrying costs. Stockout costs are not considered in the basic economic order quantity model and shall be discussed in a later section. There are three approaches available to determine the economic order quantity-the graphic approach, the tabular approach, and the formula approach.

The Graphic Approach

Orders of large quantity are desirable because they enable managers to reduce the order-placing costs incurred in a given period. However, the purchase of a large quantity of items at one time raises inventory carrying costs because of the increased size of the average inventory held. Thus as inventory ordering costs increase, inventory carrying costs will decrease, and a decrease in ordering costs accompanies an increase in carrying costs. Management would like to find the balance between ordering costs and carrying costs that will minimize their total over a period of time.

The number of orders placed during a given period is equal to total demand (D) for the period divided by the size of order quantity (Q), or (D/Q). The total ordering cost per period is therefore equal to the cost of placing an order (P) multiplied by the number of orders per period (D/Q); i.e., (P) x (D/Q). As the order size increases, fewer orders are required to meet the demand for a period, and consequently the total ordering costs will decrease. The total ordering costs may be represented by the downward sloping cost curve shown in Illustration 14-1.

The total carrying costs are equal to the cost of carrying one item per period (C) multiplied by the average inventory (Q/2) if the usage rate is constant. As the order size Q increases, carrying cost will increase as shown in Illustration 14-1.

The total cost curve in Illustration 14-1 simply represents the sum of ordering costs and carrying costs at each order size. The most economical order size, which results in a minimum total inventory cost per period, occurs at the lowest point on the total cost curve. This is represented by point A shown in Illustration 14-1. It should be noted that the total costs are always lowest when the ordering costs and the carrying costs are equal.

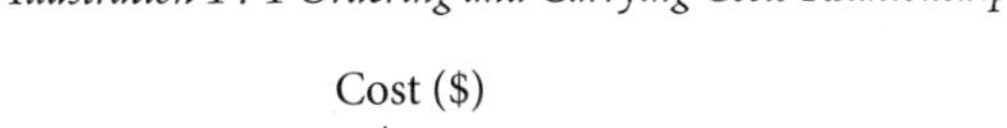

Illustration 14-1 Ordering and Carrying Costs Relationship

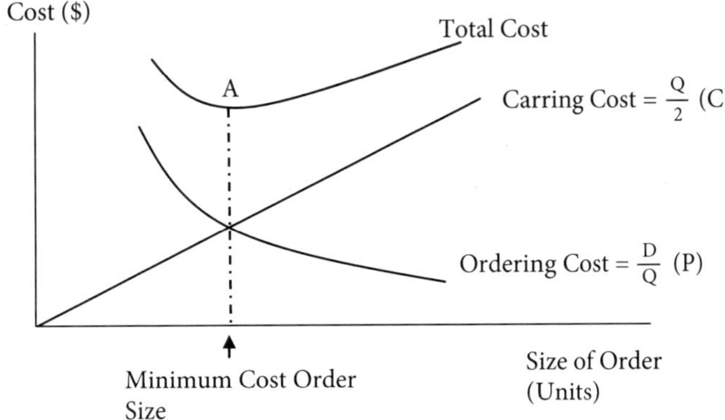

THE TABULAR APPROACH

A simple example problem will serve as the best vehicle for understanding the tabular approach to computing the economic order quantity. Assume that the Golden Company's annual demand of an item is 1,000 units. The ordering cost is $10 per order. The annual carrying cost is $2 per unit. In this case, the relevant parameters for the problem are:

D = 1,000 units
P = $10 per order
C = $2 per average unit per year

Ordering cost, carrying cost, and total cost associated with various order sizes can be developed to show the relationships between the parameters and to determine the economic order quantity. Illustration 14-2 presents such a tabulation for the example problem.

As shown in Illustration 14-2, the economic order quantity for our example problem is 100 units per order. This order size will result in the lowest total costs among the given sizes of order. The approach is conceptually sound, but a drawback is that the accountant may have to try many calculations to determine the precise economic order quantity.

THE FORMULA APPROACH

The tabular approach involves experimentation and the calculation of total costs in order to arrive at the economic order quantity. Instead of performing the tabular procedures, it is less time-consuming to find the EOQ using the formula approach. The formula used to compute the EOQ is usually expressed as follows:

$$Q = \sqrt{\frac{2PD}{C}} \tag{1}$$

This EOQ formula can be derived by two different methods.

Method 1—Minimization of total costs.

The total cost (TC) is equal to the sum of the ordering cost, (D/Q) x P, and carrying cost, (Q/2) x C. Therefore, in equation form the total cost is:

$$TC = \frac{D}{Q}(P) + \frac{Q}{2}(C) \tag{2}$$

The objective is to find the Q which minimizes TC. To accomplish this, one can first differentiate TC with respect to Q. Then the result is set to equal zero and solved for Q as follows:

Illustration 14-2 Tabular Approach for Determining EOQ

Size of Order (Q)	*Number of Orders Per Year (P/D)*	*Annual Ordering Cost (P)(D/Q)*	*Annual Carrying Costs (C)(Q/2)*	*Total Costs*
1,000	*1*	*$10*	*$1,000*	*$1,010*
500	*2*	*20*	*500*	*520*
250	*4*	*40*	*250*	*290*
200	*5*	*50*	*200*	*250*
100	*10*	*100*	*100*	*200* ←
50	*20*	*200*	*50*	*250*

$$\frac{d(TC)}{d(Q)} = \frac{-PD}{Q^2} + \frac{C}{2} = 0$$

$$\frac{PD}{Q^2} = \frac{C}{2}$$

$$Q^2 = \frac{2PD}{C}$$

$$Q = \sqrt{\frac{2PD}{C}}$$

Method 2—Equality of ordering costs and carrying costs

As noted before, the total costs are always lowest at the point where the ordering costs and the carrying costs are equal. Therefore, the EOQ formula can be derived by solving the following equation for Q:

$$\frac{D}{Q}(P) = \frac{Q}{2}(C)$$

$$Q^2 = \frac{2PD}{C}$$

$$Q = \sqrt{\frac{2PD}{C}}$$

After solving Q from equation (1), the optimal number of orders (N) can be determined as follows:

$$N = \frac{D}{Q} \tag{3}$$

Using the data in our example problem, the EOQ, the optimal number of orders, and the associated total inventory costs are calculated as follows:

$$Q = \sqrt{\frac{2PD}{C}} = \sqrt{\frac{2(10)(1{,}000)}{2}} = 100\ units$$

$$N = \frac{1{,}000}{100} = 10\ orders$$

$$TC = \frac{1{,}000}{100}(\$10) + \frac{100}{2}(\$2) = \$200$$

Assumptions of the Basic EOQ Model

The basic EOQ model is relatively easy to understand and apply. An understanding of the assumptions underlying the model is necessary to avoid misapplications and poor results. The assumptions underlying the basic EOQ model are:

1. Deterministic demand—The demand for the period is assumed to be known with certainty.
2. Constant usage rate—The rate at which the inventory quantities are depleted is assumed to be constant. This assumption allows the use of Q/2 for the average inventory in the basic EOQ model.
3. Instantaneous ordering and receiving time—It is assumed that replenishment orders are made whenever the inventory level reaches zero, and that the items ordered are received and are available for use immediately.
4. No stockout—It is assumed that the stockout cost is infinite. Therefore, an implicit assumption is that no stockout is allowed.
5. Constant purchase, ordering, and carrying costs—It is assumed that the unit purchase price is unchanged regardless of the quantity ordered. Inventory carrying costs such as insurance, storage, and interest are assumed to be independent of inventory level. In addition, the cost of placing an order is assumed to be constant regardless of the size or value of the order.

In practice, situations that meet the assumptions of the basic EOQ model are very rare. In the following discussion, some of the assumptions will be modified to make the model more consistent with actual inventory situations.

Reorder Point, Lead Time, and Safety Stock

One of the most serious limitations of the basic EOQ model is its assumption that inventory can be replaced instantaneously. This assumption can be relaxed by considering the *lead time* for delivery, which is the time between placing and receiving an order. The lead time can be used to determine when the new order should be placed. For example, if the daily usage is known to be 50 units and 10 working days of lead time are required before an order can be filled, then 10 times the daily usage, 10 x 50 = 500 units, must be in stock when the order is placed. In other words, the *reorder point* is when the inventory level reaches 500 units. Illustration 14-3 provides a graphic illustration of the reorder point.

If the daily usage and lead time are not constant, *safety stocks* may be necessary to protect against the possibility of a stockout. In that case, the reorder point will be equal to the expected usage during the lead time plus the desired safety stock. The introduction of a safety stock will increase carrying costs and decrease the costs of stockouts. Therefore, the desired safety stock is the quantity where the sum of the safety stock carrying costs and the expected stockout costs is a minimum. For example, assume that a firm has determined the basic EOQ to be 8,320 units which at normal usage will last 80 working days. The expected daily demand would be 8,320/80 or 104 units. Three orders will be placed each year. According to the firm's accounting records, the following discrete probabilities are assigned to the possible lead times and various levels of daily demand.

Illustration 14-3 Determining the Reorder Point - Constant Usage Rate

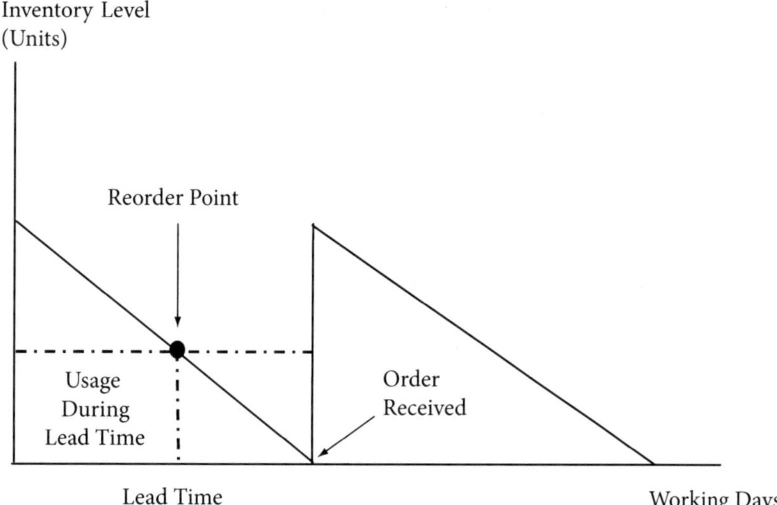

Lead time	Probability
9 days	0.50
10 days	0.50
1.00	

The expected value of the lead time is 9(.5) + 10(.5) = 9.5 days.

Daily Demand	*Probability*
90 units	.20
100 units	.50
120 units	.30
	1.00

The expected value of daily demand is (90)(0.20) +(100)(0.50) +(120)(0.30) = 104 units.

Without safety stock, the reorder point is equal to the average demand during the expected lead time. In our example, it is 104 x 9.5 = 988 units. For purposes of illustration, assume that four safety stock policies (0, 12, 92, and 212 units) are under consideration and the firm wants to select the one that will result in minimum cost. The carrying cost is $20 and stock out cost is $30 per unit. The total expected costs associated with each safety stock policy, assuming five possible lead time demand quantities and their associated probabilities, are calculated in Illustration 14-4. The costs of ordering and of carrying other inventory, not considered safety stock, are excluded from this analysis because they do not affect the safety stock level.

Column 1 lists the number of units of safety stock for each safety stock policy. Column 2 contains some possible demand quantities which may occur during the lead time, and column 5 shows their associated probabilities. Column 3 is the expected lead time (in days) multiplied by the expected daily demand. In column 4, the possible shortage is derived by comparing column 2 with the sum of columns 1 and 3. If the contents of column 2 is greater than the sum of the contents of columns 1 and 3, then lead time demand exceeds the reorder point and a shortage is

Illustration 14-4 Calculation of Total Expected Costs for Each Safety Stock Policy

(1)	(2)	(3)	(4)	(5)	* (6)	** (7)	*** (8)
Safety Stock	Possible Demand During the Lead Time	Average Demand During the Lead Time	Possible Shortage	Probability	Expected Annual Costs of Shortag	Annual Safety Stock Carrying Costs	Total Expected Costs of (6) + (7)
0	810	988	0	.10	0		
0	900	988	0	.35	0		
0	1000	988	12	.25	3 x 12 x 30 x (.25) = 270		
0	1080	988	92	.15	3 x 92 x 30 x (.15) = 1242		
0	1200	988	212	.15	3x 212 x 30 x (.15) = 2862		
				1.00	$4374	0	$4374
12	810	988	0	.10	0		
12	900	988	0	.35	0		
12	1000	988	0	.25	0		
12	1080	988	80	.15	3 x 80 x 30 x (.15) = 1080		
12	1200	988	200	.15	3x 200 x 3o x (.15) = 2700		
				1.00	$3780	20x12 =$240	$4020
92	810	988	0	.10	0		
92	900	988	0	.35	0		
92	1000	988	0	.25	0		
92	1080	988	0	.15	0		
92	1200	988	120	.15	3 x 120 x 30 x (.15) = 1620		
				1.00	$1620	20x92 =$1840	$3460
212	810	988	0	.10	0		
212	900	988	0	.35	0		
212	1000	988	0	.25	0		
212	1080	988	0	.15	0		
212	1200	988	0	.15	0		
				1.00	0	20x212 =$4240	$4240

* Number of orders per year x shortage in units x stockout cost per unit x probability.
** (Carrying cost per unit) x (Units in safety stock).
*** Expected annual costs of shortage + Annual safety stock carrying costs.

expected. Formulas to determine the contents of columns 6, 7, and 8 are given in the footnote of Illustration 14-4. The following probability tree illustrates the calculations for columns 2 and 5.

From the probability tree, the following probabilities can be computed for each possible demand during lead time. Note that the probability of a demand for 900 units is (.25 + .10) = .35.

Possible Demand During the Lead Time	Probability
810 units	.10
900 units	.35
1,000 units	.25
1,080 units	.15
1,200 units	.15

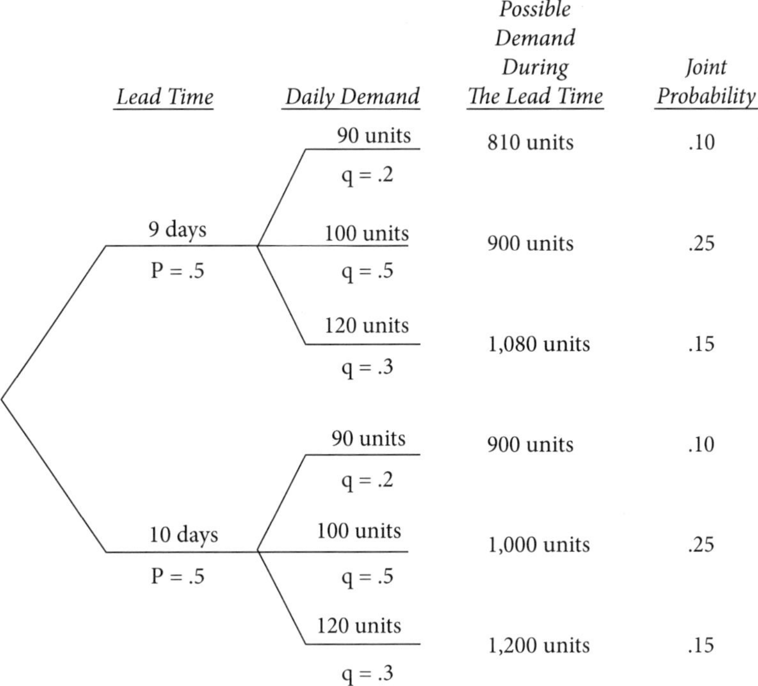

As shown in Illustration 14-4, the policy of carrying 92 units of safety stock will result in a total expected cost of $3,460, which is lower than the total expected cost required by each of the other three policies. Therefore, the reorder point in the example problem is:

Average demand during the Lead Time	988 units
+ Desired safety stock	92
	1,080 units

The Effect of Stockouts on the EOQ Model

One of the assumptions of the basic EOQ model is that the stockout cost is infinite. Thus, no stockouts are permitted in the model. It may be modified to expand its applicability to the situation when stockouts are permitted. If a firm permits stockouts and customers are willing to accept a backorder when an item is not on hand, then the backorder will be filled as soon as the items are received. In this case, the number of units being stored (S) will be less than the order quantity (Q). The difference between the number of units ordered and the number of units stored is (Q – S) which is the number of units backordered. Illustration 14-5 shows how inventory quantities vary in such a system. In this diagram, T represents the time between two successive orders, t_1 is the period of time before a stockout, and t_2 represents the time after a backorder has occurred.

During the time period t_1, the firm is carrying an average inventory of S/2 units. During the time period t_2, the firm has an average stockout of (Q – S)/2 units. Since t_1 and t_2 are parts of the entire inventory planning horizon T, the firm will carry an average inventory of S/2 units over

Illustration 14-5An Inventory System with Stockouts

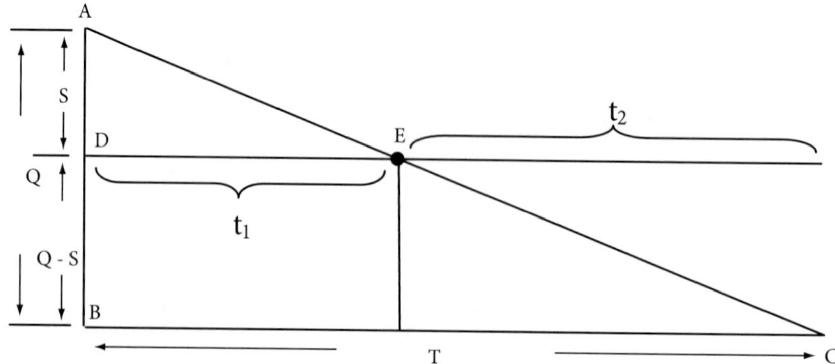

t_1 /T of the planning horizon and will have an average stockout of (Q – S)/2 units over t_2 /T of the planning horizon. Furthermore, since DABC and DADE in Illustration 14-5 are two similar triangles, we know t_1 /T = S/Q.

The average inventory over the entire planning horizon T will be

$$\frac{S}{2}\times\frac{t_1}{T}=\frac{S}{2}\times\frac{S}{Q}=\frac{S^2}{2Q}$$

Similarly, the average stockout over the entire planning horizon T will be

$$\frac{Q-S}{2}\times\frac{t_2}{T}=\frac{Q-S}{2}\times\frac{T-t_1}{T}=\frac{Q-S}{2}\times\left(1-\frac{t_1}{T}\right)=\frac{Q-S}{2}\left(1-\frac{S}{Q}\right)=\frac{(Q-S)^2}{2Q}$$

If stockout costs are B per average unit of stockout, the total cost related to the inventory system will be:

TC = Ordering Costs + Carrying Costs + Stockout Costs

$$TC=\frac{D}{C}(P)+\frac{S^2}{2Q}(C)+\frac{(Q-S)^2}{2Q}(B) \qquad (4)$$

The lowest cost order quantity Q and inventory level S can be found from the following equations:

$$Q^\circ=\sqrt{\frac{2PD}{C}}\times\sqrt{\frac{C+B}{B}} \qquad (5)$$

$$S=\sqrt{\frac{2PD}{C}}\times\sqrt{\frac{B}{B+C}} \qquad (6)$$

Here Q* refers to the lowest cost order quantity when stockouts are permitted.

For purposes of illustration, assume that the Golden Company estimates a stockout cost of $4 per unit per year in the earlier example. From equations (5), (6), and (4), Q*, S, and TC are determined in the following:

$$Q^{\circ} = \sqrt{\frac{2PD}{C}} \times \sqrt{\frac{C+B}{B}} = \sqrt{\frac{2(10)(1{,}000)}{2}} \times \sqrt{\frac{6}{4}} = 122 \text{ units}$$

$$S = \sqrt{\frac{2PD}{C}} \times \sqrt{\frac{B}{B+C}} = \sqrt{\frac{2(10)(1{,}000)}{2}} \times \sqrt{\frac{4}{6}} = 82\ units$$

$$TC = \frac{1{,}000}{122}(10) + \frac{(82)^2}{2(122)}(2) + \frac{(40)^2}{2(122)}(4) = 82 + 55 + 26 = \$163$$

The minimum cost policy for the Golden Company is to replenish inventory with orders of 122 units, and to issue backorders for customers of up to 40 units. The total cost associated with this inventory policy is \$163.

Quantity Discounts

The basic EOQ model assumes that the price of an item is constant, regardless of the size of an order. In practice, discounts on large-quantity orders are common. When quantity discounts are available, the unit purchase cost of inventory becomes relevant and must be considered in determining the order quantity. One approach compares the total costs resulting from the basic EOQ with those resulting from a quantity discount. For example, suppose the Big Sky Company's demand for an item is 10,000 units. Each unit costs \$100. But on orders of 1,000 units or more, the firm receives a 5% discount. Ordering costs are \$50 per order and the inventory carrying cost is 4% per unit per year. To determine the optimal ordering policy, the total costs with the basic EOQ must be compared with those under the quantity discount.

Using equation (1), the basic EOQ is determined as:

$$EOQ = \sqrt{\frac{2(50)(10{,}000)}{4}} = 500\ units$$

The total annual costs under this policy are:

Annual purchase price of units = \$100(10,000)	\$1,000,000
Annual inventory carrying cost = \$4(500/2) =	1,000
Annual ordering cost = \$50(10,000/500) =	1,000
Total Annual Costs	\$1,002,000

If the firm decides to buy 1,000 units in each order to take the purchase discount, the total annual cost would be:

Annual purchase price of units = \$95(10,000)	\$ 950,000
Annual carrying cost = \$95(4%)(1,000/2) =	1,900
Annual ordering cost = \$50(10,000/1,000) =	500
Total Annual Costs	\$ 952,400

The total cost under the basic EOQ is higher than that with the quantity discount. Therefore, the optimum order quantity is 1,000 units. A question which may be asked is: Why is the optimum order quantity not some other quantity over 1,000 units? First, any order quantity over 1,000 units would result in carrying costs which exceed any savings in ordering costs. Secondly, no additional price discounts are allowed for quantities above 1,000, such as purchases of 1,500 or 2,000 units.

Difficulties of Cost Estimation and Insensitivity of the EOQ Model

Estimation of cost parameters for the EOQ model may be difficult. Determination of the carrying cost is usually complicated because of the difficulty in computing the opportunity cost of funds invested in inventories. The opportunity cost is measured by the interest cost of carrying inventory. The proper interest cost should be based on future investment opportunities available to the firm; however, the estimation of future investment returns is very difficult. In practice, the interest cost is usually approximated by current borrowing rates or the firm's average cost of capital.

The costs of placing and receiving an order are a part of the ordering cost. In many cases, these costs are difficult to measure because the personnel who process and receive purchase orders usually have a number of other duties.

Stockout costs are also difficult to estimate. A stockout may result in two different types of cost: (1) additional costs of processing and shipping backorders and (2) foregone profit because of customer dissatisfaction and sales lost. These costs are usually not easy to identify. Even if they can be identified, their measurement may be subject to debate.

If the estimated cost items for the EOQ model are inaccurate, the inventory policy resulting from the model will not minimize the total inventory costs. Therefore, a related and interesting question that may be asked is: What is the effect on the optimal inventory policy of inaccuracies in the cost estimates? Sensitivity analysis can be utilized to answer this question. For purposes of illustration, assume that for the Golden Company the actual carrying cost per unit is $3 (instead of $2) and all other predictions are accurate. In this case, the actual model parameters are as follows:

P = Ordering cost per order = $10
D = Annual demand = 1,000 units
B = Stockout cost per unit = $4
C = Carrying cost per unit = $3

Using Q* = 122 units and S = 82 units from the original estimates (P = 10, D = 1,000, B = 4, and C = 2), the actual total inventory cost would be:

$$TC = \frac{D}{Q^\circ}(P) + \frac{S^2}{2Q^\circ}(C) + \frac{(Q^\circ - S)^2}{2Q^\circ}(B)$$

$$= \frac{1{,}000}{122}(10) + \frac{(82)^2}{2(122)}(3) + \frac{(40)^2}{2(122)}(4)$$

$$= \$191 \text{ per year}$$

However, given that the actual C is $3 instead of $2, the expost optimal Q* and S are:

$$Q^{\circ} = \sqrt{\frac{2PD}{C}} \times \sqrt{\frac{C+B}{B}}$$

$$= \sqrt{\frac{2(10)(1{,}000)}{3}} \times \sqrt{\frac{3+4}{4}} = 18\, units$$

$$S = \sqrt{\frac{2PD}{C}} \times \sqrt{\frac{B}{C+B}}$$

$$= \sqrt{\frac{2(10)(1{,}000)}{3}} \times \sqrt{\frac{4}{3+4}} = 61\, units$$

The total minimum inventory cost for the expost inventory policy is:

$$TC = \frac{1{,}000}{108}(10) + \frac{(61)^2}{2(108)}(3) + \frac{(108-61)^2}{2(108)}(4)$$

$$= \$186 \text{ per year}$$

Therefore, a 50% error in predicting the carrying cost per unit results in an additional inventory cost of $5. This additional cost is less than 3% of the expost total cost. Thus, the variance in total inventory cost caused by the error in predicting the carrying cost is relatively insignificant.

A similar analysis can show the effect of predicting errors in other cost items on the inventory policy and the total inventory cost. To provide another illustration, assume that the true cost of a stockout in the example is $8 instead of $4 per unit per year and that all other predictions are correct. Using the original Q* = 122 units and S = 82 units, actual total inventory cost would be:

$$TC = \frac{1{,}000}{122}(10) + \frac{(82)^2}{2(122)}(2) + \frac{(40)^2}{2(122)}(8)$$

$$= \$189 \text{ per year}$$

However, given that the actual B = $8, the expost optimal Q* and S would be:

$$Q = \sqrt{\frac{2(10)(1{,}000)}{2}} \times \sqrt{\frac{2+8}{8}} = 112\, units$$

$$S = \sqrt{\frac{2(10)(1{,}000)}{2}} \times \sqrt{\frac{8}{2+8}} = 89\, units$$

The minimum cost for this inventory policy would be:

$$TC = \frac{1{,}000}{112}(10) + \frac{(89)^2}{2(112)}(2) + \frac{(23)^2}{2(112)}(8)$$

$$= \$179 \text{ per year}$$

In this example, the excess total inventory cost caused by an error of 100% in stockout cost is only $10. This variance is only 6% of the expost total inventory costs, and again is relatively insignificant. The total inventory costs are relatively insensitive to variations in cost estimates. This phenomenon can also be seen in the total inventory cost curve of Illustration 14-1. As shown in the figure, the curve is flat and U-shaped. The flatness of the curve implies that the total inventory costs are affected very little by errors in cost estimates. Because of this characteristic, extreme accuracy in cost estimates is not necessary in order to develop a meaningful inventory policy. A reasonable estimation of cost parameters will produce useful results with the EOQ model.

Summary

Inventories are necessary in almost all business firms. In inventory management, a manager is concerned with finding that inventory level which minimizes the total costs of ordering and carrying inventory. In order to maintain inventory at this optimum level, a manager needs information on how much to order and when to order. Several inventory models to address these questions have been discussed.

This chapter began with a discussion of costs required in maintaining inventory. First, the basic EOQ model which minimizes ordering costs and carrying costs in determining the optimum order quantity was developed. The assumptions of the basic EOQ model were then examined to show the limitations of the model. Modifications of the basic EOQ model in terms of lead time, nonconstant usage rate, stockout, and purchase discounts were demonstrated to make the model more realistic and to broaden its area of applications. Difficulties in estimating certain inventory costs and the insensitivity of the EOQ model were discussed to show the merit of the model. The discussion of this chapter provides an illustration of how the costs resulting from maintaining inventories influence the optimal inventory policy.

Key Definitions

Carrying (or Holding) costs	Costs associated with holding the inventory; i.e., storage costs, spoilage and shortage costs, capital costs, insurance and taxes.
Economic order quantity model	An equation used to determine the order quantity that minimizes the total inventory costs.
Lead time	The elapsed time between placing an order and receiving it.
Ordering costs	Costs associated with the acquisition of the inventory; i.e., the costs of placing and receiving an order of inventory.
Reorder point	The inventory level at which a new order should be placed.

Safety stocks Additional inventory held to protect against the possibility of a stockout.

Stockout costs Costs associated with not holding sufficient inventories, including cost of lost sales, loss of goodwill, and additional cost to process backorders.

Questions

14-1 Define the following terms:
Economic order quantity, Reorder point, Lead time, Safety stock, and Stockout costs.

14-2 True or False—Indicate "true" or "false" for each of the following statements and explain why.

(1) If the lead time of delivery is known with certainty, no safety stock would be needed.
(2) An increase in annual demand would increase the reorder point proportionally.
(3) A decline in selling price with all other items (including carrying costs) remaining constant would not affect the EOQ if stockouts are permitted.
(4) A reduction in the prime interest rate has no effect on economic order quantity.
(5) The safety stock is equal to the expected demand during lead time.
(6) Perfect inventory control is to keep detailed records on each item carried in inventory and bring the records up to date.
(7) The larger the quantity ordered, the higher the total inventory cost.
(8) A decline in the investment in inventory is an indicator of good inventory management.

14-3 Why is inventory management important to a firm? How do modern managers exercise effective management over the investment in inventories?

14-4 What is the optimal inventory level in a firm?

14-5 What information is useful to managers in properly planning and controling inventory?

14-6 Briefly discuss and compare three methods of determining the economic order quantity.

14-7 Discuss the trade-offs in costs involved in determining the economic order quantity.

14-8 What are the assumptions underlying the basic economic order quantity model?

14-9 Why are quantity discounts important in inventory management decisions?

Problems

14-10 *Basic Terms and Concepts*

Inventories usually are an important asset for both manufacturing and merchandising firms. A proper balance of inventory quantities is desirable from several standpoints. Maintaining such a balance is dependent upon a number of factors including ordering at the proper time and in the correct lot size. Serious penalties may attend both overstocking and stockout situations.

Required:

a. In connection with inventory ordering and control, certain terms are basic. Explain the meaning of each of the following:
1. Economic order quantity.
2. Reorder point.
3. Lead time.
4. Safety stock.

b. 1. What are the costs of carrying inventories? Explain.
2. How does overstocking add to the cost of carrying inventories?

c. 1. What are the consequences of maintaining minimal or inadequate inventory levels?
2. What are the difficulties of measuring precisely the costs associated with understocking?

d. Discuss the propriety of including carrying costs (of normal inventory, overstocking and understocking) in the inventory cost:
1. For external reporting.
2. For internal decision making.

(*AICPA adapted*)

14-11 *Estimation of Carrying Costs*

The following data refer to various annual costs relating to the inventory of a single-product company:

	Cost per Unit
Transportation-in on purchases	$.20
Storage	12
Insurance	10

	Total per Year
Interest that could have been earned on alternate investment of funds	$ 800
Units required	10,000

Required:

What is the annual carrying cost per unit?

(*AICPA adapted*)

14-12 *Average Inventory and Annual Ordering Costs*

Expected annual usage of a particular raw material is 2,000,000 units, and the standard order size is 10,000 units. The invoice cost of each unit is $500, and the cost to place one purchase order is $80.

Required:

Determine:

(1) The average inventory.

(2) The estimated annual order cost.

(AICPA adapted)

14-13 *Calculation of EOQ*

Barter Corporation has been buying Product A in lots of 1,200 units which represents a four months' supply. The cost per unit is $100; the order cost is $200 per order; and the annual inventory carrying cost for one unit is $25. Assume that the units will be required evenly throughout the year.

Required:

What is the economic order quantity?

(AICPA adapted)

14-14 *EOQ and Annual Inventory Expenses*

Brady Sporting Goods Incorporated buys baseballs at $20 per dozen from its wholesaler. Brady will sell 36,000 dozen baseballs evenly throughout the year. Brady desires a 10% return on its inventory investment. In addition, rent, insurance, taxes, etc., for each dozen baseballs in inventory is $.40. The administrative cost involved in handling each purchase order is $10.

Required:

(1) What is the economic order quantity?

(2) Assuming that Brady ordered in order sizes of 800 dozen evenly throughout the year, what would be the total annual inventory expenses to sell 36,000 dozen baseballs?

(AICPA adapted)

14-15 *Minimizing Annual Inventory Costs*

The Polly Company wishes to determine the amount of safety stock that it should maintain for Product D that will result in the lowest cost. The following information is available:

Stockout cost	$80 per occurrence
Carrying cost of safety stock	$ 2 per unit
Number of purchase orders	5 per year

The available options open to Polly are as follows:

Units of Safety Stock	*Probability of Running Out of Safety Stock*
10	50%
20	40%
30	30%
40	20%
50	10%
55	5%

Required.

Determine the number of units of safety stock that will result in the lowest annual cost.

(*AICPA adapted*)

14-16 Determining Optimal Inventory Policy

The Thornton Company has found that its ordering cost of a raw material is $20 and the carrying cost is $1 per average unit of inventory per year. The company uses 10,000 units of raw material per year.

Required:

(1) Determine the optimal order quantity.

(2) Calculate the annual inventory cost of the optimal inventory policy.

(3) How many times should the raw material be ordered in a year?

14-17 Determining EOQ and Reorder Point

The W & S Department Store has a requirement for a product line that amounts to 40,000 units per year. The unit purchase cost of the product is $4. The manager of the store estimates the cost of storage and the loss due to deterioration at 10 cents per unit per month. The store expects 15 percent of return on investment per year. Lead time is 15 days. Ordering and receiving costs are estimated to be *$20* per order.

Required:

(1) Determine the optimal order quantity.

(2) Determine the reorder point.

(3) What additional cost is incurred if the firm orders in lots of 2,000 units?

14-18 Determining Safety Stock and Reorder Point

The average lead time for delivery of a raw material used by the Nell Company is 10 days. The average use of the material is 18 units per day. The carrying cost per unit of average inventory is $10 per year. The following information is available through an analysis of the company's accounting records:

Usages During Lead Time	*Probability of the Usage*
150 units	.05
160 units	.10
170 units	.20
180 units	.30
190 units	.20
200 units	.15
	1.00

The optimum number of orders is 10 per year. The stockout cost is $20 per unit. The manager is considering whether to carry a safety stock of 0, 10, 15, or 20 units.

Required:

(1) Determine the level of safety stock that should be carried assuming the pattern of usage during lead time will remain the same as before.
(2) Determine the reorder point.

14-19 *Purchase Discount*

The Green Grass Company uses $1,000,000 of widgets per year. The unit cost of the widgets is $20. The company's ordering cost is $40 per order and the carrying cost is $1 per unit of average inventory. The company has used the basic EOQ model with no stockouts to determine the optimal order quantity. Recently, the company has been offered by the supplier a one percent discount if the company purchases an equal quantity weekly.

Required:

Should the company accept the offer of a purchase discount?

14-20 *EOQ and Purchase Discount*

The Treasure Manufacturing Company uses 100,000 units of Material M a year. It costs the company $2 a year to carry a unit of the material, and $20 to process a purchase order. Material M can be purchased from a supplier according to the following price schedule:

0	- 1,999 units	$10.00 per unit
2,000	- 3,999 units	9.80 per unit
4,000	- 5,999 units	9.60 per unit
6,000	- 7,999 units	9.40 per unit
8,000	- 9,999 units	9.20 per unit
10,000 or more units		9.00 per unit

Required.

Determine the optimal order quantity.

14-21 *Analysis of Two Price Alternatives*

The manager of the Old Dominion Company is considering an offer of quantity discounts on an item from its vendor. The company's requirement for the item is 8,000 units a year. Carrying cost is estimated to be $2 per year and ordering cost is $40 per order. Currently, the firm purchases in lots of 400 units at a unit cost of $5. The quantity discount from the vendor is $3.60 per unit if orders are in lots of 1,000 units.

Required.

(1) Should the manager accept the offer from the vendor?

(2) At what discount unit price would the company be indifferent between purchases in lots of 400 units and 1,000 units?

14-22 *EOQ with Stockouts*

The estimated demand for a product at the Little Jimmy Store is 4,000 units per year. The estimated ordering cost is $30 per order and the estimated carrying cost is $5 per unit per year. The stockout cost is estimated to equal $10 per unit. The manager of the store has used the estimated data and the EOQ model with stockouts to determine the optimal order quantity

Required:

(1) What is the optimal order quantity and how much is the expected total inventory cost of the optimal inventory policy?

(2) Calculate the value of the perfect information for the true carrying cost of $4 instead of $5 per unit [assume: (1) all estimates except the carrying cost are correct, and (2) without the knowledge of the true carrying cost, the manager's original solution will be implemented for a full year].

14-23 *EOQ, Reorder Point, and Problems in Applying the EOQ Formula*

The Robney Company is a restaurant supplier that sells a number of products to various restaurants in the area. One of their products is a special meat cutter with a disposable blade.

The blades are sold in packages of twelve for $20.00 per package. After a number of years, it has been determined that the demand for the replacement blades has a constant rate of 2,000 packages per month. The packages cost the Robney Company $10.00 each from the manufacturer and require a three-day lead time from date of order to date of delivery. The ordering cost is $1.20 per order and the carrying cost is 10% per annum.

Robney is going to use the economic order quantity formula:

$$EOQ = \sqrt{\frac{2(Annual\ Requirements)(Cost\ Per\ Order)}{(Price\ Per\ Unit)(Carrying\ Cost)}}$$

Required:

a. Calculate:

1. The economic order quantity.
2. The number of orders needed per year.
3. The total cost of buying and carrying blades for the year.

b. Assuming there is no reserve (e.g., safety stock) and that the present inventory level is 200 packages, when should the next order be placed? (Use 360 days equal one year.)

c. Discuss the problems that most firms would have in attempting to apply this formula to their inventory problems.

(IMA adapted)

14-24 *Determining Safety Stock and Reorder Point*

The Starr Company manufactures several products. One of its main products requires an electric motor. The management of Starr Company uses the economic-order-quantity formula (EOQ) to determine the optimum number of motors to order. Management now wants to determine how much safety stock to order.

Starr Company uses 30,000 electric motors annually (300 working days). Using the EOQ formula, the company orders 3,000 motors at a time.

The lead time for an order is five days. The annual cost of carrying one motor in safety stock is $10. Management has also estimated that the cost of being out of stock is $20 for each motor they are short.

Starr Company has analyzed the usage during past reorder periods by examining the inventory records. The records indicate the following usage patterns:

Usage During Lead Time	*Number of Times Quantity Was Used*
440	6
460	12
480	16
500	130
520	20
540	10
560	6
	200

Required:

(1) Using an expected-value approach, determine the level of safety stock for electric motors that Starr Company should maintain in order to minimize costs.

(2) What would be Starr Company's new reorder point?

(3) What factors should Starr Company have considered to estimate the out-of-stock costs?

(IMA adapted)

14-25 *Determining Annual Inventory Expenses, Reorder Point, and Stockout Costs*

You have been engaged to install an accounting system for the Kaufman Corporation. Among the inventory control features Kaufman desires as a part of the system are indicators of "how much" to order and "when" to order. The following information is furnished for one item, called a komtronic, which is carried in inventory:

a. Komtronics are sold by the gross (twelve dozen) at a list price of $800 per gross F.O.B. shipper. Kaufman receives a 40% trade discount off list price on purchases in gross lots.

b. Freight cost is $20 per gross from the shipping point to Kaufman's plant.

c. Kaufman uses about 5,000 komtronics during a 259-day production year and must purchase a total of thirty-six gross per year to allow for normal breakage and usage. Minimum and maximum usages are 12 and 28 komtronics per day, respectively.

d. Normal delivery time to receive an order is twenty working days from the date a purchase request is initiated. A rush order in full gross lots can be received by air freight in five working days at an extra cost of $52 per gross. A stockout (complete exhaustion of the inventory) of komtronics would stop production, and Kaufman would purchase komtronics locally at list price rather than shut down.
e. The cost of placing an order is $10; the cost of receiving an order is $20.
f. Space storage cost is $12 per year per gross stored.
g. Insurance and taxes are approximately 12% of the net delivered cost of average inventory and Kaufman expects a return of at least 8% on its average investment (ignore return on order and carrying cost for simplicity).

Required:

(1) Prepare a schedule computing the total annual cost of komtronics based on uniform order lot sizes of one, two, three, four, five and six gross of komtronics. (The schedule should show the total annual cost according to each lot size.) Indicate the economic order quantity (economic lot size to order).
(2) Prepare a schedule computing the minimum stock reorder point for komtronics. The komtronics inventory should not fall below this point without reordering, so as to guard against a stockout. Factors to be considered include average lead-period usage and safety stock requirements.
(3) Prepare a schedule computing the cost of a stockout of komtronics.

Factors to be considered include the excess costs for local purchases and for rush orders.

(*AICPA adapted*)

14-26 *Economic Order Quantity*

EDP Associates, a small data processing company, is a wholly owned subsidiary of Norbrook Inc. EDP Associates provides data processing services to the parent company and many small outside businesses. Bill Kamp, President of EDP Associates, employs a small staff to conduct the data processing activities of the company.

Waring Paper Products, a regional distributor of paper products, has proposed a quantity discount on one type of computer paper purchased by EDP Associates. Kamp currently pays $12 per carton for this paper and uses 15,000 cartons of the paper annually. Waring has offered a 5% cash discount on all quantity orders in excess of 1,000 cartons, (i.e., Kamp would pay the full price of $12 per carton on the first 1,000 cartons and the price on any cartons ordered in excess of 1,000 would be $11.40 each).

Kamp believes that any opportunity to save money would be worthwhile and is considering ordering larger quantities of paper to take advantage of the quantity discount. He has contacted John Barzoni in the controller's office of Norbrook for advice. Barzoni cautions Kamp not to act too quickly in taking the quantity discount. Barzoni points out that there are other relevant costs which must be considered before a decision is made regarding the optimum order quantity of computer paper. He indicates that the order quantity that will minimize the following cost formula must be determined.

$$TC = PD + O\frac{D}{Q} + PC\frac{Q}{2}$$

TC = total inventory-related costs
D = annual demand

Q = quantity ordered at one time
P = purchase price of a carton of paper
O = cost of placing an order
C = annual cost of carrying one carton in inventory

Together Kamp and Barzoni have been able to determine cost factors which may have an effect on the total inventory related costs. They are as follows:

(i) The cost to place an order is $64.80.
(ii) Imputed interest cost of inventory is 15% of the purchase price per carton.
(iii) Inventory storage cost is 5% of the purchase price per carton.

Required:

(a) Compute the optimum number of cartons of paper EDP Associates should be ordering currently without consideration of the quantity discount.
(b) Explain what effect the quantity discount offered by Waring Paper Products will have on the total cost of computer paper to EDP Associates.
(c) 1. Explain how EDP Associates should proceed to determine the economic order quantity when the quantity discount is considered. 2. Calculate the economic order quantity which will minimize the company's relevant paper cost.
(d) Without prejudice to your answers for Requirements (a) and (c), assume that EDP Associates is currently using an economic order quantity of 1,000 cartons and has decided to increase their order quantity to 5,000 cartons to take advantage of the quantity discount offered by Waring Paper. Determine the net increase or decrease this new course of action will have on the annual paper costs of EDP Associates.

14-27 *JIT and the EOQ Model*

TexTec Inc. is a manufacturer of computer disk drives. It currently operates a traditional factory which is divided into departments and allocates overhead based on direct labor hours.

Recently, the management of the company has been disrupted by a disagreement between the young, aggressive marketing manager, Alice Waterman, and the controller of many years, Jim Bob Johnson. Alice knows that some competitors have changed to just-in-time (JIT) production and believes that this has given them a competitive edge. She has studied the subject and understands the objectives and philosophy of a JIT production system.

Jim Bob studied inventory control in school many years ago and believes that TexTec's inventory policies, based on the EOQ model, are ideal. The EOQ model, he argues, decreases total costs by balancing the costs of ordering and carrying inventories. He believes that changing to JIT production will increase costs because it results in more frequent orders to suppliers. Jim Bob agrees that a JIT system will lower inventory carrying costs, but he is convinced that this cost savings will be lost because of the higher ordering costs.

Alice is puzzled by all this. She doesn't understand how, if what Jim Bob says is true, that TexTec's competitors can sell disk drives at a price below TexTec's own costs.

Alice suspects that the problem is with the EOQ model and has suggested that there are many inventory carrying costs that the EOQ ignores. Jim Bob acknowledges that there may be additional costs. But since these are not direct manufacturing costs, he responds, generally accepted accounting principles does not recognize them as costs of the product.

Required:

a. Identify the kinds of expenditures that are identified as inventory carrying costs by the OQ model.
b. Suggest some other expenditures that occur as a result of carrying inventories. These may include facilities, operations, and administrative costs.
c. How could a nontraditional cost accounting system associate these costs with TexTec's products?

15

1. *To understand quality and quality cost.*
2. *To discuss the classification and measurement of quality costs.*
3. *To study and understand quality cost reporting.*
4. *To use various quality cost analysis.*
5. *To learn how to use quality cost information for continuous quality improvement.*

Measuring, Reporting, and Controlling Product Quality Costs

In the past three decades, US firms have faced increased competition of high quality products at lower prices from foreign firms and markets. In order to compete and survive in the modern business environment, manufacturing firms are always looking for ways to become more competitive in terms of quality, price, and delivery. This is known as total quality management (TQM), which is one of the most important current management trends. TQM is a management philosophy that aims to eliminate defects, wastes, and non-value-added activities in production processes. This management system promotes and seeks continuous quality improvement by creating an environment that requires all employees in an organization to understand and participate in manufacturing zero-defect products and meeting total customer satisfaction.

For effective implementation of TQM, management needs information about quality costs and performance of quality improvement programs. This chapter discusses important topics on quality management such as measurement, reporting, and control of quality costs. First, we will define quality and quality costs. Then, we will discuss the classification and measurement of typical quality costs. Finally, quality cost reports and uses of quality cost information for continuous quality improvement will also be discussed in this chapter.

Definition of Quality

There are two ways to define product quality: design quality and conformance quality. Design quality is determined at the stage of product development and design. It is the specification of product performance standards. In contrast, conformance quality is determined by the degree that a product meets its designed quality standards or specifications. If a product meets every aspect of its designed specifications, it is considered total conformance to the design quality. This is what a product quality control program should strive to achieve after a product quality standard is specified. It should be noted that, after a product quality is specified or designed in, quality of conformance is the main concern of management in quality assurance. In this chapter, we refer product quality to the quality of conformance not quality of design in our discussion of measuring, reporting, and analyzing product quality costs. It is important to note that the degree of quality conformance is a measure of how a product conforms to meet its specification for customer expectations. A defective product is the one that does not meet its design specification and customer expectations. On the other hand, a non-defective product is the one that meets its design specification and satisfies or exceeds its customer expectations.

Definition of Quality Costs

In a competitive business environment, quality products or services are demanded by customers and produced by firms. In order to meet customer demand for quality products or services, manufacturing firms need to perform quality management activities, which require effort and consumption of scarce resources. Thus, quality costs are those costs incurred for the achievement or non-achievement of designed product quality. In other words, quality costs refer to all of the costs that are incurred to prevent quality defects or that result from defects in product. These quality costs are often grouped into four categories: prevention costs, appraisal costs, internal failure costs, and external failure costs. Prevention and appraisal costs are incurred to prevent quality defects, while internal failure and external failure costs are incurred because defective products are made. They are discussed in more detail below.

Classification of Quality Costs

As identified above, quality costs can be classified into four categories: prevention, appraisal, internal failure, and external failure. Each is further explained below with examples.

Prevention Costs

An effective way to assure the product quality is to avoid producing the defective products in the first place. It is important to note that normally it costs less to prevent a defective product than to correct the defective one. Therefore, prevention costs are incurred to prevent the production of defective products or services. Typical examples of prevention costs are: quality engineering, quality training, quality records and reports, quality circles, quality improvement programs, quality audits, vendor certification, and statistical process control.

Appraisal Costs

While preventive activities are generally more effective for quality management, quality inspection activities are necessary to identify any defective part or product as early as possible in the production process. Appraisal costs are incurred to evaluate and identify defective parts or products in the production process before customers receive the defective products. Typical examples of appraisal or inspection costs are: inspection materials, inspection of prototype, inspection of work-in-process, inspection of final products, and supplies, labor, and depreciation on all testing equipment.

Internal Failure Costs

Failure costs are costs incurred because a product does not meet its design specifications or customer needs. Depending upon when the defective products are discovered, failure costs may be divided into two types, internal failure costs and external failure costs. If a defective product is discovered before it is delivered to the customer, it is considered an internal failure cost. Good examples of internal failure costs include: scrap, rework cost, retesting and re-inspection cost, failure analysis, disposal of defective product, repairs and downtime due to defective process.

External Failure Costs

If the customer discovers a defective product, the cost of dealing with the defective unit is considered an external failure cost. Those costs are incurred because a product does not conform to quality requirements or satisfy customer expectations after the customer receives the product. External failure costs include: warranty repairs and replacements, returns and allowances, complaint adjustments and discounts, product recalls, lost sales, market share loss, product liabilities and lawsuits, customer dissatisfaction and credibility lost.

Illustration 15-1 summarizes the four categories of quality costs with some typical examples.

Distribution of Quality Costs

The four categories of quality costs discussed earlier may be further grouped into "quality control costs" and "quality failure costs". Prevention costs and appraisal costs are quality control

Illustration 15-1 Categories of Quality Costs

Prevention Costs	Internal Failure Costs
Quality engineering	Scrap
Quality training	Rework and repair costs
Quality records and reports	Retesting and re -inspection costs
Quality improvement programs	Disposal of defective products
Quality circles	Downtime due to defective process
Quality audits	Failure analysis
Vendor certification	
Statistical process control	
Appraisal Costs	**External Failure Costs**
Inspection materials	Warranty repairs and replacements
Inspection of prototype	Discounts and adjustments
Inspection of work-in-process	Returns and allowances
Inspection of final products	Product recalls
Testing supplies and labor	Sales lost
Depreciation on testing equipment	Market share loss
	Product liabilities and lawsuits
	Credibility

costs. Internal failure costs and external failure costs are quality failure costs. It is interesting to note that there is a trade-off between quality control costs and quality failure costs. As quality control costs increase, quality failure costs should decrease because more prevention and appraisal efforts would reduce the production and delivery of defective products to customers. Therefore, as long as the decrease in failure costs is greater than the increase in control costs, management should continue increasing its efforts to prevent and detect the production of defective units.

Traditional Quality Cost Function

The traditional acceptable quality level (AQL) approach suggests that quality control efforts should increase to a point where total control costs are equal to total failure costs. This is the optimal balance between quality control costs and quality failure costs. Illustration 15-2 presents the graphical relationship between control costs and failure costs.

Two quality cost functions (control costs and failure costs) are combined into the total quality cost function in Illustration 15-2. The control cost function assumes that the percentage of defective units decreases as the amount of control costs increases. On the other hand, the failure cost function assumes that the amount of failure costs increases as the percentage of defective units increases. Because of the trade-off between control costs and failure costs, the total quality costs decrease as the quality level increases up to the optimal balance point. At this optimal point, total control costs equal to total failure costs. After that point, additional quality improvements would require more control costs than savings in failure costs.

Illustration 15-2 Traditional Quality Cost Functions

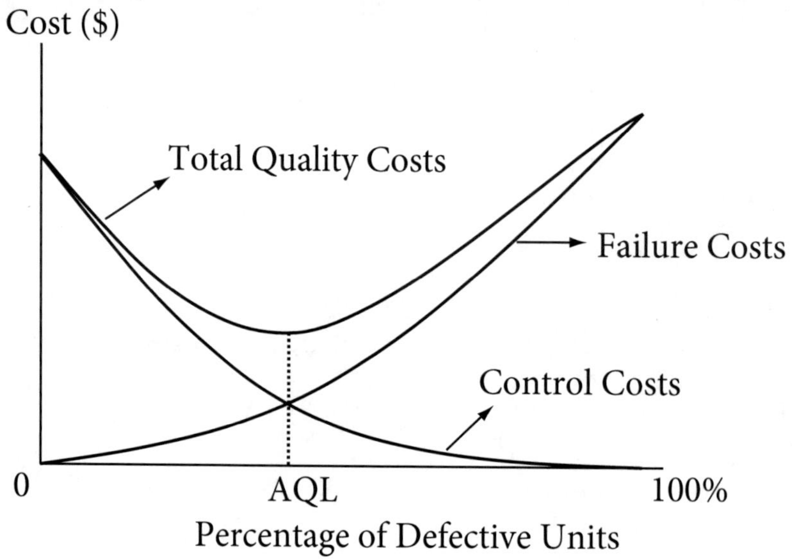

Contemporary Quality Cost Function

The traditional acceptable quality level approach permits the production of a given number of defective units. This approach was popular for many years before the late 1970s. However, some quality control experts in the 1980s challenged the traditional approach with the zero-defect approach. Those experts believe that the total quality cost is not minimized until the product quality is 100% perfect and there are no defective units produced. Indeed, many firms have found that the total quality costs seem to continue decreasing even as the product quality approaches 100% perfect. Actually, what happens in those firms is that as they increase their control costs and reduce their failure costs, they observe that they can even cut back on their control costs because of the continuing effects of the earlier quality control efforts. Therefore, what initially believed to be a trade-off between control costs and failure cost turns out to be a permanent reduction in all quality cost categories. The contemporary zero-defects experts believe that control costs do not increase without limit and they may first increase and then decrease because of their continuing effects of control efforts. Also, failure costs can be driven down to zero by effective control efforts. Illustration 15-3 presents the contemporary quality cost functions.

Measurement of Quality Costs

Most of the quality costs are easy to determine because they are available from a firm's accounting records. Normally, quality cost data are scattered in various departments in a firm. All cost data should be recorded with established procedures and guides. The objective is to collect quality costs with a high degree of validity, reliability, and verifiability. Some typical sources of quality cost data include:

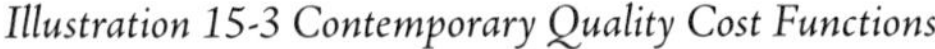

Illustration 15-3 Contemporary Quality Cost Functions

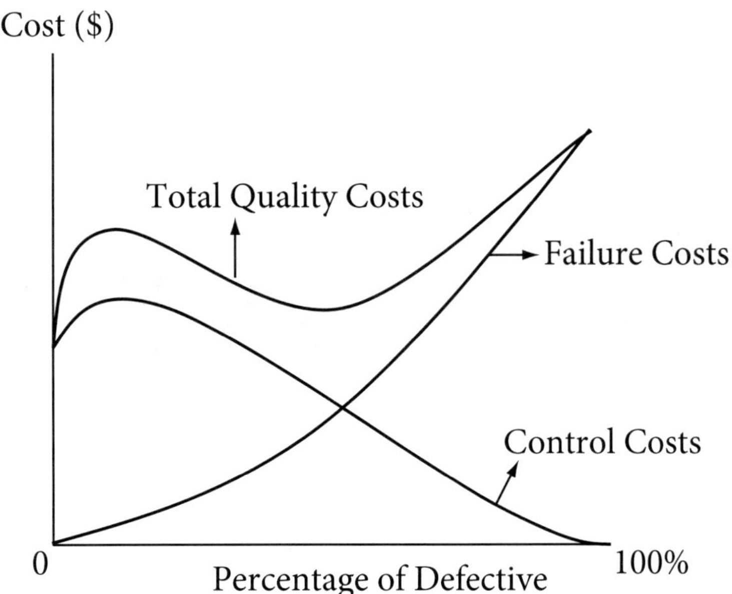

- Payroll records
- Material receiving records
- Inspection reports
- Scrap reports
- Rework reports
- Manufacturing expense reports
- Field repair, replacement, and warranty cost reports

However, some external failure costs such as customer dissatisfaction, lost sales, and market share loss are difficult to measure because they are not recorded in an accounting system. These failure costs are sometimes referred to as hidden quality costs. In some cases, these hidden quality costs can be substantial and important. Thus, they should be estimated or forecast for quality management decisions. Three methods have been suggested for estimating hidden quality costs: (1) the multiplier method, (2) the market survey method, and (3) the Taguchi quality loss function method.

The Multiplier Method

Given that some of the external failure costs can be readily determined from accounting records; this method assumes that the total external failure cost is a multiple of the recorded failure costs. Stated in an equation, it is:

Total External Failure Cost = k (Recorded External Failure Costs)

In this equation, "k" is the multiplier and can be estimated based on past experience. Once "k" is determined, the total external failure costs can be calculated and the hidden quality costs can be derived by subtracting recorded external failure costs from the total external failure costs. For example, if the recorded external failure costs are \$100,000 in a period and the past experience indicates a multiplier effect of 3 (i.e., k = 3), then the hidden quality costs can be determined as following:

Hidden quality costs = Total external failure costs – recorded external failure costs
= (3 x \$100,000) – \$100,000
= \$ 200,000.

The Market Survey Method

This method uses market surveys and interviews to estimate the hidden quality costs. Market surveys and interviews may be conducted on customers and the firm's own sales force to provide an estimate of the potential loss on sales and market share due to poor quality products.

Results from such periodic market surveys and interviews can be used to project future sales loss due to poor product quality.

The Taguchi Loss Function Method

Unrecorded failure costs of a product are hidden quality costs. In some cases, they are the largest contributor to the total product quality costs. Thus, it is vital for firms to measure, analyze, and control all tangible as well as intangible quality costs. A Taguchi quality loss function (TQLF) has been proposed and used in accounting for estimating the hidden quality costs. The TQLF approach assumes that loss occurs when a product quality deviates from a specification value regardless of whether it falls inside or outside the specification limits. This concept is different from the traditional defective-nondefective dichotomy approach. The dichotomy approach assumes no hidden quality costs for all products falls inside the specification limits and a certain hidden quality cost for all products falls outside the specification limits. Furthermore, the Taguchi approach assumes that loss continually increases as the actual quality deviates further from the target quality. Illustration 15-4 compares the Taguchi quality loss function and the traditional dichotomy loss function.

As shown in Illustration 15-4, Taguchi quality loss function is an asymmetry parabola curve that is tangent to the horizontal axis at the target quality value (T). It is a quadratic loss function and suggests that the loss is zero when a product meets the target value. However, the loss becomes quadruple if the deviation from the target value is doubled. If the deviation is tripled, the loss increases 9 times. For example, if a deviation of 0.1mm from the target generates a $10 loss, then a $40 loss occurs for a deviation of 0.2mm and a $90 loss for a deviation of 0.3mm.

Thus, the TQLF measures the loss as a quadratic function of the deviation of the actual value of quality characteristics from the target value of a product quality characteristic. Mathematically, the unit loss is determined by:

$$L(y) = k(y - T)^2 \quad (15 - 1)$$

Where k = a proportionality constant which is dependent upon the firm's failure cost structure,

y = actual value of quality characteristic,

T = target value of quality characteristic.

Before we can use Equation 15-1 to calculate the loss of a product, the value of the proportionality constant (k) must be first estimated. The larger the k means the more sensitive the loss function or the steeper the parabola. Therefore, the size of k determines the slope of the loss function. If the deviation of the actual quality characteristic value from the target value of quality characteristic (d) and its associated loss (c) are given, the value of k can be estimated by dividing the loss by the squared deviation of the actual quality value from the target value. That is,

Illustration 15-4 Traditional vs. Taguchi Quality Loss Functions

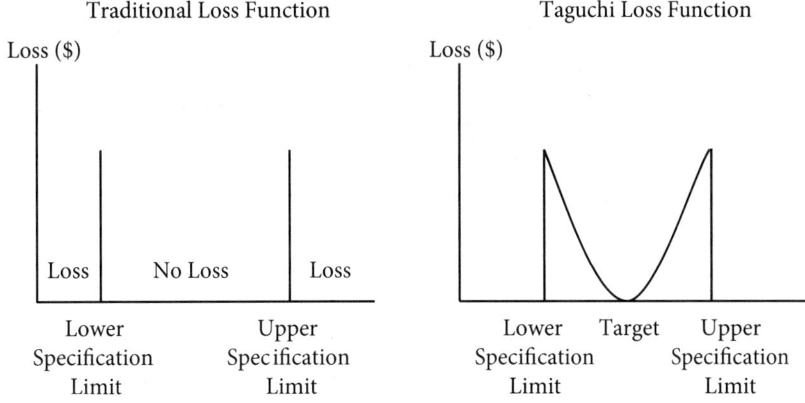

$$k = c / d^2 \quad (15\text{-}2)$$

Although the quadratic loss function illustrated above may provide good approximations of hidden quality costs in some cases, it is not a law of nature. Also, it should be noted that the successful application of the Taguchi's approach rests significantly on an accurate estimate of c. The value of c represents intangible quality costs due to a deviation between the actual quality and the target quality. As indicated before, the intangible quality costs are difficulty to quantify, they should be estimated by management based on their past experience or market surveys.

For purposes of illustration, a simple example is given below to estimate the unit hidden quality loss using the Taguchi method:

Assume that a firm has determined the target quality value for a product is 10mm (i.e., T =10mm). Analysis of the firm's records indicates that the loss associated with an actual quality value of 10.2mm is $40 (i.e., c = $40 when y = 10.2mm). If a particular unit of this product is produced with an actual quality value of 10.5mm, what is the hidden quality loss for this unit of the product?

Since d = 10.2 – 10 = .2 and $k = c / d^2 = \$40 / .2^2 = \$1{,}000$, the hidden quality loss for the unit of the product can be computed as follows:

$$L\,(y = 10.5) = \$\,1{,}000\,(10.5 - 10)^2 = \$250.$$

Quality Cost Reports

Once the quality cost data are collected, reports must be prepared to meet the needs of managers. Quality cost reports should be designed to identify problems for further analysis and opportunities for improvements. Two types of quality cost reports provide insights for controlling quality costs: (1) current quality cost reports and (2) quality cost performance reports. Quality cost reports are prepared to assess the magnitude and distribution of a period's quality costs by the category. In contrast, quality cost performance reports are prepared to compare between actual and budgeted quality costs for measuring the progress of a quality improvement program.

Current Quality Cost Report

This quality cost report shows the quality costs incurred in a period by individual items in each category. It also provides information regarding current distribution of quality costs by reporting these costs as a percentage of total sales as well as total quality costs in the period. Furthermore, additional ratios relating quality costs to total manufacturing costs and total sales may be calculated to provide additional insights of current quality costs. Illustration 15-5 presents the Big Q Company's current quality cost report for the period ended June 30, 20X5.

Additional Ratios:

Appraisal costs to total manufacturing costs: 60,000/2,000,000 = 3%.
Internal failure costs to total manufacturing costs: 260,000/2,000,000 = 13%.
External failure costs to total sales: 100,000/5,000,000 = 2%.
Total quality costs to total sales = 500,000/5,000,000 = 10%.

Quality Performance Reports

In our illustrative example, the Big Q Company's quality costs for period ended June 30, 20X5 represent 10% of its total sales. This information may be compared to the company's long-range goal of quality policy to see how much to improve its quality costs. If the goal is 3% of sales, the company has plenty of room to improve its quality costs. Also, the report shows that the company incurred more internal and external failure costs than prevention and appraisal costs. This may indicate the opportunity for further improving its quality costs.

Illustration 15-5 Big Q Company Quality Cost Report for the Period Ended June 30, 20X5

	Quality Costs	Percentage of of Total Sales	Percentage of of Total Quality Costs
Prevention Costs:			
Quality Administration	$ 40,000		
Quality Training	40,000		
Total	80,000	1.6%	16%
Appraisal Costs:			
Materials Inspection	20,000		
Testing	10,000		
Product inspection	30,000		
Total	60,000	1.2%	12%
Internal Failure Costs:			
Scrap	100,000		
Rework	130,000		
Re-inspection	30,000		
Total	260,000	5.2%	52%
External Failure Costs:			
Customer Complaints	20,000		
Warranty Repairs	50,000		
Product Replacement	30,000		
Total	100,000	2.0%	20%
Total Quality Costs	$ 500,000	10.0%	100%
Total Manufacturing Costs	$ 2,000,000		
Total Sales	$ 5,000,000		

Quality performance reports compare actual with budgeted quality costs for controlling quality costs and measuring the progress of a quality improvement program. Depending upon what budgeted quality costs (the current period's budget or the total quality control budget) are used, two types of quality performance reports may be prepared for management control of quality costs: (1) current quality performance reports and (2) total quality performance reports. In a current quality performance report, we compare the actual and budgeted quality costs for the current period. On the other hand, in a total quality performance report, we compare the current period's actual quality costs with the costs that a firm eventually plans to achieve for total quality control.

Generally speaking, in preparation of quality performance reports, a budget formula for each quality cost item must be first developed. The flexible budget concept serves well in developing quality cost formula. First, the behavior pattern of each quality cost item must be identified. Some quality costs vary with sales and others remain constant within a relevant range of sales. For example, the Big Q Company has the following variable and fixed quality costs:

	Fixed Costs per Period	Variable Costs (As % of Sales)
Prevention Costs:		
Quality Administration	$ 40,000	------
Quality Training	35,000	------
Appraisal Costs:		
Materials Inspection	------	0.3%
Testing	------	0.6%
Product Inspection	------	0.1%
Internal Failure costs:		
Scrap	------	2.2%
Rework	------	2.5%
Re-inspection	------	0.4%
External Failure Costs:		
Customer Complaints	20,000	------
Warranty Repairs	-------	0.5%
Product Replacement	-------	0.5%

Current Quality Performance Report

At the end of each period, a current quality performance report is prepared to reveal quality improvement achieved in the period. Based on the budget formula for each quality cost, budgeted costs are first determined and then compared against the actual quality costs incurred in the period to calculate a quality cost variance for the current period. Illustration 15-6 presents the Big Q Company's current quality performance report for the period ended June 30, 20X5.

The current quality performance report for the Big Q Company shows that the overall quality performance in the period is fairly close to what was budgeted. It shows that $500,000 of total actual quality costs compared to $450,000 of total budgeted quality costs. However, there is a $50,000 unfavorable variance resulting mainly from failure costs that may warrant management attention.

Total Quality Performance Reports

Quality improvement is a continual process. In addition to an ongoing evaluation of each period's quality performance, it is also necessary to evaluate the quality performance in terms of total quality standard (or zero-defect standards). This is shown in a total quality performance report where the current period's quality costs are compared with the costs allowed under total quality standard. It should be noted that under total quality control, internal and external failure costs should be non-existent. However, prevention and appraisal costs would not be ever totally eliminated. In fact, emphasis on total quality control would still incur the cost of prevention although appraisal costs may be expected to decrease. Illustration 15-7 presents the Big Q Company's total quality performance report for the period ended June 30, 20X5. Note that there are no budgeted internal and external failure costs and budgeted prevention and appraisal costs are the company's planned costs at total quality control for total sales of $5,000,000.

Illustration 15-6 Current Quality Performance Report For the Period Ended June 30, 20X5

	Actual Costs	Budgeted Costs	Variance
Prevention Costs:			
Qulity Administration	$ 40,000	$ 40,000	$ 0
Quality Training	40,000	35,000	5,000 U
Total	80,000	75,000	5,000 U
Appraisal Costs:			
Materials Inspection	20,000	15,000	5,000 U
Testing	30,000	30,000	0
Product Inspection	10,000	5,000	5,000 U
Total	60,000	50,000	10,000U
Internal Failure costs:			
Scrap	100,000	110,000	10,000
Rework	130,000	125,000	5,000 U
Reinspection	30,000	20,000	10,000 U
Total	260,000	255,000	5,000 U
External Failure Costs:			
Customer Complaints	20,000	20,000	0
Warranty Repairs	50,000	25,000	25,000 U
Product Replacement	30,000	25,000	5,000 U
Total	100,000	70,000	30,000 U
Total Quality Costs	$500,000	$450,000	$50,000 U
Percentage of Total Sales ($5m)	10%	9%	1%

The total quality performance report in Illustration 15-7 reveals that the Big Q Company incurred excessive quality costs particularly in the failure costs. In other words, the company is still not producing total quality product in the first time. The total unfavorable quality cost variance of $390,000 or 7.8% of sales indicate that the company has a large room for quality improvement.

Additional Quality Cost Analyses

In addition to the quality cost reports and quality performance reports discussed above, two additional quality cost comparisons and analyses may be useful for management control of quality improvements. They are discussed below.

Trend Analysis

Total quality costs or each quality cost component (prevention, appraisal, internal failure, and external failure) incurred in the current period may be compared with that incurred in some previous periods to show the trend of quality costs. The trend analysis should be provided periodically in terms of a fraction of some meaningful bases (such as sales or total production costs). Any trend developed in total quality costs or a quality cost component may inform management about the effectiveness and problems of quality control programs.

Illustration 15-8 presents a trend analysis of total quality costs and individual quality cost component in a graphic form.

Illustration 15-7 Total Quality Performance Report for the Period Ended June 30, 20X5

	Actual Costs	Budgeted Costs	Variance
Prevention Costs:			
Quality Administration	$ 40,000	$ 30,000	$ 10,000 U
Quality Training	40,000	30,000	10,000 U
Total	80,000	60,000	20,000 U
Appraisal Costs:			
Materials Inspection	20,000	15,000	5,000 U
Testing	30,000	30,000	0
Product Inspection	10,000	5,000	5,000 U
Total	60,000	50,000	10,000 U
Internal Failure costs:			
Scrap	100,000	0	100,000 U
Rework	130,000	0	130,000 U
Re-inspection	30,000	0	30,000 U
Total	260,000	0	260,000 U
External Failure Costs:			
Customer Complaints	20,000	0	20,000 U
Warranty Repairs	50,000	0	50,000 U
Product Replacement	30,000	0	30,000 U
Total	100,000	0	100,000 U
Total Quality Costs	$500,000	$110,000	$390,000 U
Percentage of Total Sales ($5m)	10%	2.2%	7.8%

Pareto Analysis

An important advantage of quality cost reporting is to facilitate an analysis in identifying key problem areas for improvements. Pareto analysis summarizes possible factors contributing to a particular quality cost component (or activity) and ranks them according to the magnitude of their contributions to the quality cost component. In many cases, a small number of factors contribute a large portion of a quality cost component. For example, Illustration 15-9 presents an analysis of internal failure costs showing the costs contributed by each of the five possible factors, with scrap contributing the largest portion. Also, Illustration 15-10 presents a further analysis of scrap costs contributed by different departments. With such information, the key problem area of internal failure costs can be identified for further improvements. Pareto analysis provides information regarding how efforts and resources should be directed to provide the largest quality improvements.

Uses of Quality Cost Information

The primary objective of measuring and reporting quality costs is to improve product quality and overall firm's performance. A quality cost report has many advantages:

1. Quality cost information offers financial consequence of defective products or services.
2. Quality cost reports help management understand the distribution of quality costs by items and categories.
3. Quality cost reports help management see the trade-off between the quality control costs and the quality failure costs.

Illustration 15-8 Graphic Trend Analysis of Total Quality Costs and Individual Cost Component

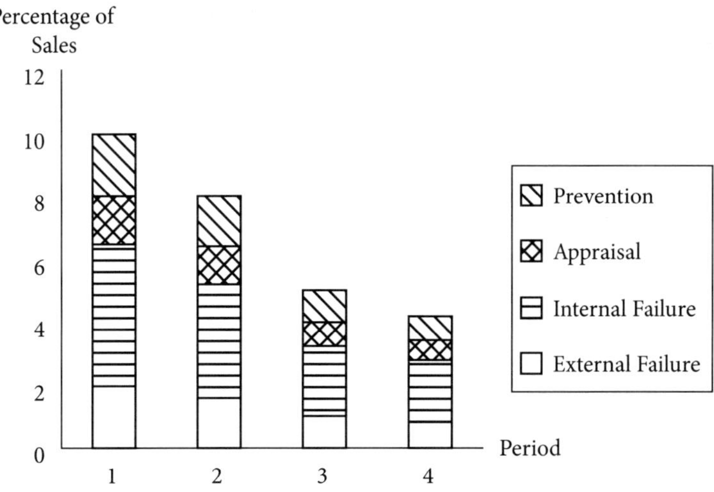

Illustration 15-9 Pareto Analysis of Internal Failure Costs

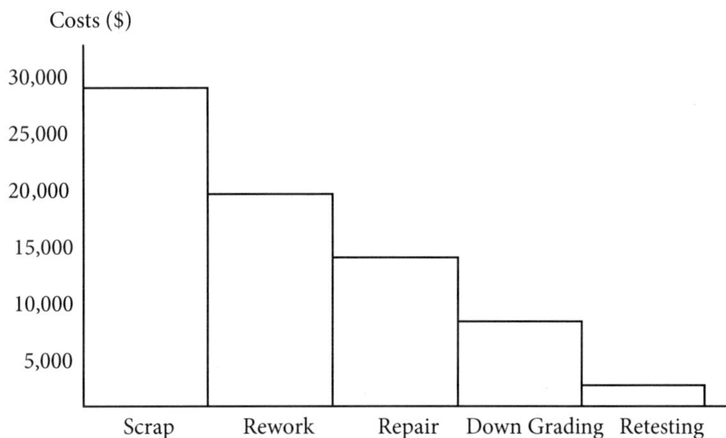

Illustration 15-10 Pareto Analysis of Scrap Costs

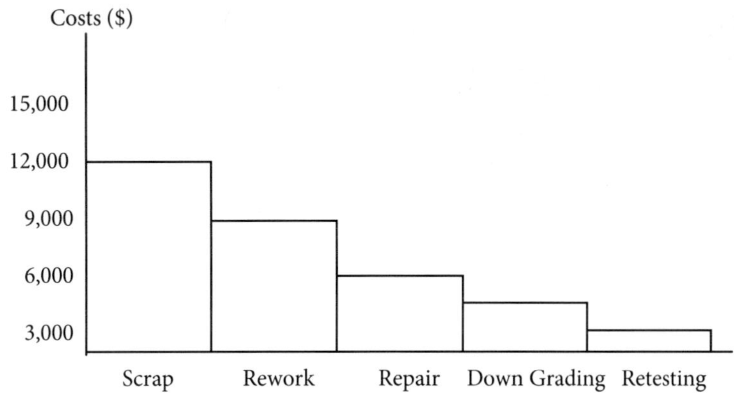

4. Quality cost reports provide information about the relative importance and the trend of each category of quality costs.
5. Quality cost reports provide information for assessing the effectiveness of quality improvement programs.

Summary

A firm needs to be competitive not only in price but also in quality and delivery. In modern highly competitive business environment, product quality is one of the key performance measures in all firms. In order to achieve a high quality performance, management needs information about quality costs and the performance results of their quality assurance programs.

This chapter has discussed quality cost concepts and measurement and reporting of quality costs. Quality costs can be classified into four categories: prevention costs, appraisal costs, internal failure costs, and external failure costs. Prevention costs are incurred to prevent the production of defective products. Appraisal costs are incurred to evaluate and identify defective products in the production process before customers receive them. Internal failure costs are incurred as a consequence of detecting defective products before customers received them. External failure costs are incurred as a consequence of delivering defective products to customers. Quality experts believe that management should focus on quality prevention activities to reduce appraisal costs and costs of internal and external failures.

Quality cost reports provide information about the size and distribution of a period's quality costs. On the other hand, quality performance reports provide information about quality performance in a period and in terms of total quality control. In addition, quality cost analysis such as the trend analysis and the Pareto analysis identify problem areas to assist management of quality assurance program.

Key Definitions

Appraisal Costs — Cost incurred to measure, evaluate, and monitor products to assure conformance to quality standard and performance requirements.

Current Quality Performance Report — A report prepared to compare actual and budgeted quality costs for the current period.

External Failure Costs — Costs incurred after a nonconforming product is delivered to the customer.

Internal Failure Costs — Costs incurred because of nonconformance of quality before product delivery and shipment.

Pareto Analysis — A summary with ranking of possible factors contributing to a particular quality cost component (or activity).

Prevention Costs — Costs incurred to prevent poor quality in products.

Quality Costs — Costs incurred for the achievement or non-achievement of product quality.

Quality Cost Report — A report prepared to assess the size and distribution of a period's quality costs by category.

Quality Loss Function — A quadratic function represents loss for a product quality deviating from a specification value.

Quality of Conformance — The degree that a product meets its designed specifications.

Quality of Design — The specification of a product's standard which is determined at the stage of product development and design.

Total Quality Performance Report — A report prepared to compare the current period's actual quality costs with the costs that a firm plans to achieve for total quality control.

Trend Analysis — A comparison of costs incurred in the current period with those incurred in some previous periods to show the trend of quality costs.

Questions

15-1 How are quality of design and quality of conformance related and distinguished?

15-2 Identify and discuss four quality cost components.

15-3 What quality costs are incurred before and after product is delivered to the customer?

15-4 Explain the difference between the traditional view and the modern view of optimal quality costs.

15-5 Explain the difference between the designed in and the inspected in product quality.

15-6 Identify typical sources of quality cost data.

15-7 Describe and illustrate Taguchi quality loss function.

15-8 Explain why successful applications of Taguchi quality loss function is dependent upon an accurate estimate of loss associated with the specification limit.

15-9 What are the key assumptions of Taguchi quality loss function?

15-10 What is the purpose of quality costs reports?

15-11 What are the purposes of current and total quality performance reports?

15-12 How is a trend analysis useful in quality improvement?

15-13 How is a pareto analysis useful in quality improvement?

15-14 Explain why all purchases orders should be inspected for quality assurance.

15-15 Explain why prevention costs and appraisal costs are related.

Problems

15-16 *Quality Cost Classification*

Classify each of the following items as prevention, appraisal, internal failure, and external failure costs:

a. Product warranty costs
b. Vendor survey and review
c. Design of product test equipment
d. Rework done by local distributor
e. Set-up for product tests
f. Preparation of quality manual
g. Preparation of quality cost report
h. Expenses of attending quality improvement convention
i. Replacement of defect parts at dealer's location
j. Scrap and rework
k. Inspection of incoming materials
l. Supplier evaluations and certification
m. Expenses of handling a product liability law suit
n. Expenses of handling consumer's complaints

15-17 *Total Quality Control*

Management of Top-Quality Company has set a goal of total quality control that specifies annual quality costs to be 3% of total revenue and an equal balance between prevention costs and appraisal costs. Determine the budgeted prevention costs and appraisal costs for a total quality performance report with total sales of $1,000,000.

15-18 *Distribution of Quality Costs*

During 20X5, Benson recorded the following quality costs when it had total sales of $5,000,000:

Prevention costs	$100,000
Appraisal costs	200,000
Internal failure costs	200,000
External failure costs	300,000
Total quality costs	$800,000

Required:

1. Determine the relative distribution of Benson's quality costs by component.
2. Compute the individual quality cost to sales rations and the total quality costs to sales ratio.
3. Comment on the distribution of Benson's quality costs in 20X5.

15-19 *Quality Performance Report*

Recently Kent Company instituted a quality improvement program. Kent's actual and budgeted quality costs for 20X5 are summarized below: (The actual sales for 20X5 are $1,000,000)

	Actual	Budgeted
Supplier survey	$25,000	$20,000 per year
Quality training program	10,000	10,000 per year
Consumer complaints	25,000	20,000 per year
Lost sales due to mislabeling	12,000	1% of sales
Scrap	25,000	2% of sales
Rework	15,000	2%of sales
Testing & inspection of products	15,000	1% of sales
Warranty repairs	10,000	0.5% of sales
Product replacement	8,000	0.5% of sales

Required:

Prepare a quality cost performance report for 20X5.

15-20 *Estimating Intangible Quality Loss*

Radford Manufacturing Company's specification states a target weight of 10 oz. for its product. Based on past experience, management estimated that loss associated with the specification limit at 9.5 oz. is about $50 per unit.

Required:

Using the Taguchi QLF, estimate the intangible quality loss of the product when its actual weight is 9.8 oz.

15-21 *Estimating Intangible Quality Costs*

Fine Product Company manufactures a product with a feature that has a target value of 18 grams. The company has set specification limits for the product equal to the target value plus or minus 0.5 grams. The estimated intangible quality loss at the upper or lower specification limits (18.50 grams or 17.50 grams) is $10. During the past month, a batch of 1,000 units of the product was produced. Five of the units produced were sampled for the weight quality of the batch. The weights of these 5 units are given as below:

Sample #	Weight (grams)
1	18.10
2	18.30
3	17.80
4	17.20
5	18.60

Required:

1. Applying the Taguchi quality loss function, calculate the proportionality constant (K).
2. Based on the sample weights, calculate the average quality loss per unit of the batch produced.
3. Estimate the total intangible quality loss for the batch.

15-22 Actual Quality Cost Reports and Quality Performance Reports

Teresa Company has recently launched a product quality improvement program. For the current year 20X5, its goal is to reduce quality costs to 10% of sales revenues. The company's actual and budgeted sales and quality costs for 20X5 are summarized as follows:

	Actual	Budgeted
Sales	$500,000	$600,000
Quality Costs:		
Raw materials inspection	4,000	0.5% of sales
Rework	4,000	1.5% of sales
Scrap	5,000	0.8% of sales
Quality planning & training	10,000	$8,000 per year
Product warranty	10,000	1.5% of sales
Finished product inspection	5,000	1.0% of sales
Quality reporting & administration	2,000	$3,000 per year
Customer complaints	10,000	$8,000 per year
Work-in-process inspection	4,000	0.7% of sales
Supplier review & evaluation	6,000	$5,000 per year

Required:

1. Prepare an actual quality cost report for the company, classifying costs by item and category.
2. Prepare a quality performance report to assess the company's quality improvement in 20X5.
3. Comment on Teresa Company's quality performance in 20X5.

15-23 *Quality Costs and Profit Improvement*

Anderson Company reported sales of $5,000,000 in 20X5. During the year, Anderson included the following quality costs:

Appraisal costs	$ 70,000
Prevention costs	140,000
Internal failure costs	210,000
External failure costs	280,000
Total quality costs	$700,000

Required:

1. Compute the quality cost as a percentage of total quality costs by category.
2. Compute the quality cost as a percentage of total sales by category.
3. Estimate the company's profit improvement ($) if quality costs are reduced to 10% of sales.
4. Comment on Anderson Company's quality cost distribution in 20X5.

15-24 *Trend Analysis of Quality Costs*

Calco Electronics Company's quality improvement program requires a trend analysis of its quality costs every year. At the end of 20X4, Calco's records show the following quality costs and sales for the past five years:

	Prevention	Appraisal	Internal Failure	External Failure	Sales
20X4	$20,000	$30,000	$15,000	$15,000	$800,000
20X5	14,000	26,000	10,000	20,000	650,000
20X6	12,000	20,000	12,000	20,000	500,000
20X7	10,000	15,000	15,000	20,000	500,000
20X8	10,000	10,000	20,000	15,000	450,000

Required:

1. Calculate the quality cost as a percentage of sales for each category of quality costs and total costs for each year.
2. Prepare a graph to show the trend of Calco's quality costs by category and total costs in the past five years.

15.25 *Pareto Analysis*

Terry Taylor's quality improvement program includes a pareto analysis each period to identify key quality cost components for management attention and action. For the past accounting period, Taylor's records show the following internal failure costs:

Rework costs	$20,000
Scrap costs	15,000
Down Grading Costs	12,000
Retesting costs	10,000

A further analysis of rework costs revealed that each of the company's five product lines incurred the following rework costs in the period:

Product A	$ 8,000
Product B	6,000
Product C	3,000
Product D	2,000
Product E	1,000
Total rework costs	$20,000

Required:

1. Prepare a pareto analysis of internal failure costs and identify the main contributor of the internal failure costs in the company.
2. Prepare a pareto analysis of rework costs and identify the key contributor of the rework costs in the company.

15-26 *Classification and Calculation of Quality Costs*

During November and December 20X7, Watella Company incurred the following costs of quality:

	November	December
Inspection materials	$ 5,000	$ 6,000
Product design	20,000	22,000
Scrap	4,000	5,000
Rework	15,000	18,000
Testing supplies	3,000	4,000
Quality training	3,000	2,000
Product recalls	8,000	9,000
Warranty replacements	25,000	20,000

Required:

1. Calculate the following quality costs for each month:
2. Total prevention costs.
3. Total appraisal costs.
4. Total internal failure costs.
5. Total external failure costs.

15-27 *Taguchi Loss Function*

Acadia Company manufactures and sells a special product. Based on the marketing manager's past experience, the target value of product quality characteristic is 0.10 and the average cost for warranty repair associated with an actual value of quality characteristic of 0.12 is $100 per unit.

Required:

1. Determine the value of d and k.
2. Determine the estimated loss when the actual value of quality characteristic is 0.11.
3. Determine the estimated loss when the actual value of quality characteristic is 0.105.
4. Determine the amount of the estimated loss when the deviation of the actual value from the target value of quality characteristic doubled.

1. *To understand the concept of the time value of money.*
2. *To discuss the principal data required to make capital budgeting decisions.*
3. *To study and apply various criteria and methods used in project evaluation.*
4. *To examine the effects of income taxes and inflation on capital budgeting decisions.*
5. *To discuss the lease-or-buy decision.*
6. *To understand the significance of uncertainty in the capital budgeting process.*

16

Capital Budgeting Decisions

Among the most important decisions that management makes in an organization are those which involve capital budgeting. Capital budgeting concerns the process of planning and financing capital outlays whose returns are expected over several years in the future. The characteristics and data requirements of capital budgeting decisions, the concept of the time value of money, and the alternative capital budgeting approaches in general use will be discussed and evaluated in this chapter. The effects of income taxes and inflation on capital budgeting decisions, the lease-or-buy decision, and capital budgeting analysis under conditions of uncertainty will also be discussed.

Characteristics of Capital Investments

The business world is dynamic. In the long run, a company can maintain a competitive edge only if it continues to develop and produce products to meet changing demand. In order to accomplish this objective, companies must continue to develop, upgrade and/or modify their facilities. "When", "what", and "how" to do this constitute capital investment decisions. Two major types of capital investment decisions are:

1. Expansion decisions—For example, should a firm buy an additional piece of equipment, or build a new plant to meet expected increase in demand? Should the current facilities be expanded or modified to produce new products?

2. Replacements decisions—Should a firm replace present equipment with new and more efficient equipment in order to reduce costs?

These capital investments or expenditures are different from operating expenditures in two ways:

1. they are usually large in amount, and
2. they are made in expectation of benefits to be received over a number of years in the future.

Therefore, capital investments are major long-term commitments of funds that will affect a firm's long-run profitability.

Data Requirements for Capital Budgeting Decisions

Capital investments are usually made if their expected returns are large enough to cover their anticipated expenses in the future and the risks of committing funds to them in the present. In evaluating individual investment projects, the following quantitative data may be relevant:

1. Expected future revenues (or benefits) from the project,
2. Expected costs and expenses required by the project,
3. The expected life of the project,
4. Estimated salvage value,
5. Tax expenses or benefits,
6. The minimum desired rate of return.

In the entire process of capital budgeting, probably nothing is more important than reliable estimates of the necessary data. Reliable data depend on good judgment in estimating and forecasting. These are not routine clerical tasks, but require continuous evaluation by qualified personnel such as accountants, economists, cost analysts, engineers and managers.

The Concept of the Time Value of Money

Cash in hand today is more valuable than an equal amount of cash to be received a year from today. This results from the opportunity cost of the interest which could be earned on it during the year. Since capital investments are long-term commitments of funds, and money has a time value, managers need a method of determining if a capital investment made now can be justified by expected receipts from the projct in the future. Managers need means to convert future receipts and expenses into present values so that net expected cash inflows can be compared with the present cash outlays on an equivalent basis. Compound interest theory provides managers with the technique to make the comparison. In the following section, four basic formulas for calculating the time value of money will be discussed.

FUTURE VALUE OF A SINGLE PRESENT AMOUNT

The future value of a single present amount is the amount of cash that will be received after n periods from an investment made now. The formula to compute the future value of a single present amount is:

$$FV = PV\,(1+i)^n \tag{1}$$

where
PV = Principal (i.e., the present amount invested now),
i = the rate of interest,
n = number of periods from now.

For example, if a person deposits \$100 today in a savings account paying five percent interest, the amount to be received by the person from the bank would be \$105 a year from now and \$110.25 two years from now. These amounts are determined as follows:

1. one year from now:
   $\$100\,(1 + .05) = \$105.$
2. two years from now:
   $\$100\,(1 +.05)^2$
   $= \$105(1+.05)$
   $= \$110.25.$

Illustration 16-1 shows the future value of a deposit of \$100 for one year and two years at a five percent rate of interest. The interest for the first year is \$5 and for the second year is \$5.25. More interest is earned in the second year because the \$5 earned in the first year is added to the original principal of \$100 in computing interest for the second year. This is known as compounded interest.

PRESENT VALUE OF A SINGLE FUTURE AMOUNT

When a single amount of cash, FV, is to be received n periods into the future, the present value of that amount is:

$$PV = \frac{FV}{(1+i)^n} \tag{2}$$

Illustration 16-1 Future Value of a Single Present Amount

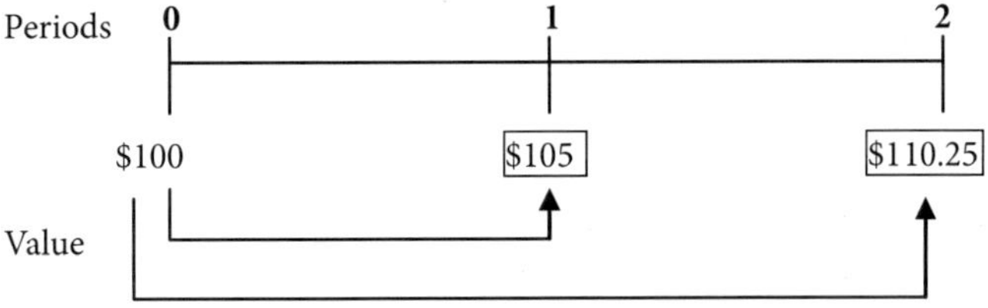

In this equation, i is the interest rate at which funds can currently be invested. Equation (2) is simply a transformation of Equation (1). In the previous example, FV = \$110.25, i = 5%, and n = 2, the present value can be determined from Equation (2) as follows:

$$PV = \frac{\$110.25}{(1+0.05)^2} = \frac{\$110.25}{1.1025} = \$100$$

As shown in this calculation, \$100 is the present value of \$110.25 two years from now at a five percent interest rate. Illustration 16-2 shows the relationship between the present value of \$100 and the future value of \$110.25 two years from now.

Future Value of an Annuity

An annuity is defined as a series of payments (or receipts) of a fixed amount for a specified number of years. The future value of an annuity is the amount that will be available n periods in the future when an amount (A) is invested at the end of each period. The formula to compute the future value of an annuity is:

$$FV_n = A(1+i)^{n-1} + A(1+i)^{n-2} + \ldots\ldots + A(1+i) + A \qquad (3)$$
$$= A\left[\frac{(1+i)^n - 1}{i}\right]$$

As shown in the formula, the first deposit is made at the end of the first year and earns interest for n – 1 periods, the second deposit is made at the end of the second year and earns interest for n – 2 periods, and the last deposit is made at the end of the nth period and earns no interest. For example, if a person deposited \$100 in a savings account paying five percent interest at the end of each year for three years, how much would be available to the person at the end of three years? Using Equation (3), we can determine the future value for the annuity as follows:

$$\$100(1+.05)^2 + \$100(1+.05) + \$100$$
$$= \$110.25 + \$105 + \$100$$
$$= \$315.25,$$

Or

$$\$100\left[\frac{(1+.05)^3 - 1}{.05}\right]$$
$$= \$100\ (3.1525)$$
$$= \$315.25.$$

Illustration 16-3 shows the calculation of the future value of a deposit of \$100 at a five percent interest rate at the end of each year for three years.

Illustration 16-2Present Value of a Single Future Amount

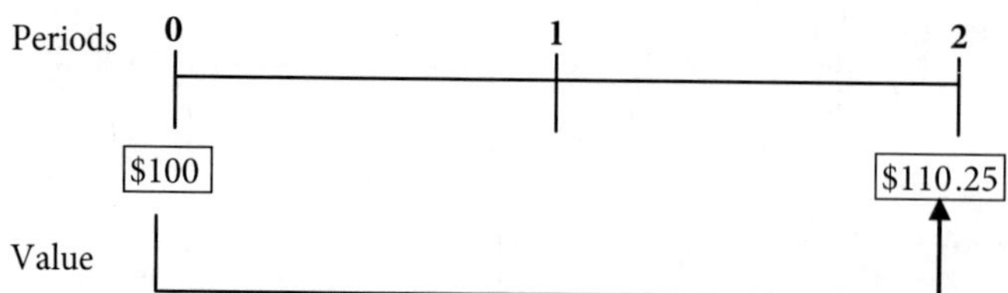

Illustration 16-3 Future Value of an Annuity

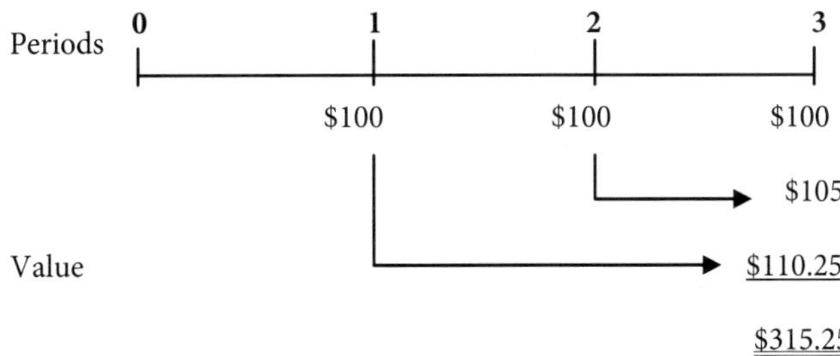

Present Value of an Annuity

When an annuity of amount A is to be received at the end of each period for n periods, the present value of the annuity is:

$$PV_n = \frac{A}{(1+i)} + \frac{A}{(1+i)^2} + \ldots\ldots + \frac{A}{(1+i)^n}$$

$$= A\left[\frac{1-(1+i)^{-n}}{i}\right] \tag{4}$$

As shown in the formula, payments are assumed to be made at the end of each period. In the present value calculations, future values are discounted back to the present. For example, what is the present value of an annuity of a payment of $100. at the end of each year for three years at an interest rate of five percent? Using Equation (4), we can determine the present value of this annuity as follows:

$$\frac{\$100}{(1+.05)} + \frac{\$100}{(1+.05)^2} + \frac{\$100}{(1+.05)^3}$$

$$= \$95.24 + \$90.70 + \$86.38$$
$$= \$272.32,$$

or

$$\$100\left[\frac{1-(1+.05)^{-3}}{.05}\right]$$

$$= \$100\ (2.7232)$$
$$= \$272.32.$$

Illustration 16-4 shows the calculation for the example.

Illustration 16-4 Present Value of an Annuity

Periods 0 1 2 3

$100 $100 $100

Value $90.70

$86.38

$272.32

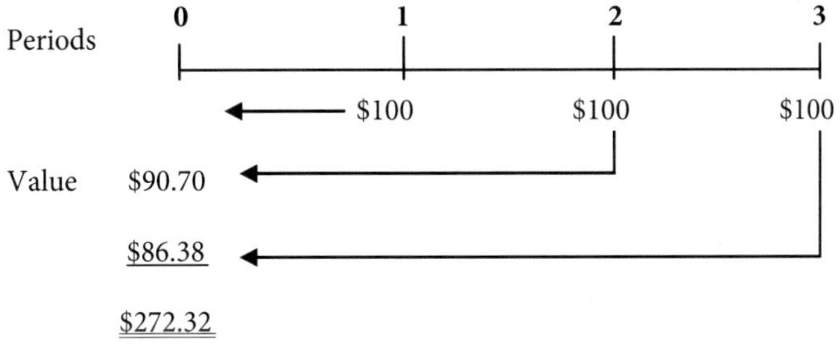

Compound Interest and Present Value Tables

Four basic formulas for calculating the time value of money have been discussed. Because some of these formulas are difficult to remember, they are seldom used in practice. Compound interest and present value tables are normally used instead. These tables, which are included in an appendix to this chapter, show present or future values for an amount of $1 at various interest rates over different time periods.

Table 16-1 contains the future value of a single present amount of $1. For an interest rate i, the value of $1 at the end of n periods into the future can be read from the body of the table. From these factors, the future value of any other amount can be calculated. For example, the future value of $100 in 10 years invested now at an interest rate of 6% is:

$$\begin{aligned} FV &= \$100\ (\text{FV of } \$1) \\ &= \$100\ (1.7908) \\ &= \$179.08 \end{aligned}$$

Table 16-2 shows the present value of a single future amount of $1 to be received n periods in the future. From the discount factors in the body of the table, the present value of other amounts can be calculated. As an example, the present value of $100 to be received in 10 years at an interest rate of 6% is determined as follows:

$$\begin{aligned} PV &= \$100\ (\text{PV of } \$1) \\ &= \$100\ (.558) \\ &= \$55.80 \end{aligned}$$

The future value of an annuity of $1 over various periods and at several interest rates is shown in Table 16-3. The compound interest factors in this table are used like those in the previous tables. An annuity of $100 per year invested for 10 years at an interest rate of 6% will have the future value:

$$\begin{aligned} FV_{10} &= \$100\ (\text{FV of annuity of } \$1) \\ &= \$100\ (13.1808) \\ &= \$1{,}318.08 \end{aligned}$$

The final table, Table 16-4, contains the present value of an annuity of $1 given the time period covered by the annuity and the interest rate. The present value of other amounts are likewise calculated from these discount factors. A series of payments of $100 for each of the next 10 years has the following present value at an interest rate of 6 percent:

$$\begin{aligned} PV_{10} &= \$100\ (\text{PV of annuity of } \$1) \\ &= \$100\ (7.360) \\ &= \$736.00. \end{aligned}$$

The present value tables, Table 16-2 and Table 16-4, are commonly used by businesses in evaluating capital investment projects. They enable the cost accountant to easily state future cash inflows and outflows in terms of their values at the present time. These can then be compared to the present cash outflows required by the investment, and the desirability of the investment determined. The approach to evaluating capital investments in this way utilizes *discounted cash flow* methods, and will be described in detail later in this chapter.

Project Evaluation Methods

In a business firm, since funds available for long-term capital investments are limited, an investment project available to management is usually competing with other projects available at the same time. Therefore, all projects under consideration should be evaluated, ranked, and chosen in terms of their relative benefits and costs. Benefits may be measured in different ways by different companies at different times and situations. For example, a firm's objective in a particular situation may be to avert risk, to improve long-run profitability, or to improve short-run earnings per share. A number of different approaches have been developed to measure different benefits. The three most commonly used methods of evaluating capital investment projects are: (1) Payback period, (2) Accounting rate of return, and (3) Discounted cash flow. Each of these methods has its advantages and disadvantages. The selection of an approach or approaches depends upon management's objectives.

The Payback Period

The payback period method evaluates projects in terms of the length of time required to recover the initial investment outlays. The formula to calculate the payback period of a project with uniform cash inflows is:

$$P = \frac{I}{C} \tag{5}$$

Where
P = Payback period,
I = Initial investment outlay,
C = Net annual cash inflows (or cash savings).

The payback period is the period required for the net cash inflows from a project to recover the initial investment outlays. For example, assume that a company is considering a project costing $10,000 with a life of five years and expected annual cash inflows of $2,500. In this example, the payback period is

$$P = \frac{\$10,000}{\$2,500} = 4\ Years$$

If the annual cash inflows are not the same each year, the preparation of a schedule of cumulative cash inflows is used in determining the payback period. Assume that the Diamond Company is considering a project costing $10,000, the life of the project is five years, and the expected net annual cash inflows are $3,000, $3,000, $4,000, $3,000, and $3,000 in each year. Illustration 16-5 provides a schedule of cumulative cash inflows for the project.

In this example, the payback period of the project is three years. The initial investment of $10,000 will be fully recovered during the third year.

Payback Reciprocal The payback reciprocal is sometimes used because it measures the annual cash inflow as a percent of the initial investment. It is computed in the following manner:

$$Payback\ Reciprocal\ = \frac{1}{P} = \frac{C}{I}$$

The payback reciprocal approximates the rate of return on a project whenever its life is at least twice the payback period, and when uniform cash inflows are expected. The rate of return

Illustration 16-5 The Diamond Company Schedule of Cumulative Cash Inflows

Year	Net Cash Inflows	Cumulative Cash Inflows
1	$ 3,000	$3,000
2	3,000	6,000
3	4,000	10,000
4	3,000	13,000
5	3,000	16,000

will be described later in this chapter. For example, consider a project with an investment of $25,000 generating annual net cash inflows of $5,000 for 10 years. In this example, the payback period is $25,000/$5,000 = 5 Years and the payback reciprocal is $5,000/$25,000 = 20%. The 20 percent provides a reasonable approximation to the true rate of return.

The payback method is simple to compute and easy to understand. It places a high degree of emphasis on liquidity, and is useful when the danger of obsolescence is great. This approach is often used by companies with weak financial positions, who wish to limit capital investments to those projects that promise a rapid payback. This method has been criticized as a misleading method for capital budgeting because it ignores the time value of money and the over-all profitability of the project. However, some adjustments can be made to improve payback analysis in this respect. The following discussions show how this is done.

Payback Analysis and the Time Value of Money The concept and importance of the time value of money in capital budgeting has been discussed in an earlier section of this chapter. The payback period can readily be modified to reflect the timing differences in cash flows. Let's revisit the Diamond Company problem. If the company's cost of capital is 10 percent, then the schedule of cumulative cash inflows in Illustration 16-5 can be restated to show the present values of these inflows. This is done in Illustration 16-6.

When the time value of money is considered, the payback period of the project is almost four years rather than three years as calculated previously. This example demonstrates how considering the time value of money can lead to a different decision from that which would be made using the simple payback period.

Payback Analysis and the Salvage Value Traditional payback analysis determines how long it will take for the cash required for an investment to be recovered by the net cash flows from it. A more fundamental question concerns the time period over which an investment outlay will be recovered when the salvage value of the investment is also considered. The method which considers the salvage value of a project in the payback calculation is called the *bail-out method.* This modification represents an improvement because it provides a better measure of the overall cash return from thepro-ject. Moreover, the salvage value of a project may reflect the value of the future cash flows generated by the project. The bail-out method effectively adjusts

Illustration 16-6 The Diamond Company Schedule of Cumulative Present Value of Cash Inflows

Year	Cash Inflows	Present Value (i=10%)	Cumulative Present Value of Cash Inflows
1	$3,000	$2,727	$ 2,727
2	3,000	2,479	5,206
3	4,000	3,005	8,211
4	3,000	2,049	10,260
5	3,000	1,862	12,123

the measure of return to reflect a project's profitability beyond its payback period. The bail-out period is reached when the present value of the cumulative cash flows plus the present value of the salvage value is equal to the initial investment outlay.

In the Diamond Company problem, assume that the salvage value of the project at the end of each year is as follows:

Year	Salvage value
1	$6,000
2	5,000
3	4,000
4	3,000
5	2,500

The calculations using the bail-out method for the project are given in Illustration 16-7. The bail-out payback period in this example is less than three years.

Accounting Rate of Return (Unadjusted Rate of Return)

The accounting rate of return is calculated by dividing the average annual net income from a project by either the original investment or by the average investment of the project. The formulas to calculate the accounting rates of returns are:

1. Based on the original investment:

$$R = \frac{\begin{array}{l}\text{Average annual net income (or savings)}\\ \text{after taxes and depreciaton}\end{array}}{\text{Original Investment}} \tag{6}$$

2. Based on the average investment:

$$R = \frac{\begin{array}{l}\text{Average annual net income (or savings)}\\ \text{after taxes and depreciaton}\end{array}}{(\text{Original Investment} + \text{Salvage Value})/2} \tag{7}$$

Assume that a company expects a total net income of $500,000 after taxes and before depreciation from a project over a ten-year period.

Illustration 16-7 The Diamond CompanySchedule of the Sum of Cumulative Present Value of Cash Inflows and Present Value of the Salvage Value at the End of the Year

Year	(1) Cumulative Present Value of Cash Inflows (from Illustration 16-6)	(2) Salvage Value at End of Each Year	(3) Present Value of Salvage Value	(4) Cumulative Present Value of Cash Inflows and Salvage Value
1	$ 2,727	$6,000	$5,454	$ 8,181
2	5,206	5,000	4,130	9,336
3	8,211	4,000	3,003	11,214
4	10,260	3,000	2,049	12,309
5	12,123	2,500	1,553	13,676

The original investment for the project is $200,000 with an expected salvage value of $40,000 at the end of ten years. In this example, the accounting rate of return would be computed as:

Total net income over ten years before depreciation	$500,000
Less: Total depreciation ($200,000-$40,000)	160,000
Total net income after taxes and depreciation	$340,000
Average annual net income after taxes and depreciation =	$340,000/10
	= $ 34,000
Accounting rate of return based on original investment =	$ 34,000/$200,000
	= 17%
Accounting rate of return based on average investment	$= \frac{\$34,000}{(\$200,00 + 40,000)/2}$
	= 28.33%

The method is simple to calculate and easy to understand. As a measure of rate of return, it places the emphasis on the profitability of the project rather than on liquidity as does the payback period. However, the accounting rate of return considers the average net income regardless of how far into the future that it may be realized, and the time value of money is not considered. The approach is also referred as the "unadjusted rate of return".

Discounted Cash Flow

Discounted cash flow methods focus on flows of cash instead of revenue and expenses, and consider the time value of money. Two discounted cash flow methods used in capital budgeting are the net present value approach and the internal rate of return approach.

Net Present Value Approach This approach computes the present value of all expected future cash flows at a minimum desired rate of return. This minimum desired rate is sometimes called the *cost of capital.* Their total present value is then compared with the initial cash outlay to determine the net present value of the project. If the net present value is zero or positive, the project is acceptable. If the net present value is negative, the project is not desirable because its expected return is less than the minimum desired return. For example, the Sunflowers Company is considering buying a $90,000 machine which has an expected useful life of five years. The new machine is expected to generate net cash inflows of $25,000 per year with no salvage value. The company's minimum desired rate of return is 10 percent. Should the new machine be purchased? Illustration 16-8 shows the calculation of the net present value for the machine.

According to the analysis in Illustration 16-8, the project is acceptable because its net present value is $4,775.

A variation on the net present value approach utilizes the *present value index* (also known as the profitability index). The present value index may be computed with the data used for the present value calculations. It is computed as follows:

$$\textit{Present Value Index} = \frac{\textit{Total Present Value of Cash Flows}}{\textit{Initial Cash Outlay}}$$

In the Sunflowers Company problem, the total present value was $94,775 and the initial outlay was $90,000. The present value index is $94,775/$90,000 = 1.053.

A project is considered acceptable when its present value index is greater than or equal to one. When the present value index is less than 1, the net present value is negative and the

Illustration 16-8 Sunflowers Company Calculation of Net Present Value

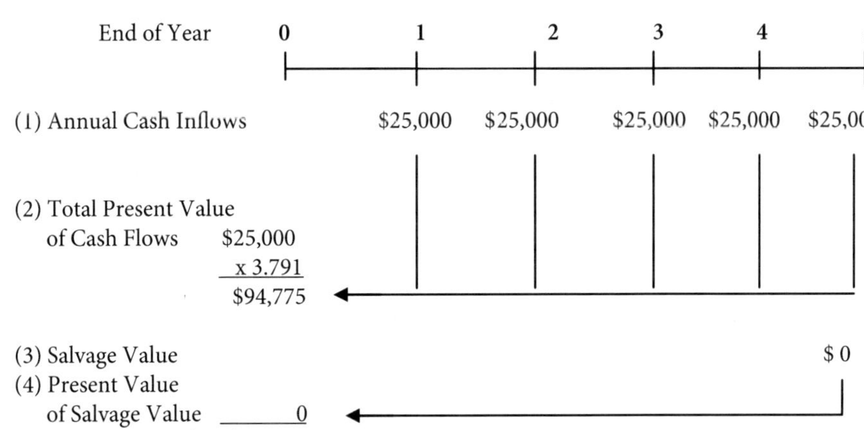

Total Present Value $94,775
Initial Outlay (90,000)
Net Present Value $ 4,775

project is not acceptable. In comparing two or more projects, the project having the larger present value index is more desirable.

Internal Rate of Return (Time Adjusted Rate of Return) Approach The internal rate of return is the rate of interest at which the present value of expected net cash flows from a project equals its initial cash outlays. Mathematically, the internal rate of return is the interest rate i in the following equation:

$$\sum_{t=1}^{n}[NCI_t(1+i)^{-t}] = Initial\ outlays$$

where
NCI_t = the net cash flows from the project in period t
n = the expected life of the project.

In evaluating a proposed investment, the internal rate of return is compared to the minimum desired rate of return to determine whether a project should be accepted. If the internal rate of return is equal to or greater than the minimum desired rate of return, the project is desirable. If the internal rate of return is less than the minimum desired rate of return, the project is not desirable. The internal rate of return for the new machine considered by the Sunflowers Company can be determined by setting:

$$\sum_{t=1}^{5}[\$25{,}000(1+t)^{-t}] = \$90{,}000$$

$$\frac{\$25{,}000}{(1+i)^5} + \frac{\$25{,}000}{(1+i)^4} + \frac{\$25{,}000}{(1+i)^3} + \frac{\$25{,}000}{(1+i)^2} + \frac{\$25{,}000}{(1+i)} = \$90{,}000$$

or

$$\$25{,}000\left[\frac{1-(1+i)^{-5}}{i}\right] = \$90{,}000$$

so $$\frac{1-(1+i)^{-5}}{i} = 3.6$$

The value 3.6 is the discount factor which is used to determine the internal rate of return i. In a problem with uniform expected annual cash inflows, the discount factor is simply equal to initial outlays divided by annual cash inflows. The discount factor is then located in a table of present values for an annuity of $1. In the Sunflowers example, the discount factor of 3.6 equates a five-year series of $25,000 annual cash inflows with the initial outlays of $90,000. Referring to Table 16-4, we find that a factor of 3.6 represents a 12 percent rate of return for n = 5. Therefore, the internal rate of return of the new machine is 12 percent. Since the internal rate of return exceeds the firm's minimum desired rate of return, 10 percent, the project is desirable.

The example just given assumes uniform annual cash inflows. If annual cash inflows are not uniform, a trial-and-error method must be used to calculate the internal rate of return. Choose a reasonable interest rate and compute the present value of the cash inflows. If this present value does not equal the initial outlay, continue selecting rates until they are equal. This may require interpolating to obtain values of i not shown in the present value table. The interest rate at which the net present value of future cash inflows equals the initial outlay for the project is its internal rate of return.

In the Sunflowers Company problem, assume that there is an expected salvage value of $10,000 at the end of five years, the annual cash inflows would be as follows:

Year	*Cash Inflows*
1	$25,000
2	25,000
3	25,000
4	25,000
5	25,000 + 10,000 = 35,000

If an interest rate of 20 percent is used to discount the expected cash inflows, the present value of the expected cash inflows is $78,770.

Year	*Expected Cash Flows*	*Present Value Factor (20%)*	*Present Value*
1	$25,000	.833	$20,825
2	25,000	.694	17,350
3	25,000	.579	14,475
4	25,000	.482	12,050
5	35,000	.402	14,070
		Total Present Value	$78,770

If an interest rate of 10 percent is used, the present value of the cash inflows is $100,960.

Year	*Expected Cash Inflows*	*Present Value Factor (10%)*	*Present Value*
1	$25,000	.909	$ 22,725
2	25,000	.826	20,650
3	25,000	.751	18,775
4	25,000	.683	17,075
5	35,000	.621	21,735
		Total Present Value	$100,960

Therefore, the internal rate of return is somewhere between 10 percent and 20 percent. The internal rate of return can be reasonably approximated by straight-line interpolation as follows:

	Interest Rate		*Total Present Value*		
at	10	percent	$100,960		
				10,960	
at	?	percent	90,000		22,190
				11,230	
at	20	percent	78,770		

The approximate internal rate of return is:

$$= 10\% + \frac{10\%}{22,190}(10,960) = 14.94\%$$

or

$$= 20\% - \frac{10\%}{22,190}(11,230) = 14.94\%$$

Effects of Income Taxes and Inflation on Capital Budgeting Decisions

The preceding discussion has ignored the effects of income tax and inflation on capital budgeting decisions. Income taxes are an important aspect of business life, and their effect on investment decisions is usually significant. An investment decision may be affected by many income tax factors, for example, short-term and long-term gains, loss carrybacks and carryforwards, alternative depreciation methods, and special tax incentives allowed in the past. Because income tax implications may be very complex, professional tax accountants are usually consulted regarding them. Similarly, inflation reduces the general purchasing power of the monetary unit and inflates future cash flows of capital investments. As a result, inflation affects capital budgeting decisions through its impact on the present value of cash flows. In this section, we will discuss some effects of income taxes on the determination of cash flows for capital budgeting decisions. We will also discuss the impact of inflation on capital budgeting decisions.

Income Taxes and Cash Flows

The payment of income taxes represents a cash outflow, and a tax saving represents a cash inflow. If a firm has an income-tax rate of 40 percent, each dollar of the firm's cash revenue would generate only $.60 net cash inflow after tax. Similarly, each dollar of the firm's cash expense would represent only $.60 net cash outflow after tax. For example, consider a firm that has cash sales of $20,000 and cash expenses of $10,000 each month. Further assume that the firm's income tax rate is 40 percent.

The firm's after-tax net cash inflow may be computed as follows:

Sales	$20,000
Expenses	10,000
Cash Inflow (before tax)	$10,000
Income Taxes (40%)	4,000
Net Cash Inflow (after tax)	$6,000

A formula can be developed to compute the after-tax net cash inflow for the above example as follows:

1. After-tax Cash Inflow = Cash Revenues x (1- Income-tax rate) =	$20,000(1-.4)
=	$12,000
2. After-tax Cash Outflow = Cash Expenses x (1- Income-tax rate) =	$10,000(1- .4)
=	$ 6,000
3. Net Cash Inflow (after-tax) = (1) – (2) = $12,000 – $6,000 =	$ 6,000

Depreciation and the Tax Shield

The foregoing example assumes that all expenses are represented by cash expenditures. Other expenses, such as depreciation and amortization, represent expenses in determining taxable income but do not entail cash outlays. When calculating net cash inflows, depreciation and amortization must be added back to net income to determine the after-tax net cash inflow. Depreciation and amortization provide a shield against tax payments. The following illustration will demonstrate the tax shielding effects of noncash expenses.

Corona Company is considering the purchase of a new machine for $11,000. The machine has an expected life of five years and a salvage value of $1,000 at the end of its life. The new machine will provide cash cost savings of $4,000 per year. The income-tax rate is 40 percent. The after-tax net cash inflow for the example may be computed as follows:

Annual cash cost savings (before subtraction of depreciation)	$4,000
Less: depreciation (straight-line)	2,000
Incremental income subject to tax	$2,000
Income tax (.4)	800
Net income	$1,200
Add: depreciation	2,000
After-tax net cash inflow	$3,200

Inflation and Cash Flows

Inflation is the decline in the general purchasing power of the monetary unit. In the past three decades, the average annual inflation rate was about 3%. Even with this low average annual rate of inflation, the purchasing power of the monetary unit will still be significantly reduced over the long term. It is, therefore, critical to take into account the inflation effect on cash flows associated with capital budgeting decisions.

There are two methods that can be used to incorporate the inflation effect in capital budgeting decisions, namely nomimal method and real method. Since data on cash flows and nominal interest rate are readily available from existing accounting systems, managers prefer nominal method to real method. However, these two methods produce identical results.

Nominal method uses a nomimal interest rate to discount cash flows represented in nominal dollars. In contrast, real method uses a real interest rate to discount cash flows represented in real dollars. A nominal interest rate is calculated as the sum of a real interest rate plus an inflation premium as follows:

Norminal interest rate = Real interest rate + Inflation premium
= Real interest rate + Inflation rate
+ Real interest rate x Inflation rate
or = [(1+Real interest rate)x(1+Inflation rate)]-1

where a real interest rate consists of risk free rate (i.e., the interest rate on risk-free long-term government bonds) and risk premium (i.e., the premium needed for bearing risk). That is, a real interest rate is the rate of return required to cover investment risk and the decline in purchasig power of the monetary unit as a result of inflation.

To illustrate the application of these two methods, let's assume that Canyon Company is considering the purchase of a new machine costing $10,000. The new machine is to be depreciated on the sum-of-the-years'-digits method. The salvage value at the end of 4 years is zero. The estimated annual pre-tax incomes from the new machine are $5,000. The company's income tax rate is 25% and required rate of return is 10%. If the annual inflation rate is expected to be 3% for the next 4 years, the company's estimated cash flows for the next 4 years can be summarized in illustration 16-11.

Nominal Method

Under the nominal method, the present value for Canyon Company is shown in Illustration 16-12.

Illustration 16-11 Cash Flows Canyon Company

Year	After-Tax Income*	Depreciation	Tax Shield***	After-Tax Cash Flows
0	$(10,000)	--	--	$(10,000)
1	3,750	4,000**	1,000	4,750
2	3,750	3,000	750	4,500
3	3,750	2,000	500	4,250
4	3,750	1,000	250	4,000

* After-tax cash flows =$5,000 x (1 -25%) = $3,750 for years 1 through 4.

** Depreciation = $10,000 x (4/(1+2+3+4)) = $4,000

*** Tax shield = Depreciation x 25%

Illustration 16-12 Cash Flows Canyon Company

Year	After-Tax Cash Flows	PV Factor*	Present Value**
0	$(10,000)	1.0000	$(10,000)
1	4,750	0.8826	4,192
2	4,500	0.7790	3,506
3	4,250	0.6876	2,922
4	4,000	0.6068	2,427
NPV			$ 3,047

* PV factor is based on nominal interest rate 13.3% ([=(1+10%)x(1+3%) -1]).

** Present value = Total after tax cash flows x PV factor

Illustration 16-13 Cash Flows Canyon Company

Year	After-Tax Incomes	Cumulative Inflation Rate	After-Tax Real Dollars	PV Factor*	Present Value
0	$(10,000)	1.0000	$(10,000)	1.0000	$(10,000)
1	4,750	(1.03)=1.0300	4,612	0.9091	4,193
2	4,500	$(1.03)^2$ =1.0609	4,242	0.8264	3,505
3	4,250	$(1.03)^3$ =1.0927	3,889	0.7513	2,922
4	4,000	$(1.03)^4$ =1.1255	3,554	0.6830	2,427
NPV					$ 3,047

* PV factor is based on the required rate of return 10%

Real Method

The real method involves two steps. Step 1 converts the nominal dollars into real dollars and step 2 discounts the real dollars using the real interest rate. Illustration 16-13 reports the present value for Canyon Company using the real method.

As can be seen from the results of illustrations 16-12 and 16-13, the net present value (NPV) under both methods is identical, $3,047.

Summary

Capital budgeting involves the process of planning and financing capital outlays, which is one of the most important and difficult problems facing management. Before a capital investment decision can be made, the benefits expected from a project should be estimated and evaluated. Usually a decision to make a capital investment is dependent upon whether the future benefits expected from the project are large enough to cover the present cash outlays. The four most frequently used capital investment evaluation techniques are the payback period, accounting rate of return, net present value, and internal rate of return. The selection of a method to be used is usually dependent upon the overall objectives of the firm.

Income taxes in most cases play an important role in capital budgeting decisions and must be considered in the analysis. Depreciation and amortization expenses do not require cash outflows but are deductible for tax shield against tax payments. Since inflation reduces the general purchasing power of the monetary unit, it has a significnat impact on the present value of cash flows associated with capital budgeting. Uncertainty may affect capital budgeting analysis through the estimates of future events. The uncertain nature of future estimates makes capital budgeting a difficult but challenging area.

Key Definitions

Accounting rate of return	A measure of profitability for an investment project. It is determined by dividing the average annual net income from the project by the original investment or the average investment of the project.
Annuity	A series of payments or receipts which are incurred for a specified number of years.
Capital budgeting	The process of determining how to allocate a firm's resources to proposed projects.
Cost of capital	The minimum rate of return which is required by a firm for an investment project.
Inflation	The decline in the general purchasing power of the monetary unit.
Internal rate of return	The interest rate which, when used to discount cash flows, will make the present value of cash inflows equal to the present value of cash outflows for a project.
Net present value	An approach used to evaluate investment projects which discounts all cash inflows and outflows of a project back to the present period. The cost of capital is used as the discount rate.
Nominal interest rate	The sum of a real interest rate plus an inflation premium.
Payback period method	A technique used to evaluate alternative projects in terms of the length of time required to recover the initial cash outlays.
Payback reciprocal	Is equal to annual cash inflow divided by initial investment. It approximates the true rate of return when the project life is at least twice the payback period and cash flows are uniform.
Real interest rate	The rate of return required to cover investment risk and the decline in purchasing power of the monetary unit because of inflation.

Appendix A

The Lease-or-Buy Decision

Leasing is a special form of financing. In recent years, leasing some types of assets, such as automobiles, buildings, and machine tools, has become a common practice. Some of the advantages of leasing are the following:

1. A lease contract usually covers maintenance and servicing of the asset being leased.
2. A lease eliminates a large amount of the initial cash outlay required to purchase the asset.
3. Leasing removes or reduces the economic risk of owning an asset.

Lease agreements can be classified into two types: capital leases and operating leases. A capital lease is a lease agreement that is non-cancellable. It requires lease payments over the entire lease period even though the lessee may not continue to use the leased asset. An operating lease is a lease agreement that is cancellable at the option of the lessee or the lessor at certain times specified in the contract. Since capital leases are non-cancellable and require lease payments over the lease period, the decision to lease or to purchase can be considered a capital budgeting decision. The choice between a lease and a purchase can be analyzed by comparing cash flows for leasing and cash flows for owning an asset. The project evaluation methods discussed earlier in this chapter can be used to make the cash flow comparison and obtain a desirable choice. The following examples illustrates this type of analysis.

Houston Company considers obtaining communication equipment from one of two vendors: outright purchase from P Company and lease from L Company. Information pertaining to the equipment offered is:

Purchase:
Purchase price (including installation) $24,000
Estimated maintenance, taxes, and insurance .... $ 4,000 per year
Miscellaneous expenses .... $ 3,000 per year
Expected useful life .... 5 years
Expected salvage value .... $ 1,000
Depreciation method: Straight-line
Lease:
Annual lease payment (including maintenance, taxes, and insurance) .... $ 8,000
Installation charge .... $ 3,000
Miscellaneous expenses .... $ 2,500 per year

If the Houston Company purchases the equipment, it will pay cash. The Company's desired rate of return is 12 percent. The Company's income tax rate is 48 percent. The lease contract is non-cancellable and runs for five years.

Illustration 16-14 analyzes the relevant annual cash outflows for each proposal assuming a depreciation basis of $23,000. The difference in annual cash outflows between the two proposals is summarized in Illustration 16-15.

Illustration 16-15 shows that an additional cash outlay of $22,440 is required by the purchase proposal in year 0. It also shows that annual cash outflows of leasing are less than the annual cash outflows of purchasing. The difference in annual cash outflows represents a cost savings in

Illustration 16-14 Houston Company Annual Cash Outflows for Purchase and Lease Proposals

	Start-up	*Year 1*	*Year 2*	*Year 3*	*Year 4*	*Year 5*
Purchase						
Tax Deductible Expenses:						
Depreciation	$0	$4,600	$4,600	$4,600	$4,600	$4,600
Maintenance, Taxes, and Insurance	0	4,000	4,000	4,000	4,000	4,000
Miscellaneous Expenses	0	3,000	3,000	3000	3000	3000
Total Tax Deductible Expenses	0	$11,600	$11,600	$11,600	$11,600	$11,600
Less: Tax Effects:						
Income Tax Savings (11,600x.48)	0	-5,568	-5,568	-5,568	-5,568	-5,568
Expenses After Tax Effects	0	$6,032	$6,032	$6,032	$6,032	$6,032
Purchase Costs	24,000	0	0	0	0	0
Less: Salvage Value	0	0	0	0	0	-1,000
Less: Depreciation	0	-4,600	-4,600	-4,600	-4,600	-4,600
Net Cash Outflows	$24,000	$1,432	$1,432	$1,432	$1,432	$432
Lease						
Tax Deductible Expenses:						
Lease Payment	$0	$8,000	$8,000	$8,000	$8,000	$8,000
Installation Charge	3,000	0	0	0	0	0
Miscellaneous	0	2 500	2 500	2 500	2,500	2 500
Total Tax Deductible Expenses	3,000	10,500	10,500	10.5	10,500	10,500
Less: Income Tax Savings (.48)	-1,440	-5,040	-5,040	-5,040	-5,040	-5,040
Net Cash Outflows	$1,560	$5,460	$5,460	$5,460	$5,460	$5,460

Illustration 16-15 Houston Company Comparison of Net Cash Outflows Between Purchase and Lease Proposals

Year	*Purchase*	*Lease*	*Difference*	*Cumulative*
0	*$24,000*	*$1,560*	$22,440	$22,440
1	*$1,432*	*$5,460*	($4,028)	18,412
2	$1,432	$5,460	($4,028)	14,384
3	$1,432	$5,460	($4,028)	10,356
4	$1,432	$5,460	($4,028)	6,328
5	$432	$5,460	($5,028)	1,300
Total	$30,160	$28,860	$1,300	

Illustration 16-16 Houston Company The Present Value of Annual Cash Outflows for the Two Proposals (i =12%)

Year	*Purchase*	*Lease*	*Difference*	*Cumulative*
0	$24,000.00	$1,560.00	$22,440.00	$22,440.00
1	$1,278.78	$4,875.78	($3,597.00)	$18,843.00
2	$1,141.30	$4,351.62	($3,210.32)	$15,632.68
3	$1,019.58	$3,887.52	($2,867.94)	$12,764.74
4	$910.75	$3,472.56	($2,561.81)	$10,202.94
5	$244.94	$3,095.82	($2,850.88)	$7,352.06
Total	$28,595.36	$21,243.30	$7,352.06	

the amount of $1,300 over the 5 year period in favor of leasing. This can be seen in Illustration 16-15 where the cumulative difference in cash outflows remains a positive amount overall when comparing leasing to purchasing. Thus, leasing is more desirable than purchasing.

The form of analysis described above is known as traditional payback analysis. As discussed in an earlier section of this chapter, this approach does not take the time value of money into consideration. However, the time value of money is an important factor and should be considered in capital budgeting decisions. Illustration 16-16 summarizes the present value of the difference and the cumulative difference in annual cash outflows between the two proposals. Illustration 16-16 shows that the cumulative difference of the present value of annual cash outflows is a positive amount of $7,352.06. This means that, when the time value of money is considered, the company cannot expect to recover the total additional initial outlay of $22,440 from the savings in annual cash outflows due to purchasing rather than leasing. The $7,352.06 also represents the difference in the present value of total cash outflows between the two proposals over the life of the equipment. This can be verified by subtracting the total present value of cash outflows under leasing from the total present value of cash outflows under purchasing, i.e., $28,595.36 – $21,243.30 = $7,352.06. Therefore, according to the net present value analysis and the payback analysis when the time value of money is considered, the lease proposal is more desirable than the purchase alternative.

Appendix B

Conflicts in Project Rankings

The net present value (NPV) method and the internal rate of return (IRR) method are two of the most common approaches for evaluating investment projects. The NPV method provides a relatively straight-forward rule for investment decisions: accept a project if the net present value is positive. Using the IRR method, a project should be accepted if the internal rate of return *is* greater than the cost of capital. When a single investment project is being considered, these two methods will lead to the same decision.

However, in a decision involving the selection of the best single project or group of projects from a set of project alternatives, the NPV method and the IRR method may provide different rankings of the desirability of projects. This contradiction is caused by different assumptions concerning the reinvestment rate made by each method. In this Appendix, we will first discuss the nature and problems of this conflict in ranking. Then an approach to reconcile the problem of different rankings will be presented.

To illustrate the nature of the problem, assume a firm is considering two mutually exclusive investment projects that are expected to generate cash flows as given in Illustration 16-17.

In this example, the internal rates of return for projects A and B are 22 percent and 47 percent, respectively. If the firm's cost of capital is 10 percent, the net present value of projects A and B are $984 and $500, respectively. Thus, project A is preferred if the NPV method is used while project B is preferred if the IRR is used.

Illustration 16-17 Cash Flows, Net Present Values, and Internal Rates of Return of Projects A and B

Year	Project A	Project B
	Cash Flows	
1	0	2,200
2	0	0
3	0	0
4	0	0
5	4,000	0
Present Value of Cash Inflows at 10%	$2,484	$2,000
Less: Initial Outlay ($1,500)	1,500	1,500
Net Present Value	$ 984	$ 500
Internal Rate of Return	22%	47%

Illustration 16-18 Comparison of Assumptions of the Reinvestment Rate of Return Between the Two Methods for Projects A and B

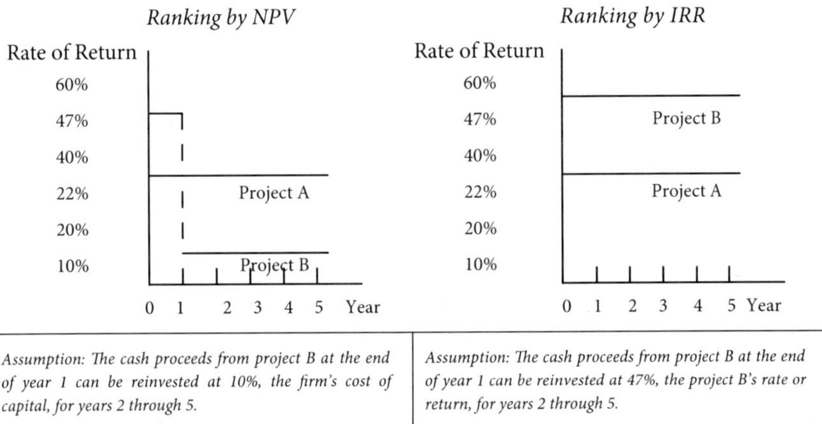

Assumption: The cash proceeds from project B at the end of year 1 can be reinvested at 10%, the firm's cost of capital, for years 2 through 5.	*Assumption: The cash proceeds from project B at the end of year 1 can be reinvested at 47%, the project B's rate or return, for years 2 through 5.*

As stated above, the conflict of rankings between the two methods is caused by different assumptions about the reinvestment rate of return on cash proceeds from the projects.[1] Under the IRR method, the reinvestment is assumed to earn the same rate of return as the original project. Under the NPV method, the reinvestment rate of return is the cost of capital. In the problem of Illustration 16-17, the reinvestment rate of return on the cash proceeds from project B under the NPV method is 10 percent, the firm's cost of capital. Under the IRR method, the reinvestment rate of return is the same as project B's rate of return, 47 percent. Because of their different assumptions of the reinvestment rate of return, the two methods give different rankings of investment projects. This difference is shown graphically in Illustration 16-18.

The reason for different rankings of investment projects under different discounted cash flow models has been discussed. A question that needs to be addressed concerns which method—the NPV method or the IRR method—should be used for ranking investment projects. In the example problem, what is the appropriate reinvestment rate of return for the cash proceeds

1 Similar conflicting results can occur when the terminal dates are the same but the investment outlays are different. In such cases, the conflict is caused by different assumptions about the rate of return on the difference between the amounts of investment required by the projects.

from project B for years 2 through 5? Is the appropriate reinvestment rate of return equal to the firm's cost of capital or project B's rate of return? Obviously, neither one is absolutely correct. The cash proceeds from project B at the end of year I would be reinvested in another project, which would earn a rate greater than the firm's cost of capital and may be different from project B's rate of return. The valid comparison is not simply between two projects, projects A and B, but between two alternative courses of action.[2]

One course of action is to accept project A; the other course of action is to accept project B plus another project after year 1. Accordingly, the ultimate criterion should be the terminal value[3] that the firm can expect from each alternative course of action. The ideal solution to the problem is to predict the reinvestment rate of return for the cash proceeds from project B for years 2 through 5. Then the terminal value of the course of action is calculated on the basis of the predicted reinvestment rate of return and compared to the terminal value from project A. The practical difficulties are in predicting the reinvestment rates of return for future projects, which are much greater than those for immediate projects.

The choice of a reinvestment rate depends upon the rate of return at which the cash proceeds from project B can be reinvested for years 2 through 5. If future reinvestment opportunities may be foreseen and measured, then their expected rate(s) of return can be used in the analysis. For example, if the reinvestment rate of return for the cash proceeds from project B in years 2 through 5 is 40 percent, then the terminal value of the course of action of project B plus another project will be $\$2,200\ (1 + 40\%)^4 = \$8,451.52$. This amount can be compared to the terminal value of project A, \$5,000, at the end of year 5 to determine the desirability of each course of action.

Future investment opportunities are usually not foreseeable with certainty and most likely change over time. Thus, the prediction of reinvestment rates for future unforeseeable projects is very difficult. But, generally, since no project will be accepted if it yields less than the firm's cost of capital, the reinvestment rate of return can be expected to be greater than the cost of capital. The reinvestment rate of return can be reasonably assumed to be greater than the cost of capital with a certain probability, for example 99 percent. Furthermore, from the firm's long-range and short-range profit planning and control budgets, the firm's expected rate of return for the period under consideration may be obtained. This expected rate of return may be considered as the mean value of the investment rates of return for the projects expected by the firm during the period. Therefore, although the future projects may not be foreseeable, the minimum value and the mean value of the investment rate of return for the period under consideration can still be estimated. Given the minimum value and the mean value of the reinvestment rate, a simulation model may be used to generate random reinvestment rates for the future projects if the statistical distribution of the rates of return is known. These random reinvestment rates can then be used in the problem to determine the terminal value of a course of action.

The proposed approach described above may be summarized in the following steps:

1. Consider the reinvestment rate of return to be greater than the firm's cost of capital with a certain probability, for example 99.74 percent.

2 Ezra Solomon, "Arithmetic of Capital Budgeting Decisions," *Journal of Business, XXIX*, No. 2, p. 127.

3 Terminal value is the total wealth that the firm can expect from a course of action by the terminal date of the longer-lived project.

2. Based on the firm's profit planning and control budgets, the expected rate of return for the period is determined. This expected rate of return is then used as the mean value of the reinvestment rate of return for the projects expected by the firm during the period.
3. Determine the statistical distribution of the firm's investment rates of return based on the historical data.
4. Employ a simulation model to generate random reinvestment rates of return for the period under consideration.
5. Calculate the terminal value for each course of action based on the random reinvestment rates of return generated in step 4.

In order to illustrate this approach, the following assumptions are added to the example problem described in Illustration 16-17.

1. The firm's reinvestment rate of return is greater than the cost of capital, 10 percent, for years 2 through 5 with a probability of 99.74 percent.
2. The firm's expected rate of return for years 2 through 5 is 31 percent.
3. The firm's investment rates of return are described statistically by a normal distribution.

It should be noted that different costs of capital and different expected rates of return can be assumed for each year during the period. The assumption of a normal distribution for investment rates of return is made for the reasons of simplicity; other types of distribution are likely to be found in practice.

Given the distribution for the investment rates of return, the mean value of 31 percent, and the minimum value of 10 percent with a probability of 99.74 percent standard deviation of the investment rates of return for the period under consideration can be estimated as:[4]

$$\sigma = \frac{31\% - 10\%}{3} = 7\%$$

Based on the mean value of 31 percent and the standard deviation of 7 percent, 1,000 normal random investment rates of return were generated for the projects expected during the period. The terminal value of the course of action of project B plus another project or other projects during the period is then calculated based on the above generated random rates of return. The mean value and the standard deviation of the terminal value of the course of action are calculated as $6,611.54, and $1,369.07, respectively. The calculated mean value and standard deviation of the terminal value of the action can thus be compared to the terminal value from project A to determine the ranking of the alternatives.

4 The area under the normal curve between the points obtained by moving three standard deviations in each direction from the mean is 99.74 percent.

Appendix C

Uncertainty in the Capital Budgeting Process

Estimates of cash inflows and outflows for future periods are usually subject to a certain degree of uncertainty. The capital budgeting analysis in this chapter so far has assumed certain estimates of cash inflows and outflows. The actual cash flows may prove to be different from the estimated amounts. These differences may arise due to changes in the salvage value of the project, the expected life of the project, or income tax rates. While various approaches have been developed to deal with problems of uncertainty in capital budgeting analysis, this appendix will discuss the expected value approach to highlight the effects of uncertainty on the capital budgeting process. The expected value is determined from a set of estimates about the probability of all possible outcomes. For purposes of illustration, cash flows will be treated as non-constant estimates in the following discussion. The determination of the expected value of cash inflows in a period can be illustrated by considering the following example.

Assume that a manager has considered the risks associated with his operation and derived the following possible cash flows for a project with the probability that the event will occur in a particular year:

Probability (P)	*Cash Inflow (A)*
0.10	*$10,000*
0.15	15,000
0.20	20,000
0.30	25,000
0.15	30,000
0.10	40,000

The expected value of cash inflows for a period can be determined by the following formula:

$$E(A) = \sum_{i=1}^{n} (A_i P_i) \qquad (8)$$

Where

E(A) = the expected value of cash flows for the year,

A_i = the amount of the ith possible cash flow,

P_i = the probability of occurrence of the ith possible cash flow.

In our current example, the expected value of cash flows for the year is:

E(A) = 0.1($10,000) + 0.15($15,000) + 0.2($20,000) + 0.3($25,000) + 0.15($30,000)
+ 0.1($40,000)
= $23,250.

The standard deviation which measures the dispersion of the probability distribution of cash flows for a period can be determined from the following formula:

$$\sigma = \sqrt{\sum_{i=1}^{n} [(A_i - E(A))]^2 P_i} \qquad (9)$$

For our current example, the standard deviation of the cash flows for the year is calculated as follows:

$$\sigma^2 = 0.1(10{,}000\text{-}23{,}250)^2 + 0.15(15{,}000\text{-}23{,}250)^2 + 0.2(20{,}000\text{-}23{,}250)^2$$
$$+ 0.3(25{,}000\text{-}23{,}250)^2 + 0.15(30{,}000\text{-}23{,}250)^2 + 0.1(40{,}000\text{-}23{,}250)^2$$
$$= \$65{,}691{,}025$$
$$\sigma^2 = \sqrt{65{,}691{,}025}$$
$$\sigma = \$8{,}105.$$

When uncertainty is considered in capital budgeting analysis, the payback period, accounting rate of return, net present value, and internal rate of return will not be known with certainty. For purposes of illustration, the following example will be used to demonstrate the calculation of the expected value and the standard deviation of net present value.

Assume that a company is considering buying a $100,000 machine which has an expected life of three years. The company has estimated the expected value of cash inflows and its related standard deviation for each year for the new machine as shown in the following table. The company's minimum desired rate of return is 10 percent.

	Cash Inflows (at end of each year)	
Year	*Expected Value*	*Standard Deviation*
1	*$40,000*	$2,000
2	60,000	3,000
3	50,000	2,000

The expected present value of the project is:

$$\$40{,}000(1+.10)^{-1} + \$60{,}000(1+.10)^{-2} + \$50{,}000(1+.10)^{-3}$$
$$= \$36{,}360 + 49{,}560 + 37{,}550$$
$$= \$123{,}470.00.$$

Therefore, the expected net present value is equal to $123,470.00 – $100,000 = $23,470.

The present value of the standard deviation for the project is:

$$= \sqrt{2{,}000^2(1+.10)^{-1} + 3{,}000^2(1+.10)^{-2} + 2{,}000^2(1+.10)^{-3}}$$
$$= \sqrt{3{,}636{,}000 + 7{,}434{,}000 + 3{,}004{,}000}$$
$$= \sqrt{14{,}074{,}000}$$
$$= \$3{,}752.$$

The resultant expected value ($23,470) and standard deviation ($3,752) of the net present value of the project can then be used to derive some probability statements concerning net present value intervals. For example, if the distribution of the net present value is normal, the company can expect a probability of 95.5 percent that the net present value of the project will be between $23,470 – 2($3,752) = $15,966 and $23,470 + 2($3,752) = $30,974.

Appendix D

Compound Interest and Present Value Tables

Table 16-1 Future value of $1.00

$$FV = PV(1 + i)^n$$

n	2%	2.5 %	3%	4%	5%	6%	8%	10%
1	1.0200	1.0250	1.0300	1.0400	1.0500	1.0600	1.0800	1.1000
2	1.0404	1.0506	1.0609	1.0816	1.1025	1.1236	1.1664	1.2100
3	1.0612	1.0769	1.0927	1.1249	1.1576	1.1910	1.2597	1.3310
4	1.0824	1.1038	1.1255	1.1'699	1.2155	1.2625	1.3605	1.4641
5	1.1041	1.1314	1.1593	1.2167	1.2763	1.3382	1_4693	1.6105
6	1.1262	1.1597	1.1941	1.2653	1.3401	1.4185	1.5869	1.7716
7	1.1487	1.1887	1.2299	1.3159	1.4071	1.5036	1.7138	1.9438
8	1.1717	1.2184	1.2668	1.3686	1.5775	1.5938	1.8509	2.1436
9	1.1951	1.2489	1.3048	1.4233	1.5513	1.6895	1.9990	2.3589
10	1.2190	1.2801	1.3439	1.4802	1.6289	1.7908	2.1589	2.5938
11	1.2434	1.3121	1.3842	1.5395	1.7103	1.8983	2.3316	2.8532
12	1.2682	1.3449	1.4258	1.6010	1.7959	2.0122	2.5182	3.1385
13	1.2936	1.3785	1.4685	1.6651	1.8856	2.1329	2.7196	3.4524
14	1.3195	1.4130	1.5126	1.7317	1.9799	2.2609	2.9372	3.7976
15	1.3459	1.4483	1.5580	1.8009	2.0709	2.3966	3.1722	4.1774
16	1.3728	1.4845	1.6047	1.8730	2.1829	2.5404	3.4259	4.5951
17	1.4002	1.5216	1.6528	1.9479	2.2920	2.6928	3.7000	5.0545
18	1.4282	1.5597	1.7024	2.0258	2.4066	2.8543	3.9960	5.5600
19	1.4568	1.5987	1.7535	2.1068	2.5270	3.0256	4.3157	6.1160
20	1.4859	1.6386	1.8061	2.1911	2.6533	3.2071	4.6610	6.7276
22	1.5460	1.7216	1.9161	2.3699	2.9253	3.6035	5.4365	8.1404
24	1.6084	1.8087	2.0328	2.5633	3.2251	4.0489	6.3412	9.8498
26	1.6734	1.9003	2.1566	2.7725	3.5557	4.5494	7.3964	11.9183
28	1.7410	1.9965	2.2879	2.9987	3.9201	5.1117	8.6271	14.4211
30	1.8114	2.0976	2.4273	3.2434	4.3219	5.7435	10.0627	17.4495
32	1.8845	2.2038	2.5751	3.5081	4.7649	6.4534	11.7371	21.1140
34	1.9607	2.3153	2.7319	3.7943	5.2533	7.2510	13.6901	25.5479
36	2.0399	2.4325	2.8983	4.1039	5.7918	8.1473	15.9682	30.9130
38	2.1223	2.5557	3.0748	4.4388	6.3855	9.1543	18.6253	37.4047
40	2.2080	2.6851	3.2620	4.8010	7.0400	10.2857	21.7245	45.2597
42	2.2972	2.8210	3.4607	5.1928	7.7616	11.5570	25.3395	54.7643
44	2.3901	2.9638	3.6715	5.6165	8.5572	12.9855	29.5560	66.2648
46	*2.4866*	*3.1139*	*3.8950*	*6.0748*	*9.4343*	*14.5905*	*34.4741*	*80.1804*
48	*2.5871*	*3.2715*	*4.1323*	6.5705	10.4013	16.3939	40.2106	97.0181
50	2.6916	3.4371	4.3839	7.1067	11.4674	18.4202	46.9016	117.3920
60	3.2810	4.3998	5.8916	10.5196	18.6792	32.9877	101.2571	304.4846

Table 16-2 Present value of $1.00

$$PV = FV(1 + i)^{-n}$$

n	2%	4%	6%	8%	10%	12%	14%	16%	18%	20%	22%	24%	26%	28%	30%	40%	50%
1	0.980	0.962	0.943	0.926	0.909	0.893	0.877	0.862	0.847	0.833	0.820	0.806	0.794	0.781	0.769	0.714	0.667
2	0.961	0.925	0.890	0.857	0.826	0.797	0.769	0.743	0.718	0.694	0.672	0.650	0.630	0.610	0.592	0.510	0.444
3	0.942	0.889	0.840	0.794	0.751	0.712	0.675	0.641	0.609	0.579	0.551	0.524	0.500	0.477	0.455	0.364	0.296
4	0.924	0.855	0.792	0.735	0.683	0.636	0.592	0.552	0.516	0.482	0.451	0.423	0.397	0.373	0.350	0.260	0.197
5	0.906	0.822	0.747	0.681	0.621	0.567	0.519	0.476	0.437	0.402	0.370	0.341	0.315	0.291	0.269	0.186	0.131
6	0.888	0.790	0.705	0.630	0.564	0.507	0.456	0.410	0.370	0.335	0.303	0.275	0.250	0.227	0.207	0.133	0.088
7	0.871	0.760	0.665	0.583	0.513	0.452	0.400	0.354	0.314	0.279	0.249	0.222	0.198	0.178	0.159	0.095	0.059
8	0.853	0.731	0.627	0.540	0.467	0.404	0.351	0.305	0.266	0.233	0.204	0.179	0.157	0.139	0.123	0.068	0.039
9	0.837	0.703	0.592	0.500	0.424	0.361	0.308	0.263	0.225	0.194	0.167	0.144	0.125	0.108	0.094	0.048	0.026
10	0.820	0.676	0.558	0.463	0.386	0.322	0.270	0.227	0.191	0.162	0.137	0.116	0.099	0.085	0.073	0.035	0.017
11	0.804	0.650	0.527	0.429	0.350	0.287	0.237	0.195	0.162	0.135	0.112	0.094	0.079	0.066	0.056	0.025	0.012
12	0.788	0.625	0.497	0.397	0.319	0.257	0.208	0.168	0.137	0.112	0.092	0.076	0.062	0.052	0.043	0.018	0.008
13	0.773	0.601	0.469	0.368	0.290	0.229	0.182	0.145	0.116	0.093	0.075	0.061	0.050	0.040	0.033	0.013	0.005
14	0.758	0.577	0.442	0.340	0.263	0.205	0.160	0.125	0.099	0.078	0.062	0.049	0.039	0.032	0.025	0.009	0.003
15	0.743	0.555	0.417	0.315	0.239	0.183	0.140	0.108	0.084	0.065	0.051	0.040	0.031	0.025	0.020	0.006	0.002
16	0.728	0.534	0.394	0.292	0.218	0.163	0.123	0.093	0.071	0.054	0.042	0.032	0.025	0.019	0.015	0.005	0.002
17	0.714	0.513	0.371	0.270	0.198	0.146	0.108	0.080	0.060	0.045	0.034	0.026	0.020	0.015	0.012	0.003	0.001
18	0.700	0.494	0.350	0.250	0.180	0.130	0.095	0.069	0.051	0.038	0.028	0.021	0.016	0.012	0.009	0.002	0.001
19	0.686	0.475	0.331	0.232	0.164	0.116	0.083	0.060	0.043	0.031	0.023	0.017	0.012	0.009	0.007	0.002	
20	0.673	0.456	0.312	0.215	0.149	0.104	0.073	0.051	0.037	0.026	0.019	0.014	0.010	0.007	0.005	0.001	
21	0.660	0.439	0.294	0.199	0.135	0.093	0.064	0.044	0.031	0.022	0.015	0.011	0.008	0.006	0.004	0.001	
22	0.647	0.422	0.278	0.184	0.123	0.083	0.056	0.038	0.026	0.018	0.013	0.009	0.006	0.004	0.003	0.001	
23	0.634	0.406	0.262	0.170	0.112	0.074	0.049	0.033	0.022	0.015	0.010	0.007	0.005	0.003	0.002		
24	0.622	0.390	0.247	0.158	0.102	0.066	0.043	0.028	0.019	0.013	0.008	0.006	0.004	0.003	0.002		
25	0.610	0.375	0.233	0.146	0.092	0.059	0.038	0.024	0.016	0.010	0.007	0.005	0.003	0.002	0.001		
26	0.598	0.361	0.220	0.135	0.084	0.053	0.033	0.021	0.014	0.009	0.006	0.004	0.002	0.002	0.001		
27	0.586	0.347	0.207	0.125	0.076	0.047	0.029	0.018	0.011	0.007	0.005	0.003	0.002	0.001	0.001		
28	0.574	0.333	0.196	0.116	0.069	0.042	0.026	0.016	0.010	0.006	0.004	0.002	0.002	0.001	0.001		
29	0.563	0.321	0.185	0.107	0.063	0.037	0.022	0.014	0.008	0.005	0.003	0.002	0.001	0.001	0.001		
30	0.552	0.308	0.174	0.099	0.057	0.033	0.020	0.012	0.007	0.004	0.003	0.002	0.001	0.001			
40	0.453	0.208	0.097	0.046	0.022	0.011	0.005	0.003	0.001	0.001							
50	0.372	0.141	0.054	0.021	0.009	0.003	0.001	0.001									

Table 16-3 Future value of annuity of $1.00

$$FV_n = \frac{(1 + i)^n - 1}{i}$$

n	2%	2.5%	3%	4%	5%	6%	8%	10%
1	1.0000	1.0000	1.0000	1.0000	1.0000	1.0000	1.0000.	1.0000
2	2.0200	2.0250	2.0300	2.0400	2.0500	2.0600	2.0800	2.1000
3	3.0604	3.0756	3.0909	3.1216	3.1525	3.1836	3.2464	3.3100
4	4.1216	4.1525	4.1836	4.2465	4.3101	4.3746	4.5061	4.6410
5	5.2040	5.2563	5.3091	5.4163	5.5256	5.6371	5.8666	6.1051
6	6.3081	6.3877	6.4684	6.6330	6.8019	6.9753	7.3359	7.7156
7	7.4343	7.5474	7.6625	7.8983	8.1420	8.3938	8.9228	9.4872
8	8.5830	8.7361	8.8923	9.2142	9.5491	9.8975	I0.6366	U.4360
9	9.7546	9.9545	10.1591	10.5828	11.0266	11.4913	12.4876	13.5796
10	10.9497	11.2034	11.4639	12.0061	12.5779	13.1808	14.4866	15.9376
11	12.1687	12.4835	12.8078	13.4864	14.2068	14.9716	16.6455	18.5314
12	13.4121	13.7956	14.1920	15.0258	15.9171	16.8699	18.9771	21.3846
13	14.6803	15.1404	15.6178	16.6268	17.7130	18.8821	21.4953	24.5231
14	15.9739	16.5190	17.0863	18.2919	19.5986	21.0151	24.2149	27.9755
15	17.2934	17.9319	18.5989	20.0236	21.5786	23.2760	27.1521	31.7731
16	18.6393	19.3802	20.1569	21.8245	23.6575	25.6725	30.3243	35.9503
17	20.0121	20.8647	21.7616	23.6975	25.8404	28.2129	33.7502	40.5456
18	21.4123	22.3863	23.4144	25.6454	28.1324	30.9057	37.4502	45.6001
19	22.8406	23.9460	25.1169	27.6712	30.5390	33.7600	41.4463	51.1601
20	24.2974	25.5447	26.8704	29.7781	33.0660	36.7856	45.7620	57.2761
22	27.2990	28.8629	30.5368	34.2480	38.5052	43.3923	55.4568	71.4041
24	30.4219	32.3490	34.4265	39.0826	44.5020	50.8156	66.7648	88.4989
26	33.6709	36.0117	38.5530	44.3117	51.1135	59.1564	79.9544	109.1835
28	37.0512	39.8598	42.9309	49.9676	58.4026	68.5281	95.3388	134.2119
30	40.5681	43.9027	47.5754	56.0849	66.4388	79.0582	113.2832	164.4962
32	44.2270	48.1503	52.5028	62.7015	75.2988	90.8898	134.2135	201.1402
34	48.0338	52.6129	57.7302	69.8579	85.0670	104.1838	158.6267	245.4796
36	51.9944	57.3014	63.2759	77.5983	95.8363	119.1209	187.1021	299.1302
38	56.1149	62.2273	69.1594	85.9703	107.7095	135.9042	220.3159	364.0475
40	60.4020	67.4026	75.4013	95.0255	120.7998	154.7620	259.0565	442.5974
42	64.8622	72.8398	82.0232	104.8196	135.2318	175.9505	304.2435	537.6428
44	69.5027	78.5523	89.0484	115.4129	151.1430	199.7580	356.9496	652.6478
46	74.3306	84.5540	96.5015	126.8706	168.6852	226.5081	418.4261	791.8039
48	79.3535	90.8596	104.4084	139.2632	188.0254	256.5645	490.1322	960.1827
50	84.5794	97.4843	112.7969	152.6671	209.3480	290.3359	573.7702	1163.9209
60	114.0515	135.9916	163.0534	237.9907	353.5837	533.1282	1253.2133	3034.8470

Table 16-4 Present value of an annuity of $1.00

$$PV_n = \frac{1-(1+i)^{-n}}{i}$$

n	2%	4%	6%	8%	10%	12%	14%	16%	18%	20%	22%	24%	25%	26%	28%	30%	40%	50%
1	0.980	0.962	0.943	0.926	0.909	0.893	0.877	0.862	0.847	0.833	0.820	0.806	0.800	0.794	0.781	0.769	0.714	0.667
2	1.942	1.886	1.833	1.783	1.736	1.690	1.647	1.605	1.566	1.528	1.492	1.457	1.440	1.424	1.392	1.361	1.224	1.111
3	2.884	2.775	2.673	2.577	2.487	2.402	2.322	2.246	2.174	2.106	2.042	1.981	1.952	1.923	1.868	1.816	1.589	1.407
4	3.808	3.630	3.465	3.312	3.170	3.037	2.914	2.798	2.690	2.589	2.494	2.404	2.362	2.320	2.241	2.166	1.849	1.605
5	4.713	4.452	4.212	3.993	3.791	3.605	3.433	3.274	3.127	2.991	2.864	2.745	2.689	2.635	2.532	2.436	2.035	1.737
6	5.601	5.242	4.917	4.623	4.355	4.111	3.889	3.685	3.498	3.326	3.167	3.020	2.951	2.885	2.759	2.643	2.168	1.824
7	6.472	6.002	5.582	5.206	4.868	4.564	4.288	4.039	3.812	3.605	3.416	3.242	3.161	3.083	2.937	2.802	2.263	1.883
8	7.325	6.733	6.210	5.747	5.335	4.968	4.639	4.344	4.078	3.837	3.619	3.421	3.329	3.241	3.076	2.925	2.331	1.922
9	8.162	7.435	6.802	6.247	5.759	5.328	4.946	4.607	4.303	4.031	3.786	3.566	3.463	3.366	3.184	3.019	2.379	1.948
10	8.983	8.111	7.360	6.710	6.145	5.650	5.216	4.833	4.494	4.192	3.923	3.682	3.571	3.465	3.269	3.092	2.414	1.965
11	9.787	8.760	7.887	7.139	6.495	5.988	5.453	5.029	4.656	4.327	4.035	3.776	3.656	3.544	3.335	3.147	2.438	1.977
12	10.575	9.385	8.384	7.536	6.814	6.194	5.660	5.197	4.793	4.439	4.127	3.851	3.725	3.606	3.387	3.190	2.456	1.985
13	11.343	9.986	8.853	7.904	7.103	6.424	5.842	5.342	4.910	4.533	4.203	3.912	3.780	3.656	3.427	3.223	2.468	1.990
14	12.106	10.563	9.295	8.244	7.367	6.628	6.002	5.468	5.008	4.611	4.265	3.962	3.824	3.695	3.459	3.249	2.477	1.993
15	12.849	11.118	9.712	8.559	7.606	6.811	6.142	5.575	5.092	4.675	4.315	4.001	3.859	3.726	3.483	3.268	2.484	1.995
16	13.578	11.652	10.106	8.851	7.824	6.974	6.265	5.669	5.162	4.730	4.357	4.033	3.887	3.751	3.503	3.283	2.489	1.997
17	14.292	12.166	10.477	9.122	8.022	7.120	6.373	5.749	5.222	4.775	4.391	4.059	3.910	3.771	3,518	3.295	2.492	1.998
18	14.992	12.659	10.828	9.372	8.201	7.250	6.467	5.818	5.273	4.812	4.419	4.080	3.928	3.786	3.529	3.304	2.494	1.999
19	15.678	13.134	11.158	9.604	8.365	7.366	6.550	5.877	5.316	4.844	4.442	4.097	3.942	3.799	3.539	3.311	2.496	1.999
20	16.351	13.590	11.470	9.818	8.514	7.469	6.623	5.929	5.353	4.870	4.460	4.110	3.954	3.808	3.546	3.316	2.497	1.999
21	17.011	14.029	11.764	10.017	8.649	7.562	6.687	5.973	5.384	4.891	4.476	4.121	3.963	3.816	3.551	3.320	2.498	2.000
22	17.658	14.451	12.042	10.201	8.772	7.645	6.743	6.011	5.410	4.909	4.488	4.130	3.970	3.822	3.556	3.323	2.498	2.000
23	18.292	14.857	12.303	10.371	8.883	7.718	6.792	6.044	5.432	4.925	4.499	4.137	3.976	3.827	3.559	3.325	2.499	2.000
24	18.914	15.247	12.550	10.529	8.985	7.784	6.835	6.073	5.451	4.937	4.507	4.143	3.981	3.831	3.562	3.327	2.499	2.000
25	19.523	15.622	12.783	10.675	9.077	7.843	6.873	6.097	5.467	4.948	4.514	4.147	3.985	3.834	3.564	3.329	2.499	2.000
26	20.121	15.983	13.003	10.810	9.161	7.896	6.906	6.118	5.480	4.956	4.520	4.151	3.988	3.837	3.566	3.330	2.500	2.000
27	20.707	16.330	13.211	10.935	9.237	7.943	6.935	6.136	5.492	4.964	4.524	4.154	3.990	3.839	3.567	3.331	2,500	2,000
28	21.281	16.663	13.406	11.051	9.307	7.984	6.961	6.152	5.502	4.970	4.528	4.157	3.992	3.840	3.568	3.331	2.500	2.000
29	21.844	16.984	13.591	11.158	9.370	8.022	6.983	6.166	5.510	4.975	4.531	4.159	3.994	3.841	3.569	3.332	2.500	2.000
30	22.396	17.292	13.765	11.258	9.427	8.055	7.003	6.177	5.517	4.979	4.534	4.160	3.995	3.842	3.569	3.332	2.500	2.000
40	27.355	19.793	15.046	11.925	9.779	8.244	7.105	6.234	5.548	4.997	4.544	4.166	3.999	3.846	3.571	3.333	2.500	2.000
50	31.424	21.482	15.762	12.234	9.915	8.304	7.133	6.246	5.554	4.999	4.545	4.167	4.000	3.846	3.571	3.333	2.500	2.000

Questions

16-1 Define capital budgeting.

16-2 What major factors must be considered in evaluating capital investment projects?

16-3 Why is one dollar today worth more than one dollar to be received a year from now?

16-4 Discuss the major advantage of the discounted cash flow method in evaluating capital investment projects.

16-5 Explain why depreciation is a tax shield against taxes.

16-6 How does depreciation affect capital investment decisions?

16-7 Explain how income taxes affect capital investment decisions.

16-8 Explain how inflation affects capital investment decisions.

16-9 Under what conditions can the payback reciprocal be used to approximate the internal rate of return?

16-10 Discuss how uncertainty affects capital budgeting analysis.

16-11 Why are accelerated methods of depreciation more desirable than the straight-line depreciation method? Discuss your answer from an income tax point of view.

16-12 Discuss the effect of each of the following cases on a capital investment proposed for a new machine. Consider each case separately.

(1) An expected increase in interest rate on long-term debt.

(2) A new requirement on pollution control is passed by the Congress.

(3) An increase of the unit selling price of the company's product (sales volume is not affected).

(4) The company's income taxes are expected to increase from 46 percent to 50 percent.

(5) A new product promoted by a competitor seems to be a good substitute for the product produced by the machine (the market demand is not unlimited).

(6) A special promotion is required to introduce the product into the current market.

Problems

16-13 *Determining Cash Flows*

Posa Co. is planning to invest $40,000 in a three-year project. Posa's expected rate of return is 10 perent. The present value of $1 at 10 percent for one year is .909, for two years is .826, and for three years is .751. The cash flow, net of income taxes, will be $15,000 for the first year (present value of $13,635) and $18,000 for the second year (present value of $14,868). Assuming the rate of return is exactly 10 percent, what would the cash flow, net of income taxes, be for the third year?

(AICPA adapted)

16-14 *Determining Cash Flows*

The Herb Company acquired a new machine for $16,000 which it will depreciate on a straight-line basis over a ten year period. A full year's depreciation was taken in the year of acquisition. The accounting (book value) rate of return is expected to be 12 percent on the initial increase in required investment. If we assume a uniform cash inflow, what will be the annual cash flow from operations, net of income taxes?

(AICPA adapted)

16-15 *Impact of Different Depreciation Methods on Cash Flows*

Freedom Corporation acquired a fixed asset at a cost of $100,000. The estimated life was four years, and there was no estimated salvage value. Assume a relevant interest rate of 8 percent and an income tax rate of 40 percent. The present value of $1 at 8 percent is as follows:

Number of Periods	Present Value
1	.926
2	.857
3	.794
4	.735

Required.

What is the present value of the tax benefits resulting from using sum-of-the-years'-digits depreciation as opposed to straight-line depreciation on this asset?

(AICPA adapted)

16-16 *Ranking Alternatives with NPV and IRR*

Given below is cash flow information pertaining to three alternative investment projects. The cost of capital is 12 percent.

Project	Period A	B	C
0	$(40,000)	$(40,000)	$(40,000)
1	16,000	0	28,000
2	16,000	0	28,000
3	16,000	0	0
4	16,000	72,000	0

Required:

(1) Rank these projects according to the net present value and the internal rate of return.

Explain the difference in the rankings.

16-17 *Replacement Analysis*

A Company bought Machine M on March 5, 20X4 for $5,000 cash.The estimated salvage was $200 and the estimated life was eleven years. On March 5, 20X5, the company learned that it could purchase a different machine for $8,000 cash. The new machine would save the company an estimated $250 per year compared to Machine A. The new machine would have no estimated salvage and an estimated life of ten years. The company could get $3,000 for Machine A on March 5, 20X5.

Required:

Ignore income taxes: should the company purchase the new machine if th e cost of capital is 16 percent?

(*AICPA adapted*)

16-18 *Determining Useful Life and Net Book Value*

The Happy Valley Company is planning to purchase a new machine. The payback period is estimated to be six years. The cash flow from operations, net of income taxes, is estimated to be $2,000 a year for each of the first three years and $3,000 for eah of the next three years. Depreciation of $1,5000 will be charged to income each year. The salvage value is estimated to be $3,000 at the end of the life of the machine.

Required:

Determine the estimated useful like of the machine and the net book value of the machine at the end of six years.

16-19 *Computing Payback Period*

A new machine costing $60,000 will result in the following net cash inflows. The desired rate of return on investment is 10 percent.

Year	Net Cash Inflows
1	$30,000
2	20,000
3	10,000
4	20,000

Required:

1) Compute the payback period for the investment (ignore the time value of money).

2) Compute the payback period for the investment (consider the time value of money).

16-20 *Computing Payback Periods and Internal Rates of Return*

Two investment projects are being considered by the Gem Company. Project A, costing $16,000 with an estimated useful life of three years, will earn a net cash inflow of $8,000 per year. Project B, costing *$29,000* with an expected useful life of four years, will earn a net cash inflow of *$12,000* per year.

Required:

1. Calculate the payback period (consider the time value of money, i=10%) for each project.
2. Calculate the internal rate of return for each project.
3. The company has the following policies for evaluating alternative projects:

(a) The payback period should not be greater than 75 percent of the estimated useful life of the project.

(b) The project with the largest internal rate of return is considered to be the most desirable.

Which project is most desirable?

16-21 *Computing Payback Period, Net Present Value, Internal Rate of Return, and Accounting Rate of Return*

A machine costing $50,000 is expected to provide the following net cash flows:

Year	*Cash Savings*
1	$20,000
2	5,000
1	5,000
4	0,000

The expected salvage value of the machine at the end of four years is $5,000. The company's minimum desired rate of return is 12 percent.

Required:

Compute:

(1) The payback period (consider the time value of money).

(2) The net present value.

(3) The internal rate of return.

(4) The accounting rate of return.

16-22 *Determining Net Present Value*

Jack, Jones, and Johnson, three franchised home appliance dealers, have requested short-term financing from their company. The dealers have agreed to repay the loans within three years, and to pay Benjamin Industries 6 percent of net income over the three year period for the use of the funds. The following table summarizes by dealer the financing requested and the total remittance (principal plus 6% of net income) expected at the end of the each year:

	Jack	*Jones*	*Johnson*
Financing requested	$ 80,000	$40,000	$30,000
Remittances expected			
Year 1	$ 10,000	$25,000	$10,000
Year 2	40,000	30,000	15,000
Year 3	70,000	5,000	15,000
	$120,000	$60,000	$40,000

Management believes these financing requests should be granted only if the annual pre-tax return to the company exceeds the target internal rate of 22 percent on investment.

Required:

Prepare a schedule to compute the net present value of the investment opportunities of financing Jack, Jones, and Johnson. The schedule should determine if the discounted cash flows expected from (1) Jack, (2) Jones, and (3) Johnson would be more or less than the amount of Benjamin Industries' investments in loans to each of the three dealers.

(*AICPA adapted*)

16-23 Computing Net Present Value and Internal Rate of Return

The Aloha Company is considering the purchase of a piece of equipment. Thee following information is available:

The cost of the equipment	$100,000
Annual net cash inflow expected from the use of the equipment	30,000
Salvage value at the end of five years	1,000

The company's minimum desired rate of return is 12 percent.

Required:

(1) If the net present value method is used to evaluate the project, should the equipment be purchased?

(2) Compute the internal rate of return for the investment.

16-24 Impact of Depreciation on Capital Budgeting Decisions

The Aloha Company is considering the purchase of a machine costing $200,000. The estimated net incomes from the machine are:

Year	*Net Income Before Tax*
1	$50,000
2	60,000
3	50,000
4	60,000
5	40,000
6	30,000
7	20,000
8	20,000

The machine is to be depreciated on the sum-of-the-years'-digits method. The salvage value at the end of eight years is zero. The company's income tax rate is 40 percent and desired rate of return is 10 percent. Assume that the machine has a depreciation base of $200,000.

Required:

Calculate

(1) Payback period (consider the time value of money),

(2) Accounting rate of return on initial investment,

(3) Net present value,

(4) Internal rate of return.

16-25 *Uncertain Sales Estimates and Cash Flow Calculations*

Vernon Enterprises designs and manufactures toys. Past experience indicates that the product life cycle of a toy is three years. Promotional advertising produces large sales in the early years, but there is a substantial sales decline in the final year of a toy's life. Consumer demand for new toys on the market tends to fall into three classes. About 30 percent of the new toys sell well above expectations, 60 percent sell as anticipated, and 10 percent have poor consumer acceptance.

A new toy has been developed. The following sales projections were made by carefully evaluating consumer demand for the new toy:

		Estimated Sales in Thousand Dollars		
Consumer Demand for New Toy	Chance of Occurring	Year 1	Year 2	Year 3
Above average	30%	$1,200	$2,500	$600
Average	60	700	1,700	400
Below average	10	200	900	150

Variable costs are estimated at 30 percent of the selling price. Special machinery must be purchased at a cost of $860,000 and will be installed in an unused portion of the factory that Vernon has been unsuccessfully trying to rent to someone for several years at $50,000 per year; there are no prospects for future utilization. Fixed expenses (excluding depreciation) of a cash-flow nature are estimated at $50,000 per year on the new toy. The new machinery will be depreciated by the sum-of-the-years'-digits method with an estimated salvage value of $110,000 and will be sold at the beginning of the fourth year. Advertising and promotional expenses will be incurred uniformly and will total $100,000 the first year, $150,000 the second year, and $50,000 the third year. These expenses will be deducted as incurred for income tax reporting.

Vernon believes that state and federal income tax will total 60 percent of income in the foreseeable future and may be assumed to be paid uniformly over the year income is earned.

(1) Prepare a schedule computing the probable sales of this new toy in each of the three years, taking into account the probability of above average, average, and below average sales occurring.

(2) Assume that the probable sales computed in (1) are $900,000 in the first year, $1,800,000 in the second year, and $410,000 in the third year. Prepare a schedule computing the probable net income for the new toy in each of the three years of its life.

(3) Prepare a schedule of net cash flows from sales of the new toy for each of the years involved and from disposition of the machinery purchased. Use the sales data given in (2).

(4) Assuming a minimum desired rate of return of 10 percent, prepare a schedule of the present value of the net cash flows calculated in (3). The following data are relevant:

Year	Present value of $1.00 due at the end of each year discounted at 10%	Present value of $1.00 earned uniformly throughout the year discounted at 10%
1	.91	.95
2	.83	.86
3	.75	.78

(*AICPA adapted*)

16-26 *Determining Cash Inflows, Payback Period, and Net Present Value*

The Baxter Company manufactures short-lived fad-type items. The R & D Department has developed an item that would be an interesting promotional gift for office equipment dealers. Aggressive and effective efforts by Baxter's sales personnel have resulted in almost firm commitments for this product for the next three years. It is expected that demand for the product will be exhausted by that time.

In order to produce the quantity demanded, Baxter will need to buy additional machinery and rent 12,500 square feet of additional space. There is another 12,500 square feet of space adjoining the Baxter facility which Baxter will rent for 3 years at $4 per square foot per year if it decides to make this product.

The equipment will be purchased for about $900,000. It will require $30,000 in modification, $60,000 for installation, and $90,000 for testing; all of these activities will be done by a firm of engineers hired by Baxter. All of the expenditures will be paid for on January 1, 20XX.

The equipment should have a salvage of about $180,000 at the end of the third year. No additional general overhead costs are expected to be incurred.

The following estimates of revenues and expenses for this product for the three years have been developed:

	20XX	20XY	20XZ
Sales	$1,000,000	$1,600,000	$800,000
Material, labor, and additional factory overhead	$ 400,000	$ 750,000	$350,000
Assigned general overhead	77,500	112,500	72,500
Rent (12,500 square feet of space x $4)	50,000	50,000	50,000
Depreciation	450,000	300,000	150,000
Total expenses	$ 977,500	$1,212,500	$622,500
Net income before income tax	$ 22,500	$ 387,500	$177,500
Income tax (40%)	9,000	155,000	71,000
Net income	13,500	$ 232,500	$106,500

Required:

(1) A schedule showing the net increase in aftertax cash inflow for this project.

(2) A decision (with supporting computations) as to whether this project should be untaken if thc Baxter Company requires a two-year payback period for its investment.

(3) The after-tax average annual return on average investment for the project.

(4) A decision (with supporting computations) as to whether the project will be accepted if the company sets a required 20 percent aftertax rate of return. (A newly hired business school graduate recommends that the Baxter Company consider using net present value analysis to evaluate this project.)

(*IMA adapted*)

16-27 *Inflation and Cash Flows*

Drexel Company is considering the purchase of a new machine costing $15,000. The new machine is to be depreciated on the sum-of-the-years'-digits method. The salvage value at the end of 5 years is zero. The estimated annual pre-tax incomes from the new machine are $5,000. The company's income tax rate is 25% and required rate of return is 10%. Assume that the annual inflation rate is expected to be 3% for the next 5 years.

Required:

(a) Calculate the net present value of the purchase of the new machine using the nominal method.

(b) Calculate the net present value of the purchase of the new machine using the real method.

16-28 *Lease or Buy*

Madisons, Inc. has decided to acquire a new machine either by an outright cash purchase at $25,000 or by leasing alternative of $6,000 per year for the life of the machine. Other relevant information is:

Purchase price due at time of purchase	$25,000
Estimated useful life	5 years
Estimated salvage value if purchased	$3,000
Annual cost of maintenance contract to be acquired with either lease or purchase	$500

Additional information:

(a) Assume a 40 percent income tax rate and the use of the straight-line method of depreciation.

(b) Assume that the taxing authorities will permit taxation of the lease agreement as a lease.

(c)The company's cost of capital is 10 percent.

Required:

(1) Determine the present value of the purchase price of the new machine.

(2) Under the purchase alternative, what is the present value of the estimated salvage value?

(3) Under the purchase alternative, what is the annual tax reduction (cash inflow) related to depreciation?

(4) Under the purchase alternative, what is the annual aftertax cash outflow for maintenance?

(AICPA adapted)

16-29 *House Financing Analysis*

Bart Mover, CPA, has been asked for advice by a client wishing to sell her home. The client has found a buyer who has agreed to the following terms of sale:

Selling price $150,000
Down payment....................25%
Interest rate..........................12.5%
Length of mortgage ....20 years.

However, the client's attorney has advised her that any interest rate in excess of 10 percent is usurious and should be avoided. The client will accept a 10 percent mortgage interest rate from the buyer, but would like to increase the selling price of the home by a corresponding amount.

Required:

Ignoring tax effects, by what amount should the selling price be increased to compensate Mover's client for the lower interest rate? (Hint: the monthly payment for a loan of $1 over 20 years at 12.5% is $.0113615; at 10% it is $.0096504.)

16-30 *Replacement Analysis*

The management of Essen Manufacturing Company is currently evaluating a proposal to purchase a new and innovative drill press as a replacement for a less efficient piece of similar equipment which would then be sold. The cost of the equipment including delivery and installation is $175,000. If the equipment is purchased, Essen will incur costs of $5,000 in removing the present equipment and revamping service facilities. The present equipment has a book value of $100,000 and a remaining useful life of ten years. Due to new technical improvements which have made the equipment outmoded, it presently has a resale value of only $40,000.

Additional information:

1. Management has provided you with the following comparative manufacturing cost tabulation:

	Present Equipment	*New Equipment*
Annual production units	400,000	500,000
Annual costs:		
Labor	$ 30,000	$ 25,000
Operating costs:		
Depreciation 10% of asset book value	10,000	17,500
Other	48,000	20,000
	58,000	37,500
Total	$ 88,000	$ 62,500

2. Management believes that if the present equipment is not replaced now, it will have to wait seven years before replacement is justifiable.
3. Both pieces of equipment are expected to have a negligible salvage value at the end of ten years.
4. If the new equipment is purchased, the management of Essen would require a 15 percent return on the investment before income taxes.
5. The following table lists the present value of an ordinary annuity of $1 at 15 percent:

Period	Present Value
1	0.870
2	1.626
3	2.283
4	2.855
5	3.352
6	3.784
7	4.160
8	4.487
9	4.772
10	5.019

Required:

In order to assist the management of Essen in reaching a decision on the proposal, prepare schedules showing the computation of the following:
(a)Net initial outlay before income taxes.
(b) Net present value of investment before income taxes.
(2) Would you recommend this investment, and why?
Note:Ignore any effects of net incremental cash flow from increased sales of units produced by the new machine.

(AICPA adapted)

16-31 *Accounting Rate of Return*

Amex Company is considering the introduction of a new product which will be manufactured in an existing plant; however, new equipment costing $150,000 with a useful life of five years (no salvage value) will be necessary. The space in the existing plant to be used for the new product is currently used for warehousing. When the new product takes over the warehouse space, on which the annual depreciation is $20,000, Amex Company will rent warehouse space at an annual cost of $25,000. An accounting study produces the following estimates on an average annual basis:

Sales	$500,000
Cost of merchandise sold (excluding depreciation)	385,000
Depreciation of equipment (straight-line)	30,000
Marketing expense	10,000

Amex requires an accounting rate of return of 11 percent (after income taxes) on average investment proposals. The effective income tax rate is 46 percent. Ignore the time value of money.

Required:

(a) Determine the average annual increase in costs (including income taxes) associated with the proposed product.

(b) Determine the minimum annual increase in net income needed to meet the company's requirements for this investment.

(AICPA adapted)

17-32 Earnings per Share: Debt Financing or Equity Financing

The Morton Company is planning to invest $10,000,000 in an expansion program which is expected to increase earnings before interest and taxes by $2,500,000. The company currently is earning $5 per share on 1,000,000 shares of common outstanding. The capital structure prior to the investment is:

Debt	$ 10,000,000
Equity	30,000,000
	$ 40,000,000

The expansion can be financed by sale of 200,000 shares at $50 net each or by issuing long-term debt at a 6 percent interest cost. The firm's recent profit and loss statement was as follows:

Sales		$101,000,000
Variable cost	$60,000,000	
Fixed cost	30,500,000	
		90,500,000
Earnings before interest and taxes		$ 10,500,000
Interest		500,000
Earnings before taxes		$ 10,000,000
Taxes (50%)		5,000,000
Earnings after taxes		$ 5,000,000

Required:

Assuming the firm maintains its current earnings and achieves the anticipated earnings from the expansion, what will be the earnings per share if the expansion is financed by (a) debt? (b) equity?

16-33 Determining NPV of Alternative Investments

Thorne Transit, Inc. has decided to inaugurate express bus service between its headquarters city and a nearby suburb (one-way fare of $.50) and is considering the purchase of either 32- or 52-passenger buses, on which pertinent estimates are as follows:

	32-Passenger Bus	52-Passenger Bus
Number of each to be purchased.............	6	4
Useful life...	8 years	8 years
Purchase price of each bus (paid on delivery)........................	$80,000	$110,000
Mileage per gallon	10	7.5
Salvage value per bus..............................	$ 6,000	$ 7,000
Drivers' hourly wage..............................	$ 3.50	$ 4.20
Price per gallon of gasoline	$ .40	$ .40
Other annual cash expenses.....................	$ 4,000	$ 3,000

During the daily rush-hour period (which totals four hours), all buses would be in service and are expected to operate at full capacity (state law prohibits standees) in both directions of the route, each bus covering the route 12 times (6 round trips) during that period. During the remainder ofthe 16 hour daily service period, 500 passengers would be carried and Thorne would operate four buses on the route. Part-time drivers (paid at the regular rate) would be employed to drive during the rush hours. A bus traveling the route all day would go 480 miles and one traveling only during rush hours would go 120 miles a day during the 260-day year.

Required.

(a) Prepare a schedule showing the computation of estimated annual revenue of the new route for both alternatives.

(b) Prepare a schedule showing the computation of estimated annual drivers' wages for both alternatives.

(c) Prepare a schedule showing the computation of estimated annual cost of gasoline for both alternatives.

(d) Assuming that a minimum rate of return of 12 percent before income taxes is desired and that all annual cash flows occur at the end of the year, prepare a schedule showing the computation of the present values of net cash flows for the eight year period; include the cost of buses and the proceeds from their disposition under both alternatives, but disregard the effect of income taxes. Round all calculations to the nearest dollar.

(*AICPA adapted*)

16-34 *Lease or Purchase*

The Gercken Corporation sells computer services to its clients. The company completed a feasibility study and decided to acquire an additional computer on January 2, 20X5. Information regarding the new computer follows:

1. The purchase price is $230,000. Maintenance, property taxes, and insurance will be $20,000 per year. If the computer is rented, the annual rent will be $85,000 plus 5 percent of annual billings. The rental price includes maintenance. The rent is due on the last day of each year.
2. Due to competitive conditions, the company feels it will be necessary to replace the computer at the end of three years with one which is larger and more advanced. It is estimated that the computer will have a resale value of $110,000 at that time.

3. The income tax rate is 50 percent. If the computer is purchased, sum of-the-years'-digits depreciation will be used for tax purposes.
4. The estimated annual billing for the services of the new computer will be $220,000 during the first year and $260,000 during each of the second and third years.
5. The estimated annual expense of operating the computer is $80,000 in addition to the previously mentioned expense. Additional start-up expenses of $10,000 will be incurred during 20X5.
6. If the computer is purchased, the Gercken Corporation will borrow the purchase price from a local bank with interest at 8 percent. The principal and interest will be repaid as follows:

Date	*Principal*	*Interest*
12/31/20X5	$ 30,000	$18,400
12/31/20X6	100,000	16,000
12/31/20X7	100,000	8,000

7. The company has a cost of capital of 14 percent.

Required:

Should Gercken purchase the computer with borrowed funds or lease it? Round all calculations to the nearest dollar.

(*AICPA adapted*)

16-35 *Purchase, Lease, or Build Equipment*

The Edwards Corporation is considering adding a new stapler to one of its product lines. More equipment will be required to produce the new stapler. There are three alternative ways to acquire the needed equipment: (1) purchase general purpose equipment, (2) lease general purpose equipment, (3) build special purpose equipment. A fourth alternative, purchase of the special purpose equipment, has been ruled out because it would be prohibitively expensive.

The general purpose equipment can be purchased for $125,000. The equipment has an estimated salvage of $15,000 at the end of its useful life of ten years. At the end of five years the equipment can be used elsewhere in the plant or be sold for $40,000.

Alternatively, the general purpose equipment can be acquired by a five year lease for $40,000 annual rent. The lessor will assume all responsibility for taxes, insurance and maintenance.

Special purpose equipment can be constructed by the contract equipment department of the Edwards Corporation. While the department is operating at a level which is normal for the time of year, it is below full capacity. The department could produce the equipment without interfering with its regular revenue producing activities.

The estimated departmental costs for the construction of the special purpose equipment are:

Materials and parts	$ 75,000
Direct labor (DL)	60,000
Variable overhead (50% of DL$)	30,000
	$165,000

However, the cost of the equipment for depreciation purposes is $180,000, a full cost basis. This full cost includes $15,000 of fixed overhead which would be incurred regardless of whether or not the equipment was constructed.

Engineering and management studies provide the following revenue and cost estimates (excluding lease payments and depreciation) for producing the new stapler, depending upon the equipment used:

	General Purpose Equipment		
	Leased	*Purchased*	*Self-Constructed*
Unit selling price	$ 5.00	$ 5.00	$ 5.00
Unit production costs:			
Materials	$ 1.80	$1.80	$ 1.70
Conversion costs	1.65	1.65	1.40
Total unit production costs	$ 3.45	$3.45	$ 3.10
Unit contribution margin	$ 1.55	$1.55	$ 1.90
Estimated unit volume	40,000	40,000	40,000
Estimated total contribution margin	$62,000	$62,000	$76,000
Other costs:			
Supervision	$16,000	$16,000	$18,000
Taxes and insurance	0	3,000	5,000
Maintenance	0	3,000	2,000
Total	$16,000	$22,000	$25,000

The company will depreciate the general purpose machine over ten years on the sum-of-the-years'-digits (S-Y-D) method. At the end of five years the accumulated depreciation will total $80,000. (The present value of this amount for the first five years is $62,100). The special purpose machine will be depreciated over five years on the S-Y-D method. Its salvage value at the end of that time is estimated to be $30,000.

The company uses an after tax cost of capital of 10 percent. Its marginal tax rate is 40 percent.

Required:

Calculate which of the three options would be the best using the net present value method.

(*IMA adapted*)

1. *To describe how cost accounting systems can provide information for motivation and control.*
2. *To discuss how a responsibility accounting system functions.*
3. *To describe the difficulties in designing an effective responsibility accounting system.*
4. *To discuss the concepts of controllable and uncontrollable costs.*
5. *To introduce the concept of participative budgeting.*

17

Responsibility Accounting and Performance Reporting

Management is provided with a means of controlling operations by a well-designed system of budgeting and performance reporting. The purpose of this chapter is to describe a type of cost accounting system in which budgets and performance reports are provided at each managerial level in the organization. Because each manager is held responsible for the amount by which his or her actual performance differs from that budgeted, these are commonly referred to as *responsibility accounting* systems.

How Responsibility Accounting Works

Responsibility accounting systems have achieved wide acceptance because they provide an effective method of motivating individual managers and evaluating their performance. Prior to the beginning of the budgetary year, budgets are developed which indicate cost and (sometimes) revenue objectives for each manager in the organization. In a properly designed system, these objectives provide goals for achievement and serve to motivate managers to increase revenues or to decrease costs. Periodically during the year, usually on a monthly basis, each manager receives a performance report disclosing how well he or she is achieving the objectives. These monthly performance reports provide a means of feedback to managers, allowing them to investigate problem areas or to adjust operations for improved performance in subsequent months. These performance measures also are examined by each manager's superiors in the organization, and year-end performance reports frequently are used as a basis for determining bonuses or selecting managers for promotion. It is not surprising that the structure of a responsibility accounting system is of considerable interest to the managers utilizing it as well as to the cost accountants who develop and implement it.

Responsibility Accounting Structure

An effective responsibility accounting system is developed around the structure of the organization in which it is implemented. The organization is divided into units of management responsibility, sometimes referred to as *responsibility centers.* In many cases, a responsibility center is simply a cost center. However, a manager's decisions may also affect revenues, investments, assets, or liabilities, and this fact is frequently recognized in the responsibility accounting system. The system traces all costs, and revenues if appropriate, to a responsibility center using the chart of accounts. Ideally, costs and revenues are traced to the responsibility center of the manager who is best able to influence them. When actual costs and revenues are compared with those budgeted for the responsibility center, the manager in charge can be held responsible for deviations from the budget.

Organizations themselves exist in many different forms and are governed by widely varying managerial styles. However, an effective responsibility accounting system can be developed for any organization in which (1) a distinct delegation of authority exists and (2) the level of authority given at any level is commensurate with the responsibilities assigned.

A common organization structure is shown in Illustration 17-1. The organization is constructed as a hierarchy, in which a manager at any level has several subordinates who may themselves function in a managerial capacity. In this example, Departments A, B and X all represent production cost centers for product costing purposes. But, in the responsibility accounting system, they are considered to be responsibility centers. Other responsibility centers at an equivalent level in the hierarchy might consist of specific product divisions in the marketing branch, or of the general accounting, cost accounting and budgeting, and tax accounting

Illustration 17-1 Partial Organization Structure, Alpha Manufacturing Company

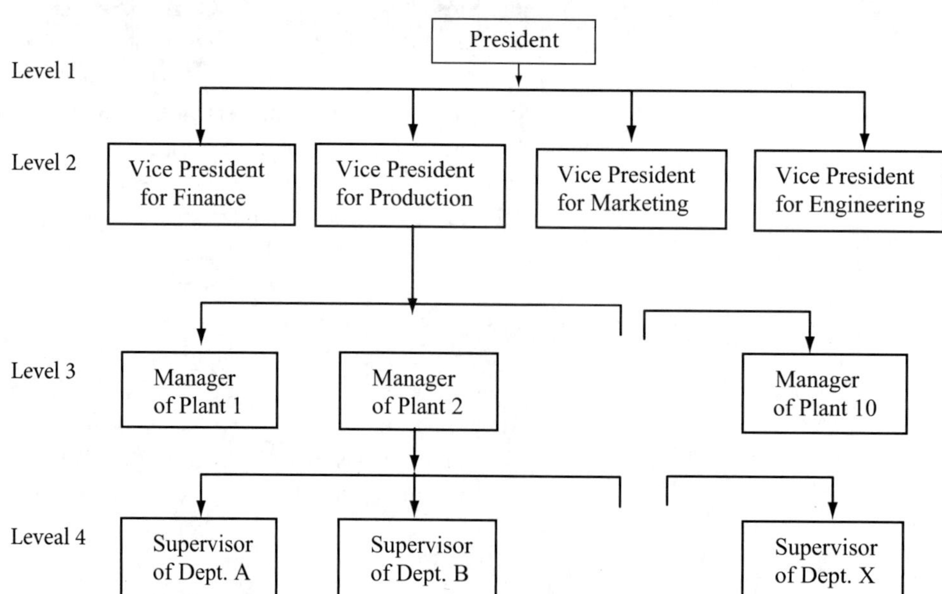

sections in the financial segment of the business. Supervisors in these responsibility centers can be held responsible for the costs and, if appropriate, revenues incurred in these centers. Annual budgets would be developed for each center and monthly performance reports would be produced to disclose deviations from the budget.

Several of these supervisors will report to a single manager at the next highest level in the hierarchy. Level 3 managers in this example might be the manager of Plant 2, the controller, the corporate treasurer, and the managers of major product lines. Each would be held responsible for the performance of his or her subordinates, and the responsibility accounting system would report budgeted costs and revenues and deviations from budget for each subordinate at that level. Similar budgets and performance reports could be produced at Level 2, the vice presidential level, showing the performance of the subordinates to each vice president, and at Level 1 which summarizes the performance of the organization as a whole.

In this manner a responsibility accounting system develops budgeting and performance reporting processes around the structure of the organization in which it operates. Examples of a series of monthly performance reports consistent with this hierarchical organization are shown in Illustration 17-2.

Typically, performance reports will disclose the actual costs incurred, the budgeted costs, and *a variance,* which is the difference between the actual and budgeted amounts. Normally these amounts will be summarized by the responsibility center for the month being reported and also for the current year-to-date.

Difficulties with Responsibility Accounting

Responsibility accounting is a conceptually appealing tool for providing motivation and controlling operations throughout an organization. However, many systems in practice do not adequately achieve these objectives. The major difficulties in implementing a successful responsibility accounting system result from the mass of data which must be accumulated and from the need to develop appropriate performance measures.

Data Accumulation

Responsibility accounting requires that the accounting system be capable of recording costs and revenues for each responsibility center in an organization. This is accomplished by a modification of the organization's chart of accounts, such that each responsibility center has in effect its own chart of accounts. Subsidiary revenue and expense accounts are created for each center, which enables accounting transactions to be recorded not only by revenue and expense category, but also by the responsibility center incurring the transaction. The accounting system can then summarize transactions by descriptive category for public reporting purposes, and by responsibility center for purposes of performance evaluation. Illustration 17-2 indicates how, at the lowest reporting level in an organization, performance reports show costs incurred in a division by descriptive category. At higher reporting levels, summaries reflect total costs incurred in subordinate responsibility centers. A chart of accounts structure which makes possible recording and summarizing at these various levels of detail is described in Illustration 17-3.

Cost accumulation at such a detailed level throughout an organization is made practicable by the use of computer-based cost accounting systems. Computer programs can quickly

Illustration 17-2 PerformanceReports, Alpha Manufacturing Company

Level 1 Report to President

Alpha Manufacturing Company Percformance Report-April 20XX All divisions						
	Current Month			Year-to-Date		
	Actual	Budget	Varience	Actual	Budget	Varience
Finance	XXX	XXX	XXX	XXX	XXX	XXX
Marketing	XXX	XXX	XXX	XXX	XXX	XXX
Engineering	XXX	XXX	XXX	XXX	XXX	XXX
Production	$52,110	53,619	1,509	202,581	210,697	8,116
R & D	XXX	XXX	XXX	XXX	XXX	XXX
Total	XXX	XXX	XXX	XXX	XXX	XXX

Level 2 Report to V.P. - Production

Alpha Manufacturing Company Percformance Report-April 20XX All Production Centers						
	Current Month			Year-to-Date		
	Actual	Budget	Varience	Actual	Budget	Varience
Plant 1	XXX	XXX	XXX	XXX	XXX	XXX
Plant 2	15,509	16,110	601	62,855	59,004	(3,851)
.						
.						
Plant 10	XXX	XXX	XXX	XXX	XXX	XXX
Total	$52,110	$53,619	$1,509	$202,581	$210,697	$8,116

Level 3 Report to Plant Manager

Alpha Manufacturing Company Percformance Report-April 20XX All Departments, Plant 2						
	Current Month			Year-to-Date		
	Actual	Budget	Varience	Actual	Budget	Varience
Department A	XXX	XXX	XXX	XXX	XXX	XXX
Department B	4,226	4,155	(71)	14,040	14,621	581
.						
.						
.						
Department C	XXX	XXX	XXX	XXX	XXX	XXX
Total	$15,509	$16,110	$601	$62,855	$59,004	($3,851)

Level 4 Report to Dept. Supervisor

Alpha Manufacturing Company Percformance Report-April 20XX Department B						
	Current Month			Year-to-Date		
	Actual	Budget	Varience	Actual	Budget	Varience
Direct Material	XXX	XXX	XX	XXX	XXX	XX
Direct Labor	XXX	XXX	XX	XXX	XXX	XX
Supplies	XXX	XXX	XX	XXX	XXX	XX
Rework	XXX	XXX	XX	XXX	XXX	XX
Setup	XXX	XXX	XX	XXX	XXX	XX
Supervision	XXX	XXX	XX	XXX	XXX	XX
Total	$4,226	$4,155	($71)	$14,040	$14,621	$581

Illustration 17-3 Example Chart of Accounts, Responsibility Accounting System

Account Number Structure: A-BB-CC-DDDD

A - one digit number for each major segment of the organization, identifying decision centers at Level 2.

1 - Vice President, Finance
2 - Vice President, Production
.
.

BB - two digit number uniquely identifying each decision center at Level 3.

2-01 - Manager of Plant 1
2-02 - Manager of Plant 2
.
.
2-10 - Manager of Plant 10

CC - two digit number uniquely identifying each cost center, or decision center at Level 4.

2-02-01 - Supervisor of Department A in Plant 2
.
.
2-02-24 - Supervisor of Department X in Plant 2

DDDD four digit number for each revenue and cost category

2-02-01-7010 - Direct materials, Department A, Plant 2
2-02-01-7020 - Direct labor, Department A, Plant 2
2-02-01-7030 - Applied overhead, Department A, Plant 2

summarize costs for each descriptive category for purposes of product costing and producing a traditional income statement. Similar programs can summarize costs by responsibility center and generate the associated performance reports. Thus, the problem of data accumulation, although a substantial one, can now be overcome through the use of computer technology. As a result, the problem of developing appropriate performance measures has become the more difficult one to resolve.

Measuring Management Performance

As has been discussed, a properly functioning responsibility accounting system can serve both as a motivator of managers and as a means of controlling their performance. Motivation is provided by incorporating the responsibility accounting system into the budgetary process. Control is improved by the ability to compare actual results with those budgeted on a periodic basis. A failure of responsibility systems to achieve these objectives is usually a result of the choice of inappropriate or inadequate performance measures.

The budgets utilized in such a system are intended to provide cost and revenue goals for each individual manager in the organization. However, the goals provided in the budget by an improperly designed system may not be those which encourage a manager to actively pursue the best interests of the organization as a whole. To some degree this lack of goal congruence is present in any budgetary system, but in a well-designed one it will be minimized. For example, a production manager who wishes to minimize costs may defer repairs and maintenance to equipment. This action may in turn decrease the useful life and productive capacity of the machinery. Although this may produce lower short-term costs and acceptable performance reports, the effect on the company owning the machinery is detrimental. Similarly, a manager of a sales decision center may be under budgetary pressure to increase revenues even though in the process profits are decreased. A method of developing appropriate performance measures will be described in the next chapter. For a budgetary system to serve as an effective means of control, cost and revenue goals must be adopted by each manager and accepted as individual objectives. This is most likely to occur when budgeted goals are reasonable and realistically attainable, and yet challenging enough that the manager feels a sense of accomplishment in reaching them. An individual manager will be motivated to minimize budget variances when he or she has some control over the actual costs incurred and some input to the process of developing the budget. Effective motivation and control based on appropriate performance measures does not occur by accident, but must be carefully considered during the design of the responsibility accounting system.

Design of a Responsibilty Accounting System

Responsibility accounting systems assign the responsibility for all costs and revenues to the specific individual in charge of a responsibility center. As has been discussed, the effectiveness of a system for motivation and control depends on three factors in its design. These relate to the controllability of costs, the manager's degree of participation in the budgeting process, and the characteristics of the performance reports.

Controllability of Costs

In designing the system, each type of cost assigned to a responsibility center should be categorized as either a controllable cost or an uncontrollable one. *Controllable costs* are those which can be regulated by the manager of the responsibility center within the performance reporting period. Examples of costs usually considered controllable include direct materials, direct labor, and operating supplies. Controllable costs should be disclosed on the performance report because the manager is responsible for variances from their budgeted amounts.

Uncontrollable costs of a responsibility center are those which the manager cannot regulate within the reporting period. Frequently they may result from long-term choices made in the past and their existence can no longer be affected by the manager's decisions, such as rentals resulting from lease agreements. Other uncontrollable costs may arise from the existence of the responsibility center but can be changed only at higher levels of management authority, for example insurance and depreciation on equipment. Some costs may be affected by the decisions of a manager, but they are subject to factors outside the managers discretion to such an extent that they are classified as uncontrollable. Costs allocated to a responsibility center from service departments by the methods discussed in Chapter 7 are of this type. For example, when factory maintenance costs are allocated to a producing department, the amount allocated is subject to decisions by the producing department supervisor, the maintenance department supervisor, and the cost accountant who chooses the allocation method.

Opinions differ regarding the disclosure of uncontrollable costs on performance reports. Some accountants advocate that they not be disclosed because they are not subject to a manager's discretion, and he or she should not be held responsible for them. Their inclusion, these people argue, would cause the manager to question the validity of the performance measures and to distrust the performance reporting system. As a result, it would decrease the effectiveness of the system as a motivator. Others argue that uncontrollable costs should be disclosed because they are incurred for the benefit of the responsibility center and the manager should be made aware of them. Furthermore, although such costs cannot be regulated by the manager, all are controllable at some level in the organization and the manager has some indirect influence over their incurrence. Proponents of disclosure generally agree that if they are included, uncontrollable costs should be designated as such, clearly distinguished from controllable costs, and the manager should not be held responsible for them. Promotions and year-end bonuses should be based only on variances arising from controllable costs.

Just as responsibility accounting systems differ in their treatment of uncontrollable costs, there are also differing opinions regarding the extent to which managers should participate in the development of the budgeted performance measures. This issue is discussed in the next section of this chapter.

Participative Budgeting

Responsibility accounting systems provide an effective means for motivation and control whenever managers accept their budgeted performance measures as personal goals and thus will work to attain them. Most managers will be more responsive to a budget which they have helped to develop. In practice, there are many different degrees to which the manager of a responsibility center may participate in the budgeting process. Two extremes in this respect are sometimes referred to as authoritative budgeting and participative budgeting.

In authoritative budgeting, cost and revenue goals are established for the entire organization by top management. These goals are then subdivided in order to provide goals for responsibility centers at progressively lower levels in the organization. Budgets are established so that if each manager at the operating level achieves his or her budget, then the budgeted cost and revenue targets of the entire organization will be met. Authoritative budgets are so called because budget goals are developed at the top management level and are imposed on managers of lower level responsibility centers. They utilize very little consultation with the operating managers who are responsible for achieving the goals.

Authoritative budgets are primarily advocated by those who function at the top management level and feel the need to demonstrate continuing improved performance to owners or stockholders. The method ensures that improvements considered desirable for the entire organization are translated into budgets at the lowest levels of an organization. Frequently top management will consider that an authoritative budget should be an ideal, a goal toward which all employees should be striving. They may consider a budget which is attainable to represent their acceptance of less than maximum effort by subordinates. However, operating managers may recognize that such a budget is unrealistic and impossible to attain, and any efforts to achieve budgeted goals will be unenthusiastic. Such a budget may achieve the desired motivation objective for only a short period of time.

A radically different approach is sometimes termed *participative* budgeting. In its purest form, the budget of each responsibility center is produced by a process of negotiation between its manager and his or her immediate superior. Discussions of proposed budgets continue at all levels of the organization, until cost and revenue targets are agreed upon by all the parties involved. For example, prior to the beginning of a budgetary year, the manager of Plant 2 will hold separate meetings with the supervisors of all the subordinate production departments. Annual budget proposals will be drawn up for each, which can be summarized as a proposed budget for Plant 2. The plant manager will then meet with the vice president for production and attempt to gain approval for it. The vice president for production will summarize budget proposals from all subordinate managers into a budget for the production responsibility center, and attempt to gain approval for it from the president. Several revisions and further meetings with lower level managers may be necessary before a budget is developed which is acceptable to the supervisors, the plant manager, the vice president, and the president.

The purely participative budget is characterized by the fact that cost and revenue objectives are developed first at the operating level, and are combined at successively higher levels into an overall organization budget. All managers are involved in the process and are satisfied that the budgeted amounts are reasonable and attainable. Therefore each manager is more likely to actively pursue the goals, and to accept the resulting performance measures as equitable. In the negotiations between each superior and subordinate, a certain amount of *padding* of the budget can be expected to result. The existence of this slack in the budget, together with the time-consuming nature of the process, are the major disadvantages of participative budgeting. Yet many organizations feel that these are more than compensated for by the improved motivation which is achieved.

In practice, a budgetary system which is designed to be participative may evolve into one which is more authoritative in its nature. Because of time pressures, a strong-willed superior, or other factors, the negotiating process may become more like a dictatorial one. Subordinate managers are rarely deceived by the formalities of the process when their inputs at budget meetings are never accepted.

Characteristics of Performance Reports

To be effective for motivation, a responsibility accounting system must incorporate a properly designed set of performance reports. The performance reports may have a significant impact on the attitudes and aspirations of managers in the organization. They provide the means of communication between individual responsibility centers and top management, and thus should be clear, concise, and understandable by all using them. By providing feedback on the results of past actions, performance reports enable managers to adjust plans for future actions to correct past deficiencies.

Because of their importance for motivation and control, performance reports should reflect the following four characteristics.

1. **Implement Management by Exception**. Performance reports should be designed to direct the attention of managers to exceptional or unusual items that may affect future activities. Any significant variation from the budget should indicate a need for investigation, regardless of whether the variance is favorable or unfavorable. Unfavorable variances may signal problems that require management attention, or may result from an unrealistic budget. Favorable variances may justify praise from higher management, or may result from a permissive budget.
2. **Satisfy Requirements of the User**. Differing levels of management have differing needs for information, and this should be reflecting in the performance reports. Supervisors and foremen usually constitute lower level management. They are primarily concerned with daily operations. The performance reports designed for their use should be limited to the items controlled by their individual responsibility centers, and should be presented in great detail. Middle management is generally considered to be those in charge of a firm's major subdivision. These managers are responsible for carrying out the guidelines and policies determined by top management. Their reports should include summary data pertaining to the departments within the division and details of their daily operations. Top management, not as concerned with the control and coordination of day-to-day

operations, requires summarized reports highlighting the overall operations and major events. These summaries must be accompanied by sufficient supporting details so that the sources of unfavorable situations may be traced.

3. **Simple and Relevant**. Since the user of the performance report is usually not an accountant, performance reports should be kept simple and relevant and the terminology should not be too technical. Bulky or complicated reports tend to discourage management use and careful attention. Titles and headings should be descriptive and clearly identify the data. Only absolutely essential information needs to be included so that waste of time and confusion can be minimized. Furthermore, performance reports should be standardized so that users can become familiarized with the format, terminology, and location of specific items of interests. This not to say that performance reports should never change; indeed, constant attention should be given to improving them with proper planning and timing. Changes should be made with a minimum of confusion.
4. **Timely**. Timeliness in preparation and presentation of performance reports is crucial. Management has the responsibility to make prompt decisions concerning problem areas. Obviously the sooner they receive the reports, the earlier they can formulate a plan of corrective action and render decisions. The time span between performance reporting and decision making must be minimized for several reasons. First, management is most concerned with problems when they occur, not after time has passed and new problems have arisen. Secondly, the company loses money as long as a problem situation remains uncorrected. Finally, after passage of time, management tends to become tolerant of inefficiencies.

The characteristics of a responsibility accounting system which effectively achieves the dual objectives of motivating employees and providing control of operations are summarized in Illustration 17-4.

Illustration 17-4 Characteristics of an Effective Responsibility Accounting System

Data accumulation
- by descriptive category; e.g., direct materials, insurance, depreciation
- by responsibility center; e.g., supervisor of department, regional manager, vice president

Performance measures
- revenues generated (if appropriate)
- controllable costs

Budget development
- participative
- attainable

Performance reports
- implement management by exception
- satisfy requirements of user
- simple and relevant
- timely

Role of the Cost Accountant

This chapter has described the mechanics of a responsibility accounting system, and the design considerations which are needed to make the system effective. However, the role fulfilled by the cost accountant in responsibility accounting should be emphasized.

Probably the most significant contribution which a cost accountant can make to such a system is during its design. Responsibility accounting requires that for each responsibility center appropriate performance measures be developed. The cost accountant is in a position to identify those performance measures and to isolate the costs incurred in each responsibility center. These costs must then be categorized as controllable and uncontrollable before the reporting structure is developed. These decisions will have a lasting impact on the effectiveness of the system.

On an ongoing basis, cost accountants are usually involved in the budgeting process. In an authoritarian system, they usually provide the detailed analysis to support the budget objectives developed by top management. In a participative system, their function is to provide the necessary information and to summarize the results of the negotiating processes which take place. Frequently responsibility accounting systems are used in conjunction with standard costs, in which a major responsibility of the cost accountant is the development of standards and their interpretation. This extremely valuable function will be described in detail in the next chapter.

Summary

Responsibility accounting systems are utilized to provide information for the motivation of employees and for the control of operations. They employ a method of budgeting and performance reporting created around the structure of the organization utilizing it. Individual managers are held responsible for the amount by which actual costs and revenues deviate from those budgeted, called the budget variance. To achieve its objectives effectively, the system should hold a manager accountable for only those costs which are controllable by the manager. Furthermore, managers should be involved in developing the budgeted measures by which their performances are evaluated.

Key Definitions

Authoritative budgeting — A method of developing a budget in which goals are established by top management with very little input from lower level managers.

Budget slack — A result of participatory budgets when subordinates overestimate expected costs and underestimate expected revenues in order to make goals easier to attain.

Controllable costs — Those costs which can be regulated by the manager of a decision center within a budgetary reporting period.

Decision center An area of management responsibility, which may be a cost center at the operating level or a higher level manager to which other managers report.

Participative budgeting A method of developing a budget in which goals are established by a process of negotiation between superiors and subordinates at all levels of the organization.

Performance report A report produced for each decision center which discloses budgeted and actual performance measures and variances from the budget.

Responsibility accounting system A method of budgeting and performance reporting which assigns responsibility to individual managers for all costs and revenues incurred by an organization.

Uncontrollable costs Those costs which cannot be regulated by the manager of a decision center within a budgetary reporting period.

Variance The difference between budgeted costs or revenues and actual costs or revenues during a budgetary reporting period.

Questions

17-1 What is a decision center?

17-2 How can a budgetary system be used for purposes of motivation?

17-3 How can a budgetary system be used for purposes of control?

17-4 What factors affect the extent to which a manager can control costs in a department?

17-5 What are the arguments for including uncontrollable costs on a manager's performance report? What are the arguments against?

17-6 When uncontrollable costs are included on a performance report, how should they be disclosed?

17-7 How does a participative budgetary system improve the effectiveness of a budget as a motivator?

17-8 Why do some organizations use authoritarian budgetary methods?

17-9 What is meant by "budgetary slack?"

17-10 What knowledge should a cost accountant have who participates in the design of a responsibility accounting system?

17-11 What is a variance? For what purpose is it used?

Problems

17-12 *Controllable and Uncontrollable Costs*

The following expenses are incurred in a shipping department. Identify those costs which are controllable by the manager of the department.

(a) supplies
(b) shipping clerk's salary
(c) depreciation on equipment
(d) electric power
(e) shipping manager's salary
(f) allocated portion of plant manager's salary
(g) building rent
(h) property taxes.

17-13 *Cost Controllability by Level*

For each of the following examples of factory costs, indicate whether each most likely is controllable by the plant manager (P), the supervisor of repair and maintenance (R), or the foreman of the machining department (M).

(a) depreciation on machining equipment
(b) machining direct labor
(c) labor for repairs on machining department equipment
(d) repair supplies
(e) heat in machining department
(f) overtime for machining department labor
(g) repair and maintenance costs allocated to machining department
(h) labor fringe benefits.

17-14 *Performance Report*

Jefferson Corp. uses a responsibility accounting system. The following are the budgeted and actual costs incurred in Department A for the month of August.

Direct materials:.. $13,000 budgeted, $13,600 actual.
Direct labor: .... $15,000 budgeted, $16,000 actual.
Electric power:.. $500 budgeted and actual.
Depreciation:.. $3,000 budgeted and actual.
Allocated plant office costs:........................ $2,400 budgeted and actual.
Property taxes:.. $250 budgeted and actual.
Supplies:.. $600 budgeted, $500 actual.

From this data, prepare a performance report for Department A in good form.

17-15 *Responsibility for Variances*

Responsibility accounting systems provide improved control when specific managers can be held responsible for variances, The following represent possible sources of cost variances in a production department. For each possible source, determine who in an organization exerts the most direct control over it.

(a) excessive use of labor for work performed
(b) rejected units due to spoilage
(c) excessive cost of direct materials used
(d) using highly paid labor for a job requiring little skill
(e) substitution of low quality material
(f) excessive labor costs due to pay raise
(g) excessive price paid for direct materials.
(h) poor workmanship resulting in high spoilage rates
(i) idle workers
(j) excessive costs for indirect materials.

From this data, prepare a performance report for Department A in good form

17-16 *Levels of Performance Reports*

Ajax Manufacturing Corp. utilizes a responsibility accounting system which discloses the uncontrollable costs for each decision center on its performance reports. The following data reflects the budgeted and actual costs in the Seattle Plant during March.

	Seattle Plant					
	Department A		*Department B*		*Plant Office*	
	Budgeted	*Actual*	*Budgeted*	*Actual*	*Budgeted*	*Actual*
Direct materials..	$ 5,000	$ 4,800	$ 2,000	$ 2,100	-	-
Direct labor.........	3,600	3,400	4,700	5,000	-	-
Supplies	600	650	300	350	$ 400	$ 410
Rent (allocated)..	1,000	1,000	700	700	300	300
Power..................	450	500	300	320	150	180
Depreciation	3,000	3,000	1,500	1,500	500	500
Clerical salaries..	500	500	500	500	2,500	2,500
Total..............	$14,150	$13,850	$10,000	$10,470	$3,850	$3,890

Prepare in good form performance reports covering the month of March for:
(a) Department A, and
(b) the Seattle Plant.

17-17 *Budgeting Procedures*

Deborah Dashley, young president of VIP Corp., has described her company's budgeting procedures in the following way.

Our controller is a real go-getter so I just turn the budgeting process over to him. He has access to all the past sales records so he can prepare a sales forecast as well as anybody in the company. And he is excellent with figures, so he can develop the budgeted costs much faster than any of our operating people. He develops the master budget and submits it to me. I make any changes I think are necessary and turn it back to him. From then on his people can develop the departmental budgets for the rest of the company. I have thought about letting the operating people get involved, but that would distract them from more productive work. As long as the budget goals are difficult to attain, our workers will be motivated to improve their performances.

Comment on any problems which you perceive might result from the above procedures. What improvements can you suggest?

17-18 *Critique of a Performance Report*

Randolph Corporation utilizes a nationwide sales organization for marketing its line of consumer products. Year-end bonuses are awarded to managers based on annual profit improvement. The manager of the Denver Sales Region has just received the following profit report for the month of November.

Randolph Corporation
Denver Sales Region
Profit Report for November
(in 000's)

	Current Month	*Previous Month*	*Same Month, Previous Year*
Sales revenues	$16,000	$17,150	$15,200
Cost of goods sold	11,200	12,005	9,880
Gross margin	4,800	5,145	5,320
Less other costs:			
Salaries and commissions	200	210	200
Travel and entertainment	15	20	16
Promotions	45	60	44
Data processing	210	245	210
Advertising	600	600	580
Allocated corporate overhead	530	585	510
Net Income	$ 3,200	$ 3,425	$ 3,760
As % of sales	20%	20%	25%

Selling prices are set nationally by the corporate office in New York. Individual sales managers are allowed to establish promotional activities (coupons, rebates, etc.) within their regions; however, major advertising campaigns are authorized only at corporate headquarters. Data processing costs are allocated to each sales region based on its usage relative to other sales regions. Other corporate costs are allocated to sales regions based on sales percentages.

(a) Consider yourself as manager of the Denver sales region. How would you react to being evaluated by this profit report?

(b) What suggestions for improvement in this performance evaluation system can you make?

17-19 *Responsibility Accounting*

An important concept in management accounting is the concept of "responsibility accounting."

Required:

(a) Define the term "responsibility accounting."

(b) What are the conditions that must exist for there to be effective "responsibility accounting"?

(c) What benefits are said to result from "responsibility accounting?"

(d) Listed below are three charges found on the monthly report of a division which manufactures and sells products primarily to outside companies. Division performance is evaluated by the use of return on investment. You are to state which, if any, of the following charges are consistent with the "responsibility accounting" concept. Support each answer with a brief explanation.

1. A charge for general corporation administration at 10% of division sales.
2. A charge for the use of the corporate computer facility. The charge is determined by taking actual annual computer department costs and allocating an amount to each user on the ratio of its use to total corporation use.
3. A charge for goods purchased from another division. The charge is based upon the competitive market price for the goods.

(*IMA adapted*)

17-20 *Controllable Costs*

The Fillep Co. utilizes a responsibility accounting system. The variances for each department are calculated and reported to the department manager. It is expected that the manager will use the information to improve his operations and recognize that it is used by his superiors when they are evaluating his performance.

John Smith was recently appointed manager of the assembly department of the company. He has complained that the system as designed is disadvantageous to his department. Included among the variances charged to the departments is one for rejected units. The inspection occurs at the end of the assembly department. The inspectors attempt to identify the cause of the rejection so that the department where the error occurred can be charged with it. Not all errors can be easily identified with a department. These are totalled and apportioned to the departments according to the number of identified errors. The variance for rejected units in each department is a combination of the errors caused by the department plus a portion of the unidentified causes of rejects.

Required:

(a) Is John Smith's claim valid? Explain the reason(s) for your answer?

(b) What would you recommend the company do to solve its problem with John Smith and his complaint?

(*IMA adapted*)

17-21 *Budgets for Motivation*

The Parsons Co. compensates its field sales force on a commission and year-end bonus basis. The commission is 20% of standard gross margin (planned selling price less standard cost of goods sold on a full absorption basis) contingent upon collection of the account. Customer's credit is approved by the company's credit department. Price concessions are granted on occasion by the top sales management, but sales commissions are not reduced by the discount. A year-end bonus of 15% of commissions earned is paid to salesmen who equal or exceed their annual sales target. The annual sales target is usually established by applying approximately a 5% increase to the prior year's sales.

Required:

(a) What features of this compensation plan would seem to be effective in motivating the salesmen to accomplish company goals of higher profits and return on investment? Explain why.

(b) What features of this compensation plan would seem to be countereffective in motivating the salesmen to accomplish the company goals of higher profits and return on investment? Explain why.

(*IMA adapted*)

17-22 *Authoritarian Budgeting*

Argon County Hospital is located in the county seat. Argon County is a well-known summer resort area. The county population doubles during the vacation months (May to August), and hospital activity more than doubles during this time. The hospital is organized into several departments. Although it is a relatively small hospital, its pleasant surroundings have attracted a well-trained and competent medical staff.

An administrator was hired a year ago to improve the business activities of the hospital. Among the new ideas introduced is responsibility accounting. This program was announced along with quarterly cost reports to be supplied to department heads. Previously, cost data were presented to department heads infrequently. Excerpts from the announcement and the report received by the laundry supervisor are presented as follows:

The hospital has adopted a "responsibility accounting system." From now on you will receive quarterly reports comparing the costs of operating your department with budgeted costs. The reports will highlight the differences (variations) so that you can zero in on the departure from budgeted costs. (This is called "management by exception.") Responsibility accounting means you are accountable for keeping the costs in your department within the budget. The variations from the budget will help you identify which costs are out of line, and the size of the variation will indicate which ones are the most important. Your first such report accompanies this announcement.

Argon County Hospital
Performance Report—Laundry Department
July–September, 20X1

	Budget	Actual	(Over) Under Budget	Percent (Over) Under
Patient days	9,500	11,900	(2,400)	(25)
Pounds process-laundry	125,000	156,000	(31,000)	(25)
Costs:				
Laundry labor	$ 9,000	$12,500	($3,500)	(39)
Supplies ;	1,100	1,875	(775)	(70)
Water, water heating, & softening	1,700	2,500	(800)	(47)
Maintenance	1,400	2,200	(800)	(57)
Supervisor's salary	3,150	3,750	(600)	(19)
Allocated administration costs	4,000	5,000	(1,000)	(25)
Equipment depreciation	1,200	1,250	(50)	(4)
	$21,550	$29,075	($7,525)	(35)

Administrator's comments: Costs are significantly above budget for the quarter. Particular attention needs to be paid to labor, supplies, and maintenance.
The annual budget for 20X1 was constructed by the new administrator. Quarterly budgets were computed as one-fourth of the annual budget. The administrator compiled the budget from analysis of costs over the prior three years. The analysis showed that all costs increased each year and that the increases were more rapid between the second and third years. The administrator considered establishing the budget at an average of the prior three years' costs, hoping that the installation of the system would reduce costs to this level. However, in view of the rapidly increasing prices, 20X0 costs less 3 percent were finally chosen for the 20X1 budget. The activity level measured by patient days and pounds of laundry processed was set at 20X0 volume, which was approximately equal to the volume of each of the past three years.

Required:

(a) Comment on the method used to construct the budget.
(b) What information should be communicated by variations from budgets?
(c) Does the report effectively communicate the level of efficiency of this department? Give reasons for your answer.

(*IMA adapted*)

17-23 Data Accumulation

Ollie Mace has recently been appointed controller of a family owned manufacturing enterprise. The firm, S. Dilley & Co., was founded by Mr. Dilley about 20 years ago, is 78% owned by Mr. Dilley, and has served the major automotive companies as a parts supplier. The firm's major operating divisions are heat treating, extruding, small parts stamping, and specialized machining. Sales last year from the several divisions ranged from $150,000 to over $3,000,000. The divisions are physically and managerially independent except for Mr. Dilley's constant surveillance. The accounting system for each division has evolved according to the division's own needs and to the abilities of individual accountants or bookkeepers. Mr. Mace is the first controller in the firm's history to have responsibility for overall financial management. Mr. Dilley expects to retire within six years and has hired Mr. Mace to improve the firm's financial system. Mr. Mace soon decides that he will need to design a new financial reporting system that will:

1. Give managers uniform, timely, and accurate reports on business activity. Monthly divisional reports should be uniform and available by the 10th of the following month. Company wide financial reports also should be prepared by the 10th.
2. Provide a basis for measuring return on investment by division. Divisional reports should show assets assigned each division and revenue and expense measurement in each division.
3. Generate meaningful budget data for planning and decision-making purposes. The accounting system should provide for the preparation of budgets which recognize managerial responsibility, controllability of costs, and major product groups.
4. Allow for a uniform basis of evaluating performance and quick access to underlying data. Cost center variances should be measured and reported for operating and non-operating units including headquarters. Also questions about levels of specific cost factors or product costs should be answerable quickly.

A new chart of accounts, as it appears to Mr. Mace, is essential to getting started on other critical financial problems. The present account codes used by divisions are not standard.

Mr. Mace sees a need to divide asset accounts into six major categories, i.e., current assets, plant and equipment, etc. Within each of these categories, he sees a need for no more than 10 control accounts. Based on his observations to date, 100 subsidiary accounts are more than adequate for each control account.

No division now has more than five major product groups. The maximum number of cost centers Mr. Mace foresees within any product group is six, including operating and non-operating groups. He views general divisional costs as a non-revenue producing product group. Altogether, Mr. Mace estimates that about 44 natural expense accounts plus about 12 specific variance accounts would be adequate.

Mr. Mace is planning to implement the new chart of accounts in an environment that at present includes manual records systems and one division which is using an EDP system. Mr. Mace expects that in the near future most accounting and reporting for all units will be automated. Therefore, the chart of accounts should facilitate the processing of transactions manually or by machine. Efforts should be made, he believes, to restrict the length of the code for economy in processing and convenience in use.

Required.

(a) Design a chart of accounts coding system that will meet Mr. Mace's requirements. Your answer should begin with a digital layout of the coding system. You should explain the coding method you have chosen and the reason for the size of your code elements. Explain your code as it would apply to *asset* and *expense* accounts.

(b) Use your chart of accounts coding system to illustrate the code needed for the following data:

1. In the small parts stamping division, $100 was spent by foreman Bill Shaw in the polishing department of the Door Lever Group on cleaning supplies. Code the expense item using the code you developed above.
2. A new motorized sweeper has been purchased for the maintenance department of the extruding division for $3,450. Code this asset item using the code you developed above.

(*IMA adapted*)

17-24 *Budgets for Performance Evaluation*

The Noton Company has operated a comprehensive budgeting system for many years. This system is a major component of the company's program to control operations and costs at its widely scattered plants. Periodically the plants' general managers gather to discuss the overall company control system with the top management.

At this year's meeting, the budgetary system was severely criticized by one of the most senior plant managers. He said that the system discriminated unfairly against the older, well-run and established plants in favor of the newer plants. The impact was lower year-end bonuses and poor performance ratings. In addition, there were psychological consequences in the form of lower employee morale. In his judgment, revisions in the system were needed to make it more effective. The basic factors of Noton's budget include:

1. Announcement of an annual improvement percentage target established by top management.
2. Plant submission of budgets implementing the annual improvement target.
3. Management review and revision of the proposed budget.
4. Establishment and distribution of the final budget.

To support his argument, he compared the budget revisions and performance results. The older plants were expected to achieve the improvement target but often were unable to meet it. On the other hand, the newer plants were often excused from meeting a portion of this target in their budgets. However, their performance was usually better than the final budget.

He further argued that the company did not recognize the operating differences which made attainment of the annual improvement factor difficult, if not impossible. His plant has been producing essentially the same product for its 20 years of existence. The machinery and equipment, which underwent many modifications in the first five years, have had no major changes in recent years. Because they are old, repair and maintenance costs have increased each year, and the machines are less reliable. The plant management team has been together for the last ten years and works well together. The labor force is mature, with many of the employees having the highest seniority in the company. In his judgment, the significant improvements have been "wrung out" of the plant over the years and that merely keeping even is difficult.

For comparison he noted that one plant opened within the past four years would have an easier time meeting the company's expectations. The plant is new, containing modern equipment that is in some cases still experimental. Major modifications in equipment and operating systems have been made each year as the plant management has obtained a better understanding of the operations. The plant's management, although experienced, has been together only since its opening. The plant is located in a previously nonindustrial area and therefore has a relatively inexperienced work force.

Required:

(a) Evaluate the manufacturing manager's views.
(b) Equitable application of a budget system requires the ability of corporate management to remove "budgetary slack" in plant budgets. Discuss how each plant could conceal "slack" in its budget.

(*IMA adapted*)

17-25 Evaluating Managers by Division Performance

George Johnson was hired on July 1, 2009, as assistant general manager of the Botel Division of Staple, Inc. It was understood that he would be elevated to general manager of the division on January 1, 2011, when the current general manager retired; this was duly done. Besides becoming acquainted with the division and the general manager's duties, Mr. Johnson was charged specifically with the responsibility for development of the 2010 and 2011 budgets. As general manager in 2011, he obviously was responsible for the 2012 budget.

Staple, Inc. is a multiproduct company that is highly decentralized. Each division is quite autonomous. The corporation staff approves operating budgets prepared by the divisions but seldom makes major changes in them. The corporate staff actively participates in decisions requiring capital investment (for expansion or replacement) and makes the final decisions. The division management is responsible for implementing the capital investment program. The major method used by Staple, Inc. to measure division performance is contribution return on division net investment. The budgets below were approved by the corporation. (Revision of the 2012 budget is not considered necessary, even though 2011 actually departed from the approved 2011 budget.)

Staple, Inc.
Comparative Profit Report
($000 omitted)

	Actual			Budget	
Botel Division	2009	2010	2011	2011	2012
Sales	$1,000	$1,500	$1,800	$2,000	$2,400
Less: Division variable costs:					
Material and labor	250	375	450	500	600
Repairs	50	75	50	100	120
Supplies	20	30	36	40	48
Less: Division managed costs:					
Employee training	30	35	25	40	45
Maintenance	50	55	40	60	70
Less: Division commited costs:					
Depreciation	120	160	160	200	200
Rent	80	100	110	140	140
Total	600	830	871	1,080	1,223
Division net contribution	$ 400	$ 670	$ 929	$ 920	$1,177
Division investment:					
Accounts receivable	100	150	180	200	240
Inventory	200	300	270	400	480
Fixed assets	1,590	2,565	2,800	3,380	4,000
Less: Accounts and wages payable	(150)	(225)	(350)	(300)	(360)
Net investment	$1,740	$2,790	$2,900	$3,680	$4,360
Contribution return on investment	23%	24%	32%	25%	27%

Required:

(a) Identify Mr. Johnson's responsibilities under the management and measurement program described above.

(b) Appraise the performance of Mr. Johnson in 2011.

(c) Recommend to the president any resident any changes in the responsibilities assigned to managers or in the measurement methods used to evaluate division management based upon your analysis.

(*IMA adapted*)

17-26 Participative Budgeting

Scott Weidner, the Controller in the Division of Social Services for the state, recognizes the importance of the budgetary process for planning, control and motivation purposes. He believes that a properly implemented participative budgeting process for planning purposes and a management by exception reporting procedure based upon the participative budget will motivate his subordinates to improve productivity within their particular departments. Based upon this philosophy, Weidner has implemented the following budget procedures.

- An appropriation target figure is given to each department manager. This amount is the maximum funding that each department can expect to receive in the next fiscal year.
- Department managers develop their individual budgets within the following spending constraints as directed by the controller's staff.

(1) Expenditure requests cannot exceed the appropriation target.
(2) All fixed expenditures should be included in the budget. Fixed expenditures would include such items as contracts and salaries at current levels.
(3) All government projects directed by higher authority should be included in the budget in their entirety.

- The controller's staff consolidates the departmental budget requests from the various departments into one budget that is to be submitted for the entire division.
- Upon final budget approval by the legislature, the controller's staff allocates the appropriation to the various departments on instructions from the division manager. However, a specified percentage of each department's appropriation is held back in anticipation of potential budget cuts and special funding needs. The amount and use of this contingency fund is left to the discretion of the division manager.
- Each department is allowed to adjust its budget when necessary to operate within the reduced appropriation level. However, as stated in the original directive, specific projects authorized by higher authority must remain intact.
- The final budget is used as the basis of control for a management by exception form of reporting. Excessive expenditures by account for each department are highlighted on a monthly basis. Department managers are expected to account for all expenditures over budget. Fiscal responsibility is an important factor in the overall performance evaluation of department managers.

Weidner believes his policy of allowing the department managers to participate in the budget process and then holding them accountable for their performance is essential, especially during these times of limited resources. He further believes the department managers will be motivated positively to increase the efficiency and effectiveness of their departments because they have provided input into the initial budgetary process and are required to justify any unfavorable performances.

Required:

(a) Explain the operational and behavioral benefits that generally are attributed to a participative budgeting process.
(b) Identify deficiencies in Scott Weidner's participative budgetary policy for planning and performance evaluation purposes. For each deficiency identified, recommend how the deficiency can be corrected.

17-27 *Responsibility Accounting System*

Kelly Petroleum Company has a large oil and natural gas project in Oklahoma. The project has been organized into two production centers (petroleum production and natural gas production) and one service center (maintenance).

Maintenance Center Activities and Scheduling: Don Pepper, maintenance center manager, has organized his maintenance workers into work crews that serve the two production centers. The maintenance crews perform preventive maintenance and repair equipment both in the field and in the central maintenance shop.

Pepper is responsible for scheduling all maintenance work in the field and at the central shop. Preventive maintenance is performed according to a set schedule established by Pepper and approved by the production center managers. Breakdowns are given immediate priority in scheduling so that downtime is minimized. Thus, preventive maintenance occasionally must be postponed, but every attempt is made to reschedule it within three weeks.

Preventive maintenance work is the responsibility of Pepper. However, if a significant problem is discovered during preventive maintenance, the appropriate production center supervisor authorizes and supervises the repair after checking with Pepper.

When a breakdown in the field occurs, the production centers contact Pepper to initiate the repairs. The repair work is supervised by the production center supervisor.

Machinery and equipment sometimes need to be replaced while the original equipment is repaired in the central shop. This procedure is followed only when the time to make the repair in the field would result in an extended interruption of operations. Replacement of equipment is recommended by the maintenance work crew supervisor and approved by a production center supervisor.

Routine preventive maintenance and breakdowns of automotive and mobile equipment used in the field are completed in the central shop. All repairs and maintenance activities taking place in the central shop are under the direction of Pepper.

Maintenance Center Accounting Activities: Pepper has records identifying the work crews assigned to each job in the field, the number of hours spent on the job, and the parts and supplies used on the job. In addition, records for the central shop (jobs, labor hours, parts and supplies) have been maintained. However, this detailed maintenance information is not incorporated into Kelly's accounting system.

Pepper develops the annual budget for the maintenance center by planning the preventive maintenance that will be needed during the year, estimating the number and seriousness of breakdowns, and estimating the shop activities. He then bases the labor, part, and supply costs on this plans and estimates and develops the budget amounts by line item. Because the timing of the breakdowns is impossible to plan, Pepper divides the annual budget by 12 to derive the monthly budget.

All costs incurred by the work crews in the field and in the central shop are accumulated monthly and then allocated to the two production cost centers based upon the field hours worked in each production center. This method of cost allocation has been used on Pepper's recommendation because he believed that it was easy to implement and understand. Furthermore, he believed that a better allocation system was impossible to incorporate into the monthly report due to the wide range of salaries paid to maintenance workers and the fast turnover of materials and parts.

The November cost report for the maintenance center that is provided by the accounting department is shown below.

Oklahoma Project
Maintenance Center Cost Report
For the Month of November 20X9
(in thousands of dollars)

	Budget	*Actual*	*Petroleum Production*	*Natural Gas*
Shop hours	2,000	1,800	--	--
Field hours	8,000	10,000	6,000	4,000
Labor:				
Electrical	$ 25.0	$ 24.0	$ 14.4	$ 9.6
Mechnical	30.0	35.0	21.0	14.0
Instrumentation	18.0	22.5	13.5	9.0
Automotive	3.5	2.8	1.7	1.1
Heavy equipment	9.6	12.3	7.4	4.9
Equipment operation	28.8	35.4	21.2	14.2
General	15.4	15.9	9.6	6.3
Parts	60.0	86.2	51.7	34.5
Supplies	15.3	12.2	7.3	4.9
Lubricants and fuels	3.4	3.0	1.8	1.2
Tools	2.5	3.2	1.9	1.3
Accounting and data processing	1.5	1.5	.9	.6
Total	$213.0	$254.0	$152.4	$101.6

Production Center Manager's Concerns: Both production center managers have been upset with the method of cost allocation. Furthermore, they believe the report is virtually useless as a cost control device. Actual costs always seem to deviate from the monthly budget and the proportion charged to each production center varies significantly from month-to-month. Maintenance costs have increased substantially since 20X6, and the production managers believe that they have no way to judge whether such an increase is reasonable.

The two production managers, Pepper, and representatives of corporate accounting have met to discuss these concerns. They concluded that a responsibility accounting system could be developed to replace the current system. In their opinion, a responsibility accounting system would alleviate the production managers' concerns and accurately reflect the activity of the maintenance center.

Required:

(a) Explain the purposes of a responsibility accounting system, and discuss how such a system could resolve the concerns of the production center managers of Kelly Petroleum Company.

(b) Describe the behavioral advantages generally attributed to responsibility accounting systems that the management of Kelly Petroleum Company should expect if the system were effectively introduced for the maintenance center.

(c) Describe a report format for the maintenance center that would be based upon an effective responsibility accounting system, and explain which, if any, of the maintenance center's costs should be charged to the two production centers.

(IMA adapted)

1. *To illustrate the difficulties in accounting for management control in decentralized organizations.*
2. *To describe methods of segment profit reporting and managerial performance evaluation in decentralized organizations.*
3. *To discuss three methods of segment performance evaluation, return on investment, residual income and economic value added.*
4. *To discuss the problems and illustrate the methods of accounting for sales between divisions.*
5. *To introduce the balanced scorecard.*

18 Divisional Performance Measurement

As an organization grows, its activities become more diversified and increasingly difficult to control. Many large companies have found that control over operations is improved by dividing the organization into divisions or segments, and placing an individual manager in charge of each segment. This individual is then given decision-making authority and responsibility over the activities of the division, and is held accountable for its performance. Such a decentralized company may be segmented by product line, by geographical region, by industry classification, or in very large companies by some combination of these methods. The performance of each division is evaluated in comparison to the other divisions by its contribution to the overall objectives of the company.

Divisions or segments may be classified into three types: cost centers, profit centers, and investment centers. A cost center is a division where performance is measured by comparing actual costs with budgeted costs for a specified period of time. Activities often associated with a cost center include accounting, personnel, legal, data processing, engineering, and public relations. A profit center is a division of a firm where performance measurement is based on the division's net income. An investment center is a division of a firm where performance is measured by relating its net income to the capital investment in the division. The performance measurement system useful for evaluating the performance of a cost center has been discussed in chapter 17.

The problem of developing an accounting system that provides appropriate measures of divisional performance is a difficult one, and no standardized preferred method has been created. The greatest difficulty is one of maintaining *goal congruence*, in which each division is motivated to pursue the best interests of the company as a whole rather than those of the division alone. In this chapter, a commonly used approach to measuring segment profitability will be illustrated.

Then methods of evaluating a division's ability to provide a return to the company on invested capital are described. Solutions to the problem of accounting for interdivision sales are also discussed in this chapter. Finally, the balanced scorecard is introduced.

Reporting Segment Profitability

In most businesses, a major objective is the maintenance of an adequate level of profitability. In a decentralized company, each division is expected to contribute to this objective. Because of its advantages for internal reporting, the direct costing approach to income determination is frequently used in measuring the profitability of individual segments. Each segment is considered to be an individual profit center and a measure of net income is determined for each in a manner similar to that used for the company as a whole.

Separable and Common Costs

One advantage of the direct costing approach is that it isolates fixed costs. In a decentralized company, some of these fixed costs are incurred at the divisional level while others are incurred for the benefits of all divisions. Costs which are attributable to an individual division are called *separable* costs, and may or may not be controllable by the manager in charge of the division. When computing net income for the division, these are subtracted from the division's contribution to give the division's *segment margin.* The segment margin measures the divisions contribution to the company's profits and to the recovery of the company's *common costs.*

Common costs are those fixed costs incurred for all the divisions in common. They are not traceable to any individual segment, but are most often incurred at the corporate office and may include executive salaries, clerical and administrative costs, and legal and public relations expenses. In some organizations common costs may be allocated to segments in order to make divisional managers aware of them; however, because they are not controllable at the segment level, and because the methods of making such allocations are disputable, allocations of common costs should not be used in evaluating segment performance. An example of a segment profitability report in which common costs are not allocated is contained in Illustration 18-1.

Illustration 18-1 Direct Costing Approach to Measuring Segment Profitability

International Industries, Inc.
Division Profit Report

20xx (Stated in 1,000's)	Division A	Division B	Company Total
Sales Revenue	$60,000	$40,000	$100,000
Variable Cost of Goods Sold	(30,000)	(15,000)	(45,000)
Contribution	30,000	25,000	55,000
Separable Fixed Costs	(20,000)	(15,000)	(35,000)
Segment Margin	$10,000	$10,000	$20,000
Unallocated Common Costs			(1,000)
Net Income			$19,000

SEGMENT PROFITABILITY AND MANAGERIAL PERFORMANCE

Control is established in decentralized organizations by assigning responsibility for an operating division to the manager in charge of it. However, a distinction should be made between evaluating the profitability of a division and evaluating the performance of its manager. As has been discussed in the chapter on responsibility accounting, a manager's performance should be evaluated by his or her ability to achieve the cost and revenue targets incorporated in a budget. These costs should include only those costs which are controllable at the manager's level in the organization. Of the separable costs attributable to a division, many will not be controllable by the division manager. These include costs such as depreciation on equipment, property taxes, or interest costs on external financing. Also, a division may operate in an industry or geographic area where profits are very difficult to achieve. This fact can be considered in developing the division's budget, but is not reflected in a divisional performance report such as that of Illustration 18-1. Although a segment's profitability may indeed result from good (or poor) managerial performance, segment profit reporting is not a substitute for a system of budgeting and responsibility reporting.

When a manager is responsible for the profitability of a division, segment profit reporting can be integrated into the system of responsibility reporting. The segment profit report in this case is a responsibility report at the division level, and should distinguish between costs controllable and uncontrollable by the manager. An example of such a report is contained in Illustration 18-2. An additional item, the *performance margin*, is calculated which can be used to evaluate the performance of the manager. The segment margin as before reflects the profitability of the division.

Illustration 18-2 Segment Responsibility and Profit Report International Industries, Inc. Division A Profit Report 20XX (stated in 1,000's)

International Industries, Inc.
Division A Profit Report
20xx
(stated in 1,000's)

	Actual	*Budget*	*Variance*
Sales Revenue	$60,000	$65,000	$(5,000)
Variable Cost of Goods Sold:	24,000	26,000	(2,000)
Manufacturing			
Selling	6,000	7,000	(1,000)
Total	30,000	33,000	(3,000)
Contribution	30,000	32,000	(2,000)
Controllable Fixed Costs:			
Salaries	4,000	4,000	--
Advertising	5,000	6,000	(1,000)
Total	9,000	10,000	(1,000)
Performance Margin	21,000	22,000	(1,000)
Uncontrollable Fixed Costs:	10,000	10,000	
Depreciation			
Property Taxes	1,000	1,000	
Total	11,000	11,000	
Segment Margin	$10,000	$11,000	

The profitability of each division is always of concern to a decentralized company. Yet in evaluating divisional performance, a measure of income such as the segment margin is inadequate. Segment margin fails to consider the amount of capital required by the segment to achieve a level of profitability. More appropriate measures of segment performance recognize that a division should provide its parent company with a fair return on the capital employed by the division.

Evaluating Segment Performance

Decentralized companies, as part of their capital budgeting procedures, distribute funds to operating divisions for further investment by the divisions. For this purpose each segment is considered an investment center, because the segment itself represents an investment by the parent company. Often capital funds are distributed to investment centers based on their past performance, in which those segments with better performance are allocated more funds. A parent company which desires the greatest return on its invested capital will evaluate segment performance utilizing a measure that considers the return on that capital. Three commonly used such measures are *return on investment, residual income, and economic value added.*

Return on Investment

A division's return on investment (ROI) is a measure of the division's efficiency in the use of its invested capital. Stated as a percentage, the return on investment is computed from the following relationship:

$$ROI = \frac{Income}{Invested\ Capital}$$

It is sometimes useful to express ROI as the product of two other ratios of managerial interest as follows:

ROI = capital turnover x income as a percent of sales

$$ROI = \underbrace{\frac{Sales}{Invested\ Capital}}_{capital\ turnover} \times \underbrace{\frac{Income}{Sales}}_{income\ as\ \%\ of\ sales}$$

Return on investment can be used to compare divisions as investments by comparing the ROI of each division. It can be used to identify segments not contributing sufficiently to company profitability by comparing each division's ROI to that of the company as a whole. These applications of ROI are demonstrated in Illustration 18-3. It is sometimes used by a segment to evaluate individual capital investments such as a new plant or machine, although the discounted cash flow methods discussed in Chapter 16 are preferable for this purpose.

ROI is calculated in widely differing ways by different companies, depending on the definition of invested capital used. These alternative methods will be discussed in a later section of this chapter. In comparing performance between divisions, it is necessary that the calculation for each division be performed using the same definition.

The manager of a division can improve its ROI in at least one of the two ways. First, segment margin can be increased by either decreasing costs, or by increasing sales without a

Illustration 18-3 Segment Performance Evaluation by Return on Investment

International Industries, Inc.
Division Performance Summary
20XX
(stated in 1,000's)

	Division A	*Division B*	*Company*
Sales Revenue	$ 60,000	$40,000	$100,000
Income	$ 10,000	$10,000	$ 19,000
Invested Capital*	$100,000	$50,000	$155,000
Return on Investment	10%	20%	12.2%

* Company-invested capital may differ from the total of its divisions because of assets held at the corporate office.

corresponding increase in costs. This type of endeavor is also encouraged by a well-designed responsibility accounting system, and is in most instances consistent with the objectives of the entire company. Secondly, the manager may improve ROI by decreasing the invested capital of the segment. This may be accomplished in many cases by disposing of the divisions assets which are less efficient or less profitable, or have been depreciated to a value below their market value. The effect of such an action on ROI is shown in Illustration 18-4. Disposal may not be in the best interests of the company as a whole, particularly if the action hinders the ability of the division to provided needed services or materials to other divisions of the company. Actions of this kind are encouraged whenever segment performance is used as a measure of managerial performance. If managerial bonuses, promotions, and salary increases are determined based on the manager's ability to achieve budgeted objectives instead of segment performance, goal congruence between the manager and the company may be improved. Self-serving actions by managers to the detriment of the company are discouraged.

The use of return on investment for segment performance evaluation may also result in its misuse in evaluating capital expenditures. A divisional manager intent on maximizing segment ROI may invest only in projects, plants, or equipment which individually provide an ROI greater than that of the division. This may cause the manager of a division with a high ROI to reject an investment which would be accepted by a division with a lower ROI, and which would be beneficial to the company as a whole. This is an objection which causes some companies to prefer residual income as a measure of segment performance.

Residual Income

As a measure of segment performance, residual income is less commonly used than return on investment. Like ROI, the calculation of residual income considers the capital invested in a division. Some companies consider it preferable to ROI because residual income is stated in monetary units rather than a percentage, and the attention of managers is thus directed toward increasing the dollars contributed by the segment. Residual income is computed from the following relationship:

RI = Net income – Cost of capital x Invested Capital

In this equation, the cost of capital is stated as a percentage and invested capital is measured in monetary units. The second term represents the company's minimum desired return on

Illustration 18-4 Effect of Disposal of Assets on ROI

Assume International Industries, Inc. evaluates the performance of its division managers based on divisional return on investment. During the year 20xx, the manager of Division A is concerned about an expected low ROI in the division for the year. Divisional contribution is expected to be $30,000, and the separable fixed costs of $20,000 include 11,000 of depreciation and property taxes on equipment. Investment capital totals $100,000 for the division. The manager can dispose of equipment with a net book value of $50,000, thereby cutting depreciation and property taxes by $5,000 with no effect on contribution. Compute the ROI for each of the following four cases:

(a) without disposal of the equipment;

(b) the equipment is sold for $50,000;

(c)the equipment is sold for $60,000;

(d) the equipment is sold for $40,000.

Solution	(a)	(b)	(c)	(d)
Contribution	$30,000	$30,000	$30,000	$30,000
Less: Separable Fixed Costs	20,000	15,000	15,000	15,000
Net	10,000	15,000	15,000	15,000
Plus: Gain on Sale	0	0	10,000	(10,000)
Segment Margin	$10,000	$15,000	$25,000	$5,000
Invested Capital	$100,000	$100,000	$110,000	$90,000
ROI	10%	15%	22.7%	5.6%

The manager would maximize ROI by selling the equipment for as much as possible in excess of its book value.

investment from a segment, measured in dollars. A positive residual income signifies that this minimum return is being attained, and is evidence of satisfactory segment performance.

The cost of capital is an imputed interest rate and represents the cost to the company of having funds invested in the segment. It may be the company's current interest rate for borrowed funds, or it may be the expected return on investment of an alternative use of the funds. Frequently the cost of capital used in computing residual income may be different for each division in the company. A segment's cost of capital may be the ROI of another company operating in the same industry. It may be the company's cost of borrowed funds adjusted in proportion to the perceived riskiness associated with the division. A segment operating in a high risk industry or geographical area may be expected to achieve a higher return to compensate for the increased risk. When used in this way, the degree of risk to the company is incorporated into the performance measure for the division.

An example of the use of residual income as a means of segment performance evaluation is presented in Illustration 18-5. From this and the previous illustrations, it can be seen that considerations of invested capital and segment risk can radically alter the measured relative performance of divisions in a decentralized company. The manner in which invested capital is computed can also affect the measure of performance of a division.

Illustration 18-5 Segment Performance Evaluation by Residual Income

International Industries, Inc.
Division Performance Summary
20xx
(stated in 1,000's)

	Division A	Division B	Company
Sales Revenue	$ 60,000	$40,000	$100,000
Income	$ 10,000	$10,000	$ 19,000
Invested Capital	$100,000	$50,000	$155,000
Cost of Capital	5%	15%	10%
Residual Income	$ 5,000	$ 2,500	$ 3,500

Concepts of Invested Capital

Companies which utilize return on investment or residual income use varying methods of computing the amount of invested capital. Variations exist in the choice of an investment base, in the method of valuation for the investment base, and in whether or not common assets are allocated to operating divisions. These alternatives will now be described.

Choice of the Investment Base

Invested capital may consist of the monetary equivalent of all or a portion of the assets of a segment, or it may be the equity interest of the company in a segment. The choice of an appropriate investment base depends upon the preference of company management and their expectations of the company's segments.

The most frequently used method is to consider invested capital as the monetary equivalent of the *total assets available* to the division. This includes both the current and the fixed assets assigned to the division. Companies using this approach reason that all assets represent an investment by the company, and that they all should be employed as efficiently as possible in contributing to company profit objectives.

Other companies recognize that some assets of a segment are not productive. Nonproductive assets may include idle facilities, investments in land or securities, construction in progress, or current assets such as cash or accounts receivable. When nonproductive assets are excluded, the investment base becomes the *total assets employed.* Performance measures based on this concept of invested capital evaluate a division based on its ability to utilize those assets that may be reasonably expected to contribute to company profits.

Another method recognizes that of all the assets of a segment, some are contributed by the segment's short-term creditors. Proponents of this method feel that these assets should be excluded from the measure of capital invested by the company. Using *net working capital plus fixed assets* accomplishes this purpose by excluding from the investment base the amount of total assets which exist due to current liabilities.

A final investment base is the *stockholders equity* of the segment. This approach may be appropriate when the segment is a wholly or partially owned subsidiary of a parent company. The performance measure then indicates the return provided by the segment to its owners. The characteristics of these four alternative investment bases are summarized in Illustration 18-6.

Illustration 18-6 Alternative Investment Bases in the Computation of Invested Capital

Investment Base	Distinguishing Concepts
Total Assets Available	Monetary value of all assets assigned to segment
Total Assets Employed	Monetary value of all productive assets utilized by segment
Net Working Capital Plus Fixed Assets	Monetary value of all assets not provided by short-term creditors
Stockholders Equity	Ownership interest in the segment

Choice of the Valuation Method

Since invested capital is the monetary equivalent of an investment base, a method must be chosen to establish the monetary equivalent. Valuation methods used for this purpose may be based on historical cost or may attempt to determine current values.

Historical costs are those used in income determination for external reporting. Stockholders equity is always, by definition, valued at historical cost when this base is used in computing invested capital. Values for asset bases also may utilize historical costs. Fixed assets may be stated at *gross book value,* which are their original costs, or at *net book value,* which is original cost less accumulated depreciation.

Gross book value has the advantage of being objective, unchanging over the life of the asset, and easy to determine. The use of net book value is consistent with the valuation of assets used in external reporting. However, when the physical asset base remains constant over a period of years, use of net book value results in a periodic decrease in the monetary equivalent of the assets. This would cause a periodic increase in the computed ROI or residual income over the same period, when all other factors are unchanged. Thus, a perceived improvement in the performance measure will result, not from improved performance, but rather from the method of valuation selected. Performance measures tend to lose their significance when affected by such factors.

Some companies prefer to value assets at their current replacement costs. The replacement cost is the cost to obtain a similar asset that would produce the same cash inflows as an existing asset. *Market values* are the preferred source of replacement costs when they are available. However, because of technological innovations, many fixed assets such as certain types of machinery cannot be replaced by a similar one. Any new asset of this type would be significantly different in operating costs and cash inflows. In such a situation, the *present value of future cash inflows* from the existing asset may be used to approximate its market value. Another approach is to restate historical costs to the current price level using an index of inflation. These *price level adjusted costs* are more objective than replacement costs but may be misleading if the index used is not appropriate for the asset being valued. Replacement costs, when available, represent current conditions and are preferable for comparing the current performance of operating divisions. These alternative valuation methods are summarized in Illustration 18-7.

Choice of Allocation Methods

Most decentralized companies maintain a corporate office independent of the various operating segments. The corporate office has associated with it certain assets which represent invested capital, such as cash, receivables, equipment and buildings. Because these common assets exist for the benefit of the operating divisions, sometimes a company will allocate them to divisions when computing their invested capital. When this is done, an allocation base must be chosen

Illustration 18-7 Alternative Valuation Methods in the Computation of Invested Capital

Valuation Methods	Distinguishing Concepts
Historical Cost Method	
Gross Book Value	Monetary equivalents stated at original purchase cost
Net Book Value	Monetary equivalents stated at original purchase cost less accumulated depreciation
Current Value Methods	
Market Value	Monetary equivalents stated at cost of a similar asset producing identical cash flows
Present Value of Future Cash Inflows	Monetary equivalents which approximate market values if they are not available
Price Level Adjusted Cost	Monetary equivalents stated at original cost adjusted by an appropriate index of inflation

for each asset. Ideally, an allocation base is measurable within each segment and is related to the benefit received by the segment from the asset. Some types of common assets and frequently used allocation bases are described in Illustration 18-8.

When segment reporting is used strictly as a historical measure of performance, some form of common asset allocation may be beneficial. The practice makes operating managers aware of common assets, and to the extent that operating managers can influence them, may provide some control over the use of capital to acquire them. However, when segment reporting is used in allocating capital to divisions for further investment, no allocation at all is preferable to allocation using a base which is questionable. For example, allocating common cash based on sales billed may motivate a manager to manipulate billings in order to alter allocated cash, thus achieving a desired ROI during a reporting period. The dangers of using allocation methods as a basis for managerial decisions were discussed in Chapter 13.

Economic Value Added

Another performance measure for a business segment is the economic value added (EVA). EVA has been adopted by many well-known companies such as AT&T, J.C. Penney, Coca-Cola, Briggs & Stratton, etc. Like RI, EVA is stated as a dollar amount calculated as the segment's net income after tax and required investment return have been deducted as follows:

EVA = Net income after tax – Required investment return

The required investment return in the context of EVA is determined differently from that in residual income. Specifically, EVC considers the cost of long-term capital instead of a minimum rate of return on investment. The cost of long-term capital measures a weighted average of the cost of a segment's two key long-term financing sources such as long-term debts and equity. Under such a case, the required investment return is calculated as the investment base (e.g., debt and equity capital) times the weighted average cost of capital (WACC) as follows:

Required investment return = (Long-term debts + Market value of equity) x WACC = Investment base x WACC

where WACC = (After-tax cost of long-term debts x Long-term debts) + (Cost of equity x Market value of equity) / (Long-term debts + Market value of equity)

Illustration 18-8 Alternative Allocation Methods for Common Assets in the Computation of Invested Capital

Common Assets	*Basis for Allocation to Segments*
Cash	Sales billed Cost of goods sold Standard percentage of sales or cost of goods sold Budgeted cash requirements
Accounts Receivable	Sales billed Sales weighted by payment terms
Raw Materials Inventories	Raw materials consumed Budgeted raw materials
Fixed Assets	Actual usage measures Budgeted usage measures Depreciation of segment assets Segment fixed assets

Note that while the investment base of equity used in the calculation of WACC is the market value of equity many managers prefer to use the book value because the market value has high variability. When the book value is used in the calculation of WACC, the emphasis of EVA becomes the evaluation of how efficient and effective a segment is using its working capital and fixed assets supported by the long-term capital to generate profits. This idea is that the investment base is now equal to total assets minus current liabilities.

Consider Dessert Company for which the following information is available for year 20X7:

Current assets	$ 200,000
Fixed assets	800,000
Total assets	$1,000,000
Current liabilities	$ 200,000
Long-term debts	200,000
Owners' equity	600,000
Total liabilities and owners' equity	$1,000,000

Desert Company had income before tax $180,000 for year 20X7. The cost of capital for long-term debts and owners' equity is 10% and 15%, respectively. Assume that the income tax rate is 30% and the market value of owners' equity is the same as its book value. The WACC can then be calculated as follows:

WACC = [$200,000 x (1-30%) + $600,000 x 15%] / ($200,000+$600,000)
= $104,000 / $800,000
= 13%

Thus, the EVA can be calculated as follows:

EVA = $180,000 x (1-30%) – ($1,000,000-$200,000) x 13%
= $126,000 – $104,000
= $22,000

Pricing Interdivision Sales

Determining segment profitability and adequate measures of segment performance are always difficult problems. These problems become more complex when segments within a decentralized company provide goods or services to other segments within the same company.

Because each segment is a profit center, each would like to maximize profit on such a transaction and seeks to establish a price for the goods or services accordingly. This price is frequently called the *transfer price* because it is the selling price at which goods are transferred between segments. From the point of view of the company, the transfer price has no direct effect on profits since it results from an internal transaction, and interdivisional sales are eliminated when determining income for external reporting.

The complexities of transfer pricing illustrate the difficulty of maintaining goal congruence in a decentralized organization. Each profit center has an objective to increase its income. When interdivisional sales exist, an increase in income for one division occurs at the expense of another. Transfer prices must be set in order to achieve a desired profit level for the entire company; this objective may conflict with those of the individual segments making the transfer. In most situations internal transfers of goods are beneficial to the company. An internal supplier provides some control over costs, quality, and the availability of goods required by other divisions. When an internal supplier exists, transfers from it rather than purchases from an external supplier aid in the recovery of the company's fixed costs. In many situations, such transfer may not be desirable either to the transferring division or to the receiving division. This will be true when such a transfer adversely affects a division's segment margin.

A system of transfer pricing in a decentralized organization attempts to achieve the following objectives:

1. Provide a price which is fair to each segment and consistent with the objectives of the entire company;
2. Provide an accurate measure of the performance that each division is contributing to company profitability;
3. Motivate each division manager to control costs within the division; and
4. Maintain the autonomy of each division as a profit center.

No method of setting transfer prices fully achieves all of these objectives. Four methods of transfer pricing will be discussed and will be illustrated by the example situation in Illustration 18-9.

Transfer at Market Price

When one or more external suppliers exist for the goods being transferred, an external market also exists for the goods. The normal selling price in this external market can be adopted as the transfer price between divisions. This method has the advantage of objectivity because prices are set outside the company. When divisions are fully autonomous a division has the option of purchasing either from the supplying division within the company or from an external source. Thus, the supplying division is motivated to control costs in order to stay competitive. The performance of each division is evaluated as if each were a separate company dealing in an open market.

When market prices exist, they provide a method which achieves most of the objectives of transfer pricing. However, market-based transfer prices are not always available and may

Illustration 18-9 Transfer Pricing Example

> Brilliant Paint Company manufactures a variety of colors of house paint for sale through its chain of retail outlets. The company consists of three divisions which are each autonomous profit centers. The Pigment Division manufactures the color pigment which gives each shade of paint its characteristic tint. The Blending Division blends pigments with other ingredients and packages the pro-duct in one gallon containers. The Retail Division purchases paint at wholesale prices for resale to customers.
>
> The Pigment Division produces at a standard variable cost of $20 per gallon of pigment. Its standard fixed factory overhead rate is $5 per gallon. The Blending Division can purchase identical pigment from the ABC Color Co. at a cost of $23 per gallon.
>
> Brilliant management prefers that materials be obtained from within the company. What price should Blending pay Pigment for its product?

not serve the best interests of the company as a whole. In the example of Illustration 18-9, a transfer price of $23 per gallon could be selected based on the external market price. When the Pigment Division is operating at normal activity with unused capacity, then $2 per gallon of fixed manufacturing costs will not be recovered. If the Pigment Division could reduce its costs to below the market price, it could sell either to the Blending Division or in the external market and still earn a profit. This illustrates how market-based transfer prices provide motivation for cost control.

Transfer at Cost

Many companies establish a policy of transferring goods from one profit center to another at some measure of cost. The cost could be either the variable unit cost or the full (absorption) unit cost, and could be either standard or actual. Cost-based transfer pricing offers the advantage of simplified accounting, because it creates no interdivision profits which must be eliminated for external reporting. A variation of this approach sets transfer prices at full cost plus some agreed-upon percentage as a profit to the supplying division. A major disadvantage of any of these methods is that it guarantees cost recovery to the supplier, who as a result is not motivated to control costs.

In Illustration 18-9 the transfer price could be set at the full cost of $25 per gallon, or at this cost plus a reasonable profit percentage. A cost-plus arrangement might be satisfactory to the Pigment Division but not to the Blending Division, which could obtain equivalent raw material at a lower price elsewhere. Using full cost would probably satisfy neither, because Pigment earns no profit on the transaction and Blending pays an inflated price. Neither method produces a measure of income which adequately reflects divisional performance.

Negotiated Transfer Prices

Divisional managers are sometimes allowed to negotiate a transfer price. This maintains a degree of segment autonomy and makes each manager responsible for costs within his or her division. Negotiated transfer prices provide motivation for cost control and produce fair measures of segment performance. However, such negotiations may be time-consuming and require frequent revisions. Sometimes divisions are unable to agree upon a price, and negotiations are terminated. Then company management must either arbitrate a transfer price, decreasing divisional autonomy, or allow use of an external supplier which may be detrimental to company profits.

In the example situation, a negotiated transfer price may be possible. If the Pigment Division has idle capacity, its manager may be willing to transfer a fixed quantity of pigment as a special order in excess of the $20 variable cost. And the Blending manager may be able to obtain the order at less than the market price of $23 per gallon. Such an agreement would not be acceptable to the Pigment Division on a continuous basis since it does not provide for a profit. Arbitration by the management of Brilliant would be necessary to prevent the Blending Division from buying externally.

Dual Transfer Prices

Organizational conflicts between divisions may be minimized by using dual transfer prices, with separate prices recorded by the consuming and producing segments. The consuming division records the transfer at a price set by company policy, which typically would be the variable unit cost plus a portion of fixed costs. Thus, it is motivated to purchase internally, an action desirable from the viewpoint of the entire company. The producing division records the sale at full cost plus a fair profit, also determined by company policy. The sale is then recorded at a price which reflects favorably on both the producing and consuming divisions in performance evaluation.

When dual pricing is used, total company profit will be less than the sum of the profits of the divisions. The profit of the producing divisions must be eliminated in determining company net income for external reporting. Furthermore, divisional autonomy is lost because the prices are set by company policy, and neither division is motivated to control costs within the division. Because of these disadvantages, dual pricing is seldom used in practice.

In the example situation of Illustration 18-9, dual pricing could be implemented in the following manner. In the Pigment Division, a sale to Blending could be recorded at a transfer price of $27 per gallon, which is full cost plus a profit of $2 per gallon. The Blending Division could record the purchase at $22 per gallon, a savings of $1 over the market price. Each manager would be satisfied with the transaction but the resulting segment incomes would reflect the transfer pricing method rather than divisional performance. The Pigment manager would not be motivated to cut production costs, nor would the Blending manager have reason to look for a lower price.

The choice of a transfer pricing method is indeed a complex one, requiring an understanding of cost behavior, human motivation, and requirements for external reporting. No single approach is preferable in all situations. Transfer prices are determined as a result of management philosophy regarding decentralization, individual production and market situations, and the manner in which segment performance measures are utilized by company management.

The Balanced Scorecard

Today firms are operating in a rapidly changing business environment. In such a dynamic environment, firms must find efficient and effective ways of producing and delivering products and services to customers in order to maintain the competitive edge. To accomplish this, each business segment or strategic business unit (SBU) of the firm needs to understand and focus on the linkage among all parties in its value chain.

In Chapter eight, we discussed how activity-based management (ABM) can assist managers of a business unit better understand and manage the cost of activities. It should be noted that the traditional financial-based system is useful for firms operating in a stable business environment. However, it may not be suitable for those firms operating in a dynamic environment where continuous improvement processes are critical factors for the success of the firm.

While the activity-based management offers significant improvement in responsibility assignment, performance measurement and rewards over the financial-based management control system, it has some limitations in achieving the overall goal of a firm. The most significant limitation is that continuous improvement processes are often fragmented and not connected with a firm's vision and strategy. When continuous improvement activities are not directed to a firm's vision, expected strategic successes will not materialize. What is needed in this case is a strategic-based management control system that requires continuous improvement activities connected to the strategy and vision of the firm.

A strategic-based management control system may take different forms and approaches. The balanced scorecard is one of the most common strategic control systems developed in the past decade. In this section, we will discuss the basic concepts and commonly adopted performance measures of the balanced scorecard for effective management of a firm's strategy.

Strategy Translation

The balanced scorecard (BSC), developed by Kaplan and Norton, is a performance measurement and strategic management systems that helps an organization create a strategic focus by translating its vision and strategy into operational objectives and performance measures classified in four different perspectives: (1) financial, (2) customer, (3) internal process, and (4) learning and growth. Illustration 18-10 presents the strategy translation process of the balanced scorecard approach.

As shown in illustration 18-10, the organization's strategy defines management's desired relationships among the four perspectives. After defining the organization's strategy, management translates the defined strategy into objectives and measures for each perspective. Each of the four perspectives is discussed below with corresponding commonly used performance measures summarized in Illustration 18-11.

1. *Financial Perspective*

The financial perspective focuses on the value creation for shareholders. The balanced scorecard retains the financial perspective from the traditional management control systems because financial measures are valuable information in reporting the measurable economic consequences of management actions. Such financial performance measures indicate whether strategy implementation and execution are effectively contributing to the financial achievement. Financial objectives are typically related to profitability and measured by operating income, return on investment, residual income, and economic value added. Depending on management's desired strategies, alternative financial objectives could be sales growth, dividend yield, and generation of cash flow. Therefore, once operational objectives are defined, performance measures can be developed and executed.

Illustration 18-10 Strategy Translation Process

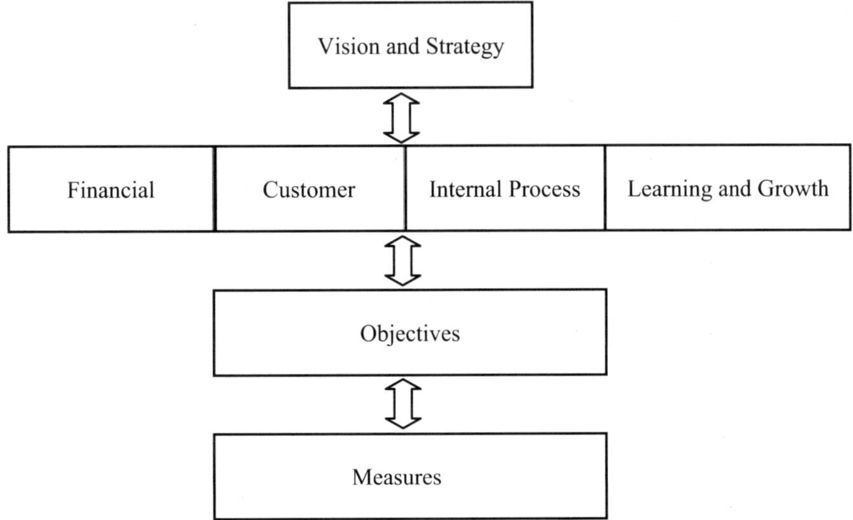

2. Customer Perspective

The customer perspective entails customer satisfaction. It identifies customers and market segments in which a business unit should compete. Once the customers and segments are identified, key objectives and performance measures can be developed for implementation. Key objectives typically include customer acquisition, customer retention, customer satisfaction, customer profitability, and market share. Possible key outcome measures for these objectives are number of new customers, percentage of repeating customers, ratings and feedback from customer satisfaction surveys, individual customer and segment profitability, number of customer complaints, time taken to fulfill customers' order, and percentage of market share.

3. Internal Process Perspective

The internal process perspective identifies critical business processes required to provide values for customers and shareholders of the firm. Each organization has its unique set of business processes for creating value for customers and shareholders. A general value chain model, however, provides a framework that is useful for firms to develop their own objectives and performance measures for this perspective. The general value chain consists of three inter-related business processes: (1) the innovative process, (2) the operations process, and (3) the post-sales service process.

(1) The Innovative Process

The innovative process involves the identification of the emerging and potential needs of customers and the introduction of new products and services to meet their needs. This process represents the long wave of value creation because firms first identify new market, new customers, and new needs of existing customers and then design and develop new products and services for them. Objectives for this process include increase in the number of new products, increase in percentage of revenues from new products, and decrease in the time to develop new products. Related performance measures are number of new products developed, percentage of revenues from new products, time taken to develop new products.

Illustration 18-11 Summary of Commonly Used Performance Measures in the Balanced Scorecard

Perspectives	Performance Measures
1. Financial	Sales growth Operating income Return on investment Residual income Economic value added (EVA) Cash flows
2. Customer	Market share On-time delivery Number of new customers Customer and segment profitability Customer retention Customer satisfaction
3. Internal Process	
(1) For Innovations	New products developed New product development time
(2) For Operations	Manufacturing cycle time Velocity
(3) For Post-Sales Services	Service cost trends Service cycle time
4. Learning and Growth	Employee training hours Employee turnover Employee suggestions Store computerization Real-time feedback capabilities Employees with graduate degrees

(2) The Operations Process

The operations process produces and delivers existing products and services to customers. It represents the short wave of value creation. The process begins with the receipt of a customer order and ends with delivery of the product or service to the customer. It emphasizes efficient, consistent, and timely delivery of products and services to customers. Thus, objectives for this process include increase in process quality, increase in process efficiency, and decrease in process time. Possible performance measures for process quality are product quality costs, yields, and percentage of defective units. Examples of process efficiency measures are process productivity and process costs. Typical process time measures are cycle time, velocity, and manufacturing cycle efficiency (MCE).

"Cycle time" is the time it takes a firm to respond to a customer order. Manufacturing cycle (throughput) time is the time required to produce a product for a customer order. "Velocity" is the number of output units that can be produced in a given time period (i.e., units produced per hour). Manufacturing cycle efficiency is a measure of processing time as a percentage of total production time. The production processing time is considered value added time. The total production time includes value added time and non-value added time such as move time, inspection time, waiting time, and other non-productive time. Thus,

MCE = Value added time / (Value added time + Non-value added time).

(3) The Post-Sales Service Process

The post-sales service process provides critical services to customers after the product or service has been delivered. Such services include warranty and repair activities, handling defects returns and customer complaints, and invoicing and processing of payments. Therefore, increasing service quality, increasing service efficiency, and decreasing service process time are objectives of the post-sales service process. Service quality may be measured by the percentage of customer requests resolved by a single service call. Service efficiency may be measured by service cost trends and service productivity while service time may be measured by service cycle time.

4. Learning and Growth Perspective

The learning and growth perspective supports continuous improvements in the internal processes to create future value. It identifies the infrastructure factors and capabilities that an organization needs to create long-term growth and improvement. Organizational learning and growth come from three operational sources: people, systems, and organizational motivation and empowerment. Therefore, this perspective has three major objectives, namely increase in employee capabilities, increase in information system capabilities, and increase in organizational motivation and empowerment.

Outcome measurements for employee capabilities are employee satisfaction, retention, training, and productivity. Information system capabilities refer to providing accurate and timely information to employees to facilitate and improve their performance. Possible measures include real-time feedback capabilities, store computerization, and on-line accessibilities to customers and product information. Organizational motivation and empowerment are critical in alignment of employee incentives with overall organizational goal. They can be measured by employee suggestion and suggestions implemented.

STRATEGY MAPPING

An essential aspect of the balanced scorecard lies in its articulation of the linkage between performance measures and business strategy. A business strategy is a set of testable plans that specify on how a firm can do to leverage resources and capabilities in order to achieve its objectives. Thus, a business strategy provides directions for operations and offers guidelines for making decisions.

To help managers understand the strategic linkage, Kaplan and Norton suggest that the BSC be graphically represented in a "strategy map". The map provides a visual representation of the critical objectives and clarifies to employees how their jobs are linked to organizational objectives.[11] It also emphases the notion that financial performance is the ultimate goal of the firm since no business can survive without making profits in the long run.

1 Kaplan, R. and D. Norton, "Having trouble with your strategy? Then map it," Harvard Business Review, Vol. 28, 2000, pp. 167-176.

As shown in Illustration 18-12, the map begins at the lowest level with the identification of learning and growth objectives such as employee satisfaction and number of new patents. These objectives support objectives at the next highest level in the map, the internal process objectives such as yields and defect rates. The objectives in the internal process perspective in turn support the objectives in the customer perspective. Finally, the customer objectives such as market share and customer satisfaction support the highest level in the map, the financial objectives such as sales and earnings.

Features for a Properly Designed Scorecard

A properly designed scorecard should help an organization eventually become a good place for its employees to work, a good place for its customers to shop, and a good place for its investors to invest. Thus, a properly designed balanced scorecard typically possesses the following features:

1. The scorecard facilitates the communication of the firm's business strategy to its employees by linking the performance to the business strategy so that everyone has a clear understanding on what to do to achieve the firm's objectives. It should also articulate a cause effect relation between performance and outcome.
2. The scorecard is in balance between the four different perspectives of the scorecard, between financial and non-financial measures, between short-term and long-term objectives, between leading and lagging indicators, and between stakeholders, including shareholders, customers, employees and society.
3. The scorecard contains only those measures critical to the implementation of the firm's business strategy so as to help managers and employees focus their attentions on measures that are linked to the strategy.

Constraints of the Balanced Scorecard

While the balanced scorecard can help a firm implement its business strategy effectively, managers need to be aware of the following two main constraints.

1. Each business segment of a firm may have its unique scorecard. As a result, comparing performance across different business segments becomes a complex and challenging task due to the lack of a common ground or basis for comparison. That is why many organizations have their business segments set up targets and evaluate their performance relative to pre-set targets.
2. The BSC requires data on non-financial measures. However, many of these non-financial measures are not readily available from existing management control systems; thus, the reliability and timeliness of availability of the non-financial information have been a primary challenge of implementing the BSC.

Summary

This chapter has described some of the unique problems and issues in accounting for decentralized organizations. Such organizations are composed of autonomous or semi-autonomous profit centers called segments or divisions. Methods of segment profit reporting were described

Illustration 18-12 Strategy Map

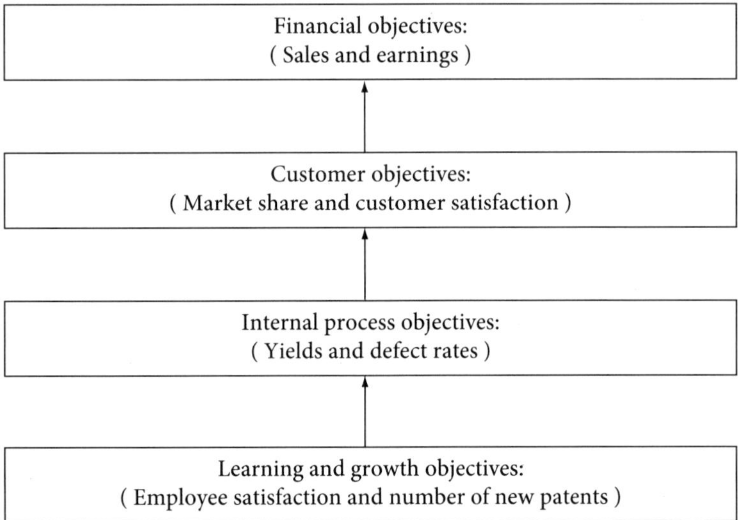

which utilize the direct costing approach to income determination. Three methods of evaluating segment performance were discussed. These were the return on investment, the residual income, and the economic value added. The difficulties in accounting for interdivisional sales, and various methods of transfer pricing, were also discussed. Finally, the balanced scorecard is introduced.

Key Definitions

Balanced scorecard A performance measurement and strategic management systems that help an organization create a strategic focus by translating its vision and strategy into operational objectives and performance measures classified in four different perspectives: (1) financial, (2) customer, (3) internal process, and (4) learning and growth.

Common costs and assets Those costs and assets which are not associated with any individual division in a decentralized company. They exist because of all divisions.

Cost of capital An imputed interest rate representing the cost of having funds invested in a division or asset.

Economic value added A segment's net income after tax and required investment return have been deducted.

Invested capital	Funds of a decentralized company which are not available for other use as a result of the existence of an operating division.
Investment base	The investment in assets or equity for which company capital has been used.
Investment center	An operating division to which funds are allocated for further investment.
Performance margin	The difference between divisional revenues and the total variable costs plus the controllable fixed costs of a division. It can be used to evaluate the divisional manager's performance.
Profit center	An operating division which generates its own revenues and costs, and is expected to contribute to overall company profits.
Residual income	A method of segment performance evaluation which measures a division's performance by its contribution to company profits in excess of a minimum expected return.
Return on investment	A method of segment performance evaluation which measures a division's efficiency in its use of invested capital.
Segment margin	The contribution of an operating division to company profits and to the recovery of common costs.
Separable costs	Costs which are incurred by, and directly as a result of, an operating division.
Transfer price	The value placed upon the goods or services transferred between profit centers of a decentralized company.

Questions

18-1 Many organizations evaluate the performance of a manager in charge of a division by the performance of the division. What potential problems exist in doing this?

18-2 Distinguish between (a) contribution margin, (b) segment margin, and (c) performance margin. Why should such a distinction be made in performance reporting?

18-3 Describe how the use of return on investment as a measure of managerial performance can result in a lack of goal congruence.

18-4 What are the components of the return on investment? How do these components point to methods of improving ROI?

18-5 Return on investment is sometimes used to evaluate opportunities for capital investment. Why are discounted cash flow methods (net present value, internal rate of return) preferable for this purpose?

18-6 Both return on investment and residual income require a determination of the amount of invested capital. Distinguish between four methods of establishing an investment base in determining this amount.

18-7 Describe five ways of placing a monetary value on the investment base in arriving at a measure of invested capital.

18-8 What is meant by "economic value added"?

18-9 One division in a decentralized company sometimes sells goods or services to another division in the same company. What are the advantages of this practice? the disadvantages?

18-10 What are four methods of establishing prices for interdivisional transfers of goods or services?

18-11 What method of pricing interdivisional sales best achieves the objective of: (1) fairness to each division; (2) measuring divisional performance; (3) motivation for cost control; (4) maintaining divisional autonomy?

18-12 What is the balanced scorecard?

18-13 List three performance measures for each of the four perspectives in the balanced scorecard.

18-14 What is a business strategy?

18-15 What are the features of a properly desinged scorecard?

Problems

18-16 *Separable and Common Costs*

A decentralized company utilizes each of the following account descriptions for certain of its expense accounts. Identify each account as either a separable cost/asset or a common cost/asset.

(a) Officer's salaries
(b) Property and equipment, Division A
(c) Direct labor
(d) Corporate public relations
(e) Data processing
(f) Accounts receivable, corporate
(g) Indirect labor
(h) Buildings, corporate

18-17 *Performance and Segment Margin*

Division X of Competitive Corp. had sales of $4,000,000 during the third quarter of 20X2. The following costs were recorded for Division X during the same period. All amounts are stated in thousands of dollars.

Manufacturing: $1,500 variable, $1,000 fixed including $400 of controllable costs and $600 of uncontrollable costs.

Selling: $800, including $500 of variable costs and $300 of controllable fixed costs.

Administrative: $250 in fixed costs, of which *$200* are controllable by the division manager.

Common costs allocated from corporate headquarters: $500

Prepare a profit report for Division X that discloses the actual:
(a) Performance margin, and (b) Segment margin.

18-18 *ROI and the Investment Base*

The Southeastern Division of the Worldwide Company is operated as an investment center. During 20X1 the Division had income (before tax) of $250,000, and the following balance sheet shows its financial position at the end of the year.

Current Assets:		Current Liabilities:	
Cash	$ 20,000	Accounts Payable	$ 50,000
Accounts Receivables	50,000	Note Payable	100,000
Inventory	230,000		150,000
	300,000		
Fixed Assets		Long-Term Loan	500,000
Equipment	550,000	Stockholders Equity:	
Buildings	750,000	Common Stock	1,000,000
Land	400,000	Retained Earnings	350,000
	1,700,000		1,350,000
Total Assets	$2,000,000	Total Liabilities and Stockholders Equity	$2,000,000

The Division currently owns a plant in Mobile which is not in operation and is expected to be sold during the next year. The Mobile plant has land, buildings and equipment with a book value of $200,000. Worldwide Company uses return on investment to evaluate the performance of its divisions.

Required:

From the above data, determine the ROI of the Southeastern Division for 20X1 if invested capital is based on:
(a) Total assets available;
(b) Total assets employed;
(c) Net working capital plus other assets;
(d) Stockholders equity.

18-19 *Divisional Performance Evaluation and the Cost of Capital*

Buckeye Enterprises is composed of two major divisions. Division I is a relatively new manufacturer of electronic subassemblies for the computer industry. Although its market is highly competitive, potential technological developments from the division's research staff may soon provide Division I with a new product unavailable from any other source. Because of the high risks involved, Buckeye assigns a cost of capital to Division I of 30%. Its other major segment, Division II, has been Buckeye's major source of revenue for many years. Division II manufactures automobile components that are sold primarily to Gigantic Motors Corp. Because it has no longterm debt and is relatively secure in its market, Division II is assigned a cost of capital of 15%.

Buckeye has a limited amount of capital available for re-investment, and will allocate it to the two divisions based on their performance. During the previous year, Division I earned $600,000 on its invested capital of $2,400,000. Over the same period, Division II had income of $1,500,000 with invested capital of $8,000,000.

Required:

Evaluate the performance of each division using: (a) return on investment, and (b) residual income. What other factors might affect this capital allocation decision?

18-20 *Valuation Methods for Invested Capital*

Major Manufacturing Co. is a producer and distributor of a wide variety of consumer products. Major is a decentralized corporation, and evaluates the performance of its segments using return on investment as a performance measure. Invested capital is defined as the total assets available to a division valued at the assets' historical costs. Major is currently attempting to evaluate the performance of the Food Products Division over the past three years, and the Controller has prepared the following summary of operating results.

	Food Products Division (000 omitted)		
	20X1	20X2	20X3
Segment margin............................	$ 200	$ 190	$ 180
Current assets................................	40	40	40
Equipment and buildings............	1,000	1,000	1,000
Less: Accumulated depreciation	(300)	(400)	(500)
Net book value..............................	700	600	500
Land	960	960	960
Total assets....................................	$1,700	$1,600	$1,500

Required:

Using the data provided,

(a) Compute ROI for each year for the Food Products Division if:

(1) Assets are valued at gross book value;

(2) Assets are valued at net book value.

(b) What criticism of these methods can you offer the management of Major Manufacturing?

18-21 *Divisional Performance and Capital Budgeting Decisions*

Drexell Industries is a medium-sized diversified manufacturing company which operates subsidiaries in several different industries. Top management has established corporate goals which include a target return on shareholders' investment (before tax) of 25%. The performance of each subsidiary is evaluated using return on investment, and is considered satisfactory whenever ROI during a year is in excess of this amount.

The manager of the Small Valve Division, Sally Hardsell, has been quite proud of her division's performance. During the most recent year this division had a ROI of 30%, and Sally is determined to maintain this above average record of profitability.

Sally is considering the purchase of a new piece of equipment, a computer-controlled multi-spindle lathe, which promises to increase productivity at a substantial savings in labor cost. The lathe has an original cost of $300,000 but will provide incremental benefits totaling $96,000 per year over its five year useful life. It will be obsolete at the end of that time and will have no salvage value.

Required:

(a) In evaluating this capital investment for the Small Valve Division, determine its

(1) return on investment (more properly known as the accounting rate of return);

(2) internal rate of return.

(b) Should the lathe be purchased? Explain the reason(s) for your answer.

18-22 *Return on Investment, Residual Income and Economic Value Added*

Agnes Company has the following data available for two of its segments for year 20X9:

	Segment A	Segment B
Operating income	$50,000	$60,000
Operating assets	250,000	400,000

The company's weighted average cost of capital and target ROI is 18% and 12%, respectively.

Required:

(a) Compute the following for each segment:
(1) ROI
(2) RI
(3) EVA
(b) Briefly explain which segment performs better.

18-23 *Return on Investment, Residual Income, and Economic Value Added*

Anne Company has two divisions for which the following data is available for year 20X8:

	Division X	Division Y
Income before taxes	$ 200,000	$ 300,000
Total assets	1,000,000	1,200,000
Current liabilities	400,000	300,000
Tax rate	30%	35%
Weighted average cost of capital	15%	20%

Anne Company's cost of capital is 15%.

Required:

(a) Compute the following for each division:
(1) ROI
(2) RI
(3) EVA
(b) Briefly explain which division performs better.

18-24 *Transfer Prices and Goal Congruence*

Mar Company has two decentralized divisions, X and Y. Division X has always purchased certain units from Division Y at $75 per unit. Because Division Y plans to raise the price to $100 per unit, Division X desires to purchase these units from outside suppliers for $75 per unit. Division Y's costs follow:

Y's variable costs per unit	$70
Y's annual fixed costs	$15,000
Y's annual production of these units for X	1,000 unit

If Division X buys from an outside supplier, the facilities Division Y uses to manufacture these units would remain idle.

Required:

(a)What is the full (absorption) cost per unit in Division Y?
(b) Of the alternatives available, which transfer price would
(1) produce the greatest profit for Division X?
(2) produce the greatest profit for Division Y?
(3) produce the greatest profit for Mar Company?

(4) provide incentive for cost control?
(5) allow the most divisional autonomy?
(6) satisfy each manager simultaneously?

(AICPA adapted)

18-25 *Cost, Profit, and Investment Centers*

Elwood Bank is a large municipal bank with several branch offices. The bank has a computer department which handles all data processing for the bank's operations. In addition, the bank acts as a service bureau by selling its expertise in systems development and excess machine time to several small business firms.

The computer department currently is treated as a cost center of the bank. The manager of the computer department prepares an expense budget annually for approval by senior bank officials. Monthly operating reports compare actual and budgeted expenses. Revenues from the department's service bureau activities are treated as "other income" by the bank and are not reflected on the computer department's operating reports. The costs of serving these clients are included in departmental reports, however.

The manager of the computer department has proposed that the bank management convert the computer department to a profit or investment center.

(a) Describe the characteristics which differentiate:
(1) a cost center,
(2) a profit center, and
(3) an investment center from each other.
(b) Would the manager of the computer department be likely to conduct the operations of the department differently if the department were classified as a profit center or an investment center rather than as a cost center? Explain your answer.

18-26 *Segment Performance by Product Line*

Bundt Foods Company produces and sells many products in each of its 35 different product lines. From time to time a product or an entire product line is dropped because it ceases to be profitable. The company does not have a formalized program for reviewing its products on a regular basis to identify those products which should be eliminated.

At a recent meeting of Bundt Foods' top management, one person stated that there probably were several products or possibly a product line which was unprofitable or producing an unsatisfactory return on investment. After considerable discussion, management decided that Bundt foods should establish a formalized product discontinuance program. The purpose of the program would be to review the company's individual products and product lines on a regular and on-going basis to identify problem areas.

The vice president of finance has proposed that a person be assigned to the program on a full-time basis. This person would work closely with the marketing and accounting departments in determining (1) the factors which indicate when a product's importance is declining and (2) the underlying data that would be required in evaluating whether a product line should be discontinued.

Required:

(a) Identify and explain briefly the benefits, other than the identification of unprofitable products or product lines, Bundt Foods Company can derive from a formalized product discontinuance program.

(b) In developing Bundt Foods Company's product discontinuance program:

(1) Identify the factors which would indicate that a product's or product line's importance is diminishing.

(2) Identify the data which the accounting department would be able to provide which would be useful in evaluating a product or product line.

(IMA adapted)

18-27 *Difficulties with Transfer Pricing*

The Ajax Division of Gunnco, operating at capacity, has been asked by the Defco Division of Gunnco Corporation to supply it with Electrical Fitting No. 1726. Ajax sells this part to its regular customers for $7.50 each. Defco, which is operating at 50 percent capacity, is willing to pay $5.00 each for the fitting. Defco will put the fitting into a brake unit which it is manufacturing on essentially a cost plus basis for a commercial airplane manufacturer.

Ajax has a variable cost of producing fitting No. 1726 of $4.25. The cost of the brake unit as being built by Defco is as follows:

Purchased parts—outside vendors	$ 22.50
Ajax fitting—1726	5.00
Other variable costs	14.00
Fixed overhead and administration	8.00
	$49.50

Defco believes that obtaining the price concession from Ajax is necessary if the sale of the brake units is to be made.

The company uses return on investment and dollar profits in the measurement of division and division manager performance.

Required:

(a) Consider that you are the division controller of Ajax. Would you recommend that Ajax supply fitting 1726 to Defco? (Ignore any income tax issues.) Why or why not?

(b) Would it be to the short-run economic advantage of the Gunnco Corporation for the Ajax division to supply Defco division with fitting 1726 at $5.00 each? (Ignore any income tax issues.) Explain your answer.

(c) Discuss the organizational and manager behavior difficulties, if any, inherent in this situation. As the Gunnco controller, what would you advise the Gunnco Corporation president do in this situation?

(IMA adapted)

18-28 *Operating Ratios as Performance Measures*

A common measure of a management's performance is "return on net worth." This is a particularly important measure from the shareholder's point of view. This ratio can be expressed as the product of three other ratios as shown below:

$$\text{Return on Net Worth} = \frac{\text{Net Income}}{\text{Net Worth}} = \overset{\text{I}}{\frac{\text{Net Income}}{\text{Sales}}} \times \overset{\text{II}}{\frac{\text{Sales}}{\text{Assets}}} \times \overset{\text{III}}{\frac{\text{Assets}}{\text{Net Worth}}}.$$

Required:

(a) Discuss the "return on net worth" as a management goal and as a measurement of management performance.

(b) What management activities are measured by each of the ratios I, II, III?

(c) Would separation of the "return on net worth" into the three ratios and use of these ratios for planning targets and performance measures result in goal congruence (or improvement toward goal congruence) among the responsible managers? Explain your answer.

(*IMA adapted*)

18-29 *Divisional Profit Planning*Western Company recently acquired Papion Men's Clothing Company which now operates as a western subsidiary. Papion offers dress, casual, and sports clothing and related incidental accessories. The clothing is manufactured at several plants throughout the United States. The company's different lines are sold through company-owned stores and other retailers.

Western exercises close control over its subsidiaries. Western's management expects the subsidiaries' reports to present the proposed operating plans and to evaluate past performance in order to provide a foundation for this degree of control. However, Western's controller failed to provide Papion management with complete specifications regarding the format and the content of the reports because he had been devoting all of his energies to the final details of the acquisition.

The Annual Operating Plan Report presented on the next page for Papion is the first report prepared and submitted to Western since the acquisition. Papion's management developed its own format for the report. The report includes the proposed budget for 20X2 and related remarks regarding past and future operations.

Required:

(a) Would the proposed budget and accompanying remarks included in Papion Men's Clothing Company's Annual Operating Plan Report fulfill the needs of Western Company's management to exercise close control? Explain your answer.

(b) Irrespective of your answer to (a) what changes would you recommend in this report to improve its effectiveness for communicating the 20X2 plans of Papion Men's Clothing Company?

Papion Men's Clothing Company 20X2 Annual Operating Plan Report

The Papion Men's Clothing Company expects the operating results for 20X2 to be better than last year. Several actions have been taken which will improve sales and solve problems that affected operations last year. Sales should increase substantially due to the introduction of a new line of women's sportswear to be distributed through company-owned stores. Progress also was made last year in attracting other retailers to handle Papion's lines. Additional sales increases can be expected this year if negotiations to induce a major chain to distribute Papion lines are successful. The budget includes the sales expected to be made through this large chain retailer.

Operating costs should be lower this year. A new production facility should be completed in February to replace an older plant. This older plant has caused production shortages due to frequent equipment breakdowns. Also, labor problems which existed at the midwest plant have been resolved. Thus, the lower output and higher costs of the midwest plant should be corrected.

Original Budget for 20X1
Forecast of Actual Operations for 20X1
Proposed Budget for 20X2 (000 omitted)

	Budget 20X1	*Forecast Actual 20X1*	*Budget 20X2*
Sales	$10,000	$8,500	$12,000
Cost of goods sold:			
Material	$ 1,050	$ 975	$ 1,260
Labor	1,400	1,400	1,680
Factory overhead	1,750	1,600	1,800
Selling expenses:			
Sales force	500	425	600
Advertising and promotion	600	500	950
Company stores	1,000	950	1,100
General administration	750	755	825
Total expenses	$ 7,050	$6,605	$ 8,215
Net income before taxes	$ 2,950	$1,895	$ 3,785

Required:

Prepared and submitted: October, 20X1

18-30 *Multiple Criteria for Performance Evaluation*

Berton Inc. is a large, decentralized electronics firm. Berton uses a multiple criteria performance evaluation system in measuring the achievements of its divisions. The criteria used to evaluate performance are as follows:

1. Profitability.
2. Market position.
3. Productivity.
4. Product leadership.
5. Personnel development.
6. Strengthening of employee attitudes.
7. Public responsibility.
8. Balance between short-range and long-range goals.

Required:

(a) Identify and briefly discuss the advantages of a multiple criteria performance system over a single criterion performance system.

(b) The maintenance of "goal congruence" is a management problem that is often associated with large, complex organizations.

What is meant by the term "goal congruence?"
Will a multiple criteria performance evaluation system lead to goal congruence? Explain your answer.

(c) Suppose management wishes to combine the multiple criteria described above into a single index which would be used to evaluate overall performance. Identify and explain briefly the difficulties in developing and employing such an index or measure to evaluate performance.

(IMA adapted)

18-31 *Segment Income Statement*—Caprice Company manufactures and sells two products: a small portable office file cabinet that it has made for over 15 years and a home/travel file introduced more recently. The files are made in Caprice's only manufacturing plant. Budgeted variable production costs per unit of product are as follows.

	Office File	*Home/Travel File*
Sheet metal	$ 3.50	--
Plastic	--	$3.75
Direct labor (@ $8 per DLH)	4.00	2.00
Variable manufacturing overhead (@ $9 per DLH)	4.50	2.25
	$12.00	$8.00

Variable manufacturing overhead costs vary with direct labor hours. The annual fixed manufacturing overhead costs are budgeted at $120,000. A total of 50% of these costs are directly traceable to the office file department and 22% of the costs are traceable to the home/travel file department. The remaining 28% of the costs are not traceable to either department.

Caprice employs two full-time salespersons—Pam Price and Robert Flint. Each salesperson receives an annual salary of $14,000 plus a sales commission of 10% of his/her total gross sales. Travel and entertainment expense is budgeted at $22,000 annually for each salesperson. Price is expected to sell 60% of the budgeted unit sales for each file and Flint the remaining 40%. Caprice's remaining selling and administrative expenses include fixed administrative costs of $80,000 that cannot be traced to either file plus the following traceable selling expenses.

	Office File	*Home/Travel File*
Packaging expenses per unit	$ 2.00	$ 1.50
Promotion	$30,000	$40,000

Data regarding Caprice's budgeted and actual sales for the fiscal year ended May 31, 20XX, are presented in the following schedule. There were no changes in the beginning and ending balances of either finished goods or work in process inventories.

	Office File	*Home/Travel File*
Budgeted sales volume in units	15,000	15,000
Budgeted and actual unit sales price	$29.50	$19.50
Actual unit sales:		
Pam Price	10,000	9,500
Robert Flint	5,000	10,500
Total units	15,000	20,000

Data regarding Caprice's operating expenses for the year ended May 31, 20XX, follow. There were no increases or decreases in raw materials inventory for either sheet metal or plastic and there were no usage variances. However, sheet metal prices were 6% above budget and plastic prices were 4% below budget.

The actual direct labor hours worked and costs incurred were as follows.

	Hours	Amount
Office file	7,500	$ 57,000
Home/travel file	6,000	45,600
	13,500	$102,600

Fixed manufacturing overhead costs attributable to the office file department were $8,000 above the budget. All other fixed manufacturing overhead costs were incurred at the same amounts as budgeted, and all variable manufacturing overhead costs were incurred at the budgeted hourly rates.

All selling and administrative expenses were incurred at budgeted rates or amounts except the following items.

Non-traceable administrative expenses		$ 34,000
Promotion:		
Office files	$32,000	
Home/travel files	58,000	90,000
Travel and entertainment:		
Pam Price	24,000	
Robert Flint	28,000	52,000
		$176,000

Required:

(a) Prepare a segmented income statement of Caprice Company's actual operations for the fiscal year ended May 31, 20XX. The report should be prepared in a contribution margin format by product and should reflect total income (loss) for the company before income taxes.

(b) Identify and discuss any additional analyses that could be made of the data presented that would be of value to Caprice Company.

(*IMA adapted*)

18-32 *Evaluating Managers by Division Performance*

The Texon Co. is organized into autonomous divisions along regional market lines. Each division manager is responsible for sales, cost of operations, acquisition and financing of divisional assets and working capital management.

The vice president of general operations for the company will retire in September 2012. A review of the performance, attitudes, and skills of several management employees has been undertaken. Interviews with qualified outside candidates also have been held. The selection committee has narrowed the choice to the managers of Divisions A and F.

Both candidates were appointed division managers in late 2008. The manager of Division A had been the assistant manager of that division for the prior five years. The manager of Division F had served as assistant division manager of Division B before being appointed to his present post. He took over Division F, a division newly formed in 2007 when its first manager left to join a competitor. The financial results of their performance in the past three years is reported below:

Required:

(a) Texon Co. measures the performance of the divisions and the division managers on the basis of their return on investment (ROI). Is this an appropriate measurement for the division managers? Explain.

(b) Many believe that a single measure, such as ROI, is inadequate to fully evaluate performance. What additional measure(s) could be used for performance evaluation? Give reasons for each measure listed.

(c) On the basis of the information given, which manager would you recommend for vice president of general operations? Present reasons to support your answer.

Texon Co.

	Division A			*Division F*		
	2009	*2010*	*2011*	*2009*	*2010*	*2011*
		(000 omitted)			(000 omitted)	
Estimated industry sales-market area	$10,000	$12,000	$13,000	$5,000	$6,000	$6,500
Division sales	$ 1,000	$ 1,100	$ 1,210	$ 450	$ 600	$ 750
Variable costs	$ 300	$ 320	$ 345	$ 135	$ 175	$ 210
Managed costs	400	405	420	170	200	230
Committed costs	275	325	350	140	200	250
Total costs	$ 975	$ 1,050	$ 1,115	$ 445	$ 575	$ 690
Net income	$ 25	$ 50	$ 95	$ 5	$ 25	$ 60
Assets employed	$ 330	$ 340	$ 360	$ 170	$ 240	$ 300
Liabilities incurred	103	105	115	47	100	130
Net investment	227	235	245	123	140	170
Return on investment	11%	21%	39%	4%	18%	35%

(*IMA adapted*)

18-33 *Divisional Autonomy, Transfer Prices, and Performance Evaluation*

A.R. Oma, Inc. manufactures a line of men's perfumes and after-shaving lotions. The manufacturing process is basically a series of mixing operations with the addition of certain aromatic and coloring ingredients; the finished product is packaged in a company produced glass bottle and packed in cases containing 6 bottles.

A.R. Oma feels that the sale of its product is heavily influenced by the appearance and appeal of the bottle and has, therefore, devoted considerable managerial effort to the bottle production process. This has resulted in the development of certain unique bottle production processes in which management takes considerable pride.

The two areas (i.e., perfume production and bottle manufacture) have evolved over the years in an almost independent manner, in fact, a rivalry has developed between management personnel as to "which division is the more important" to A.R. Oma. This attitude is probably intensified because the bottle manufacturing plant has purchased intact 10 years ago and no real interchange of management personnel or ideas (except at the top corporate level) has taken place.

Since the acquisition, all bottle production has been absorbed by the perfume manufacturing plant. Each area is considered a separate profit center and evaluated as such. As the new corporate controller you are responsible for the definition of a proper transfer price to use in crediting the bottle production profit center and in debiting the packaging profit center.

At your request, the Bottle Division General Manager has asked certain other bottle manufacturers to quote a price for the quantity and sizes demanded by the perfume division. These competitive prices are:

Volume	*Total Price*	*Price per Case*
2,000,000 eq. cases*	$ 4,000,000	$2.00
4,000,000	$ 7,000,000	$1.75
6,000,000	$10,000,000	$1.67

*An "equivalent case" represents 6 bottles each.

A cost analysis of the internal bottle plant indicates that they can produce bottles at these costs.

Volume	*Total Price*	*Cost per Case*
2,000,000 eq. Cases	$3,200,000	$1.60
4,000,000	$5,200,000	$1.30
6,000,000	$7,200,000	$1.20

(Your cost analysts point out that these costs represent fixed costs of $1,200,000 and variable costs of $1.00 per equivalent case.)

These figures have given rise to considerable corporate discussion as to the proper value to use in the transfer of bottles to the perfume division. This interest is heightened because a significant portion of a division manager's income is an incentive bonus based on profit center results.

The perfume production division has the following costs in addition to the bottle costs:

Volume	*Total Cost*	*Cost per Case*
2,000,000 cases	$16,400,000	$8.20
4,000,000	$32,400,000	$8.10
6,000,000	$48,400,000	$8.07

After considerable analysis, the marketing research department has furnished you with the following price-demand relationship for the finished product:

Sales Volume	*Total Sales Revenue*	*Sales Price per Case*
2,000,000 cases	$25,000,000	$12.50
4,000,000	$45,600,000	$11.40
6,000,000	$63,900,000	$10.65

(a) The A.R. Oma Company has used market price transfer prices in the past. Using the current market prices and costs, and assuming a volume of 6,000,000 cases, calculate the income for

(1) the bottle division.

(2) the perfume division.

(3) the corporation.

(b) Is this production and sales level the most profitable volume for

(1) the bottle division?

(2) the perfume division?

(3) the corporation?

Explain your answer.

(c) The A.R. Oma Company uses the profit center concept for divisional operation.

(1) Define a "profit center."

(2) What conditions should exist for a profit center to be established?

(3) Should the two divisions of the A.R. Oma Company be organized as profit centers?

(IMA adapted)

18-34 *Budgets for Divisional Performance Evaluation*

Clarkson Company is a large multi-division firm with several plants in each division. A comprehensive budgeting system is used for planning operations and measuring performance. The annual budgeting process commences in August five months prior to the beginning of the fiscal year. At this time the division managers submit proposed budgets for sales, production and inventory levels, and expenses. Capital expenditure requests also are formalized at this time. The expense budgets include direct labor and all overhead items which are separated into fixed and variable components. Direct materials are budgeted separately in developing the production and inventory schedules. The expense budgets for each division are developed from its plants' results, as measured by the percent variation from an adjusted budget in the first six months of the current year, and a target expense reduction percentage established by the corporation. To determine plant percentages the plant budget for the just completed half-year period is revised to recognize changes in operating procedures and costs outside the control of plant management (e.g., labor wage rate changes, product style changes, etc.). The difference between this revised budget and the actual expenses is the controllable variance, and is expressed as a percentage of the actual expenses. This percentage is added (if unfavorable) to the corporate target expense reduction percentage. A favorable plant variance percentage is subtracted from the corporate target. If a plant had a 2% unfavorable controllable variance and the corporate target reduction was 4%, the plant's budget for next year should reflect costs approximately 6% below this year's actual costs.

Next year's final budgets for the corporation, the divisions, and the plants are adopted after corporate analysis of the proposed budgets and a careful review with each division manager of the changes made by corporate management. Division profit budgets include allocated corporate costs, and plant profit budgets include allocated division and corporate costs.

Return on assets is used to measure the performance of divisions and plants. The asset base for a division consists of all assets assigned to the division, including its working capital, and an allocated share of corporate assets. For plants the asset base includes the assets assigned to the plant plus an allocated portion of the division and corporate assets. Recommendations for promotions and salary increases for the executives of the divisions and plants are influenced by how well the actual return on assets compares with the budgeted return on assets.

The plant managers exercise control only over the cost portion of the plant profit budget because the divisions are responsible for sales. Only limited control over the plant assets is exercised at the plant nt level.

The manager of the Dexter Plant, a major plant in the Huron division, carefully controls his costs during the first six months so that any improvement appears after the target reduction of expenses is established. He accomplishes this by careful planning and timing of his discretionary expenditures. During 20X1 the property adjacent to the Dexter Plant was purchased by Clarkson Company. This expenditure was not included in the 20X1 capital expenditure budget. Corporate management decided to divert funds from a project at another plant since the property appeared to be a better longterm investment.

Also during 20X1 Clarkson Company experienced depressed sales. In an attempt to achieve budgeted profit, corporate management announced in August that all plants were to cut their annual expenses by 6%. In order to accomplish this expense reduction, the Dexter Plant manager reduced preventive maintenance and postponed needed major repairs. Employees who quit were not replaced unless absolutely necessary. Employee training was postponed whenever possible. The raw materials, supplies and finished goods inventories were reduced below normal levels.

Required:

(a) Evaluate the budget procedure of Clarkson Company with respect to its effectiveness for planning and controlling operations.

(b) Is the Clarkson Company's use of return on assets to evaluate the performance of the Dexter Plant appropriate? Explain your answer.

(c) Analyze and explain the Dexter Plant Manager's behavior during 20Xl.

(*IMA adapted*)

18-35 *Evaluating Investment Opportunities*

During your examination of the financial statements of Benjamin Industries, the president requested your assistance in the evaluation of several financial management problems in his home appliances division which he summarized for you as follows:

1. Management wants to determine the best sales price for a new appliance which has a variable cost of $4 per unit. The sales manager has estimated probabilities of achieving annual sales levels for various selling prices as shown in the following chart:

Sales Level (Units)	*Selling Price*			
	$4	$5	$6	$7
20,000		--	20%	80%
30,000	--	10%	40%	20%
40,000	50%	50%	20%	--
50,000	50%	40%	20%	--

2. The division's current profit rate is 5% on annual sales of $1,200,000; an investment of $400,000 is needed to finance these sales. The company's basis for measuring divisional success is return on investment.
3. Management is also considering the following two alternative plans submitted by employees for improving operations in the home appliances division:

Green believes that sales volume can be doubled by greater promotional effort, but his method would lower the profit rate to *4%* of sales and require an additional investment of $100,000.

Gold favors eliminating some unprofitable appliances and improving efficiency by adding *$200,000* in capital equipment. His methods would decrease sales volume by 10% but improve the profit rate to *7%*.

Required:

(a) Prepare a schedule computing the expected incremental income for each of the sales prices proposed for the new product. The schedule should include the expected sales levels in units (weighted according to the sales manager's estimated probabilities), the expected total monetary sales, expected variable costs and the expected incremental income.

(b) Prepare schedules computing (1) the company's current rate of return on investment in the home appliances division, and the anticipated rates of return under the alternative suggestions made by (2) Green and (3) Gold.

(AICPA adapted)

18-36 *Measuring Segment Profitability*

The Justa Corporation produces and sells three products. The three products: A, B, and C, are sold in a local market and in a regional market. At the end of the first quarter of the current year, the following income statement has been prepared:

	Total	*Local*	*Regional*
Sales	$1,300,000	$1,000,000	$300,000
Cost of goods sold	1,010,000	775,000	235,000
Gross margin	$ 290,000	$ 225,000	$ 65,000
Selling expenses	$ 105,000	$ 60,000	$ 45,000
Administrative expenses	52,000	40,000	12,000
	$ 157,000	$ 100,000	$ 57,000
Net income	$ 133,000	$ 125,000	$ 8,000

Management has expressed special concern with the regional market because of the extremely poor return on sales. This market was entered a year ago because of excess capacity. It was originally believed that the return on sales would improve with time, but after a year no noticable improvement can be seen from the results as reported in the above quarterly statement.In attempting to decide whether to eliminate the regional market, the following information has been gathered:

	Products		
	A	B	C
Sales	$500,000	$400,000	$400,000
Variable manufacturing expenses as a percentage of sales	60%	70%	60%
Variable selling expenses as a percentage of sales	3%	2%	2%

	Sales by Markets	
Product	*Local*	*Regional*
A	$400,000	$100,000
B	300,000	100,000
C	300,000	100,000

All administrative expenses and fixed manufacturing expenses are common to the three products and the two markets and are fixed for the period. Remaining selling expenses are fixed for the period and separable by market. All fixed expenses are based upon a prorated yearly amount.

Required:

(a) Prepare the quarterly income statement showing contribution margins by markets.

(b) Assuming there are no alternative uses for the Justa Corporation's present capacity, would you recommend dropping the regional market? Why or why not?

(c) Prepare the quarterly income statement showing contribution margins by products.

(d) It is believed that a new product can be ready for sale next year if the Justa Corporation decides to go ahead with continued research. The new product can be produced by simply converting equipment presently used in producing Product C. This conversion will increase fixed costs by $10,000 per quarter. What must be the minimum contribution margin per quarter for the new product to make the changeover financially feasible?

18-37 *Transfer Pricing*

DePaolo Industries manufactures carpets, furniture, and foam in three separate divisions. DePaolo's operating statement for 20XX is reproduced below.

Additional information regarding DePaolo's operations are as follows:

Included in foam's sales revenue is *$500,000* in revenue that represents sales made to the furniture division that were transferred at manufacturing cost.

The cost of goods sold is composed of the following costs.

	Carpet	*Furniture*	*Foam*
Direct material	$ 500,000	$1,000,000	$1,000,000
Direct labor	500,000	200,000	1,000,000
Variable overhead	750,000	50,000	1,000,000
Fixed overhead	250,000	50,000	0
Total cost of goods sold	$2,000,000	$1,300,000	$3,000,000

Administrative expenses include the following costs.

	Carpet	*Furniture*	*Foam*
Segment expenses:			
Variable	$ 85,000	$140,000	$ 40,000
Fixed	85,000	210,000	120,000
Home office expenses (all fixed):			
Directly traceable	100,000	120,000	200,000
General (allocated on sales dollars)	30,000	30,000	40,000
Total	$300,000	$500,000	$400,000

Selling expense is all incurred at the segment level and is *80%* variable for all segments. John Sprint, manager of the foam division, is not pleased with DePaolo's presentation of operating performance. Sprint claimed, "The foam division makes a greater contribution to the company's profits than what is shown. I sell foam to the furniture division at cost and it gets our share of the profit. I can sell that foam on the outside at my regular markup, but I sent to furniture for the well-being of the company. I think my division should get credit for those internal sales at market. I think we should also revise our operating statements for internal purposes. Why don't we consider preparing these internal statements on a contribution approach reporting format showing internal transfers at market?"

DePaolo Industries
Operating Statement
For the Year Ended December 31, 20XX

	Carpet Division	*Furniture Division*	*Foam Division*	*Total*
Sales revenue	$3,000,000	$3,000,000	$4,000,000	$10,000,000
Cost of goods sold	2,000,000	1,300,000	3,000,000	6,300,000
Gross profit	$1,000,000	$1,700,000	$1,000,000	$ 3,700,000
Operating expenses:				
Administrative	$ 300,000	$ 500,000	$ 400,000	$ 1,200,000
Selling	600,000	600,000	500,000	1,700,000
Total operating expenses	$ 900,000	$1,100,000	$ 900,000	$ 2,900,000
Income from operations before taxes	$ 100,000	$ 600,000	$ 100,000	$ 800,000

Required:

(a) John Sprint believes that the intra-company transfers from the foam division to the furniture division should be at market rather than manufacturing cost for divisional performance measurement.

1. Explain why Sprint is correct.
2. Identify and describe two approaches used for setting transfer prices other than manufacturing cost (used by DePaolo Industries) and market price (as recommended by Sprint).

(b) Using the contribution approach and market based transfer prices, prepare a revised operating statement by division for DePaolo Industries for 20XX that will promote the evaluation of divisional performance.